Understanding

Adam-God

Teachings

Drew Briney

Table of Contents

β

Introduction

~   A Note to the Reader   i

~   A Note to Members of the LDS Church   viii

~   Adam-God Teachings: A Few Observations   xii

Abbreviations & Format   xxix

Acknowledgments   xxxii

Adam

1   Adam as God the Father   1

2   Adam as Father of Our Spirits   33

~   God as Father of Our Spirits   41

~   God as Father of Our Bodies   44

3   Adam as Father of Christ   51

~   God as Father of Christ   60

~   Christ as Father of Righteous   68

4   Adam as Michael the Archangel   79

~   Scriptures & Lore: Michael   89

5   Adam as Ancient of Days   94

6   Adam as Creator of this Earth   118

7   Adam Presides Over Our Spirits & has the Keys   124

Eve

8   Eve as the Mother of All Living   136

9   Eve as a Plural Wife During This Probation   150

10   Eve as a Plural Wife in the Eternities   154

11   Mary Sealed to Adam   157

12   Eve as Adam's Daughter   161

Adam & Eve: The Creation, Fall, & Atonement

13   Adam & Eve: Immortal & Exalted Before the Fall   165

14   Adam & Eve not Formed from the Dust of this Earth   178

15   Adam & Eve Knew They Would Fall   188

16   Partaking of the Forbidden Fruit   193

17   Partaking of the Seeds of Death   200

18   Procreation: Mortal & Spiritual Offspring   208

19   Adam's Death - Translation   227

20   Does the Atonement Pertain to Adam & Eve?   233

The Cycle of the Gods

21	The Faithful Become Gods: Becoming an Adam/Eve	242
22	The Creation: Modus Operandi	263
23	Gods Continually Learn & Progress	283
24	Eternal Progression	291
~	The Good Samaritan	294
25	Adam & His Associates	298
26	The Royal Order of Saviors	305

Titles & Offices

27	Jehovah	327
~	Who is Jehovah?	332
~	Jehovah is God	347
~	Jehovah is Christ	366
~	Scriptures: Jehovah is Christ	372
~	Jehovah is not Christ	375
~	Scriptures: Jehovah	408
~	Jehovah is not Adam	410
28	Elohim	424
29	God & god	431
30	Adam & Eve	442
31	Angels & Archangels	446

Miscellaneous Controversies

32   Did Joseph Smith Introduce Adam-God Teachings?   452

33   Was Brigham Young Misquoted?   474

34   Was Brigham Young Speculating?   484

~   False Prophecy & False Gods   510

35   Statements of Unbelief   514

~   Orson Pratt   519

~   Scott Anderson   540

~   Edward Bunker   544

Important Accounts

36   Joseph's First Vision   552

37   Journal of Discourses 1:50-51   575

38   Millennial Star 15:801-804   584

39   Brigham Young's October 8, 1854 Discourse   592

~   Other Accounts of the 1854 Discourse   612

40   The Lecture at the Veil   618

41   The Women of Mormondom   626

Epilogue

Annotated Bibliography

Introduction

β

A Note to the Reader

~

This volume is over four years in the making and has two primary purposes. The first purpose of *Understanding Adam-God Teachings* is to provide a comprehensive doctrinal resource for the interested reader to study Adam-God teachings within a sensitive reading environment. I have tried to make each statement as short as practically reasonable (while preserving the context) because some lengthy quotes address multiple doctrinal issues and therefore appear in multiple sections[1] and subsections.[2] I hope that this facilitates the reader's ability to quickly find the portion of the statement that directly addresses the issue at hand while simultaneously keeping this book from being too bulky. Additionally, in most cases, I have italicized the phrases within each statement that are relevant to the topic wherein the statement is found so that the reader may quickly find the language that teaches the principle of any given topic.

I have placed all commentary on a given issue *after* all statements from the early brethren

---

[1] Throughout this volume, I refer to "sections" and "subsections" instead of chapters as a matter of organizational convenience. The sections are identified in the table of contents by their encasement in lines and are further identified throughout the book via the headers at the top of each right-hand page. Subsections are identified in the table of contents by a number or the symbol "~" and are not identified in the headers throughout this volume.

[2] The reader is advised that some subsections are highly repetitive in documenting some issues (e.g., "Adam as God the Father"; "Adam as Ancient of Days"); while this does not make particularly engaging reading material, I believe that this serves three purposes. First, it definitively dispels with the popular notion that there are only "a half a dozen" statements about Adam-God teachings. Second, it serves to demonstrate that these teachings were not unusual, speculative aberrations - these teachings were systematically taught and represented a cohesive, complex, and thorough theology. Lastly, the repetition offers the reader a comprehensive source of statements about any given issue so all known Adam-God materials are readily available in one volume.

on a given topic have been presented. My analyses therefore take a secondary seat behind the teachings of the early brethren - besides, in many instances, commentary seems superfluous after reading all of the primary sources. Therefore, my analysis has often been primarily textual rather than doctrinal, which fits my personal beliefs anyway - it is the responsibility of the priesthood heads to reveal doctrines from the heavens - our responsibility is to hear, to understand, to analyze, and ultimately to believe and adhere to their true teachings. My commentary therefore is of much less import than the primary accounts of the words of the prophets themselves - and in some cases my commentary is very brief and simplistic.[3] However, I have compiled these resources and written my commentary in this way in an effort to create an objective research environment for the reader. Nevertheless, despite my attempts to provide the reader an unbiased presentation of Adam-God teachings (apart from the commentary), some subjectivity is unavoidable. I have therefore come short of my purpose in at least five ways:

1

Categorizing the original sources by topic necessitates a certain degree of interpretation. However, I have tried to place each source in as many topics as I could reasonably read into the statement. I have also included as many topics as I could discover were taught by the early brethren.[4] In this way, the reader can decide whether or not a given statement applies to a given subsection. Due to these methodological decisions, the reader may note that some statements will be more convincing and/or more authoritative in their respective sections than other statements. This is an important point for the reader to keep in mind because, although most statements are straightforward and directly on point, occasional statements found within any given section do not have an immediately evident correlation to the materials in that section. However, these occasional statements may be particularly insightful to Adam-God adherents who hold doctrinal

---

[3] The reader should note that much of my analyses offer different and conflicting interpretations of Adam-God teachings. I have done this because I intend this book to be used as a resource for study, not as a compendium of "true doctrine" as accepted by the author. Further, when considering varying interpretations, one is able to understand how others may believe and is therefore able to communicate and debate with persons who believe in teachings contrary to the reader's belief. Lastly, I am of the belief that these teachings are not of a nature that they should be systematically spoon-fed to the reader. I have tried to arrange the material topically in a fashion that hopefully will help readers to learn each principle fairly systematically. However, the analyses are meant to further instigate thoughtful prayer and research, not to teach any specific beliefs about the statements themselves. The Spirit should teach – the book should facilitate the reader to know what to ask so that the Spirit can answer.

[4] There are some teachings *tangentially related* Adam-God teachings that I have not included. If, as I argue later in this volume, the plan of salvation is inseparably connected to Adam-God teachings in general, then I could not possibly include *all* related materials.

assumptions that may not be shared with each individual reader.

2

I have placed each statement chronologically within each subsection. This, of course, is a pragmatic issue - I had to place the teachings in some order - by author (subjective by illuminating authors in some order of prominence - or completely objective - if it is simply random or alphabetical), source (subjective or objective for similar reasons), pertinence (clearly subjective), or by date (quasi-objective at worst). Organizing the citations chronologically made the most sense to me - as a historian, this method allows the reader to "objectively" analyze any "evolution" in these teachings as well - no other organization seems to have a similar benefit. When I have been entirely unable to ascertain a date for a statement, I have placed this citation at the end of the pertinent month, year, or section (if I have been unable to ascertain the date for a given periodical, I have placed it at the last year that that periodical was printed to minimize its incorrect chronological placement; alternatively, if the author of the statement died before the publication was discontinued, I have placed the statement at the year of the author's death whenever that date is known). I realize that this likely places any such statement out of chronological context, but it avoids a subjective chronological placement.

3

Understanding Adam-God Teachings excludes virtually all statements by modern leaders of the LDS Church. In a nutshell, modern leaders either teach that:

~ Adam-God was never taught - Brigham Young was merely misquoted, or

~ Brigham Young was only speculating about Adam,[5] and/or

~ Brigham Young was simply mistaken.

Regardless of which approach is taken, modern leaders conclude by informing us that Adam-God teachings are deadly heresies. Because none of these propositions do anything to illuminate Adam-God teachings (which is the primary purpose of this volume as the title indicates), apart from claiming that they are manifestly false, they are not included herein. Previous authors have gone to great lengths to provide several statements from later brethren discounting, discrediting, and otherwise disparaging Adam-God teachings by denying that anyone besides enemies of the Church ever taught such doctrines in an effort to destroy the credibility of the modern brethren. I personally feel that this has done little but increase animosity between these two competing factions of Mormonism. I have included some very few representative statements from this genre

---

[5] This proposition has been coupled with the inaccurate statement that these teachings were never considered doctrine and/or were never considered binding upon the Church.

of statements to demonstrate that this is the modern LDS Church's position but I have only sparsely acknowledged these references to minimize this arena of contentious academia.[6]

4

I have italicized pertinent phrases within each topic. I realize that I could have avoided this problem by not providing italics. However, I have found that several statements are not obvious upon the first reading. In pre-publishing studies, I have found that some people read the same statement multiple times before they found the pertinent language of important statements. Therefore, I thought that this help would be more worthwhile than the bias it could engender. Further, I have tried to minimize the number of statements within any given section by selecting only the most "on point" statements so the influence of bias in this regard should be fairly minimal.

5

In the first few sections of this volume ("Adam", "Eve", "Adam & Eve"), I have made conscientious efforts to organize materials in as unbiased of a manner as possible by organizing the statements in very narrow categories. However, when I arranged some of the materials in later sections in this same fashion, I found that it made the concepts found in those respective sections more difficult to grasp. Whenever this became an issue, I did not organize the materials in as unbiased of a manner as possible for two reasons:

first, I did not want the reader to have to read multiple topics in order to piece together one basic concept and

second, after reading these first few sections, even the most discriminating, objective, reader will have to acknowledge that Adam-God teachings were abundant and well-developed. Thus, I found less need to cater to the skeptical reader in later portions of the volume and found more need to cater to those readers who are sincerely interested in learning what the early brethren had to teach on these issues.

There are approximately fifty issues and topics covered in this volume. I have generally tried to arrange the sections and topics in a fashion that allows the reader to read the most basic, fundamental materials first. However, after many attempts to organize the

---

[6] I have also chosen to do this out of respect for the modern LDS position; some early brethren felt that Adam-God teachings were a pearl of great price that needed to be retracted from general Church membership due to their unbelief - this keeps the general Church membership out of condemnation; I believe therefore that these various denials are a legitimate posture for the modern Church to take - see Mark 10:1-5 for an analogous situation and note that Jesus did not condemn Moses for his teachings that were contrary to a higher law.

material in a doctrinally systematic fashion, I found that this general arrangement of materials was not entirely consistent with this attempt to present the basic materials first and the deeper doctrines last. Therefore, I want to alert the reader that the following subsections are more advanced and ought to be read by the reader only after he/she has a firm grasp and understanding of most of the other Adam-God teachings presented in this volume:

Does the Atonement Pertain to Adam & Eve?
Adam and His Associates
The Royal Order of Saviors

While these topics are very interesting, a basic understanding of Adam-God teachings is requisite to fully grasp the concepts presented therein. The reader unacquainted with Adam-God teachings will probably find that reading the other materials in the order that they are presented in this volume will generally build line upon line and precept upon precept.

On the other hand, members of the LDS Church may find that reading the section "Titles & Offices" may be particularly helpful if any other section is somewhat confusing or if Adam-God teachings become generally perplexing to their theological world-view. The confusion with Adam-God teachings is generally due to the fact that the LDS Church began teaching that Jehovah was the pre-existent Jesus Christ in the early 1880's. Adam-God teachings are not consistent with the teaching that Jesus Christ was Jehovah in the pre-existence so these teachings can be very confusing without the information found in that section.

The second and primary purpose of *Understanding Adam-God Teachings* is to explore the implications of Adam-God teachings from a doctrinal perspective. Although this can feasibly be accomplished within the sterile confines of the primary materials provided in each section, I have included textual analysis from other Adam-God authors and from myself in the sections entitled "Analysis & Observations" that follow each major section to further expand upon our understanding of these teachings as they fell from the lips of the early brethren. The reader prone to believe that accepting or rejecting Adam-God teachings is of little salvific importance because they do not significantly modify our understanding of foundational doctrinal issues may be starkly awakened by the numerous implications entailed by Adam-God teachings. They may further be surprised to find multiple statements proclaiming the profound effects the acceptance of these teachings have made upon the lives of those who have invested the time and energy to study these teachings.

I have made extensive efforts to accumulate diverse understandings of Adam-God teachings from various fundamentalist sources (both historical and contemporary) but have largely limited the commentary that I found within this volume to previously published materials and to my own observations; I have found little expansion upon Adam-God teachings in modern times apart from a few teachings that appear to not only contradict the bulk of Mormon scriptural resources but also contradict the teachings of the early brethren as well (e.g., Adam became the Holy Ghost after the fall).

While most Adam-God teachings found within this volume are basic enough that most adherents are in agreement concerning the correct interpretation of each Adam-God topic, there are a few topics that are less clear. I have included in this volume every topic of this nature that I am aware of - whether or not I personally believe certain interpretations presented in each topic.[7] Additionally, I have cross-referenced each section that may be relevant to that topic as well. If the reader does not believe in any or all of these more controversial "grey areas," he/she is free to ignore these cross-references and topics. However, I felt compelled to cross-reference these topics for the benefit of those persons seeking a greater understanding of any given controversial topic.

Lastly, I am aware that my subtitle "A Comprehensive Resource of Adam God Materials" is somewhat misleading. There are some "available" sources that I have not thoroughly researched. For instance, I have not gone to BYU to read all available, post-1880, volumes of the Millennial Star and I have not sought out unpublished journals buried somewhere in Special Collections or in the Church Historical Archives in order to find previously unpublished Adam-God materials. Further, there are scriptures and statements where Adam-God teachings can be "read into" the text for deeper doctrinal understandings that have not been included in this volume. Frankly, the author simply did not have the time, initiative, or resources to rectify the former deficiency. The latter

---

[7] I'm confident that some readers will readily object to this assertion given the fact that I have not addressed multiple mortal probations. Unless one interprets this teaching to mean that each god or goddess will have multiple probations as an Adam or as an Eve (in addition to the sole mortal probation that we are now experiencing), I think that this issue is generally too tangential for consideration in this volume – although there are some few teachings about multiple mortal probations that are directly related to Adam-God teachings (and that expound upon Adam-God teachings), there are only a few statements that support these teachings and these few statements require interpolations and explanations that were not clearly set forth by the early brethren; as I have intended this volume to be a resource of Adam-God materials as taught by the early brethren, these few teachings are outside of the scope of the purpose of this volume as well.

deficiency is likely without any foreseeable end as it requires a subjective analysis of primary texts. I have taken over four years to compile and finish this volume and the project needed completion so I will leave these remaining endeavors to future authors - or a second edition - to complete this task.[8]

I hope that *Understanding Adam-God Teachings* may serve not only as an exhaustive reference book on Adam-God teachings but that it may serve to deepen the reader's doctrinal understanding of those teachings and that it may thereby facilitate and engender a more profound, healthy, and intimate relationship between the reader and Adam, our common Father and God.

---

[8] Additionally, in subsections where the modern LDS Church has not significantly changed the doctrines as they were taught by the early brethren, I have not included exhaustive references to support the statements found within this volume (e.g., "God as Father of Our Spirits", etc.) because 1) since these statements are not subject to controversy, there is no need to provide significant documentation "proving" that they were presented as doctrine by the early brethren and 2) since these teachings are relatively easy to understand, I thought it was a superfluous endeavor to compile further statements.

~ A Note to Members of the LDS Church

All previously published Adam-God publications have spent a significant amount of time trying to indoctrinate the reader in one way or another. That is, either the author has been a fundamentalist trying to prove that the Adam-God "doctrine" was taught by Brigham Young and that the LDS Church has lost this light and knowledge or the author has been a member of the LDS Church trying to prove that the Adam-God "theory" is either a false doctrine or an unfortunate speculative deviancy briefly put forth by President Brigham Young. While both positions have merit for different reasons, I believe that this dialogue has been largely unproductive; without having any delusions of a widespread resolution to this debate between fundamentalists and members of the LDS Church, I aspire to at least bridge the gap of understanding between these two opposing viewpoints as much as I can - in other words, we don't have to agree but at least we can acknowledge and understand one another's positions well enough to have a constructive dialogue.

In virtually every book, article, or pamphlet that has been published, the author has, in some way, misunderstood the position of the opposing party and made arguments and/or assertions that were fundamentally flawed because the *assumptions behind the arguments* have not been acceptable to the opposing party. For instance, fundamentalist authors have frequently pointed out that an unembodied spirit (Jesus) could not have eaten a meal with Jacob, created an earth out of physical (as opposed to spiritual) elements, etc. to prove that the Jehovah of the Old Testament could not have been Jesus Christ. These arguments are flawed because there is no doctrine in the modern LDS Church that would disallow these behaviors from a disembodied spirit - sure, if you think about it, you need to wonder how an unembodied spirit can eat mortal food,[9] but a member of the LDS Church can feasibly argue that there is no reason why a spirit cannot create a physical earth when the materials making up a physical earth are more base than (and therefore inferior to) elements of spirit. Similarly, members of the LDS Church try to discredit Adam-God teachings by pointing out statements from Brigham Young and others that distinguish Jehovah from Adam. As I explain in the section "Jehovah is not Adam", and unbeknownst to these LDS authors, these statements are not problematic for fundamentalists and do nothing to discredit their position.

This genre of misunderstanding has largely impeded the dialogue between fundamentalists and members of the LDS Church.[10] While I feel indebted to the scholarship put forth by both sides, I believe that the above positions have added unnecessary stumbling blocks for readers unacquainted with Adam-God teachings. That is, trying to overlook these authors' biases and flawed arguments has largely prevented the average reader from being able to decipher the teachings of the early brethren in a way that allows the reader to come to his/her own conclusions.

After reading all Mormon publications available on Adam-God teachings, I found that:

1

There was a wide discrepancy between the teachings of each publication and that many of these teachings were entirely irreconcilable;

2

None of these publications contained all available Adam-God teachings (some appear to deliberately exclude significant material);

3

As a member of the LDS Church, Adam-God teachings presented me with the difficult challenge of confronting the fact that modern LDS Church leaders were either:

~ deliberately hiding these teachings from members of the mainstream LDS Church in order to protect them from condemnation or

~ uninformed about these teachings or

---

[9] And, as shown later in this volume, there are doctrinal statements that support the fundamentalist position that an unembodied spirit cannot eat mortal food.

[10] This is not to mention that excommunications for believing and/or teaching Adam-God teachings have not exactly helped to create a healthy or constructive dialogue between the parties involved.

~ lying about these teachings.

After a thorough reading of the historical background of Adam-God teachings, I found the latter position to be manifestly unfair. However, the remaining prospects still presented a difficult challenge that was compounded by the additional confusion of the conflicting interpretations that I found in these publications - not to mention the frequently argumentative and contentious postures held by the authors.

After sorting through all of these issues, it became apparent to me that there was a significant need for a book like *Understanding Adam-God Teachings* both in mainstream LDS academia and in fundamentalist academia.

Because acceptance of Adam-God teachings as a doctrine often leads to other fundamentalist beliefs, other Adam-God publications have covered many tangential issues - issues that are not necessarily directly correlated to Adam-God (e.g., the Church is in some sort of apostasy, plural marriage is essential to salvation, one should not blindly follow a prophet, etc.). While these issues may be of interest to the reader, I have completely avoided commenting on these issues in this volume. Where I have addressed these issues by citing the words of the early brethren,[11] I have limited my commentary to how these statements can be read to substantiate or expound upon various Adam-God teachings as taught by the early brethren. I hope that preparing this volume in this way will further my purpose in presenting members of the LDS Church with a sterile environment in which to study Adam-God teachings should they desire to do so.

Of the some fifty doctrinal issues addressed in *Understanding Adam-God Teachings*, the reader may notice that a significant number of these doctrines are still taught by the LDS Church - although they are taught as doctrines distinct from Adam-God teachings (e.g., "God as Father of Christ", "Adam as Michael the Archangel", "Adam as Ancient of Days", etc.). I have addressed these topics in this volume because these teachings were taught in connection with Adam-God teachings and because they shed further insight into our eternal progression as an Adam or Eve on other earths.

Lastly and perhaps most importantly, how should you deal with the inherent stress that occurs when you learn about these teachings? Once you have read a significant portion of this volume, you will be confronted with some uncomfortable questions – do the

---

[11] The subsection entitled "Eve as a Plural Wife" necessarily implicates plural marriage; the subsection "Jehovah" tangentially refers to a few of these topics because references to Jehovah are in the context of a variety of teachings.

brethren know about this? If so, why have the brethren consistently claimed that Brigham Young was misquoted? Are these teachings reconcilable with the scriptures? If Adam-God teachings are true, are there other true teachings that have been taken away from the Church? What are those doctrines? Perhaps, you may even question your testimony as to whether or not the Church is "true".

As you confront these and similar questions, I invite you to remember the promise of Moroni and to kneel down before your Maker in solemn prayer – let the Father guide you to all truth. I would also suggest one more thing for those readers prone to feeling betrayed by their Church leaders after reading these teachings: as Jesus did *not* condemn Moses for allowing the Israelites to divorce even though Jesus *did* condemn divorce as it was allowed by Moses (Deuteronomy 24:1; Mark 10:1-5), I would suggest that we should be cautious in how we speak of the Lord's anointed – who have led or who currently lead the LDS Church – despite their various weaknesses and/or failings. At least consider this question: were the brethren inspired in reclaiming this pearl of great price from the members of the Church as Moses was inspired to reclaim the higher laws of marriage from the Israelites to keep them from being under greater condemnation? If so, what should you do with these newly found truths?

The path to accepting Adam-God teachings is difficult for members of the LDS Church, not because these teachings are false, but because tradition and teachings within the LDS Church have taught you doctrines that are not compatible with Adam-God teachings – just as Moses' law of divorce was not compatible with the teachings in Genesis (as Jesus taught in Mark 10:1-5). If you can keep this in mind and ward off any contentious feelings of criticism against the brethren, you may find your soul expanding and your breast swelling with the Spirit as it did once, perhaps long ago, as you discovered some other great truth through the witness of the Holy Ghost.

Adam-God

~ # Teachings

A Few Observations

Since its inception, Adam-God teachings have been a great source of controversy. Members of the Church in Brigham Young's day had a difficult time accepting the doctrine; apparently the same was true in the days of Joseph as well - Adam-God teachings were a source of controversy in the Nauvoo Expositor. Accordingly, the brethren addressed the concerns that members of the Church had in an effort to help them accept these teachings as a doctrine of the Church. The following quotes[12] are statements made by the early brethren that address the issues of accepting deeper doctrines, the importance of knowing who God is, and the importance of accepting Adam-God teachings generally. For a more detailed listing of comments addressing specific concerns, see "Statements of Unbelief".

Accepting Deeper Doctrines

Brigham Young   *10/9/1859*

JD 7:284

All truth is for the salvation of the children of men- for their benefit and learning - for their furtherance in the principles of divine knowledge; and divine knowledge is any matter of fact - truth; and *all truth* pertains to divinity.

---

[12] The reader may note that the statements in this subsection are not in chronological order - this is because I have tried to organize these statements in an order that teaches a continuation of principles and because chronological order is not of significant importance in this subsection.

George Q. Cannon   *1957*

Gospel Truth 1:330-31

There are differences in spirits. There are different grades of intelligences among the spirits of men. We are not all on a dead level. ... But the Lord deals with His children mercifully. He gives them intelligences according to their capacity to receive it. Therefore, wise men such as Joseph and others give the counsel that is *adapted* to the conditions and circumstances of the people though they may see that it is not exactly what ought to be. *Better to give the people something they will obey, if it is not the fullness of the law of God*; better to lead them on until their capacity is enlarged and they are prepared to receive higher principles and truths. *That is* the way God has done with His people.

There are many [things] that the leading men of this Church can see and understand that they cannot impart to the people nor ask the people to do. Why? Because they know that the people would not come up to the requirement and that therefore they would be disobedient. *Better to give them line upon line*, precept upon precept, here a little and there a little *than to give them something that they could not receive* and that they would rebel against. *That is* the main manner in which wise men inspired of the Lord deal with their fellow men.

Speaking as a First Presidency, if we could have our way, there are *many changes that we would make*; but you know how difficult it is to have people see alike upon many points.

Brigham Young   *Sunday p.m. 6/8/1873*

DN 22:308

Is it a mystery to the Christian world that Jesus is the Son of God, and still the son of man? Yes it is, it is hidden from them, and this fulfills the Scripture - `If our gospel be hid, it is hid to them that are lost,' who have no faith, and who pay no attention to the Spirit of God. These things are *called mysteries* by the people *because they know nothing about them* ... I told the people that as true as God lived, *if they would not have truth they would have error sent unto them, and they would believe it*. What is the mystery of it?

Samuel W. Richards   *Saturday 12/17/1853*

MS 15:825

Many principles have been revealed from time to time, which have proved a source of trouble to some, *not because they were untrue*, but because the Saints would indulge in fear lest those principles might be untrue, while they knew very well that their anxiety of mind could not affect the results of those principles in the least degree.

Whatever may prove to be the facts in the case it certainly would exhibit a great degree of weakness on the part of anyone to indulge in fears and anxieties about that which he has no power to control. Facts still remain facts whether kept or revealed. ... It should be borne in mind that *these wonderful mysteries, as they are supposed to be, are only mysteries because of the ignorance of men*; and when men and women are troubled in spirit over these things which come to light through the proper channel of intelligence, they only betray their weakness, ignorance, and folly.

Joseph Smith   *5/7/1843*

TPJS, 305

I could explain a hundred fold more than I ever have of the glories of the kingdom manifested to me in the vision where I permitted and were people prepared to receive them. The Lord deals with this people as a tender parent with a child, communicating light and intelligence and the knowledge of his ways *as they can bear it*.

Joseph Smith   *1/20/1844*

TPJS, 331

[T]here has been a great difficulty in getting anything into the heads of this generation. It has been like splitting hemlock knots with a corn-dodger for a wedge, and a pumpkin for a beetle. *Even the Saints are slow to understand*. I have tried for a number of years to get the minds of the Saints prepared to receive the things of God; but we frequently see some of them after suffering all they have for the work of God, will fly to pieces like glass as soon as anything comes that is *contrary to their traditions*; they cannot stand the fire at all.

Brigham Young   *4/4/1860*

Minutes of Meeting at Historian's Office

Joseph could not reveal what was revealed to him ... .

Joseph Smith   *5/25/1862*

JD 9:294

Brother Brigham, if I was to reveal to this people what the Lord has revealed to me, *there is not a man or a woman would stay with me*.

Wilford W. Woodruff   *4/9/1857*

JD 5:83-84

The fact is, there are a great many things taught in the building up of this kingdom which seem strange to us, being contrary to our traditions, and are calculated to try men. Brother Joseph ... taught a great many things which, in consequence of tradition, required prayer, faith, and a testimony from the Lord, before they could be believed by many of the Saints. His mind was opened by the visions of the Almighty, and the Lord taught him many things by vision and revelation that were never taught publicly in his days; for the people could not bear the flood of intelligence which God poured into his mind.

Brigham Young   *3/25/1855*

Journal of Samuel W. Richards 2:215
The Lord had to give but little at a time as much could not be received, and *it is our duty to use that little so as to profit by it and be prepared for more when God should be willing to impart it to us.*

Brigham Young   *4/25/1855*

MABY
If I should undertake to tell the people what I believe in my heart and what seemeth ... to me to be eternal truth, *how would they know* unless *they* had the spirit of *revelation to say to them* whether it was a truth or untruth?

Brigham Young   *8/29/1852*

JD 6:280-82
If it was necessary to write [revelations], we would write all the time. *We would rather the people, however, would live so as to have revelations for themselves*, and then do the work we are called to do: that is enough for us. Can any of you think of any revelations you have received that are not written? You can.

Orson Pratt   *1/29/1860*

DN 9:51
God placed Joseph Smith at the head of this church. God has likewise placed Brigham Young at the head of this church. ... We are commanded to give heed to their words in all things, and receive their words as from the mouth of God, in all patience and faith. When we do not do this, we get into darkness.[13]

Brigham Young   *4/7/1862*

JD 9:279
We often hear it said that the living oracles must be in the Church, in order that the Kingdom of God may be established and prosper on the earth. I will give another version of this sentiment. I say that the living oracles of God, or *the Spirit of revelation*

---

[13] See "Statements of Unbelief: Orson Pratt" below - Orson knew these things from personal experience.

must be in each and every individual, to know the plan of salvation and keep in the path that leads them to the presence of God.

Heber C. Kimball	*1957*

Life of Heber C. Kimball, 460-61

To meet the difficulties that are coming, it will be necessary for you to have a knowledge of the truth of this work *for yourselves*. The difficulties will be of such a character that the man or woman who does not possess this personal knowledge or witness will fall. If you have not got the testimony, live right and call upon the Lord and cease not till you obtain it. *If you do not you will not stand*. Remember these sayings, for many of you will live to see them fulfilled. The time will come when no man or woman will be able to endure on borrowed light. Each will have to be guided by the light within himself.

Brigham Young	*8/19/1877*

JD 19:96-97

Our motive is to make *every* man and woman to know just as much as we do; this is the plan of the gospel, and this is what I would like to do. I would like *all* the Latter Day Saints to come up to this standard, and know as much as I do, and then just as much more as they can learn, and if they can get ahead of me, all right. I can then have the privilege of following after them. If they keep up close to me, so that they will understand as I do the workings of the spirit, they will do a good deal better than they do now. But the beauty and excellency of the wisdom that god has revealed to us is to fill everybody with wisdom, bringing them up to the highest standard of knowledge and wisdom, purifying us and preparing us to enter into the highest state of glory, knowledge and power, that we may become fit associates of the gods and be prepared to dwell with them.

Knowing God

John 17:3	

And this is life eternal, that they might know thee the only true God, and Jesus Christ, whom thou hast sent.

D&C 132:24	*7/12/1843*

This is eternal lives - to know the only wise and true God, and Jesus Christ, whom he hath sent.

Brigham Young   *2/8/1857*

JD 4:215-16

It is one of the first principles of the doctrine of salvation to become acquainted with our Father and our God. The scriptures teach that this is eternal life, to "know Thee, the only true God, and Jesus Christ whom thou hast sent;" this is as much as to say that *no man can enjoy or be prepared for eternal life without that knowledge.*

Joseph Smith   *8/5/1844*

TPJS, 343, 346

If men do not comprehend the character of God, they do not comprehend themselves. ... It is the *first principle* of the Gospel to know *for a certainty* the Character of God, and to know that we may converse with him as one man converses with another, *and that he was once a man like us*; yea, that God himself, the Father of us all, dwelt on an earth, the same as Jesus Christ himself did and I will show it from the Bible.

Joseph Smith   *circa 1834*

LF

[T]hree things are necessary, *in order that any rational and intelligent being may exercise faith in God* unto life and salvation ... [This includes a] *correct idea of his character,* perfections and attributes.

Brigham Young   *4/17/1853*

JD 2:123

[E]ven the best of the Latter-day Saints have but *a faint idea* of the attributes of the Deity. Were the former and Latter-day Saints, with their Apostles, Prophets, Seers, and Revelators collected together to discuss this matter, I am led to think there would be found a great variety in their views and feelings upon this subject, without direct revelation from the Lord.

John Taylor   *3/31/1867*

JD 11:341

We believe that this gospel will redeem all men who believe in it, and that it will elevate them to a knowledge of the true god, *whom to know is life eternal.*

Adam-God Teachings

The early brethren spoke about this topic fairly regularly because of the controversy that arose with the public pronouncement of this teaching in April conference, 1852. Their responses to the saints that struggled with these teachings fall into two basic categories:
1) testimonials regarding the truthfulness of Adam-God teachings and
2) advice on how to deal with people who disbelieved these teachings.
The following statements are therefore generally arranged to reflect these two genres of responses:

Brigham Young   *4/25/1855*

MABY

It is a subject I am aware that does not appear so close to our understandings at present as we could wish it or as it will be some day, and it is one that *should not trouble us at all,* all such things will become more clear to your minds bye and bye. ... I do not tell it because that I wish it established in the minds of others; though to me this is as clear as the sun, it is as plain as my alphabet. *I understand it as I do the path to go home. I did not understand so until my mind became enlightened with the spirit and by the revelations of God; neither will you understand until our Father in Heaven reveals all things unto you.* To my mind and to my feelings those matters are all *plain* and *easy* to be understood.

Lorenzo Snow   *10/12/1897*

Brigham Young Jr. diary, Church Archives

At meeting of all the apostles except Grant and Merill, Pres. Snow let out on *Adam being our father and God. How beautiful the thought - it brot* [sic] *God nearer to us.* Bro Franklin [D. Richards] said it *made him thrill through his whole body - it was new & it was inspiring.* I followed.

Elders' Journal

This is precisely what constitutes the "fall of *Adam*" ... *It represents in every meaningful way a sacrifice on the part of a loving father for his children.*

George Q. Cannon   *Sunday p.m. 5/4/1884*

JD 25:155

My brethren and sisters, *it is a glorious truth* that has been taught to us, that we are literally the children of God, that we are his literal descendants, as Jesus was literally descended from Him, and that He is our Father as much as our earthly parent is our father, and *we can go to Him with a feeling of nearness, knowing this*, understanding it by the revelations which God has given to us.

J.F. Gibbs   *11/--/1884*

Contributor 6:76

To the intelligent Latter-day Saint [the phrase, "Our Father which art in Heaven"] *emits a world of light and comfort*. It enunciates a principle that indissolubly links the immortal past to the mortal present, and this life to the glorious and infinite future.

Franklin D. Richards   *12/18/1897*

Letter of F. D. Richards to President E. H. Nye

Dear Brother:

… *This*, like many other points of more advanced doctrine, *is too precious a pearl to be cast before swine*. But when the swine get hold of them, let us rescue them by the help of the Spirit as best we can.

Perhaps Eliza R. Snow, an adamant Adam-God adherent, had Adam-God teachings in mind when she wrote these lines to "O My Father":

I had learned to call thee Father

Through thy Spirit from on high

But until the key of knowledge

Was restored, I knew not why.

The following statements are advisory in nature; at times, they seem to reflect a frustrated priesthood leadership that could not understand why these teachings were so difficult for the saints to grasp. They also reflect a variety of leadership styles: while some chastised the saints for their unbelief, others tried to redirect the saints to study other, more simple, doctrines that would be easier for them to grasp.

Brigham Young   *4/9/1852*

JD 1:51

Now, *let all who may hear these doctrines, pause before they make light of them, or treat them with indifference, for they will prove their salvation or damnation.*[14]

---

[14] This statement is frequently used to support Adam-God teachings and I have followed this pattern; however, although it appears clear to fundamentalists who have studied Adam-God teachings that Brigham Young intended this statement to specifically refer to Adam-God doctrines, the context of the statement could allow a different reading. See "Journal of Discourses 1:50-51."

Samuel W. Richards   *Saturday 11/26/1853*

MS 15:780

The Extract from the Journal of Discourses (1:50) *may startle some of our readers*, but we would wish them to recollect that in this last dispensation God will send forth, by his servants, things *new*[15] as well as old, until man is perfected in the truth.

Elders Hall, Little, & Richards   *6/--/1854*

MS 16:483 - Elder Joseph Hall:

Relative to the principles recently revealed, we have not the least difficulty. If Adam's being our Father and God *cannot be proved by the Bible, it is all right*.

MS 16:530 - Elder James A. Little:

I believe in the principle of obedience; and *if I am told that Adam is our Father and our God, I just believe it*. Brethren, I feel well, and have felt well all the time.

MS 16:534 - Franklin D. Richards:

Concerning the item of doctrine alluded to by Elder Caffall and others, viz., that Adam is our Father and our God, I have to say *do not trouble ourselves, neither let the Saints be troubled about that matter*. The Lord has told us in a revelation which he gave through the Prophet Joseph, Jan. 19, 1841 - "I design to reveal unto my Church t*hings which have been kept hid from before the foundation of the world*, things that pertain to the dispensation of the fullness of times." (D&C 124:41) I would like to know *where you will find scriptures to prove those things, by which have never before been revealed*.

Some feel their bounded duty to prove everything which belongs to our faith from the Bible, but I do not, and *I will excuse you from all obligation to prove this from the Old Scriptures, for you cannot, if you try*. You may bring much collateral evidence from the Bible and other revelations that will dissipate objections, and serve to strengthen the position, but to directly and substantially prove it, as the world requires, and as we can the first principles, it will puzzle you to do it, and from henceforth we may expect more and more of the word of the Lord giving us instructions which are nowhere written in the Old Scriptures. If we feel ourselves, and teach the Saints or the people generally, that we are only to believe that which can be proved from the scriptures, we shall never know much of the Lord ourselves, nor be able to teach the children of men to any very considerable extent.

If as Elder Caffall remarked, there are those who are waiting at the door of the Church for this objection to be removed, tell such, the prophet and apostle *Brigham has declared it, and that is the word of the lord*. That is vastly stronger proof than Christendom can

---

[15] HC 4:209-10 & D&C 124:41

give for much that they profess to believe. Tell the Saints that *if this stone does not seem to fit into the great building of their faith just now, to roll it aside.* You can help them roll it out of their way so that *they will be but a short time till they will find a place in their building where no other stone will fit;* then it will be on hand all right, and will come into its place in the building without the sound of hammer or chisel.

Abraham B. Smoot   *6/8/1868*

Minutes of the School of the Prophets, 37-40

The doctrine preached by Pres. Young for a few years back, wherein he says that *Adam is our God* - the God we worship - that *most of the people believe this* - some believe it because the President says so - others because they can find testimony in the Book of Mormon and Book of Doctrine and Covenants. ... This is not the way to act. *We should not suffer ourselves to entertain one doubt.* We are not accountable on points of doctrines if the President makes a statement. It is not our prerogative to dispute it. He is only accountable in points of doctrine. I have heard President Young avow the truth of *Adam being our Father and God* but have never heard him argue the question at all.

Brigham Young   *5/18/1873*

JD 16:46

Where is the divine who knows the least thing about that Being who is the Father of our spirits and the author of our bodies? ... *I have had many revelations; I have seen and heard for myself, and know these things are true, and nobody on earth can disprove them.* ... What I know concerning God, concerning the earth, concerning government, *I have received from the heavens*, not alone through my natural ability, and I give God the glory and the praise.

First Presidency   *6/--/1865*

JD 11:122

With regard to the quotations and comments in the Seer as to Adam's having been formed "out of the ground," and "from the dust of the ground," & c., *it is deemed wisest to let that subject remain without further explanation at present,* for it is written that we are to receive "line upon line," according to our faith and capacities, and the circumstances attending our progress.

Brigham Young   *10/6/1870*

JD 13:263

But I will give a caution to my brethren the Elders - *never undertake to teach a thing that you do not understand.* Such things will come into your minds; but without launching out on such subjects, questions may be asked and answered, and we gain knowledge from each other. There is plenty within the scope of our own brains that, by the assistance of the Spirit of the Lord, will enable us to tell many things - more than the world or even *more than the Saints can receive.* Suppose a man should come here and tell you the very nature of our Father Adam - tell precisely how he was organized, his height, his proportions, the extent of his knowledge, tell you the agreement that was entered into, the amount of knowledge he had to forget to reduce himself to the capacity of a corruptible being! Suppose this could all be told to the congregations of the Saints, *what would they know about it? Very little.* There may be some minds which could grasp some things pertaining to it, but others could not. *The spirit of revelation can reveal these things to the people, but unless they live so as to have the revelations of the Lord Jesus Christ, they will remain a mystery,* for there is a veil before the minds of the people, and they cannot be understood. Some of these principles have been taught to the Latter-day Saints, but who can understand them?

Brigham Young	1/8/1865

JD 11:42

I would exhort my brethren to read the Scriptures, and seek earnestly for the Spirit of the Almighty to understand them; and this great subject [the nature of God], at which I have merely glanced, *will appear to them in all it simplicity and grandeur.*

First Presidency	11/--/1909

MFP 4:199-200

The Lord must reveal Himself, or remain unrevealed; and the same is true of the facts relating to the origin of Adam's race - God alone can reveal them. *Some* of these facts, however, *are already known,* and what has been made known *it is our duty to receive* and retain.

Brigham Young	10/8/1854

MABY

I wish you should understand well the position I have taken, and the nature of the remarks I have made. Profit by them, both saints and sinners. You have had things laid before you that does not belong to the world, nor to men and women, who calculate to apostatize. *They belong to the wise; to those who are serving God with all their hearts.*

Brigham H. Roberts	1903

Mormon Doctrine of Deity, 42-43

Some of the sectarian ministers are saying that we "Mormons" are ashamed of the doctrine announced by President Brigham Young to the effect that Adam will thus be God of this world. No, friends, *it is not that we are ashamed of that doctrine*. If you see any change come over our countenances when this doctrine is named, *it is surprise, astonishment, that anyone* at all capable of grasping the largeness and extent of the universe - the grandeur of existence and the possibilities in man for growth, for progress, *should be so lean of intellect*, should have such a paucity of understanding, *as to call it in question at all*. That is what our change of countenance means - not shame - for the doctrine Brigham Young taught.

Samuel W. Richards   *Saturday 12/17/1853*

MS 15:825

It has been said that Adam is the God and Father of the human family, and persons are perhaps in fear and great trouble of mind, lest they have to acknowledge him as such in some future day. For our part we would much rather acknowledge Adam to be our Father than hunt for another and take up with the devil. Whoever is acknowledged Father must have the rights and honor that belong to him. No man may ever expect to attain to more than he is willing others should enjoy. *If these things have power to disturb the pure mind, we apprehend that even greater troubles than these may arise before mankind learn all the particulars of Christ's incarnation.*

Brigham Young   *6/27/1860*

DN

And I will say, as I have said before, if guilt before my God and my brethren rests upon me in the least, it is in this one thing, that *I have revealed too much concerning God and his kingdom,* and the designs of our Father in heaven. If my skirts are stained in the least with wrong, it is because *I have been too free in telling who God is*, how he lives, the nature of his providences and designs in creating the world, in bringing the human family on the earth, his designs concerning them, etc. If I had, like Paul, said - "But if any man be ignorant, let him be ignorant,"[16] perhaps it would have been better for the people.

Brigham Young   *10:30 a.m. 10/8/1861*

Brigham Young Papers

I will give you a few words doctrine, upon which there has been much inquiry, and with regard to which considerable ignorance exists. Brother Watt will write it, but it is not my intention to have it published; therefore pay good attention, and store it up in your memories. Some years ago, I advanced a doctrine with regard to Adam being our

---

[16] 1 Corinthians 14:38

Father and God. *That will be a curse to many of the Elders of Israel, because of their folly with regard to it. They yet grovel in darkness - and will. It is one of the most glorious revelations* [concerning] the economy of heaven, yet the world hold it [in] derision. Had I revealed the doctrine of Baptism for the Dead instead of Joseph Smith, there are men around me who would have ridiculed the idea until dooms day. But they are ignorant and stupid like the dumb ass.

Francis M. Lyman   *2/15/1862*

MS 24:100

Persons sometimes say that they have enjoyed the spirit of the work as much since they were cut off as while they were in the Church. Have they enjoyed the Spirit? Yes. Why? Simply because they were wrongfully cut off. They were cut off in such a way that it did not take the Spirit of God from them. And the reason why they were cut off was because they did not come up to the particular standard of perfection of those who dealt with them, or they did not come up to their feelings.

I have heard of a man who was cut off because he would not believe that Adam was our Father and God. "Well, but was it not so?" Its being so does not change the fact that we are sinners and need salvation, and *such preaching does not help men and women to repent of their sins. ...*

As for believing that Adam was our God, I do not know but that we are gods; only, if it is so, we are very young yet. But could we ever feel that we are the children of a God who watches over us with more care and solicitude than we can bestow upon the little ones who call us fathers here on the earth, would not our desires and object be to win the continued love of such a Parent by leaving off everything wrong, while we would seek to fill up the whole aggregate of our judgments with knowledge that is pure and holy, that we might become like that Father and be prepared to dwell with him. Then it is well to think that God is our Father; and whether it be Adam or anyone else, ever struggle upwards, upwards; always keep your hearts and faces upwards, and let every struggle you make be to carry you to the harbour of rest, the haven of peace, where you may enjoy the felicity awaiting the faithful children of our God. May the Lord bless you. Amen.

President Jensen   *2/24/1880*

Minutes of the High Priests Quorum

The point in *dispute* being, was Adam our God, some taking the affirmation and some the negative of the question. *This was not right.* We ought to allow these matters to rest until our minds were better informed regarding them. *Contention leads to strife and ill feelings and eventually into apostasy.* Hence how careful we ought to be in these regards.

Wilford W. Woodruff & George Q. Cannon   *6/11/1892*

Diary of Charles Lowell Walker 2:740-41

Showed the folly of some men because they cannot look up and prove by the Bible the glorious Revelations that God has given they receive them doubtfully. Showed that God had, and would yet, reveal many glorious things that men could not prove, and Search out of the old Bible. Pres Cannon said that *it was not necessary* that we should or endorse the doctrine that some men taught that *Adam was the Father of Jesus Christ.*

Bishop Heber Bennion   *1920*

Supplement to Gospel Problems, 8-9, 13

It seems strange that people will believe that `as man now is, God once was, and that as God now is, man may be'; that `God is an exalted man' *and still repudiate the doctrine of Adam-God.* These incredulous people believe that Elohim, Jehovah and Michael (Adam) the `Father of all living,' created the world and yet cannot believe that He is the God of this world. It seems presumptuous indeed for them to ever aspire to be the God of anything, if Adam cannot be the God of the world he created and peopled. If a man is not to become the God of his own posterity what will he be the God of?

Analysis & Observations

β

It appears that Brigham Young did not expect that his public announcement of Adam-God teachings would lead to such an intense controversy that it would eventually lead Adam-God teachings to rank highly among the list of deep and "mysterious" doctrines in both Christendom and Mormonism. Undoubtedly, this was astonishing to the man who most likely would have offered a resounding "Amen" to Cannon's statement that the glorious truths in Adam-God teachings generate "a feeling of nearness" in the breast of those who learn them. Nevertheless, after immediate controversy and unbelief, the early brethren discovered and began teaching that Adam-God teachings were only meant for the worthy saints who were capable of receiving the spirit of revelation and who were capable of accurate discernment.

Extensive efforts were made to reclaim this precious pearl from the world - and later from the saints themselves. I have not given much attention to this "devolution" of

Adam-God teachings as Tholson, Christensen, and others have. A thorough reading of the material that has been compiled by these authors on this issue will show the reader that the leaders of the LDS Church took Adam-God teachings away from the general membership because most members of the Church were unable to accept these teachings as doctrine. I believe that this was done to keep members of the Church from being under condemnation for rejecting such sacred light and knowledge. President Woodruff, under great pressure to explain the growing theological discrepancies originating from this changing policy denying Adam-God teachings and originating from the new teaching that Jesus was Jehovah,[17] recognized that a satisfactory answer was not feasibly forthcoming for the saints. Said he on one occasion:

Wilford Woodruff   *4/7/1895*

CD 4

I want to say this to all Israel: *Cease troubling yourselves about who God is*; who Adam is, who Christ is, who Jehovah is. For heaven's sake, let these things alone.

Given the history behind this issue, the author is of the opinion that Franklin D. Richards' advice to Elder Nye remains the most sound advice for all persons engaged in Adam-God discussions to remember - Adam-God teachings are pearls that should not be cast before the swine.[18] This theological propaganda battle has largely been won by the modern LDS Church and despite any contrary efforts (whether fundamentalist, academic, or anti-

---

[17] Boyd Kirkland, in his ground breaking article "Elohim and Jehovah in Mormonism and the Bible", which was printed in Dialogue 19:77 #1, noted that the current position of the LDS Church regarding the status of Jehovah "*took official form in "The Father and the Son: A Doctrinal Exposition by the First Presidency and the Twelve" (1916) as the culmination of five major stages of theological development in Church history (Kirkland 1984):* 1. Joseph Smith, Mormonism's founder, originally spoke and wrote about God in terms practically indistinguishable from then-current protestant theology. He used the roles, personalities, and titles of the Father and the Son interchangeably in a manner implying that he believed in only one God who manifested himself as three persons. The Book of Mormon, revelations in the Doctrine and Covenants prior to 1835, and Smith's 1832 account of his First Vision all reflect "Trinitarian" perceptions. He did not use the title Elohim at all in this early stage and used Jehovah only rarely as the name of the "one" God. ... 5. To achieve some semblance of harmony between these widely varying ideas, as well as to quell external attacks from anti-Mormon critics at the "Adam-God" doctrine, *Mormon leaders carefully reformulated Mormon theology around the turn of the century and articulated it in 1916 (Kirkland 1984, 39-41). These adjustments remain as the current doctrine of the Church today.*" (Kirkland, 77-78); while his observation is probably accurate as to the "official" *position* of the LDS Church, the initial *efforts* to formulate this new theology began in approximately 1885. See "Jehovah is Christ" below.

[18] While the reader may find this an odd position for the author of this exhaustive volume to take, he/she may note that I have focused my distribution and sale of this volume to fundamentalists and academic Mormons and that I have prepared this volume for the use of members of the LDS Church who have already stumbled upon Adam-God teachings and who need help understanding them.

Mormon), I believe the Church will continue to be successful in this divine game of hide-and-seek. If the reader is interested in learning more about the "devolution" of Adam-God teachings, I would encourage them to read Christensen, Tholson, or Buerger. Christensen's material is less thorough than Tholson's material but it kindly treats both the LDS Church's position and Brigham Young's position. Tholson's material is the most thorough but his tone is chronically critical of the LDS Church. Buerger's material is fairly concise but it is somewhat critical of Brigham Young.

A few of the statements above explain that sometimes the prophets give the saints preparatory truths that do not always coincide with absolute truths because the saints are neither ready to understand nor to accept absolute truth. As in the case of Moses and divorce, we may therefore rest assured that inconsistent teachings do not prove that a prophet has fallen (though this could be a possibility). Rather, inconsistent teachings could mean a variety of things. Christensen explained it well when he stated that "[a]s one progresses in knowledge, many previous assumptions consistent with a former state of progression may no longer be consistent." AGM, 18. For instance, Joseph publicly taught the saints in Nauvoo that plural marriage was not acceptable before God - and yet, he had privately been living this principle for over a decade before he made these statements. Individuals who had been thusly taught undoubtedly discovered (when Joseph later introduced them to plural marriage) that some assumptions that they had made about plural marriage were no longer consistent with the new knowledge that Joseph had given them.

It is for this reason that Adam-God adherents are not overly concerned with the fact that the abundance of scriptures do not overtly proclaim Adam-God teachings - nor are they concerned when confronted with scriptures that overtly appear to contradict Adam-God teachings. Brigham Young, while not prepared to call Moses a liar for his allegorical account of Eve's creation out of Adam's rib, was perfectly comfortable with the fact that there were statements in the Bible that were patently inaccurate - he concurred in the principle of prophets offering the saints preparatory teachings. Said he: "'But Brother Brigham, would you make it appear that Moses did not tell the truth?' Not a particle more than I would that your mother did not tell the truth, when she told you that little Billy came from a hollow toad stool. I would not accuse your mother of lying, any more than I would Moses; the people in the days of Moses wanted to know things that was not for them, the same as your children do, when they want to know where their little brother came from, and he answered them according to their folly, the same as you did your children."

Christensen (AGM, 237-38) pointed out that this principle was taught by the early Christian church by citing the following statements:

Testament of Our Lord Jesus Christ, 18
_____
These teachings are only for the tried and worthy; preach other words to the churches.

Ignatius
_____
Epistle to the Trallians, chapter 5
I would like to write to you of heavenly things (or of things more full of mystery), but I fear to do so, lest I should inflict injury on you who are but babes ... you would be strangled by such things.

We read of this principle in the Book of Mormon as well:

3 Nephi 26:18
_____
And many of them saw and heard unspeakable things, which are not lawful to be written.[19]

For these (and perhaps other) reasons, Adam-God adherents are not bothered by statements contradicting Adam-God teachings made by the early brethren because they believe that any contrary statement was either made in error or was made to an audience unprepared for these higher teachings - this stance typically includes the prophet Joseph Smith's statements as well. Similarly, statements made in the scriptures that appear to contradict Adam-God teachings are not looked upon with grave concern. For this reason, I have not significantly addressed scriptural objections to Adam-God teachings throughout this volume.

_____

[19] Why were these things not lawful to be written? While we do not specifically know what teachings are being kept secret here, clearly some of the saints were worthy to hear and learn of them - while others may have been harmed by the disclosures of these teachings.

Abbreviations &
Format

AGM	Adam God Maze
DJJS	Diaries and Journals of Joseph Smith
E&MS	Evening and Morning Star
HC	History of the Church
JD	Journal of Discourses
LF	Lectures on Faith
M&A	Messenger and Advocate
MABY	Manuscript Addresses of Brigham Young
MCD	The Mormon Conception of Deity
MFP	Messages of the First Presidency
MS	Millennial Star
Papers JS	Papers of Joseph Smith
T&S	Times & Seasons
TPBY	Teachings of the Prophet Brigham Young
TPJS	Teachings of the Prophet Joseph Smith
WJS	Words of Joseph Smith

There are several non-substantive, pragmatic, format changes that have been made throughout this volume. They are as follows:

Of greatest importance for the reader to note is that throughout this volume, I have retained the original spelling and punctuation of each statement in every instance. Proof sheets returned by every independent proofreader of this text has shown that proofreaders had a difficult time getting accustomed to this format decision - and I understand that many readers prefer to read edited, and therefore more easily understood, materials - but given the chronic nature and the chronic barrage of allegations that are placed against fundamentalist authors for supposedly altering the meaning of this genre of text, I have chosen to leave the materials in their purist form possible.[20] Besides, it is charming betimes to see the various and creative ways that the pioneers spelled words.

Paragraphs have been altered in many instances because citations have been shortened and because some paragraphs were very long in the original format - in no case have I attempted or noticed a change in meaning and/or interpretation by making these changes.

In many resources that I have used, I have discovered many statements that use parenthesis to indicate additions by an editor. As an academic matter, this is improper — editor additions should be in brackets - [ ]. I have made efforts in every instance to rectify these additions either by putting in brackets or by deleting the parenthetical additions; however, because some sources are essentially unavailable to verify these markings, I have potentially left some materials in parenthesis that ought to have been placed in brackets.

All scripture references have been standardized within the statements whenever possible (e.g., a statement reading "verse 3 sec. fourteen of the Doc. & Covenants" would have been changed to D&C 14:3 for easier reading and reference. I did this because I have met many individuals who cannot readily find scriptures when they are in some format varying from the current LDS Church's format.

All publications marked with a number followed by a colon and another number (1:50) refer to the volume and page number. If these numbers are further followed by a "#" marking, this refers to the publication number. In order to make the format of this volume easily readable, I have only included a brief version of any given citation with each statement. For a more complete citation (and occasionally for explanatory notes and references - some of which make the statement more meaningful: e.g., the statement was made in the temple at a meeting of apostles, etc.), see the annotated bibliography at

---

[20] I bring to the reader's attention the fact (also noted above) that I have not independently verified the precise text in several of the journals, minutes, etc. that are very difficult to get access to. Therefore, it is possible that some of the misspellings found in this volume are perpetuated scrivener's errors made by previous authors. However, I have not taken the prerogative to make any specific assumptions that produced any textual changes in this matter when I have been unable to verify the spelling with the original source.

the end of this volume.

Lastly, and perhaps most importantly, I have not engaged in any significant debate as to whether or not any of the statements are true and/or accurate. If Wilford Woodruff states in his journal that Brigham Young said something, I have listed Brigham Young as the author of that statement. If an apostate states that Orson Pratt said something, I have listed Orson Pratt as the author of that statement. Unquestionably, academics may challenge the authenticity of some of these statements.[21] This has been a common technique to challenge Adam-God teachings throughout most of the twentieth century. Candidly, this volume ought to dispel with most challenges as to the authenticity of many of these statements because the evidence provided herein is too academically overwhelming to casually brush aside. In other words, suggesting that a given statement attributed to Heber C. Kimball is falsely attributed to him because, as they say, he never would have agreed to the Adam-God doctrinal faux-pas found within that statement is no longer academically credible when one considers the evidence in this volume documenting the broad expanse of statements supporting teachings related to Adam-God.[22]

---

[21] I personally believe that some few statements in this volume were likely poorly transcribed, understood, transmitted, or communicated.

[22] Of course, such an argument would be circular in its nature anyway — however, this type of rhetoric is largely successful within the confined walls of the modern LDS Church.

Acknowledgements

Authoring *Understanding Adam-God Teachings* was possible only because previous authors have pioneered this field by compiling many different statements on Adam-God teachings. There are so many sources available now that the author is not burdened with the necessity of forcefully arguing that Brigham Young was not misquoted and/or of arguing that he really did put forth Adam-God teachings as doctrine - though I have tangentially addressed these topics in the "Miscellaneous Controversies" section. Although many statements have been quoted by multiple Adam-God authors, I have gone to the effort to verify the vast majority of all statements that have been previously published. However, I have not verified (by finding the original source) a significant (though small minority) portion of the information found within the covers of this volume; specifically, I have not gone to various archives to verify previously published statements from personal journals and/or out of print newspapers and/or minute books. I understand that this is sloppy as an academic matter; however, given the extreme difficulty of obtaining many of these very obscure resources and given the very improbable likelihood that any substantive transmission error has occurred,[23] and given the fact that it has taken over four years of my spare time to compile the materials in this volume, and given my audience, I chose negligence in this fashion over having to make

---

[23] Although fundamentalists are notorious for their lackadaisical manner of citing sources and for their habitual ability to publish incorrect citations while managing to produce a substantively accurate and verifiable statements - largely due to the fact that until recently, most early resources have not been available for the general public to research and/or analyze - I have, perhaps naively, trusted that any author who had the ambition to go to these archives would accurately portray the information cited inasmuch as anti-fundamentalist authors are ever eager to disprove any fundamentalist author's assertions. As no such expose has been forthcoming over the last few decades and as other mainstream LDS authors have published similar and substantiating materials, I have presumed that these materials are likely substantively accurate.

these materials available at a much later date. Given that disclosure and admission, I freely take all responsibility for any errors produced and/or perpetuated herein and would welcome any corrections - this subject deserves an error free treatment so I will be happy to publish any substantive errors in this book online so that the record can be clear and available for everyone. I would also welcome any academic criticism and/or references to materials that I may have missed (email: drewbriney@hotmail.com).

Further, my analysis & observations subsections are largely the result of the comments of various authors and individuals who have shared their perspectives on these teachings.

Although I have used many resources in compiling this volume, I have relied more heavily upon the following resources:

The Adam-God Maze by Culley K. Christensen
Adam-God by Craig Tholson
The Position of Adam in Latter-day Saints Scripture and Theology by Rodney Turner
Gospel Link
http://www.spires.net (a private website with resources on multiple, obscure Mormon issues)
http://relarchive.byu.edu/19th/description.html (BYU's online, PDF, resource of 19th Century Mormon publications)

A few individuals have significantly assisted me in compiling materials for this book and in helping me to verify the accuracy of hundreds of citations that I have produced in this book. I would like to particularly thank Robert Marck Jr. for his help in compiling hundreds of statements for the "Jehovah" subsection of this volume and to Chris M. Hansen for sharing decades of his personal research with me for the sole purpose of making sure that this volume included every citation available at the time of its printing. A few other persons have generously helped me in various ways to edit this volume; however, out of respect for their privacy and out of a desire to keep their names out of publications for various personal and legal reasons, my only expressions of appreciation in this volume must remain anonymous - but my gratitude for their help is no less sincere.

Adam

$$\frac{}{\beta}$$

1

Adam as God the Father

Zebedee Coltrin   *9/21-22/1827*

UR 2:55 par. 33-38[24]

Joseph said, "Let's us kneel down here and pray." After prayer Joseph stretched himself upon his back upon a grassy spot with his arms extended like one upon the cross. He told me to lie by his side and Oliver in like manner on the other side. We did, all three of us looking heavenward. As I looked I saw the blue sky open; I beheld a throne [where] sat a man and woman. Joseph asked us if we knew who they were; we answered, "*That is Father Adam and Mother Eve.*" And their faces shown with immortal youth.

Joseph Smith   *11/8/1832*

HC 1:296; 2:428; 7:558

[After Brigham Young spoke in tongues, some members thought it was "of the devil" but Joseph] told them it was the pure *Adamic* language [or the] *language of God.*[25]

---

[24] This account was related by Joseph's mother in 1845. The first few quotes here presented are the least clear of any of the following statements. The italicized distinction is at the end of each account. The following account appears to corroborate some of these initial accounts as well:

Heber C. Kimball   *3/17/1861*

JD 9:41

This brings to mind the vision that Joseph Smith had, when he saw Adam open the gate of the Celestial city and admit the people one by one. He then saw Father Adam conduct them to the throne one by one, when they were crowned Kings and Priests of God.

Joseph Smith et al.   *5/7/1834*

Salt Lake School of the Prophets, Minutes, 69-70[26]

Once after returning from a mission, he [Zebedee Coltrin] met Bro. Joseph in Kirtland, who asked him if he did not wish to go with him to a conference at New Portage. The party consisted of Prests. Joseph Smith, Sidney Rigdon, Oliver Cowdery and myself. Next morning at New Portage, he noticed that Joseph seemed to have a far off look in his eyes, or was looking at a distance, and presently he, Joseph, stepped between Brothers Cowdery, and Coltrin and taking them by the arm, said, "lets take a walk." They went to a place where there was some beautiful grass, and grapevines and swampbeech interlaced. President Joseph Smith then said, "Let us pray." They all three prayed in turn--Joseph, Oliver and Zebedee. Bro. Joseph then said, "now brethren we will see some visions." Joseph lay down on the ground on his back and stretched out his arms and the two brethren lay on them. The heavens gradually opened, and they saw a golden throne, on a circular foundation, something like a light house, and on the throne were two aged personages, having white hair, and clothed in white garments. They were the two most beautiful and perfect specimens of mankind he ever saw. Joseph said, *They are our first parents, Adam and Eve.* Adam was a large broad shouldered man, and Eve as a woman, was as large in proportion.

President Peterson   *5/7/1834*

Journal of Abraham H. Cannon 13:89[27]

UR 2:66 par. 1-6

In a meeting held in the year 1832, on the occasion of Elder Brigham Young speaking in tongues, the Prophet being present; it was the first time that the exercise of this gift had come under his notice. The congregation was at the time in a kneeling posture. As soon as Brother Brigham had concluded his prayer, the Prophet rose to his feet and invited them to rise and be seated. Joseph then addressed them, and said; "Brethren, this tongue that we have heard is the gift of God, for He has made it known unto me, and I shall never oppose anything that comes from Him. I feel the spirit that Brother Brigham has manifested in this gift of tongues, and I wish to speak myself in the tongue that it will please the Lord to give me; He accordingly spoke in what may be called an open and fluent language; more so than was commonly heard. He occupied some minutes in the exercise of the gift. After he had concluded he said, "Brethren, this is the *language of our father Adam* while he dwelt in Eden; and the time will again come, that when the Lord brings again Zion, the Zion of Enoch, this people will then all speak the language which I have just spoken.

[26] This was recorded in records circa 1883.

Pres. Peterson told of an incident which he often heard Zebedee Coltrin relate. One day the Prophet Joseph asked him and Sidney Rigdon to accompany him into the woods to pray. When they had reached a secluded spot, Joseph laid down on his back and stretched out his arms. He told the brethren to lie one on each arm, and then shut their eyes. After they had prayed he told them to open their eyes. They did so and saw a brilliant light surrounding a pedestal which seemed to rest on the earth. They closed their eyes and again prayed. They then saw, on opening them, *the Father* seated upon a throne; they prayed again and on looking saw *the Mother* also; after praying and looking the fourth time they saw *the Savior* added to the group. He had ___ brown, rather long, wavy hair and appeared quite young.

Parley P. Pratt   *1/1/1844*

The Angel of the Prairies

On entering this room, a vast and extensive hall was opened before me, the walls of which were white, and ornamented with various figures which I did not understand. In the midst of this hall was a vast throne and white as ivory, and ascended by seventy steps, and on either side of the throne, and of the steps leading to it, there were seats rising one above another. On this throne was seated an aged, venerable looking man. His hair was white with age, and his countenance beamed with intelligence and affection indescribable as if he were the father of the kingdoms and the people over which he reigned. He was clad in robes of dazzling whiteness, while a glorious crown rested upon his brow: and a pillar of light above his head seemed to diffuse over the whole scene a brilliance of glory and grandeur indescribable. There was something in his countenance which seemed to indicate that he had passed long years of struggle and exertion in the achievement of some mighty revolution, and been a man of sorrows and acquainted with grief. But, like the evening sun after a day of clouds and tempest, he seemed to smile with the dignity of repose. In connection with this venerable personage sat two others scarcely less venerable, and clad and crowned in the same manner, on the next seat below were twelve personages, much of the same appearances and clad in the same manner, with crowns upon their heads; while the descending seats were filled with some thousands of noble and dignified personages, all enrobed in white and crowned with authority, power and majesty, as kings and presiding among the Sons of God. 'You now behold,' said the Angel of the Prairies, 'the Grand Presiding Council organized in wisdom, and holding the keys of power to bear rule over all the earth in righteousness. And of the increase and glory of their kingdoms there shall be no end.'

---

[27] This was recorded on the date 8/25/1890; Critics have suggested that President Peterson confused the individuals involved in this event. However, it is worth noting that he states that he "often heard" this account related to him; it is also worth noting that the accounts are otherwise generally consistent.

… The venerable council which you beheld enthroned in majesty and clad in robes of white, with crowns upon their heads, is the order of the Ancient of Days, before whose august presence thrones have been cast down, and tyrants have ceased to rule.

6/7/1844

Nauvoo Expositor 1:2, Resolution #2

Inasmuch as we have for years borne with the individual follies and iniquities of Joseph Smith, Hyrum Smith, and many of the official characters, and having labored with them repeatedly with all Christian love, meekness, and humility, yet to no effect, we feel as if forbearance has ceased to be a virtue and hope of reformation vain. And inasmuch as they have introduced false and damnable doctrines into the church such as; a plurality of Gods above the God of this universe; and *his liability to fall with all of His creations*; the plurality of wives; unconditional sealing up.

Brigham Young   *Friday 4/9/1852*

JD 1:50

Now hear it, O inhabitants of the earth, Jew and Gentile, Saint and sinner! When our father Adam came into the garden of Eden, he came into it with a celestial body, and brought Eve, one of his wives, with him. He helped to make and organize this world. He is Michael, the Archangel, the Ancient of Days! About whom holy men have written and spoken - *He is our father and our God, and the only God with whom we have to do.*

Brigham Young   *Friday 4/9/1852*

Journal of Wilford Woodruff

Our Father begot all the spirits that were before any tabernacle was made. When our Father came into the Garden He came with his Celestial body & brought one of his wives with him and ate of the fruit of the Garden until He could beget a Tabernacle. And *Adam is Michael God and all the God that we have anything to do* with. They ate of this fruit & formed the first Tabernacle that was formed. And when the Virgin Mary was begotten with child it was by the Father and in no other way only as we were begotten. I will tell you the truth as it is in God. The world don't know that Jesus Christ our Elder Brother was begotten by our Father in Heaven. Handle it as you please, it will either seal the damnation or salvation of man. He was begotten by the Father & not by the Holy Ghost.

Brigham Young   *Friday 4/9/1852*

Journal of Hosea Stout 2:435

Another meeting this evening. President B. Young taught that *Adam was* the father of Jesus and *the only God to us*. That he came to this world in a resurrected body, etc. More hereafter.

Heber C. Kimball   *Saturday 4/10/1852*

Journal of Wilford Woodruff

Some have said that I was very presumptuous to say that Brother Brigham was my God and Savior. Brother Joseph was his God. The one that gave Joseph the keys of the Kingdom was his God,[28] which was Peter. Jesus Christ was his God and *the God and Father of Jesus Christ was Adam*.

Brigham Young   *Friday 4/16/1852*

Journal of Samuel Holister Rogers 1:179

Conference commenced on the 6 and continued until the 11, it was held in the new tabernacle, adjourned until the 6 of next October We had the best Conference that I ever attended during the time of the Conference President Brigham Young said that our spirits ware begotten before that Adam came to the Earth and that Adam helped to make the Earth, that he had a Celestial body when he came to the Earth and that he brought his wife or one of his wives with him, and that Eave was also a Celestial being, that they eat of the fruit of the ground until they begat children from the Earth, he said that *Adam was the only God that we would have*, and that Christ was not begotten of the Holy Ghost, but of the Father Adam, that Christ, was our elder brother.

Orson Pratt   *9/30/1852*

Thomas Evans Jeremy Sr Journal

Brother Orson Pratt preached on the subject of the resurrection of the dead, that they are to come out of their graves, but said that he did not know how the power of God would operate to raise them up from their graves. Also he did not believe that Father Adam had flesh and bones, when he came to the garden of Eden, but he and his wife Eve were spirits, and that God formed their bodies out of the dust of the ground, and the (sic) became a living souls. He also said that he believed that Jesus Christ and Adam are brothers in the Spirit, and that *Adam is not the God* that he is praying unto.[29]

---

[28] See "Titles & Offices: God & god" for an explanation of this statement.

[29] Throughout this volume, I have included occasional statements of *unbelief* in various subsections. I have done this primarily because these statements serve to substantiate the position that a given doctrine *was* taught - there would have been no statements opposing a doctrine if it was never taught. These statements generally do not directly help us to *understand* any given doctrine but they do help us to understand the dynamics of responses found in contemporary audiences who heard these teachings in person.

Samuel W. Richards   *1853*

MS 15:iii (index)

Adam, our Father and our God 769

Do.[30] the Father and God of the Human Family 801

Samuel W. Richards   *Saturday 11/26/1853*

MS 15:769 #48

ADAM, OUR FATHER AND GOD[31]

Samuel W. Richards ·   *Saturday 12/10/1853*

MS 15:801-04

ADAM, THE FATHER AND GOD OF THE HUMAN FAMILY

The above sentiment appeared in Star No. 48, a little to the surprise of some of its readers; and while the sentiment may have appeared blasphemous to the ignorant, it has no doubt given rise to some serious reflections with the more candid and comprehensive mind. A few reasonable and scriptural ideas upon this subject may be profitable at the present time. Then *Adam is really God!* And why not? If there are Lords many and *Gods many*, as the scriptures inform us, *why not our Father Adam be one of them?* ...

With these considerations before us, we can begin to see how it is that we are under obligations to our father *Adam, as to a God.* ...

Then why may not *Adam be a God*, as well as any of his sons, inasmuch as he has performed the work to which the Great Eloheim appointed him? ... This is the hope of all Saints who have a just conception of the future; and why should we not be willing for father Adam to inherit all things, as well as for ourselves? He is the first, the Father of all the human family, and his glory will be above all, for *he will be God over all*, necessarily, standing as he will through all eternity at the head of those who are the redeemed of his great family.

...

It is upon this foundation that the throne of *Michael is established as* Father, Patriarch, *God*; and it is for all his children who come into this world, to learn and fully understand the eternity of that relationship.

...

While the God of unnumbered worlds is acknowledged to be his God and Father,

---

[30] "Do." stands for "ditto".

[31] The article that follows under this heading is a reprint of JD 1:50-51; see "Important Accounts" for the complete article and commentary.

Adam still maintains his exalted position at the head of all those who are saved from among the whole family of man; and *he will be God over all those who are made Gods from among men ... .* As the great Elohim is supreme and Almighty over all His children and kingdoms, *so is Adam as great a ruler, or God, in his sphere*, over his children, and the kingdom which they possess. The earth and all things upon it were created for Adam, and it was given to him of his Father to have dominion over it.

...

Then shall the nations know that [*the Ancient of Days*] *is* their Judge, their Lawgiver, and *their God*, and upon his decree hangs the destiny of the assembled dead.

Samuel W. Richards　　　　　　　　　　　　　*Saturday 12/17/1853*
MS 15:824

It has been said that *Adam is the God and Father of the human family*, and persons are perhaps in fear and great trouble of mind, lest they have to acknowledge him as such in some future day. For our part we would much rather acknowledge Adam to be our Father than hunt for another and take up with the devil.

Brigham Young　　　　　　　　　　　　　　　*2/19/1854*
MABY

Who was it that spoke from the heavens and said "This is my beloved son hear ye him?" Was it God the Father? It was. ... Who did beget [Jesus]? His Father, and his father is our God, and the Father of our spirits, and he is the framer of the body, *the God and Father of our Lord Jesus Christ. Who is he? He is Father Adam*; Michael; the Ancient of Days.

Brigham Young　　　　　　　　　　　　　　　*2/19/1854*
Journal of Wilford Woodruff

He [Brigham Young] said that *our God was Father Adam.* He was the Father of the Savior Jesus Christ - *Our God was no more or less than Adam*, Michael the Archangel.

Elders Cafall, Hall, Little, & Richards　　　　　　　*6/--/1854*
MS 16:482 - Elder Thomas Cafall:

They (the members of the district) are lacking faith on one principle - the last "cat that was let out of the bag." Polygamy has been got over pretty well; that cloud has vanished away, but they are troubled about *Adam being our Father and God.* There is a very intelligent person investigating our principles, and who has been a great help to the Saints; he has all the works, and can get along with everything else but the last "cat," and as soon as he can see that clearly, he will become a "Mormon." I instructed him to write to Liverpool upon it.

MS 16:483 - Elder Joseph Hall:

Relative to the principles recently revealed, we have not the least difficulty. If *Adam's being our Father and God* cannot be proved by the Bible, it is all right.

MS 16:530 - Elder James A. Little:

I believe in the principle of obedience; and if I am told that *Adam is our Father and our God*, I just believe it. Brethren, I feel well, and have felt well all the time.

MS 16:534 - F. D. Richards:

Concerning the item of doctrine alluded to by Elder Caffall and others, viz., that *Adam is our Father and our God*, I have to say do not trouble ourselves, neither let the Saints be troubled about that matter.

Missionaries   *6/--/1854*

MS 16:629

Beloved President ... It has fallen to your lot to preside over the British Saints at a time and under circumstances unparalleled in the history of the work in this country. The introduction of the Law of Celestial Marriage, which, in its operations, will revolutionize all our political, religious, and domestic arrangements; and the announcement of the position which *Adam, our great progenitor, occupies among the Gods*; have marked your Presidency as a special epoch in the history of the British Mission.

Brigham Young   *9/17/1854*

Journal of Wilford Woodruff

Some of his (Orson Pratt's) doctrines as contained in the Seer were being discussed. Brother Pratt also thought that Adam was made of the dust of the earth. Could not believe that *Adam was our God* or the Father of Jesus Christ. President Young said that He came from another world & made this. Brought Eve with him, partook of the fruits of the earth, begat children & they were earthly & had mortal bodies & if we were faithful, we should become Gods as He was.

Brigham Young   *10/6/1854*

Journal of Joseph Lee Robinson, 102-03

Attended conference. A very interesting conference; for at this meeting President Brigham Young said thus: That Adam and Eve were the names of the first man and woman of every earth that was ever organized. And that Adam and Eve were the natural Father and Mother of every spirit that comes to this planet or that receives tabernacles on this planet. Consequently we are brothers and sisters. And that *Adam was God our Eternal Father.*

Brigham Young	Sunday 10/8/1854

John Pulsipher Papers, 37

[W]hen this work was made - *our God who is Adam* came & commenced the peopling of it ... There are Lords many & Gods many But *the God that we have to account to, is the father of our Spirits - Adam.*

Brigham Young	Sunday 10/8/1854

MABY

Father Adam, and Mother Eve had the children of the human family prepared to come here and take bodies; and when they come to take bodies, they enter into the bodies prepared for them, and that body gets an exaltation with the spirit, when they are prepared to be crowned in *Father's Kingdom.* *"What, into Adam's Kingdom?"* Yes. ... *I* tell you, when you see your *Father in the Heavens, you will see Adam*; when you see your Mother that bore your spirit, you will see Mother Eve. ... What will become of the world then? It will be baptized with fire. It has been baptized with water, and it will then be cleansed by fire, and become like a sea of glass, and be made Celestial; and Jesus Christ our Elder Brother will take the whole of the Earth, with all the Saints and go with them to *the Father, even to Adam.*

Brigham Young	Sunday 10/8/1854

John Pulsipher Papers, 35-37

So we had a grandfather & great-great-great-great-great grandfather So far back there is no beginning - They always Existed on some world - & when this work was made - our God who is *Adam* came & commenced the peopling of it - Tho *he is God* & had lived & died & been reserected on some other plannet - & obtained his exaltation & begat the Spirits of children enough people this world he came down & brot some of the animal & vegetable productions of some other world so that they might grow & increase here - He by eating the mortal fruits of the Earth, it caused & produced mortal children or commenced the increase of men on the Earth which is the bodies for the Spirits to live in There never was a time when Worlds were not created - The work of creation was always in Progress - An Adam & Eve is necesary for every world The oldest Son, if faithful, is the Saviour of the family - There are Lords many & Gods many But *the God that we have to account to, is the father of our Spirits - Adam.*

Eliza R. Snow	1/9/1855

MS 17:320

Father Adam, our God,

let all Israel extol,
And Jesus, our Brother,
who died for us all.

Franklin D. Richards   *3/31/1855*

MS 17:194-96

The Mosaic account of the creation states that, after the earth had been prepared, 'there was not a man to till the ground.' This was not the only, nor perhaps the greatest, deficiency. There was no one to commence and carry out the order of the higher spheres. There was no one to partake of mortality, and propagate the race of the Gods in a descending scale, that their spiritual children might become beings of tabernacle, and receive all knowledge in a school of experience. It is evident that for this great purpose Adam and Eve were placed upon the earth, from the fact, that the first and most prominent command given them was to increase and multiply.

…

While there is nothing to refute, the whole tenor of revelation substantiates, the supposition, that Adam has continued to bear rule over the earth, and control the destinies of his never ending posterity. From the time he received his commission in the Garden of Eden, he has been laboring diligently to fulfill the instructions there given him by the Lord God concerning his dominions, and to bring them under subjection to his will. This will be fully accomplished when every knee shall bow, and every tongue confess that *he is the God of the whole earth*. Then will the words of the Prophet Brigham, *when speaking of Adam*, be fully realized - '*He is our Father and our God, and the only God with whom we have to do.*'

Having now observed how *Adam*, the first man, *became God*, we inquire why may not millions of his children receive the same Godlike knowledge and power? The Apostles, Prophets, and Seers, who have lived on the earth since the days of Adam, have been a succession of intelligences, who by doing the will of the Father receive of His glory, and become the heirs of His increasing dominions.

…

[Brigham Young] declared that Jesus Christ is the actual spirit and mortal son of Michael *Adam God*; that Michael *Adam is the supreme god* and father of the spirits of our mortal world.

Brigham Young   *4/25/1855*

MABY

When we come to that great and wise and glorious being that the children of Israel were afraid of whose countenance shone so that they could not look upon him. I say when we get to him whom they could not look upon, to that man, that is I conclude he was a man for it says that he had hands and you know men have hands. And it says that he put his hands out before Moses in the cleft of the rock until his glory passed by and would not suffer Moses to see his face but his parts only. Seeing then that he had parts I conclude that he was a man. When we can see that very character and talk and live with him in our tabernacles, if we are so fortunate as to get there into his society, then we can say that to us *there is but one living and true God*, and he is the father of our Lord Jesus Christ and of our spirits. And when we get back to him and learn that *he is actually our father*, we shall not feel any anxiety to call upon anybody else for the blessings we are in need of. It is a subject I am aware that does not appear so close to our understandings at present as we could wish it or as it will be some day, and *it is one that should not trouble us at all*, all such things will become more clear to your minds bye and bye. I tell you this as my belief about that personage who is called *the Ancient of Days*, the Prince and so on …

F. D. Richards	12/15/1855

MS 17:785-86

Not only do the Old and New Testament, and other ancient and modern revelations through the Holy Priesthood assert the fact but mankind of every grade, condition, and religion, whether Christian, Jew, Mohamedan, or Pagan, all believe in leading personages or influences which are the sources of good and evil. One of these is *God the Father, Michael or Adam*, from whose loins the earth is peopled, and who is now laboring for the redemption of his children. The great captain of evil is Satan, formerly Lucifer, but now a fallen "Son of the Morning" who with his followers are diligently laboring to destroy the works of God by reducing them to a like condition with themselves.

Samuel W. Richards	3/11/1856

History of Samuel W. Richards, 15
Orson Pratt does not understand how *Adam could be God*.

Heber C. Kimball	6/29/1856

JD 4:1

I have learned by experience that there is but one God that pertains to this people, and *He is the God* that pertains to this earth - *the first man*.[32] That first man sent his own Son to redeem the world, to redeem his brethren; his life was taken, his blood shed, that

---

[32] See TPJS, 167; HC 4:207; D&C 84:16; Moses 1:34; Abraham 1:3; HCK Journal 10/28/1854.

our sins might be remitted.

John Jacques   *1856*

Sacred Hymns #306
WE BELIEVE IN OUR GOD

We believe in our God, the great Prince of his race,
The Archangel, Michael, the Ancient of Days,
Our own Father Adam, earth's Lord is his plane,
Who'll counsel and fight for his children again.

We believe in his Son Jesus Christ, who in love
For his brothers and sisters, came down from above;
To die to redeem them from death, and to teach
To mortals and spirits the Gospel we preach.

Brigham Young   *2/8/1857*

JD 4:217-19

Whether *Adam is the personage that we should consider our heavenly Father*, or not, is considerable of a mystery to a good many. I do not care for one moment how that is; it is no matter whether we are to consider Him our God, or whether His Father, or His Grandfather, for in either case we are of one species - of one family - and Jesus Christ is also of our species.

Brigham Young   *Wednesday p.m. 10/7/1857*

JD 5:331-32

Some have grumbled because *I believe our God to be so near to us as Father Adam*. There are many who know that doctrine to be true. Where was Michael in the creation of this earth? Did he have a mission to the earth? He did. Where was he? In the Grand Council, and performed the mission assigned him there. Now if it should happen that we have to pay tribute to Father Adam what a humiliating circumstance it would be! Just wait till you pass Joseph Smith; and after Joseph lets you pass him, you will find Peter; and after you pass the Apostles and many of the Prophets, you will find Abraham, and he will say, 'I have the keys, and except you do thus and so, you cannot pass;' and after awhile you come to Jesus; and when you at length meet Father Adam, how strange it will appear to your present notions. If we can pass Joseph and have him say, 'Here; you have been faithful, good boys' I hold the keys of this dispensation; I will let you pass.' Then we shall be very glad to see the white locks of Father Adam.

Wilford W. Woodruff   *3/24/1858*

Wilford W. Woodruff Journal

Orson Pratt promises not to oppose Brigham Young's doctrine that Adam is our God.

Orson Pratt & Brigham Young   *4/4/1860*

Minutes of Meeting at Historian's Office

I would like to enumerate items, firstly - preached & publish, that Adam is the fa[ther] of our spirits, & father of Spirit & father of our bodies - When I read the Rev given to Joseph I read directly the opposite - Lord spake to Adam, which Man eventually became Adam's (3 blank lines)

B.Y.: Your statements tonight, You come out to night & place them as charges, & have as many against me as I have you. One thing I have thought that I might still have omitted. It was Joseph's doctrine that *Adam was God* &c When in Luke Johnson's at O. Hydes the power came upon us, or shock that alarmed the neighborhood. God comes to earth & eats & partakes of fruit. Joseph could not reveal what was revealed to him, & if Joseph had it revealed, he was not told to reveal it. The Spirit is sent when the mother feels earth, God put it into his mouth, & when God, to translate he had the power. Not a contradictory thing in what I have said.

Orson Hyde & Orson Pratt   *4/5/1860*

Minutes of the Meeting of the Council of the Twelve

O. Hyde:

Who is our Heavenly Father. I would as soon it was Father Adam, or any other good and lawful being. I shall see him some time, if I do right. What do I know about Adam, in the Councils of the Great God before he came here, or his privileges. I don't know. ...

O. Pratt:

[I]n regard to *Adam being our Father and our God*, I have not published it, although I frankly say, I have no confidence in it, although advanced by bro. Kimball in the stand, and afterwards approved by bro. Brigham. ...

George Q. Cannon   *9/4/1860*

Journal of Wilford Woodruff

Brother Cannon said there was a learned Doctor that wanted to be baptized. ... He (the doctor) is satisfied that the doctrine of the plurality of God and that *Adam is our Father* is a true doctrine revealed from God to Joseph & Brigham. For this same doctrine is taught in some of the old Jewish records which have never been in print and I know Joseph Smith nor Brigham Young have had access to, and the Lord has revealed this doctrine unto them or they could not have taught it. President Young said if all that God had revealed was in fine print it would more than fill this room but very little is written or printed which the Lord has revealed.

Brigham Young   *Sunday 2/3/1861*

A Mormon Chronicle - The Diaries of John D. Lee 1:293
Evening I attended Prayer meeting & instruct the Saints on the points of Doctrine referred to by the true Latter-day Saints Herald & their Bombarding Pres. B. Young for saying that *Adam is all the God* that we have to do with & those that know no better, it is quite a stumbling Block & all Enemies to the cause.

Brigham Young   *10:30 a.m. 10/8/1861*

Brigham Young Papers
Some years ago, I advanced a doctrine with regard to *Adam being our Father and God*. That will be a curse to many of the Elders of Israel, because of their folly with regard to it.

W. W. Phelps   *1/20/1862*

Letter to President Brigham Young
To end the whole matter, we must be heard by the Gods; fearing: and, according to the commandments, watch, - for this sustained *Adam our Father, who is the Almighty* before mentioned. When Israel was in the Wilderness, they kept the word of wisdom, as died like Achan for stealing, god and garments. My voice is Virtue and Victory. Amen!

Francis M. Lyman   *2/15/1862*

MS 24:99-100
I have heard of a man who was cut off because he would not believe that *Adam was our Father and God*. ... As for believing that *Adam was our God*, I do not know but that we are gods ... Then it is well to think that God is our Father; and whether *it be Adam* or anyone else, ever struggle upwards, upwards; always keep your hearts and faces upwards ...

Heber C. Kimball   *4/30/1862*

Heber C. Kimball, Memorandum
The Lord told me that *Adam* was my father and that He *was the God and father* of all the inhabitants of this earth.

Brigham Young   *11/30/1862*

MABY

[E]ach person who we crown in the celestial kingdom of God will be a father of fathers, a king of kings, a lord of lords, a *god of gods* ... Each person will reign over his posterity. *Adam*, Michael, the Ancient of Days, will sit as the judge of the quick and dead, for he is the father of all living, and Eve is the mother of all living, pertaining to the human family, and *he is* their king, their Lord, *their God*, taking and holding his position in the grand unbroken chain of endless increase, and eternal progression.

Brigham Young   *1/8/1865*

JD 11:41-42

No mortal man has ever seen God in His glory at any time and lived. We may have seen the Lord and angels many times, and did not know it. I will be satisfied with seeing and associating with His children whom I now behold, for there is not a son or daughter of *Adam* and Eve before me today but what is the offspring of that God we worship. *He is our Heavenly Father; He is also our God*, and the Maker and upholder of all things in heaven and on earth. ...

One of the prophets describes *the Father of us all*, saying, "I beheld till the thrones were cast down, and the *Ancient of days* did sit, whose garment was white as snow, and the hair of his head like the pure wool; his throne was like the fiery flame," etc. The prophet further says, "thousand thousands ministered unto him, and ten thousand times ten thousand stood before him," etc. Again "and, behold, one like the Son of Man came with the clouds of heaven and came to the Ancient of days, and they brought him near before him." Now, *who is the Ancient of days?* You may answer this question at your pleasure, I have already told the people. But *the Savior would answer* the question as to the appearance of the Father of us all, *by saying*, "Look at me, for *I am the very express image of my Father.*"

W. W. Phelps   *Monday 10 a.m. 10/9/1865*

General Conference Report, "The Spirit"

O may the Saints be perfect
As *God our Father* was,
When he *got back to Eden*,
By her celestial laws.

W. W. Phelps   *5/6/1867*

Letter from W. W. Phelps
Pres. Young. ...

"And it shall come to pass, that I the Lord God will send one mighty and strong, holding the sceptre of power in his hand, clothed with light for a covering; whose mouth shall utter words, eternal words, while his laurels shall be a fountain of truth: - to set in order the house of God, and to arrange by lot the inheritance of the saints, etc. etc. while that man who was called of God, and appointed that put forth his hand to steady the Ark of God, shall fall by the shaft of death" - etc. now this revelation was sent to me in Zion, and has reference to the time when *Adam our father and God*, comes at the beginning of our Eternal Lot of inheritance, - according as our names are found in the Law of the Lord, while the fools that received the priesthood, like the fool that took his "one Talent" and hid it; - or reached out to steady the ark, will find themselves where the rich man did - in hell, with plenty of fire - but no water. Love begets lives eternal; our grace begets glory, but sin seeks secession, where goats and skunks can enjoy the lower room fog of a more dismal prison, than the nether room of Noah's Ark. Now should I be wrong in my belief as to these quotations: - please let me have your views, for I am for God, light and life as his "steward"

yours etc.
/s/ W. W. Phelps

Brigham Young	*12/16/1867*

Wilford Woodruff Journal

At meeting of School of the Prophets: President Young said Adam was Michael the Archangel, & he was the Father of Jesus Christ & was our God & that Joseph taught this principle.

Wilford W. Woodruff	*1/24/1868*

The School of the Prophets

I feel thankful for the privilege of speaking a few words to this school. I wish to refer to the first doctrine preached that *Adam was our Father & God* in the revelation called the olive leaf it says that "the devil gathered together the hosts of hell and Michael the ark angel gathered together the hosts of heaven and he overcame the devil & his angels & this is the battle of *the great God*" who is this Michael the ark angel it is Adam who was Michael in the creation of the world.

Elders McDonald & Bywater	*6/8/1868*

Minutes of the School of the Prophets, 37-42

The doctrine preached by Pres. Young for a few years back, wherein he says that *Adam is our God* - the God we worship - that most of the people believe this - some believe it because the President says so - others because they can find testimony in the Book of Mormon and Book of Doctrine and Covenants. ... I have heard President Young avow the truth of *Adam being our Father and God* but have never heard him argue the question at all.

A. F. McDonald:

I thought I would speak briefly in relation to *Adam being our God*. Since the year 1852 when the President first spoke on this subject, I have frequently endeavored to reconcile what I have read with regard to this matter. I believe what the President says on the subject although it comes in contact with all our tradition. I have not any doubt in my mind but that *Adam is our God*. Who his God and Father may be, I have no knowledge. President Kimball spoke on this question recently and very plainly illustrated the character and relationship of our Father and God.

George G. Bywater:

I am not disposed to question the discrepancies on this question of doctrine; if we live faithful all will become clear to us. We cannot become united only as we get united in understanding. When I first heard the doctrine of *Adam being our Father and God*, I was favorably impressed - enjoyed, and hailed it as a new revelation. It appeared reasonable to me, as the Father of our spirits that he should introduce us here. And what we do not see is only evidence that we have not the light necessary.

George Q. Cannon   *10/15/1870*

Meeting of the School of the Prophets

[George Q. Cannon] fully endorsed the doctrine that father *Adam was our God* and Father - or as He in many places is called, Michael the great prince - the Arch Angel, Ancient of Days, & c. It was not only wisdom, but perfectly consistent, that Adam & Eve should partake of the forbidden fruit and start the work of increase of their species. The above doctrine had been revealed to him, so that he knew it was true.

Daniel H. Wells et al.   *10/15/1870*

Salt Lake School of the Prophets Minute Book (as cited in Buerger, 63)

Daniel Wells of the First Presidency asked his colleagues whether they endorsed the "doctrine pertaining to Adam being our Father & our God." He personally "bore a powerful testimony to the truth of the doctrine, remarking that if ever he had received a testimony of any doctrine in this church he had of the truth of this. The Endowments plainly teach it and the Bible & other revelations are full of it." Others who "approved or endorsed" the doctrine at the meeting were Henry Grow, D. B. Huntington, John Lyon, George B. Wallace, and Joseph F. Smith, the latter stating that "the enunciation of that doctrine gave him great joy."

Joseph F. Smith   *10/15/1870*

Journal of Joseph F. Smith, Church Archives

School of the prophets - opening prayer by bro. W. Woodruff, who spoke a short time on the Subject of Adam being Michael, the arch-Angel & c referred to D&C p. 79 & Dan. 7 ch. See also D&C p. 106 sec. 50, p. 200. Bro. Cannon made a few remarks on the Same Subject. bro [sic] Henry said he felt like shouting "Glory Hallelujah." ... Prest. Young spoke on the subject of *Adam and God*, "whom to know is life eternal" - who knows him? It is certainly important to know. He wanted the brethren to meditate on the subject, pray about it and keep it to themselves.

Orson Hyde   *Wednesday 1/25/1871*

Jans Christian Anderson Weibye Daybooks

I attended meeting, Orson Hyde preached to us, and he told us that what we heard before that *Adam is our God*, we had a splendid good meeting. At Manti, Jan 25th Orson Hyde preached to us here in Manti, that, *Adam is our God* for this planet (Earth).

Brigham Young   *Sunday p.m. 6/18/1873*

DN 22:308

I frequently think, in my meditations, how glad we should be to instruct the world with regard to the things of God, if they would hear, and receive our teachings in good and honest hearts and profit by them. ... How pleased we would be to place these things before the people if they would receive them! How much unbelief exists in the minds of the Latter-day Saints in regard to one particular doctrine which I revealed to them, and which God revealed to me - namely that *Adam is our father and God*.

T. B. H. Stenhouse [an apostate]   *1873*

The Rocky Mountain Saints, 92, 492

Orson [Pratt]'s submission [to the twelve] was painful to his friends, but the thoughtful hoped for the growth and development of his soul outside the iron cast of infallible priesthood. From the hour of that trial he was silently accounted an "Apostate"... . He bore it all in silence, and returned to Utah determined to stand by his convictions of truth against the *Adam deity*. ...

Orson Pratt, for presuming to teach a *deity contrary to Brigham's Adam*, was for years upon the point of being severed from the Church; at last, ten years ago, he was tried for rebellion. ...

[T]he mass of the Mormon people do not believe the doctrine of the Adam deity.

Brigham Young   *5/14/1876*

Journal History

Is there in the heaven of heavens a leader? Yes, and we cannot do without one and that being the case, whoever [t]his is may be called God. Joseph said that *Adam was our Father and God*.

The Lecture at the Veil   *Tuesday 2/7/1877*

Journal of L. John Nuttall

Adam was an immortal being when he came. On this earth he had lived on an earth similar to ours he had received the Priesthood and the Keys thereof. and had been faithful in all things and gained his resurrection and his exaltation and was crowned with glory immortality and eternal lives and *was numbered with the Gods* for such he became through his faithfulness.

Byron Allred   *3/1/1877*

Jans Christian Anderson Weibye Daybooks

Byron Allred preaches at Manti on *Adam as God*, with the following remarks in part: Adam was buried by God (God his Father) and was only dead like a twinkling of an eye, and his God exalted him immediately. Mary was sealed to Adam, and was his wife when she had Jesus. Mary will be the Queen to people another world; Mary was the second wife to Adam; and unless we have two wives, we can never be Gods. Adam will worship his God and *we will worship Adam*, and our children will worship us.

Edward Tullidge   *3/--/1877*

Women of Mormondom, 179, 191

"*Adam is our Father and God. He is the God of the earth*." So says Brigham Young. Adam is the great archangel of this creation. He is Michael. He is the Ancient of Days. He is the father of our elder brother, Jesus Christ - the father of him who shall also come as Messiah to reign. He is the father of the spirits as well as the tabernacles of the sons and daughters of man. Adam! ...

Brightest among these spirits, and nearest in the circle to *our Father* and Mother *in heaven* (*the Father being Adam*), were Seth, Enoch, Noah and Abraham, Moses, David, and Jesus Christ - indeed that glorious cohort of men and women, whose lives have left immortal records in the world's history. ... These are the sons and daughters of *Adam - the Ancient of Days - the Father and God of the whole human family*. These are the sons and daughters of Michael, who is Adam, the father of the spirits of all our race. These are the sons and daughters of Eve, the Mother of a world.

Edward Tullidge   *3/--/1877*

Women of Mormondom, 193-94

The oracle of this last grand truth of women's divinity and of her eternal Mother as the partner with the Father in the creation of worlds, is none other [than] the Mormon Church. It was revealed in the glorious theology of Joseph and established by Brigham in the vast patriarchal system which he has made firm as the foundations of the earth, by proclaiming *Adam as our Father and God*. The Father is first in name and order, but the Mother is with him - these twain, one from the beginning.

Edward Tullidge   *3/--/1877*

Women of Mormondom, 200

The Mormons exalt the grand parents of our race. Not even is the name of Christ more sacred to them than the names of Adam and Eve. It was to them the poetess and high priestess addressed her hymn of invocation; and Brigham's proclamation that *Adam is our Father and God* is like a hallelujah chorus to their everlasting names. The very earth shall yet take it up; all the sons and daughters of Adam and Eve shall yet shout it for joy, to the ends of the earth, in every tongue!

Eliza R. Snow   *1877*

The Ultimatum of Human Life

Adam, your God, like you on earth, has been
Subject to sorrow in a world of sin:
Through long gradation he arose to be
Cloth'd with the Godhead's might and majesty.
And what to him in his probative sphere,
Whether a Bishop, Deacon, Priest, or Seer?
Whate'er his offices and callings were,
He magnified them with assiduous care:
By his obedience he obtain'd the place
Of God and Father of this human race.

...

Life's ultimatum, unto those that live
As saints of God, and all my pow'rs receive;
Is still the onward, upward course to tread -
To stand as Adam and as Eve, the head
Of an inheritance, a new-form'd earth,

And to their spirit race, give mortal birth -
Give them experience in a world like this;

Then lead them forth to everlasting bliss,
Crown'd with salvation and eternal joy
Where full perfection dwells, without alloy.

Shortened Lecture at the Veil *between 1877-1894*

He [*Adam*] had been true and faith in all things and gained his resurretin and exaltation.
He was crowned ~~in which~~ with glory, immortality and eternal lives and was *numbered
with the Gods* - for such he became through his faithfulness.

L. John Nuttall *3/6/1879*

L. John Nuttall Journal, 254
Attended fast day Meeting [sic]. several [sic] spoke and the question as to *Adam being our
Father & God* was presented. I explained this matter as I got it from Prest B [sic] Young
and as I understand it - this question has been on the minds of several of the brethren
since Bro. Wandel Mace spoke on it about a Month [sic] ago and gave a wrong
impression [sic] I spoke to correct him & set the people right - which correction he
accepted.

Court: Lake County, Ohio *2/23/1880*

The Reorganized Church of Jesus Christ of Latter Day Saints v. Lucien Williams,
Joseph Smith, Sarah F. Videon, Mark H. Forscutt, the Church in Utah of which John
Taylor is President and commonly known as the Mormon Church, and John Taylor,
President of said Utah Church
The following are the findings of the Court in which the late suit of the Reorganized
Church for the quieting the title to the Kirtland Temple, was tried. ...
That the church in Utah, the Defendant of which John Taylor is President, has
materially and largely departed from the faith, doctrines, laws, ordinances and usages of
said original Church of Jesus Christ of Latter Day Saints, and has incorporated into its
system of faith the doctrines of Celestial Marriage and a plurality of wives, and the
doctrine of Adam-God worship, contrary to the laws and constitution of said original
Church.

President Jensen *2/24/1880*

Minutes of the High Priests Quorum
Pres. Jensen referred to the condition of some of the High Priests in the Malad Ward

who were contending one with another concerning some point of doctrine, which they did not understand. The point in dispute being, was *Adam our God*, some taking the affirmation and some the negative of the question.

Scott Anderson   *9/22/1884*

Letter to Pres. John Taylor

I joined your Church on the 20th of May 1879 and during the first 2 years of my membership I faithfully adhered to it and would have given my life to defend it, during all this time I never heard of *Adam being God*, never heard of Blood Atonement, never heard of polygamy being required of all men before they could attain to highest glory. Never dreamed that Brigham Young or any one else coolly threw the Bible overboard and preached whatever they pleased which I was bound to accept as the revelations of God. ...

What did I find? I found that God, the God of the Bible is not even worshiped by the Church over which you preside, *the God you worship is Adam*. Brigham Young teaches [sic] his words, "When our Father *Adam* came into the Garden of Eden, he came into it with a celestial body and brought Eve one of his wives with him. *He is our Father and our God* and the only God with whom we have to do." At first I could not bring myself to believe that this doctrine was accepted by the Church, but on careful enquiry found to my horror and astonishment that it was really so. It is true a great many know nothing about it and are simply in ignorance. Those who do know accept it as far more to be relied on than any portion of the Bible, for say they the Bible has been translated over and over again and may be wrong but this is the direct teaching of a Great Prophet. I reject this as abominable and horrible idolatry and give it as one reason why I cannot remain in your Church. ...

As I have shown *Adam is made God* but you do not give him much power or rather leave him much for you do teach that he has given you the power to wield, that however matters little you hold it and he has parted with it. that is my point you teach that. If a faithful son of Adam's is called behind the veil and has no priesthood God (Adam) cannot give him any. He must wait until he gets it from the earth where you have all the power. If he has no wife or wives (and you teach that he must have at least three or he cannot have the highest glory) *God (Adam)* is utterly unable to help him You have the keys and he must wait your leisure and pleasure.

Brigham Young (as quoted by Scott Anderson)   *9/22/1884*

Letter to Pres. John Taylor

One morning about three or four, a vision of the pre-existence, and the future was shown me. It was all so clear. My parents were my brother and sister. They were simply a medium in helping *God (which is Adam)* in bringing his children from the spirit to the mortal stage. This is necessary that we might have the opportunity to being celestial beings like the Father. If I could so conduct myself in this stage of action, to be worthy of the celestial kingdom with eternal increase, then and only *then, would I gain an inheritance of my own to be as a Father Adam, and my wife, a mother Eve.*

George Q. Cannon   *4/7/1889*

MS 51:278

We believe that *we are the literal offspring of Deity*. We have descended from the great Being who formed this earth, and from Him we have inherited the glorious aspirations to be like unto Him. ... We believe in a God of revelation, who will give more and more light to us til we can become like Him. We worship the Being who has revealed Himself to us. It was necessary at the outset of this work to have a revelation from Him. There were many erroneous ideas about God, and the first revelation to Joseph Smith was the appearance of the Father and the Son. I have heard that there are some among us who say that both are one person. This is a fallacy. There are two personages, the Father and the Son. *God is the Being who walked in the Garden of Eden,* and who talked with the Prophets. This revelation came to us in certainty.

George Q. Cannon   *6/23/1889*

Journal of Abraham H. Cannon

He (George Q.) believes that Jesus Christ is Jehovah, and that *Adam is His Father and our God*: that under certain unknown conditions the benefits of the Savior's atonement extend to our entire solar system. ... He asked me what I understood concerning Mary conceiving the Savior; and as I found no answer, he asked what was to prevent Father Adam from visiting and overshadowing the mother of Jesus. Then said I: "he must have been a resurrected Being." "Yes," said he, "and though Christ is said to have been the first fruits of them that slept, yet the Savior said he did nothing but what He had seen His Father do, for He had power to lay down His life and take it up again. Adam, though made of dust, was made, as President Young said, of the dust of another planet than this." I was very much instructed by the conversation and this days services.

11/8/1890; 5/22/1890

Manuscript History of St. George Stake

Myron Abbott, counselor to Bishop Edward Bunker, Jr., stated that for a number of years, questions on church teachings have been agitated in Bunkerville Ward. Bishop Bunker had stated he did not believe *Adam was our God*, and Bishop Bunker had expressed his opinion that some teachings in the Temples were wrong, notably part of the lecture at the veil. ...As a result of the investigation the following was passed as the action of the Council: It is the sense of this Council that it is an error to teach that Adam was not an immortal or resurrected being, when he came to this earth, also, that we pray to *Adam as our God*; and it is wrong to teach that *Adam is one of the Godhead.*

5/26/1892

Journal of Abraham H. Cannon 16:119

At two o'clock I was at my Quorum meeting where were present all the Presidency and myself, as also Bro. Lyman; Geo. Gibbs, clerk. Bro. Jos. F. Smith was mouth in prayer. Thereafter some conversation followed as to whether *Adam is our God* or not. There are some in the Church who do not accept of the statement of Pres. Young that such is the case, but to me it seems reasonable to think that Adam has at least much to do with our present condition, and will control greatly our future destiny.

Lorenzo Snow   *10/12/1897*

Brigham Young Jr. diary

At meeting of all the apostles except Grant and Merill, Pres. Snow led out on *Adam being our father and God*. How beautiful the thought - it brot [sic] God nearer to us. Bro Franklin [D. Richards] said it made him thrill through his whole body - it was new & it was inspiring. I followed.

Franklin D. Richards   *Thursday 12/16/1897*

Journal of Franklin D. Richards

At 11 at Council with WW GQC &JFS - LS, FDR, BY, J.H.S., G.T., HJG, AH Lund. ... Letter & Article by E. H. Nye was read & highly approved but no action as to the dealing with *Adam our F. & God* subject.

Brigham Young, Jr.   *Thursday 12/16/1897*

Brigham Young, Jr. Journal

Adam is our father and God and no use to discuss it with Josephites or any one else. Gave in my report on Bluff, that city will be maintained for the present.

George Q. Cannon   *11/28/1898*

Proceedings of the First Sunday School Convention

Many questions come up from theological classes - questions that are, to say the least, somewhat abstruse, and concerning which there is no written revelation; questions, too, that are not pertinent at all to the work of the schools. I was stopped yesterday afternoon by a young man, who wanted to know whether *Adam* was the father of our Lord and Savior - *whether he was the being we worshiped*, etc. ... Concerning the doctrine in regard to Adam and the Savior, the Prophet Brigham taught some things concerning that; but the First Presidency and the Twelve do not think it wise to advocate these matters.

A. T. Schreader, ed. [anti-Mormon]   *circa 1899*

Zion - Lucifer's Lantern 4: 65

If I can get any intelligent idea of the after life of mormons by the study of there inane sermons it is something like this: There are two resurrections one of the spirit, the other of the flesh. After the second resurrection the spirit and the body are united and transplanted to some place in the universe where they gather up enough raw planetary material out of which to "organize a world."

To this world the resurrected man now [sic] himself and by virtue of the "sealing power" of the Mormon priesthood all the women who have been "sealed" to him for eternity are attracted or transplanted to this same planet. Here they set up housekeeping as Adam did in the Garden of Eden, and they will live eternal lives unless some walking or talking snake should put up a jot on them as it did on Eve.

To this world of his own creation the man will be the God, even as *Adam in Mormon theology is the God* of this world. He is the King and his wives queens. Their kingdom will consist of their own "eternal progeny." Hence polygamy is essential because the extent and glory of every man's kingdom in the hereafter must depend on the number of wives sealed to him for eternity.

Edward Bunker   *2/9/1902*

President Joseph F Smith

Dear Bro.

One of our recently returned missionary from the North Western States is advicating [sic] the Doctorn [sic] that *Adam is the very eternal Father in the Godhead* and the Father of Jesus Christ and that Pres Kelch so taught the Elders in that mission. I say the Doctorn is Faulse and while every Person enjoying the spirit of the Lord may know of a Doctorn whether it is true or faulse; but that they have no right (Except the President of the Church) to advance any Doctorn not clearly set forth and defined in the written Law, and in doing so they stand on dangerous ground, and until we are able to live up to the reveled Law in the spirit thereof, can we hope to enjoy suficient of the spirit of the

Lord to understand fully the plan of life and salvation. As a Bp my position cared if not where in am I in error. Your answer through the meidim of the Juvenil instructor or other wise will be greatly apreasiated by your Brothr in the Gospel.

Edw Bunker Jr

B. H. Roberts   *1903*

The Mormon Doctrine of Deity, 11, 42-43

Dr. Paden ... After calling attention to the material view of God as set forth in these teachings, the speaker said that he thought he could see a tendency towards a more spiritual idea of God among the younger and more enlightened members of the dominant church, and noticed this in the writings of Dr. Talmage especially. Referring to *the Adam-God idea*, the speaker said that he had not investigated it much, but thought that the "Mormon" Church was ashamed of such an idea. He placed special stress on the idea that when men attempted to give God a human form they fashioned him after their own weaknesses and frailties. ...

I take it that we may classify under three heads the complaints here made against us with reference to the doctrine of Deity.

First, we believe that God is a being with a body in form like man's; that he possesses body, parts and passions; that in a word, God is an exalted, perfected man.

Second, we believe in a plurality of Gods.

Third, we believe that somewhere and some time in the ages to come, through development, through enlargement, through purification until perfection is attained, man at last, may become like God - a God.[33]

I think these three complaints may be said to cover the whole ground of what our reverend critics regard as our error in doctrine on the subject of Deity. ...

Some of the sectarian ministers are saying that we "Mormons" are ashamed of the doctrine announced by President Brigham Young to the effect that *Adam will thus be God of this world.* No, friends, it is not that we are ashamed of that doctrine. If you see any change come over our countenances when this doctrine is named, it is surprise, astonishment, that anyone at all capable of grasping the largeness and extent of the universe - the grandeur of existence and the possibilities in man for growth, for progress, should be so lean of intellect, should have such a paucity of understanding, as to call it in question at all. That is what our change of countenance means - not shame -

---

[33] Note that none of these deny Adam-God teachings and that they suggest that these three issues are really what Adam-God teachings are all about. It is not unreasonable therefore to suggest that when Joseph taught these principles to the saints, they understood that he was in fact promoting Adam-God teachings. More on this will be discussed later in this volume.

for the doctrine Brigham Young taught.

Orson F. Whitney   *1904*

Elias, an Epic of the Ages, 18, 76, 77

"Father!" - the voice like music fell,
Clear as the murmuring flow
Of mountain streamlet, trickling down
From heights of virgin snow -
"Father," it said, "since One must die
Thy children to redeem,
Whilst Earth - as yet unformed and void -
With pulsing life shall teem;

"And thou, great Michael, foremost fall[34]
That mortal man may be,
And chosen Savior yet must send,
Lo, here am I, send me![35]
I ask - I seek no recompense,
Save that which then were mine;
Mine be the willing sacrifice,
The endless glory - Thine!"
...
One are the human twain, as sheath and sword--
Woman and man, the lady and the lord;
Each pair the Eve and Adam of some world,
Perchance unborn, into space unhurled.
...
Chosen, omniscient, children of the Sun,
Offspring of Adam, Michael, Ancient One,
Who comes anon his fiery throne to rear,

---

[34] Gospel Themes, 19-20: In 1914, Orson F. Whitney changed lines 5-9 as follows:
"Father," it said, "Since one must die,
Thy children to redeem,
From spheres all formless now and void,
Where pulsing life shall teem:

"And mighty Michael foremost fall.
[35] Isaiah 6:8; 2 Nephi 16:8; Moses 4:1; Abraham 3:27

His council summoning from far and near.
Ten thousand times ten thousand bow the knee,
And "Father" hail him, "King," eternally.

Brigham H. Roberts   *circa 1905*
Defense of the Faith and the Saints 2:268
In fact, the Mormon Church teaches that God the Father has a material body of flesh
and bone's; that Adam is the God of the human race; that this Adam-God was physically
begotten by another God; that the Gods were once as we are now; that there is a great
multiplicity of Gods …

W. W. Phelps   *1912*
Sacred Hymns, 327-28 #283

Come to me; here are *Adam and Eve* at the head
Of a multitude quickened and raised from the dead;
Here's the knowledge that was, or that is, or will be,
In the gen'ral assembly of worlds. Come to me.

Come to me; here are mysteries man hath not seen,
Here's our *Father in heaven, and Mother, the Queen,*
Here are worlds that have been, and the worlds yet to be,
Here's eternity endless; amend. Come to me.

Bishop Heber Bennion   *1920*
Supplement to Gospel Problems, 8-9
The Mosaic account of the creation states that, after the earth had been prepared,
`there was not a man to till the ground.' This was not the only, nor perhaps the
greatest, deficiency. There was no one to commence and carry out the order of the
higher spheres. There was no one to partake of mortality, and propagate the race of the
Gods in a descending scale, that their spiritual children might become beings of
tabernacle, and receive all knowledge in a school of experience. It is evident that for
this great purpose Adam and Eve were placed upon the earth, from the fact, that the
first and most prominent command given them was to increase and multiply.
After Adam and Eve had partaken of the seeds of mortality, it appears from the
Scriptures that the Gods held a council on the subject. We read in Gen. 3:22: `And the
Lord God said, Behold, the man has become as one of us, to know good and evil.'
From this we learn that Adam was not only in form like unto the Gods, as previously

stated, but that this knowledge of good and evil was that which would exalt him among the Gods; and then that his resemblance to the Gods might be complete, the Lord God bestowed the right to exercise full power and dominion over the earth, and all its creations. 'And God said unto them, Be fruitful, and multiply, and replenish the earth, and subdue it: and have dominion over the fish of the sea, and over the fowl of the air; and over every living thing that moveth upon the earth.' (Gen. 1:28.) If the Lord God has ever withdrawn from Father Adam the authority here bestowed upon him, He has not seen fit to make it known to the world.

While there is nothing to refute, the whole tenor of revelation substantiates, the supposition, that *Adam* has continued to bear rule over the earth, and control the destinies of his never ending posterity. From the time he received his commission in the Garden of Eden, he has been laboring diligently to fulfill the instructions there given him by the Lord God concerning his dominions, and to bring them under subjection to his will. This will be fully accomplished when every knee shall bow, and every tongue confess that *he is the God of the whole earth*. Then will the words of the Prophet Brigham, when speaking of Adam, be fully realized - '*He is our Father and our God, and the only God with whom we have to do.*'

Having now observed how Adam, the first man, became God, we inquire why may not millions of his children receive the same Godlike knowledge and power? The Apostles, Prophets, and Seers, who have lived on the earth since the days of Adam, have been a succession of intelligences, who by doing the will of the Father receive of His glory, and become the heirs of His increasing dominions. ...

It seems strange that people will believe that 'as man now is, God once was, and that as God now is, man may be;' that 'God is an exalted man' and still repudiate the *Doctrine of Adam God*. ... It seems presumptuous indeed for them to ever aspire to be the God of anything, if Adam cannot be the God of the world He created and peopled. If a man is not to become the God of His own posterity, what will he be the God of? .... *The whole superstructure for a plurality of the Gods is based upon this doctrine of Adam God, and must stand or fall together.*

Bishop Heber Bennion   *1920*

Supplement to Gospel Problems, 8-9, 13

It seems strange that people will believe that 'as man now is, God once was, and that as God now is, man may be'; that 'God is an exalted man' and still repudiate the doctrine of *Adam-God*. These incredulous people believe that Elohim, Jehovah and Michael (Adam) the 'Father of all living,' created the world and yet cannot believe that He is the God of this world. It seems presumptuous indeed for them to ever aspire to be the God of anything, if Adam cannot be the God of the world he created and peopled. If a man is not to become the God of his own posterity what will he be the God of? Evidently, if God the Father of Jesus Christ was once a man like ourselves, he had a father as we have, a God to pray to, and that God in turn, was once a man also, and so on ad infinitum, without beginning or end. As Brigham Young says, 'there never was a time when men were not passing through this ordeal in preparation to become Gods.' Joseph Smith says, 'Wherever was there a father without first being a son?' Jehovah means son, and is used interchangeably as the Son and a son.

In the dedicatory prayer of the Kirtland Temple the Prophet Joseph repeatedly applies the name of Jehovah to the Father whom he is addressing, as any one may see by careful perusal of the prayer as recorded in the Doctrine and Covenants, Sec. 109. Elohim may signify the Father or Grandfather, or Great Grandfather - God or the Council of the Gods, and Jehovah may be applied to any of them in the capacity or relationship of a son, as they all are, for 'where was there ever a father without first being a son?' (Joseph Smith in Church History, 6:476.) Adam is in line with his progenitors, the Gods, and by the genealogical record cannot be deposed from his position as the God of this world under the council and direction of the Gods above him, 'intelligences one above another without end.' (D&C 78) The whole superstructure for a plurality of the Gods is based upon this doctrine of *Adam-God*, and must stand or fall together. ...

T[he unbelieving gentiles] mocked at Brigham Young, *Adam-God*, and we seek to molify and pacify them by telling them that is not the doctrine of the Church, but only the doctrine of Brigham Young. But we are making matters worse, for next we will have to explain that it was only an idea of Joseph Smith, and the Prophet Daniel, and of Jesus Christ, for Jesus gave this revelation to Joseph Smith. 'Adam-ondi-Ahman, because, said he, it is the place where Adam shall come to visit his people, or the Ancient of Days shall sit, as spoken of by Daniel, the prophet.' - D&C 116.

Now let us turn to Daniel, and see what he says about the *Adam-God doctrine*. 'I beheld till the thrones were cast down, and the Ancient of Days did sit, whose garments were white as snow, and the hair of his head like the pure wool; his throne was like the fiery flame, and his wheels as burning fire. A fiery stream issued and came forth from before him; thousands ministered unto him, and ten thousand times ten thousand stood before him; and the judgment was set, and the books were opened.' - Daniel 7:9, 10. The above revelation of Joseph Smith, together with the prophecy of Daniel seems to corroborate Brigham Young's doctrine of *Adam-God* - beyond question.

J. Arthur Horne, Patriarch   *5/28/1963*

C. Jess Gorewsbeck's Elder's Journal 1:291

Elder Horne and I chatted again tonight about the Gospel and the *Adam-God Doctrine*, as we have done many times before. Brother Horne, who grew up in Salt Lake City and was the son of Richard Horne and grandson of Joseph Horne said, in reference to the *Adam-God Doctrine*, that when he first went through the Temple [Salt Lake] for his Endowment in 1902 before going on his mission he was surprised to hear the teachings during the Temple ceremony [in the Sermon before the veil] that, `Adam was our God' and that "he came here with Eve, one of his wives'. Also, it was taught that 'Eve bore our spirits.'

Merle H. Graffam   *Fall 1982*

Dialogue 15:4-5 #3

I found one further link which no one to my knowledge has previously explored in the "Grammar and Alphabet of the Egyptian Language" attributed by many to Joseph Smith, Jr. The document consists of a series of lists of glyphs (not really hieroglyphs) which were purportedly the working sheets Joseph Smith used in his translation of the papyrus found on mummies in his possession.

The glyphs appear in the left column, followed by lines of explanation to the right, supposedly translations of the strange markings. If one checks the list it will be found that one glyph appears to be a kind of checkmark stroke written backwards. In the several lists the explanatory note appears similar but with more information as the lists develop.

For this glyph the notes give the following information:

(glyph represented) = Phah-eh:

the first man-Adam, first father

(glyph represented) =Ah lish:

the first being clothed with supreme glory (supreme power)

(glyph represented) =Ah lish:

the first being - supreme intelligence; supreme power; supreme glory - supreme justice; supreme mercy without beginning of life or end of life; comprehending all things, seeing all things - the invisible and eternal godhead.

All of these notes occur after the same glyph represented in each list. It can be seen that *the glyph representing Adam also represents the eternal godhead and the first being, supreme intelligence*. It must be said, also, however that another glyph also represents "Adam or the first man, or first king."

This document needs, however, to be further studied in light of the question of whether Joseph and Brigham taught the same doctrine (however secretly) about Adam being God. Photocopies of the "Egyptian Grammar" are, of course, obtainable at some Salt Lake City bookstores.

Analysis & Observations

β

At first blush, it may appear that since this first section only addresses a very simple and concise doctrinal concept (viz., Adam is God the Father), there could only be a trivial amount of commentary worthy of placement here. If commentary were relegated only to a textual analysis, this would quite possibly be true. However, beyond that textual analysis, little could be further from that initial first blush impression.

Learning this basic doctrinal concept is merely the picayune beginnings of understanding this controversial teaching. A belief that Adam is our God leads us to understand that our Heavenly Father is both our spiritual and physical father, which belief is inclined to engender a feeling of familial intimacy with our God that is unparalleled by any existing or historical theological dogma. New light bursts upon us, the cycle of creation begins to unfold, humanity's divine potential opens to the envisioning soul, familial ties and genealogies begin to unfurl with cosmic consequences, and our hearts soften as we, in humility, must recognize the sacrifice of our heavenly parents - and not the Father only, for mother Eve gave up her comforts and chose suffering and sacrifice so that we might have the opportunity to progress. As these and many other doctrinal concepts slowly emerge from other teachings, dogmas, philosophies and precepts of men and the mysterious haze obscuring God's true identity begins to dissipate, dozens of theological questions begin to follow.

Indeed, upon acceptance of Adam-God teachings, all previous theological concepts require significant review. Consideration of only some highly related theological issues is what gave rise to this volume and will undoubtedly continue to inspire other authors to further plow this fallow field of theology. In sum, while the above statements may be deconstructed into on short sentence: "Adam is God," the repercussions of that sentence are not only of vast religious import - they are also of considerable academic and theological significance as well. And thus begins our journey into our understanding of Adam-God teachings …

2 Adam as Father of Our Spirits

See also
God as Father of Our Bodies
Adam Presides Over Our Spirits & has the Keys
Procreation: Mortal & Spiritual Offspring
Jehovah is the Father of Our Spirits

Joseph Smith   *Monday 10/5/1840*

TPJS, 167

Commencing with *Adam*, who was the first man, who is spoken of in Daniel as being the "Ancient of Days," or in other words, the first and oldest of all, the great, grand progenitor of whom it is said in another place he is Michael, because he was the first and *father of all*, *not only by progeny*, but the first to hold the spiritual blessings, to whom was made known the plan of ordinances for the salvation of his posterity unto the end, and to whom Christ was first revealed, and through whom Christ has been revealed from heaven, and will continue to be revealed from henceforth.

Brigham Young   *4/9/1852*

Journal of Wilford Woodruff

Our Father begot all the spirits that were before any tabernacle was made. *When our Father came into the Garden* He came with his Celestial body & brought one of his wives with him and ate of the fruit of the Garden until He could beget a Tabernacle. And Adam is Michael God and all the God that we have anything to do with. They ate of this fruit & formed the first Tabernacle that was formed.

Brigham Young   *8/28/1852*

JD 6:274-75

After men have got their exaltations and their crowns - have become Gods, even the sons of God - are made Kings of kings and Lords of lords, they have the power then of propagating their species in spirit; and that is the first of their operations with regard to organizing a world. Power is then given to them to organize the elements, and then commence the organization of tabernacles. How can they do it? Have they to go to that earth? Yes, and *Adam will have to go there*, and *he cannot do without Eve*; he must have Eve to commence the work of generation, and they will go into the garden, and continue to eat and drink of the fruits of the corporeal world, until this grosser matter is diffused sufficiently through their celestial bodies to enable them, according to the established laws, *to produce mortal tabernacles for their spiritual children*. This is a key for you. The faithful will become Gods, even the sons of God; but this does not overthrow the idea that we have a father.

Brigham Young   *2/19/1854*

TPBY 3:252

Who did beget [Jesus]? His Father, and his Father is our God, and *the Father of our spirits*, and He is the framer of the body. The God and Father of our Lord Jesus Christ - *Who is He? He is Father Adam* - Michael - the Ancient of Days.

Brigham Young   *10/6/1854*

Diary, Joseph Lee Robinson, 102-03

Attended conference. A very interesting conference; for at this meeting President Brigham Young said thus: That Adam and Eve were the names of the first man and woman of every earth that was ever organized. And that *Adam and Eve were the natural Father and Mother of every spirit that comes to this planet* or that receives tabernacles on this planet. Consequently we are brothers and sisters. And that Adam was God our Eternal Father.

Brigham Young   *Friday 10/6/1854*

Journal of the Southern Indian Mission - Diary of Thomas D. Brown, 87- 89

[T]he *Father of our Spirits* is the Father of Jesus Christ: He is the Father of Jesus Christ, Spirit & Body and he *is the beginner of the bodies of all men*. ... *Adam & Eve had children in the spirit* - and their children married - brother & sister - then the bodies followed.

Brigham Young   *Sunday 10/8/1854*

John Pulsipher Papers, 37

[W]hen this work was made - our God who is Adam came & commenced the peopling of it - Tho he is God & had lived & died & been reserected on some other plannet - &

obtained his exaltation & *begat the Spirits of children enough people this world* he came down & brot some of the animal & vegetable productions of some other world so that they might grow & increase here - He by eating the mortal fruits of the Earth, it caused & produced mortal children or commenced the increase of men on the Earth which is the bodies for the Spirits to live in ... There are Lords many & Gods many But the God that we have to account to, is the father of our Spirits - Adam.

Brigham Young   *Sunday 10/8/1854*

MABY

I tell you more, *Adam is the father of our spirits* ... [O]ur spirits and *the spirits of all the heavenly family were begotten by Adam*, and born of Eve.

Brigham Young   *3/31/1855*

MS 17:195-96

[Brigham Young] declared that Jesus Christ is the actual spirit and mortal son of Michael Adam God; that Michael *Adam is* the supreme god and *father of the spirits* of our mortal world.

Brigham Young   *4/25/1855*

MABY

We begin with t*he father of* our Lord Jesus Christ, and of o*ur spirits - who is he?* Do you know anything about him? Can you find out who he is? ... If we can get to him, *the Ancient of Days* whose hair is like wool, a man of age, a man of experience, and can learn of him to understand, I am that I am, we shall then hear him say, *I am your father* and leader, I will be your front and your rearward ... When we can see that very character and talk and live with him in our tabernacles, if we are so fortunate as to get there into his society, then we can say that to us there is but one living and true God, and *he is the father of* our Lord Jesus Christ and of *our spirits.* And when we get back to him and learn that he is actually our father, we shall not feel any anxiety to call upon anybody else for the blessings we are in need of. It is a subject I am aware that does not appear so close to our understandings at present as we could wish it or as it will be some day, and it is one that should not trouble us at all, all such things will become more clear to your minds bye and bye.

Brigham Young   *2/8/1857*

JD 4:217-18

Things were first created spiritually; *the Father actually begat the spirits*, and they were brought forth and lived with Him. *Then He commenced the work of creating earthly tabernacles,* precisely as He had been created in this flesh himself, *by partaking of the course material* that was organized and composed this earth, *until His system was charged with it,* consequently the tabernacles of His children were organized from the course materials of this earth.

Brigham Young	*10/9/1859*

JD 7:290
Adam and Eve are the parents of all pertaining to the flesh, and I would not say that they are not also the parents of *our spirits.*

Orson Pratt	*7 p.m. 4/4/1860*

Minutes of Meeting at Historian's Office, Great SLC
I would like to enumerate items, firstly - preached & published, that *Adam is the fa[ther] of our spirits*, & father of Spirit & father of our bodies - When I read the Rev given to Joseph I read directly the opposite - Lord spake to Adam, which [sic] Man eventually became Adam's (3 blank lines)

Orson Pratt	*10 a.m. 4/5/1860*

Minutes of the Meeting of the Council of the Twelve
I have heard brother Brigham say that *Adam is the Father of our Spirits*, and he came here with his resurrected body, to fall for his own children; and I said to him, it leads to an endless number of falls, which leads to sorrow and death.

George G. Bywater	*6/8/1868*

Minutes of the School of the Prophets, 40-42
I am not disposed to question the discrepancies on this question of doctrine; if we live faithful all will become clear to us. We cannot become united only as we get united in understanding. When I first heard the doctrine of *Adam* being our Father and God, I was favorably impressed - enjoyed, and hailed it as a new revelation. *It appeared reasonable to me, as the Father of our spirits that he should introduce us here.* And what we do not see is only evidence that we have not the light necessary.

Brigham Young	*12/11/1869*

Journal History, 131, School of the Prophets
Some may think what I have said concerning Adam strange, but the period will come when the people will be willing to adopt Joseph Smith as their prophet, Seer, and

Revelator and God! but not *the Father of their spirits, for that was our Father Adam.*

Brigham Young *12/11/1869*

Wilford Woodruff Journal

Some have thought it strange what I have said concerning Adam. But the period will come when this people, if faithful, will be willing to adopt Joseph Smith as their Prophet, Seer, Revelator, and God, but not *the Father of their spirits, for that was our Father Adam.*

Gilbert Belnap *1870*

Autobiography of Gilbert Belnap, 23

When contrasting the present conditions of the inhabitants of the earth with their primeval state in the Garden of Eden, the period *when the Father of our spirits condescended that through the partaking of the fruits of the earth* that man might be … I am caused to mourn.

Brigham Young *Sunday p.m. 6/18/1873*

DN 22:308

My brother said that God is as we are. He did not mean those words to be literally understood. He meant simply, that in our organization we have all the properties in embryo in our bodies that our Father has in his, and that literally, morally, socially, *by the spirit and by the flesh we are his children.* Do you think that God, who holds the eternities in his hands and can do all things at his pleasure, is not capable of sending forth his own children, and forming this flesh for his own offspring? Where is the mystery in this? We say that Father Adam came here and helped to make the earth. Who is he? He is Michael, a great prince, and it was said to him by Elohim: Go ye and make an earth." What is the great mystery about it? He came and formed the earth. … Adam found it in a state of chaos, unorganized and incomplete. … Adam came here and got it up in a shape that would suit him to commence business. Father Adam came here, and then they brought his wife. "Well," says one, "Why was Adam called *Adam?*" He was the first man on the earth, and its framer and maker. He with the help of his brethren, brought it into existence. Then he said," *I want my children who are in the spirit world to come and live here.* I once dwelt upon an earth something like this, in a mortal state, I was faithful, I received my crown and exaltation. I have the privilege of extending my work, and to its increase there will be no end. *I want my children that were born to me in the spirit world* to come here and take tabernacles of flesh, that their spirits may have a house, a tabernacle or a dwelling place as mine has, and where is the mystery?

The Lecture at the Veil   *Tuesday 2/7/1877*

Journal of L. John Nuttall

Adam was an immortal being when he came. On this earth he had lived on an earth similar to ours he had received the Priesthood and the Keys thereof. and had been faithful in all things and gained his resurrection and his exaltation and was crowned with glory immortality and eternal lives and *was numbered with the Gods* for such he became through his faithfulness. and had *begotten all the spirit* that was to come to this earth. and *Eve our common Mother who is the mother of all living bore those spirits* in the celestial world. And when this earth was organized by Elohim. Jehovah & Michael who is Adam our common Father. Adam & Eve had the privilege to continue the work of Progression. consequently came to this earth and commenced the great work of forming tabernacles for those spirits to dwell in.

Shortened Lecture at the Veil   *between 1877-1894*

[*Adam*] *had begotten all the spirits* that was to come to/this earth, and *Eve*, our common mother - who is the mother of *all* living - *bore our spirits* in the celestial world. And when this *earth was organized by* Elohim, Jehovah and *Michael - who is Adam* our common father - Adam and Eve had the privilege to continue the work of progression. They consequently came to this earth and commenced the great work of forming tabrnacles for those spirits to dwell in.

Edward Tullidge   *3/--/1877*

Women of Mormondom, 179-80, 191

"*Adam* is our Father and God. ... He *is the father of the spirits* as well as the tabernacles of the sons and daughters of man. Adam! ...
These were *father* and mother *of a world of spirits* who had been born to them in heaven.
...
These are the sons and daughters of Adam - the Ancient of Days - the Father and God of the whole human family. These are the sons and daughters of Michael, who is *Adam, the father of the spirits of all our race.* These are the sons and daughters of Eve, the Mother of a world.

Eliza R. Snow   *1877*

THE ULTIMATUM OF HUMAN LIFE

Life's ultimatum, unto those that live

As saints of God, and all my pow'rs receive;
Is still the onward, upward course to tread -
To stand as *Adam and as Eve,* the head
Of an inheritance, a new-form'd earth,
And to their spirit race, give mortal birth -
Give them experience in a world like this.

John Taylor   *1/13/1880*

L. John Nuttall Papers
Adam is the father of our bodies. Who is to say he is not the father of our spirits.

Edward Stevenson   *3/7/1880*

Edward Stevenson Diary; Davis Stake Conference
[T]herefore *Adam is the Father of my Spirit* & also of my body, the body being Bone of his Bone & Flesh of his Flesh. I Spoke 45 Minutes & Bp. Hess said that he could endorse all that had been said although he did not understand all, yet it made him feel good & like living his religion.

Joseph E. Taylor   *12/29/1888*

Deseret Weekly News 38:27
I think these two quotations[36] from such a reliable authority fully solve the question as to the relationship existing between Father Adam and the Savior of the world, and prove beyond question the power that *Adam* possessed in regard to taking his body [up] again after laying [it] down - which power he never could have attained unless he had first a resurrection from the grave to a condition of immortality. We further say that this power was not forfeited when as a celestial being he *voluntarily partook of the forbidden fruit and thereby rendered his body mortal in order that he might become the father of mortal tabernacles, as he was already the father of immortal spirits* - thus giving opportunity to the offspring of his own begotten to pass through the ordeals necessary to prepare them for a resurrection from the dead, a celestial glory.

Myron Abbott   *12/13/1890*

St. George Stake High Council Minutes
[Spirits] were begotten in the spirit world the same as we are begotten here and that *Adam is the father of our spirits.*

---

[36] TPJS 346-47; HC 5:426.

Analysis & Observations

β

As with the preceding section, there is little specific textual analysis to grace these pages. All of the more interesting textual analysis concerning the above statements appears more properly in other sections of this volume.

The reader may note that this subsection could have been significantly larger; if one accepts Adam-God teachings, the materials under "God as Father of our Bodies" are doctrinally identical to this subsection and those statements ought to be studied in connection with this section. However, for academic reasons noted in that subsection, these two subsections have been separated in this book.

God as Father of Our Spirits

~

See also
Procreation: Mortal & Spiritual Offspring

Joseph Smith   *circa 1834-35*

LF 3:6

Having previously been made acquainted with the way the idea of his existence came into the world, as well as the fact of his existence, we shall proceed to examine his character, perfections, and attributes, in order that this class may see, not only the just grounds which they have for the exercise of faith in him for life and salvation, but the reasons that all the world, also, as far as the idea of his existence extends, may have to exercise faith in him, *the Father of all living*.

Brigham Young   *Friday 4/9/1852*

JD 1:50

Our *Father in Heaven begat all the spirits* that ever were, or ever will be, upon this earth; and they were born spirits in the eternal world. *Then the Lord by His power and wisdom organized the mortal tabernacle of man*. We were made first spiritual, and afterwards temporal.

Brigham Young   *Sunday 10/8/1854*

MABY

I tell you simply, He is our Father; the God and Father of our Lord Jesus Christ, and the *Father of our spirits*. Can that be possible? Yes, it is possible. He is the *Father of all the spirits* of the human family. All things are first made spiritual, and brought forth into His kingdom. *The spirits of all the human family were begotten by one Father*. Now be watchful, for if I have time, and feel able, I shall communicate something with this you are not expecting. Yes, every son and daughter of Adam according to the flesh can claim one parentage; the Heathen, and the Christian, the Jew and the Gentile, the high and the low, the king and the beggar, the black and the white, all who have sprung from Adam and Eve have one father. "... The God and Father of our Lord Jesus Christ is the *Father of our spirits.*

Brigham Young   *2/8/1857*

JD 4:218-19

The Savior was begotten by the Father of His spirit, by *the same Being who is the Father of our spirits*, and that is all the organic difference between Jesus Christ and you and me. And a difference there is between our Father and us consists in that He has gained His exaltation, and has obtained eternal lives.

Brigham Young   *6/18/1865*

JD 11:122-23

I am quite satisfied to be made aware by the scriptures, and by the Spirit of God, that *He is not only the God and Father of Jesus Christ, but is also the Father of our spirits and the Creator of our bodies* which bear His image as Seth bore the image of his father Adam.

Brigham Young   *8/4/1867*

Utah Historical Quarterly 29:68

Do you believe that He is the God whom Moses followed and by whom he was directed? "Yes," says the whole house of Israel. Well, that is the very God that we - the Latter-day Saints - are serving. He is our Father, He is our God and Father of our Lord Jesus Christ - whom the tribe of Judah discard, heaping ridicule upon his name. *He is the Father of our Spirits*, everyone of us, Jew and Gentile, bond or free, white or black.

Brigham Young   *7/10/1870*

JD 14:71-72

But the fact exists that the Father, the Divine Father, whom we serve, the God of the Universe, the *God and Father of our Lord Jesus Christ, and the Father of our spirits*, provided this sacrifice and sent his Son to die for us; and it is also a great fact that the Son came to do the will of the Father, and he has paid the debt, in fulfillment of the Scripture which says, 'He was the Lamb slain from the foundation of the world.' Is it so on any other earth? On every earth. ... Sin is upon every earth that was ever created. ... Consequently every earth has its redeemer, and every earth has its tempter; and every earth, and the people thereof, in their turn and time, receive all that we receive, and pass through all the ordeals that we are passing through.

Analysis & Observations

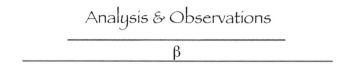

β

The doctrine presented in this chapter remains a well accepted LDS Church doctrine so I have not taken the time to create an exhaustive representation of this issue - surely there are dozens, if not hundreds of statements from the early brethren proclaiming this doctrine to be true. However, the few statements above are helpful in creating an important syllogism for the reader new to Adam-God teachings:

Adam is the father of our spirits
The father of our spirits is God
Therefore: Adam is God

While this is more simply stated in the many statements in the first section of this volume, this and the previous section (through the above syllogism) help to strengthen the witness that the early brethren did teach that Adam was and is God the Father.

God as Father of Our Bodies

~

See also
Adam as Father of Our Spirits
Procreation: Mortal & Spiritual Offspring

Brigham Young   *Friday 10/6/1854*

Journal of the Southern Indian Mission, 87- 89
[T]he *Father of our Spirits* is the Father of Jesus Christ: He is the Father of Jesus Christ, Spirit & Body and he *is the beginner of the bodies of all men.*

Brigham Young   *Sunday 10/8/1854*

John Pulsipher Papers, 36-37
God is the father of spirits of all the people of this world - *he is the father of the bodies also* of the first inhabitants of the Earth also the father of the body of Jesus Christ.

Brigham Young   *Sunday 10/8/1854*

MABY
He is the *God and Father* of our Lord Jesus Christ, both body and spirit; and He is the Father of our spirits. You may add these words to it, or let it alone, it is all the same to me, that *He is not only the Father of our spirits, but also of our flesh, He being the founder of that natural machinery through which we all have obtained our bodies.*

Heber C. Kimball   *Sunday a.m. 11/8/1857*

JD 6:31
Now, brethren, you have got a spirit in you, and that spirit was created and organized - was born and begotten by our Father and *our God* before we ever took these bodies; and

these bodies were formed by him, and through him, and of him, just as much as the spirit was; for I will tell you, he commenced and brought forth spirits; and then, when he completed that work, he commenced and brought forth tabernacles for those spirits to dwell in. *I came through him, both spirit and body*. God made the elements that they are made of, just as much as he made anything.

George Q. Cannon   *10/12/1861*

MS 23:654

President Young, in the foregoing passages,[37] while substantiating the fact of the union of man's preexisting spirit with a bodily product of the "dust of the ground," enters more particularly into the modus operandi of that union. He unmistakably declares man's origin to be altogether of a celestial character - that *not only is his spirit of heavenly descent, but his organization too, - that the latter is not taken from the lower animals, but from the originally celestial body of the great Father of humanity*.

Brigham Young   *6/18/1865*

JD 11:122-23

I am quite satisfied to be made aware by the scriptures, and by the Spirit of God, that He is not only the God and Father of Jesus Christ, but is also *the Father of our spirits and the Creator of our bodies* which bear His image as Seth bore the image of his father Adam.

Brigham Young   *9/25/1870*

JD 13:250

He is our Father; He is our God, *the Father of our spirits; He is the framer of our bodies*, and set the machine in successful operation to bring forth these tabernacles that I now look upon in this building, and all that ever did or ever will live on the face of the whole earth.

Brigham Young   *11/13/1870*

JD 13:306

Our Spirits are His; He begot them. We are his children; *He set the machine in motion to produce our tabernacles*.

Brigham Young   *5/21/1871*

JD 14:136

God notices this world. He organized it, and brought forth the inhabitants upon it. *We*

---

[37] JD 1:50-51; 6:275.

are his children, literally, spiritually, naturally, and in every respect. We are the children of our Father; Jesus is our elder brother, ready to save all who will come to him.

Brigham Young   *Sunday p.m. 6/18/1873*

DN 22:308

My brother said that God is as we are. He did not mean those words to be literally understood. He meant simply, that in our organization we have all the properties in embryo in our bodies that our Father has in his, and that *literally, morally, socially, by the spirit and by the flesh we are his children.*

Daniel H. Wells   *Saturday p.m. 8/9/1873*

JD 16:127

It has been revealed in our day who we are, and the relationship we hold to God. We have learned that God is our Father, and that we are his children, bona fide his children. *Not in a spiritual sense alone, but when we say, "Our Father who are in heaven," we mean just what we say.*

Brigham Young   *7/19/1874*

JD 17:143

All those who are counted worthy to be exalted and to become Gods, even the sons of God, will go forth and have earths and worlds like those who framed this and millions on millions of others. *This is our home, built expressly for us by the Father of our spirits, who is the Father, maker, framer and producer of these mortal bodies* that we now inherit, and which will go back to mother earth. When the spirit leaves them they are lifeless.

John Taylor   *7/29/1877*

JD 19:79

God, it is true, *is the Father* and Spirit *of all flesh*; God, it is true, has a right to demand obedience from his children, and the observance of the laws he has given unto them; but that right has been contested from the very first.[38]

George Q. Cannon   *Sunday p.m. 5/4/1884*

JD 25:155

My brethren and sisters, it is a glorious truth that has been taught to us, that we are literally the children of God, that *we are his literal descendants, as Jesus was literally*

---

[38] Grammar makes this difficult to understand but it seems to suggest the doctrine put forth in this subsection - context does not help.

descended from Him, and that He is our Father as much as our earthly parent is our father, and we can go to Him with a feeling of nearness, knowing this, understanding it by the revelations which God has given to us.

J. F. Gibbs   *11/--/1889*
Contributor 6:78

The Being that has organized the world; and placed upon it the germs of animated nature; *is the one most entitled to furnish mortal bodies for his spiritual children.* And when the great drama of life is finished and he with his children are redeemed and glorified, is he not entitled, as the head of an innumerable posterity, to be recognized as a Father and God to those that will rise up and call Him blessed?

George Q. Cannon   *4/7/1889*
MS 51:278

We believe that we are the *literal* offspring of Deity. *We have descended from the great Being who formed this earth*, and from Him we have inherited the glorious aspirations to be like unto Him.

Benjamin F. Johnson   *circa 1903*
Letter from Benjamin F. Johnson to G. S. Gibbs, 18-19

In teaching us the "Fatherhood of God, and the Brotherhood of Man", we could begin to see why we should "love God supremely, and our brothers as ourselves," He [Joseph Smith] taught us that *God was the great head of human procreation - was really and truly the father of both our spirits and our bodies*; that were but parts of a great whole, mutually and equally dependent upon each other, according to condition.

First Presidency   *11/--/1909*
MFP 4:199, 206

The Church of Jesus Christ of Latter-day Saints, basing its belief on divine revelation, ancient and modern, proclaims *man to be the direct and lineal offspring of Deity.* God Himself is an exalted man, perfected, enthroned, and supreme. ...

Man is the child of God, formed in the divine image and endowed with divine attributes, and even as the infant son of an earthly father and mother is capable in due time of becoming a man, so the undeveloped offspring of celestial parentage is capable, by experience through ages and aeons, of evolving into a God.

Priesthood Course of Study, "The Creation of Man"
Man has descended from God: In fact, he is of the same race as the Gods. His descent has not been from a lower form of life; in other words, man is, in the most literal sense, a child of God. *This is not only true of the spirit of man, but of his body also.*

Analysis & Observations

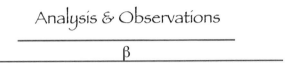

As a preliminary note, many fundamentalists may wonder why the following material has been set aside as a topic of its own - after all, if God is the Father of our bodies, doesn't that clearly implicate that Adam is God the Father? The reasonable, rational, and logical answer to members of the modern LDS Church unfamiliar with Adam-God teachings may well be "No." While not systematically taught in the modern LDS Church, its members often believe that God was the literal father of Adam and that Adam was therefore immortal before he came to this earth.[39] Although the early brethren clearly taught otherwise (see "Procreation: Mortal & Spiritual Offspring"), I have made every effort to make this first section on Adam as LDS friendly as possible - I have therefore separated these two topics. If the reader does not accept the doctrines as put forth in the subsection "Procreation: Mortal & Spiritual Offspring", then the reader would not find that the following material is appropriately placed under any of the previous subsections of this volume - hence the necessity for this subsection.

Lest the fundamentalist be misled, members of the modern LDS Church have reasonable means to believe in this reading of the above statements - especially given Brigham Young's statement wherein he averred:

Brigham Young   *4/17/1870*

JD 13:311
We are all the children of Adam and Eve, and *they and we* are the offspring of Him who dwells in the heavens.

He made other statements that seem to indicate this viewpoint as well:

---

[39] It is important for fundamentalists to remember at this point that members of the modern LDS Church do not always equate an immortal body with a resurrected body.

Brigham Young   *2/23/1862*

JD 9:283

Our Heavenly Father orders all things that pertain to this earth and to multitudes of worlds of which we are ignorant. We are *as much the children of this great Being as we are the children of our mortal progenitors.* We are flesh of his flesh, bone of his bone, and the same fluid that circulates in our bodies, called blood, once circulated in his veins as it does in ours.

Although this last statement is somewhat vague and implies an accord with Adam-God teachings, it stops short of this assertion to a modern member of the LDS Church because they believe that God the Father once lived on an earth as well - and that He was mortal - so the allusion to the "same fluid ... called blood" is not quite as specific as most fundamentalists are prone to believe. The terminology here says "as much ... as," which could be read to indicate that God the Father and Adam are not the same individual - hence the uncertainty of this statement.

Two other statements of interest that carry some interest as it pertains to this doctrine but that retain enough vagueness to keep them from being definitive statements are as follows:

Brigham Young   *6/19/1859*

JD 6:332

The Apostles and Prophets, when speaking of our relationship to God, say that *we are flesh of his flesh and bone of his bone.* God is our Father, and Jesus Christ is our Elder Brother, and both are our everlasting friends. This is Bible doctrine.

Brigham Young   *10/7/1860*

JD 8:236

[The Lord] said, "Have you confidence in me, my son Abraham?" "Yes," said Abraham. "Well, I will prove you. Bring up your son Isaac to Mount Moriah, build an altar there, place the wood on the altar and bind your son and place him on the altar and sacrifice him to me, and this will prove whether you have faith in me or not." The sacrifice was offered and accepted, and the Lord provided a way whereby Isaac could live. We are just so foolish, and unwise and shortsighted, and so wanting in philosophy that we actually believe God told Abraham to do this very thing. *Who is that God? He is my Father. He is your Father; we are His offspring.*

Under either theological view, Mormons have an intimate concept of their relationship with deity that is not shared with any other religion. From a certain perspective, fundamentalists only disagree with modern members of the LDS Church in a matter of degree: both believe we are physically and spiritually descended from God the Father; fundamentalists merely define this relationship one generation closer than the modern Latter-day Saint. Perhaps then, from a simplistic point of view, an outsider may view the Adam-God controversy as one of relative insignificance. If the entire controversy was limited to the issue described directly above, this could be true. However, the details that are generated from this one distinction are what creates the wide divide. That is, fundamentalists cannot accept Adam as merely a spiritual brother (even one of a valiant, prophetic nature - but who is also inferior to Jesus Christ under modern LDS theology) and mainstream Latter-day Saints cannot accept Adam as God. Therefore, even ignoring the numerous other implications that proceed from Adam-God teachings, this one generation of difference creates an inseparable gulf between the fundamentalist Mormon and mainstream Mormon theologies.

3

Adam as Father of Christ

See also
Adam Presides Over Our Spirits & has the Keys
Procreation: Mortal & Spiritual Offspring

Brigham Young   *Friday 4/9/1852*

JD 1:50

He [Adam] is our Father and our God, and the only God with whom we have to do. ...
When the Virgin Mary conceived the child *Jesus, the Father had begotten him* in his own
likeness. He was not begotten by the Holy Ghost. *And who is the Father? He is the first of
the human family*; and when he took a tabernacle, it was begotten by his Father in
heaven, after the same manner as the tabernacles of Cain, Abel, and the rest of the sons
and daughters of Adam and Eve; from the fruits of the earth, the first earthly
tabernacles were originated by the Father, and so on in succession. ... What a learned
idea! *Jesus*, our elder brother, *was begotten in the flesh by the same character that was in the
garden of Eden*, and who is our Father in Heaven.

Brigham Young   *Friday 4/9/1852*

Journal of Wilford Woodruff

When our Father came into the garden He came with his celestial body & brought one
of his wives with him and ate of the fruit of the garden until He could beget a
tabernacle. And *Adam is Michael or God* and all the God that we have anything to do
with. They ate of this fruit & formed the first tabernacle that was formed. And *when the
Virgin Mary was begotten with child it was by the Father* and in no other way only as we
were begotten. I will tell you the truth as it is in God. The world don't know that Jesus
Christ our elder brother was begotten by our Father in Heaven. Handle it as you
please, it will either seal the damnation or salvation of man. He was begotten by the

Father & not by the Holy Ghost.

Brigham Young *Friday 4/9/1852*

Journal of Hosea Stout 2:435

President B. Young taught that *Adam was the father of Jesus* and the only God to us. That he came to this world in a resurrected body, etc. More hereafter.

Heber C. Kimball *Saturday 4/10/1852*

Journal of Wilford Woodruff

The one that gave Joseph the keys of the Kingdom was his God,[40] which was Peter. Jesus Christ was his God and *the God and Father of Jesus Christ was Adam.*

Brigham Young *Friday 4/16/1852*

Journal of Samuel Holister Rogers 1:179

[H]e said that Adam was the only God that we would have, and that *Christ was not begotten of the Holy Ghost, but of the Father Adam*, that Christ, was our elder brother.

Brigham Young *2/19/1854*

TPBY 3:251-52

I will notice another idea touching the Holy Ghost begetting the Son of God. Who was it that spoke from the heavens and said, "This is my beloved Son, hear ye him"? Was it God the Father? It was. The Apostles bear testimony that such a voice was actually heard, "This is my beloved Son," and if it is true [that] the Holy Ghost begat him, I would add, "which was begotten by one of my neighbors, hear ye him." Who was the Saviour begotten by? Oh, by his Father or his brother, or some other person. So the Holy Ghost begetting the Saviour looks to me. It makes me think of a story I heard in a dramatical performance once, that a certain individual was born of one of his aunts but he had no mother. It appears as reasonable to me to say a cousin or a fellow laborer of the Saviour begat him, as to say the Holy Ghost begat him. Who did beget him? His Father, and his Father is our God, and the Father of our spirits, and He is the framer of the body. *The God and Father of our Lord Jesus Christ - Who is He? He is Father Adam - Michael - the Ancient of Days.* Has he a Father? He has! Has he a Mother? He has! Now to say that the Son of God was begotten by the Holy Ghost, is to say the Holy Ghost is God the Father, which is inconsistent, and contrary to all the revelations of God, both modern, and ancient. ...

I will however, add, that Jesus Christ is the Son of God as I am the son of my father,

---

[40] See "Titles & Offices: God & god" for an explanation of this statement.

and was born of the virgin Mary. On this all Christians have stumbled and fallen in ignorance, and they will remain until they are willing to admit the truth. In Jesus Christ we have God manifest in the flesh, He was the only one begotten of the Father full of grace and truth; was born in humble circumstances, placed in a manger, grew up to manhood, preached the Gospel, established His Church, suffered martyrdom and went back to the Father.

Brigham Young   *2/19/1854*

Journal of Wilford Woodruff

He (BY) said that our God was Father *Adam*. He *was the Father of the Savior Jesus Christ -* Our God was no more or less than Adam, Michael the Archangel.

Orson Pratt   *9/17/1854*

Journal of Wilford Woodruff

Some of his [Orson Pratt's] doctrines as contained in the Seer were being discussed. Brother Pratt also thought that Adam was made of the dust of the earth. Could not believe that *Adam was our God or the Father of Jesus Christ.*

Brigham Young   *Friday 10/6/1854*

Journal of the Southern Indian Mission, 87- 89

[T]he *Father of our Spirits is the Father of Jesus Christ: He is the Father of Jesus Christ, Spirit &* *Body* and he is the beginner of the bodies of all men. ... There is no time when worlds have not been created and exalted; there have always been an Adam and an Eve - the first man and woman, and *their oldest son is heir*, and should be our Savior. ... When Jesus has done his work he will take this planet back to his Father.

Brigham Young   *3/31/1855*

MS 17:195-96

[Brigham Young] declared that *Jesus Christ is the actual spirit and mortal son of Michael* *Adam God*; that Michael Adam is the supreme god and father of the spirits of our mortal world.

Brigham Young   *4/25/1855*

MABY

We begin with the father of our Lord Jesus Christ, and of our spirits - who is he? Do you know anything about him? Can you find out who he is? Suppose we go to the scriptures and enquire who he is. At one time he says "I am that I am," at another time when the question was proposed by somebody, he replied, "I am the Lord your God";

at another time he is spoken of as a Man of War, a General and so on. You may trace the scriptures through, and you will find that he is known to one people by one title today, and tomorrow by another, and the next day by another, and there he leaves it ... When we can see that very character [*Michael*] and talk and live with him in our tabernacles, if we are so fortunate as to get there into his society, then we can say that to us there is but one living and true God, and he *is the father of our Lord Jesus Christ* and of our spirits. And when we get back to him and learn that he is actually our father, we shall not feel any anxiety to call upon anybody else for the blessings we are in need of. ... [when we] get there into his society then we can say that to us there is but one living and true *God* and he is the *father of our Lord Jesus Christ* and of our spirits. I tell you this as my belief about that personage *who is called the Ancient of Days*, the Prince, and so on.

Heber C. Kimball   *6/29/1856*

JD 4:1

That first man[41] *sent his own Son to redeem the world*, to redeem his brethren; his life was taken, his blood shed, that our sins might be remitted.

John Jacques   *1856*

Sacred Hymns #306
WE BELIEVE IN OUR GOD

We believe in our God, the Prince of his race,
The archangel Michael, the Ancient of Days
Our own *Father Adam*, earth's Lord as is plain,
Who'll counsel and fight for His children again.

We believe in *His Son, Jesus Christ* who in love
To His brothers and sisters came down from above,
To die, to redeem them from death, and to teach
To mortals and spirits the gospel we preach.

Brigham Young   *2/8/1857*

JD 4:217-18

Things were first created spiritually; the Father actually begat the spirits, and they were brought forth and lived with Him. Then He commenced the work of creating earthly tabernacles, precisely as He had been created in this flesh himself, by partaking of the

---

[41] This must be Adam - see TPJS, 167; HC 4:207; D&C 84:16; Moses 1:34; Abraham 1:3; HCK Journal 10/28/1854.

course material that was organized and composed this earth, until His system was charged with it, consequently the tabernacles of His children were organized from the course materials of this earth. When the time came that *His first-born, the Savior*, should come into the world and take a tabernacle, the Father came Himself and favored that spirit with a tabernacle instead of letting any other man do it. *The Savior was begotten by the Father of His spirit*, by the same Being who is the Father of our spirits, and that is all the organic difference between Jesus Christ and you and me. And a difference there is between our Father and us consists in that He has gained His exaltation, and has obtained eternal lives.

Heber C. Kimball   *3/11/1857*

Journal of Heber C. Kimball 20:17
The Lord told me that *Jesus Christ was the son of Adam.*[42]

Brigham Young   *1/8/1865*

JD 11:41-42
One of the prophets describes the *Father of us all*, saying, "I beheld till the thrones were cast down, and the *Ancient of days* did sit, whose garment was white as snow, and the hair of his head like the pure wool; his throne was like the fiery flame," etc. The prophet further says, "thousand thousands ministered unto him, and ten thousand times ten thousand stood before him," etc. Again "and, behold, one like the Son of Man came with the clouds of heaven and came to the *Ancient of days*, and they brought him near before him." Now, who is the *Ancient of days?* You may answer this question at your pleasure, I have already told the people. But the Savior would answer the question as to the appearance of the *Father of us all*, by saying, "Look at me, for I am the very express *image of my Father.*"

Brigham Young   *12/16/1867*

Journal of Wilford Woodruff
President Young said *Adam* was Michael the Archangel, & he *was the Father of Jesus Christ & was our God & that Joseph taught this principle.*[43]

---

[42] Musser, 49 adds that J. Golden Kimball testified on February 10, 1931 that he had read this statement in his father's (Heber C. Kimball) Journal.

[43] This is the twelfth statement by Brigham Young in this subsection that declares that Jesus Christ was the son of Adam. Compare this observation with the following statement by Joseph Fielding Smith: "President Brigham Young did not believe and did not teach, that Jesus Christ was begotten by Adam." Mechizedek Priesthood Manual, "Answers to Gospel Questions," 22; 1972.

Lecture at the Veil   *Tuesday 2/7/1877*

Journal of L. John Nuttall 1:18-21
Father *Adam's oldest son* (*Jesus* the Savior), who is the heir of the family is *Father Adams first begotten in the spirit World*, who according to the flesh is the only begotten as it is written. In his divinity he having gone back into the spirit world, and come in the spirit to Mary and she conceived ...

Byron Allred   *3/1/1877*

Jans Christian Anderson Weibye Daybooks 5:20-22
Mary was sealed to Adam, and was his wife when she had Jesus.

Edward Tullidge   *3/--/1877*

Women of Mormondom, 179
"*Adam* is our Father and God. He is the God of the earth." So says Brigham Young. Adam is the great archangel of this creation. He is Michael. He is the Ancient of Days. He *is the father of our elder brother, Jesus Christ* - the father of him who shall also come as Messiah to reign.

Joseph E. Taylor   *6/2/1888*

Deseret Weekly News 38:19-27
It is recorded in the fifth chapter of Genesis that Adam died at the advanced age of 930 years. But it is often asked, `Did Adam lie in the grave until he was redeemed therefrom through the death and resurrection of the Only Begotten?' I will ask a question in reply: `Did Jesus have power to lay down his life and take it up again?' He so declared.[44] It might be well at this point to inquire *who was the Savior of the world; and what relation did he bear to our father Adam?* For the veil of the mysterious past has been lifted just a little to enable us to see within. I will first quote from a discourse preached by President Brigham Young, in Salt Lake City, April 9th, 1852.
[He here quotes JD 1:50-51.]
We will now quote some of the sayings of Joseph Smith upon this point, as uttered by him in Nauvoo, April 6, 1844. `It is the first principle of the Gospel to know for a certainty the character of God, and to know that we may converse with Him, as one man converses with another, and that he was made a man like us. Yea, that God Himself, the Father of us all, dwelt on our earth the same as Jesus Christ did. ... What did Jesus say? ... `As the Father hath power in himself, so hath the Son power.' To do what? Why, what the Father did. The answer is obvious, in a manner, to lay down his

---

[44] John 10:18.

body and take it up again. `Jesus, what are you going to do?' `To lay down my life and take it up again.' Do you believe it? If you do not believe it, you do not believe the Bible. The Scriptures tell it, and I defy all the learning and wisdom of all the combined powers of earth and hell together to refute it. What did Jesus do? Why, `I do the thing I saw my Father do when worlds came rolling into existence. My Father worked out His Kingdom with fear and trembling; and I must do the same; and when I get my kingdom, I shall present it to my Father, so that He may obtain kingdom upon kingdom and it will exalt Him in glory. He will then take a higher exaltation and I take His place, and thereby become exalted myself'; so that Jesus treads in the track of his Father and inherits what God did before.'[45]

I think these two quotations from such a reliable authority fully solve the question as to the relationship existing between Father Adam and the Savior of the world, and prove beyond question the power that Adam possessed in regard to taking his body again after laying it down - which power he never could have attained unless he had received first a resurrection from the grave to a condition of immortality.

George Q. Cannon   *6/23/1889*

Journal of Abraham H. Cannon

He [George Q.] believes that *Jesus Christ* is Jehovah, and that *Adam is His Father* and our God: that under certain unknown conditions the benefits of the Savior's atonement extend to our entire solar system. ... He asked me what I understood concerning Mary conceiving the Savior; and as I found no answer, he asked what was to prevent *Father Adam from visiting and overshadowing the mother of Jesus.* Then said I: "he must have been a resurrected Being." "Yes," said he, "and though Christ is said to have been the first fruits of them that slept, yet the Savior said he did nothing but what He had seen His Father do, for He had power to lay down His life and take it up again. Adam, though made of dust, was made, as President Young said, of the dust of another planet than this." I was very much instructed by the conversation and this days services.

George Q. Cannon   *6/11/1892*

Diary of Charles Lowell Walker 2:740-41

Pres Cannon said that it was not necessary that we should or endorse the doctrine that some men taught that *Adam was the Father of Jesus Christ.*

---

[45] TPJS 345, 346, 347; HC 6:305, 306; JD 6:3.

George Q. Cannon   *11/28/1898*

Proceedings of the First Sunday School Convention

I was stopped yesterday afternoon by a young man, who wanted to know whether *Adam was the father of our Lord and Savior* - whether he was the being we worshiped, etc. … Concerning the doctrine in regard to Adam and the Savior, the Prophet Brigham taught some things concerning that; but the First Presidency and the Twelve do not think it wise to advocate these matters.

Edward Bunker   *2/9/1902*

Letter to President Joseph F Smith

Dear Bro.

One of our recently returned missionary from the North Western States is advicating [sic] the Doctorn [sic] that *Adam is the* very eternal Father in the Godhead and *the Father of Jesus Christ* and that Pres Kelch so taught the Elders in that mission.

Brigham H. Roberts

Defense of the Faith and the Saints 2:268

In fact, the Mormon Church teaches that God the Father has a material body of flesh and bones; that *Adam is the God* of the human race … that *Jesus Christ was physically begotten by* the *Heavenly Father* of Mary, His wife; that, as we have a Heavenly Father, so also we have a Heavenly Mother …

Analysis & Observations

β

The above statements give greater meaning to passages of scripture that refer to Jesus as the "Son of Man", an appellation that refers to Christ in over eighty New Testament passages and in over a dozen more modern scriptural passages.[46] Via the exegetical lens

---

[46] It also shows up many times in connection with various prophets (especially Ezekiel). Christensen noted in AGM, 154, that "Under Adam, the Interpreter's Dictionary of the Bible, 1:42, states: '… the word adham occurs well over five hundred times in the Old Testament with the meaning `man' or `mankind.' This generic term is used only rarely as a proper name for the first man.'"

The following is a list of all occurrences of "son of man" or "Son of Man" in the standard works:

of Adam-God teachings, these statements help us to understand that Jesus is the Only Begotten in the flesh because he is the only child of Adam, physically born on this earth, to be sired while Adam was an immortal, glorified personage. As many authors have noted, Mary gave Christ the seeds of death that allowed Christ to sacrifice his life for us. In contrast, Adam passed on the seeds of godhood to Jesus so that Jesus could fill his office as the Messiah, Redeemer, and Savior. While the above statements explicitly focus on Adam as Christ's father and on the eternal nature of the procreation process, they also *adamantly refute* the sectarian notion of the immaculate conception that Christianity glibly adopted from other ancient pagan mythologies.

When viewed from the perspective of Adam-God teachings, the literal fatherhood of Jesus by Adam brings a much more personal application to the related teaching that those who accept the fullness of the gospel are the literal descendants of Jesus Christ (see "Christ as Father of Righteous"). Thus, Adam is not only their mortal physical father from nearly six thousand years ago, Adam is their immortal physical father through Christ himself - two thousand years ago. Thus, the nearness of godhood and royalty are not so far removed from us as sectarians and modern Mormons would have us believe. Understanding these principles can help Christ's descendants to approach the Father, in the name of Jesus Christ (also their father), in an intimate fashion that is not possible under any other belief system.

Numbers 23:19; Job 25:6; 35:8; Psalms 8:4; 80:17; 144:3; 146:3; Isaiah 51:12; 56:2; Jeremiah 49:18; 50:40; 51:43; Ezekiel 2:1-8; 3:1-10, 17, 25; 4:1, 16; 5:1; 6:2; 7:2; 8:5-17; 11:2-15; 12:2-18; 12:22, 27; 13:2, 17; 14:3, 13; 15:2; 16:2; 17:2; 20:3-4, 46; 21:2-19, 28; 22:2, 18, 24; 23:2, 36; 24:2, 16, 25; 25:2; 26:2; 27:2; 28:2, 12, 21; 29:2, 18; 30:2, 21; 31:2; 32:2, 18; 33:2, 7, 10, 12, 24, 30; 34:2; 35:2; 36:1, 17; 37:3, 9, 11, 16; 38:2, 14; 39:1, 17; 40:4; 43:7-10, 18; 44:5; 47:6; Daniel 7:13; 8:17

Matthew 8:20; 9:6; 10:23; 11:19; 12:8; 13:37-41; 16:13, 27-28; 17:9-12, 22; 18:11; 19:28; 20:18, 28; 24:27-44; 25:13, 31; 26:2, 24, 45; 26:64 (JST - Matthew 26, 36-43, 48); Mark 2:10, 28; 8:31, 38; 9:9-12, 31; 10:33, 45; 13:26, 34; 14:21, 41, 62; Luke 5:24; 6:5; 7:34; 9:22-26, 44, 56-58; 11:30; 12:8-10, 40; 17:22-30; 18:8, 31; 19:10; 21:27, 36; 22:22, 48, 69; 24:7; John 1:51; 3:13-14; 5:27; 6:27, 53, 62; 8:28; 12:23, 34; 13:31; Acts 7:56; Hebrews 2:6; Revelation 1:13; 14:14

2 Nephi 8:12
D&C 45:39; 49:6, 22; 58:65; 61:38; 63:53; 64:23; 65:5; 68:11; 76:16; 109:5; 122:8; 130:12-17
Moses 1:12; 6:57; 7:24, 47, 54-59; Abraham 3:27

With an Adam-God perspective (and knowing that the Hebrew term for "man" is "adham"), one understands that these passages referring to Christ as the Son of Man are not merely presenting descriptive appellations of Christ - they are literal declarations that Christ is the son of Adam.

God as Father of
Christ

~

See also
Procreation: Mortal & Spiritual Offspring

1842

MS 2:184

The Old and New Testament everywhere reveals a God with body, parts, and passions. The following are a few of the many texts which speak of his body and parts:

Image	Genesis. 1:27
Eyes	Proverbs 15:3
Mouth	Isaiah 55:11
Nose	Isaiah 65:5
Lips and tongue	Isaiah 30:27
Ear	2 Kings 19:16
Soles of his feet	Ezekiel 43:7
Arm	Jeremiah 21:5
Finger	Exodus 31:18
Fingers	Psalms 8:3
Loins	Ezekiel 1:27
Heart	Genesis 6:6
Nostrils	Exodus 15:8
Hand, face, and back parts	Exodus 33:22

The foregoing abundantly show that *the Father of our Lord Jesus Christ had both body and parts*, to say nothing of Jesus Christ. ... Hence, what can we say of this sectarian "God without body, parts, or passions!!!" as compared with Jehovah and Jesus Christ, or with Scripture and reason.

1842

MS 2:187

Let us now inquire after *the true God* and after the manner of worshipping him. The eternal Jehovah has revealed himself to man as enthroned in the heavens while the earth is his footstool, and *Jesus Christ as his son* seated at his right hand.

Joseph Smith   *6/16/1844*

TPJS, 372

My object was to preach the scriptures, and preach the doctrine they contain, there being a *God* above, *the Father of our Lord Jesus Christ*.

Joseph Smith   *6/16/1844*

TPJS, 373

If Abraham reasoned thus - If *Jesus Christ was the Son of God*, and John discovered that God the Father of Jesus Christ had a Father,[47] you may suppose that He had a Father also. Where was there ever a son without a father? And where was there ever a father without first being a son? Whenever did a tree or anything spring into existence without a progenitor? And everything comes in this way. Paul says that which is earthly is in the likeness of that which is heavenly, Hence *if Jesus had a Father*, can we not believe that He had a Father also? I despise the idea of being scared to death at such a doctrine, for the Bible is full of it.

Brigham Young   *7/24/1853*

JD 1:238

[T]he *Father* came down from heaven, as the Apostles said he did, and *begat the Savior* of the world; for he is the only-begotten of the Father, which could not be if the Father did not actually beget him in person. ... I believe *the Father came down in His tabernacle and begat Jesus Christ*.

Orson Pratt   *10/--/1853*

The Seer, 1:158-59

God, the Father of our spirits, became the Father of our Lord Jesus Christ according to the flesh. Hence, the Father saith concerning him, "Thou art my Son, this day have I begotten thee." We are informed in the first chapter of Luke, that Mary was chosen by the

---

[47] Revelation 1:6.

Father as a choice virgin, through whom He begat Jesus. The angel said unto the Virgin Mary, "The Holy Ghost shall come upon thee, and the power of the Highest shall overshadow thee; therefore, also, that holy thing which shall be born of thee shall be called the Son of God." After the power of the Highest had overshadowed Mary, and she had by that means conceived, she related the circumstance to her cousin Elizabeth in the following words: "He that is Mighty hath done to me great things; and holy is His name."

It seems from this relation that the Holy Ghost accompanied "the Highest" when He overshadowed the Virgin Mary and begat Jesus; and from this circumstance some have supposed that the body of Jesus was begotten of the Holy Ghost without the instrumentality of the immediate presence of the Father. There is no doubt that the Holy Ghost came upon Mary to sanctify her, and make her holy, and prepare her to endure the glorious presence of "the Highest," that when "He" should "overshadow" her, she might conceive, being filled with the Holy Ghost; hence the angel said, as recorded in Matthew, "That which is conceived in her is of the Holy Ghost;" that is, the Holy Ghost gave her strength to abide the presence of the Father without being consumed; but it was the personage of the Father who begat the body of Jesus; and for this reason Jesus is called "the Only Begotten of the Father;" that is, the only one in this world whose fleshly body was begotten by the Father.

There were millions of sons and daughters whom He begat before the foundation of this world, but they were spirits, and not bodies of flesh[48] and bones; whereas, both the spirit and body of Jesus were begotten by the Father - the spirit having been begotten in heaven many ages before the tabernacle was begotten upon the earth. The fleshly body of Jesus required a Mother as well as a Father. Therefore, the Father and Mother of Jesus, according to the flesh, must have been associated together in the capacity of Husband and Wife; hence the Virgin Mary must have been, for the time being, the lawful wife of God the Father; we use the term lawful Wife, because it would be blasphemous in the highest degree to say that He overshadowed her or begat the Saviour unlawfully. It would have been unlawful for any man to have interfered with Mary, who was already espoused to Joseph; for such a heinous crime would have subjected both the guilty parties to death, according to the law of Moses.[49] But God

---

[48] This subsection implicitly rejects Adam-God teachings by noting that we are only the spirit children of God, while Christ is both the physical and spirit child of God.

[49] Apparently, Orson Pratt is referring to Deuteronomy 22:23-24 - however, this scripture requires that both parties be caught in their relationship. Alternatively, Orson Pratt could be referring to Leviticus 20:10-11; although if he was referring to this scripture, he would have been in error because Mary would not have been considered a wife under Mosaic law as other laws specifically distinguish between a betrothed woman and a married woman and as this distinction provides for different punishments (although, see Deuteronomy 22:24 for an exception; Deuteronomy generally represented legal reform, so

having created all men and women, had the most perfect right to do with His own creation, according to His holy will and pleasure; He had a lawful right to overshadow the Virgin Mary in the capacity of a husband, and beget a Son, although she was espoused to another; for the law which He gave to govern men and women was not intended to govern Himself, or to prescribe rules for his own conduct. It was also lawful in Him, after having thus dealt with Mary, to give her to Joseph her espoused husband. Whether God the Father gave Mary to Joseph for time only, or for time and eternity, we are not informed.[50] Inasmuch as God was the first husband to her, it may be that He only gave her to be the wife of Joseph while in this mortal state, and that He intended after the resurrection to again take her as one of his own wives to raise up immortal spirits in eternity.[51]

As God the Father begat the fleshly body of Jesus, so He, before the world began, begat his spirit. As the body required an earthly Mother, so his spirit required a heavenly Mother. As God associated in the capacity of a husband with the earthly mother, so likewise He associated in the same capacity with the heavenly one.

Brigham Young	*Sunday 10/8/1854*

MABY

He is the God and Father of our Lord Jesus Christ, both body and spirit; and He is the Father of our spirits.

Brigham Young	*2/8/1857*

JD 4:217-19

You may hear the divines of the day extol the character of the Saviour, undertake to exhibit his true character before the people, and give an account of his origin, and were

---

one could feasibly argue that this law provided that a woman should always be considered married if she was betrothed). Alternatively, Orson could be referring to Deuteronomy 22:22 but this law requires that the parties be caught in the act - or else only the woman is stoned. Deuteronomy 22:20-21 informs us that the woman would be stoned for not being a virgin on her wedding night; Leviticus 19:20 specifically informs us that neither of them would be put to death but that both would be scourged - but this law probably would not have applied because it specifically refers to a betrothed bondmaid - and Mary was a free woman; similarly, Leviticus 18:20 informs us that this is breaking a commandment (if Mary was considered Joseph's wife) but it does not provide for a punishment; and Numbers chapter five provides for a remedy that Joseph could have put into place if Mary were considered his wife under this law - but this would not require the death penalty. While these appear to be the only laws that Orson could have been referring to and as none of them would be correctly applied in his instance, the intent behind these laws does seem to support his position.

[50] As a side note, this is one of the many evidences that Joseph taught that some sealings are for mortality only and that other sealings are for time and all eternity.

[51] See "Mary as a Daughter of Adam".

it not ridiculous, I would tell what I have thought about their views. Brother Kimball wants me to tell it, therefore you will excuse me if I do. I have frequently thought of mules, which you know are half horse and half ass, when reflecting upon the representations made by those divines. I have heard sectarian priests undertake to tell the character of the Son of God, and they make him half of one species and half of another, and I could not avoid thinking at once of the mule, which is the most hateful creature that ever was made, I believe. You will excuse me, but I have thus thought many a time.

Now to the facts in the case; all the difference between Jesus Christ and any other man that ever lived on the earth, from the days of Adam until now, is simply this, the Father, after He had once been in the flesh, and lived as we live, obtained His exaltation, attained to thrones, gained the ascendancy over principalities and powers, and had the knowledge and power to create - to bring forth and organize the elements upon natural principles. This He did after His ascension, or His glory, or His eternity, and was actually classed with the Gods, with the beings who create, with those who have kept the celestial law while in the flesh, and again obtained their bodies. Then He was prepared to commence the work of creation, as the scriptures teach. It is all here in the Bible; I am not telling you a word but what is contained in that book.

Things were first created spiritually; the Father actually begat the spirits, and they were brought forth and lived with Him. Then He commenced the work of creating earthly tabernacles, precisely as He had been created in this flesh himself, by partaking of the course material that was organized and composed this earth, until His system was charged with it, consequently the tabernacles of His children were organized from the course materials of this earth.

When the time came that His first-born, the Savior, should come into the world and take a tabernacle, the Father came Himself and favored that spirit with a tabernacle instead of letting any other man do it. The Savior was begotten by the Father of His spirit, by the same Being who is the Father of our spirits, and that is all the organic difference between Jesus Christ and you and me. And a difference there is between our Father and us consists in that He has gained His exaltation, and has obtained eternal lives. ... I know my heavenly Father and Jesus Christ whom He has sent, and this is eternal life.

Brigham Young   *10/9/1859*

JD 7:286

The Being whom we call Father was the Father of the spirit of the Lord Jesus Christ, and he was also his Father pertaining to the flesh.

| Brigham Young | 6/18/1865 |

JD 11:123

I am quite satisfied to be made aware by the scriptures, and by the Spirit of God, that He is not only the God and Father of Jesus Christ, but is also the Father of our spirits and the Creator of our bodies which bear His image as Seth bore the image of his father Adam.

| Brigham Young | 8/4/1867 |

Utah Historical Quarterly 29:68

Do you believe that He is the God whom Moses followed and by whom he was directed? "Yes," says the whole house of Israel. Well, that is the very God that we - the Latter-day Saints - are serving. He is our Father, He is our God and Father of our Lord Jesus Christ - whom the tribe of Judah discard, heaping ridicule upon his name. He is the Father of our Spirits, everyone of us, Jew and Gentile, bond or free, white or black.

| Brigham Young | Sunday p.m. 6/18/1873 |

DN 22:308

What is the mystery in Jesus being the Son of God and at the same time the son of the Virgin Mary?

| Brigham Young, Jr. | 5/14/1876 |

L. John Nuttall Papers

Have we learned the character of the Son of God? Yes we know that he is the son of the living God Jesus could not have redeemed this earth had he been begotten of earthly parents.[52] No; he must be begotten of an eternal parent being. so as to have the power of redemption. if Christ had been a son born of earthly parents natural father he could not have saved us. Who is the father? He is the living God & we know that much more than the Christian world.

| Brigham Young, Jr. | 5/14/1876 |

Charles L. Walker Journal, 95-96

Said that the Father of Jesus Christ's spirit, was the same that begat him in the Flesh. Showed that had he been all human He would not have had power to make the atonement and Redeem the world.

---

[52] Alma 34:9.

George Q. Cannon   *Sunday p.m. 5/4/1884*

JD 25:155

My brethren and sisters, it is a glorious truth that has been taught to us, that we are literally the children of God, that we are his literal descendants, as *Jesus was literally descended from Him*, and that He is our Father as much as our earthly parent is our father, and we can go to Him with a feeling of nearness, knowing this, understanding it by the revelations which God has given to us.

Joseph F. Smith   *12/20/1914*

Box Elder News[53]

[*T*]*he Father of Jesus Christ in the flesh is the God of Heaven.* ... We want to try to make it appear that God does not do things in the right way, or that he has another way of doing things than what we know, we must come down to the simple fact that *God Almighty was the Father of His Son Jesus Christ.* Mary, the virgin girl, who had never known mortal man, was his mother. *God by her begot His son Jesus Christ*, and He was born into the world with power and intelligence like that of His Father.

Analysis & Observations

β

Some may question why this subsection was included in this book - clearly, if Adam is God the Father, and if Adam is the father of Christ, then it is more than obvious that God is the father of Christ. They may argue that this was established in the preceding subsections and that this subsection is therefore nothing more than a redundant echo - not to mention the fact that this subsection is far from being a thorough compilation of teachings on this particular doctrine. Further, we cannot glean any new truth from this subsection that was not already treated in the above subsections (apart from a few details that are not crucial to the purposes of this volume).

While these observations have merit when considered in this larger context, this subsection was included primarily for the benefit of the LDS reader. Previous fundamentalist authors have essayed to use the teachings in this subsection to prove that

---

[53] There has been some controversy over this particular source because it has previously been published with an incorrect publication date and source. The above source is correct and the correct publication date is 1/28/1915.

Adam is God the Father; however, this argumentation is embarrassingly circular because they rely upon the assumption that Adam is the God referred to as the father of Christ in order to show that Adam must be the father of Christ. Because the teaching that God the father is the literal father of Christ is still a solid doctrine in the modern LDS Church, these statements are not even remotely convincing when presented to members of the LDS Church as proof that Adam is the father of Christ. Thus, in order to avoid the perpetuation of this inane effort and in order to alert future fundamentalist authors of this incommodious, troubling, and faulty effort of persuasion, I have distinguished this subsection as a large academic footnote. As fundamentalists arguments are typically unpersuasive to the vast majority of Mormonism in general, they ought to be more careful in presenting their position if they have a desire to be persuasive - especially when putting forth arguments in favor of foundational teachings regarding Adam-God.

That noted, it may be of interest to the member of the LDS Church to note that the same rhetoric and argumentation is behind both of these teachings. This subsection and the preceding subsection both have statements that discuss the purpose behind these teachings - at the most basic level, they were used to prove that Jesus literally had the seeds of godhood in him and that Jesus was not begotten by the Holy Ghost as sectarians believed at that time. Some of the statements in this subsection (notably, the October 8, 1854 discourse) were in the larger context of Adam-God teachings but did not specifically identify Adam as the father of Christ. It appears that this was not done out of an intent to distinguish these two individuals - rather, it was a rhetorical/grammatical choice that avoided redundant usage of a proper noun: "Adam." That said, a thorough reading of the statements in this subsection, compared with a thorough reading of the statements in the preceding subsection will produce many similarities in style and in doctrine that may be useful to the member of the modern LDS Church in coming to understand that the voices behind these statements understood these teachings to be one and the same - that is, when they said God was the father of Christ, they understood that God to be our common father Adam.

Christ as Father of Righteous

~

While one could easily justify an extensive discussion on the necessity of plural marriage in connection with the below references, I have chosen not to do so. While plural marriage increases a man's capacity to raise up righteous seed, there is some theological justification to argue that the commandment to multiply and replenish the earth is not precisely synonymous with the commandment to live plural marriage - although there are substantial positions that persuasively argue that they are inextricably intertwined. The following selection of statements are presented here to show that the early brethren (and other theologians) taught that Christ had children[54] and that the early brethren taught that the believers in the fullness of the gospel were the literal descendents of Christ and these children.

Geneva Bible   *1599*

Psalms 45:6
Kings daughters were among thy honorable wives.

Church of England Bible   *1636*

Psalms 45:6
Kings daughters were among thy honorable wives.

Joseph Smith

Oliver B. Huntington Journal, 259
While visiting with Zina, she related a conversation that occurred between her and a Sister Repshire upon events in Nauvoo, where this Prophet Joseph Smith sealed her,

---

[54] I have excluded statements that only declare that Jesus was married as these do not logically force the conclusion that he had children.

Sister Repshire, to a Judge Adams of Springfield, Illinois. The Prophet stated to her (Repshire) that *Judge Adams was a literal descendant of Jesus Christ*. The judge died in Nauvoo and Sister Repshire, his wife, who had been married before to Repshire, died at Hill Creek, Utah. ...

The offspring from such a union, being the children of a perfect being, would almost certainly be uniquely endowed with an inclination towards righteousness, and a rare degree of spiritual strength, not often seen amongst other mortals. What a loss it would be to the world if they were to go unrecognized, but this is not a danger us Latter-day Saints need fear of, for the early prophets and apostles of this dispensation declared - through use of their revelatory skills - that indeed, *the sons of the Messiah did walk amongst the Saints.* Joseph Smith being the first to reveal this truth, when he informed the plural wife of Elder Judge Adams, that the Apostle "*was a literal descendant of Jesus Christ.*"

"Omega"	*5/16/1842*

T&S 3:801 #14

[W]e shall be enabled to resist disease; and wisdom will crown our councils, and our bodies will become strong and powerful, our progeny will become mighty, and will rise up and call us blessed; *the daughters of Jesus will be beautiful*, and her sons the joy of the whole earth.

Hyrum Smith	*6/1/1842*

T&S 3:801 #15

Let these things be adhered to; let the saints be wise; let us lay aside our folly and abide by the commandments of *God*; so shall we be blessed of the great Jehovah in time and in eternity: we shall be healthy, strong and vigorous: we shall be enabled to resist disease; and wisdom will crown our councils, and our bodies will become strong and powerful, our progeny will become mighty, and will rise up and call us blessed; *the daughters of Jesus will be beautiful,* and her sons the joy of the whole earth; we shall prepare ourselves for the purposes of Jehovah for the kingdom of God for the appearance of Jesus in his glory; "out of Zion the perfection of beauty," God will shine; Zion will be exalted, and become the praise of the whole earth."

Brigham Young	*2/27/1853*

JD 1:119

A great promise was made to Abraham, which was - *you shall have seed*, and unto your increase there shall be no end. *The same promise was made unto the Savior*, and unto every true and faithful man who serves God with all his heart, and whose delight is in keeping the law of the Lord, obeying the behests of Jehovah, and building up His kingdom upon the earth.

Samuel W. Richards   *Saturday 12/17/1853*

MS 15:825

If these things have power to disturb the pure mind, we apprehend that even greater troubles than these may arise before mankind learn all the particulars of Christ's incarnation - how and by whom he was begotten; the character of the relationships formed by that act; *the number of wives and children he had*, and all other circumstances with which he was connected, and by which he was tried and tempted in all things like unto man. Whatever may prove to be the facts in the case, it certainly would exhibit a great degree of weakness on the part of anyone to indulge in fears and anxieties about that which he has no power to control. Facts still remain facts, whether kept or revealed. If there is a way pointed out by which all beings who come into this world can lay the foundation for rule, and a never-ending increase of kingdoms and dominions, by which they can become Gods, we are as willing the Lord Jesus Christ should enjoy them all as any other being, and we believe *the descendants of such a sire* would glory in ascribing honor and power to him as their God. The Apostle informs us that those who are redeemed shall be like Jesus; *not say*, however, that they shall be wifeless and *childless*, and without eternal affections.

Orson Pratt   *circa 1853*

The Seer, 169-71

Inasmuch as the Messiah was to have a "plurality of wives," will they not all be Queens? Yes; but there will be an order among them. One seems to be chosen to stand at his right hand; perhaps she may have merited that high station by her righteous acts, or by the position she had previously occupied. It seems that she was one of the daughters of a king; for in the same Psalm it says, "The king's daughter is all glorious within; her clothing is of wrought gold. She shall be brought unto the King in raiment of needle work; the virgins her companions that follow her shall be brought unto Thee. With gladness and rejoicing shall they be brought; they shall enter into the King's palace." (verses 13-15) It must be recollected that "kings' daughters were among Thine honorable Wives." The kings here spoken of were no doubt those who through obedience to the gospel became kings and priests forever; for we cannot suppose that Christ would marry the daughters of the kings of this world who only reign under the pretended name of kings for this short life; such are not worthy to be called kings. Some of the daughters of those kings who are to reign on the earth forever and ever, and who are in reality kings, will be among His "honorable wives," one being chosen to stand as Queen at His right hand and worship Him, unto whom is made the following promise: "*Instead of thy fathers shall be thy children*, whom thou mayest make Princes in all the earth. I will make thy name to be remembered in all generations; therefore, shall the people praise thee forever." (verses 16, 17)

We are not informed at what time Jesus was to be married to this king's daughter or to any of the rest of His wives. But from what John the Baptist says, He may have been married to some of them previous to that prophet's martyrdom. The passage is as follows: "He that hath the Bride is the Bridegroom; but the friend of the Bridegroom, which standeth and heareth Him, rejoiceth greatly because of the Bridegroom's voice; this my joy therefore is fulfilled. He must increase, but I must decrease." (John 3:29, 30) And again, "Jesus said unto them, *Can the children of the bridechamber mourn* as long as the Bridegroom is with them? But the days will come, when the Bridegroom shall be taken from them, and then shall they fast." (Matt. 9:15) John represents Jesus as already in the possession of the Bride; while the Savior confirms what John says, by calling Himself "the Bridegroom," and the disciples "*the children of the Bridechamber*," but who the Bride was neither of them informs us.

Orson Hyde   *Friday 10/6/1854*

JD 2:79-80, 82-83

He being married, we would expect him to have lived up to all of the God-given responsibilities that come with such a union, chief among these being the *commandment to bring spirit children into the world through the means of procreation*. Once again God's apostles and prophets proclaimed that this was not just a possibility that he might do so, but a necessity:

Did the Savior of the world consider it to be his duty to fulfill all righteousness? You answer, yes. Even the simple ordinance of baptism he would not pass by, for the Lord commanded it, and therefore it was righteousness to obey what the Lord had commanded, and he would fulfill all righteousness. Upon this hypothesis I will go back to the beginning, and notice the commandment that was given to our first parents in the Garden of Eden. The Lord said unto them, "Multiply and replenish the earth. ..." Our first parents, then, were commanded to multiply and replenish the earth; and if the Savior found it his duty to be baptized to fulfill all righteousness, a command of far *less importance than that of multiplying his race*, (if indeed there is any difference in the commandments of Jehovah, for they are all important, and all essential,) would he not find it his duty to join in with the rest of the faithful ones in replenishing the earth? "Mr. Hyde, do you really wish to imply that *the immaculate Savior begat children*? It is a blasphemous assertion against the purity of the Savior's life, to say the least of it. The holy aspirations that ever ascended from him to his Father would never allow him to have any such fleshly and carnal connexions, never, no never." This is the general idea;

but the Savior never thought it beneath him to obey the mandate of his Father; he never thought this stooping beneath his dignity; he never despised what God had made; for they are bone of his bone, and flesh of his flesh; kindred spirits, that once basked in rays of immortality and eternal life. When he found them clothed upon and surrounded with the weaknesses of mortal flesh, would he despise them? ...

We say it was Jesus Christ who was married, to be brought into the relation whereby he could see his seed, before He was crucified. "Has he indeed passed by the nature of angels, and taken upon himself the seed of Abraham, to *die without leaving a seed* to bear his name on the earth?" *No*. But when the secret is fully out, *the seed of the blessed shall be gathered in*, in the last days; and he who has not the blood of Abraham flowing in his veins, who has not *one particle of the Savior's* in him, I am afraid is a stereotyped Gentile, who will be left out and not be gathered in the last days; for I tell you it is the chosen of God, *the seed of the blessed*, that shall be gathered. ...

Well, then, *he shall see his seed*, and who shall declare his generation, for he was cut off from the earth? I shall say here, that before the Savior died, *he looked upon his own natural children*, as we look upon ours; *he saw his seed*, and immediately afterwards he was cut off from the earth; but who shall declare his generation?[55] They had no father to hold them in honorable remembrance; they passed into the shades of obscurity, never to be exposed to mortal eye as *the seed of the blessed one*. For no doubt had they been exposed to the eye of the world, those infants might have shared the same fate as the children in Jerusalem in the days of Herod, when all the children were ordered to be slain under such an age, with the hopes of slaying the infant Savior.

Thomas D. Brown   *Friday 10/6/1854*

Journal of the Southern Indian Mission, 87- 89
Conference assembled, in the afternoon being called on by President Bm. Young I addressed the numerous saints assembled in the Tabernacle, gave them an account of our mission so far, and had liberty. On the evening of this day elder O. Hyde delivered an excellent discourse proving that *Jesus Christ was a married man - and children besides*.

Orson Hyde   *3/18/1855*

JD 2:210
I discover that some of the Eastern papers represent me as a great blasphemer, because I said, in my lecture on Marriage, at our last Conference, that Jesus Christ was married at Cana of Galilee, that Mary, Martha, and others were his wives, and *that he begat children*. All that I have to say in reply to that charge is this - they worship a Savior that

---

[55] Isaiah 53:7.

is too pure and holy to fulfil the commands of his Father. I worship one that is just pure and holy enough "to fulfil all righteousness;" not only the righteous law of baptism, but the still more righteous and important law "to *multiply and replenish the earth*." Startle not at this! for even the Father himself honored that law by coming down to Mary, without a natural body, and begetting a son; and *if Jesus begat children*, he only "did that which he had seen his Father do."

1855

MS 17:784

I would be a "Mormon"
I would with the "Mormons" reside in that land
Bless'd by *Jehovah*, where *Jesus* shall stand
When he descends, with his glorious train,
Long on the earth with his people to reign.

Heber C. Kimball   *3/1/1857*

JD 4:248

Are you ever going to be prepared to see God, Jesus Christ, His angels, or comprehend His servants, unless you take a faithful and prayerful course? Did you actually know Joseph Smith? No. Do you know Brother Brigham? No. Do you know Brother Heber? No, you do not. Do you know the Twelve? You do not; if you did, you would begin to know God, and learn that those men who are chosen to direct and counsel you are *near kindred to God and Jesus Christ*, for the keys, power, and authority of the kingdom of God are in that lineage.

Orson Hyde   *3/1/1857*

JD 4:259-60

Is there no way provided for those to come into this covenant relation who may not possess, in their veins, any of the blood of Abraham or of Christ? Yes! By doing the works of Abraham and of Christ.... . At this doctrine the long-faced hypocrite and the sanctimonious bigot will probably cry, blasphemy! Horrid perversion of God's word! Wicked wretch! He is not fit to live! &c, &c. But the wise and reflecting will consider, read, and pray. If God be not our Father, grandfather, or great grandfather, or some kind of a father in reality, in deed and in truth, why are we taught to say, "Our Father who art in heaven?" How much soever of holy horror this doctrine may excite in *persons not impregnated with the blood of Christ*, and whose minds are consequently dark and benighted, it may excite still more when they are told that if none of the *natural blood of Christ flows in their veins*, they are not the chosen or elect of God. Object not, therefore, too strongly against the marriage of Christ, but remember that in the last days, secret and hidden things must come to light, and that *your life also (which is in the blood)* is hid with Christ in God. Abraham was chosen of God for the purpose of raising up a chosen seed, and a peculiar people unto His name. Jesus Christ was sent into the world for a similar purpose, but upon *a more extended scale.* Christ was the seed of Abraham, so reckoned. To these, great promises were made; one of which was, that in Abraham and in his seed, which was Christ, all the families of the earth should be blessed. When? When the ungodly or those not of their seed should be cut off from the earth, and no family remaining on earth *except their own seed.* Then in Abraham *and in Christ*, all the families and kindreds of the earth will be blessed - Satan bound, and the millenium fully come. Then the meek will inherit the earth, and God's elect reign undisturbed, at least, for one thousand years.

Brigham Young	*11/13/1870*

JD 13:309

The Scripture[56] says that he, the Lord, came walking in the Temple, with his train; I do not now who they were, *unless his wives and children... .*

George Q. Cannon & Lorenzo Snow

Journal of Pres. Rudger Clawson, 374-75

There are those in this audience who are descendants of the old Twelve Apostles - and shall I say it, yes, *descendants of the Savior Himself. His seed* is represented in this body of men.

Following Pres. Cannon, President Snow arose and said that what Bro. Cannon had stated respecting the *literal descendants* among this company *of* the old apostles and *the Savior himself* is true - *the Savior's seed* is represented in this body of men.

George Q. Cannon

Anthony W. Ivins Journal, 21

There are men in this congregation who are *descendants of* the ancient Twelve Apostles and shall I say it, of *the Son of God Himself, for he had seed*, and in the right time they shall be known.

John Taylor	*5/18/1884*

JD 25:181

God is interested in the dead as well as the living. *Adam, who is the Ancient of Days and*

---

[56] Isaiah 6:1.

the father of the human family; Seth, Enos, Enoch, Mahalaleel, Methuselah, Noah, and all the prominent leading men of God, as well as Abraham, Isaac, Jacob, Moses, the Prophets, *Jesus* and His Apostles, together with the Prophets and Apostles who lived on this continent, and who stood at the various times or epochs as the representatives of the nations, and as thousands of these peoples have passed away having held and now holding the Priesthood; all these ancient fathers feel interested in this great work, and their hearts are turned toward the children, being interested in their welfare, happiness and exaltation; and *their children* who now have received the Gospel have their hearts, through this instrumentality, and the keys and principles which were introduced by Elijah, turned towards the fathers through the inspiration of the same Gospel, which Gospel as spoken of in the Scriptures, is an everlasting Gospel, being associated with the everlasting covenant, which principle wherever it has existed, brought life and immortality to light.

Orson F. Whitney   *1888*

Life of Heber C. Kimball, 185

A rare scene, indeed, and a suggestive one, for the parallel of which the mind must leap backward nigh two thousand years:

"On the next day much people that were come to the feast, when they heard that Jesus was coming to Jerusalem, took branches of palm trees, and went forth to meet Him, and cried, Hosanna; Blessed is the King of Israel that cometh in the name of the Lord. "The Pharisees therefore said among themselves, Perceive ye how ye prevail nothing? Behold, the world is gone after him." ... There was divine harmony in all this. In Heber, his character, manner and methods - we say it reverently - there was much of the Christ; the might of the lion, with the meekness of the lamb. *His, also, was the Savior's lineage*; in his heart a kindred spirit, *in his veins the self-same blood*. Where causes are similar, should there not spring similar results?

Joseph F. Smith   *circa 1900*

MS 62:97

Jesus Christ *never omitted the fulfillment of a single law* that God had made known for the salvation of the children of men. It would not have done for him to have come and obeyed one law and neglected or rejected another. He could not do that and then say to mankind, "Follow me!"

Sacred Hymns, 17 #12

Ere long the veil will rend in twain,
The King descend with all His train;
The earth shall shake with awful fright,
And all creation feel His might.

M. Zvi Udley, Th.M., Ph.D.

(As cited in Kraut's *Jesus Was Married*)
Jesus said once that he came to fulfill the Law: the first positive commandment of the Bible according to rabbinic understanding (Maimonides, Minyan ha-Mitzvet, 212) is that dealing with the *propagation of the human race* (Genesis 1:28); thus it has been considered the duty of every member of the House of Israel to marry at an early age.

Did Jesus have children? There seems to be evidence that such was the case; in 1873 M. Clermont Gannau discovered near Bethany on the mount of Offence certain sarchepphagi of extremely ancient times." Dr. Udley goes on to say that one of the tombstones there was the name "Simeon, son of Jesus" and that the other names on the tombstones bore the names of the persons mentioned in the Gospels near the site of the village of Bethany. This Simeon was at one time the Bishop of Jerusalem,[57] and Dr. Udley concludes: "In all probability Simeon was a son of Jesus and Martha and was that child who appeared at the crucifixion.

Rabbi Emil Hirsch   *1925*

My Religion, 43-44
Now as the life of Jesus is pictured in the New Testament, there are certain peculiar defects in that life from a Jewish point of view. His teachings are the ideal teachings of Judaism; they are not new teachings, nor new revelations. They are confirmations of Jewish thought and life. But his personal life - I am speaking respectfully; I do not think anyone should think I cast any shadow on the beauty and perfection of that life, but I can take it as it is pictured - you know he was not married and from the Jewish point of view, that is a defect. The Jewish morality insists that a man who does not assume the social responsibility for *the continuation of society*, lives a life that is not complete.

---

[57] circa 100 A.D.

Greenstone
The Messiah Idea in Jewish History, 147

The Messiah will die, and *his son* will become king in his stead, and there will be no immortality, but the people will live much longer... .

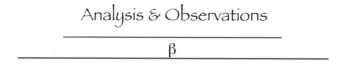

Analysis & Observations

β

Although this topic is not immediately identifiable as an Adam-God teaching, it has profound significance *in light of* Adam-God teachings and it has profound significance *upon* Adam-God teachings. When a believer accepts Adam as their immortal, physical father - albeit some six thousand years (or more) removed - they are initiated into a realm of increased understanding as to whom they are in relation to their Father in Heaven - a relationship that is much more intimate than that taught by mainstream Mormons. However, as many fundamentalists consider themselves the seed of Christ in accordance with the teachings found above, and as they accept Adam as the father of Christ, they view their relationship with their God in an intimate fashion yet one more profound level deeper. When viewed from the perspective of the teachings within this subsection, Adam is their immortal physical father through Christ only two millennia past. Thus, the nearness of godhood and royalty is not so far removed and their ability to approach their God in this very personal fashion is of paramount importance to their claims.

Apart from Adam-God teachings, the belief that some people are the literal descendants of Jesus Christ would certainly lead the believer to adopt a stronger personal relationship with our Savior and Redeemer. However, in light of Adam-God teachings, the believer has reason to cherish these teachings as a pronouncement of their profoundly personal relationship with Deity. As fundamentalists believe in the words of the early brethren declaring that the most righteous spirit children were favored to be born into the lineage of Abraham, the teaching that they were also favored to be born into the lineage of the Savior necessarily leads them to believe that they must have been especially valiant in the pre-existence - and therefore, they may have greater confidence in their ability to continue on in their righteous endeavors in this probation. Consider how George Q. Cannon expressed his feelings about these teachings:

JD 25:155

My brethren and sisters, *it is a glorious truth* that has been taught to us, that we are literally the children of God, that we are his literal descendants, as Jesus was literally descended from Him, and that He is our Father as much as our earthly parent is our father, and we can go to Him with *a feeling of nearness*, knowing this, understanding it by the revelations which God has given to us.

For more detailed information on this subject, the reader is invited to read Drama of the Lost Disciples and/or Holy Blood, Holy Grail and their progeny as they explore this issue quite thoroughly. More recently, the Divinci Code (fiction) has engendered vociferous opposition to the idea that Jesus had any children, which has produced several reactionary volumes disputing the claims of Holy Blood, Holy Grail and all related historical research. For further scriptural suggestions that Jesus had children, see: Isaiah 11:1, 10; 53:8, 10; Luke 23:27-29; Acts 8:33; Hebrews 1:8; 2:16; 1 Timothy 3:2,12; D&C 13:1-2.

4 Adam as Michael the Archangel

See also
Angels & Archangels

Joseph Smith   *7/--/1839*

MFP 1:113[58]

The Priesthood was first given to *Adam*; he obtained the First Presidency, and held the keys of it from generation to generation. He *obtained it in the Creation*, before the world was formed, as in Gen. 1:26-28. He had dominion given him over every living creature. He *is Michael the Archangel*, spoken of in the Scriptures. Then to Noah, who is Gabriel; he stands next in authority to Adam in the Priesthood; he was called of God to *this office*, and was the father of all living in his day, and to him was given the dominion. These men held keys first on earth, and then in heaven.[59] The Priesthood is an everlasting principle, and existed with God from eternity, and will to eternity, without beginning of days or end of years. The keys have to be brought from heaven whenever the Gospel is sent. When they are revealed from heaven, it is by Adam's authority. Daniel in his seventh chapter speaks of the Ancient of Days; he means the oldest man, our *Father Adam, Michael*, he will call his children together and hold a council with them to prepare them for the coming of the Son of Man.

Joseph Smith   *Monday 10/5/1840*

---

[58] JD 6:237-38 has the date for this discourse as June 2, 1839.

[59] This is a curious statement - first, Joseph suggests that Adam obtained the keys "in the Creation," and then he states that he obtained these keys "first on earth, and then in heaven." This appears to be a contradiction. However, the statements are so close together that it seems that there would be some better explanation - although none is given.

TPJS, 167-68

Commencing with *Adam*, who was the first man, who is spoken of in Daniel as being the "Ancient of Days," or in other words, the first and oldest of all, the great, grand progenitor of whom it is said in another place he *is Michael*, because he was the first and father of all, not only by progeny, but the first to hold the spiritual blessings, to whom was made known the plan of ordinances for the salvation of his posterity unto the end, and to whom Christ was first revealed, and through whom Christ has been revealed from heaven, and will continue to be revealed from henceforth. Adam holds the keys of the dispensation of the fullness of times; i.e., the dispensation of all the times have been and will be revealed through him from the beginning to Christ, and from Christ to the end of all the dispensations that are revealed. ...These angels are under the direction of *Michael or Adam*, who acts under the direction of the Lord.

Brigham Young   *2/5/1852*

Speech at the territorial legislature

After the deed was done, the Lord enquired for Abel, and made Cain own what he had done with him. Now says the grandfather, I will not destroy the seed of *Michael* and his wife, and Cain I will not kill you, nor suffer anyone else to kill you, but I will put a mark upon you.

Brigham Young   *Friday 4/9/1852*

JD 1:50

Now hear it, O inhabitants of the earth, Jew and Gentile, Saint and sinner! When our father *Adam* came into the garden of Eden, he came into it with a celestial body, and brought Eve, one of his wives, with him. He helped to make and organize this world. He *is Michael*, the Archangel, the Ancient of Days!

Brigham Young   *Friday 4/9/1852*

Journal of Wilford Woodruff

And *Adam is Michael God* and all the God that we have anything to do with.

Franklin D. Richards   *Saturday 12/10/1853*

MS 15:802-04

It is upon this foundation that the throne of *Michael* is established as *Father*, Patriarch, God; and it is for all his children who come into this world, to learn and fully understand the eternity of that relationship.

...

Again, the word of the Lord through the Prophet Joseph, gives additional importance, if possible, to the part which *Adam* acts relating to his children, which reads as follows - 'But, behold, verily I say unto you, before the earth shall pass away, *Michael*, mine archangel, shall sound his trump, and then shall all the dead awake, for their graves shall be opened, and they shall come forth; yea, even all.'[60]

…

In relation to this earth alone and its inhabitants, *Michael* and Gabriel have perhaps held the greatest keys of dominion and power. They were, both in their day, Fathers of all living, and had dominion given unto them over all things. Gabriel, or Noah, held the keys of this power under *Michael*, and to him he will render an account of all things before *Michael* renders an account of his stewardship to Him whose dominion reaches over many worlds, and who is God over all Gods. These two important personages have ever been watchful of the interests of their children, hence we find them ministering from time to time to holy men upon the earth - Gabriel often appearing unto Daniel, and opening to his view the most wonderful visions of the future, by which he could act as a God to the people, outvie the wisdom of the astrologers, and so control the elements that the burning furnace could have no power over him; *Michael* also coming to the release of Gabriel, when he was withstood one and twenty days from answering Daniel's prayer.

We also read of *Michael* disputing with the Devil about the body of Moses, probably because the Devil was not willing that Moses should be translated, inasmuch as he had sinned; but even in this, *Michael* was the great deliverer. Again we read that Michael shall stand up for the children of his people in a time of trouble such as never was since there was a nation, and at that time every one that shall be found written in the book shall be delivered, and those who sleep in the dust of the earth shall awake.

From these and many other Scriptures, we find that those important personages are clothed upon with no mean authority, and that *Michael* has power to deliver men from the power of the Devil, which is death; that by the sound of his own trump-the trump of the archangel, the nations of the dead shall awake and come forth to judgment, and there render an account to the Ancient of Days seated upon his burning throne. Then shall the nations know that he is their Judge, their Lawgiver, and their God, and upon his decree hangs the destiny of the assembled dead. Yes, our Judge will be a kind and compassionate Father, by whom none can pass, but through whom all glory, dominion, and power, will be ascribed to the great ETERNAL.

---

[60] D&C 29:26

Brigham Young   *2/19/1854*

Journal of Wilford Woodruff

Our God was no more or less than Adam, *Michael the Archangel*.

Brigham Young   *2/19/1854*

TPBY 3:251-52

The God and Father of our Lord Jesus Christ - Who is He? He is Father *Adam - Michael* – the Ancient of Days.

Brigham Young   *Friday 10/6/1854*

Journal of the Southern Indian Mission, 87- 89

Eloheim spoke, "Yehovah, Michael - see matter all around, go and organize a world," Yehovah Michael went and carried material: Then Michael came down with his wife, & began to people it. *Michael* had his body from the dust of the planet he was begotten on, he obeyed his Lord, was faithful and obedient, died and was resurrected, he did not resurrect himself.

Brigham Young   *3/31/1855*

MS 17:195-96

[Brigham Young] declared that Jesus Christ is the actual spirit and mortal son of *Michael Adam* God; that *Michael Adam* is the supreme god and father of the spirits of our mortal world.

Brigham Young   *4/25/1855*

MABY

I will tell you what I think about some who will have something to do with us by and by. When *Michael* blows his trumpet and calls the world together, we shall then be before him and we shall be perfectly satisfied that he can pass all the judgment that we shall want, and that the dominions of the wicked will want, and I have no doubt but the Saints that live and have lived from the days of Adam will be satisfied that he can give them kingdoms and power, thrones and dominions and influence in eternity. And when they get all that he can give, they will be satisfied and say it is enough.

Franklin D. Richards   *Saturday 12/15/1855*

MS 17:785-86

… *God the Father, Michael or Adam*, from whose loins the earth is peopled, and who is now laboring for the redemption of his children.

Franklin D. Richards   *Saturday 12/15/1855*

MS 17:787

We read in Jude 9: "Yet Michael the archangel, when contending with the devil he disputed about the body of Moses, durst not bring against him a railing accusation, but said, The Lord rebuke thee." Before leaving this part of our subject, we will add, that in reviewing it, it is evident that the mission of Satan on the earth is a necessary one, that he has been especially raised up to fill the place which he now occupies, that the great plan of redemption and exaltation of man could not have existed according to the order of creation without him, and that he is one of the dignitaries against whom men should not bring a railing accusation, lest they partake of his spirit.

John Jacques   *1856*

Sacred Hymns #306

WE BELIEVE IN OUR GOD

We believe in *our God*, the great Prince of his race,
The Archangel, *Michael, the Ancient of Days*,
Our own Father *Adam*, earth's Lord is his plane,
Who'll counsel and fight for his children again.

Brigham Young   *10/7/1857*

JD 5:331-32

Where was *Michael* in the creation of this earth? Did he have a mission to the earth? He did. Where was he? In the Grand Council, and performed the mission assigned him there. Now, if it should happen that we have to pay tribute to *Father Adam*, what a humiliating circumstance it would be! Just wait till you pass Joseph Smith; and after Joseph lets you pass him, you will find Peter; and after you pass the Apostles and many of the Prophets, you will find Abraham, and he will say, "I have the keys, and except you do thus and so, you cannot pass"; and after a while you come to Jesus; and when you at length meet *Father Adam*, how strange it will appear to your present notions. [fn: notice that this passage indicates a progression of hierarchy and Adam is at the top of this hierarchy above Christ] If we can pass Joseph and have him say, "Here; you have been faithful, good boys; I hold the keys of this dispensation; I will let you pass"; then we shall be very glad to see the white locks of *Father Adam*.

Brigham Young   *1/27/1860*

Minutes of a meeting of the First Presidency

Michael was a resurrected Being and he left Elohim and came to this earth & with an immortal body, & continued so till he partook of earthly food *and begot children who were mortal*.

Brigham Young   *11/30/1862*

MABY

[E]ach person who we crown in the celestial kingdom of God will be a father of fathers, a king of kings, a lord of lords, a god of gods ... Each person will reign over his posterity. *Adam, Michael*, the Ancient of Days, will sit as the judge of the quick and dead, for he is the father of all living, and Eve is the mother of all living, pertaining to the human family, and he is their king, their Lord, their God, taking and holding his position in the grand unbroken chain of endless increase, and eternal progression.

Brigham Young   *12/16/1867*

Journal of Wilford Woodruff

At meeting of School of the Prophets: President Young said *Adam was Michael the Archangel,* & he was the Father of Jesus Christ & was our God & that Joseph taught this principle.

Wilford W. Woodruff   *1/24/1868*

The School of the Prophets

I feel thankful for the privilege of speaking a few words to this school. I wish to refer to the first doctrine preached that *Adam was our Father & God* in the revelation called the olive leaf it says that "the devil gathered together the hosts of hell and Michael the ark angel gathered together the hosts of heaven and he overcame the devil & his angels & this is the battle of *the great God*" *who is this Michael the ark angel it is Adam who was Michael* in the creation of the world.

Orson Pratt   *10/7/1869*

JD 13:187

Adam is called an Archangel - yet he is a God.

George Q. Cannon   *10/15/1870*

Meeting of the School of the Prophets

[George Q. Cannon] fully endorsed the doctrine that father *Adam* was our God and Father - or as He in many places *is called, Michael* the great prince - the Arch Angel, Ancient of Days, &c.

Joseph F. Smith 10/15/1870

Journal of Joseph F. Smith

School of the prophets - opening prayer by bro. W. Woodruff, who spoke a short time on the Subject of *Adam being Michael, the arch-Angel* & c referred to D&C p. 79[fn: It is unclear which version of the D&C he is refering to here; however, this doctrine is taught in D&C 27:11; 107:54; and 128:21] & Dan. 7 ch. See also D&C p. 106 sec. 50, p. 200.

Wilford W. Woodruff 10/15/1870

I dug potatoes in the forenoon & attended the School of the Prophets in the Afternoon President Yo[un]g asked me to speak upon the Character of Adam who he was I proved that *Adam was Michael the Archangel*, the Seventh Angel, & the Ancient of Days, the Father of all & the prince of All. [sic] Daniel 7:9-14 D&C 79 page 28 paragraph 106 page 35 p 201 p 2d Paragraph I was followed by G Q Cannon President Yg & G.A. Smith

Brigham Young *Sunday p.m. 6/18/1873*

DN 22:308

We say that Father *Adam* came here and helped to make the earth. *Who is he? He is Michael*, a great prince, and it was said to him by Elohim: "Go ye and make an earth." What is the great mystery about it?

The Lecture at the Veil *Tuesday 2/7/1877*

Journal of L. John Nuttall

And when *this earth was organized by* Elohim. Jehovah & *Michael who is Adam* our common Father.

Edward Tullidge *3/--/1877*

Women of Mormondom, 179, 191

Adam is the great archangel of this creation. He *is Michael*. He is the Ancient of Days. He is the father of our elder brother, Jesus Christ - the father of him who shall also come as Messiah to reign. He is the father of the spirits as well as the tabernacles of the sons and daughters of man. Adam! ...

These are the *sons and daughters of Adam* - the Ancient of Days - the Father and God of the whole human family. These *are the sons and daughters of Michael, who is Adam*, the father of the spirits of all our race. These are the sons and daughters of Eve, the Mother of a world.

Edward Stevenson   *2/28/1896*
Edward Stevenson Diary

Certainly Eloheim, and Jehovah stands [sic] before Adam, or else I am very much mistaken. Then 1st Eloheim, 2nd Jehovah, 3d Michael-Adam, 4th Jesus Christ, Our Elder Brother, in the other World from whence our spirits came ... Then Who is Jehovah? The only begotten Son of Eloheim on Jehovah's world.

Benjamin F. Johnson   *circa 1903*
My Life's Review, 35-36

When, after a few days, the Prophet accompanied us to this spot, and pointed out those rocks as the ones of which *Adam* built an altar and offered sacrifice upon this spot, where he stood and blessed the multitude of his children, when they called him *Michael*, and where he will again sit as the Ancient of Days, then I was not envious of anyone's choice for a city lot in Adam-ondi-Ahman.

E. L. T. Harrison   *1912*
Sacred Hymns, 375-75 #316
SONS OF MICHAEL, HE APPROACHES

Sons of *Michael*, he approaches!
Rise; *the Eternal Father* greet;[61]
Bow, ye thousands, low before him;
Minister before his feet;
Hail, hail the Patriarch's glad reign,
Hail, hail the Patriarch's glad reign,
Spreading over sea and main.

Sons of *Michael*, 'tis his chariot
Rolls its burning wheels along!
Raise aloft your voices million
In a torrent power of song:
Hail, hail our Head with music soft!
Hail, hail our Head with music soft!
Raise sweet melodies aloft!

Mother of our generations,
Glorious by great *Michael's* side,

---

[61] This has been changed to read "Rise; the ancient Father greet" in the current hymnal.

Take thy children's adoration;
Endless with thy Lord preside;[62]
Lo, lo, to greet thee now advance,
Lo, lo, to greet thee now advance
Thousands in the glorious dance!

Raise a chorus, sons of *Michael*,
Like old Ocean's roaring swell,
Till the mighty acclamation
Through rebounding space doth tell
That, that the Ancient One doth reign,
That, that the Ancient One doth reign
In his Paradise again![63]

Orson F. Whitney

ELIAS, AN EPIC OF THE AGES, 18, 51, 76, 77

"Father!" - the voice like music fell,
Clear as the murmuring flow
Of mountain streamlet, trickling down
From heights of virgin snow -
"Father," it said, "since One must die[64]
Thy children to redeem,
Whilst Earth - as yet unformed and void -
With pulsing life shall teem;

And thou, great Michael, foremost fall
That mortal man may be,
And chosen Savior yet must send,
Lo, here am I, send me![65]

---

[62] This has been changed to read "Endless with thy seed abide" in the current hymnal.

[63] This has been changed to read "In his Father's house again!" in the current hymnal.

[64] Gospel Themes, 19-20 In 1914, Orson F. Whitney changed lines 5-9 as follows:
"Father," it said, "Since one must die,
Thy children to redeem,
From spheres all formless now and void,
Where pulsing life shall teem:
"And mighty Michael foremost fall,

[65] Isaiah 6:8; 2 Nephi 16:8; Moses 4:1; Abraham 3:27

I ask - I seek no recompense,
Save that which then were mine;
Mine be the willing sacrifice,
The endless glory - Thine!

…

Michael, the Prince,
the Monarch of our race,
Sire of a world from dust and spirit sprung;
Here sits he, throned in fire; before His face,
Ten thousand times ten thousand throng the judgment place.
…[Michael] The God of Gods, Supreme Magnificence.

…

One are the human twain, as sheath and sword -
Woman and man, the lady and the lord;
Each pair the Eve and Adam of some world,
Perchance unborn, into space unhurled.

…

Chosen, omniscient, children of the Sun,
Offspring of *Adam, Michael, Ancient One,*
Who comes anon his fiery throne to rear,
His council summoning from far and near.
Ten thousand times ten thousand bow the knee,
And "Father" hail him, "King," eternally.

Mighty Michael. *Michael the Archangel,* leader of the host of Heaven … *became Adam* and fell from an immortal to a mortal state that he might become the progenitor of the human family.

UR 2:153 par. 8
Here, in the times of restitution, when all things in Christ are gathered in one, *Adam, Michael,* the great Prince, Ancient of Days, is to come in power and glory, revisiting the scenes of his earthly pilgrimage.

~ ### Scriptures & Lore: Michael

Jude 1:9

Yet Michael the archangel, when contending with the devil he disputed about the body of Moses, durst not bring against him a railing accusation, but said, The Lord rebuke thee.[66]

Revelation 12:77   _circa 90 A.D._

And there was war in heaven: Michael and his angels fought against the dragon; and the dragon fought and his angels.

_D&C 27:11_   _8/--/1830_

And also with Michael, or Adam, the father of all, the prince of all, the ancient of

---

[66] AGM, 289: "Jude 9 ... is often cited as an example of Michael's limited powers over Satan because he "durst" not bring a railing accusation against him. ... The difficulty with this passage lies in the interpretation of the word "durst" which is assumed to mean "dare" as though to say that Michael was intimidated by Lucifer's powers. The word "durst" is more accurately interpreted as "did not presume" as is brought out by the context of immediate passages in Jude. The verse of Jude 9 is sandwiched between two verses which decry the ungodliness of men who speak evil of dignities, and speak evil of those things which they know not. Michael in verse 9 is singled out as an example of righteousness for not having brought a railing accusation against Satan. The New English translation clearly defines the doctrine under consideration to be one of railing insults and not of power and authority." In support of Christensen's position, consider D&C 50:31-33: Wherefore, it shall come to pass, that if you behold a spirit manifested that you cannot understand, and you receive not that spirit, ye shall ask of the Father in the name of Jesus; and if he give not unto you that spirit, then you may know that it is not of God. And it shall be given unto you, power over that spirit; and you shall proclaim against that spirit with a loud voice that it is not of God. _Not with railing accusation_, that ye be not overcome, neither with boasting nor rejoicing, lest you be seized therewith.

days.[67]

D&C 29:26   *9/--/1830*

But, behold, verily I say unto you, before the earth shall pass away, Michael, mine archangel, shall sound his trump, and then shall all the dead awake, for their graves shall be opened, and they shall come forth - yea, even all.[68]

D&C 78:15-16   *3/--/1832*

That you may come up unto the crown prepared for you, and be made rulers over many kingdoms, saith the Lord God, the Holy One of Zion, who hath established the foundations of Adam-ondi-Ahman; Who hath appointed Michael your prince, and established his feet, and set him upon high, and given unto him the keys of salvation under the counsel and direction of the Holy One, who is without beginning of days or end of life.[69]

D&C 88:112-15   *12/27/1832*

And Michael, the seventh angel, even the archangel, shall gather together his armies, even the hosts of heaven. And the devil shall gather together his armies; even the hosts of hell, and shall come up to battle against Michael and his armies. And then cometh the battle of the great God; and the devil and his armies shall be cast away into their own place, that they shall not have power over the saints any more at all. For Michael shall fight their battles, and shall overcome him who seeketh the throne of him who sitteth upon the throne, even the Lamb.[70]

D&C 107:54   *3/28/1835*

And the Lord appeared unto them, and they rose up and blessed Adam, and called him

---

[67] Referring to this scripture, Rodney Turner noted that "It was only about five months after the Church was organized on April 6, 1830 that Joseph Smith received a revelation from God identifying Adam as Michael, the Archangel, the Ancient of days."

[68] AGM, 155: "'For the Lord himself shall descend from heaven with a shout, with the voice of the archangel, and with the trump of God; and the dead in Christ shall rise first' (1 Thessalonians 4:16). The word of the Lord in the 29th section of the Doctrine and Covenants confirms Paul's teachings with the clarification that Michael is the archangel referred to by Paul. Furthermore, what Paul describes as God's trump, the Lord describes as Michael's trump. Assuming exclusive ownership of the trump, Michael is God by reason of parallel description."

[69] The old footnote "n" explained that the "Holy One" in verse 16 is the "Holy One of Zion" in verse 15. see AGM, 291. Christensen further points out that Ether 3:15 definitively tells us that this could not have been the Savior and therefore was someone else.

[70] Note that it is Michael that overcomes Lucifer in this passage.

Michael, the prince, the archangel.

D&C 128:21 9/6/1842

And again, the voice of God in the chamber of old Father Whitmer, in Fayette, Seneca county, and at sundry times, and in divers places through all the travels and tribulations of this Church of Jesus Christ of Latter-day Saints! And the voice of Michael, the archangel; the voice of Gabriel, and of Raphael, and of divers angels, from Michael or Adam down to the present time, all declaring their dispensation, their rights, their keys, their honors, their majesty and glory, and the power of their priesthood; giving line upon line, precept upon precept; here a little, and there a little; giving us consolation by holding forth that which is to come, confirming our hope!

See also Daniel 10:13, 21; 12:1; Revelation 10:1, 6; 12:7-9; Abraham 3:24-26 (Michael means "one like god")

Analysis & Observations

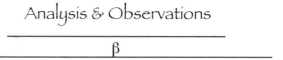

β

There are several textual issues regarding the statements from the early brethren above that are worthy of note. However, all of these textual issues are dealt with in other portions of this volume so they are not included in this section of this volume. Analysis of the history and lore of Michael the archangel is a different matter. Interest in the archangel Michael has long engaged Jewish, Christian, and Islamic thought. Without exaggeration, one could write an entire book on Michael's presence in scripture and religious mythology. For purposes of this volume, a quick overview of this subject will suffice. Christensen, in Adam-God Maze, compiled a significant amount of research regarding Adam's position as Michael the Archangel and summarized it very succinctly and well in that volume. Rather than replicate his research and writings, I have excerpted the following material from pages 159-161:

"Michael is styled as the "general" or the "chief Captain" (2 Enoch 22:6; 33:10), and his name is emblazoned on the escutcheon of one of the four divisions (tower) of the troops of God (1QM IX, 14-16; The Interpreter's Bible Dictionary 3:373). This last observation, that Michael is the captain of the Lord's hosts, is consistent with his role in defeating Satan as depicted in the Doctrine and Covenants, section 88. A more complete understanding of Michael as the captain of the Lord's host can be gleaned from Joshua 5:13-15. As recorded by Joshua, the "Captain of the Host of the Lord" appeared to Joshua as a man with a drawn sword. This being is identified as a physical being. Furthermore, upon learning his identity, Joshua fell on his face to the earth, and did "worship" him. This being was no commonplace angel or messenger, but a deity worthy of worship. This is evidenced by the "captain's" command that Joshua loose the shoes from off his feet "for the place whereon thou standest is holy" - precisely what the Lord told Moses. Thus, the Joshua account documents the "captain of the Lord's hosts" as a physical being - a resurrected deity. As seen above, this "captain" is identified as Michael or Adam. Further evidence that the "captain of the Lord's hosts" is "Michael" the "prince" surfaced with the recently discovered Ebla documents written in old Canaanite about 2400 B.C. The Ebla account of Joshua's experience identifies the "captain of the hosts of the Lord" or the commander of the army of Yahweh by the term "Prince," another of Michael's titles (G. Pettinato, "The Royal Archives of Tell Mardikh-Ebla," Biblical Archaeology 39:50 [1976]).

If Michael is the great prince denoted in Daniel 12:1, then he may be the God denoted as the "Prince of Princes" in Daniel 8:25 who in the last days will break "the king of fierce countenance" who destroyed the holy people. The holy people, according to this verse, are to be prevailed against and destroyed by peace and prosperity. Might this king also be the same "horn" seen in Daniel 7:21-22 that made war with the saints and prevailed against them until the Ancient of Days (the Prince of Princes) came? Thus we see Adam's continued intervention as Michael, the patron of Israel.

It is also of interest to note that the Canaanites, in adopting their religious concepts, worshiped the God "Mikal" which is derived from the root ykl which means "to be powerful," "powerful one," or "conqueror" (The Anchor Bible, the Book of Daniel, 282). Where would the Canaanites get such a notion that Michael was God?

Michael's role as the God and lawgiver to Israel is further brought out by identifying the God with whom Moses on Mt. Sinai spoke. The Exodus account identifies this being as the "God of thy fathers, the God of Abraham, the God of Isaac, and the God of Jacob," whereas, in Acts 7:38, we are told that Moses spoke with an angel on Mt. Sinai. This apparent discrepancy is resolved by the apocalypses wherein Moses is identified as speaking with, and receiving the law on Mt. Sinai from, "Michael" the "archangel" (Greek Apocalypse of Moses; Jubilee. 1:27; 2:1; Ascension of Isaiah 11:21; The Shepherd of Hermas Visions VIII. 3:3; Palestinian Targum; Deuteronomy Rabbah 11:10). ...

Of Michael another author writes: Michael ("who is a God") - in Biblical and post-Biblical lore - Michael ranks as the greatest of all angels, whether in Jewish, Christian, or Islamic writings, secular or religious. He derives originally from the Chaldeans by whom he was worshipped as something of a god. He is chief of the order of virtues, chief of archangels, prince of the presence, angel of repentance, righteousness, mercy, and sanctification; also ruler of the 4th Heaven, tutelary sar (angelic prince) of Israel, guardian of Jacob, conqueror of Satan ... His mystery name is Sabbathiel. In Islamic writings he is called Mika'il. As the deliverer of the faithful, he accords, in the Avesta, with Saosyhant the Redeemer. Midrash Rabba (Exodus 18) credits Michael with being the author of the whole of Psalm 85. In addition, he has been identified with the angel who destroyed the hosts of Sennacherib (a feat also ascribed to the prowess of Uriel, abriel, Ramiel) and as the angel who stayed the hand of Abraham when the latter was on the point of sacrificing his son Isaac. ... In Jewish lore (Ginzberg, The Legends of the Jews 2:303) "the fire that Moses saw in the burning bush had the appearance of Michael, who had descended from Heaven as the forerunner of Shekinah." ... According to Talmud Berakot 35, where the comment is on Genesis 18:1-10, Michael is recognized by Sarah as one of 3 "men" whom Abraham entertained unawares. Legend speaks of Michael having assisted 4 other great angels - Gabriel, Uriel, Raphael, Metatron - in the burial of Moses, Michael disputing with Satan for possession of the body ... . In mystic and occult writings, Michael has often been equated with the Holy Ghost, the Logos, God, Metatron, etc. In Baruch 3, Michael "holds the keys of the kingdom of heaven (David Gustav, A Dictionary of Angels, 193-94)." Legends of the Jews by Ginzberg has much more information on Michael in Jewish legend and contains material worthy of the reader's attention should he/she be interested in learning more about Michael's role in extra-biblical sources. While many of these legends are tangentially related to Adam-God teachings, they are too tangential for consideration in this volume.

5   Adam as Ancient of Days

See also
Did Joseph Smith Introduce Adam-God Teachings?

Daniel 7:9-22

I beheld till the thrones were cast down, and the *Ancient of days* did sit, whose garment was white as snow, and the hair of his head like the pure wool: his throne was like the fiery flame,[71] and his wheels as burning fire. A fiery stream issued and came forth from before him: thousand thousands ministered unto him, and ten thousand times ten thousand stood before him: the judgment was set, and the books were opened. I beheld then because of the voice of the great words which the horn spake; I beheld even till the beast was slain, and his body destroyed, and given to the burning flame. As concerning the rest of the beasts, they had their dominion taken away: yet their lives were prolonged for a season and time. I saw in the night visions, and, behold, one *like* the Son of man came[72] with the clouds of heaven, and came to the *Ancient of days*, and

---

[71] Notice the parallels between Daniel's description and the following:

D&C 110:3   *4/3/1836*

His eyes were as a flame of fire; the hair of *his head was white like the pure snow; his countenance shone above the brightness of the sun*; and his voice was as the sound of the rushing of great waters, even the voice of Jehovah.

Consider also the following series of scriptures:
Psalms 2:6-7; Ezekiel 8:2; Acts 2:33-34; 1 Corinthians 15:24; Ephesians 1:20-22; Hebrews 1:1-3, 13; 8:1; 10:12-13; 12:2; 1 Peter 3:22; Revelation 1:14-15; 4:2-3,5-6, 8, 11
This pseudepigraphal work is also worthy of comparison here: Book of Enoch, 14:15-23.

[72] A second hand account claims that Joseph Smith taught that this personage was Adam's savior or "Michael's Christ." See the Contribtor statement below.

they brought him near before him. And there was given him dominion, and glory, and a kingdom, that all people, nations, and languages, should serve him: his dominion is an everlasting dominion, which shall not pass away, and his kingdom that which shall not be destroyed.

I Daniel was grieved in my spirit in the midst of my body, and the visions of my head troubled me. I came near unto one of them that stood by, and asked him the truth of all this. So he told me, and made me know the interpretation of the things. These great beasts, which are four, are four kings, which shall arise out of the earth. But the saints of the most High shall take the kingdom, and possess the kingdom for ever, even for ever and ever. Then I would know the truth of the fourth beast, which was diverse from all the others, exceeding dreadful, whose teeth were of iron, and his nails of brass; which devoured, brake in pieces, and stamped the residue with his feet; And of the ten horns that were in his head, and of the other which came up, and before whom three fell; even of that horn that had eyes, and a mouth that spake very great things, whose look was more stout than his fellows. I beheld, and the same horn [If this is Lucifer or Satan, then this is parallel to D&C 88:112-15 where Michael battles Lucifer until his defeat is certain.] made war with the saints, and prevailed against them; Until the *Ancient of days* came, and judgment was given to the saints of the most High; and the time came that the saints possessed the kingdom.

Book of Enoch[73] 55:1,2

And after that the *Head of Days* repented and said ... I destroyed all who dwell on the earth. And he sware by His great name: "Henceforth I will not do so to all who dwell on the earth, and I will set a sign in the heaven: and this shall be a pledge of good faith between me and them forever so long as heaven is above the earth."

The Messiah Texts, 13-14

I saw in a night vision, and, behold, with the clouds of heaven came one like unto a son of man Jesus, [fn: see also Abraham 3:27], and he went to the Ancient One and he was brought near before him. And to him was given dominion and glory and kingship, and all the peoples, nations, and languages will serve him. His dominion shall be an everlasting dominion which shall not pass away, and his kingdom shall not be destroyed.

D&C 27:11   *8/--/1830*

And also with Michael, or *Adam*, the father of all, the prince of all, the *ancient of days;*

---

[73] The reader may note that there are other versions of the Book of Enoch; see also D&C 107:57.

D&C 116:1   *5/19/1838*

Spring Hill is named by the Lord Adam-ondi-Ahman, because, said he, it is the place where *Adam* shall come to visit his people, or the *Ancient of Days* shall sit, as spoken of by Daniel the prophet.

D&C 138:38   *10/31/1918*

Among the great and mighty ones who were assembled in this vast congregation of the righteous were Father *Adam*, the *Ancient of Days* and father of all.

Orson Pratt   *5/--/1834*

E&MS 2:154 #20

According to Daniel, he was to come to the *ancient of days*: here he is said to reign before his ancients, that is, all the saints from our father *Adam*, down; for who could the *ancient of days* be but our father *Adam*? surely none other: he was the first who lived in days, and must be the ancient of days. And to whom would the Savior come, but to the father of all the race, and then receive his kingdom, in which he was to reign before, or with his ancients gloriously? Let it here be remarked, that it is said to be in mount Zion, and in Jerusalem, where the Lord is to reign before his ancients gloriously.

Joseph Smith   *6/2/1839*

JD 6:237-39

Daniel 7 speaks of the *Ancient of Days*. He means the oldest man - our Father Adam (Michael). He will call his children together and hold a council with them to prepare them for the coming of the Son of Man. He (Adam) is the Father of the human family, and presides over the spirits of all men; and all that have had the keys must stand before him in this grand council. This may take place before some of us leave this stage of action. The Son of Man stands before him, and there is given him glory and dominion. Adam delivers up his stewardship to Christ - that which was delivered to him as holding the keys of the universe, but retains his standing as head of the human family. ...

These men are in heaven, but their children are on earth. Their bowels yearn over us. God sends down men for this reason. (Matthew 13:41) "And the Son of Man shall send forth his angels, &c." All these authoritative characters will come down and join hand in hand in bringing about this work. ... When these things are done, the Son of Man will descend - the *Ancient of Days* sit; we may come to an innumerable company of angels - have communion with and receive instruction from them. ...

The horn made war with the Saints and overcame them, &c., until the *Ancient of Days* came; judgment was given to the Saints of the Most High from the *Ancient of Days*; the time came that the Saints possessed the kingdom. ...

When wars come, we shall have to flee to Zion. The cry is to make haste. The last revelation says, "Ye shall not have time to have" gone over the earth, until these things come. It will come as did the cholera, war, fires, and earthquakes, one pestilence after another, &c., until the *Ancient of Days* come; then judgment will be given to the Saints.

Joseph Smith	*Monday 10/5/1840*

TPJS, 167

Commencing with *Adam*, who was the first man, who is spoken of in Daniel as being the "*Ancient of Days*," or in other words, the first and oldest of all, the great, grand progenitor of whom it is said in another place he is Michael ... .

Joseph Smith	*Wednesday 5/4/1842*

TPJS, 237

I spent the day in the upper part of the store, that is in my private office ... in council with [several individuals] instructing them in the principles and order of the Priesthood, attending to washings, anointings, endowments and the communication of keys pertaining to the Aaronic Priesthood, and so on to *the highest order* of the Melchizedek Priesthood, setting forth the order *pertaining to the Ancient of Days*, and all those plans and principles by which any one is enabled to secure the fullness of those blessing which have been prepared for the Church of the Firstborn, and come up and abide in the presence of the Eloheim in the eternal worlds. In this council was instituted the ancient order of things for the first time in these last days. And the communications I made to this council were of things spiritual, and to be received only by the spiritual minded: and there was nothing made known to these men but what will be made known to all the Saints of the last days, so soon as they are prepared to receive, and a proper place is prepared to communicate them, even to the weakest of the Saints.

Mr. Adams[74]	*7/--/1842*

T&S 3:835

On Sunday Mr. Adams lectured ... . In the course of the lecture he threw much light on the subject of the *Ancient of Days, showing* him not to be the Lord Jesus Christ, nor God the Father, but *that he is Father Adam*, who shall sit as a great patriarch at the head of the whole family; when the second Adam, the Lord from heaven, the Son of Man shall come with the clouds, and come to the *Ancient of Days*, and the saints should take the kingdom, and the greatness of the kingdom, under the whole heaven, according to

---

[74] *Rodney Turner suggests this was George J.*

Daniel 7.

Orson Pratt   *5/15/1843*

T&S 4:203-04

In this wonderful vision he saw the *Ancient of Days* sit, clothed in great power and majesty; he was attended by unnumbered millions from the heavenly worlds - a grand council was organized upon the earth, over which he presided - the books were opened, and among the most important business which came before them, was the condemnation and judgment of some of the corrupt powers of the earth, and also the confirming of more power upon the Saints, that they might be prepared for the reception of their Great King - the Son of Man, who was to come and take the kingdom, and reign in the greatness of his splendour, in the midst of his people for ever. The Great King, having sent forth the *Ancient of Days*, with the grand council of heaven as messengers, to set all things in their most perfect order, at length appears in the clouds of heaven. He comes in royal splendour, and in the greatness of his strength to the *Ancient of Days*, who delivers up the kingdom into his hands, and henceforth all people, nations, and languages serve and obey him. O glorious period! O happy time! How these glorious visions must have cheered the heart of Daniel in his long captivity! And how blessed, and how inexpressibly happy will that people be who inherit the earth in that day!

But who is this *Ancient of Days* that is to act this glorious and conspicuous part in the grand councils of the last days, and finally deliver up the kingdom organized and prepared, into the hands of the Great King? It cannot be the Son of God, for he afterwards comes to the *Ancient of Days*. It cannot be the Father, for if the Saints were prepared to meet the Father and set [sic] in council with him, they would also be prepared to meet the Son, for the glory of the Father is equal to that of the Son. ... The *ancient of Days then, is Adam* - the great progenitor of the human race.

Parley P. Pratt   *1/1/1844*

The Angel of the Prairies

On entering this room, a vast and extensive hall was opened before me, the walls of which were white, and ornamented with various figures which I did not understand. In the midst of this hall was *a vast throne* and white as ivory, and ascended by seventy steps, and on either side of the throne, and of the steps leading to it, there were seats rising one above another. On this throne was seated *an aged, venerable looking man*. His *hair was white with age*, and his countenance beamed with intelligence and affection indescribable as if he were *the father of the kingdoms and the people over which he reigned*. He was clad in robes of dazzling whiteness, while a glorious crown rested upon his brow: and a pillar of light above his head seemed to diffuse over the whole scene a brilliance of glory and grandeur indescribable. There was something in his countenance which seemed to indicate that he had passed long years of struggle and exertion in the achievement of some mighty revolution, and been a man of sorrows and acquainted with grief.[75] But, like the evening sun after a day of clouds and tempest, he seemed to smile with the dignity of repose. In connection with this venerable personage sat two others scarcely less venerable, and clad and crowned in the same manner, on the next seat below were twelve personages, much of the same appearances and clad in the same manner, with crowns upon their heads; while the descending seats were filled with some thousands of noble and dignified personages, all enrobed in white and crowned with authority, power and majesty, as kings and presiding among the Sons of God. `You now behold,' said the Angel of the Prairies, `*the Grand Presiding Council* organized in wisdom, and holding the keys of power to bear rule over all the earth in righteousness. And of the increase and glory of their kingdoms there shall be no end.' ... The *venerable council* which you beheld enthroned in majesty and clad in robes of white, with crowns upon their heads, *is the order of the Ancient of Days*, before whose august presence thrones have been cast down, and tyrants have ceased to rule.

Franklin D. Richards   *12/10/1853*

MS 15:803-04

Hear what the Prophet Daniel says upon this subject - [quotes Daniel 7:9, 10, 13, 14.] Again, the word of the Lord through the Prophet Joseph, gives additional importance, if possible, to the part which *Adam* acts relating to his children, which reads as follows - [quotes D& C 29:26.]

From the foregoing we are enabled to draw important conclusions, that before the coming of the Lord Jesus in the clouds of heaven, to take the reins of government upon the earth, *Adam* comes and gathers around him all that have ever held keys of power under him upon the earth, in *any* of the dispensations thereof to man; he *calls forth the dead from their graves, at the sound of his trump*; he brings them to judgment, and they render unto him an account of their several stewardships; the books are opened that a righteous judgment may be rendered by him who now sits upon his throne, not only as the Father, but the Judge, of men; and in that capacity thousands minister unto him. An august assemblage are now gathered in one grand council around the great Patriarch of all Patriarchs, consisting of his sons, who have been faithful in that which was committed to them; and all this preparatory to that great event, when the greatness of the kingdom under the whole heaven should be given to the Saints of the Most High.

---

[75] In this context, consider Isaiah 53:3 "He is despised and rejected of men; a man of sorrows, and acquainted with grief" and John 14:9 "Jesus saith ... he that hath seen me hath seen the Father."

Daniel saw that the Saints possessed the kingdom, by virtue of which *Adam* was once more in possession of the dominion given unto him before the fall, which was over every living thing that moved upon the earth, which rendered him the universal Sovereign and Lord of *all*.

At this important period, when *Adam is reinstated* with full power upon the earth, seated upon his throne, as Daniel saw him - *a glorious and an immortal God*, one like the Son of Man comes in the clouds of heaven (as oftimes represented by the Apostles), to the *Ancient of days*, and receives from him dominion, glory, and a kingdom; or in other words, Michael, having accomplished the work committed to him, pertaining to this world, delivers up an account of his stewardship over the same, to that character represented as Yahovah[76] in the creation of the world, who reigns in unison with those upon the earth, until his work is fully accomplished - till the last great contest with the enemy, who has been released for a little season, is won; then he in turn delivers up the kingdom to the great Eloheim, that in the language of the Apostle, 'God may be all in all.'

This final surrender, we are to bear in mind, does not detract from the God-like power and dominion of our first Parent, nor of our Lord Jesus Christ. In the Patriarchal order of government, each and every ruler is independent in his sphere, his rule extending to those below, and not to those above him, in the same order. ...

[W]e find that ... *Michael has power to deliver men from the power of the Devil*, which is death; that by the sound of his own trump - the trump of the archangel, the nations of the dead shall awake and come forth to judgment, and there render an account to the *Ancient of Days* seated upon his burning throne. Then shall the nations know that he is their Judge, their Lawgiver, and *their God*, and upon his decree hangs the destiny of the assembled dead. Yes, our Judge will be a kind and compassionate Father, by whom none can pass, but through whom all glory, dominion, and power, will be ascribed to the great ETERNAL.

Brigham Young	*2/19/1854*

TPBY 3:251-52

He is Father *Adam* - Michael - the *Ancient of Days*.

First Presidency	*4/10/1854*

MFP 2:135

Then haste, ye Elders, to the work which lies before you; and let all the Saints go to with their mights to prepare for the great day of power and devastation which will

---

[76] This is not referring to Jesus; see "Titles & Offices: Jehovah".

assuredly come upon the whole earth, for the day when the Son of Man shall appear, the *Ancient of Days* shall sit in judgment; and each and every one will be required to render a faithful and true account of his stewardship.

Brigham Young   *4/25/1855*

MABY[77]

We begin with the father of our Lord Jesus Christ, and of our spirits - who is he? Do you know anything about him? Can you find out who he is? Suppose we go to the scriptures and enquire who he is. ... "This is eternal life, to know thee, the only true God, and Jesus Christ whom thou hast sent." Well, *how can we learn by reading the history of Adam and Eve to know the Lord*? If you were to hear the footsteps of the Lord, would you know from the history of Adam and Eve that it was the Lord coming? They knew his voice and his footsteps for they had lived with him. And what I have upon this subject I now say; Adam had been with the Lord and had lived with him upon an earth like this and had been faithful and overcome, and had received his body and was resurrected and was well acquainted with the Lord and was one of his mess mates. He had eaten and drank with him and had lived with him from generation to generation and in many worlds, probably while many had come into and gone out of existence. And he helped to make this earth and brought the seeds with him that you see springing up spontaneously, and when he called, the elements came rolling together.
Well, you see from this that when you and I have been with and lived with the Lord, we shall know his voice. If father Adam were to come into this house and you were to see him go back and forth, would you know him? No, you would never mistrust it was him unless he revealed himself. But by the time that you have lived with him as long as Adam had before he came here, you will know him and recognize his footsteps, but reading the history will not teach you these things. Consequently I come right down to ourselves and say we cannot know the only wise God and Jesus Christ whom he has sent. No man can have this knowledge but those to whom God reveals it. Has he revealed it to you, who he is, what he has to do with this world and the relationship that he sustains to it? You must not be astonished when I tell you that the whole world, with the exception of the Latter-day Saints, for they do know something about God, but the whole world besides are as far from that knowledge as the east is from the west. Though they read it in the Bible, yet it never enters into their hearts that the apostle told the truth when he says, "There is but one living and true God, the father of our spirits." Well now, who is the father of our spirits?
I will tell you what I think about some who will have something to do with us by and

---

[77] The Deseret News, on May 2, 1855 reported that "President Brigham delivered a lengthy and interesting lecture on theology, which was listened to with profound attention by the audience."

by. When Michael blows his trumpet and calls the world together, we shall then be before him and we shall be perfectly satisfied that he can pass all the judgment that we shall want, and that the dominions of the wicked will want, and I have no doubt but the Saints that live and have lived from the days of Adam will be satisfied that he can give them kingdoms and power, thrones and dominions and influence in eternity. And when they get all that he can give, they will be satisfied and say it is enough. If we can get to *him, the Ancient of Days*, whose hair is like wool, a man of age, a man of experience, and can learn of him to understand "I am that I am," we shall then hear him say, "I am your father and leader. I will be your front and your rearward. I understand what this world is. I understand all about it. I have the government of the world in my hands, although to a certain extent my opposer, my enemy, has gained a certain influence in the world."

You will hear him say, "I am in the whirlwind at my pleasure. I ride upon the storms and I govern worlds. I set up one king and put another down and organize empires and overthrow them at my pleasure. I the Lord do all these things." When we come to that great and wise and glorious being that the children of Israel were afraid of, whose countenance shone so that they could not look upon him, I say when we get to him whom they could not look upon, to that man … . When we can see that very character and talk and live with him in our tabernacles, if we are so fortunate as to get there into his society, then we can say that to us there is but one living and true God and he is the father of our Lord Jesus Christ and of our spirits. And when we get back to him and learn that he is actually our father, we shall not feel any anxiety to call upon anybody else for the blessings we are in need of. It is a subject I am aware that does not appear so clear to our understandings at present as we could wish it or as it will some day, and it is one that should not trouble us at all. All such things will become more clear to your minds by and by.

I tell you this as my belief about that personage who is called the *Ancient of Days*, the Prince and so on, but I do not tell it because that I wish it to be established in the minds of others, though to me this is as clear as the sun, it is as plain as my alphabet. I understand it as I do the path to go home. I did not understand so until my mind became enlightened with the Spirit and by the revelations of God, neither will you understand until our Father in Heaven reveals all these things unto you. To my mind and to my feelings those matters are all plain and easy to be understood.

John Jacques   *1856*

Sacred Hymns #306
WE BELIEVE IN OUR GOD

We believe in our God, the great Prince of his race,
The Archangel, Michael, the *Ancient of Days*,
Our own Father *Adam*, earth's Lord is his plane,
Who'll counsel and fight for his children again.

Parley P. Pratt   *before 1857*
Voice of Warning, 100

I now no longer marvel, when I call to mind that Abraham counted himself a stranger
and pilgrim, seeking a better country, and a city whose builder and maker is God. And
according to the scriptures, *Adam our Father, the Ancient of Days*, is to sit; the Lord is to
come; the earth is to be renewed; and then after this restoration there will be but one
more change necessary, in order to fit the earth for man's eternal inheritance; and that
change is to take place at the last day, after man has enjoyed it in peace a thousand
years. We have now discovered the great secret, which none but the saints have
understood (but was well understood by them in all ages of the world), which is this,
that man is to dwell in the flesh, upon the earth, with the Messiah, with the whole
house of Israel and with all the saints of the Most High, not only one thousand years,
but forever and ever.

There again our father *Adam*, whose hair is white like the pure wool, will sit enthroned
in dignity as the *Ancient of Days*, the great Patriarch, the mighty Prince; while again
thousands of thousands stand before him, and ten thousand times ten thousand minister
to him; there he will hail all his children, who died in the faith of the Messiah; while
Abel, Enoch, Noah, Abraham, Job, and Daniel with all the prophets and apostles, and
all the saints of God of all ages, hail each other in the flesh. Jesus the great Messiah will
stand in the midst, and, to crown the whole, will gird himself, and administer bread
and wine to the whole multitude, and he himself will partake of the same with them on
the earth, all being clothed in fine linen, clean and white. This is the marriage supper of
the Lamb. Blessed are they who partake thereof.

Brigham Young   *6/27/1860*
DN

We talk in this ignorant age, of children becoming of age, as it is called; and we
consider when they are of age they are free from the authority of their father. But no
such rule is known in the celestial law and organization, either here or hereafter. By
that law a son is subject to his father forever and ever, worlds without end. ...
His most gracious and venerable majesty, King Adam, with his royal consort, Queen
eve, will appear at the head of the whole great family of the redeemed, and will be
crowned in their midst as a King and Priest forever after the [Order of] Son of God.

They will then be arrayed in garments white as snow and will take their seats on the throne, in the midst of the paradise of God on the earth, to reign forever and ever. While thousands of thousands stand before him, and ten thousand times ten thousand minister unto him. And if you will receive it, this is the order of the *Ancient of days* - the kingdom prepared and organized to meet Jesus when he comes.

This venerable patriarch and sovereign [Adam] will hold lawful jurisdiction over Abel, Enoch, Noah, Abraham, Isaac, Jacob, Joseph, Moses, the prophets, apostles, Saints of all ages and dispensations, who will all reverence and obey him as their venerable father and lawful sovereign. They will then be organized, each over his own department of the government, according to their birthright and office, in their families, generations and nations. Each one will obey and be obeyed according to the connection which he sustains as a member of the great celestial family. Thus the graduation will descend in regular degrees from the throne of the *Ancient of days* with his innumerable subjects, down to the least and last Saint of the last days who may be counted worthy of a throne and scepter, although his kingdom may, perhaps, only consist of a wife and single child. Such the order and organization of the celestial family, and such the natures of the thrones, principalities and powers, which are the rewards of diligence. [fn: see Parley P. Pratt, MS 5:189] If we are crowned to become lords of lords, and kings of kings, it will be to rule and reign over our own posterity pertaining to this flesh - these tabernacles - this commencement in our finite state of being. When I reign King of Kings, and lord of lords, over my children, it will be when my first, second, third, fourth, and so on, son rises up and counts thousands and millions of his posterity, and is king over them; then I am a king of these kings. Our Father, who is Lord of all, will reign a King of kings and Lord of lords over all his children.

Brigham Young   *11/30/1862*
MABY

[E]ach person who we crown in the celestial kingdom of God will be a father of fathers, a king of kings, a lord of lords, a god of gods ... Each person will reign over his posterity. *Adam*, Michael, the *Ancient of Days*, will sit as the judge of the quick and dead, for he is the father of all living, and Eve is the mother of all living, pertaining to the human family, and he is their king, their Lord, their God, taking and holding his position in the grand unbroken chain of endless increase, and eternal progression.

Brigham Young   *1/8/1865*
JD 11:41-42

One of the prophets describes the Father of us all, saying, "I beheld till the thrones were cast down, and the *Ancient of days* did sit, whose garment was white as snow, and the hair of his head like the pure wool; his throne was like the fiery flame," etc. The prophet further says, "thousand thousands ministered unto him, and ten thousand times ten thousand stood before him," etc. Again "and, behold, one like the Son of Man came with the clouds of heaven and came to the *Ancient of days*, and they brought him near before him." Now, who is the *Ancient of days*? You may answer this question at your pleasure, I have already told the people. But the Savior would answer the question as to the appearance of the Father of us all, by saying, "Look at me, for *I am the very express image of my Father*."

Brigham Young   *1/13/1867*

JD 11:283

When Jesus comes to reign King of nations as he now reigns King of Saints, he will not apostatize although the whole world will be at his command; and when the *Ancient of Days* shall come and sit upon his throne to bring to judgment the vast family of man, he will not apostatize.

Brigham Young   *2/10/1867*

JD 11:327

They will come up tribe by tribe, and the *Ancient of Days*, He who led Abraham, and talked to Noah, Enoch, Isaac, and Jacob, that very Being will come and judge the twelve tribes of Israel.

George Q. Cannon   *10/15/1870*

Meeting of the School of the Prophets

[George Q. Cannon] fully endorsed the doctrine that father *Adam* was our God and Father - or as He in many places is called, Michael the great prince - the Arch Angel, *Ancient of Days*, &c.

Wilford W. Woodruff   *10/15/1870*

I dug potatoes in the forenoon & attended the School of the Prophets in the Afternoon President Yo[un]g asked me to speak upon the Character of Adam who he was I proved that *Adam was* Michael the Archangel, the Seventh Angel, & the *Ancient of Days*, the Father of all & the prince of All. [sic] Daniel 7:9-14 D&C 79 page 28 paragraph 106 page 35 p 201 p 2d Paragraph I was followed by G Q Cannon President Yg & G.A. Smith

JD 17:185-87

Having made these few preliminary remarks in regard to the judgment of the children of men, let us now refer again to the passage contained in the seventh chapter of Daniel - Says that ancient Prophet - "I beheld till the thrones were cast down, and the *Ancient of days* did sit, whose garment was white as snow, and the hair of his head like the pure wool; his throne was like the fiery flame, and his wheels as burning fire. A fiery stream issued and came forth from before him; thousand thousands ministered unto him, and ten thousand times ten thousand stood before him: the judgment was set and the books were opened."

How many are ten thousand times ten thousand. One hundred millions. That would be a larger congregation than you or I ever saw, and larger, probably, than any congregation that has ever been collected together upon this earth at any one time. They would occupy a vast region of country, even for a foothold. A hundred million people stood before this personage - the *Ancient of days*. Who was this personage called the *Ancient of days*? We are told by the Prophet Joseph Smith ... that the *Ancient of days* is the most ancient personage that ever had an existence in days here on the earth. And who was he? Why, of course, old father Adam, he was the most ancient man that ever lived in days that we have any knowledge of. He comes, then, as a great judge, to assemble this innumerable host of which Daniel speaks. He comes in flaming fire. The glory and blessing and greatness of this personage it would be impossible even for a man as great as Daniel fully to describe. He comes as a man inspired from the eternal throne of Jehovah himself. *He comes to set in order the councils of the Priesthood pertaining to all dispensations, to arrange the Priesthood and the councils of the Saints of all former dispensations in one grand family and household.*

What is all this for? Why all this arrangement? Why all this organization? Why all this judgment and the opening of the books? It is to prepare the way for another august personage whom Daniel saw coming with the clouds of heaven, namely the Son of Man, and these clouds of heaven brought the Son of Man near before the *Ancient of days*. And when the Son of Man came to the *Ancient of days*, behold a kingdom was given to the Son of Man, and greatness and glory, that all people, nations and languages should serve him, and his kingdom should be an everlasting kingdom, a kingdom that should never be done away.

This explains the reason why our father *Adam* comes as the *Ancient of days* with all these numerous hosts, and organizes them according to the records of the book, every man in his place, preparatory to the coming of the Son of Man to receive the kingdom. Then every family that is in the order of the Priesthood, and every man and every woman, and every son or daughter whatever their kindred, descent or Priesthood, will know their place.

Where will this great conference take place? The Lord has revealed this also. ... I say that [Joseph Smith], by the power of the Holy Ghost, and the spirit of revelation, revealed the very place where this great assemblage of ten thousand times ten thousand of the righteous shall be gathered together when the books are opened. It will be on one of the last places of residence of our father Adam here on the earth, and it is called by revelation Adam-ondi-ahman, which, being interpreted, means the valley of God where Adam dwelt, the words belonging to the language which was Spoken by the children of men before the confusion took place at Babel. In that valley Adam called together Seth, Enos, Cainan, Mahalaleel, Jared, Enoch, Methusaleh and all the high Priests and righteous of his descendants for some seven or eight generations. Three years before his death he there stood up, being bowed with age, and preached to that vast assembly of people, and pronounced upon them his great and last patriarchal blessing, and they rose up by the authority and power and revelation of the holy Priesthood which they held, and pronounced their blessing upon their great common progenitor Adam, and he was called the Prince of Peace, and the Father of many nations, and it was said that he should stand at the head of and rule over his people of all generations, notwithstanding he was so aged. That was the blessing pronounced, three years before his death, upon the great head, Patriarch and Prophet of this creation, the man whom God chose to begin the works of this creation, in other words to begin the peopling of this earth.

Where was that valley in which that grand patriarchal gathering was held? It was about fifty, sixty or seventy miles north of Jackson County, Missouri, where the Zion of the latter days will be built. Where the garden of Eden was is not fully revealed; where Adam ate the forbidden fruit is not revealed so far as I know, that is, the particular location on the earth, no revelation informs us where he passed the first few centuries of his life; but suffice it to say that, when Adam was about six or seven hundred years old there was a great gathering of the people Enoch, the seventh from Adam, who lived contemporary with his old ancestor, and others who were called by him, went forth and gathered out the righteous from all the nations, and as there was no Atlantic Ocean in those days rolling between the eastern and western continents, they could gather together by land from Asia, Africa and Europe. In those days the earth was not divided as it was after the flood, in the days of Peleg. In that gathering many came from the ends of the earth. Adam might have been among the emigrating companies, if not, then, he most probably had his residence at that central place of gathering.

Let this be as it may, it is not revealed. There is a place, however, where this great Conference took place in ancient times, where the Lord revealed himself to that vast assembly, and stood in their midst, and instructed them with his own mouth, and they saw his face. There is the place where it was ordained that *Adam* should have the power, as the *Ancient of Days*, after a certain period and dispensations had rolled away, to come in his glory accompanied by the ancient Saints, the generations that should live after him and should take up their abode upon that land where they received their last blessing, there in the valley of Adam-ondi-ahman. This man, will sit upon his throne, and ten thousand times ten thousand *immortal beings - his children -* will stand before him, with all their different grades of Priesthood, according to the order which God has appointed and ordained. Then every quorum of the Priesthood in this Latter-day Saint Church will find its place, and never until then. If we go behind the vail we will not see this perfect organization of the Saints of all generations until that period shall arrive. That will be before Jesus comes in his glory. Then ... all the various quorums and councils of the Priesthood in every dispensation that has transpired since the days of Adam until the present time will find their places, according to the callings, gifts, blessings, ordinations and keys of Priesthood which the Lord Almighty has conferred upon them in their several generations. This, then, will be one of the grandest meetings that has ever transpired upon the face of our globe.

Brigham Young	*5/14/1876*

L. John Nuttall Papers

The Savior comes to the father, the *Ancient of Days*, and presents to the Father the kingdoms of this world all in a saved condition except the sons of perdition and he says, "Here, Father, here they are and I with them" Then he is prepared to go forth and fill up his kingdom, and so he goes on.

John Taylor	*12/31/1876*

JD 18:329-30

In speaking with the Prophet Joseph once on this subject, he traced it from the first down to the last, until he got to the *Ancient of Days*. He wished me to write something for him on this subject, but I found it a very difficult thing to do. He had to correct me several times. We are told that the "judgment shall sit and the books be opened." He spoke of the various dispensations and of those holding the keys thereof, and said there would then be a general giving up or "accounting for." I wrote that each one holding the keys of the several dispensations would deliver them up to his predecessor, from one to another, until the whole kingdom should be delivered up to the Father and then God would be "all in all." Said he, "That is not right." I wrote it again, and again he said it was not right. It is very difficult to find language suitable to convey the meaning of spiritual things. The idea was that they should deliver up or give an account of their administrations, in their several dispensations, but that they would all retain their several positions and priesthood.

Orson Pratt   *Sunday p.m. 2/25/1877*

JD 18:342-43

Who would be the most likely person to fill this important position? He is called the *Ancient of Days.* ... This place, Spring Hill, is alluded to by the Lord, in this revelation, as being anciently called Adam-ondi-Ahman, because it is the place where *Adam* shall come to visit his children, or the place where the *Ancient of Days* shall sit. ... We have then an understanding that it was the place where Adam dwelt.

John Taylor   *1/13/1880*

L. John Nuttall Papers

I heard Joseph say that *Adam* was the *ancient of Days* spoken of by Daniel.

John Taylor   *5/18/1884*

JD 25:181

God is interested in the dead as well as the living. *Adam, who is the Ancient of Days* and the father of the human family; Seth, Enos, Enoch, Mahalaleel, Methuselah, Noah, and all the prominent leading men of God, as well as Abraham, Isaac, Jacob, Moses, the Prophets, Jesus and His Apostles, together with the Prophets and Apostles who lived on this continent ... all these ancient fathers feel interested in this great work, and their hearts are turned toward the children, being interested in their welfare, happiness and exaltation.

Orson F. Whitney   *8/--/1885*

Contributor 6:403

The central point was called Spring Hill by the people of that neighborhood, but Joseph rechristened it Adam-ondi-Ahman, having been informed by the Lord that it was the identical spot where *Adam*, the father of the human family, would come to visit his people in the last days, in other words, where the *Ancient of Days* would sit, as foretold by the Prophet Daniel. This fact was made known on the nineteenth of May, 1838.

Joseph Smith   *5/--/1886*

Contributor 7:286 #8

Joseph also referred to Michael's Christ's future coming to this same Valley: He shall "*come to the Ancient of Days and shall give to Him dominion and Glory,* and issue a Decree that all people shall serve and obey Him."

My Life's Review, 35-36

On our arrival at Diahman, our camp was pitched upon the town plat which had just been surveyed by direction of the Prophet, and of course each one was anxious to obtain the most eligible, or first choice of lots. As I was young and unmarried my choice would come near the last under the rule of "oldest served first." So when it was my choice I found I must take the top lot on the promontory overlooking the Grand River valley, or go farther away and lower down than I wished to. So I chose the upper, which at first appeared rocky, but which made the other lots appear almost enviable. When, after a few days, the Prophet accompanied us to this spot, and pointed out those rocks as the ones of which *Adam* built an altar and offered sacrifice upon this spot, where he stood and blessed the multitude of his children, when they called him Michael, and where he will again sit as the *Ancient of Days*, then I was not envious of anyone's choice for a city lot in Adam-ondi-Ahman. Yet I would not have it inferred that my inheritance there, or those given me elsewhere are to be especially guaranteed to have in future.

ELIAS, AN EPIC OF THE AGES, 51

Ancient of Days here sits, as at the first,
When time and earth and *Adam's* race were young;
When, bowed with age, a great soul's sunset burst
In blessings on his seed. Prophetic tongue,
Thy patriarchal tone through time hath rung!

Michael, the prince, the monarch of our race,
Sire of a world from dust and spirit sprung;
Here sits he, throned in fire; before his face
Ten thousand times ten thousand throng the judgment place.

Sacred Hymns, 375-75 #316
SONS OF MICHAEL, HE APPROACHES

Sons of *Michael*, he approaches!
Rise; *the Eternal Father* greet;
Bow, ye thousands, low before him;

Minister before his feet; [78]
Hail, hail the Patriarch's glad reign,
Hail, hail the Patriarch's glad reign,
Spreading over sea and main.

Sons of *Michael*, 'tis his chariot
Rolls its burning wheels along!
Raise aloft your voices million[79]
In a torrent power of song:
Hail, hail our Head with music soft!
Hail, hail our Head with music soft!
Raise sweet melodies aloft!

Mother of our generations,
Glorious by great *Michael's* side,
Take thy children's adoration;
Endless with thy Lord preside;
Lo, lo, to greet thee now advance,
Lo, lo, to greet thee now advance
Thousands in the glorious dance!

Raise a chorus, sons of *Michael*,
Like old Ocean's roaring swell,
Till the mighty acclamation
Through rebounding space cloth tell
That, that the Ancient One doth reign,
That, that the Ancient One doth reign
In his Paradise again!

Bishop Heber Bennion   *1920*

Supplement to Gospel Problems, 13
T[he unbelieving gentiles] mocked at Brigham Young, Adam-God, and we seek to

---

[78] The first verse has been changed to read:
Sons of Michael, he approaches!
Rise; the ancient Father greet;
Bow, ye thousands, low before him;
Minister before his feet.
[79] Could this be an allusion to Daniel 7 given this allusion and the reference to "thousands" above and below?

molify and pacify them by telling them that is not the doctrine of the Church, but only the doctrine of Brigham Young. But we are making matters worse, for next we will have to explain that it was only an idea of Joseph Smith, and the Prophet Daniel, and of Jesus Christ, for Jesus gave this revelation to Joseph Smith. Adam-ondi-Ahman, because, said he, it is the place where *Adam* shall come to visit his people, or the *Ancient of Days* shall sit, as spoken of by Daniel, the prophet.' - D&C 116.

Now let us turn to Daniel, and see what he says about the Adam-God doctrine. `I beheld till the thrones were cast down, and the *Ancient of Days* did sit, whose garments were white as snow, and the hair of his head like the pure wool; his throne was like the fiery flame, and his wheels as burning fire. A fiery stream issued and came forth from before him; thousands ministered unto him, and ten thousand times ten thousand stood before him; and the judgment was set, and the books were opened.' - Daniel 7:9, 10. The above revelation of Joseph Smith, together with the prophecy of Daniel seems to corroborate Brigham Young's doctrine of Adam-God - beyond question.

Brigham H. Roberts

Seventy's Course in Theology 3:91

"We have reason to believe that the Britons inhabited England not long after the days of Noah. We might therefore expect to find resemblances between their religion and the religion of other ancient peoples; and we are not disappointed. There is a striking correspondence between the system of the ancient Britons and those of the Hebrew patriarchs, the Brahmins of India, the Magi of Persia, and the Greek priests. It was one system that was finally conveyed to these different parts of the globe. Take, as a single instance of the many points of comparison, their idea of God. Among their names for the supreme God which they had in use before the introduction of Christianity, were terms which have been literally translated, "God," "Distributor," "Governor," the "Mysterious One," the "Eternal," "He that pervadeth all things," "the Author of Existence," "*the Ancient of Days.*" These expressive appellations sufficiently indicate their views of the moral character and attributes of God."[80]

Brigham H. Roberts

CHC 1:421-22

The upper settlement on Grand river was called "Adam-ondi-Ahman," generally abbreviated to "Di-Ahman." ... A number of families of saints had been settled at this point for several months before the arrival of Joseph Smith who called the place "Spring Hill;" "but by the mouth of the Lord," said the Prophet, "it was named Adam-ondi-

---

[80] He is here citing: The World's Worship - Dobbins, 188.

Ahman" "because" said he, "it is the place where *Adam* shall come to visit his people or the *Ancient of Days* shall sit as spoken of by Daniel the prophet." A short distance south of Spring Hill, or Adam-ondi-Ahman, was the home of Lyman Wight, at the foot of "Tower Hill," a name given to the place by Joseph Smith "in consequence of the remains of an old Nephite altar or tower," he explains, "that stood there." A photogravure of Wight's house is published in this chapter, being the only "Mormon" home left standing in "Di-Ahman," or its vicinity. It may also be said to be a typical Missouri house of the period.

Brigham H. Roberts

CHC 2:134-35

THE FIRST "ENDOWMENT HOUSE"

This contemplated order of things so pressed upon President Joseph Smith's mind that apparently he could not wait for the completion of the temple in Nauvoo, but improvised the means of introducing this foreshadowed ritual by arranging rooms in the upper story of his brick store standing near the banks of the Mississippi river on Water street, and there, on the fourth of May, 1842, began the introduction of the said ritual, General James Adams, of Springfield, Patriarch Hyrum Smith, Bishops Newel K. Whitney and George Miller; also Brigham Young, Heber C. Kimball, and Willard Richards of the quorum of the twelve apostles, being present. The Prophet's Journal for the 4th of May says that he spent the day instructing these men "in the principles and order of the priesthood, attending to washings, anointings, endowments and the communication of keys pertaining to the Aaronic priesthood, setting forth the order of the '*Ancient of Days*,' and so on to the highest order of the Melchizedek priesthood, setting forth the order pertaining to the '*Ancient of Days*,' and all those plans and principles by which any one is enabled to secure the fulness of those blessings which have been prepared for the 'Church of the First Born,' and come up and abide in the presence of the Elohim in the eternal worlds." He continues his record of the 4th of May as follows: "In this council was instituted the ancient order of things for the first time in these last days. And the communications I made to this council were things spiritual, and to be received only by the spiritually minded: and there was nothing made known to these men but what will be made known to all the saints of the last days, so soon as they are prepared to receive, and a proper place is prepared to communicate them, even to the weakest of the saints; therefore let the saints be diligent in building the temple, and all houses which they have been, or shall hereafter be, commanded of God to build; and wait their time with patience in all meekness, faith, perseverance unto the end, knowing assuredly that all these things referred to in this council are always governed by the principle of revelation.

Orson Pratt

UR 1:91 par. 45-49

Again, my servant Daniel was shown a vision of my coming in a cloud to take the dominion of the earth; and that all kingdoms should serve and obey me. But before I came he saw my kingdom organized in its beauty by the Ancient of Days, and all prepared to receive me. Know ye therefore, O inhabitants of the earth, that all these, and many other scriptures must be fulfilled in connection with my coming; And that I cannot come till the times of restoration are fulfilled, and till the circumstances and preparations are complete as it is written; And that when all things are prepared I will come, and bring all the Saints with me to reign on the earth.

UR 2:153 par. 8

Here, in the times of restitution, when all things in Christ are gathered in one, Adam, Michael, the great Prince, *Ancient of Days*, is to come in power and glory, revisiting the scenes of his earthly pilgrimage.

Analysis & Observations

β

In contrast to teachings that Adam is the father of Jesus Christ and the father of our spirits, the teaching that Adam is the Ancient of Days referred to in Daniel 7 is not a shocking revelation to members of the modern LDS Church. Many of the members of the LDS Church already believe this to be true - and they subsequently do not see any correlation to Adam-God teachings. In contrast, fundamentalists perceive this teaching as proof not only of Adam-God teachings, but as proof that Joseph Smith originated Adam-God doctrines. The above statements do little to resolve that conflict. However, the information below may be helpful in bridging this academic gap a little better.

The statements that follow[81] inform us of two things: First, a now classic biblical

---

[81] These statements represent a compilation of sources that I received from at least three Internet sources and two written sources. I have not been able to identify which author or authors originally performed the research that follows so I am unable to give them the credit they deserve. Further, I have not taken the time to verify which edition most of these statements were found in.

commentary authored by Adam Clark (a Hebrew scholar and Methodist minister) and used by Joseph Smith proclaims that the Ancient of Days was God the Father. Second, representative commentaries from various Jewish, Catholic, and Christian sects all concur that the Ancient of Days was God the Father.

1706

Matthew Henry Bible Commentary
The Judge is the Ancient of days himself, God the Father, the glory of whose presence is here described. He is called the Ancient of days, because his is God from everlasting to everlasting.

circa 1754

John Wesley's Explanatory Notes on the Whole Bible
God the king, and judge of all, called the Ancient of days, because of his eternal deity.

Adam Clark   *circa late 1700s*

Clark's Commentary of the Bible, Daniel 7-9
[The] Ancient of Days is God Almighty. ... This is the only place in the sacred writings where God the Father is represented in human form. ... Hence Abraham worshipped the Ancient of Days.

The Jewish Encyclopedia 1:571-572
The Ancient of Days is a poetical epithet for God. ... [Daniel uses the title Ancient of Days to describe] the venerable character of the being whose name the author hesitates to mention.

circa 1823

Matthew Easton's Bible Dictionary
Ancient of Days - an expression applied to Jehovah three times in the vision of (Daniel 7:9, 13, 22) in the sense of eternal. In contrast with all earthly kings, his days are past reckoning.

1871

Commentary Critical and Explanatory on the Whole Bible
Ancient of days - "The everlasting Father" (Isaiah 9:6). He is the Judge here, as the Son does not judge in His own cause.

The Catholic Encyclopedia 1:463
The Ancient of Days is a name given to God by the Prophet Daniel. ... It is from these descriptions of the Almighty that Christian art derived its general manner of representing the first person of the Holy Trinity.

Erdman's Commentary of the Bible, 480
The Ancient of Days is the description given by Daniel, who pictures God on His throne of judgment, judging the great world empires. ... This title alternates with the 'Most High.'

The Anchor Bible 23:217-218
Even though God is not explicitly mentioned by name, every reader would at once recognize as God 'the Ancient One' who presides at this celestial tribunal. ... The term 'the Ancient One' is used of God, though not found in older Biblical literature is partly based on the ... popular notion of God as an old man.

The Zondervan Pictorial Encyclopedia of the Bible 1:156
This expression [Ancient of Days] occurs only in Daniel 7:9, 13, 22. ... It is an elegant Semitic expression to designate an old man. ... Although the passage does not directly say so, the numerous commentators unite to take it at once to be a euphemistic term for God.

That all of these statements concur in their belief that the Ancient of Days was God the Father is significant because it strongly *suggests* that the early saints, upon hearing Joseph proclaim that Adam was the Ancient of Days, would have been aware of the implications of this doctrine. However, what fundamentalists often tend to overlook when arguing this point is that these early saints *could* have understood these proclamations by Joseph to mean that Joseph was contradicting *all* of these sectarian teachings about the identity of the Ancient of Days[82] - after all, Joseph commonly contradicted a vast amount of teachings promoted by competing sects of his day (e.g., baptism by immersion, the laying on of hands, the gathering, plural marriage, plurality of gods, differing degrees of glory, etc.). Therefore, on their own, the above statements, along with the Bible

---

[82] Consider the 1842 Mr. Adams quote as an example.

commentaries, do little to convince us as to whether or not the early saints believed that these teachings were in fact, pronouncements that Adam is God the Father. Nevertheless, when the above information is analyzed as a whole with the information found in the subsection "Did Joseph Smith Introduce Adam-God Teachings?" and the "Millennial Star 15:801-04" subsection along with its analysis, the fundamentalist position that the early saints understood this teaching as a pronouncement that Adam is God the Father is much more defendable. If the reader is interested in researching the position as to whether or not the early saints understood these Ancient of Day teachings to be Adam-God pronouncement, he/she is advised to read those sections and compare all of that information conglomerately.

6 Adam as Creator of this Earth

Brigham Young   *Sunday 4 p.m. 3/14/1852*

Historian's Office Journal, 106 [fn: I found the following explanation of the format of this quote on the internet but was unable to ascertain who produced this information: CR/100/1/Reel #1. The words in parenthesis are transcribed Pitman shorthand entries that I am sure of the transcription. Portions of words in brackets are filled out as context seems to intend. Shorthand entries I could not transcribe are indicated by (sh). Once in the text I have (s) because the shorthand indicated merely the letter s. It should not be considered a mistake in typing (s) instead of (sh). It is not a short-form either for a word I could fit into the context or one with which I am familiar. The blank space after the first time the word Adam appears is in the original. Typed as in the original with no punctuation or capitalization supplied.]

BY, HCK, WR OP WW GAS TB EH DH Wells TOA. WWO. (met) (in) (the) (temple) rooms (and) prayed T B. O Pratt (sh) mouths conversed about O Pratt's discourse (in) (the) endowment rooms yesterday B Y rolled out rev.n (upon) rev.n (in) regard (to) (the) crea(tion).n [sic] (of) (the) world *Adam came (to) (the) E[arth] when (he) assisted (to) form (it)* (sh) (he) then partook (of) (the) fruits (of) (the) E[arth] (and) Became Earthy (and) (they) (which) are (the) (s) (after) (sh) rece[ive] our resurrected bodies (and) (shall) (all) (have) (the) priv[ilege] (of) going (as) Adam's form (an) E[arth] (and) do likewise.

Brigham Young   *Friday 4/16/1852*

Journal of Samuel Holister Rogers, 1:179

[O]ur spirits ware begotten before that Adam came to the Earth and that *Adam helped to make the Earth*, that he had a Celestial body when he came to the Earth and that he brought his wife or one of his wives with him ...

Brigham Young   *Friday 10/6/1854*

Journal of the Southern Indian Mission, 87- 89

Eloheim spoke, "Yehovah, Michael - see matter all around, go and organize a world," Yehovah Michael went and carried material: Then Michael came down with his wife, & began to people it.

Brigham Young   *Sunday 10/8/1854*

MABY

Eloheim looks round upon the eternity of matter, and said to His associates, and those that He was pleased to call upon at that time for His counselors, with regard to the Elements, Worlds, Planets, Kingdoms and Thrones; said He: "Yahovah Michael, see that Eternal Matter on all sides, this way and that way; we have already created Worlds upon Worlds, shall we create another World? Yes, go and organize the elements in yonder space" ... "Yahovah *Michael, go and create a world*, make it, organize it, form it; and then put upon it everything in all the variety that you have seen, that you have been in the habit of being associated with in other worlds, of beasts, birds, fowls, fish, and every insect, and creeping thing, and finally, when the whole eternity of element is full of life, bring it together and make of it living creatures." Yahovah Michael goes and does as he is told. What I am now going to tell you, will no doubt astonish the whole of you. When Yahovah Michael had organized the world, and brought from another kingdom the beasts, fish, fowl, and insects, and every tree, and plant with which we are acquainted, and thousands we never saw - when He had filled the Earth with animal and vegetable life - Michael or Adam goes down to the new made world, and there he stays.

Brigham Young   *5/6/1855*

Wilford Woodruff Journal

Adam assisted in forming this earth & agreed to fall when he came here, & he fell that man might be...

Brigham Young   *4/20/1856*

JD 3:319-20

Though we have it in history that our father *Adam* was made of the dust of this earth, and that he knew nothing about his God previous to being made here, yet it is not so; and when we learn the truth we shall see and understand that he helped to make this world, and *was the chief manager in that operation. He was the person who brought the animals and the seeds from other planets to this world*, and brought a wife with him and stayed here. You may read and believe what you please as to what is found written in the Bible.

Heber C. Kimball	6/12/1860

JD 8:243-44

The religion of Jesus Christ, of angels, of Brigham, and of all good men is to take care of and improve and adorn the earth as *Adam* did. *When he planted the garden, he planted it with seeds he brought with him; and he also brought the animals from the earth he lived upon where his Father dwelt.*

W. W. Phelps et al.	a.m. 10/8/1861

James Beck Journal

Also the two wings north & South of our earth were inhabited. the north with the 9-1/2 tribes & the south wing by the People of Enochs City - this Earth when first created occupied a Position next to Kolob the highest in glory of all the Creations consequently on account of the high Position we once occupied we have fallen below all of the others in space - consequently our sufferings are greater - the greater the rise the greater will be the fall - when we are Redeemed we will be taken back again & Placed in our former Position.

Heber C. Kimball	6/27/1863

JD 10:235

We have been taught that our Father and God, from whom we sprang, *called and appointed his servants to go and organize an earth, and, among the rest, he said to Adam, "You go along also* and help all you can; you are going to inhabit it when it is organized, therefore go and assist in the good work." It reads in the Scriptures that the Lord did it, but the true rendering is, that the Almighty sent Jehovah and Michael to do the work.[83] *They* were also instructed to plant every kind of vegetable, likewise the forest and the fruit trees, and they actually brought from heaven every variety of fruit, of the seeds of vegetables, the seeds of flowers, and planted them in this earth on which we dwell. And I will say more, the spot chosen for the garden of Eden was Jackson County, in the State of Missouri, where Independence now stands; *it was occupied in the morn of creation by Adam and his associates who came with him for the express purpose of peopling this earth.* Father Adam was instructed to multiply and replenish the earth, to make it beautiful and glorious, to make it, in short, like unto *the garden from which the seeds were brought to*

---

[83] Perhaps this understanding is a key to reconciling the two creation accounts - in addition to the key that one account appears to be the spiritual creation while the other account is of the physical creation.

plant the garden of Eden. I might say much more upon this subject, but I will ask, has it not been imitated before you in your holy endowments so that you might understand how things were in the beginning of creation and cultivation of this earth? God the Father made Adam the Lord of this creation in the beginning, and *if we are the Lords of this creation under Adam*, ought we not to take a course to imitate our Father in heaven? Is not all this exhibited to us in our endowments: the earth made glorious and beautiful to look upon, representing everything which the Lord caused to be prepared and placed to adorn the earth.

Brigham Young   *Sunday a.m. 8/25/1867*

Minutes of Meetings Held in Provo City
Adam helped organize this world for an inheritance for himself and posterity.

Brigham Young   *8/25/1867*

MABY

While Brother Orson Pratt was telling you a good deal about this great holy wedding, the first that was ever celebrated, I thought about father *Adam*; he *helped to make the world, to organize this earth*, which was organized expressly for him.

Brigham Young   *Sunday p.m. 6/18/1873*

DN 22:308

We say that *Father Adam came here and helped to make the earth*. Who is he? He is Michael, a great prince, and it was said to him by Elohim: Go ye and make an earth." What is the great mystery about it? *He came and formed the earth*. ... Adam found it in a state of chaos, unorganized and incomplete. ... *Adam came here and got it up in a shape* that would suit him to commence business. Father Adam came here, and then they brought his wife. "Well," says one, "Why was Adam called Adam?" He was the first man on the earth, and *its framer and maker*. He with the help of his brethren, brought it into existence. Then he said," I want my children who are in the spirit world to come and live here. I once dwelt upon an earth something like this, in a mortal state, I was faithful, I received my crown and exaltation. I have the privilege of extending my work, and to its increase there will be no end. I want my children that were born to me in the spirit world to come here and take tabernacles of flesh, that their spirits may have a house, a tabernacle or a dwelling place as mine has, and where is the mystery?

Brigham Young   *Sunday 8/31/1873*

JD 16:167

When *Father Adam came to assist in organizing the earth* out of the crude material that was found, an earth was made upon which the children of men could live. After the earth was prepared Father Adam came and stayed here, and there was a woman brought to him.

Lecture at the Veil   *Tuesday 2/7/1877*

L. John Nuttall Journal

When *this earth was organized by Elohim, Jehovah and Michael* who is Adam our common father, Adam and Eve had the privilege to continue the work of progression. Consequently came to this earth and commenced the great work of forming tabernacles for those spirits to dwell in.

Edward Tullidge   *3/--/1877*

Women of Mormondom, 179

"Adam is our Father and God. He is the God of the earth." So says Brigham Young. Adam is t*he great archangel of this creation.*

Brigham H. Roberts   *5/--/1889*

Contributor 10:265-67

The Prophet Joseph Smith is credited with having said that our planet was made up of the fragments of a planet which previously existed; some mighty convulsions disrupted that creation and made it desolate. Both its animal and vegetable life forms were destroyed. And when those convulsions ceased, and the rent earth was again consolidated, and it became desirable to replenish it, the work was begun by making a mist to rise, that it might descend in gentle rain upon the barren earth, that it might again be fruitful. Then came one of the sons of God to the earth - *Adam*. A garden was planted in Eden and the man placed in it, and there the Lord brought to him every beast of the field and every fowl of the air, and Adam gave names to them all. Afterwards was brought to Adam his wife, whom since she was derived from man he named woman; and she became his helpmate, his companion, and the mother of his children. In this nothing is hinted at about man being made from the dust, and woman manufactured from a rib, a story which has been the cause of much perplexity to religious people, and a source of impious merriment to reckless unbelievers. We are informed that the Lord God made every plant of the field before it was in the earth, and every herb before it grew[84] on our planet. *As vegetation was created or made to grow upon some older earth, and the seeds thereof or the plants themselves were brought to our earth and made to grow,* so likewise man and his help-meet were brought from some older world to our own, to people it

---

[84] Genesis 2:4,5.

with their children.

Analysis & Observations

β

While the above statements generally are in no way contrary to modern LDS teachings, they generate a degree of detail about Adam's involvement in the creation of this earth that is generally not accepted by the LDS Church. While he "assisted" to make the earth, it is clear from some of the above statements that Adam was the chief organizer of this world and other "associates" were under his delegation and authority (save Elohim and Jehovah). It is this detail - and the statements showing that this earth was created for Adam's benefit - that makes this Adam-God teaching distinguishable from current LDS teachings.

7 Adam Presides Over Our Spirits

& has the Keys

D&C 78:16   *3/--/1832*

Who hath appointed *Michael* your prince, and established his feet, and set him upon high, and *given unto him the keys of salvation* under the counsel and direction of the Holy One, who is without beginning of days or end of life.

Joseph Smith   *7/2/1839*

MFP 1:113[85]

The Priesthood was first given to Adam; he obtained the First Presidency, and held the keys of it from generation to generation. He obtained it in the Creation, before the world was formed, as in Gen. 1:26-28. He had dominion given him over every living creature. He is Michael the Archangel, spoken of in the Scriptures. Then to Noah, who is Gabriel; he stands next in authority to Adam in the Priesthood; he was called of God to this office, and was the father of all living in his day, and to him was given the dominion. These men held keys first on earth, and then in heaven.

The Priesthood is an everlasting principle, and existed with God from eternity, and will to eternity, without beginning of days or end of years. The keys have to be brought from heaven whenever the Gospel is sent. *When they are revealed from heaven, it is by Adam's authority.*

Daniel in his seventh chapter speaks of the Ancient of Days; he means the oldest man, our Father Adam, Michael, he will call his children together and hold a council with them to prepare them for the coming of the Son of Man. Michael, he will call his children together and hold a council with them to prepare them for the coming of the Son of Man. *He (Adam) is the father of the human family, and presides over the spirits of all*

---

[85] cf. HC 3:385-86; TPJS, 157; JD 6:237; MS 17:310.

men,[fn: Unless we construe Christ as a non-spirit god, this must include Christ so that Adam must be in authority over Christ.] and *all that have had the keys must stand before him* in this grand council. This may take place before some of us leave this stage of action. The *Son of Man stands before him*, and there is given him glory and dominion. *Adam* delivers up his stewardship to Christ, that which was delivered to him as *holding the keys of the universe*, but retains his standing as head of the human family.

Joseph Smith *before 8/8/1839*

How have we come at the Priesthood in the last days? It came down, down, in regular succession. Peter, James, and John had it given to them and they gave it to others. Christ is the Great High Priest; *Adam next.* [86]

Joseph Smith *Monday 10/5/1840*

TPJS, 167-68

Commencing with *Adam*, who was the first man, who is spoken of in Daniel as being the "Ancient of Days," or in other words, the first and oldest of all, the great, grand progenitor of whom it is said in another place he is Michael, because *he was the first and father of all, not only by progeny, but the first to hold the spiritual blessings*, to whom was made known the plan of ordinances for the salvation of his posterity unto the end, and to whom Christ was first revealed, and *through whom Christ has been revealed from heaven, and will continue to be revealed from henceforth.*

Adam holds the keys of the dispensation of the fullness of times; i.e., the dispensation of *all* the times *have been and will be revealed through him* from the beginning to Christ, and from Christ to the end of all the dispensations that are revealed. ... He [God] set the ordinances to be the same forever and ever, and set Adam to watch over them, to reveal them from heaven to man, or to send angels to reveal them. "Are they not all ministering spirits, sent forth to minister for them who shall be heirs of salvation?" (Hebrews 1:14) These angels are under the direction of Michael or Adam, who acts under the direction of the Lord. This, then, is the nature of the Priesthood; every man holding the Presidency of his dispensation, and one man holding the Presidency of them

---

[86] Unfortunately, even The Words of Joseph Smith offers no insight into this sketchy grammar that comes from the journals of Wilford Woodruff. There are other accounts of this sermon but the other accounts do not record this significant detail. Adam-God adherents have traditionally understood this text to mean that Adam was higher in authority than Christ because the order of priesthood holders here appears to be ascending. Members of the Church have tended to read this statement to mean that Adam was lower in authority in Christ because the semicolon can be interpreted to break up the apparent hierarchy presented in this journal entry. Without the support of other teachings, either reading is rationally defendable. However, in light of the teachings within this subsection, the fundamentalist position seems to have the stronger end of this particular argument.

all,[i.e., including Christ] even Adam; and Adam receiving his Presidency and authority from the Lord, but *cannot receive a fullness until Christ shall present the Kingdom to the Father*, which shall be at the end of the last dispensation.

Joseph Smith   *6/16/1844*

TPJS, 373

I want you to pay particular attention to what I am saying. Jesus said that the Father wrought precisely in the same way as His Father had done before Him. As the Father had done before? He laid down His life, and took it up the same as His Father had done before. He did as He was sent, to lay down His life and take it up again; and *then was committed unto Him the keys.*

Samuel W. Richards   *Saturday 12/10/1853*

MS 15:803

At this important period, when Adam is reinstated with full power upon the earth, seated upon his throne, as Daniel saw him - a glorious and an immortal God, one like the Son of Man comes in the clouds of heaven (as oftimes represented by the Apostles), to the Ancient of days, and receives from him dominion, glory, and a kingdom; or in other words, *Michael*, having accomplished the work committed to him, pertaining to this world, *delivers up an account of his stewardship over the same, to that character represented as Yahovah in the creation of the world*, who reigns in unison with those upon the earth, until his work is fully accomplished - till the last great contest with the enemy, who has been released for a little season, is won; then *he in turn delivers up the kingdom to the great Eloheim*, that in the language of the Apostle, 'God may be all in all.'

Jedediah M. Grant   *2/19/1854*

JD 2:13-14

If you maintain the fact that the Priesthood of God is upon the earth, and God's representatives are upon the earth, the mouth-piece of Jehovah, the head of the kingdom of God upon earth, and the will of God is done upon earth as it is in heaven, it follows that the government of God is upon the earth. I allude to the Church which it dictates, and then to the whole earth which it will dictate, Satan may succeed for a season to curtail the extent of this government, and the free working of its machinery, but if the Lord Almighty has organized a government upon the earth, and has committed the keys and Priesthood of it to His Prophet, that *Prophet holds jurisdiction over the earth, the same as Adam did* in the beginning. And righteous men in every dispensation since the creation, if they had any keys, had the keys of the kingdom of God; and they extended over this wide world wherever God had a people and a government; and just as far as the Priesthood exercised its authority, just so far the rule of the Almighty reached.

Brigham Young   *Friday 10/6/1854*
Journal of the Southern Indian Mission, 87- 89
When Jesus has done his work *he will take this planet back to his Father.*

Brigham Young   *Sunday 10/8/1854*
MABY
'*When Christ has finished his labor and presented it to his father, then he, Adam, will receive a fullness.*' That is all easily understood by me. He cannot receive a fullness of the kingdoms He has organized until they are completed. If He sends His servants off to the right and to the left to perform a certain labor, His kingdom is not complete, until His ministers have accomplished everything to make His kingdom complete and returned home again.

Franklin D. Richards   *3/31/1855*
MS 17:194-95
We read in Gen. 3:22: 'And the Lord God said, Behold, the man has become as one of us, to know good and evil.' From this we learn that Adam was not only in form like unto the Gods, as previously stated, but that this knowledge of good and evil was that which would exalt him among the Gods; and then that his resemblance to the Gods might be complete, the Lord God bestowed the right to exercise full power and dominion over the earth, and all its creations. 'And God said unto them, Be fruitful, and multiply, and replenish the earth, and subdue it: and have dominion over the fish of the sea, and over the fowl of the air; and over every living thing that moveth upon the earth.' (Gen. 1:28.) If the Lord God has ever withdrawn from Father Adam the authority here bestowed upon him, He has not seen fit to make it known to the world. While there is nothing to refute, the whole tenor of revelation substantiates, the supposition, that *Adam has continued to* bear rule over the earth, and *control the destinies of his never ending posterity.* From the time he received his commission in the Garden of Eden, he has been laboring diligently to fulfill the instructions there given him by the Lord God concerning his dominions, and to bring them under subjection to his will. This will be fully accomplished when every knee shall bow, and *every tongue confess that he is the God of the whole earth.* Then will the words of the Prophet Brigham, when speaking of Adam, be fully realized - 'He is our Father and our God, and the only God with whom we have to do.'

Brigham Young   *10/7/1857*

JD 5:331-32

Now, if it should happen that we have to pay tribute to *Father Adam*, what a humiliating circumstance it would be! Just wait till you pass Joseph Smith; and after Joseph lets you pass him, you will find Peter; and after you pass the Apostles and many of the Prophets, you will find Abraham, and he will say, "I have the keys, and except you do thus and so, you cannot pass"; and after a while you come to Jesus; and when you at length meet Father Adam, [87] how strange it will appear to your present notions.

Brigham Young   *7/8/1860*

JD 8:118

The *Savior* has not finished his work, and cannot receive the fulness of his glory until the influence and power of the wicked are overcome and brought into subjection. When the wicked inhabitants of the earth, the beasts of the field, fowls of the air, fish of the sea, all mineral substances, and all else pertaining to this earth, are overcome, then he *will take the kingdom, present it to the Father* and say, `Here is the work you gave me to do - you made the appointment - I have wrought faithfully, and here are my brethren and sisters who have wrought with me.

Brigham Young   *11/30/1862*

MABY

You can readily see this makes our father Adam a great and mighty king. When we are crowned kings and queens, father Adam and mother Eve will be king and queen of us all. Under the Priesthood which is after the Son of God and the power of an endless life, *each father being a son, will always throughout time and eternity be subject to his father,*[If we accept the teaching that Christ is the son of Adam as taught in previous subsections, then it follows that Christ will be subject to Adam if we accept the teaching here put forth by Brigham Young.] and his king, dictator, father Lord, and God. Each son, in his own turn, becomes a father, and is entitled to the same obedience from the line of his descendants. It is by the authority and power of the Holy Priesthood alone that those in heaven and on earth can be entitled to, and secured in, the possession of the legal authority.

---

[87] Notice that this passage indicates a progression of hierarchy and Adam is at the top of this hierarchy above Christ.

Brigham Young   *Sunday p.m. 6/18/1873*

DN 22:308

Our Father *Adam* is the man who stands at the gate and *holds the keys of everlasting life and salvation* to *all* his children who have or who ever will come upon the earth.

Brigham Young   *5/14/1876*

L. John Nuttall Papers

The Savior comes to the father, the Ancient of Days, and *presents to the Father the kingdoms of this world* all in a saved condition except the sons of perdition and he says, "Here, Father, here they are and I with them" *Then he is prepared to go forth and fill up his kingdom, and so he goes on.*

Helen Mar Whitney   *9/20/1882*

Plural Marriage, as Taught by the Prophet Joseph, 30, 31, 36

Brigham Young did not happen to be the author of this doctrine [Adam-God], and to prove the truth of my assertion, I will produce some of the Prophet's teachings, given May 16, 1841.[88] These were written, together with other tings, by his clerk, William Clayton, as they were spoken, and as I had the privilege of reading them when quite a young woman, I took the liberty of copying them. The copy I have retained, and, this is what the prophet said upon this subject, commencing with the Priesthood: "The Priesthood was first given to Adam - he obtained the First Presidency *and held the keys of it from generation to generation.* He obtained it in the Creation, before the word was formed. ... He had dominion given him over every living creature; he is Michael, the Archangel spoken of in the Scriptures. Then Noah who is Gabriel - he stands next in authority to Adam in the Priesthood. He was called of God to this office, and was the father of all living in his day, and to him was given the dominion. These men held keys first on earth and then in heaven. The Priesthood is an everlasting principle, and existed with God from eternity, and will to eternity, without beginning of days or end of years. *When the keys have to be brought from heaven - it is by Adam's authority.*"[89]
When the Saints first heard this doctrine advanced it looked strange and unnatural to them; it was strong meat and required a little time before it could digested; but this was owing to the narrow, contracted ideas which had been handed down from generation to generation by our forefathers. we were like babes and had always been fed upon milk; but, as Jesus said, we have to be taught "here a little and there a little." When I was able to comprehend it, it appeared quite consistent. There is something in this doctrine that is

---

[88] She is apparently referring to HC, July 1839.
[89] TPJS, 175

very home like, grand and beautiful to reflect upon, and it is very simple and comprehensive.

Joseph E. Taylor   *6/2/1888*

Deseret Weekly News 38:19-27

'Jesus, what are you going to do?' 'To lay down my life and take it up again.' Do you believe it? If you do not believe it, you do not believe the Bible. The Scriptures tell it, and I defy all the learning and wisdom of all the combined powers of earth and hell together to refute it. What did Jesus do? Why, 'I do the thing I saw my Father do when worlds came rolling into existence. My Father worked out His Kingdom with fear and trembling; and I must do the same; and *when I get my kingdom, I shall present it to my Father, so that He may obtain kingdom upon kingdom* and it will exalt Him in glory. He will then take a higher exaltation and I take His place, and thereby become exalted myself'; so that Jesus treads in the track of his Father and inherits what God did before.[90]

Wilford Woodruff   *3/3/1889*

Deseret Weekly News 38:389

In the first place, I will say that the Prophet Joseph taught us that Father *Adam was the first man on the earth to whom God gave the keys of the Everlasting Priesthood.* He held the keys of the Presidency, and was the first man who did hold them. Noah stood next to him. These keys were given to Noah, he being the father of all living in his day, as Adam was in his day. These two men were the first who received the Priesthood in the eternal worlds, before the worlds were formed. They were the first who received the Everlasting Priesthood or Presidency on the earth. *Father Adam stands at the head*, so far as this world is concerned. Of course, *Jesus Christ is the Great High Priest* of the salvation of the human family. *But Adam holds those keys* in the world today; he will hold them to the endless ages of eternity. And Noah, and *every* man[i.e., including Christ] who has ever held or will hold the keys of Presidency of the Kingdom of God, from that day until the scene is wound up, *will have to stand before Father Adam and give an account of the keys of that Priesthood*, as we all will have to give an account unto the Lord, of the principles that we have received, when our work is done in the flesh.

Edward Stevenson   *2/28/1896*

Edward Stevenson Diary

Certainly Eloheim, and Jehovah stands [sic] before Adam, or else I am very much mistaken. Then 1st Eloheim, 2nd Jehovah, 3d Michael-Adam, 4th Jesus Christ, Our

---

[90] TPJS 345, 346, 347; HC 6:305, 306; JD 6:3.

Elder Brother, in the other World from whence our spirits came … Then Who is Jehovah? The only begotten Son of Eloheim on Jehovah's world.[91]

Montgomery   *1912*

Sacred Hymns, 107 #97 1912

See! *Jehovah's* banner's furled,
Sheathed his sword, He speaks, 'tis done;
Now the kingdoms of this world
Are the kingdoms of *His Son*.[92]

Analysis & Observations

β

This particular teaching of the early brethren has been largely ignored by previous Adam-God authors - although it has received some attention in various pamphlets in recent years. Although there are a few statements that conclusively declare that Adam has priesthood keys over Christ, most of the statements that declare Adam as *the* authority who holds all of the keys over the human family require at least one of two assumptions: 1) Adam is the father of Christ via Mary and therefore Christ is a son of Adam and therefore Christ should be considered a son of Adam in each of the statements that say that Adam has authority over *all* of his children or 2) Adam is the father of Christ because the early brethren so taught - see "Adam as Father of Christ". While neither of these two assumptions are illogical in any way, the statements in this subsection tend to be viewed as tendentious proof of Adam's authority by members of the modern LDS Church. The reason appears to be that members of the LDS Church reading the statements in this subsection tend to believe that the "all" word choice was simply a poor one - that is, they presume that each statement was simply poorly worded because they did not specifically exclude Christ. [This is of course, a loose form of circular reasoning.]

---

[91] This statement is included because it is opposed to the teachings throughout this subsection while being close enough chronologically to still be a primary source worth consideration; that noted, Adam-God teachings were being brushed aside by this date in Church history and the identity of Jehovah had been changed for over a decade so perhaps elder Stevenson was "very much mistaken."

[92] This hymn is here to show that the early saints understood that Adam was giving over his kingdom to Jesus.

This appears fairly reasonable at first glance - evidences of this genre of error in extemporaneous speeches is not too difficult to find. However, when all of the statements in this section are considered as a whole, this position becomes much less tenable. Indeed, when considered in light of the teachings found throughout this entire section of *Understanding Adam-God Teachings,* this position is simply no longer credible - the early brethren clearly believed that Adam was God the Father so the teaching that He holds the highest priesthood authority was simply a logical concluding thought.

This volume has now presented hundreds of different statements declaring various, basic Adam-God teachings. In light of this fact, the modern LDS Church position that there are only a handful of Adam-God statements can only hold the slightest speck of credibility if the vast majority of statements cited herein can be proven to be forgeries and/or poor transcriptions - this is true even if some of the subsections are totally dismissed because they remain largely accepted by mainstream Mormonism. Given the volume of evidence now available, this seems unlikely - besides, the author has retraced the steps of the vast majority of these statements to the original source and has verified the same. If the LDS reader has not found the notion that Brigham Young was misquoted somewhat specious by this point, he or she is of the highest caliber of the stalwart LDS apologists.

Having now given consideration to all basic/foundational Adam-God teachings, this volume could have followed the lead of previous Adam-God authors and ended the treatment of Adam-God teachings by addressing some few items that particularly interested the author and then finished the volume without giving any further consideration to other topics. I have chosen not to do this for one simple reason: there is so much more to study that it would be an injustice to continue to leave these topics largely unaddressed in print.[93] The remainder of this volume therefore focuses on the consequences of the basic teachings presented earlier in this volume and on various aspects of these teachings that have not been thoroughly compiled and/or researched by previous authors. Although I have continued to rely heavily on the research of other authors, the remainder of *Understanding Adam-God Teachings* is based more upon my

---

[93] That noted, many of the topics addressed in later portions of this volume have been tangentially treated by previous authors. However, the treatment has tended to be limited to only a few statements on each topic and every author has left many of these topics totally unaddressed in their writings - In so stating, I am not criticizing these authors for missing this information (much of this genre of research was not available for earlier Adam-God authors and much of the research would have been available to later authors only at significant sacrifice and some of the resources have only become available since the publication of the last Adam-God book published by Craig Tholson.

independent research than it is upon the research of others.[94] It is my aspiration that the presentation of these more advanced teachings will open the door to more extensive and thoughtful consideration of Adam-God teachings as a veritable cornerstone of Mormon theology. That is, I hope that the remainder of this volume will inspire the reader to consider the *implications* of Adam-God teachings rather than

1) simply shelving these teachings because they do not concur with the mainstream LDS position or

2) accepting these teachings as true but doing little else to try and understand the vast and profound implications that result from this bold and innovative theology advanced by the early leaders of Mormonism.

See also 1 Corinthians 15:24

---

[94] The "Miscellaneous Controversies" and "Important Accounts" sections are exceptions to this statement.

Eve

β

See also
Titles & Offices: Adam & Eve

Unfortunately, only a minimal tease of information has been revealed about Eve as an individual or as an office. As little has been revealed about our Mother in Heaven out of reverence for her, perhaps it is not unsafe to extrapolate the same motivation behind the lack of revealed word behind Eve's role as the spiritual mother of all living. Despite the paucity of information available, this portion of *Understanding Adam-God Teachings* is an attempt to address this important topic that has been largely neglected by all previous Adam-God authors. That said, the two sections entitled "Adam and Eve" (each with a different subtitle) also include significant information about Eve. However, virtually none of that material tells us anything specific about Eve that does not specifically apply to Adam as well so most of those materials are not found in the following subsections.

The importance of teachings about mother Eve should not be underestimated. Neither should they be dismissed as a modern attempt to placate the feminist agenda. If there is great value to be found in any or all revealed words of the prophets, then wouldn't a revelation about our common spiritual *and* physical parentage be of vast importance? Consider the following line of reasoning: While we are only affirmatively taught in John 17:3 that "this is life eternal, that they might know thee, the only true God," it stands to reason that there is some inherent value in knowing the only true Mother in Heaven as well - especially given the teaching (covered later in this volume) that the term "Adam" comprised both male and female; if Adam is God and we are comfortable with the teaching of a Mother in Heaven, is it much of a stretch to believe that life eternal comprises knowing about our Mother in Heaven as well?[95] If the reader accepts the perspective implicit behind these rhetorical questions, the following information will be of great value.

---

[95] One may argue that it is not as important - elsewise, why would we have such a vast amount of material teaching us about Adam when, in comparison, we have only a miniscule amount of material teaching us about Eve? However, this argument fails if this restraint in revealing information about Eve has been done out of reverence as argued above.

8   Eve as the Mother of All Living

See also
Procreation: Mortal & Spiritual Offspring

Genesis 3:20

And Adam called his wife's name Eve; because she was the mother of *all* living.

Moses 4:26

And Adam called his wife's name Eve, because she was the mother of *all* living; for thus have I, the Lord God, called the first of all women, which are many.

William Law   *2/7/1844*

Warsaw Message (Buckeye's Lament for More Wives)
There you may shine like mighty Gods,
creating worlds so fair.
At least *a world for every wife*
that you take with you there.

The man that has got ten fair wives,
Ten worlds he may create;
And he that has got less than this,
Will find a bitter fate.

The one or two that he might have,
He'll be deprived of then;
And they'll be given as talents were,
To him who has got ten.

Joseph Smith   *circa 1844*

"Sayings of Joseph the Prophet," as recorded in Anson Call's Journal

Now regarding Adam: He came here from another planet an immortalized Being and *brought his wife, Eve*, with him and by eating of the fruit of this earth became subject to death and decay, and He became of the earth, earthy, was made mortal and subject to death.

Brigham Young   *2/5/1852*

Speech at the territorial legislature, Church Archives

After the deed was done, the Lord enquired for Abel, and made Cain own what he had done with him. Now says the grandfather, I will not destroy the seed of *Michael and his wife*, and Cain I will not kill you, nor suffer anyone else to kill you, but I will put a mark upon you.

Brigham Young   *4/9/1852*

JD 1:50

When our father Adam came into the garden of Eden, he came into it with a celestial body, and *brought Eve, one of his wives*, with him.

Brigham Young   *Friday 4/9/1852*

Journal of Wilford Woodruff

When our Father came into the garden He came with his celestial body & brought *one of his wives* with him and ate of the fruit of the garden until He could beget a tabernacle. And Adam is Michael or God and all the God that we have anything to do with. They ate of this fruit & formed the first tabernacle that was formed.

Brigham Young   *Friday 4/16/1852*

Journal of Samuel Holister Rogers 1:179

Adam came to the Earth and that Adam helped to make the Earth, that he had a Celestial body when he came to the Earth and that he *brought his wife* or *one of his wives* with him, and that Eave was also a Celestial being, that they eat of the fruit of the ground until they begat children from the Earth, he said that Adam was the only God that we would have, and that Christ was not begotten of the Holy Ghost, but of the Father Adam, that Christ, was our elder brother.

Brigham Young   *8/8/1852*

JD 3:90

There is only one gospel sermon, recollect, brethren and sisters, and the time that is required to preach it is from the day of the fall, or from the day when *Adam and his wife*

Eve came here upon this planet, and from that time until Jesus Christ has subdued the last enemy, which is death, and put all things under his feet, and wound up all things pertaining to this earth. Then the gospel will have been preached, and brought up and presented, and the effects thereof, to the Father.

Orson Pratt   *3/--/1853*

The Seer 1:3

The spirits of all mankind, destined for this earth, were begotten by a father, and born of *a mother in Heaven* long anterior to the formation of this world. The personages of the father and mother of our spirits, had a beginning to their organization, but the fullness of truth (which is God) that dwells in them, had no beginning; being "from everlasting to everlasting." (Psalm 90:2).

Brigham Young   *9/17/1854*

Journal of Wilford Woodruff

Adam was our God or the Father of Jesus Christ. President Young said that He came from another world & made this. *Brought Eve* with him, partook of the fruits of the earth, begat children & they were earthly & had mortal bodies & if we were faithful, we should become Gods as He was.

Brigham Young   *10/6/1854*

Journal of Joseph L. Robinson, 102-03

President Brigham Young said thus, that Adam and Eve were the names of the first man and woman of every earth that was ever organized and that Adam and *Eve* were the natural father and mother of *every spirit* that comes to this planet, or that receives tabernacles on this planet, consequently we are brother and sisters, and that Adam was God, our Eternal Father. This as Brother Heber remarked, was letting the cat out of the bag, and it came to pass, I believed every word, for I remembered saying to the Brethren at a meeting of High Priests in Nauvoo, while I was speaking to them under the influence of the Spirit, I remarked thus, that our Father *Adam had many wives*, and that Eve was only one of them, and that she was our mother, and that she was the mother of the inhabitants of this earth.

Brigham Young   *Friday 10/6/1854*

Journal of the Southern Indian Mission, 87- 89

Michael came down with his wife, & began to people it. Michael had his body from the dust of the planet he was begotten on, he obeyed his Lord, was faithful and obedient, died and was resurrected, he did not resurrect himself. ... Adam's descent was to organize people & redeem a world, *by his wife he peopled it* by his first born he redeems. ... Adam

& Eve had children in the spirit - and their children married - brother & sister - then the bodies followed.

Brigham Young   *Sunday 10/8/1854*

MABY

I tell you more, Adam is the father of our spirits ... *our spirits and the spirits of all the heavenly family were begotten by Adam, and born of Eve.* ... I tell you, when you see your Father in the Heavens, you will see Adam; *when you see your Mother that bore your spirit, you will see Mother Eve.*

Brigham Young   *4/20/1856*

JD 3:319

[*Adam*] was the person who brought the animals and the seeds from other planets to this world, and *brought a wife* with him and stayed here.

Parley P. Pratt   *before 1857*

Key to Theology, 54-56; 1938 edition

Earth, its mineral, vegetable and animal wealth, its Paradise prepared, down comes from yonder world on high a son of God, with *his beloved spouse.* And thus a colony from heaven, it may be from the sun, is transplanted on our soil. The blessings of their Father are upon them, and the first great law of heaven and earth is again repeated, 'Be fruitful and multiply.' Hence the nations which have swarmed our earth. In after years, when Paradise was lost by sin; when man was driven from the face of his heavenly Father, to toil, and droop, and die; when heaven was veiled from view, and, with few exceptions man was no longer counted worthy to retain the knowledge of his heavenly origin; then darkness veiled the past and future from the heathen mind; man neither knew himself, from whence he came, nor whither he was bound.

Brigham Young   *10/9/1859*

JD 7:290

Adam and Eve are the parents of *all* pertaining to the flesh, and I would not say that they are not also the parents of our spirits.

Brigham Young   *1/27/1860*

Journal of Wilford Woodruff

The Seventh day is the Sabbath of the Lord. That day, you and your *wife,* and all your children - as many as will follow you - will spend in the new earth, in worship and thanksgiving. ...

Now comes the morning of the new week in which mortality must begin, and your spiritual children must be introduced into mortality. *Two* must go before them and prepare the way for them. Whom will you send? Would you not say to [your] *wife*, "Come, Mother, let *you and I* lay aside our Celestial glory for a little season and eat of the elements of this new earth. that we may again become of the earth earthy, and thereby our offspring will be mortal, and thus we will begin the begetting of mortal bodies for these, our spiritual children; and when they have grown to maturity in their mortal estate, we will command them to multiply and replenish the earth.

Brigham Young   *6/27/1860*

DN

His most gracious and venerable majesty, King Adam, with his royal *consort*, Queen eve, will appear at the head of the whole great family of the redeemed, and will be crowned in their midst as a King and Priest forever after the [Order of] Son of God.

Brigham Young   *11/30/1862*

MABY

[E]ach person who we[96] crown in the celestial kingdom of God will be a father of fathers, a king of kings, a lord of lords, a god of gods ... Each person will reign over his posterity. *Adam*, Michael, the *Ancient of Days*, will sit as the judge of the quick and dead, for he is the father of all living, and Eve is the mother of *all* living, pertaining to the human family, and he is their king, their Lord, their God, taking and holding his position in the grand unbroken chain of endless increase, and eternal progression. ... You can readily see this makes our father Adam a great and mighty king. When we are crowned kings and queens, father Adam and mother Eve will be *king and queen of us all*.

Brigham Young   *6/30/1867*

JD 12:97

Now, taking the history of creation as given by Moses, let me ask the question - "Mother Eve, did you not partake of the forbidden fruit, as also did Adam, and thus bring sin and iniquity into the world?" "O, yes," says Mother Eve. Then, why cannot you bear the affliction of it? Why not say, "If I was the cause of bringing evil into the world, I will firmly bear all that God puts upon me, and maintain His word and His law, and so work out my salvation with fear and trembling, for it is God working within me." I ask this question of you, mother Eves, every one of you. If you are not sanctified and prepared, you ought to be sanctifying and preparing yourselves for the blessings in store for you when it will be said of you, this is Mother *Eve*. Why? Because

---

[96] Brigham does not here identify who "we" are but he appears to be referring to a future time, when as an exalted being, those of use who are exalted will crown others to be a father of fathers, etc.

you are the mother of *all* living. You might as well prepare first as last. If you wish to be *Eves and mothers of human families*, you ought to bear the burden.

Brigham Young   *8/25/1867*

MABY

As to the great wedding bro. Orson has been telling us about is nothing more or less than this, Adam's father came to him, saying here is *the wife* you have had so long, now you are going to have *one wife* to take with you to yonder earth, and if any of your other wives ever go to an earth to become the mother of all living, to become an Eve, it will be to another earth, not to that one. She is called Eve because she is the mother of *all* living, and she is the queen of that earth. Adam is the Lord of the earth and the father of all living on this earth, as Eve is the mother of *all* living on this earth.

Brigham Young   *1869*

MS 31:267

Before me I see a house full of Eves. What a crowd of reflections the word Eve is calculated to bring up! Eve was the name or title conferred upon our first mother, because she was actually to be the mother of *all* the human beings who should live upon this earth. I am looking upon a congregation designed to be just such beings.

Brigham Young   *5/7/1871*

JD 14:111

Do you not all know that *you are the sons and daughters of the Almighty*? If you do not I will inform you this morning that *there is not a man or woman on the earth that is not a son or daughter of Adam and Eve.* We all belong to the races which have sprung from father Adam and mother Eve; and every son and daughter of Adam and Eve is a son and daughter of that God we serve, who organized this earth and millions of others, and who holds them in existence by law.

Brigham Young   *Sunday p.m. 6/18/1873*

DN 22:308

Our Father Adam helped to make this earth, it was created expressly for him, and after it was made he and *his companions* came here. He brought *one of his wives* with him, and she was called Eve, because she was the first woman upon the earth. ... Father Adam came here, and then they brought *his wife*.

Brigham Young   *Sunday 8/31/1873*

JD 16:167

When Father Adam came to assist in organizing the earth out of the crude material that was found, an earth was made upon which the children of men could live. After the earth was prepared Father Adam came and stayed here, and there was *a woman* brought to him. Now I am telling you something that many of you know, it has been told to you, and the brethren and sisters should understand it. There was *a certain woman* brought to Father Adam whose name was Eve, because she was the first woman, and she was given to him to be *his wife*; I am not disposed to give any farther knowledge concerning her at present.

The Lecture at the Veil   *Tuesday 2/7/1877*

Journal of L. John Nuttall
Eve our common Mother who is the mother of all living bore those spirits in the celestial world.

Byron Allred   *3/22/1877*

Jans Christian Anderson Weibye Daybooks
Byron Allred preaches at Manti on Adam as God, with the following remarks in part: Adam was buried by God (God his Father) and was only dead like a twinkling of an eye, and his God exalted him immediately. Mary was sealed to Adam, and was his wife when she had Jesus. Mary will be the Queen to people another world; Mary was the *second wife* to Adam; and unless we have two wives, we can never be Gods. Adam will worship his God and we will worship Adam, and our children will worship us.

Edward Tullidge   *3/--/1877*

Women of Mormondom, 179-181, 190-93
"In the beginning" the Gods created the heavens and the earths. In their councils they said, let us make man in our own image. So, in the likeness of the Fathers, and the Mothers - the Gods - created they man - male and female. When this earth was prepared for mankind, Michael, as Adam, came down. He brought with him *one* of his wives, and he called her name Eve. Adam and Eve are the names of the fathers and mothers of worlds. Adam was not made out of a lump of clay, as we make a brick, nor was Eve taken as a rib - a bone - from his side. They came by generation. But woman, as the wife or mate of man, was a rib of man. She was taken from his side, in their glorified world, and brought by him to earth to be the mother of a race. These were father and *mother of a world of spirits* who had been born to them in heaven. These spirits had been waiting for the grand period of their probation, when they should have bodies or tabernacles, so that they might become, in the resurrection, like Gods. When this earth had become an abode for mankind, with its Garden of Eden, then it was that the morning stars sang together, and the sons and daughters of God shouted for joy. They were coming down to earth.
The children of the sun, at least, knew what the grand scheme of the everlasting Fathers

and the everlasting Mothers meant, and they, both sons and daughters, shouted for joy.
The temple of the eternities shook with their hosannas, and trembled with divine
emotions. The father and mother were at length in their Garden of Eden. They came
on purpose to fall. They fell "that man might be; and man is, that he "might have joy."
They ate of the tree of mortal life, partook of the elements of this earth that they might
again become mortal for their children's sake. They fell that another world might have a
probation, redemption and resurrection.

The grand Patriarchal economy, with Adam, as a resurrected being, *who brought his wife
Eve* from another world has been very finely elaborated by Brigham Young from the
Patriarchal genesis which Joseph conceived.

...

God the Father and God the Mother stand, in the grand pre-existing view, as the origin
and centre of the spirits of *all* the generations of mortals who had been tabernacled on
this earth.

First and noblest of this great family was Jesus Christ, who was the elder brother, in
spirit, of the *whole* human race. These constituted a world-family of pre-existing souls.
... These are the sons and daughters of Adam - the Ancient of Days - the Father and
God of the whole human family. These are the sons and daughters of Michael, who is
Adam, the father of the spirits of all our race. These are the sons and daughters of Eve,
the Mother of a world. What a practical Unitarianism is this! ... Woman is heiress of
the Gods. She is joint heir with her elder brother, Jesus the Christ; but she inherits
from her God-Father and her God-Mother. Jesus is the "beloved" of that Father and
Mother - their well-tried Son, chosen to work out the salvation and exaltation of the
whole human family. And shall it not be said then that the subject rises from the God-
Father to the God-Mother? Surely it is a rising in the sense of the culmination of the
divine idea. The God-Father is not robbed of his everlasting glory by this maternal
completion of himself. It is an expansion both of deity and humanity. They twain are
one God! The supreme Unitarian conception is here; the God-Father and the God-
Mother! The grand unity of God is in them - in the divine Fatherhood and the divine
Motherhood - the very beginning and consummation of creation. Not in the God-
Father and the God-Son can the unity of the heavens and the earths be worked out;
neither with any logic of facts nor of idealities. In them the Masonic trinities; in the
everlasting Fathers and the everlasting Mothers the unities of creations. *Our* Mother in
heaven is decidedly a new revelation, as beautiful and delicate to the masculine sense of
the race as it is just and exalting to the feminine.

THE ULTIMATUM OF HUMAN LIFE

'Tis not for you to pry
Into the secrets of the worlds on high -
To seek to know the first, the moving Cause,
Councils, decrees, organizations, laws -
Form'd by the Gods, pertaining to this earth,
Ere your great Father from their courts came forth,

The routine of his ancestors to tread -
Of this new world, to stand the royal head. ...
Adam, your God, like you on earth, has been
Subject to sorrow in a world of sin:

Through long gradation he arose to be
Cloth'd with the Godhead's might and majesty.
And what to him in his probative sphere,
Whether a Bishop, Deacon, Priest, or Seer?
Whate'er his offices and callings were,
He magnified them with assiduous care:
By his obedience he obtain'd the place
Of God and Father of this human race.

Obedience will the same bright garland weave,
As it has done for your great Mother, Eve,
For all her daughters on the earth, who will
All my requirements sacredly fulfill.
And what to Eve, though in her mortal life,
She'd been the first, the tenth, or fiftieth wife?
What did she care, when in her lowest state,
Whether by fools, consider'd small, or great?
'Twas all the same with her - she prov'd her worth -
She's now *the* Goddess and the Queen of Earth.

Life's ultimatum, unto those that live
As saints of God, and all my pow'rs receive;
Is still the onward, upward course to tread -
To stand as Adam and as Eve, *the* head

Of an inheritance, a new-form'd earth,
And to their spirit race, give mortal birth -

Give them experience in a world like this;
Then lead them forth to everlasting bliss,
Crown'd with salvation and eternal joy
Where full perfection dwells, without alloy.

Scott Anderson   *9/22/1884*

Letter to Pres. John Taylor, SLC

Brigham Young teaches [sic] his words, "When our Father Adam came into the Garden
of Eden, he came into it with a celestial body and brought Eve *one of his wives* with him.
He is our Father and our God and the only God with whom we have to do."

H. W. Naisbitt   *Sunday p.m. 3/8/1885*

JD 26:115

The scriptures give an account simply of the woman Eve; declaring that this name was
given her of Adam, because she was "the mother of *all* living;" but outside of biblical
record there has been handed down from time immemorial the idea that Adam had two
wives, the narrators go so far, or rather so near perfecting the tradition so as to give
their names, Lilith being said to be the name of one as Eve was the name of the other,
and while it may be difficult to harmonize all the Rabbinical and Talmudic versions of
this matter, it is said that Joseph Smith the Prophet taught that Adam had two wives.

Brigham Young (as quoted by Scott Anderson)   *9/22/1884*

Letter to Pres. John Taylor, SLC

If I could so conduct myself in this stage of action, to be worthy of the celestial
kingdom with eternal increase, then and only *then, would I gain an inheritance of my own
to be as a Father Adam, and my wife, a mother Eve.*

Eliza R. Snow   *before 12/7/1888*

OH MY FATHER

In the heavens are parents single?
No; the thought makes reason stare;
Truth is reason; truth eternal,
Tells me I've *a* Mother there.

When I leave this frail existence -

When I lay this mortal by,
Father, Mother, may I meet you
In your royal court on high?

Then at length, when I've completed
All you sent me forth to do,
With your mutual approbation,
Let me come and dwell with you.

Brigham H. Roberts   *5/--/1889*

Contributor 10:265-267
Afterwards was brought to Adam *his wife*, whom, since she was derived from man, he named woman; and she became his help-mate, his companion and the mother of his children. ... We are all "formed" of the dust of the ground, though instead of being molded as a brick we are brought forth by the natural laws of procreation; so also was Adam and *his wife* in some older world. And as for the story of the rib, under it I believe the mystery of procreation is hidden.

Salt Lake Tribune   *2/12/1906*

Page 3
Especially is it taught that Adam was not made out of the dust of this earth; that he was begotten as any other man is begotten, and that when he came here he brought Eve, *one of his wives*, with him.

W. W. Phelps   *1912*

Sacred Hymns, 327-28 #283

Come to me; here are *Adam and Eve* at the head
Of a multitude quickened and raised from the dead;
Here's the knowledge that was, or that is, or will be,
In the gen'ral assembly of worlds. Come to me.

Come to me; here are mysteries man hath not seen,
Here's our *Father in heaven, and Mother, the Queen,*
Here are worlds that have been, and the worlds yet to be,
Here's eternity endless; amen. Come to me.

E. L. T. Harrison   *1912*
Sacred Hymns, 375-75 #316
SONS OF MICHAEL, HE APPROACHES

Mother of our generations,
 Glorious by great Michael's side,
 Take thy children's adoration;
 Endless with thy Lord preside;

J. Arthur Horne, Patriarch   *5/28/1963*
C. Jess Gorewsbeck's Elder's Journal 1:291
Brother Horne … when he first went through the Temple (Salt Lake) for his
Endowment in 1902 before going on his mission he was surprised to hear the teachings
during the Temple ceremony in the Sermon before the veil, that, `Adam was our God'
and that "he came here with Eve, *one of his wives*'. Also it was taught that `Eve bore our
spirits' (ie the spirits of *all* men).

Analysis & Observations

β

This teaching is fairly straightforward. If Adam is our Heavenly Father and the father of
our spirits, it stands to reason that Eve, his wife, would be our Heavenly Mother and the
mother of our spirits. However, as the doctrine of plural marriage is an essential tenet
among fundamentalist Mormons, the question often arises as to whether or not Adam
brought more than one wife with him when he came to this earth (see "Eve as a Plural
Wife in the Eternities" below). Because all of the above references allude to Eve as the
mother of *all* living or to Eve as the common mother of *all* of our spirits or something
similar, it seems evident that the early brethren consistently[97] taught that Eve was the
only wife who *came to this earth* during Adam's mortal "probation" and that any other
wives that he may have left behind in the eternities did not come at any time to be his
wife during Adam's mortal lifetime.

While this does establish the doctrine that we all share the same common spiritual lineage
that began with mother Eve, it frequently raises a concern among fundamentalists. That

---

[97] There were some few exceptions - see "Eve as a Plural Wife During This Probation" below.

is, if living the principal of celestial plural marriage is essential to exaltation, why would this not be required of Adam and Eve during *this* probation as well as any other probation?[98] One answer is that the above statements merely say that Adam *came* to this earth with one wife - there is nothing here to negate the possibility that he took other wives *while* he lived on this earth (see "Eve as a Plural Wife During This Probation", "Mary Sealed to Adam", and "Adam and His Associates" below).

Perhaps, given the understanding that Eve is our common spiritual mother, we can glean greater understanding as to why the adversary has tried so forcefully to malign her good name throughout the history of man. Although Adam and Eve, once exalted and glorified beings, sacrificed their eternal comforts and suffered nearly a millennia of heartache, toil, and fatigue so that we might have the opportunity to receive a fullness of joy, their names have nevertheless been the chiefest casualties of the malignant slanders of the adversary throughout mankind's history. Perhaps the honorable name of Mary Magdalene has achieved a close second, but even her reproach among modern Christians does not reach the degree of slander found in the reprobate teachings promulgated concerning our heavenly parents by Jew, Christian, and Muslim alike.

Among fundamentalists, it has oft been noted that Eve is called the mother of all living *before* she conceived Seth. While modern LDS apologists might argue that this is referring to the future as if it has already happened - a common happening in the scriptures - this stance is much less viable when all of the above statements are considered as a whole.

Perhaps most interestingly, this particular teaching (in connection with the subsections that follow[99]) suggests that part of Eve's sacrifice in coming down to an earth to partake of mortality for the benefit of her children is that she has to perform the law of Sarah afresh - after having the veil placed over her mind once again.[100]

Lastly, the above statements have been used as evidence that the teaching that Adam came here with "associates" was false speculation on the part of some of the early brethren (See "Adam & His Associates" below). This criticism of these teachings is unfounded when it is based upon this reasoning alone. As is shown in the "Adam & His

---

[98] Mary's sealing to Adam was not during his mortal lifetime on this earth.

[99] And with the understanding of plural marriage as the early brethren taught it.

[100] While some fundamentalist women have taken some consolation from these teachings because they suggest that they will have the opportunity to be monogamist for some short season in the eternities (and on multiple occasions), this understanding appears to be in error - though they will have the opportunity of being a first wife.

Associates" subsection below, the early brethren taught that these "associates" were Adam's children. If these children were the spirit children of our common mother, Eve from another world who were later exalted, there is no reason to conclude that these two teachings are not harmonious. Even were our lineages proven to be from one of these "associates" of Adam, we could still trace our lineage back one generation further to discover that Eve was still our spiritual "mother" as the term is used in biblical language.

9

Eve as a Plural Wife

| During this Probation |

See also
Eve as the Mother of All Living

Orson Pratt   *3/--/1853*

The Seer 1:3

The spirits of all mankind, destined for this earth, were begotten by a father, and born of *a mother in Heaven* long anterior to the formation of this world. The personages of the father and mother of our spirits, had a beginning to their organization, but the fullness of truth (which is God) that dwells in them, had no beginning; being "from everlasting to everlasting." (Psalm 90:2).

In the Heaven where our spirits were born, there are many Gods, each one of whom has his own wife *or wives* which were given to him previous to his redemption, while yet in his mortal state. Each God, through his wife *or wives*, raises up a numerous family of sons and daughters; indeed, there will be no end to the increase of his own children: for each father and mother will be in a condition to multiply forever and ever. As soon as each God has begotten many millions of male and female spirits, and his Heavenly inheritance becomes too small, to comfortably accommodate his great family, he, in connection with his sons, organizes a new world, after a similar order to the one which we now inhabit, where he sends both the male and female spirits to inhabit tabernacles of flesh and bones. Thus each God forms *a world* for the accommodation of his own sons and daughters who are sent forth in their times and seasons, and generations to be born into the same. The inhabitants of each world are required to reverence, adore, and worship their own personal father who dwells in the Heaven which they formerly inhabited.

W.W. Phelps and Brigham Young   *10/8/1861*

James Beck Journal

Joseph Smith said that Eve had twenty-eight sons and twenty-eight daughters, and that *Adam had many wives* - Brother Brigham then got into the stand and stated the same thing.

Brigham Young   *2/10/1867*

JD 11:328

Yes, [plural marriage is] one of the relics of *Adam*, of Enoch, of Noah, of Abraham, of Isaac, of Jacob, of Moses, David, Solomon, the Prophets, of Jesus, and his apostles.

Byron Allred   *3/22/1877*

Jans Christian Anderson Weibye Daybooks

Mary was sealed to Adam, and was his wife when she had Jesus. Mary will be the Queen to people another world; Mary *was the second wife to Adam*; and unless we have two wives, we can never be Gods.

Edward Tullidge   *3/--/1877*

The Women of Mormondom, Ch. 20

But from Joseph Smith, through John Taylor and many ancient records, we are told that *Michael brought three wives with him* - Eve, Sarah and Lilith. If he had not then he could not demand that his children live this same law in order to inherit his degree of Glory.

H.W. Naisbitt   *Sunday p.m. 3/8/1885*

JD 26:115

The scriptures give an account simply of the woman Eve; declaring that this name was given her of Adam, because she was "the mother of all living;" but outside of biblical record there has been handed down from time immemorial the idea that *Adam had two wives*, the narrators go so far, or rather so near perfecting the tradition so as to give their names, Lilith being said to be the name of one as Eve was the name of the other, and while it may be difficult to harmonize all the Rabbinical and Talmudic versions of this matter, it is said that Joseph Smith the Prophet taught that *Adam had two wives*.

J.F. Gibbs   *11/--/1889*

Contributor, 6:76-78

Having, *while on earth complied with the requirements of the Father in relation to Celestial Marriage*, he is thus qualified to become a "Father of spirits," and *his immortal wives become the mothers of spirits*, thus obeying the only and eternal law of reproduction. ... he is placed upon it [the world] and *with his wives* repeats the history of man on this and other planets. The Being that has organized the world; and placed upon it the germs of animated nature; is the one most entitled to furnish mortal bodies for his spiritual children. And when the great drama of life is finished and he with his children are redeemed and glorified, is he not entitled, as the head of an innumerable posterity, to be recognized as a Father and God to those that will rise up and call Him blessed?

A. T. Schreader, ed. [anti-Mormon]   *circa 1898-1900*

Zion-Lucifer's Lantern 4:65

If I can get any intelligent idea of the after life of mormons by the study of there inane sermons it is something like this: There are two resurrections one of the spirit, the other of the flesh. After the second resurrection the spirit and the body are united and transplanted to some place in the universe where they gather up enough raw planetary material out of which to "organize a world."

To this world the resurrected man now [sic] himself and by virtue of the "sealing power" of the Mormon priesthood all the women who have been "sealed" to him for eternity are attracted or transplanted to this same planet. Here they set up housekeeping as Adam did in the Garden of Eden, and they will live eternal lives unless some walking or talking snake should put up a jot on them as it did on Eve.

To this world of his own creation the man will be the God, even as Adam in Mormon theology is the God of this world. He is the King and *his wives queens*. Their kingdom will consist of their own "eternal progeny." Hence polygamy is essential because the extent and glory of every man's kingdom in the hereafter must depend on the number of wives sealed to him for eternity.

Analysis & Observations

β

The above statements have been used to support the idea that Adam had more than one wife during the period of time that he lived on this earth; this section excludes references to Mary as Adam's wife because she was not his wife during Adam's *mortal* "probation."[101]

Some few individuals have reconciled this teaching with the above statements declaring

---

[101] This issue is treated below in "Mary Sealed to Adam".

Eve to be the mother of all living by following Brigham Young's lead. As Brigham interpreted 1 Timothy 3:2 ("A bishop then must be blameless, the husband of one wife …") to mean that a bishop must be the husband of at *least* one wife, so have some fundamentalists interpreted the above statements to mean that each Adam must bring at least one wife to each earth. While this clever attempt at apologetics may be helpful to some, it begs the bigger problem: the teachings are in direct contradiction with one another because both sets of teachings specifically refer to the Adam and Eve of this earth. That said, none of the above quotes that clearly teach that Adam came to this earth with more than one wife is a direct quote from an apostle. Orson Pratt's quote, which is ambiguous at best anyway, must be suspect given his stance on Adam-God teachings in the first place; Brigham's statements can easily be read to be referring to the eternities - especially given his teachings in the earlier section; and none of the other statements are authoritative primary sources of an apostolic declaration. Given these factors, it seems that the position that Adam came to this earth with more than one wife is not credible. However, it is entirely possible that the above statements claiming that Joseph Smith personally taught that Adam *brought* other wives with him from the eternities may have been misconstrued and that Joseph may have actually taught that Adam married other women *during* this mortal probation as was suggested in the previous section.

10   Eve as a Plural Wife

| In the Eternities |

Brigham Young   *Friday 4/9/1852*

JD 1:50

When our father Adam came into the garden of Eden, he came into it with a celestial body, and brought Eve, *one of his wives*, with him.

Brigham Young   *Friday 4/9/1852*

Journal of Wilford Woodruff

When our Father came into the Garden He came with his Celestial body & brought *one of his wives* with him and ate of the fruit of the Garden until He could beget a Tabernacle.

Brigham Young   *Friday 4/16/1852*

Journal of Samuel Holister Rogers 1:179

President Brigham Young said that our spirits ware begotten before that Adam came to the Earth and that Adam helped to make the Earth, that he had a Celestial body when he came to the Earth and that he brought his wife or *one of his wives* with him, and that Eave was also a Celestial being, that they eat of the fruit of the ground until they begat children from the Earth, he said that Adam was the only God that we would have, and that Christ was not begotten of the Holy Ghost, but of the Father Adam, that Christ, was our elder brother.

Orson Pratt   *circa 1853*

The Seer, 172

We have now clearly shown that *God the Father had a plurality of wives*, one or more being in eternity, by whom He begat our spirits as well as the spirit of Jesus his First

Born, and another being upon the earth by whom he begat the tabernacle of Jesus, as His Only Begotten in this world. We have also proved most clearly that the Son followed the example of the Father and became the great Bridegroom to whom kings' daughters and many honorable wives were to be married. We have also proved that both *God the Father* and our Lord Jesus Christ *inherit their wives in eternity* as well as in time; and that God the Father has already begotten many thousand millions of sons and daughters and sent them into this world to take tabernacles; and that God the Son has the promise that "of the increase of his government there shall be no end;" it being expressly declared that the children of one of His Queens should be made Princes in all the earth. (Psalm 45:16).

Brigham Young   *10/6/1854*

Journal of Joseph L. Robinson, 102-03

I believed every word, for I remembered saying to the Brethren at a meeting of High Priests in Nauvoo, while I was speaking to them under the influence of the Spirit, I remarked thus, that our Father *Adam had many wives*, and that *Eve was only one of them*, and that she was our mother, and that she was the mother of the inhabitants of this earth.

Brigham Young   *2/10/1867*

JD 11:328

Yes, [plural marriage is] one of the relics of *Adam*, of Enoch, of Noah, of Abraham, of Isaac, of Jacob, of Moses, David, Solomon, the Prophets, of Jesus, and his apostles.

Brigham Young   *8/31/1873*

JD 16:167

There was a certain woman brought to Father Adam whose name was Eve, because she was the first woman, and she was given to him to be his wife; I am not disposed to give any farther knowledge concerning her at present. *There is no doubt but that he left many companions.*

Eliza R. Snow   *1877*

THE ULTIMATUM OF HUMAN LIFE

Obedience will the same bright garland weave,
As it has done for your great Mother, *Eve*,
For all her daughters on the earth, who will
All my requirements sacredly fulfill.
And what to Eve, though in her mortal life,

She'd been the first, the tenth, or fiftieth wife?
What did she care, when in her lowest state,
Whether by fools, consider'd small, or great?
'Twas all the same with her - she prov'd her worth -
She's now the Goddess and the Queen of Earth.

A. T. Schreader, ed. [anti-Mormon]   *circa 1898-1900*

Zion-Lucifer's Lantern 4:65

If I can get any intelligent idea of the after life of mormons by the study of there inane sermons it is something like this: There are two resurrections one of the spirit, the other of the flesh. After the second resurrection the spirit and the body are united and transplanted to some place in the universe where they gather up enough raw planetary material out of which to "organize a world."

To this world the resurrected man now [sic] himself and by virtue of the "sealing power" of the Mormon priesthood all the women who have been "sealed" to him for eternity are attracted or transplanted to this same planet. Here they set up housekeeping as Adam did in the Garden of Eden, and they will live eternal lives unless some walking or talking snake should put up a jot on them as it did on Eve.

To this world of his own creation the man will be the God, even as Adam in Mormon theology is the God of this world. He is the King and *his wives queens*. Their kingdom will consist of their own "eternal progeny." Hence polygamy is essential because the extent and glory of every man's kingdom in the hereafter must depend on the number of wives sealed to him for eternity.

Analysis & Observations

β

There is not a whole lot of insight to be found in this section. To fundamentalists who have studied the early brethren's teachings regarding plural marriage and who believe that living celestial plural marriage is an essential requirement for exaltation, there is nothing particularly noteworthy in the above statements. In contrast, modern members of the LDS Church do not universally believe that all exalted gods are polygamists and may therefore find the above section noteworthy because it gives them some insight into their spiritual (and physical) mother - that is, she *was* a plural wife.

11 Mary Sealed to Adam

See also
Adam as Father of Christ

Orson Pratt   _10/--/1853_

The Seer 1:158-59

If none but Gods will be permitted to multiply immortal children, it follows that each God must have one or more wives. God, the Father of our spirits, became the Father of our Lord Jesus Christ according to the flesh. Hence, the Father saith concerning him, "Thou art my Son, this day have I begotten thee." We are informed in the first chapter of Luke, that _Mary was chosen by the Father_ as a choice virgin, through whom He begat Jesus. The angel said unto the Virgin Mary, "The Holy Ghost shall come upon thee, and the power of the Highest shall overshadow thee; therefore, also, that holy thing which shall be born of thee shall be called the Son of God." After the power of the Highest had overshadowed Mary, and she had by that means conceived, she related the circumstance to her cousin Elizabeth in the following words: "He that is Mighty hath done to me great things; and holy is His name." It seems from this relation that the Holy Ghost accompanied "the Highest" when He overshadowed the Virgin Mary and begat Jesus; and from this circumstance some have supposed that the body of Jesus was begotten of the Holy Ghost without the instrumentality of the immediate presence of the Father. There is no doubt that the Holy Ghost came upon Mary to sanctify her, and make her holy, and prepare her to endure the glorious presence of "the Highest," that when "He" should "overshadow" her, she might conceive, being filled with the Holy Ghost; hence the angel said, as recorded in Matthew, "That which is conceived in her is of the Holy Ghost;" that is, the Holy Ghost gave her strength to abide the presence of the Father without being consumed; but it was the personage of the Father who begat the body of Jesus; and for this reason Jesus is called "the Only Begotten of the Father;"

that is, the only one in this world whose fleshly body was begotten by the Father. There were millions of sons and daughters whom He begat before the foundation of this world, but they were spirits, and not bodies of flesh and bones; whereas, both the spirit and body of Jesus were begotten by the Father - the spirit having been begotten in heaven many ages before the tabernacle was begotten upon the earth. The fleshly body of Jesus required a Mother as well as a Father. Therefore, *the Father and Mother of Jesus, according to the flesh, must have been associated together in the capacity of Husband and Wife*; hence the Virgin *Mary must have been*, for the time being, *the lawful wife of God the Father*; we use the term *lawful Wife*, because it would be blasphemous in the highest degree to say that He overshadowed her or begat the Saviour unlawfully. It would have been unlawful for any man to have interfered with Mary, who was already espoused to Joseph; for such a heinous crime would have subjected both the guilty parties to death, according to the law of Moses. But God having created all men and women, had the most perfect right to do with His own creation, according to His holy will and pleasure; He had a lawful right to overshadow the Virgin Mary in *the capacity of a husband*, and beget a Son, although she was espoused to another; for the law which He gave to govern men and women was not intended to govern Himself, or to prescribe rules for his own conduct. It was also lawful in Him, after having thus dealt with Mary, to give her to Joseph her espoused husband. Whether God the Father gave Mary to *Joseph for time only*, or for time and eternity, we are not informed. Inasmuch as God was the first husband to her, it may be that He only gave her to be the wife of Joseph while in this mortal state, and that *He intended after the resurrection to again take her as one of his own wives to raise up immortal spirits in eternity*.

As God the Father begat the fleshly body of Jesus, so He, before the world began, begat his spirit. As the body required an earthly Mother, so his spirit required a heavenly Mother. As *God associated in the capacity of a husband with the earthly mother*, so likewise He associated in the same capacity with the heavenly one. Earthly things being in the likeness of heavenly things. ... or in other words, the laws of generation upon the earth are after the order of the laws of generation in heaven.

Brigham Young   *8/19/1866*

JD 11:268

The man Joseph, the husband of Mary, did not, that we know of, have more than one wife, but *Mary the wife of Joseph had another husband*. ... That very babe that was cradled in the manger, was begotten, not by Joseph, the husband of Mary, but by another Being. Do you inquire by whom? He was begotten by God our heavenly Father.

Byron Allred   *3/22/1877*

Jans Christian Anderson Weibye Daybooks

Byron Allred preaches at Manti on Adam as God, with the following remarks in part: Adam was buried by God (God his Father) and was only dead like a twinkling of an eye, and his God exalted him immediately. *Mary was sealed to Adam, and was his wife when she had Jesus.* Mary will be the Queen to people another world; *Mary was the second wife to Adam*; and unless we have two wives, we can never be Gods.

Joseph F. Smith   *12/20/1914*

Box Elder News[102]

Now, my little friends, I will repeat again in words as simple as I can, and you talk to your parents about it, that God, the Eternal Father is literally the father of Jesus Christ. Mary was married to Joseph for time. *No man could take her for eternity because she belonged to the Father of her divine Son.*

Brigham H. Roberts

Defense of the Faith and the Saints 2:268

In fact, the Mormon Church teaches that God the Father has a material body of flesh and bone's; that Adam is the God of the human race; that this Adam-God was physically begotten by another God; that the Gods were once as we are now; that there is a great multiplicity of Gods; that Jesus Christ was physically begotten by the *Heavenly Father of Mary, His wife*; that, as we have a Heavenly Father, so also we have a Heavenly Mother.

Analysis & Observations

β

The LDS Church continues to believe that the laws of procreation were not broken when the Father sired the Son. The only distinguishing factor between the LDS Church and Adam-God teachings is that the Father here was Adam, not Elohim.

While there is only a very small sampling of statements declaring Mary to be the wife of Adam, it stands to reason that our father and God would not violate sacred laws of procreation when He Himself has declared their violation to be so heinous that they stand nigh unto murder. Further, as celestial plural marriage was declared by Brigham Young

---

[102] The publication date was 1/28/1915.

and others as the only order of Heaven, it stands to reason that Mary would have been sealed to Adam as His wife for eternity before they entered into marital relations.

Although I have not been able to credibly trace this doctrine as the source of marriages for time only, it seems that this teaching was the likely source of the rare practice of one man marrying a woman for time while that same woman was simultaneously married to another man for eternity.[103] This practice appears to have led to the martyrdom of Parley P. Pratt and should be distinguished from Levirate marriage[104] where a woman is married to a man for time while she is married to a *deceased* husband for eternity. This practice was much more common in the early Church than it is today because it is much more feasibly accomplished in a family where plural marriage is practiced and because the doctrine is esteemed as a Mosaic (and therefore fulfilled) law by the modern LDS Church - it began in full force at the death of Joseph Smith when most of his wives remarried Brigham Young or Heber C. Kimball.

---

[103] For the most thorough documentation of this practice that the author is aware of, see Todd Compton's *Sacred Loneliness*, a historical account of the lives of Joseph Smith's plural wives - the reader is alerted to the fact that Compton's writings have a somewhat anti-Mormon slant to them.

[104] See Deuteronomy 25:5-10, Genesis 38: 8, Matthew 22:23 et seq, and Ruth 4:1-12 for a few biblical references. The early brethren saw Deuteronomy 25:5-10 in a broader context than biblical scholars recognize today; that is, it was not only the duty of the *biological brother* to take care of a widow in this fashion. Relatives were under this obligation as were other "brethren" - perhaps this only pertains to those who were sealed to the deceased as a father.

12 Eve as Adam's Daughter

See also
Mary Sealed to Adam

Brigham Young   *8/31/1873*
Journal of Wilford Woodruff
In his remarks he said that a man who did not have but one wife in the resurrection that woman will not be his but taken from him and given to another. But he may be saved in the kingdom of God but be single to all eternity. *Mother Eve was the Daughter of Adam.*

Byron Allred   *3/22/1877*
Jans Christian Anderson Weibye Daybooks[105]
Mary was sealed to Adam, and was his wife when she had Jesus. *Mary will be the Queen to people another world*; Mary was the second wife to Adam; and unless we have two wives, we can never be Gods. Adam will worship his God and we will worship Adam, and our children will worship us.

Edward Tullidge   *3/--/1877*
Women of Mormondom, 180, 192
Adam and Eve are the names of the fathers and mothers of worlds. Adam was not made out of a lump of clay, as we make a brick, nor was Eve taken as a rib - a bone - from his side. They came by generation. But woman, as the wife or mate of man, was a rib of man. *She was taken from his side, in their glorified world,* and brought by him to earth to be

---

[105] This statement and the statement following do not directly state that Eve was Adam's daughter. However, they do show how a god may take a wife (in this case, Mary) from a world that he created and then later, take that wife (who has been exalted) to another world where she becomes an Eve - thereby becoming both his wife and daughter.

the mother of a race. These were father and mother of a world of spirits who had been born to them in heaven. ... Woman is heiress of the Gods. She is joint heir with her elder brother, Jesus the Christ; but she inherits from *her God-Father* and her God-Mother.

Brigham H. Roberts   *11 /--/1889*

Contributor 10:265-67

We are all "formed" of the dust of the ground, though instead of being molded as a brick we are brought forth by the natural laws of procreation; *so also was Adam and his wife in some older world. And as for the story of the rib, under it I believe the mystery of procreation is hidden.*

Analysis & Observations

β

Note that Byron Allred's statement that Eve will be a queen of another world shows how Eve can be Adam's daughter and yet be his wife. The argument runs like this:

~ Mary, through several generations of descent, was the physical "daughter" of Adam during her probation on this earth.

~ Mary was sealed to Adam sometime before she conceived Christ.

~ Therefore, Mary, a physical "daughter" of Adam, became his wife during her probation on this earth.

~ Mary will become the Eve of a future world.

~ Therefore, when Mary becomes an Eve of another world, she will be Adam's daughter, wife, and Eve.

If the above statements are accurate, then this teaching is important in context of Adam-God teachings because it suggests that our mother Eve could have been the mother of a savior of a different world - a "Mary" if we can use this name as a title. This interpretation need not presume that Adam only takes one of his daughters as a wife in each world.[106] However, it may be that the Father and God of a world only takes one of his daughters as his wife from each world - no revealed word conclusively addresses this issue. While it is ennobling to the soul to know that our spiritual heritage springs from two exalted beings, would it not be more ennobling to know that our spiritual heritage springs from a woman so choice that she was chosen over millions of other women to become the mother of the savior of her world? This belief, coupled with the belief that Adam was the savior of his world engenders an understanding that all of the people of this world live among the choicest of all lineages throughout the immensities of space.

Alternatively, the above statements could be read to mean that our mother Eve was an ordinary, valiant woman of another world created by our father Adam. After her mortal probation, Adam chose her to be one of his wives and subsequently created this earth and populated this earth with this woman, our mother Eve.

---

[106] That is, Brigham Young said that Eve was the daughter of Adam and, within the context of other statements, this means that Eve could have been a Mary of another earth because we know that the Father and God of a world is joined with one of his daughters, a Mary, to sire a savior. However, this does not preclude the possibility that the Father and God of that world could take another of his daughters from that world as a wife.

Adam & Eve

β

The Creation, Fall, & Atonement

13 Adam & Eve
Immortal & Exalted Before the Fall

See also
Adam & Eve not Formed from the Dust of this Earth

Joseph Smith   *circa 1844*

"Sayings of Joseph the Prophet," as recorded in Anson Call's Journal
Now regarding Adam: He came here from another planet *an immortalized Being* and
brought his wife, Eve, with him and by eating of the fruit of this earth became subject
to death and decay, and He became of the earth, earthy, was made mortal and subject
to death.

Orson Pratt   *3/--/1850*

MS 12:69; JD 1:329
But a universal redemption from the effects of original sin, has nothing to do with
redemption from our personal sins; for the original sin of *Adam*, and the personal sins of
his children, are two different things. The first was committed by man *in his immortal
state*; the second was committed by man in a mortal state: the former was committed in
a state of ignorance of good or evil; the latter was committed by man, having a
knowledge of both good and evil. As the sins are different, and committed entirely
under different circumstances, so the penalties are different also. The penalty of the
first transgression was an eternal separation of body and spirit, and eternal banishment
from the presence of Jehovah; while the penalty of our own transgressions does not
involve a disunion of body and spirit, but only eternal banishment.

Brigham Young   *Sunday 4 p.m. 3/14/1852*

Historian's Office Journal, 106

Adam came (to) (the) E[arth] when (he) assisted (to) form (it) (sh) (he) then partook
(of) (the) fruits (of) (the) E[arth] (and) Became Earthy (and) (they) (which) are (the) (s)
(after) (sh) rece[ive] our resurrected bodies (and) (shall) (all) (have) (the) priv[ilege]
(of) going (as) Adam's form (an) E[arth] (and) do likewise

Brigham Young   *Friday 4/9/1852*

JD 1:50

When our father *Adam came into the garden of Eden*, he came into it *with a celestial body*,
and brought Eve, one of his wives, with him.

Brigham Young   *Friday 4/9/1852*

Journal of Wilford Woodruff

Our Father begot all the spirits that were before any tabernacle was made. When our
Father came into the Garden *He came with his Celestial body* & brought one of his wives
with him and ate of the fruit of the Garden until He could beget a Tabernacle. And
Adam is Michael God and all the God that we have anything to do with. They ate of this
fruit & formed the first Tabernacle that was formed.

Brigham Young   *Friday 4/9/1852*

Journal of Hosea Stout 2:435

Another meeting this evening. President B. Young taught that Adam was the father of
Jesus and the only God to us. That he *came to this world in a resurrected body,* etc. More
hereafter.

Brigham Young   *4/16/1852*

Journal of Samuel Holister Rogers 1:179

We had the best Conference that I ever attended during the time of the Conference
President Brigham Young said that our spirits ware begotten before that Adam came to
the Earth and that Adam helped to make the Earth, that *he had a Celestial body when he
came to the Earth* and that he brought his wife or one of his wives with him, and that
Eave was allso a Celestial being, that they eat of the fruit of the ground until they begat
children from the Earth.

Orson Pratt   *7/25/1852*

JD 1:284

And what was the fullest extent of the penalty of Adam's transgression? I will tell you.

It was death. The death of what? The *death of the immortal tabernacle* - of that tabernacle where the seeds of death had not been, that was wisely framed, and pronounced very good; the seeds of death were introduced into it. How, and in what manner? Some say there was something in the nature of the fruit that introduced mortality.

Brigham Young	*8/28/1852*

JD 6:274-75

After men have got their exaltations and their crowns - have become Gods, even the sons of God - are made Kings of kings and Lords of lords, they have the power then of propagating their species in spirit; and that is the first of their operations with regard to organizing a world. Power is then given to them to organize the elements, and then commence the organization of tabernacles. How can they do it? Have they to go to that earth? Yes, and Adam will have to go there, and he cannot do without Eve; he must have Eve to commence the work of generation, and they will go into the garden, and continue to eat and drink of the fruits of the corporeal world, *until this grosser matter is diffused sufficiently through their celestial bodies* to enable them, according to the established laws, to produce mortal tabernacles for their spiritual children. This is a key for you. The faithful will become Gods, even the sons of God; but this does not overthrow the idea that we have a father.

Orson Spencer	*10/3/1852*

Journal of William Clayton

A morning meeting was held at which Orson Spencer and Orson Pratt spoke on the subject of Adam. Spencer spoke of *Adam "coming to this earth* in the morning of creation *with a resurrected body* and etc... Brother Spencer endeavors to substantiate the position taken by President Young; Viz, that *Adam came to this earth with a resurrected body*, and became mortal by eating the fruits of the earth, which was earthy.

William Clayton	*10/4/1852*

Journal of William Clayton

There is also another subject which has occupied much of the time and in which the difference in opinion seems to be wider, and more firmly established than the baby resurrection; and that is in regard to Adam's coming on this earth; whether *he came here with a resurrected body* and became mortal by eating the fruits of the earth which are earthy, or he was created direct (that is his mortal tabernacle) from the dust of the earth, according to the popular opinion of the world. On this subject brother Pratt and myself, have rather locked horns, he holding to the latter opinion, and I firmly believing the former, but there can be no difficulty between us, as he is my superior and I shall not argue against him; but if it were an equal I should be apt to speak my feelings in full. There are difficulties on both sides, take it which way we will, and he is unwilling to express anything more than his opinion on the subject.

Orson Pratt & Brigham Young   *9/17/1854*

Journal of Wilford Woodruff

Brother Pratt also thought that Adam was made of the dust of the earth. Could not believe that *Adam* was our God or the Father of Jesus Christ. President Young said that He *came from another world* & made this. Brought Eve with him, partook of the fruits of the earth, begat children & they were earthly & had mortal bodies & if we were faithful, we should become Gods as He was.

Brigham Young   *Friday 10/6/1854*

Journal of the Southern Indian Mission, 87- 89

Michael came down with his wife, & began to people it. *Michael had his body from the dust of the planet he was begotten on*, he obeyed his Lord, *was faithful and obedient, died and was resurrected*, he did not resurrect himself. ... Adam's descent was to organize people & redeem a world, by his wife he peopled it by his first born he redeems. ... Adam & Eve had children in the spirit - and their children married - brother & sister - then the bodies followed.

Brigham Young   *Sunday 10/8/1854*

John Pulsipher Papers, 37

[W]hen this work was made - our God who is Adam came & commenced the peopling of it - Tho he is God & *had lived & died & been reserected on some other plannet* - & obtained his exaltation & begat the Spirits of children enough people this world.

Brigham Young   *Sunday 10/8/1854*

MABY

I tell you more: Adam is the Father of our spirits. He lived upon an earth; he did abide his creation, and did honor to his calling and Priesthood. He obeyed his Master or Lord, and probably many of his wives did the same; they *lived and died upon an earth, and then were resurrected* again to Immortality and Eternal Life. "Did he resurrect himself?" you inquire. ... Adam, therefore, was resurrected by someone who had been resurrected. ...

I reckon that Father Adam was a resurrected being, with his wives and posterity, and in the Celestial Kingdom they were crowned with Glory, Immortality and Eternal Lives, with Thrones, Principalities and Powers: and it was said to him, "It is your right to organize the elements; and to your Creations and Posterity there shall be no end, but you shall add Kingdom to Kingdom, and Throne to Throne; and still behold the vast eternity of unorganized matter." Adam then was a resurrected being. ... When the spirit enters the body it is pure, and good, and if the body would be subject to the spirit it would always be taught to do the will of the Father in Heaven. But the spirit is interwoven with the flesh and blood; it is subjected to the body, consequently Satan has power over both. I reckon *the Father has been through all this*. ...

I commenced with Father *Adam in his resurrected state*, noticed our spiritual state, then our temporal, or mortal state, and traveled until I got back to Father Adam again.

Brigham Young   *3/25/1855*

Journal of Samuel W. Richards 2:215

Adam and Eve were made of the dust of the Earth from which they came, they brought their bodies with them. They *had lived, died and been resurrected before they came here* and they came with immortal bodies, and had to partake of the fruits of this Earth in order to bring forth mortal bodies, or natural bodies, that their seed might be of the dust of this Earth as they were of the dust of the earth from which they came.

Brigham Young   *5/6/1855*

Journal of Wilford Woodruff

Adam & Eve had lived upon another Earth, *were immortal when they came here*. Adam assisted in forming this earth & agreed to fall when he came here, & he fell that man might be & the opposite principle to good, the devil, the serpent, the evil, was placed upon the earth that man might know the good from the evil, for without an experience in these things man could not know the one from the other. As soon as the devil was on earth he sowed the seeds of death in everything so as soon as they began to eat of the fruit of the earth they received into their system the seeds of mortality & of death so their children were mortal & subject to death, sorrow, pain & wo. Then when they partook of life, joy, ease, & happiness, they would know how to prize it.

Orson Pratt   *4/13/1856*

JD 3:344

Our first parents through transgressing the law of God, brought death into the world, but through the death of Jesus Christ, life and immortality were introduced. The one brings into bondage; the other gives us hope of escape, of redemption, that we may come forth with *the same kind of body that Adam had before the fall, a body of immortal flesh and bones. Adam and Eve were immortal, the same as resurrected beings*, but previous to their transgression they had no knowledge of good and evil. After the redemption we will not only have the same kind of bodies that they possessed in the garden of Eden before the fall, but we will have a knowledge of good and evil through our experience.

Brigham Young   *2/8/1857*

JD 4:217-19

Now to the facts in the case; all the difference between Jesus Christ and any other man that ever lived on the earth, from the days of *Adam* until now, is simply this, *the Father,* after He had once been in the flesh, and lived as we live, *obtained His exaltation,* attained to thrones, gained the ascendancy over principalities and powers, and had the knowledge and power to create - to bring forth and organize the elements upon natural principles. This He did after His ascension, or His glory, or His eternity, and was actually classed with the Gods, with the beings who create, with those who have kept the celestial law while in the flesh, and again obtained their bodies. Then He was prepared to commence the work of creation, as the scriptures teach.

Brigham Young   *1/27/1860*

Minutes of a meeting of the First Presidency
Michael was a resurrected Being and he left Elohim and came to this earth & with an immortal body, & continued so till he partook of earthly food and begot children who were mortal.

Orson Pratt   *10:00 a.m. 4/5/1860*

Minutes of the Meeting of the Council of the Twelve
One [revelation] says *Adam* was formed out of the Earth, and the Lord put in his spirit; and another that he *came with his body, flesh and bones,* thus there are two contrary revelations - in the garden it is said, that a voice said to Adam, in the meridian of time, I will send my only begotten son Jesus Christ. then how can that man and Adam both be the Father of Jesus Christ? ...
I have heard brother Brigham say that *Adam* is the Father of our Spirits, and he *came here with his resurrected body,* to fall for his own children; and I said to him, it leads to an endless number of falls, which leads to sorrow and death: that is revolting to my feelings, even if it were not sustained by revelation.

George Q. Cannon   *10/12/1861*

MS 23:654

President Young, in the foregoing passages,[107] while substantiating the fact of the union

---

[107] JD 1:50-51; 6:275.

of man's preexisting spirit with a bodily product of the "dust of the ground," enters more particularly into the modus operandi of that union. He unmistakably declares man's origin to be altogether of a celestial character - that *not only is his spirit of heavenly descent, but his organization too,* - that the latter is not taken from the lower animals, but *from the originally celestial body of the great Father of humanity.* Taking the doctrine of man's origin as seen from this higher point of view, and comparing it with the low assumptive theories of uninspired men, ... how great the contrast appears! 'Look on this picture' - Man, the offspring of an ape!; 'and on this' - Man, the image of God, his Father! How wide the contrast! And how different the feelings produced in the breast!

John Burrows   *Saturday 8/12/1865*

MS 27:497

When Jehovah had finished the creation of this beautiful world, and devised laws to direct the progress of nature in the animal, vegetable and mineral kingdoms, all was order, harmony and unity, and flowers and fruits shed forth their rich perfumes. In the designs of Providence, *two intelligent beings came forth, and when they were clothed with immortality, they stood forth as king and queen of a universal Eden*; but we read that before the Lord left them, he gave unto the man the following striking commandment, "Of every tree of the garden thou mayest freely eat: but of the tree of knowledge of good and evil, thou shalt not eat ...."

W. W. Phelps   *Monday 10 a.m. 10/9/1865*

Conference Report
THE SPIRIT ...
O may the Saints *be perfect*
As God our Father was,
When he got back to Eden,
By her celestial laws.

Brigham Young   *Sunday p.m. 6/18/1873*

DN 22:308

[*Adam*] was the first man on the earth, and its framer and maker. He with the help of his brethren, brought it into existence. Then he said, "I want my children who are in the spirit world to come and live here. I *once dwelt upon an earth something like this, in a mortal state, I was faithful, I received my crown and exaltation.*

Orson Pratt   *11/22/1873*

JD 16:324

Our first parents were not mortal when they were placed on this earth, but they were as immortal as those who are resurrected in the presence of God. Death came into the world by their transgression, they produced mortality; hence this will be a complete restoration, of which I am speaking.

Orson Pratt   *9/11/1859*

JD 7:257

[S]hall we be restored into the condition *Adam* was in before he fell? I answer, you will be. What condition was he in? He *was an immortal being*, and you will be restored to immortality, whether you be Saints or sinners. The decree has gone forth that every man is to be raised to immortality. Then you will be as Adam was in the Garden of Eden before he fell.

Brigham Young   *10/9/1859*

JD 7:286

Mankind are here because they are the offspring of parents (*Adam and Eve*) who *were first brought here from another planet.*

Orson Pratt   *11/22/1873*

JD 16:324

Our first parents *were not mortal when they were placed on this earth*, but they were *as immortal as those who are resurrected* in the presence of God. Death came into the world by their transgression, they produced mortality.

The Lecture at the Veil   *Tuesday 2/7/1877*

Journal of L. John Nuttall

Adam was an immortal being when he came. On this earth he had lived on an earth similar to ours he had received the Priesthood and the Keys thereof. and had been faithful in all things and gained his resurrection and his exaltation and was crowned with glory immortality and eternal lives and *was numbered with the Gods* for such he became through his faithfulness. ... Adam & Eve when they were placed on this earth *were immortal beings* with flesh, bones and sinews.

Shortened Lecture at the Veil   *between 1877-1894*

He [Adam] had been true and faith in all things and *gained his resurretin and exaltation*. He was crowned ~~in which~~ with glory, immortality and eternal lives and was numbered with the Gods - for such he became through his faithfulness.

Edward Tullidge   *3/--/1877*
The Women of Mormondom, 199

The Mormon daughters of *Eve* have also in this eleventh hour come down to earth, like her, to magnify the divine office of motherhood. She *came down from her resurrected*, they from their spirit, *estate*.

Orson Pratt   *7/18/1880*
JD 21:288-90

There is one very important item, right here, to be understood, and should be thoroughly understood by every person desirous of knowing the truth, and that is, that when Adam and Eve were in the garden of Eden, before this transgression took place, *they were not subject to death*; they were not subject to any kind of pain, or disease, or sickness, or any of the afflictions of mortality. Now, perhaps those who are not in the habit of reflecting upon this matter, may suppose that when Adam was placed on the earth, and Eve, his wife, they were mortal, like unto us; but that was not so. God did not make a mortal being. It would be contrary to this great goodness to make a man mortal, subject to pain, subject to sickness, subject to death. ... How came, then, Adam to be mortal? How came Adam to be filled with pain and affliction and with great sorrow? It was in consequence of transgression. Hence, the Apostle Paul, in speaking upon this subject, said, that by transgression sin entered into the world, and death by sin. Death, then, instead of being something that the Lord created, instead of being something that he sent into the world, and by sin; the Lord suffered it to come upon Adam in consequence of transgression. *Two immortal beings*, then, were placed in the garden of Eden, male and female.

Charles W. Penrose   *9/--/1881*
Contributor 2:363 #12

That which was lost in *Adam* is to be regained in Christ. Through the commission of crime, death came into the world. Satan gained dominion. The earth trembled under the curse. Eden bloomed no more upon its face. The tree of life was removed. Thorns and briers and noxious weeds came up in the place of the flowers and fruits of paradise. Deity was hidden from the sight of man. Sorrow and pain and toil and travail became the heritage of mortals. Enmity arose between man and beast. Venom entered the serpent's fangs, and rage the hearts of brute and fowl and aqueous creature. Strife dwelt in the very elements and death brooded over the face of the smitten globe. *What, then, was lost? The immortality of man*; the blessed tree of life; communion with Jehovah; the companionship of angels; the purity of paradise; man's dominion over inferior creatures; freedom from Satanic influence; exemption from toil and pain; earth's affinity with perfected realms on high.

Orson Pratt   *10/3/1881*

Masterful Discourses of Orson Pratt, 346

[A]nd you will fall asleep in peace, having made sure your salvation, and having done your duty well, like those whose funeral sermon we are preaching this morning; and thus you will fall asleep, with a full assurance that you will come up in the morning of the first resurrection with an *immortal body like unto which Adam had before he partook of the forbidden fruit*. This is the promise to them that fall asleep in Jesus.

Brigham H. Roberts   *11/--/1884*

The Contributor 10:265-66

As vegetation was created or made to grow upon some older earth, and the seeds thereof or the plants themselves were brought to our earth and made to grow, so likewise *man and his helpmate were brought from some other world* to our own, to people it with their children. And though it is said that the 'Lord God formed man of the dust of the ground' - it by no means follows that he was 'formed as one might form a brick, or from the dust of this earth. We are all 'formed' of the dust of the ground, though instead of being moulded as a brick we are brought forth by the natural laws of procreation; *so also was Adam and his wife in some older world*. And as for the story of the rib, under it I believe the mystery of procreation is hidden.

Thomas W. Brookbank   *4/--/1887*

The Contributor 8:218 #6

Before Adam fell, he was a resurrected man, that is, his physical body had been disorganized, and then reorganized. The Apostle Peter tells us plainly that this earth is to be dissolved, after which a new world is to be organized. It will be resurrected as Adam was. *Between the time of Adam's resurrection and his fall afterwards*, he must have enjoyed a season of rest and peace.

Wilford W. Woodruff & George Q. Cannon   *6/11/1892*

Diary of Charles Lowell Walker, 2:740-41

Pres. Woodruff and Cannon showed in a very plain manner ... that *Adam was an immortal being when he came to this earth* and was made the same as all other men and Gods are made; and that the seed of man was of the dust of the earth, and that the continuation of the seeds in a glorified state was Eternal Lives.

Edward Stevenson   *3/3/1896*

Edward Stevenson Diary

I have more pleasure than usual with a deep talk with Pres. L. Snow on *Adam* - Jehovah - Eloheim and Jesus and Spirits, and Regarding their *immortality*, creation, &c

                                                      6/27/1908

Elders' Journal 6:33 #2

When *Adam and Eve* were first placed in the garden of Eden they *had resurrected bodies*, in which there was no blood. A spiritual fluid or substance circulated in their veins instead of blood. Consequently, they had not power to beget children with tabernacles of flesh, such as human beings possess. The fall caused a change in their bodies, which, while it rendered them mortal, at the same time gave them power to create mortal bodies of flesh, blood and bone for their offspring.

Kelly   *1912*

Sacred Hymns, 112-13 #103

O God, Thou great, Thou good, Thou wise
Eternal is Thy name;
They power hath reared the lofty skies
And build creation's frame. ...

Thou mad'st him [man] monarch of the world,
And didst his kindred own,
Until by sin down he was hurled,
And *forfeited his throne.*[108]

Orson F. Whitney   *1915*

Improvement Era 19:402-03

In order that God's spirit children might have the opportunity to take bodies and undergo experiences on this earth, two *heavenly beings came down in advance and became mortal* for our sake. This is the true significance of the fall of Adam and Eve. It was not a mere yielding to temptation - they came on a mission, to pioneer this earthly wilderness, and open the way so that a world of waiting spirits might become souls, and make a stride forward in the great march of eternal progression.

---

[108] While this statement is not as direct as the other statements, its purpose here is answered by considering "what was his throne if not immortality before the fall?"

John M. Whitaker   6/24/1921

Seminary Lectures, Lecture 10

I am going to assume responsibility for making this statement, that man came here, was placed here as an immortal, glorified, resurrected being. I want to make myself clear, because these lectures are going to the brethren, and if they want to correct them, they can. ... I believe it was that fruit that changed and modified *Adam's resurrected body*, and again made it subject to death.

Melvin J. Ballard   6/24/1921

Seminary Lectures, Lecture 11

What Brother Whitaker has said I agree with, with reference to his fall and man's coming here."

Samuel Richard's Journal

There is always an Adam & Eve as the 1st man and woman to earths. *Adam & Eve were mortals and resurrected before this earth.*

Analysis & Observations

β

Some of the above statements remain reconcilable with current, mainstream LDS theology - that is, it appears that mainstream Mormons have no difficulty accepting the teaching that Adam was immortal when he came to this earth. However, the LDS Church is not so quick to concede that Adam came to this earth with a resurrected body (which somehow is different from an immortal body). Nevertheless, as Ogden Kraut has pointed out, this position is problematic - even for the noted scholar/apostle, Bruce R. McConkie, who unintentionally conceded that Adam and Eve were resurrected beings by pointing out that "Adam and Eve, as immortal beings, were placed on earth and commanded to multiply" and then later pointing out that "immortality is to live forever in the resurrected state." (Kraut, 41, quoting pages 4 and 6 of *A Light Unto the World*). This is particularly interesting in light of the following statement by Brigham Young:

MABY

Can any man, or set of men officiate in dispensing the laws, and administering the ordinances of the Kingdom of God, or of the kingdoms and governments of the world legally, without first obeying those laws, and submitting to those ordinances themselves. Do you understand me? If a foreigner wishes to become a citizen of the United States he must first become subject to this government; must you not first acknowledge and obey the laws of this government? Certainly you must. Then, to apply this to the Kingdom of God on Earth, and ask if any man has the power, the influence, the right, the authority, to go forth and preach this gospel, and baptise for the remission of sins unless he himself has, in the first place, been baptised, ordained and legally called to that office? What would the Elders of Israel and every other sensible man say to this? They would decide at once with me, that no man can lawfully officiate in any office in the Kingdom of God, or in the government of men, he has not been called to, and the authority of which has not been bestowed upon him. I am not going to talk a thousand things to you, but *I wish to tell you a few, and desire you to understand them, and connect them together.*

This statement was given as a prelude to Brigham Young's famous and most lengthy discourse on Adam-God. Notice that Brigham particularly wanted his reader to connect the above ideas with Adam-God teachings. The message that he was giving here is very revealing when considered in the context of Adam and Eve's immortality before the fall. Father Adam had gone through and obeyed the same ordinances of the gospel that we have to obey during our mortal probation and had gained his exaltation in the same fashion that we must gain our exaltation.

Given the above statements, it seems fairly clear that the early brethren held no distinction between an immortal being and an exalted being - the terms were synonymous - so when they taught that Adam was an immortal being before the fall, they were teaching that Adam was resurrected before he came to this earth.[109] Although this particular subject could use further attention from historians/scholars, the statements in this section appear to reflect the accuracy of this observation as they seem to use the terms interchangeably.

---

[109] Again, Orson Pratt runs as the exception to this observation.

14   Adam & Eve
Not Formed from the Dust of this Earth

See also
Adam & Eve: Immortal & Exalted Before the Fall

Genesis 2:7

And the Lord *God formed man of the dust of the ground*, and breathed into his nostrils the breath of life; and man became a living soul.[110]

Orson Pratt   9/30/1852

Thomas Evans Jeremy Sr. Journal

Brother Orson Pratt preached on the subject of the resurrection of the dead, that they are to come out of their graves, but said that he did not know how the power of God would operate to raise them up from their graves. Also he did not believe that Father Adam had flesh and bones, when he came to the garden of Eden, but he and his wife Eve were spirits, and that *God formed their bodies out of the dust of the ground*,[111] and the [sic] became a living souls. He also said that he believed that *Jesus Christ and Adam are brothers in the Spirit*, and that Adam is not the God that he is praying unto.

Orson Pratt et al.   10/3/1852

Journal of William Clayton

"A morning meeting was held at which Orson Spencer and Orson Pratt spoke on the subject of Adam. Spencer spoke of Adam "coming to this earth in the morning of creation with a resurrected body and etc ... He was followed by Elder Orson Pratt on

---

[110] See also Ecclesiastes 3:20 and Isaiah 51:1 for additional usages of this idiomatic phrase.

[111] This, like many other points of doctrine promoted by Orson Pratt, appears to be the modern LDS position.

the same subject ... He takes the literal reading of the scriptures for his guide, and maintains that *God took the dust of the earth, and molded a body* into which he put the spirit of man, just as we have generally understood from the scriptures; while Brother Spencer endeavors to substantiate the position taken by President Young; Viz, that Adam came to this earth with a resurrected body, and became mortal by eating the fruits of the earth, which was earthy. The subject was finally left in so much difficulty and obscurity as it has been from the beginning ... Elder Pratt advised the Brethren to pray to God for knowledge of the true principles, and it appears evident that when ever the question is decided, it will have to be by revelation from God." At an afternoon meeting four other Elders talked on the same subject, "without, however, bringing new light in regard to it. The knowledge of the truth in relation to the whole matter, is in the bosom of God, and when he sees fit to give the key, it will be plain and easy to understand."

Brigham Young	*10/23/1853*

JD 2:6

Look for instance at Adam. Listen, ye Latter-day Saints! *Supposing that Adam was formed actually out of clay*, out of the same kind of material from which bricks are formed; that with this matter God made the pattern of a man, and breathed into it the breath of life, and left it there, in that state of supposed perfection, *he would have been an adobe to this day*. He would not have known anything. Some of you may doubt the truth of what I now say, and argue that the Lord could teach him. This is a mistake. The Lord could not have taught him in any other way than in the way in which He did teach him. *You believe Adam was made of the dust of this earth. This I do not believe,* though it is supposed that it is so written in the Bible; but it is not, to my understanding. ... I do not believe that portion of the Bible as the Christian world do. I never did, and I never want to. What is the reason I do not? Because I have come to understanding, and banished from my mind all the baby stories my mother taught me when I was a child.

Orson Pratt	*9/17/1854*

Journal of Wilford Woodruff

Brother Pratt also thought that *Adam was made of the dust of the earth.* Could not believe that Adam was our God or the Father of Jesus Christ.

Brigham Young	*Friday 10/6/1854*

Journal of the Southern Indian Mission, 87- 89

Michael came down with his wife, & began to people it. *Michael had his body from the dust of the planet he was begotten on*, he obeyed his Lord, was faithful and obedient, died and was resurrected, he did not resurrect himself.

Brigham Young   *Sunday 10/8/1854*

John Pulsipher Papers, 36

The first people of the Earth was *no more made of the dust than you are* - I would not make out that Moses lied, by no means. But *we are made of dust as much as Adam was.*

Brigham Young   *Sunday 10/8/1854*

MABY

"Then the Lord did not make *Adam out of the dust of the earth.*"

Yes he did, but I have not got to that part of my discourse yet. *Adam was made of the dust of the earth.*

"Was he made of the *dust of this earth.*"

No, but of the dust of the earth whereon he was born in the flesh; that is the way he was made; he was made of dust.

"Did the Lord put into him his spirit?"

Yes, as the Lord put into you your spirit, he was begotten of a father, and brought forth as you and I were; and so are all intelligent beings brought forth from eternity to eternity. Man was not made the same as you make an adobe and put in a wall. Moses said that *Adam was made of the dust of the ground*, but he did not say of what ground. I say *he was not made of the dust of the ground of this Earth*, but *he was made of the dust of the earth where he lived*, where he honored his calling, believed in his Saviour, or Elder Brother, and by his faithfulness was redeemed, and obtained a Glorious Resurrection. All creatures that dwell upon this Earth are made of the elements that compose it; which are organized to see if they will abide their creation, and be counted worthy to receive a resurrection.

"What, every flesh?"

Yes, every flesh, for *all flesh pertaining to this world is made of the dust of this Earth*; it is made from the same material, according to the will and pleasure of Him who dictates all things. Our bodies are composed of the same material that composes this Earth; they are composed of water, air, and solid earth, either of which will resolve back to their native fountain.

Brigham Young   *3/25/1855*

Journal of Samuel W. Richards 2:215

Adam and Eve were made of the dust of the Earth from which they came, they brought their bodies with them. They had lived, died and been resurrected before they came here and they came with immortal bodies, and had to partake of the fruits of this Earth in order to bring forth mortal bodies, or natural bodies, that *their seed might be of the dust of this Earth as they were of the dust of the earth from which they came.*

Brigham Young   *10:00 p.m. 3/11/1856*

Journal of Wilford Woodruff

… met with the Regency in the evening. The time was occupied till 10 o'clock writing lessons upon the black board. Then the subject was brought up concerning *Adam being made of the dust of the earth,* and Elder Orson Pratt pursued a course of stubbornness & unbelief in what President Young said that will destroy him if he does not repent & turn from his evil ways.

Brigham Young   *4/20/1856*

JD 3:319-20

Though we have it in history that our father *Adam was made of the dust of this earth,* and that he knew nothing about his God previous to being made here, yet it is not so; and when we learn the truth we shall see and understand that he helped to make this world, and was the chief manager in that operation. He was the person who brought the animals and the seeds from other planets to this world, and brought a wife with him and stayed here. You may read and believe what you please as to what is found written in the Bible. *Adam was made from the dust of an earth, but not from the dust of this earth.* He was made as you and I are made, and no person was ever made upon any other principle.

George Albert Smith   *4/20/1856*

Journal of Wilford Woodruff

I met with the Presidency & Twelve in the prayer-circle. Brother G. A. Smith spoke in plainness his feelings concerning some principles of Elder O Pratt's wherein he differed from President Young concerning the *creation of Adam out of the dust* of the Earth & the final consummation of knowledge & many other things.

Parley P. Pratt   *before 1857*

Key to the Science of Theology, 49-50

At length a Moses came, who knew his God, and would fain have led mankind to know Him too, and see Him face to face. But they could not receive His heavenly laws, or bide His presence. Thus the holy man was forced again to veil the past in mystery, and, in the beginning of his history, assign to man an earthly origin. *Man, moulded from the earth, as a brick!* A woman, manufactured from a rib! Thus, parents still would fain conceal from budding manhood, the mysteries of procreation, and the sources of life's ever flowing river, by relating some childish tale of new-born life, engendered in the hollow trunk of some old tree, or springing with spontaneous growth, like mushrooms, from out of the heaps of rubbish. O man! when wilt thou cease to be a child in knowledge? Man, as we have said, is the offspring of Deity. The entire mystery of the past and future, with regard to his existence, is not yet solved by mortals.

Brigham Young   *10/9/1859*

JD 7:286

Here let me state to all philosophers of every class upon the earth, *when you tell me that father Adam was made as we make adobes from the earth, you tell me what I deem an idle tale.* When you tell me that the beasts of the field were produced in that manner, you are speaking idle words devoid of meaning. There is no such thing in all the eternities where the Gods dwell. Mankind are here because they are the offspring of parents who were first brought here from another planet, and power was given them to propagate their species, and they were commanded to multiply and replenish the earth.

Orson Pratt & Erastus Snow   *10 a.m. 4/5/1860*

Minutes of the Meeting of the Council of the Twelve

O. Pratt

... One [revelation] says *Adam was formed out of the Earth*, and the Lord put in his spirit; and another that he came with his body, flesh and bones, thus there are two contrary revelations - in the garden it is said, that a voice said to Adam, in the meridian of time, I will send my only begotten son Jesus Christ. then how can that man and Adam both be the Father of Jesus Christ? ... I have heard brother Brigham say that *Adam is the Father of our Spirits*, and he came here with his resurrected body, to fall for his own children; and I said to him, it leads to an endless number of falls, which leads to sorrow and death: that is revolting to my feelings, even if it were not sustained by revelation.

E. Snow

Is there any revelation saying that the body of *Adam should return to the dust of this Earth*?

O. Pratt

if you bring Adam as a Spirit, and put him into the tabernacle, runs easy with me.

George Q. Cannon   *10/12/1861*

MS 23:653-54

The 'Wise Man' has said, in reference to the period of death, that 'Then shall the dust return to the earth as it was, and the spirit shall return unto God who gave it' (Eccles. 12:7), thus showing that while the body is of the earth, earthy, the spirit is of celestial origin, and will ultimately 'return' or be received back again into the Divine presence of Him who is, as the Apostle declars, 'the Father of spirits.' Many other texts of Scripture might be cited which plainly and unmistakably declare man's origin to be Divine.

Having a divine parentage, and being of celestial origin, as to his spiritual nature, his instincts and high physical characteristics must from the first have placed him at the head of the entire animal creation, holding supreme `dominion over every living thing.' In the New Translation of the Bible, by the Prophet Joseph Smith we find the following sentence in the 1st chapter of Genesis, in reference to the formation of the vegetables and animals of the earth, and lastly man:

`Nevertheless, all things were before created; but spiritually were they created and made according to my word.'[112] Thus showing that *although man's body or tabernacle is formed from the dust of the ground, or, in other words, is of earthly origin*, and that the latter has to be animated with the breath of physical life, in order to render it a suitable abode for the former; thus showing that *his first estate was not in the Garden of Eden, as is commonly supposed, but in a pre-existing spiritual world or sphere*. ...

[He here quotes JD 1:50-51 and 6:275.]

President Young, in the foregoing passages, while substantiating the fact of the union of man's preexisting spirit with *a bodily product of the "dust of the ground,"* enters more particularly into the modus operandi of that union. He unmistakably declares man's origin to be altogether of a celestial character - that *not only is his spirit of heavenly descent, but his organization too,* - that the latter is not taken from the lower animals, but *from the originally celestial body of the great Father of humanity.* Taking the doctrine of man's origin as seen from this higher point of view, and comparing it with the low assumptive theories of uninspired men, ... how great the contrast appears! 'Look on this picture' - Man, the offspring of an ape!; 'and on this' - Man, the image of God, his Father! How wide the contrast! And how different the feelings produced in the breast! In the one case, we instinctively shrink with dread at the bare insinuation; while in the other, the heart beats with higher and warmer and stronger emotions of love, of adoration, and

---

[112] Moses 3:7; Genesis 2:9 JST.

praise; the soul is cheered and invigorated in its daily struggles to emancipate itself from the thraldom of surrounding evils and darkness pertaining to this lower sphere of existence, and is animated with a purer and nobler zeal in its onward and upward journey to that Divine Presence whence it originally came.

First Presidency   *6/18/1865*

JD 11:122

With regard to the quotations and comments in the Seer *as to Adam's having been formed "out of the ground," and "from the dust of the ground,"* & c., it is deemed wisest to let that subject remain without further explanation at present, for it is written that we are to receive "line upon line," according to our faith and capacities, and the circumstances attending our progress.[113]

The Lecture at the Veil   *Tuesday 2/7/1877*

Journal of L. John Nuttall

We have heard a great deal about Adam and Eve. how they were formed &c some think he was made like an adobe and the Lord breathed into him the breath of life. for we read "from dust thou art and unto dust shalt thou return" Well *he was made of the dust of the earth but not of this earth.* he was made just the same way you and I are made but on another earth. *Adam was an immortal* being when he came. … when Adam and Eve got through with their Work in this earth. *they did not lay their bodies down in the dust*, but returned to the spirit World from whence they came.

Edward Tullidge   *3/--/1877*

The Women of Mormondom, 196-97

So far, it is of but trifling moment how our "first parents" were created; *whether like a brick, with the spittle of the Creator and the dust of the earth, or by the more intelligible method of generation.* The prime object of man and woman's creation was for the purposes of creation. "Be fruitful, and multiply and replenish the earth, and subdue it," by countless millions of your offspring. Thus opened creation, and the womb of everlasting motherhood throbbed with divine ecstacy. It is the divine command still. All other may be dark as a fable, of the genesis of the race, but this is not dark. Motherhood to this hour leaps for joy at this word of God, "Be fruitful;" and motherhood is sanctified - as by the holiest sacrament of nature. We shall prefer Brigham's expounding of the dark passages of Genesis. *Our first parents were not made up*

---

[113] Note that this was an unusual stance for the first presidency to take at that time because they continued to expound upon this teaching and related teachings in other public venues.

like mortal bricks. They came to be the Mother and the Father of a new creation of souls.

George Q. Cannon   *6/23/1889*

Journal of Abraham H. Cannon

Then said I: "he must have been a resurrected Being." "Yes," said he, "and though Christ is said to have been the first fruits of them that slept, yet the Savior said he did nothing but what He had seen His Father do, for He had power to lay down His life and take it up again. *Adam, though made of dust, was made, as President Young said, of the dust of another planet* than this." I was very much instructed by the conversation and this days services.

Brigham H. Roberts   *11/--/1889*

Contributor 10:265-66

A garden was planted in Eden and the man placed in it, and there the Lord brought to him every beast of the field and every fowl of the air, and Adam gave names to them all. Afterwards was brought to Adam his wife, whom since she was derived from man he named woman; and she became his helpmate, his companion, and the mother of his children. *In this nothing is hinted at about man being made from the dust*, and woman manufactured from a rib, a story which has been the cause of much perplexity to religious people, and a source of impious merriment to reckless unbelievers. We are informed that the Lord God made every plant of the field before it was in the earth, and every herb before it grew on our planet. As vegetation was created or made to grow upon some older earth, and the seeds thereof or the plants themselves were brought to our earth and made to grow, so likewise man and his helpmate were brought from some other world to our own, to people it with their children. And though it is said that *the `Lord God formed man of the dust of the ground' - it by no means follows that he was formed as one might form a brick, or from the dust of this earth*. We are all `formed' of the dust of the ground, though instead of being moulded as a brick we are brought forth by the natural laws of procreation; so also was Adam and his wife in some older world. And as for the story of the rib, under it I believe the mystery of procreation is hidden.

Wilford W. Woodruff & George Q. Cannon   *6/11/1892*

Diary of Charles Lowell Walker, 2: 740-41

Attended the High Council at Which Pres. Woodruff presided G. Q. Cannon was present also and a large body of the leading men of this Stake. Br. Edward Bunker Sen. and others of Bunkerville Nevada had been advancing false doctrine, one item … was that *Adam was made of the dust of the earth contained in the Garden of Eden*. He had also advanced some erroneous ideas concerning the resurrection. Pres. Woodruff and

Cannon showed ... that Adam was an immortal being when he came to this earth and was made the same as all other men and Gods are made; and that *the seed of man was of the dust of the earth*, and that the continuation of the seeds in a glorified state was Eternal Lives. And after this Mortal tabernacle had crumbled to dust in the grave that God would in the time of the resurrection by his Matchless Power would bring together again in the form of a glorified and an imortal [sic] to the Righteous to dwell with Him for ever. Also that those that were not righteous would also be resurrected, but not with a glorified body.

Salt Lake Tribune   *2/12/1906*

Page 3

Especially is it taught that *Adam was not made out of the dust of this earth;* that he was begotten as any other man is begotten, and that when he came here he brought Eve, one of his wives, with him.

William Halls   *March*

Era, 325

We would not expect to get a full grown tree, a hundred years old, in a second of time; neither would we expect a full grown man without a natural growth from infancy. Though the creation of Adam and the birth of Jesus may be involved in more or less mystery, the fact is, there was no exception in their cases. If Adam could have been created a full grown man with all his faculties fully developed, with a knowledge of good and evil, becoming as the Gods, without having gone through the natural stages of development, then all men might have been created in the same way, and there would have been no need of male and female, the pains of maternity, the care of infancy, our schools and all our institutions of learning.

Analysis & Observations

β

The foregoing passages as a whole appear to demonstrate that the terminology "dust of the earth" is a euphemism that refers to the procreative process rather than a special term for some other process of creation. It is interesting to note however that this teaching was taught in a rather divergent manner. That is, in some statements, the brethren appear to say that we were *not* created out of the dust of the earth; others taught that we were created out of the dust of *an* earth; while others taught that this terminology refers to procreation in veiled terms. This is worthy of note because, while some of the quotes outwardly appear to be contradictory, the message behind the contradicting terminology appears consistent over the decades. This observation may be a helpful key in resolving other teachings of the early brethren where metaphor, euphemism, or other literary devices produce similarly contradictory statements.

15

Adam & Eve Knew They Would Fall

Franklin D. Richards   *12/10/1853*

MS 15:801

Adam fell, but his fall became a matter of necessity after the woman had transgressed. Her punishment was banishment from the Garden, and Adam was necessitated to fall, and go with her, in order to obey the first great command given unto them - to multiply and replenish the earth; or, in the language of the Prophet Lehi, 'Adam fell that men might be.' The fall of Adam, therefore, was virtually required at his hands, that he might keep the first great command, and that the purposes of God might not fail, while at the same time the justice of God might be made manifest in the punishment incurred by the transgression of the woman, for whom the man is ever held responsible in the government of God.

The Scriptures inform us that Christ was as a lamb slain from before the foundation of the world. If, therefore, the plan of salvation was matured before the foundation of the world, and Jesus was ordained to come into the world, and die at the time appointed, in order to perfect that plan, we must of necessity conclude that *the plan of the fall was also matured in the councils of eternity*, and that it was as necessary for the exalting and perfecting of intelligences, as the redemption. Without it they could not have known good and evil here, and without knowing good and evil they could not become Gods, neither could their children. No wonder the woman was tempted when it was said unto her - 'Ye shall be as gods, knowing good and evil.' No wonder Father Adam fell, and accompanied the woman, sharing in all the miseries of the curse, that he might be the father of an innumerable race of beings who would be capable of becoming Gods.

Brigham Young   *Sunday 10/8/1854*

MABY

I reckon that there was a previous understanding, and *the whole plan was previously calculated,* before the Garden of Eden was made, that [Adam] would reduce his posterity to sin, misery, darkness, wickedness, wretchedness, and to the power of the Devil, that they might be prepared for an Exaltation, for without this they could not receive one.

Brigham Young   *5/6/1855*

Wilford Woodruff Journal

Adam assisted in forming this earth & *agreed to fall* when he came here, & he fell that man might be.

Brigham Young   *6/3/1855*

JD 2:302

In my fullest belief, it was the design of the Lord that Adam should partake of the forbidden fruit, and I believe that *Adam knew all about it before he came* to this earth. I believe there was no other way leading to thrones and dominions only for him to transgress, or take that position which transgression alone could place man in, to descend below all things, that they might ascend to thrones, principalities, and powers; for they could not ascend to that eminence without first descending, nor upon any other principle.

Brigham Young   *8/25/1867*

MABY

While Brother Orson Pratt was telling you a good deal about this great holy wedding, the first that was ever celebrated, I thought about father Adam; he helped to make the world, to organize this earth, which was organized expressly for him. He is the king and Lord of this earth; when *he came here he came with an understanding that he would do just as you and I do.* He would go to sleep and dream for 6 hours. What we call dreaming are the reflections of the mind in sleep that cannot be remembered at all times when in a state of wakefulness. We come to this world, forget the past and commence anew.

Brigham Young   *10/6/1870*

JD 13:263

Suppose a man should come here and tell you the very nature of our Father Adam - tell precisely how he was organized, his height, his proportions, the extent of his knowledge, tell you *the agreement that was entered into,* the amount of knowledge he had to forget to reduce himself to the capacity of a corruptible being! Suppose this could all be told to the congregations of the Saints, what would they know about it? Very little. There may be some minds which could grasp some things pertaining to it, but others could not.

Brigham Young   *8/31/1873*

JD 16:167

When Father Adam came to assist in organizing the earth out of the crude material that was found, an earth was made upon which the children of man could live. After the earth was prepared Father Adam came and stayed here, and there was a woman brought to him. Now I am telling you something that many of you know, it has been told to you, and the brethren and sisters should understand it. There was a certain woman brought to Father Adam whose name was Eve, because she was the first woman, and she was given to him to be his wife; I am not disposed to give any farther knowledge concerning her at present. There is no doubt but that he left many companions. The great and glorious doctrine that pertains to this I have not time to dwell upon; neither should I at present if I had time. *He understood this whole machinery or system before he came to this earth*; and I hope my brethren and sisters will profit by what I have told them.

Brigham Young   *Sunday a.m. 7/19/1874*

JD 17:143

It would be a task for him to tell us the distance. When the earth was framed and brought into existence and man was placed upon it, it was near the throne of our Father in heaven. And when man fell - though that was designed in the economy, there was nothing about it mysterious or unknown to the Gods, *they understood it all,* it was all planned.

Edward Tullidge   *3/--/1877*

Women of Mormondom, 180

The father and mother were at length in their Garden of Eden. *They came on purpose to fall.* They fell "that man might be;" and man is, that he "might have joy." They ate of the tree of mortal life, partook of the elements of this earth that they might again become mortal for their children's sake. They fell that another world might have a probation, redemption and resurrection.

Orson Pratt   *7/18/1880*

JD 21:288-90

Now, here arises a question. Did Adam partake of this forbidden fruit, being deceived as Eve was deceived? or *did he partake of it knowingly and understandingly?* I will give you my views upon this subject. Adam very well knew that his wife Eve, after she had partaken of the forbidden fruit, having transgressed the law of God, must die. He knew this; he knew that she would have to be cast out of the garden of Eden, from the presence of her husband; she could no longer be permitted to dwell with him. Hence, inasmuch as there was a great separation threatened between husband and wife - the wife having transgressed - he concluded that he would not be separated from the woman, and hence he was not deceived, but the woman was deceived; he partook of the forbidden fruit to prevent a separation between the two, and fell, even as the woman fell, and both were cast out together. If one only had transgressed and been cast out, the great command that had been given prior to that time - to multiply and replenish the earth - could not have been fulfilled, because of the separation. In order, therefore, that the command first given might be fulfilled, Adam, though not deceived, partook of the forbidden fruit, was cast out with Eve, and hence began, as far as possible, to fulfil the command, and to multiply his species upon this earth.

Wilford W. Woodruff   *5/14/1882*

JD 23:125

The world, more or less, has found a great deal of fault with Mother Eve and with Father Adam, because of the fall of man; what I have to say with regard to it, I express as my own opinion. *Adam and Eve came to this world to perform exactly the part that they acted in the garden of Eden; and I will say, they were ordained of God to do what they did,* and *it was therefore expected that they would eat of the forbidden fruit* in order that man might know both good and evil by passing through the school of experience which this life afford us. That is all I want to say about Father Adam and Mother Eve. Adam fell that man might be, and men are that they might have joy; and some have found fault with that. It has been said that God commanded Adam to multiply and replenish the earth; and it has been said that Adam was not under the necessity of falling in order to multiply and replenish the earth, but you will understand that the woman was deceived and not the man; and according to the justice of God she would have been cast out into the lowly and dreary world alone, and thus the first great command could not have been complied with unless Adam had partaken of the forbidden fruit.

Analysis & Observations

β

The lack of understanding this simple and narrow concept has led to the nearly ageless tradition of disparaging the names of Adam and Eve for succumbing to weakness by partaking of the forbidden fruit - or fruit of mortality as Tullidge refers to it. While this teaching continues to be accepted by the modern LDS Church,[114] a full understanding of this doctrine only comes via the exegetical lenses of Adam-God teachings. The Fall is a necessary part of the plan of salvation because it allows an immortal being to partake of mortality so that spirit children can be housed with a tabernacle of flesh. Without the Fall, Adam-God teachings are entirely without purpose - the Fall provides the whole reason behind the need for Adam-God teachings in Mormon theology. If a god did not have to fall from immortality to mortality in order to have mortal children, it seems logical that he/she would not do it - however, because a mortal body can only be born by a mortal parent[115] and because gods are immortal beings, a fall is necessary in order to effectuate the plan of salvation. It is this very foundational premise that explains the need for Adam-God teachings and that explains why current LDS theology is inadequate to deal with the deeper questions of the plan of salvation as it pertains to godhood.[116]

---

[114] To the author's knowledge, there is little preventing an active, good-standing Mormon from believing all of the teachings put forth in this subsection. Undoubtedly, there are many more statements of this nature to be found in Mormonism's wealth of theological databases. However, since this teaching is not particularly controversial and since this teaching is simple and straightforward, there seems to be little need for a thorough accounting of this teaching here.

[115] See "Procreation: Mortal & Spiritual Offspring".

[116] Without Adam-God teachings, another theological foundation would have to be developed in order to explain how mortals could ever become gods. The LDS Church has never produced an alternative theology and has left the many unanswered questions about immortality as "mysteries" that ought not to be delved into.

16 Partaking of the Forbidden Fruit

See also
Partaking of the Seeds of Death

Orson Pratt   *7/25/1852*

JD 1:284

And what was the fullest extent of the penalty of Adam's transgression? I will tell you. It was death. The death of what? The *death of the immortal tabernacle* - of that tabernacle where the seeds of death had not been, that was wisely framed, and pronounced very good; *the seeds of death were introduced into it. How*, and in what manner? Some say *there was something in the nature of the fruit* that introduced mortality.

Brigham Young   *12/27/1857*

JD 6:145

Before the gospel revealed the introduction of sin to this planet, it was a great marvel even to the most learned, and they would ask, "Why was it so? - is it not strange?" and would rest with the expression, "It was suffered to be so." While reasoning or familiarly conversing with one another, let the question be asked, "Why was Eve suffered to *partake of the forbidden fruit?*" and the invariable reply was, "I cannot answer that question: it seems that it was so, and it appears to be a great pity." That is all the knowledge there is in the world on that point. The starting point they have not learned, that no intelligent being could be exalted with the Gods without being subjected to the temptation of sin, that he might know and understand the power of the adversary, the opposite to goodness; for it is written that "there must needs be an opposition in all things." The world have not yet learned that simple truth.

Brigham Young   6/30/1867

JD 12:97

Now, taking the history of creation as given by Moses, let me ask the question - "Mother Eve, did you not *partake of the forbidden fruit,* as also did Adam, and thus bring sin and iniquity into the world?" "O, yes," says Mother Eve. Then, why cannot you bear the affliction of it? Why not say, "If I was the cause of bringing evil into the world, I will firmly bear all that God puts upon me, and maintain His word and His law, and so work out my salvation with fear and trembling, for it is God working within me." I ask this question of you, mother Eves, every one of you.   If you are not sanctified and prepared, you ought to be sanctifying and preparing yourselves for the blessings in store for you when it will be said of you, this is Mother Eve. ... If you wish to be Eves and mothers of human families, you ought to bear the burden.

Brigham Young   *Sunday a.m. 8/25/1867*

Minutes of Meetings Held in Provo City

The bodies of Adam and Eve were pure and after the Celestial order until they *partook of the forbidden fruit* when their bodies were changed with the things of this world.

George Q. Cannon   10/15/1870

Meeting of the School of the Prophets

It was not only wisdom, but perfectly consistent, that Adam & Eve should *partake of the forbidden fruit* and start the work of increase of their species. The above doctrine had been revealed to him, so that he knew it was true.

Edward Tullidge   3/--/1877

Women of Mormondom, 180

The father and mother were at length in their Garden of Eden. They came on purpose to fall. They fell "that man might be; and man is, that he "might have joy." *They ate of the tree of mortal life,* partook of the elements of this earth that they might again become mortal for their children's sake. They fell that another world might have a probation, redemption and resurrection.

Edward Tullidge   3/--/1877

Women of Mormondom, 196-98

The prime object of man and woman's creation was for the purpose of creation. `Be fruitful, and multiply, and replenish the earth and subdue it,' by countless millions of your offspring. Thus opened creation, and the womb of everlasting motherhood throbbed with divine ecstasy. ... Eve - immortal Eve - came down to earth to become the mother of a race. How become the mother of a world of mortals except by herself again becoming mortal? How becoming mortal, only by transgressing the laws of immortality? How *only by 'eating of the forbidden fruit'* by partaking of the elements of a mortal earth, in which the seed of death was everywhere scattered?

The fall is simple. Our immortal parents came down to fall; came down to transgress the laws of immortality; came down to give birth to mortal tabernacles for a world of spirits. *The 'forbidden tree,' says Brigham, contained in its fruit the elements of death, or the elements of mortality.* By eating of it blood was again infused into the tabernacles of beings who had become immortal.

Brigham Young   *Sunday p.m. 6/18/1873*

DN 22:308

Now for mother Eve. The evil principle always has and always will exist. Well, a certain character came along, and said to Mother Eve, 'The Lord has told you that you must not do so and so, for if you do you shall surely die. But I tell you that if you do not do this you will never know good from evil, your eyes will never be opened, and you may live on the earth forever and ever, and you will never know what the Gods know.' The devil told the truth, what is the mystery about it? He is doing it today. He is telling one or two truths and mixing them with a thousand errors to get the people to swallow them. I do not blame Mother Eve, *I would not have had her miss eating the forbidden fruit for anything in the world.* I would not give a groat if I could not understand light from darkness. I can understand the bitter from the sweet, so can you. Here is intelligence, but bind it up and make machines of its possessors, and where is the glory or exaltation? There is none.

Brigham Young   *6/23/1867*

JD 12:70

Do you think there is any truth in hell? Yes, a great deal, and where truth is there we calculate the Lord has a right to be. You will not find the Lord where there is no truth. The devil had truth in his mouth as well as lies when he came to mother Eve. Said he, 'If you will *eat of the fruit of the tree of knowledge of good and evil,* you will see as the Gods see.' That was just as true as anything that ever was spoken on the face of the earth. She did eat, her eyes were opened, and she saw good and evil. She gave of the fruit to her husband, and he ate too. What would have been the consequence if he had not done so? They would have been separated, and where would we have been? I am glad he did eat. I am glad the fruit was given to mother Eve, that she ate of it, and that her eyes were opened, and that my eyes are opened, that I have tasted the sweet as well as the bitter, and that I understand the difference between good and evil.

Brigham Young   *Sunday a.m. 8/15/1867*

Minutes of Meetings Held in Provo City

Pres. Young was pleased with the teachings that had been given during this conference. Refered to the fall of man. The bodies of Adam and Eve were pure and after the Celestial order until *they partook of the forbidden fruit when their bodies were changed with the things of this world.* Adam helped organize this world for an inheritance for himself and posterity.

Brigham Young   *7/11/1869*

JD 13:145

We also understand the earth, and the nature of the earth, and why God permitted *Mother Eve to partake of the forbidden fruit.* We should not have been here today if she had not; we could never have possessed wisdom and intelligence if she had not done it. It was all in the economy of heaven, and we need not talk about it; it is alright. We should never blame Mother Eve, not the least. I am thankful to God that I know good from evil, the bitter from the sweet, and the things of God from the things not of God.

Charles W. Penrose   *9/--/1881*

Contributor 2:363 #12

That which was lost in Adam is to be regained in *Christ.* Through the commission of crime, death came into the world. Satan gained dominion. The earth trembled under the curse. Eden bloomed no more upon its face. *The tree of life was removed.* Thorns and briers and noxious weeds came up in the place of the flowers and fruits of paradise.

Wilford W. Woodruff   *5/14/1882*

JD 23:125

The world, more or less, has found a great deal of fault with Mother Eve and with Father Adam, because of the fall of man; what I have to say with regard to it, I express as my own opinion. Adam and Eve came to this world to perform exactly the part that they acted in the garden of Eden; and I will say, they were ordained of God to do what they did, and it was therefore expected that *they would eat of the forbidden fruit* in order that man might know both good and evil by passing through the school of experience which this life afford us. That is all I want to say about Father Adam and Mother Eve.

Joseph E. Taylor   *6/2/1888*

Deseret Weekly News 38:19-27

I think these two quotations[117] from such a reliable authority fully solve the question as to the relationship existing between Father Adam and the Savior of the world, and prove beyond question the power that Adam possessed in regard to taking his body again after laying it down - which power he never could have attained unless he had received first a resurrection from the grave to a condition of immortality. We further say that this power was not forfeited when as a celestial being *he voluntarily partook of the forbidden fruit, and thereby rendered his body mortal* in order that he might become the father of mortal tabernacles, as he was already the father of immortal spirits - thus giving opportunity to the offspring of his own begetting to pass through the ordeals necessary to prepare them for a resurrection from the dead, a celestial glory.

John M. Whitaker   *6/24/1921*

Seminary Lectures, BYU, Lecture 10

I am going to assume responsibility for making this statement, that man came here, was placed here as an immortal, glorified, resurrected being. I want to make myself clear, because these lectures are going to the brethren, and if they want to correct them, they can. … I believe *it was that fruit that changed and modified Adam's resurrected body, and again made it subject to death.*

Melvin J. Ballard   *6/24/1921*

Seminary Lectures, BYU, Lecture 11

What Brother Whitaker has said I agree with, with reference to his fall and man's coming here."

Joseph Fielding Smith   *1940*

Church History & Modern Revelation, 231

We know that when Adam was placed on the earth it was pronounced good, and he as well as the earth was not subject to death. There was no blood in his body, but he had a spiritual body until it was changed by the fall. A spiritual body is one which is not quickened by blood, but by spirit. Before the fall, Adam had a physical, tangible body of flesh and bones, but it was not quickened by blood. *The partaking of the forbidden fruit caused blood to exist in his body* and thus the seeds of mortality were sown and his body then became temporal, or mortal.[118]

---

[117] TPJS 345, 346, 347; HC 6:305, 306; JD 6:3.

[118] This doctrine continued to be taught in the modern LDS Church for many years after Adam-God teachings were rejected. Joseph Fielding Smith, in an address given at the LDS Institute of Religion in Salt

Analysis & Observations

β

The function of this subsection is to place the traditional view of Adam and Eve's partaking of the forbidden fruit before the reader before placing the slightly more esoteric view that has been made in connection with Adam-God teachings before the reader. There are two items worth noting at this point. First, among Christendom and much of mainstream Mormonism, the partaking of the forbidden fruit has been construed as metaphorical at best. Few seem to believe that any actual fruit was eaten and if someone takes the position that they believe that some fruit was eaten, the connection between that act and the effects of the Fall are not generally construed as causative. That is, the Fall is seen as the act of God casting Adam and Eve out of the garden as opposed to a physical effect generated by the nature of the fruit itself. In contrast, the above teachings indicate that the early brethren understood that the results of eating the forbidden fruit were quite literally and physically connected with the act of eating the forbidden fruit.

The second, and perhaps more interesting point, is to note that the Hebrews chronically understood trees to symbolize people. Thus, for example, in 1 Nephi 11, an angel asks Nephi what he desires. Nephi responds that he desires to know the interpretation of the tree of life (vs. 11). In response, the angel shows Nephi a vision of Christ as a baby, declares "Behold the Lamb of God, yea even the Son of the Eternal Father!" and Nephi walks away from the experience with a clear understanding that the tree represents Christ - or the love of God. While several other examples of this symbolic usage of trees could be given, the application of this principle to the Tree of Knowledge of Good and Evil is particularly important. As this tree stands in opposition to the Tree of Life, some may find the conclusion very elementary - it was Lucifer who gave the fruit to Eve, it was he who was cast out for rebellion, it was he who planted the seeds of death into the earth, and it is he who stands in opposition to Christ - therefore, Lucifer must be the individual symbolized by the tree. It seems that, to the Hebrew mind, this conclusion

---

Lake City, on January 14, 1961 declared that Adam did not come "subject to death when he was placed upon the earth[;] there had to come a change in his body through the partaking of this element - whatever you want to call it, fruit - that brought blood into his body; and blood became the life of the body instead of spirit."

was fairly elementary as well and many of their texts bear this out. However, it also appears that they believed that it was Satan who was connected with the Tree of Knowledge of Good and Evil - and that Satan was the host of Lucifer's followers - so this issue may not be as black and white as one would expect at first blush. Regardless of the answer to this question of who the tree represented, this Hebrew symbology suggests that the fruit of the tree may represent the teachings of the individuals represented by the tree. Therefore, the temptation to eat of the fruit of the Tree of Knowledge of Good and Evil could be a veiled reference to listening to the teachings of these fallen individuals - hence these teachings bear the seeds of spiritual death as the physical fruit bore the seeds of physical death.

17 Partaking of the Seeds of Death

See also
Partaking of the Forbidden Fruit

Joseph Smith   *circa 1844*

"Sayings of Joseph the Prophet," as recorded in Anson Call's Journal
Now regarding Adam: He came here from another planet an immortalized Being and brought his wife, Eve, with him and by *eating of the fruit of this earth* became subject to death and decay, and He became of the earth, earthy, was made mortal and subject to death.

Brigham Young   *Sunday 4 p.m. 3/14/1852*

Historian's Office Journal, 106
B Y rolled out rev.n (upon) rev.n (in) regard (to) (the) crea(tion).n [sic] (of) (the) world Adam came (to) (the) E[arth] when (he) assisted (to) form (it) (sh) (he) then *partook (of) (the) fruits (of) (the) E[arth]* (and) Became Earthy (and) (they) (which) are (the) (s) (after) (sh) rece[ive] our resurrected bodies (and) (shall) (all) (have) (the) priv[ilege] (of) going (as) Adam's form (an) E[arth] (and) do likewise

---

Brigham Young   *Friday 4/9/1852*

Journal of Wilford Woodruff
Our Father begot all the spirits that were before any tabernacle was made. When our Father came into the Garden He came with his Celestial body & brought one of his wives with him and *ate of the fruit of the Garden until He could beget a Tabernacle*. And Adam is Michael God and all the God that we have anything to do with. They *ate of this fruit* & formed the first Tabernacle that was formed.

Brigham Young   *Friday 4/16/1852*

Journal of Samuel Holister Rogers 1:179

President Brigham Young said that our spirits ware begotten before that Adam came to the Earth and that Adam helped to make the Earth, that he had a Celestial body when he came to the Earth and that he brought his wife or one of his wives with him, and that Eave was also a Celestial being, that *they eat of the fruit of the ground until they begat children from the Earth*, he said that Adam was the only God that we would have, and that Christ was not begotten of the Holy Ghost, but of the Father Adam, that Christ, was our elder brother.

Brigham Young   *8/28/1852*

JD 6:274-75

After men have got their exaltations and their crowns - have become Gods, even the sons of God - are made Kings of kings and Lords of lords, they have the power then of propagating their species in spirit; and that is the first of their operations with regard to organizing a world. Power is then given to them to organize the elements, and then commence the organization of tabernacles. How can they do it? Have they to go to that earth? Yes, and Adam will have to go there, and he cannot do without Eve; he must have Eve to commence the work of generation, and they will go into the garden, and continue to *eat and drink of the fruits of the corporeal world, until this grosser matter is diffused sufficiently through their celestial bodies to enable them*, according to the established laws, *to produce mortal tabernacles for their spiritual children.*

Orson Spencer & Orson Pratt   *10/3/1852*

Journal of William Clayton

A morning meeting was held at which Orson Spencer and Orson Pratt spoke on the subject of Adam. Spencer spoke of Adam "coming to this earth in the morning of creation with a resurrected body and etc ... He was followed by Elder Orson Pratt on the same subject ... He takes the literal reading of the scriptures for his guide, and maintains that God took the dust of the earth, and molded a body into which he put the spirit of man, just as we have generally understood from the scriptures; while Brother Spencer endeavors to substantiate the position taken by President Young; Viz, that Adam came to this earth with a resurrected body, and *became mortal by eating the fruits of the earth*, which was earthy.

Orson Pratt   *3/--/1853*

The Seer 1:3

The celestial beings who dwell in the Heaven from which we came, having been raised from the grave, in a former world, and having been filled with all the fullness of these eternal attributes, are called Gods, because the fullness of God dwells in each. Both the males and the females enjoy this fullness. The celestial vegetables and fruits which grow out of the soil of this redeemed Heaven, constitute the food of the Gods. This food differs from the food derived from the *vegetables of a fallen world*: the latter *are converted into blood, which circulating in the veins and arteries, produces flesh and bones of a mortal nature,* having a constant tendency to decay: while the former, or celestial vegetables, are, when digested in the stomach, converted into a fluid, which, in its nature, is spiritual, and which, circulating in the veins and arteries of the celestial male and female, preserves their tabernacles from decay and death. Earthly vegetables form blood, and blood forms flesh and bones; celestial vegetables, when digested, form a spiritual fluid which gives immortality and eternal life to the organization in which it flows.

Brigham Young   *9/17/1854*

Journal of Wilford Woodruff

President Young said that He came from another world & made this. Brought Eve with him, *partook of the fruits of the earth, begat children & they were earthly & had mortal bodies &* if we were faithful, we should become Gods as He was.

Brigham Young   *Sunday 10/8/1854*

MABY

Adam planted the Garden of Eden, and he with his wife Eve *partook of the fruit of this Earth, until their systems were charged with the nature of the Earth,* and then they could beget bodies for their spiritual children.

Brigham Young   *Sunday 10/8/1854*

John Pulsipher Papers, 37

[W]hen this work was made - our God who is Adam … He *by eating the mortal fruits of the Earth,* it caused & produced mortal children or commenced the increase of men on the Earth which is the bodies for the Spirits to live in.

Brigham Young   *3/25/1855*

Journal of Samuel W. Richards 2:215

Adam and Eve were made of the dust of the Earth from which they came, they brought their bodies with them. They had lived, died and been resurrected before they came here and they came with immortal bodies, and *had to partake of the fruits of this Earth in order to bring forth mortal bodies, or natural bodies,* that their seed might be of the dust of this Earth as they were of the dust of the earth from which they came.

Brigham Young	*5/6/1855*

Journal of Wilford Woodruff

As soon as the devil was on earth he *sowed the seeds of death in everything* so as soon *as they began to eat of the fruit of the earth they received into their system the seeds of mortality & of death* so their children were mortal & subject to death, sorrow, pain & wo. Then when they partook of life, joy, ease, & happiness, they would know how to prize it.

Brigham Young	*2/8/1857*

JD 4:217-18

Things were first created spiritually; the Father actually begat the spirits, and they were brought forth and lived with Him. Then He commenced the work of creating earthly tabernacles, precisely as He had been created in this flesh himself, *by partaking of the course material that was organized and composed this earth, until His system was charged with it,* consequently the tabernacles of His children were organized from the course materials of this earth.

Brigham Young	*6/5/1859*

JD 7:163

The blood he (Christ) spilled upon Mount Calvary he did not receive again into his veins. That was poured out, and when he was resurrected, another element took the place of the blood. It will be so with every person who receives a resurrection: the blood will not be resurrected with the body, being designed only to sustain the life of the present organization. When this is dissolved, and we again obtain our bodies by the power of the resurrection, that which we now call the *life of the body, and which is formed from the food we eat and the water we drink,* will be supplanted by another element; for flesh and blood cannot inherit the kingdom of God.

Brigham Young	*1/27/1860*

Journal of Wilford Woodruff

Now comes the morning of the new week in which mortality must begin, and your spiritual children must be introduced into mortality. Two must go before them and prepare the way for them. Whom will you send? Would you not say to [your] wife, "Come, Mother, let you and I lay aside our Celestial glory for a little season and *eat of the elements of this new earth. that we may again become of the earth earthy,* and thereby our offspring will be mortal, and thus we will begin the begetting of mortal bodies for these, our spiritual children; and when they have grown to maturity in their mortal estate, we will command them to multiply and replenish the earth. We have passed through earth life, death and the resurrection. We have power to lay aside this Celestial Glory and we have power to take it up again."

To which she, a faithful Mother, will reply: "Yes, we will partake of the elements of this new earth. We will make this sacrifice for our spiritual children that they also may continue on in the law of everlasting progression and become like unto us, for as the Gods are, some may become."

Brigham Young   *4/4/1860*

Minutes of Meeting at Historian's Office

One thing I have thought that I might still have omitted. It was Joseph's doctrine that *Adam was God* &c When in Luke Johnson's at O. Hydes the power came upon us, or shock that alarmed the neighborhood. God comes to earth & *eats* & *partakes of fruit.*

Brigham Young   *8/25/1867*

MABY

When father Adam and mother Eve *became mortal by eating of the fruits of this earth*, they were then prepared to organize the mortal tabernacle and they were prepared to organize and form living spirits long before that. Now they are prepared to form mortal bodies for their spiritual children to dwell in. His former words and experiences Adam had forgotten a great deal of, but he once knew it all beforehand.

Brigham Young   *10/6/1870*

JD 13:263

Suppose a man should come here and tell you the very nature of our Father Adam - tell precisely how he was organized, his height, his proportions, the extent of his knowledge, tell you the agreement that was entered into, the amount of knowledge he had to forget to reduce himself to the capacity of a corruptible being![119]

Autobiography of Gilbert Belnap, 23

When contrasting the present conditions of the inhabitants of the earth with their

---

[119] This sentence suggests that the veil had to have been placed upon Adam before he began to partake of the "seeds of death" or that he had to have the veil placed over him before he was able to partake of a certain degree of the seeds of death.

primeval state in the Garden of Eden, the period when the Father of our spirits condescended that *through the partaking of the fruits of the earth that man might be ...* I am caused to mourn.

The Lecture at the Veil   *Tuesday 2/7/1877*

Journal of L. John Nuttall, 20

Adam & Eve when they were placed on this earth were immortal beings with flesh, bones and sinews, but upon *partaking of the fruits of the earth* while in the garden and cultivating the ground *their bodies became changed from immortal to mortal beings* with the blood coursing through their veins as the action of life.

Edward Tullidge   *3/--/1877*

Women of Mormondom, 197-98

Eve - immortal Eve - came down to earth to become the mother of a race. How become the mother of a world of mortals except by herself again becoming mortal? How becoming mortal, only by transgressing the laws of immortality? How only by `eating of the forbidden fruit' by *partaking of the elements of a mortal earth, in which the seed of death was everywhere scattered?*

The fall is simple. Our immortal parents came down to fall; came down to transgress the laws of immortality; came down to give birth to mortal tabernacles for a world of spirits. *The `forbidden tree,' says Brigham, contained in its fruit the elements of death, or the elements of mortality.* By eating of it blood was again infused into the tabernacles of beings who had become immortal. The basis of mortal generation is blood. Without blood no mortal can be born. Even could immortals have been conceived on earth, the trees of life had made but the paradise of a few; but a mortal world was the object of creation then. Eve, then, came down to be the mother of a world. Glorious Mother, capable of dying at the very beginning to give life to her offspring, that through mortality the eternal life of the Gods might be given her sons and daughters. Motherhood the same from the beginning even to the end! The love of motherhood passing all understanding! Thus read our Mormon sisters the fall of their mother.

Edward Stevenson   *3/7/1880*

Edward Stevenson Diary

Then by Request of One of the Presidency treated upon god as the father of our Spirits in the previous World, & then Adam our Father came down as one of the 3 that made this world & Fell that man in the Flesh might be & in order for this change to take place *Adam had to partake of the fruits of this Earth & change his system from Immortal to mortal -* changing the fluid in his veins to mortal - compatible Blood by which his Issue was mortal houses for his pure Spirits begotten in other & previous World to come & take these mortal houses Bodies of flesh & perform a mission in this Earthly house of clay & in this humiliated state like Jesus in our Judgments are taken away as the words of the poet are ... therefore Adam is the Father of my Spirit & also of my body, the body being Bone of his Bone & Flesh of his Flesh. I Spoke 45 Minutes & Bp. Hess said that he could endorse all that had been said although he did not understand all, yet it made him feel good & like living his religion.

Analysis & Observations

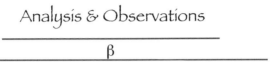

β

This section clearly lays out a teaching entirely lost to the modern LDS Church - the adversary planted seeds of death into the fruits of the earth so that when eaten, the fruits would change an immortal body into a mortal body by introducing blood into the systems of Adam and Eve. It appears from the context of these statements that this teaching was intended to be quite literal.[120] If this is correctly understood, it introduces at least two interesting questions:

1) How does this additional information coincide with the story of eating "the" forbidden fruit (singular) and "the" Tree of Knowledge of Good and Evil (also singular)?
2) Does this mean that the Fall was actually a gradual - perhaps very long - process?

I'll address each of these questions only very briefly. Unfortunately, no Adam-God teachings offer a clear interpretation as to how these questions should be answered ... the following information is therefore more of a result of speculation than it is a textual analysis. The first question strikes at the interpretation of the traditional accounts of the Fall. If the story is allegorical as far as the fruit is concerned (as suggested in the previous subsection), then the literal partaking of the seeds of death may be entirely unrelated to the partaking of the Tree of Knowledge of Good and Evil or, perhaps more likely, the partaking of the fruit of that tree represents both the literal consumption of seeds of death and the "partaking" of the spiritual seeds of death by learning to distinguish good and evil. A myriad of other interpretations may be offered but each of these alternative viewpoints suffer the trouble of reconciling the literal, physical effects of the seeds of death with the allegorical nature of the forbidden fruit or they suffer the problem of

---

[120] At a time when metaphorical teachings were being explained in simple terms, this teaching is introduced without any non-literal explanation.

reconciling the story of a single temptation of Eve with the partaking of multiple portions of the seeds of death that would have been necessary to effectuate the changes of the Fall. The latter problem may be solved by believing that, while Eve was only tempted once, she "partook" multiple times. However, this explanation is so far removed from a traditional Hebrew understanding of the symbology of trees so commonly used in Hebrew literature that it should be viewed with a healthy dose of skepticism.

The second questions is perhaps more problematic because we have even less guidance in speculative endeavors. However, if the Fall was indeed a very slow, gradual process, then the traditional, conservative Christian interpretation of the lifespan of the early patriarchs is well founded. That is, conservative Christians often believe that the earliest patriarchs lived for longer periods of time because there was less corruption and sin upon the earth - as the state of man has become more corrupt, so have the bodies of men and therefore, we live for less long periods of time. Although Christians tend to ignore the necessary assumption in this teaching, it may be significant to mention that assumption here: If the conservative Christian premise were true, then one must also accept the premise that the proportion of the seeds of death in our food supply must be steadily increasing as time passes.[121] Presumably, this would mean that the adversary is still given power to continue this planting or the seeds are of a nature that they multiply on their own. Whether or not this is true is too speculative to be worth serious consideration here. However, it does have the capacity to literally explain many historical questions presented in the Old Testament (as conservative Christians have done for centuries) - only the explanation works via an Adam-God exegetical lens.

An interesting twist that arises in connection with this speculative interpretation comes when we consider Joseph's teaching that the earth was hurled from the presence of Kolob into its current position as a result of the Fall.[122] If both teachings are believed, then it may be that the further an earth is from its Creator, the greater are the effects of the Fall.

While the author is not presenting the above items as doctrine, hopefully this line of thinking may open some reader's minds to the various considerations that ought to be addressed by Adam-God adherents if they are serious about understanding Adam-God teachings and all of their various theological implications.

---

[121] Conservative Christians, of course, would not state the assumption in this way - I'm presenting the assumption from and Adam-God perspective for purposes of illustration only.
[122] See "The Creation: Modus Operandi".

18   Procreation

| Mortal & Spiritual Offspring |

Gospel of Philip
A horse sires a horse, *a man begets a man, a god brings forth a god.*

Joseph Smith   *10/9/1843*
TPJS, 326
Flesh and blood cannot go there;[123] but flesh and bones, quickened by the Spirit of God, can.

Joseph Smith   *5/2/1844*
TPJS, 367
When our flesh is quickened by the Spirit, there will be no blood in this tabernacle.

Joseph Smith   *6/16/1844*
TPJS, 373
If Abraham reasoned thus - If Jesus Christ was the Son of God, and John discovered that God the Father of Jesus Christ had a Father, you may suppose that He had a father also. Where was there ever a son without a father? And where was there ever a father without first being a son? Whenever did a tree or anything spring into existence without a progenitor? And *everything comes in this way.*

Brigham Young   *12/6/1847*
Journal of Wilford Woodruff
We went into Council this morning. Several subjects were conversed upon. One was

---

[123] 1 Corinthians 15:50.

our posterity in this world & the offspring of celestial & resurrected beings in the world to come. President Young remarked that our children in this life did not look just like their parents but was a variety in looks etc., and *the offspring of celestial beings were spiritual bodies.*

Brigham Young   *Friday 4/9/1852*

Journal of Wilford Woodruff

When our Father came into the Garden He came with his Celestial body & brought one of his wives with him and ate of the fruit of the Garden *until He could beget a Tabernacle.* And Adam is Michael God and all the God that we have anything to do with. *They ate of this fruit & formed the first Tabernacle that was formed.* And when the Virgin Mary was begotten with child it was by the Father and in no other way only as we were begotten.

Brigham Young   *4/16/1852*

Journal of Samuel H. Rogers, 1:179

President Brigham Young said that our spirits ware begotten before that Adam came to the Earth and that Adam helped to make the Earth, that he had a Celestial boddy when he came to the Earth and that he brought his wife or one of his wives with him, and that Eave was allso a Celestial being, that *they eat of the fruit of the ground until they begat children from the Earth,* he said that Adam was the onley God that we would have, and that Christ was not begotten of the Holy Gost, but of the Father Adam, that Christ, was our elder brother. The argument that he used to shoe that Christ was not begotten by the holy gost, was a caution to the Elders that when they should go to preach the Gospel, to be careful how they laid their hands on the sisters, for the reseption of the holy Gost, lest the holy Gost should get them with Child and that it would be laid to them

---

Brigham Young   *8/28/1852*

JD 6:274-75

After men have got their exaltations and their crowns - have become Gods, even the sons of God - are made Kings of kings and Lords of lords, t*hey have the power then of propagating their species in spirit;* and that is the first of their operations with regard to organizing a world. Power is then given to them to organize the elements, and then commence the organization of tabernacles. How can they do it? Have they to go to that earth? Yes, and Adam will have to go there, and he cannot do without Eve; he must have Eve to commence the work of generation, and they will go into the garden, and continue to eat and drink of the fruits of the corporeal world, until this *grosser matter is diffused sufficiently through their celestial bodies to enable them, according to the established* *laws, to produce mortal tabernacles for their spiritual children.* This is a key for you. The faithful will become Gods, even the sons of God; but this does not overthrow the idea that we have a father.

Orson Pratt   *3/--/1853*

The Seer 1:3, 23, 24, 25

Fallen beings beget children whose bodies are constituted of flesh and bones, being formed out of the blood circulating in the veins of the parents. Celestial beings beget children, composed of the fluid which circulates in their veins, which is spiritual, therefore, their children must be spirits, and not flesh and bones. This is the origin of our spiritual organization in heaven. The spirits of all mankind, destined for this earth, were begotten by a father, and born of a mother in Heaven long anterior to the formation of this world. The personages of the father and mother of our spirits, had a beginning to their organization ....
Each God, through his wife or wives, raises up a numerous family of sons and daughters; indeed, there will be no end to the increase of his own children: for each father and mother will be in a condition to multiply forever and ever. As soon as each God has begotten many millions of male and female spirits, and his Heavenly inheritance becomes too small, to comfortably accommodate his great family, he, in connection with his sons, organizes a new world, after a similar order to the one which we now inhabit, where he sends both the male and female spirits to inhabit tabernacles of flesh and bones. Thus each God forms a world for the accommodation of his own sons and daughters who are sent forth in their times and seasons, and generations to be born into the same.

Orson Pratt   *10/--/1853*

The Seer, 1:159

Whether God the Father gave Mary to Joseph for time only, or for time and eternity, we are not informed. Inasmuch as God was the first husband to her, it may be that He only gave her to be the wife of Joseph while in this mortal state, and that He intended *after the resurrection to again take her as one of his own wives to raise up immortal spirits in eternity.*
As God the Father begat the fleshly body of Jesus, so He, before the world began, begat his spirit. As the body required an earthly Mother, so his spirit required a heavenly Mother. *As God associated in the capacity of a husband with the earthly mother, so likewise He associated in the same capacity with the heavenly one.* Earthly things being in the likeness of heavenly things. ... or in other words, *the laws of generation upon the earth are after the order of the laws of generation in heaven.*

Brigham Young   *9/17/1854*

Journal of Wilford Woodruff

President Young said that He came from another world & made this. Brought Eve with him, *partook of the fruits of the earth, begat children & they were earthly* & had mortal bodies & if we were faithful, we should become Gods as He was.

Brigham Young   *Sunday 10/8/1854*

John Pulsipher Papers, 37

[Adam] by *eating the mortal fruits of the Earth, it caused & produced mortal children* or commenced the increase of men on the Earth which is the bodies for the Spirits to live in.

Brigham Young   *Sunday 10/8/1854*

MABY

Adam was made of the dust of the earth.

"Was he made of the dust of this earth."

No, but of the dust of the earth whereon he was born in the flesh; that is the way he was made; he was made of dust.

"Did the Lord put into him his spirit?"

Yes, as the Lord put into you your spirit, he was begotten of a father, and brought forth as you and I were; and so are all intelligent beings brought forth from eternity to eternity. ... *All creatures that dwell upon this Earth are made of the elements that compose it;* which are organized to see if they will abide their creation, and be counted worthy to receive a resurrection.

"What, every flesh?"

Yes, every flesh, for *all flesh pertaining to this world is made of the dust of this Earth; it is made from the same material,* according to the will and pleasure of Him who dictates all things. Our *bodies are composed of the same material that composes this Earth;* they are composed of water, air, and solid earth, either of which will resolve back to their native fountain.

Brigham Young　　　　　　　　　　　　　　　　　*5/6/1855*

Journal of Wilford Woodruff

Adam & Eve had lived upon another Earth, were immortal when they came here.
Adam assisted in forming this earth & agreed to fall when he came here, & he fell that
man might be & the opposite principle to good, the devil, the serpent, the evil, was
placed upon the earth that man might know the good from the evil, for without an
experience in these things man could not know the one from the other. As soon as the
devil was on earth *he sowed the seeds of death in everything so as soon as they began to eat of
the fruit of the earth they received into their system the seeds of mortality & of death* so their
children were mortal & subject to death, sorrow, pain & wo.

Brigham Young　　　　　　　　　　　　　　　　　*4/20/1856*

JD 3:319

Adam was made from the dust of an earth, but not from the dust of this earth. He was
made as you and I are made, and *no person was ever made upon any other principle*.

Brigham Young　　　　　　　　　　　　　　　　　*2/8/1857*

JD 4:217-18

Thus you may continue and trace the human family back to Adam and Eve, and ask, are
we of the same species with Adam and Eve? Yes, every person acknowledges this; this
comes within the scope of our understanding. But when we arrive at that point, a vail is
dropped, and our knowledge is cut off. Were it not so, you could trace back your
history to the Father of our spirits in the eternal world. He is a being of the same
species as ourselves; He lives as we do, except the difference that we are earthly, and
He is heavenly. *He* has been earthly, and *is of precisely the same species of being that we are.*
Whether Adam is the personage that we should consider our heavenly Father, or not, is
considerable of a mystery to a good many. I do not care for one moment how that is; it
is no matter whether we are to consider Him our God, or whether His Father, or His
Grandfather, for in either case we are of one species - of one family - and Jesus Christ is
also of our species. ... Now to the facts in the case; all the difference between Jesus
Christ and any other man that ever lived on the earth, from the days of Adam until
now, is simply this, the Father, after He had once been in the flesh, and lived as we
live, obtained His exaltation, attained to thrones, gained the ascendancy over
principalities and powers, and had the knowledge and power to create - to bring forth
and organize the elements upon natural principles. This He did after His ascension, or
His glory, or His eternity, and was actually classed with the Gods, with the beings who
create, with those who have kept the celestial law while in the flesh, and again obtained
their bodies. Then He was prepared to commence the work of creation, as the

scriptures teach. It is all here in the Bible; I am not telling you a word but what is contained in that book.

Things were first created spiritually; the Father actually begat the spirits, and they were brought forth and lived with Him. Then He commenced the work of *creating earthly tabernacles, precisely as He had been created in this flesh himself*, by partaking of the course material that was organized and composed this earth, until His system was charged with it, consequently *the tabernacles of His children were organized from the course materials of this earth*.

Heber C. Kimball	*2/8/1857*

JD 4:222

Brother Brigham has talked here today[124] so plain that a little child cannot misunderstand it. He spoke about our Father and our God; I believe what he had said, in fact I know it.

Heber C. Kimball	*11/29/1857*

JD 6:101

Did God produce us? He did, and every son and every daughter of Adam upon the face of the earth; and *he produced us upon the same principle that we produce one another*. And so it is with the fruit of creation.

Parley P. Pratt	*before 1857*

Key to the Science of Theology, 49-50

At length a Moses came, who knew his God, and would fain have led mankind to know Him too, and see Him face to face. But they could not receive His heavenly laws, or bide His presence. Thus the holy man was forced again to veil the past in mystery, and, in the beginning of his history, assign to man an earthly origin. Man, moulded from the earth, as a brick! A woman, manufactured from a rib! Thus, parents still would fain conceal from budding manhood, the mysteries of procreation, and the sources of life's ever flowing river, by relating some childish tale of new-born life, engendered in the hollow trunk of some old tree, or springing with spontaneous growth, like mushrooms, from out of the heaps of rubbish. O man! when wilt thou cease to be a child in knowledge? Man, as we have said, is the offspring of Deity. The entire mystery of the past and future, with regard to his existence, is not yet solved by mortals.

We first recognize him, as an organized infdividual or intelligence, dwelling with his Father in the eternal mansions. This organized spirit we call a body, because, although

---

[124] He is referring to JD 4:217-18.

composed of the spiritual elements, it possesses every organ after the pattern, and in the likeness or similitude of the outward or fleshly tabernacles it is destined eventually to inhabit. Its organs of thought, speech, sight, hearing, tasting, smelling, feeling &c., all exist in their order, as in the physical body; the one being the exact similitude of the other. This individual, spiritual body, was begotten by the Heavenly Fahter, in his own likeness and image, and *by the laws of procreation.*

Brigham Young   *6/5/1859*

JD 7:163

The blood he spilled upon Mount Calvary he did not receive again into his veins. That was poured out, and when he was resurrected, another element took the place of the blood. It will be so with every person who receives a resurrection; the blood will not be resurrected with the body, being designed only to sustain the life of the present organization. When that is dissolved, and we again obtain our bodies by the power of the resurrection, that which we now call the life of the body, and which is formed from the food we eat and the water we drink will be supplanted by another element; for flesh and blood cannot inherit the Kingdom of God.

Brigham Young   *10/9/1859*

JD 7:285-86, 290

Our bodies are organized from the eternity of matter, from such matter as we breathe, and from such matter as is found in the vegetable and mineral kingdoms. This matter is organized into a world, with all its appendages, by whom? By the Almighty; and we see it peopled by men and women who are made in the image of God.

Here let me state to all philosophers of every class upon the earth, when you tell me that father Adam was made as we make adobes from the earth, you tell me what I deem an idle tale. When you tell me that the beasts of the field were produced in that manner, you are speaking idle words devoid of meaning. *There is no such thing in all the eternities where the Gods dwell.* Mankind are here because they are the offspring of parents who were first brought here from another planet, and power was given them to propagate their species, and they were commanded to multiply and replenish the earth. … Adam and Eve are the parents of all pertaining to the flesh, and I would not say that they are not also the parents of our spirits.

Brigham Young   *1/27/1860*

Journal of Wilford Woodruff

There never was a time or eternity but what a God did exist and *a God that had children upon the same principle that children are now begotten,* and *I was begotten by the God I worship* who reigns in the heavens and I shall also in my turn reign as a God & so will you. ... Michael was a resurrected Being and he left Eloheim and came to this earth & with an immortal body, & continued so till he *partook of earthly food and begot children who were mortal.*

Heber C. Kimball   *9/2/1860*

JD 8:211

In relation to the way in which I look upon the works of God and his creatures, I will say that *I was naturally begotten; so was* my father, and also *my Saviour Jesus Christ.* According to the Scriptures, he is the first begotten of his father in the flesh, and *there was nothing unnatural about it.*

W. W. Phelps et al.   *a.m. 10/8/1861*

James Beck Journal

The Curse Placed upon the woman is that her desire shall be to her husband she shall long & Desire for him & will not wish to be suplanted by another & in sorrow & in Pain she shall bring forth her offspring, if it was not for this curse, the woman would bring forth as easy as she would drink a glass of water. The curse upon the man is that he shall labour to support his family by the sweat of his brow &c & he has to be tormented with thorns & briars sunflowers & all kinds of noxious weeds. Is there any way for a man & his wife to committ sin in the mariage state - there is. It is for us to cultivate the Principles of life which God has Planted in us & not for us to Destroy life by an unlawfull intercourse with each other, but for us to multiply & Replenish the Earth as God has enjoined upon us.

Brigham Young   *6/181865*

JD 11:122-23

God has made His children like Himself to stand erect, and has endowed them with intelligence and power and dominion over all his works and given them the same attributes which He Himself possesses. *He created man, as we create our children; for there is no other process of creation in heaven, on the earth, in the earth, or under the earth, or in all the eternities,* that is, that were, or ever will be.

Brigham Young   *8/25/1867*

MABY

When father Adam and mother Eve became mortal by eating of the fruits of this earth, they were *then prepared to organize the mortal tabernacle* and they were prepared to organize and form living spirits long before that. Now they are prepared to form mortal bodies for their spiritual children to dwell in.

Brigham Young   *5/29/1870*

JD 13:178

All of us are in the hands of that God. We are all his children. *We are His sons and daughters naturally*, and by the principles of eternal life.

Brigham Young   *9/25/1870*

JD 13:250

He is our Father; He is our God, *the Father of our spirits; He is the framer of our bodies*, and set the machine in successful operation to bring forth these tabernacles that I now look upon in this building, and all that ever did or ever will live on the face of the whole earth.

Orson Pratt   *8/20/1871*

JD 14:242

There are no marriages among spirits, no coupling together of the males and females among them;[125] but when they rise from the grave after being tabernacled in mortal bodies, they have all the functions that are necessary to people worlds. As our Father and God begat us sons and daughters, so will we rise immortal males and females, and beget children and, in our turn, form and create worlds, and send forth our spirit children to inherit those worlds, the same as we were sent here, and thus will the works of God continue, and not only God himself, and His Son Jesus Christ have the power of endless lives, but all of His redeemed offspring.

Brigham Young   *Saturday p.m. 8/24/1872*

JD 15:137

We have not the power in the flesh to create and bring forth or produce a spirit; but we have the power to produce a temporal body. The germ of this, God has placed within us. And when our spirits receive our bodies, and through our faithfulness we are worthy to be crowned, we will then receive authority to produce both spirit and body.

---

[125] Note that this teaching contradicts Brigham's instructions nearly two decades earlier:

Brigham Young   *Friday 10/6/1854*

Journal of the Southern Indian Mission, 87- 89

Adam & Eve had children in the spirit - and their children married - brother & sister - then the bodies followed.

Orson Pratt   *11/22/1873*

JD 16:324

Our first parents were not mortal when they were placed on this earth, but they were as immortal as those who are resurrected in the presence of God. *Death came into the world by their transgression, they produced mortality*; hence this will be a complete restoration, of which I am speaking.

Brigham Young   *10/8/1876*

JD 18:258

Spirits were begotten, born and educated in the celestial world, and *were brought forth by celestial bodies*. These spirits I shall leave for the present, and refer to our first parents, Adam and Eve, who were found in the Garden of Eden, tempted and overcome by the power of evil, and consequently subject to evil and sin, which was the penalty of their transgression. *They were now prepared, as we are, to form bodies or tabernacles* for the reception of pure and holy spirits.

The Lecture at the Veil   *Tuesday 2/7/1877*

Journal of L. John Nuttall

Adam was an immortal being when he came ... and had begotten all the spirit that was to come to this earth. and Eve our common Mother who is the mother of all living bore those spirits in the celestial world. ... It is said by Moses the historian that the Lord caused a deep sleep to come upon Adam and took from his side a rib and formed the woman that Adam called Eve - this should be interpreted that the Man Adam like all other Men had the seed within him to *propagate his species.* but not the Woman. she conceives the seed but she does not produce it. consequently she was taken from the side or bowels of her father. this explains the mystery of Moses' dark sayings in regard to Adam and Eve. Adam & Eve when they were placed on this earth were immortal beings with flesh, bones and sinews. but *upon partaking of the fruits of the earth while in the garden and cultivating the ground their bodies became changed from immortal to mortal beings with the blood coursing through their veins as the action of life.*

Shortened Lecture at the Veil   *between 1877-1894*

It was said by Moses that the Lord caused a deep sleep to come upon Adam, and that he took from his side a rib and formed a woman which he called Eve. Now this should be interpreted that the man Adam - like all other men - had the seed of creation within himself to *propagate* the species, but the woman did not. She conceived the seed but did not produce it, and consequently she was taken, as it were, from the side or ribs of her father. *This explains the mystery of Mose's dark saying in regard to the creation of Eve from Adam's rib.*

Edward Tullidge   *3/--/1877*

Women of Mormondom, 198

The fall is simple. Our immortal parents came down to fall; came down to transgress the laws of immortality; *came down to give birth to mortal tabernacles* for a world of spirits. The 'forbidden tree,' says Brigham, contained in its fruit the elements of death, or the elements of mortality. By eating of it blood was again infused into the tabernacles of beings who had become immortal. *The basis of mortal generation is blood.* Without blood no mortal can be born. Even could immortals have been conceived on earth, the trees of life had made but the paradise of a few; but a mortal world was the object of creation then. Eve, then, came down to be the mother of a world. Glorious Mother, capable of dying at the very beginning to give life to her offspring, that through mortality the eternal life of the Gods might be given her sons and daughters. Motherhood the same from the beginning even to the end! The love of motherhood passing all understanding! Thus read our Mormon sisters the fall of their mother.

Orson Pratt   *7/18/1880*

JD 21:290-91

Two immortal beings, then, were placed in the garden of Eden, male and female. Was there any commandment given to those two immortal beings before the fall? There was one commandment, namely: "Be fruitful and multiply, and replenish the earth." What! Did the Lord command two immortal beings to multiply their species? He did. In meditating upon this great command given to these two immortal beings, it opens to us a field of reflection, of knowledge, concerning the great designs of the Almighty. It imparts to us a knowledge that the Lord our God intended that immortal beings should multiply their species.

Can you find any place in the book of Genesis where our first parents were commanded to *multiply after the fall?* I do not remember any such scripture. I have read the scriptures very diligently; I do not remember any such command. Yet they did so, and t*he consequences were that children of mortality were born* - mortal beings came upon the earth. Why? Because after the fall, Adam and Eve became mortal, and their species, of course, were after the order of the world, mortal in their nature. As the parents were subject to death, subject to pain, and sorrow, and distress, and all kinds of evil, so were all their posterity. *It was contrary to the law of God for mortal beings to bring forth children of immortality; it was contrary to the order of heaven for mortal beings to multiply their species in the form of immortal beings.*

But may we not suppose that it was really necessary, notwithstanding there was no command given, that the children of mortality should multiply their species? Notwithstanding the Lord said nothing to Adam and Eve upon this subject after the fall, so far as it written, yet we may suppose it was according this purpose and design that they should multiply children of mortality, even though he gave them no command after their fall to this effect. They have continued to do so, and their children after them, in all of their generations, until the present time, and will continue to do so in future generations, until the earth has filled the measure of its creation, according to the number of souls that existed before the world was organized, in the family of the two-thirds who kept their first estate.

But will the time come in the endless duration of the future, when our first parents will fulfill that command which was given to them while they were yet children of immortality? In other words will the time ever come when Adam and Eve will become immortal and carry out the command that was given to them in the days of their first immortality? I answer, yes; without this, the command of God never could be, in all respects, fulfilled. Though there should be hundreds of thousands of millions, or more, of the descendants of those mortal beings come here upon the earth, the command is not fully complied with; though he may have begotten sons and daughters, Cain, Abel, Seth and many others for some nine hundred years and upwards, yet all the sons and daughters he begat while he was mortal here upon the earth did not, in all respects, fulfill the command given to him while an immortal being.

Charles W. Penrose   *11/16/1884*

JD 26:21

God, then, the God of the Bible, who is called Jehovah, the person who manifested Himself to Israel as Jehovah, is an individual, a personality, and He made man in His image and His likeness. Now, if we are the children of God, and if Jesus Christ is the Son of God, we can upon that reasoning understand something about what God is like, for there is an eternal principle in heaven and on earth, that *every seed begets of its kind*, every seed brings forth *in its own likeness and character*. The seed of an apple, when it is reproduced, brings forth an apple, and so with a pear, and so with a plum, and so with all the varieties of the vegetable kingdom. It is the same with all the varieties of the animal kingdom. The doctrine of evolution, as it is called, is true in some respects - that is, that species can be improved, exalted, made better, but it remains of the same species. The advancement is in the same line. It is unfoldment. We do not find any radical change from one species to another. It is an eternal principle that *every seed produces its own kind, not another kind*. And as we are the children of God, we can follow out the idea and perceive what God our Father is, the Being who is the progenitor of our spiritual existence, the being from whom we have sprung. *We being the seed of God,* that Being is a personality, an individual, a being in some respects like us, or rather we are made in His image.

Brigham H. Roberts   *11/--/1884*

Contributor 10:266

The great law of nature is that every plant, herb, fish, fowl, beast and man produces his kind; though there may be slight variations from that law, those variations soon run out either by reverting to the original stock, or else by becoming incapable of producing offspring, and thus become extinct.

John Taylor   *11/--/1884*

Contributor 10:267

[A]nd if we take man, he is said to have been made in the image of God, and being His son, he is, of course, his offspring, an emanation from God, in whose likeness we are told he is made. He did not originate from a chaotic mass of matter, moving or inert, but came forth possessing, in an embryotic state, all the faculties and powers of a God. And when he shall be perfected, and have progressed to maturity he will be like his Father - a God, being indeed his offspring. As the horse, the ox, the sheep and *every living creature, including man, propagates its own species and perpetuates its own kind, so does God perpetuate His.*

Joseph E. Taylor   *6/2/1888*

Deseret Weekly News 38:22-26

I think these two quotations[126] from such a reliable authority fully solve the question as to the relationship existing between Father Adam and the Savior of the world, and prove beyond question the power that Adam possessed in regard to taking his body again after laying it down - which power he never could have attained unless he had received first a resurrection from the grave to a condition of immortality. We further say that this power was not forfeited when as a celestial being *he voluntarily partook of the forbidden fruit, and thereby rendered his body mortal in order that he might become the father of mortal tabernacles,* as he was already the father of immortal spirits - thus giving opportunity to the offspring of his own begetting to pass through the ordeals necessary to prepare them for a resurrection from the dead, a celestial glory.

---

[126] TPJS 345, 346, 347; HC 6:305, 306; JD 6:3.

George Q. Cannon *circa 1888*

Deseret Weekly News 38:675-76

We believe that *we are the literal descendants of our Eternal Father*; that we are the offspring of Deity; that those aspirations which man has, and which cause Him to perform the mighty works that we see on every hand as we travel throughout the earth, are inherited from our Eternal Father. They come to us by descent, or, to use another phrase, they are hereditary. The doctrine of heredity is manifested in the works of man. We descend from this great Father who formed the earth, and who governs this universe. Therefore, it is natural that man, being His offspring, should have these glorious aspirations which prompt him to attempt these wonderful works and to succeed in carrying them out.

This is the belief of the Latter-day Saints; and, having this belief, we should have with it a corresponding desire that, when we shall see our Father, we shall be like Him. If we have this hope within us, we will seek to purify ourselves, even as He is pure, that we may be counted worthy to come into His presence. ... A remark suggests itself to my mind which I heard a few days ago from one of our Apostles - Brother Lorenzo Snow. It was something to this effect: That as God now is, we will be; as man is, God was. It is very comprehensive. And we descend from this Father. We are His offspring.

George Q. Cannon *4/7/1889*

MS 51:278

We believe that *we are the literal offspring of Deity*. We have descended from the great Being who formed this earth, and from Him we have inherited the glorious aspirations to be like unto Him.

Brigham H. Roberts *5/--/1889*

Contributor 10:267

We are all "formed" of the dust of the ground, though instead of being molded as a brick *we are brought forth by the natural laws of procreation; so also was Adam and his wife* in some older world. And as for the story of the rib, under it I believe the mystery of procreation is hidden.

Wilford W. Woodruff & George Q. Cannon *6/11/1892*

Diary of Charles Lowell Walker 2:740-41

Pres. Woodruff and Cannon showed in a very plain manner ... that Adam was an immortal being when he came to this earth and *was made the same as all other men and Gods are made*; and that the seed of man was of the dust of the earth, and that the continuation of the seeds in a glorified state was Eternal Lives.

John Taylor   *1892*

Mediation and Atonement, 154

The *animal* and vegetable *creations are governed by certain laws*, and are composed of certain elements peculiar to themselves. *This applies to man*, to beasts, fowls, fish, and creeping things, to the insects and to all animated nature; each one possessing its own distinct features; each requiring a specific sustenance, each having an organism and faculties *governed by proscribed laws to perpetuate* its own kind.

George Q. Cannon

St. George High Council Minutes

[I testify] … in the name of Jesus Christ that *Adam was born just as we are born*. The lecture at the vail [sic] is true.

Orson F. Whitney   *1904*

ELIAS, AN EPIC OF THE AGES, 51

Ancient of Days here sits, as at the first,
When time and earth and *Adam's* race were young;
When, bowed with age, a great soul's sunset burst
In blessings on his seed. Prophetic tongue,
Thy patriarchal tone through time hath rung!

Michael, the prince, the monarch of our race,
Sire of a world from dust and spirit sprung;
Here sits he, throned in fire; before his face
Ten thousand times ten thousand throng the judgment place.

Salt Lake Tribune   *2/12/1906*

Page 3

Especially is it taught that Adam was not made out of the dust of this earth; that *he was begotten as any other man is begotten*, and that when he came here he brought Eve, one of his wives, with him.

                                                                                 6/27/1908

Elders' Journal 6:33 #2

When Adam and Eve were first placed in the garden of Eden they had resurrected bodies, in which there was no blood. A spiritual fluid or substance circulated in their veins instead of blood. Consequently, *they had not power to beget children with tabernacles of flesh*, such as human beings possess. *The fall* caused a change in their bodies, which, while it rendered them mortal, at the same time *gave them power to create mortal bodies of flesh, blood and bone for their offspring.*

1910

Divine Mission of the Savior; Course of Study for the Quorum of the Priesthood; Priests

LESSON FOURTEEN. SUBJECT: The Creation of Man.
I. *Man has descended from God*; in fact, he is of the same race as the Gods. His descent has not been from a lower form of life, but from the Highest Form of Life; in other words, *man is, in the most literal sense, a child of God*. This is not only true of the spirit of man, but of his body also. There never was a time, probably, in all the eternities of the past, when there was not men or children of God. This world is only one of many worlds which have been created by the Father through His Only Begotten. Adam, then, was probably not the first mortal man in the universe, but he was likely the first for this earth.

LESSON FIFTEEN. SUBJECT: The Creation of Adam and Eve.
II. One of the important points about this topic is to learn, if possible, how Adam obtained his body of flesh and bones. There would seem to be but one natural and reasonable explanation, and that is, that *Adam obtained his body in the same way Christ obtained his - and just as all men obtain theirs -* namely, by being born of woman.

Joseph F. Smith   *12/27/1913*
Deseret Evening News
The Son, Jesus Christ, grew and developed into manhood the same as you or I, as likewise did God, his father grow and develop to the Supreme Being that he now is. Man was born of woman; Christ the Savior, was born of woman; and *God*, the Father, *was born of woman*. *Adam*, our earthly parent, *was also born of woman into this world, the same as Jesus* and you and I.

Joseph F. Smith   *12/20/1914*
Box Elder News [127]
Well, now for the benefit of the older ones, how are children begotten? I answer just

---

[127] The publication date was 1/28/1915.

as Jesus Christ was begotten of his father. ... We want to try to make it appear that God does not do things in the right way, or that he has another way of doing things than what we know, we must come down to the simple fact that God Almighty was the Father of His Son Jesus Christ. Mary, the virgin girl, who had never known mortal man, was his mother. God by her begot His son Jesus Christ, and He was born into the world with power and intelligence like that of His Father. He was God with us, He was indeed Emmanuel for He came for a purpose and He possessed power that no human being ever possessed. He had power to lay down His life and take it up again, He had power to resist His murderers; if He had so willed it they never could have taken his life. He came for a purpose - what was it? - to redeem man from death.

Melvin J. Ballard   *circa 1919-1939*

Sermons and Missionary Experiences of Melvin J. Ballard, 239-240
What do we mean by endless or eternal increase? We mean that through the righteousness and faithfulness of men and women who keep the commandments of God they will come forth with *celestial bodies*, fitted and prepared to enter into their great, high and eternal glory in the celestial kingdom of God, and *unto them*, through their preparation, *there will come* children, who will be *spirit children*. I don't think that is very difficult to comprehend and understand.

The nature of the offspring is determined by the nature of the substance that flows in the veins of the being. When blood flows in the veins of the being, the offspring will be what blood produces, which is tangible flesh and bone, but when that which flows in the veins is spirit matter, a substance which is more refined and pure and glorious than blood, the offspring of such beings will be spirit children. By that I mean they will be in the image of the parents. They will have a spirit body and have a spark of the eternal or divine that always did exist in them.

Elders' Journal
[T]he scriptures emphatically state that "*we are the offspring of God.*"[128]

---

[128] See Acts 17:28 and others.

Analysis & Observations

β

There are basically only two principles covered in this section. Both principles are a culmination of principles presented earlier in this volume. First, the process of creating people (and other creatures) is based upon eternal principles of procreation. We do not spring from an adobe, activated by some inexplicable, magical, and mysterious process known only to God - neither are we the fortunate products of a random evolutionary process. Instead, both our spirits and our bodies are brought forth by a natural birthing process. Thus, Adam-God teachings are inherently incompatible with the nearly universally taught theory of organic evolution.[129] Although a growing number of modern members of the LDS Church are comfortable with the conceptual blending of a literal, spiritual Heavenly Father who subsequently uses organic evolution to create mankind's physical bodies, this merging of doctrines can never be acceptable to Adam-God adherents - if we are the literal descendants of God, both spirit and body, then evolution could never be a viable explanation of our origins.

The second principle outlined in the above subsection explains how one being can be both the parent of an immortal offspring and the parent of mortal offspring - and the explanation is central to the entire theology of Adam-God teachings. Immortal beings sire spirit children without exception. In order for an immortal being to sire a mortal child, blood must be (re)introduced into the body of the immortal being. Blood enters the body by partaking of the seeds of death (planted in edible vegetation by the adversary). Thus, a Fall is necessary on every earth in order for an immortal being to sire mortal children. While we are not specifically informed by the passages cited above how this biological phenomena functions, we are provided with a very clear theological explanation as to why the Fall is a necessary part of the plan of salvation - an explanation that is not satisfactorily provided by any other theology.

It also provides us with a few more philosophical questions: How much blood must be introduced into an immortal body before it can beget a mortal child? Apparently, if one parent is immortal and the other parent is mortal, the child has the choice to give up his life but he cannot be killed by another without that child's divine permission (a la the Savior). However, as previous chapters explained, Christ was able to have mortal

---

[129] This does not mean that principles of adaptive evolution are necessarily unacceptable to Adam-God adherents. In fact, these teachings implicitly seem to further the idea of evolution within a given species.

children, who probably did not have this same control over their deaths; it seems likely that some story of Christ's first generation descendants would have survived if they had lived until they affirmatively chose to pass on to the spiritual side of the veil. Even if they did have that power, at some point, their children lost that ability as no one today appears to have this option readily available. Thus, after an immortal body acquires a certain amount of blood in its system, death will be inevitable.

More questions follow: How does blood (which is referred to as the life of the body in scripture) produce death? What is the function of our organs that filter blood in an immortal body - or are they essentially without function until the next mortal probation begins? Will a sanctified individual live longer because more of the spirit flows in his/her veins?[130] Is this sanctification process part of what makes the translation of an individual possible? If the body is "quickened" by blood, then it seems reasonable to presume that spirit "quickens" the body in the same way. Does this explain the long life spans of the earliest patriarchs? In similar fashion, dozens of other interesting questions flow from these and other, related Adam-God teachings; however, there appears to be no satisfactory answers in the teachings of the early brethren.

See also 2 Nephi 2:22-23

---

[130] This assumes that the spirit of Christ moves through our bodies in the same way that blood does - see the above references by Joseph Smith for support of this position.

19 Adam's Death - Translation

Genesis 5:5

And all the days that Adam lived were nine hundred and thirty years: and *he died*.

Moses 3:7   *circa 6-10/1830*

But of the tree of the knowledge of good and evil, thou shalt not eat of it, nevertheless, thou mayest choose for thyself, for it is given unto thee; but, remember that I forbid it, for in the day thou eatest thereof *thou shalt surely die*.[131]

D&C 29:42   *9/26/1830*

But, behold, I say unto you that I, the Lord God, gave unto Adam and unto his seed, that *they should not die* as to the temporal death, *until* I, the Lord God, should send forth angels to declare unto them repentance and redemption, through faith on the name of mine Only Begotten Son.

D&C 107:42   *3/28/1835*

From Adam to Seth, who was ordained by Adam at the age of sixty-nine years, and was blessed by him three years *previous to his (Adam's) death,* and received the promise of God by his father, that his posterity should be the chosen of the Lord, and that they should be preserved unto the end of the earth;

D&C 107:53   *3/28/1835*

Three years *previous to the death of Adam,* he called Seth, Enos, Cainan, Mahalaleel, Jared, Enoch and Methuselah, who were all high priests, with the residue of his

---

[131] See also Abraham 5:13, Moses 4:9, Alma 12:23, LF 2:10.

posterity who were righteous, into the valley of Adam-ondi-Ahman, and there bestowed upon them his last blessing.[132]

Joseph Smith   *Sunday 10/2/1841*

Translated bodies cannot enter into rest until they have undergone *a change equivalent to death*. Translated bodies are designed for future missions. The angel that appeared to John on the Isle of Pathos was a translated or resurrected body (i.e. personage). Jesus Christ went in body after His resurrection, to minister to resurrected bodies.

Joseph Smith   *4/--/1844*

TPJS, 346

What did Jesus say? (Mark it, Elder Rigdon) The scriptures inform us that Jesus said, As the Father hath power in Himself, even so hath the Son power - to do what? Why, what the Father did, The answer is obvious - in a manner t*o lay down His body and take it up again.* Jesus, what are you going to do? To lay down my life as my Father did, and take it up again. Do you believe it? If you do not believe it, you do not believe the Bible.

Joseph Smith   *6/16/1844*

TPJS, 373

I want you to pay particular attention to what I am saying. Jesus said that the Father wrought precisely in the same way as His Father had done before Him. As the Father had done before? *He laid down His life, and took it up the same as His Father had done* before. He did as He was sent, to lay down His life and take it up again; and then was committed unto Him the keys.

Brigham Young   *Friday 10/6/1854*

Journal of the Southern Indian Mission, 87- 89
Adam died and was buried, where he was interred is not said.

Brigham Young   *Sunday 10/8/1854*

MABY

The inquiry will arise, among those who are strenuous, and tenacious for the account given by Moses, as to Adam: "*Did not Adam die?*" *Yes he died.* "Does not the Bible say he died?" I do not know nor care, but it would be hard I think to find where he died; or where Moses died,[133] though I have no doubt *Moses died, and Adam also.* How? *Just as you*

---

[132] See also Moses 6:35.
[133] Deuteronomy 34:7; Alma 45:19.

and I have to die, and be laid away in the bowels of Mother Earth; that, however, Moses did not see fit to tell us.

Orson Pratt & Brigham Young *5/6/1855*

Journal of Wilford Woodruff

O. Pratt asks will Adam or any God continue to make worlds, people them, *taste of death* to redeem them - Answer: I have no doubt but it is his privilege but whether He will do it is a question in my mind. How then can his seed increase to all eternity through the increase of his posterity. Many other remarks were made by the President.

Brigham Young *1/27/1860*

Journal of Wilford Woodruff

Michael was a resurrected Being and he left Eloheim and came to this earth & with an immortal body, & continued so till he partook of earthly food and begot children who were mortal (keep this to yourselves) *then they died.*

John Taylor & Orson Pratt *10 a.m. 4/5/1860*

Minutes of the Meeting of the Council of the Twelve

J. Taylor spoke again "if Christ is the first fruits of them that slept" there must be some discrepancy, he must have resumed his position, having a legitimate claim to a possession some where else, he ought not to be debarred from his rights. *the power of God was sufficient to resuscitate Jesus immediately, and also the body of Adam.* ...
O. Pratt I have heard brother Brigham say that Adam is the Father of our Spirits, and he came here with his resurrected body, to fall for his own children; and I said to him, it leads to an endless number of *falls*, which leads to sorrow and *death*: that is revolting to my feelings, even if it were not sustained by revelation.

Heber C. Kimball *Sunday 4/12/1868*

JD 12:188[134]

I have been to the altar where Adam offered sacrifices and blessed his sons and then *left them and went to heaven.*

The Lecture at the Veil *Tuesday 2/7/1877*

Journal of L. John Nuttall

[W]hen Adam and Eve got through with their Work in this earth. *they did not lay their bodies down in the dust, but returned to the spirit World from whence they came.*

---

[134] See JD 12:191 as well.

Byron Allred   *3/1/1877*

Jans Christian Anderson Weibye Daybooks 5:20

Byron Allred preaches at Manti on Adam as God, with the following remarks in part: Adam was buried by God (God his Father) and *was only dead like a twinkling of an eye, and his God exalted him immediately.*

Orson Pratt   *7/18/1880*

JD 21:290-91

That [commandment to multiply and replenish the earth] has to be fulfilled after *Adam and Eve are resurrected from the grave.* Have they yet been resurrected? I think so. There were a great many that were resurrected at the time of the resurrection of Christ. Christ was the first fruits of the resurrection, and then there were a great many Saints who came forth out of their graves and were resurrected, and permitted to enter into the celestial glory and dwell at his right hand. Among the number, I have no doubt but what our first parents Adam and Eve, were permitted to come forth and enter into celestial glory.

Joseph E. Taylor   *12/29/1888*

Deseret Weekly News 38:19-27

It is recorded in the fifth chapter of Genesis that *Adam died at the advanced age of 930 years.* But it is often asked, `Did Adam lie in the grave until he was redeemed* therefrom through the death and resurrection of the Only Begotten?' I will ask a question in reply: `Did Jesus have power to lay down his life and take it up again?' He so declared (John 10:18). It might be well at this point to inquire who was the Savior of the world; and what relation did he bear to our father Adam? For the veil of the mysterious past has been lifted just a little to enable us to see within. I will first quote from a discourse preached by President Brigham Young, in Salt Lake City, April 9th, 1852.
[He here quotes JD 1:50-51.]
We will now quote some of the sayings of Joseph Smith upon this point, as uttered by him in Nauvoo, April 6, 1844. `It is the first principle of the Gospel to know for a certainty the character of God, and to know that we may converse with Him, as one man converses with another, and that he was made a man like us. Yea, that God Himself, the Father of us all, dwelt on our earth the same as Jesus Christ did. ... What did Jesus say? ... `As the Father hath power in himself, so hath the Son power.' To do what? Why, what the Father did. The answer is obvious, in a manner, *to lay down his body and take it up again.* `Jesus, what are you going to do?' `To lay down my life and take it up again.' Do you believe it? If you do not believe it, you do not believe the Bible. The

Scriptures tell it, and I defy all the learning and wisdom of all the combined powers of earth and hell together to refute it. What did Jesus do? Why, `I do the thing I saw my Father do when worlds came rolling into existence. My Father worked out His Kingdom with fear and trembling; and I must do the same; and when I get my kingdom, I shall present it to my Father, so that He may obtain kingdom upon kingdom and it will exalt Him in glory. He will then take a higher exaltation and I take His place, and thereby become exalted myself'; so that Jesus treads in the track of his Father and inherits what God did before.'[135]

I think these two quotations from such a reliable authority fully solve the question as to the relationship existing between Father Adam and the Savior of the world, and *prove beyond question the power that Adam possessed in regard to taking his body again after laying it down - which power he never could have attained unless he had received first a resurrection from the grave to a condition of immortality.* We further say that this power was not forfeited when as a celestial being he voluntarily partook of the forbidden fruit, and thereby rendered his body mortal in order that he might become the father of mortal tabernacles, as he was already the father of immortal spirits - thus giving opportunity to the offspring of his own begetting to pass through the ordeals necessary to prepare them for a resurrection from the dead, a celestial glory.

All that Father Adam did upon this earth, from the time that he took up his abode in the Garden of Eden, was done for his posterity's sake and the success of his former mission as the savior of a world, and afterwards, or now, as the Father of a world only added to the glory which he already possessed. *If, as the savior of a world, he had the power to lay down his life and take it up again, therefore, as the father of a world which is altogether an advanced condition, we necessarily conclude that the grave was powerless to hold him after that mission was completed.* All those who have now for the first time taken upon themselves mortality, must wait for their resurrection through Him who alone possesses the power to bring it to pass. It is these, and these only, whose resurrection we here wish to consider.

Analysis & Observations

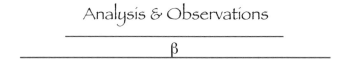

β

The first issue that this section raises is how can an immortal being die - isn't it revealed

---

[135] TPJS 345, 346, 347; HC 6:305, 306; JD 6:3.

doctrine that an immortal being is never again subject to death? This issue was so succinctly and well answered by Christensen that I will merely quote him here: "[O]ne must remember that Adam did not die as an immortal but as a mortal being. He partook of the coarser elements of this earth which subjected him to a mortal state and subsequent death." AGM, 66.

Although previous Adam-God authors have been loathe to accept the teaching that Adam died, the above statements seem to nearly uniformly declare this to be accurate doctrine. If accurately transcribed, Brigham Young even suggested that Adam was buried. And thus begins a whole string of apparent inconsistencies[136] as various brethren appeared to speculate as to who resurrected Adam - did he resurrect himself because he already held those keys as Joseph Smith seemed to suggest[137] and as Joseph E. Taylor extrapolated - or did someone else have to perform this ordinance? Or, did Adam die in the traditional sense of the word as Brigham Young taught in his October 8, 1854 discourse or was he merely translated as Heber C. Kimball and recent Adam-God authors have suggested? These questions fall among a large umber of teachings found throughout this volume - teachings that were either not fully developed, fully understood, fully recorded, or that were transcribed incorrectly. Without revelation, the reader is left to speculate the answer to these questions just as the reader is left to do so in many instances throughout this volume.

See also Alma 12:23-24; 42:6

---

[136] This conundrum is not unique to Adam-God teachings - see Deuteronomy 34:5 and Alma 35:19 for a similar inconsistency surrounding Moses' death.

[137] These statements can be read to mean that Adam had power to raise himself as the Redeemer of his world. However, Brigham Young seems to retract this teaching in his October 8, 1854 discourse and it does not necessarily follow that an Adam would have to resurrect himself - it could be done via a translation of the body or it could be done via Adam's Jehovah (his father) or some other person.

20 Does the Atonement Pertain

To Adam & Eve?

See also
The Good Samaritan

D&C 29:42   *9/26/1830*

But, behold, I say unto you that I, the Lord God, gave unto *Adam* and unto his seed, that *they should not die* as to the temporal death, *until* I, the Lord God, should send forth angels to *declare unto them repentance and redemption*, through faith on the name of mine Only Begotten Son.

Orson Pratt   *3/--/1850*

MS 12:69; JD 1:329

But a universal redemption from the effects of original sin, has nothing to do with redemption from our personal sins; for t*he original sin of Adam*, and the personal sins of his children, are two different things. The first was *committed by man in his immortal state;* the second was committed by man in a mortal state; the former was committed *in a state of ignorance of good or evil;* the latter was committed by man, having a knowledge of both good and evil. As the sins are different, and committed entirely under different circumstances, so the penalties are different also. The penalty of the first transgression was an eternal separation of body and spirit, and eternal banishment from the presence of Jehovah; while the penalty of our own transgressions does not involve a disunion of body and spirit, but only eternal banishment. The first penalty not only shut man out from the presence of God, but deprived him eternally of a body; the second penalty permits him to retain his body, though in a banished condition. As the penalties are different, so also is the redemption. Redemption from the first penalty is unconditional on the part of man; redemption from the second penalty is conditional. Unconditional redemption is universal; it takes within its scope all mankind; it is as unlimited as the fall; it redeems men from all its effects; it restores to them their bodies; it restores them to the presence of God.

Brigham Young   *1/5/1860*

JD 9:103, 105

For instance, we cannot avert the consequences of the fall as it is called, of Adam, which came through his *transgressing certain words or laws* given to him by his Father and God. ... When our first parents fell from their paradisiacal state, they were brought in contact with influences and powers of evil that are unnatural and stand in opposition to an endless life. *So far as mankind yield to those influences, they are so far removed from a natural to an unnatural state - from life to death. Adam and Eve did not sin* because it was in their nature to love sin, but, as Paul says in his Epistle to Timothy, `Adam was not deceived, but the woman being deceived was in the transgression. Notwithstanding, she will be saved in childbearing, if they continue in faith, and charity, and holiness, with sobriety.' The enemy of all righteousness deceived the woman, and Adam went with her that man might be, and that she might be saved in childbearing.

Brigham Young   *11/6/1864*

JD 10:312

Some may regret that *our first parents sinned.* This is nonsense. If we had been there, and they had not sinned, we should have sinned. I will not blame Adam or Eve. Why? Because it was necessary that sin should enter into the world; no man could ever understand the principle of exaltation without its opposite; no one could ever receive an exaltation without being acquainted with its opposite. *How did Adam and Eve sin? Did they come out in direct opposition to God* and to His government? *No.* But *they transgressed a command* of the Lord, and *through that transgression sin came into the world.* The Lord knew they would do this, and *He designed that they should.*

Brigham Young   *10/8/1876*

JD 18:258-59

Spirits were begotten, born and educated in the celestial world, and were brought forth by celestial bodies. These spirits I shall leave for the present, and refer to our first parents, Adam and Eve, who were found in the Garden of Eden, *tempted* and *overcome by the power of evil*, and consequently subject to evil and sin, which was the penalty of their transgression.

Lecture at the Veil   *Tuesday 2/7/1877*

L. John Nuttall Journal 1:18-21

Adam was not under transgression until after he partook of the forbidden fruit. This was necessary that they might be together, that man might be. *The woman was found in transgression, not the man.*

J. F. Gibbs   *11/--/1884*

Contributor 6:76-78

Having, while on earth complied with the requirements of the Father in relation to Celestial Marriage, he is thus qualified to become a "Father of spirits," and his immortal wives become the mothers of spirits, thus obeying the only and eternal law of reproduction. ... he is placed upon it [the world] and with his wives repeats the history of man on this and other planets. The Being that has organized the world; and placed upon it the germs of animated nature; is the one most entitled to furnish mortal bodies for his spiritual children. And when the great drama of life is finished and *he with his children are redeemed* and glorified, is he not entitled, as the head of an innumerable posterity, to be recognized as a Father and God to those that will rise up and call Him blessed?

Joseph E. Taylor   *6/2/1888*

Deseret Weekly News 38:19-27

It is recorded in the fifth chapter of Genesis that Adam died at the advanced age of 930 years. But it is often asked, `*Did Adam lie in the grave until he was redeemed* therefrom through the death and resurrection of the Only Begotten?' I will ask a question in reply: `Did Jesus have power to lay down his life and take it up again?' He so declared.[138] It might be well at this point to inquire who was the Savior of the world; and what relation did he bear to our father Adam? For the veil of the mysterious past has been lifted just a little to enable us to see within. I will first quote from a discourse preached by President Brigham Young, in Salt Lake City, April 9th, 1852.
[He here quotes JD 1:50-51.]
We will now quote some of the sayings of Joseph Smith upon this point, as uttered by him in Nauvoo, April 6, 1844. `It is the first principle of the Gospel to know for a certainty the character of God, and to know that we may converse with Him, as one man converses with another, and that he was made a man like us. Yea, that God Himself, the Father of us all, dwelt on our earth the same as Jesus Christ did. ... What did Jesus say? ... `As the Father hath power in himself, so hath the Son power.' To do

---

[138] John 10:18.

what? Why, what the Father did. The answer is obvious, in a manner, to lay down his body and take it up again. `Jesus, what are you going to do?' `To lay down my life and take it up again.' Do you believe it? If you do not believe it, you do not believe the Bible. The Scriptures tell it, and I defy all the learning and wisdom of all the combined powers of earth and hell together to refute it. What did Jesus do? Why, `I do the thing I saw my Father do when worlds came rolling into existence. My Father worked out His Kingdom with fear and trembling; and I must do the same; and when I get my kingdom, I shall present it to my Father, so that He may obtain kingdom upon kingdom and it will exalt Him in glory. He will then take a higher exaltation and I take His place, and thereby become exalted myself'; so that Jesus treads in the track of his Father and inherits what God did before.'[139]

I think these two quotations from such a reliable authority fully solve the question as to the relationship existing between Father Adam and the Savior of the world, and prove beyond question *the power that Adam possessed in regard to taking his body again after laying it down* - which power he never could have attained unless he had received first a resurrection from the grave to a condition of immortality. We further say that *this power was not forfeited when as a celestial being he voluntarily partook of the forbidden fruit*, and thereby rendered his body mortal in order that he might become the father of mortal tabernacles, as he was already the father of immortal spirits - thus giving opportunity to the offspring of his own begetting to pass through the ordeals necessary to prepare them for a resurrection from the dead, a celestial glory.

All that Father Adam did upon this earth, from the time that he took up his abode in the Garden of Eden, was done for his posterity's sake and the success of his former mission as the savior of a world, and afterwards, or now, as the Father of a world only added to the glory which he already possessed. *If, as the savior of a world, he had the power to lay down his life and take it up again, therefore, as the father of a world which is altogether an advanced condition, we necessarily conclude that the grave was powerless to hold him after that mission was completed.* All those who have now for the first time taken upon themselves mortality, must wait for their resurrection through Him who alone possesses the power to bring it to pass.

Melvin J. Ballard　　　　　　　　　　　　　　　　　　　　*6/24/1921*

Seminary Lectures, BYU, Lecture 11
What Brother Whitaker has said I agree with, with reference to his fall and man's coming here." Ballard then suggested that *Adam had two ways to regaining his lost immortality,* one was *by partaking of the fruit of the tree of life* and so recovering "from the

---

[139] TPJS 345, 346, 347; HC 6:305, 306; JD 6:3.

mortal condition apparently," and *the other was through the atonement* of Jesus Christ: Well, man has fallen. How can he get back? What is the antidote? The antidote was the tree of life, but he was driven out from it. Now what else? The antidote was the death of a God, and Jesus Christ was a God before he came into this world.

Joseph Fielding Smith

Doctrines of Salvation 1:114-15

I never speak of the part Eve took in the fall as a sin, *nor do I accuse Adam of a sin* ... it is not always a sin to transgress a law. ... Well, Adam's transgression was of a similar nature, that is, his transgression was in accordance with law ... . *This was a transgression of law, but not a sin* in the strict sense, for it was something that Adam and Eve had to do! *I am sure that neither Adam nor Eve looked upon it as a sin.* ... We can hardly look upon anything resulting in such benefits as being a sin, in the sense in which we consider sin.

Analysis & Observations

β

This subsection is problematic because very little guidance has been offered on this topic by the early brethren and because this is perhaps the most important issue to be addressed for those being introduced to Adam-God teachings. Although the above statements include some few references to whether or not Adam and Eve sinned in partaking of the forbidden fruit,[140] the real substantive issue that needs attention is whether or not Adam and Eve were in need of Jesus Christ's atonement whether or not they sinned in partaking of the forbidden fruit. The compound problem in answering that question is that very little has been said on the topic and none of what has been said directly answers this question. Therefore, the reader is left to conjecture an answer. However, the following insights for the reader's consideration may be of some limited help in addressing this issue.

First, the reasoning cited by Joseph E. Taylor seems to mirror the position of most Adam-God adherents. That is, Adam does not need the atonement - he had already been

---

[140] There are many more statements of this nature to be found; I have included these few representative statements to demonstrate that the early brethren and the modern brethren both appear to agree that Adam and Eve were not condemned in any fashion for effectuating the fall (again, Orson Pratt seems to be an exception to this trend).

exalted due to his obedience in a previous probation - either through the atonement of his savior or through his own merits (if one believes that Adam was the savior of his world - see "The Royal Order of Saviors").

Note that Christ had to have the seeds of godhood in him or else he could not have effectuated the atonement. If Adam is the father of Christ and if Adam is the individual who gave Christ those seeds of godhood (as opposed to Mary) then Adam was immortal when he sired Christ. Unless one believes in circular (faulty) reasoning, it stands to reason that Adam did not need the atonement of Christ to effectuate that immortality - in other words, how could Adam rely upon the atonement of someone who had not been born and who he would have to personally sire? Adam could not have had the seeds of godhood to offer had he remained in a fallen state - and the scriptures tell us that Christ was the first fruits of them that slept. If Adam was therefore already resurrected and Christ was the "first fruits," then it follows that Adam was not included underneath that statement (i.e., Adam did not die - see "Adam's Death - Translation").

In contrast, if one were to presume that Adam needed the savior's atonement, then it appears that every time an Adam enters another mortal probation, he eternally risks losing his exalted status in the event that the savior of that world fails to accomplish his mission.[141] In the alternative, an Adam requiring the atonement of his savior would have to be rendered immortal (in order to sire his savior) without the completion of his savior's atonement having been effectuated. Thus, theoretically, he could be rendered immortal based upon the contingency of an event that may or may not transpire (the atoning sacrifice of his savior). This scenario also seems implausible and, as noted above, it seems circular in its reasoning because it assumes that an atonement will be made and that this atonement can be fully efficacious upon some individuals before the atoning event transpires - in contrast, many spirits waited in prison until Christ came to liberate them during his three days in the tomb and none of the saints who lived before Christ's resurrection were allowed to be resurrected until after his atonement and resurrection were complete - why would Adam be an exception to this rule if he was subject to the savior's atonement? Lastly, some few but significant statements by the early brethren have conclusively stated that a father will always be worshipped throughout all eternities by his sons and daughters. Does it seem rational to conclude that an Adam who has need

---

[141] Although there appears to be very few statements by the early brethren suggesting that this is a possibility, some fundamentalists have understood that this is a possibility and that it accounts for the failure of some worlds to be redeemed (As is shown in "The Creation: Modus Operandi" subsection, this earth was formed out of other earths - presumably these earths were not redeemed for one reason or another and did not achieve the status of a telestial, terrestrial, or celestial orb).

of his son's atoning sacrifice could ever expect to be worshipped by that son?

Like many of the other subsections in this book, the questions that arise from the statements of the early brethren far outnumber the answers given and the reader is left to form a conclusion on their own - either by study or by prayer or by both.

The Cycle of the Gods

β

The first topic in this section is probably the most broad overview of what Adam-God teachings implicate to the believer. Many of these things are still taught in the LDS Church, albeit rarely, so members of the Church who read this section will find many things that they are already familiar with. The other topics in this section are probably the most controversial and least understood of Adam-God teachings - even among the fundamentalists who adhere to Adam-God teachings as a basic tenant of their faith. The author would therefore recommend that the reader unacquainted with basic Adam-God teachings read most of the other sections in this book before he/she attempts to digest the material in the later topics in this section.

21
The Faithful Become Gods

Becoming an Adam / Eve

This subsection could feasibly be broken up into three different subsections: God Was Once a Man Like Us, The Faithful Become Gods, and The Faithful Become Adam/Eve. Although I made meticulous and conscious efforts to make these subtle distinctions throughout the beginning portion of this volume out of sensitivity to the LDS reader, I have chosen not to do so here because I find this distinction less meaningful and significant in this section of the volume. Presuming that the reader began reading this book at the beginning and continued to read up to this section, it must be fairly evident that Adam-God teachings were quite extensive and quite developed by the early brethren. This section is devoted to some of the more deeper ramifications of these teachings so subtle distinctions of this nature are of less value. Further, I found that separating these three topics unnecessarily complicates the subject, hinders the reader's ability to grasp the full meaning of these teachings, and subjects the reader to too much repetition and redundancy. Lastly, while the distinction between becoming an Adam/Eve and becoming a god in current LDS theology is quite significant, the purpose of this section of this volume is to expound upon Adam-God teachings themselves - a purpose that is not well served by making this distinction.

W.W. Phelps   *6/--/1835*

M&A 1:30 #9

New light is occasionally bursted into our minds, of the sacred scriptures, for which I am truly thankful. We shall by and by learn that we were with God in another world, before the foundation of the world, and had our agency; that we came into this world and have our agency, in order that we may prepare ourselves for a kingdom of glory; *become archangels, even the sons of God* where the man is neither without the woman nor the woman without the man in the Lord: A consummation of glory, and happiness, and perfection so greatly to be wished, that I would not miss of it for the fame of ten worlds.

Joseph Smith   *6/11/1843*

TPJS, 312

In the resurrection, some are raised to be angels, *others are raised to become Gods.* These things are revealed in the most holy places in a Temple prepared for that purpose.

Joseph Smith   *4/7/1844*

WJS, 361; Samuel W. Richards record

God: a man like one of us, even like Adam. Not God from all Eternity. Once on a planet with flesh and blood, like Christ. As the father hath life in himself, &c. To know God learn to become God's. Exalted by the addition of subjects to his family, or kingdom.

Joseph Smith   *6/16/1844*

TPJS, 372

"I am agreed with the Father and the Father is agreed with me, and we are agreed as one." The Greek shows that it should be agreed. "Father, I pray for them which Thou hast given me out of the world, and not for those alone, but for them also which shall believe on me through their word, that they all may be agreed, as Thou, Father, are with me, and I with Thee, that they also may be agreed with us," and all come to dwell in unity, and in all the glory and everlasting burnings of the Gods; and *then we shall see as we are seen, and be as our God and He as His Father.*

Joseph Smith   *8/15/1844*

T&S; HC 6:302-03

There are but a very few beings in the world who understand rightly the character of God. ... If men do not comprehend the character of God, they do not comprehend themselves. I will go back to the beginning before the world was, to show what kind of being God is. ... *God himself was once as we are now, and is an exalted man,* and sits enthroned in yonder heavens! That is the great secret. If the veil were rent today, and the great God who holds this world in its orbit, and who upholds all worlds and all things by his power, was to make himself visible, - I say, if you were to see him today, you would see him like a man in form - like yourselves in all the person, image, and very form as a man. ... These are incomprehensible ideas to some, but they are simple. *It is the first principle of the Gospel to know for a certainty* the Character of God, and to know that we may converse with him as one man converses with another, and *that he was once a man like us*; yea, that God himself, the Father of us all, dwelt on an earth, the same as Jesus Christ himself did and I will show it from the Bible.

2/15/1845

T&S 6:808-09 #3

What shall we say then, to make Moses', Jesus' and Peter's words true? We will say that Jesus Christ had a father and mother of his Spirit, and a father and mother of his flesh; and so have all of his brethren and sisters: and *that is one reason why he said, '(ye are Gods);'* or that Isaiah prophesied:[142] 'Show the things that are to come hereafter, that we may know that *ye are Gods*; yea, do good, or do evil, that we may be dismayed, and behold it together.' In fact, '*the Gods,' in old times, was common intelligence.* Satan, in his first sectarian sermon to Adam and Eve, told them, if they would eat of the forbidden fruit, they should become as '*the Gods*,' knowing good and evil.

Brigham Young Sunday 4:00 p.m. 3/14/1852

Historian's Office Journal, 106

BY, HCK, WR OP WW GAS TB EH DH Wells TOA. WWO. (met) (in) (the) (temple) rooms (and) prayed T B. O Pratt (sh) mouths conversed about O Pratt's discourse (in) (the) endowment rooms yesterday B Y rolled out rev.n (upon) rev.n (in) regard (to) (the) crea(tion).n [sic] (of) (the) world Adam came (to) (the) E[arth] when (he) assisted (to) form (it) (sh) (he) then partook (of) (the) fruits (of) (the) E[arth] (and) Became Earthy (and) (they) (which) are (the) (s) (after) (sh) rece[ive] our resurrected bodies (and) *(shall)* *(all)* *(have)* *(the)* *priv[ilege]* *(of)* *going* *(as)* *Adam's form* (an) E[arth] (and) do likewise

Brigham Young 8/8/1852

JD 3:93-94

The Lord created you and me for the purpose of becoming Gods like Himself; when we have been proved in our present capacity, and been faithful with all things He puts into our possession. We are created, we are born for the express purpose of growing up from the low estate of manhood, *to become Gods like unto our Father in heaven.* That is the truth about it, just as it is. The Lord has organized mankind for the express purpose of increasing in that intelligence and truth, which is with God, until he is capable of creating worlds on worlds, and *becoming Gods*, even the sons of God. How many will become thus privileged? Those who honor the Father and the Son; those who receive the Holy Ghost, and magnify their calling, and are found pure and holy; they shall be

---

[142] Isaiah 41:23.

crowned in the presence of the Father and the Son. Who else? Not anybody.

Brigham Young   *8/28/1852*

JD 6:274-75

Perhaps in the case before us, as in others, we might say that men become children. We are children in the first place, then become men; and in the second place men become children in their understanding. ... But I expect, if I am faithful with yourselves, that I shall see the time with yourselves that we shall know how to prepare to organize an earth like this - know how to people that earth, how to redeem it, how to sanctify it, and how to glorify it, with those who live upon it who hearken to our counsels. The Father and the Son have attained to this point already; I am on the way, and so are you, and every faithful servant of God. ... Joseph will come up in his turn, receive his body again, and continue his mission in the eternal worlds until he carries it out to perfection, with all the rest of the faithful, to be made perfect with those who have lived before, and those who shall live after; and when the work is finished, and it is offered to the Father, then they will be crowned and receive keys and powers by which they will be capable of organizing worlds. What will they organize first?

After men have got their exaltations and their crowns - *have become Gods*, even the sons of God - are made Kings of kings and Lords of lords, they have the power then of propagating their species in spirit; and that is the first of their operations with regard to organizing a world. Power is then given to them to organize the elements, and then commence the organization of tabernacles. How can they do it? Have they to go to that earth? Yes, and Adam will have to go there, and he cannot do without Eve; he must have Eve to commence the work of generation, and they will go into the garden, and continue to eat and drink of the fruits of the corporeal world, until this grosser matter is diffused sufficiently through their celestial bodies to enable them, according to the established laws, to produce mortal tabernacles for their spiritual children. This is a key for you. *The faithful will become Gods, even the sons of God*; but this does not overthrow the idea that we have a father.

Heber C. Kimball   *11/14/1852*

JD 1:356

When we escape from this earth, do we suppose we are going to heaven? Do you suppose you are going to the earth that Adam came from? that Eloheim came from? where Jehovah the Lord came from? No. When you have learned to become obedient to the Father that dwells upon this earth, to the Father and God of this earth, and obedient to the messengers He sends - when you have done all that, remember you are not going to leave this earth. You will never leave it until *you become qualified*, and capable, and capacitated *to become* a *father of an earth yourselves.*

Orson Pratt   *3/--/1853*

The Seer 1:1, 3, 23, 24, 25, 37

The *celestial beings who dwell in the Heaven from which we came, having been raised from the grave, in a former world,* and having been filled with all the fullness of these eternal attributes, are called Gods, because the fullness of God dwells in each. Both the males and the females enjoy this fullness. ... The spirits of all mankind, destined for this earth, were begotten by a father, and born of a mother in Heaven long anterior to the formation of this world. The personages of the father and mother of our spirits, had a beginning to their organization, but the fullness of truth (which is God[143]) that dwells in them, had no beginning; being "from everlasting to everlasting." (Psalm 90:2). In the Heaven where our spirits were born, there are many Gods, each one of whom has his own wife or wives which were given to him previous to his redemption, while yet in his mortal state. Each God, through his wife or wives, raises up a numerous family of sons and daughters; indeed, there will be no end to the increase of his own children: for each father and mother will be in a condition to multiply forever and ever. As soon as each God has begotten many millions of male and female spirits, and his Heavenly inheritance becomes too small, to comfortably accommodate his great family, he, in connection with his sons, organizes a new world, after a similar order to the one which we now inhabit, where he sends both the male and female spirits to inhabit tabernacles of flesh and bones. Thus each God forms a world for the accommodation of his own sons and daughters who are sent forth in their times and seasons, and generations to be born into the same. The inhabitants of each world are required to reverence, adore, and worship their own personal father who dwells in the Heaven which they formerly inhabited.

Orson Hyde   *10/6/1853*

JD 1:123-24; DN, 78 (10/27/1853)

Says one, "If an angel from heaven would descend and bear testimony that this work was of God, I would believe it. Why may I not receive the testimony of angels, as well as Joseph Smith or any other person? for God is no respecter of persons! If I could receive it, I would be satisfied then that the work is true." But let me here remark again - suppose the Omnipotent Jehovah, that sits upon His throne of glory and power, was to descend and bear testimony, what further credence would you then want? You would want some one to tell you that it was really God Himself that had visited you,

---

[143] Brigham Young later declared this doctrine to be false.

that you might be satisfied it was not an angel of darkness in the similitude of a heavenly personage. *Remember that God, our heavenly Father, was perhaps once a child, and mortal like we ourselves,* and rose step by step in the scale of progress, in the school of advancement; has moved forward and overcome, until He has arrived at the point where He now is. "Is this really possible?" Why, my dear friends, how would you like to be governed by a ruler who had not been through all the vicissitudes of life that are common to mortals? If he had not suffered, how could he sympathise with the distress of others? If he himself had not endured the same, how could he sympathise and be touched with the feelings of our infirmities? He could not, unless he himself had passed through the same ordeal, and overcome step by step. If this is the case, it accounts for the reason why we do not see Him - He is too pure a being to show himself to the eyes of mortals; He has overcome, and goes no more out, but He is the temple of my God, and is a pillar there.

Franklin D. Richards   *12/10/1853*

MS 15:801-03

Without [the Fall] they could not have known good and evil here, and without knowing good and evil they could not *become Gods*, neither could their children. No wonder the woman was tempted when it was said unto her - `Ye shall be as gods, knowing good and evil.' No wonder Father Adam fell, and accompanied the woman, sharing in all the miseries of the curse, that he might be the father of an innumerable race of beings who would be capable of *becoming Gods*.

With these considerations before us, we can begin to see how it is that we are under obligations to our father Adam, as to a God. He endured the sufferings and the curse that we might be; and we are, that we might *become Gods*. Through him the justice of God was made manifest. Jesus came into the world, endured, and suffered, to perfect our advantages for *becoming Gods*, and through him the mercy of God abounded. ...

In ancient times they were called Gods unto whom the word of God came, because of which Moses *became a God* unto Pharaoh. The Almighty was not so jealous of His Godly title but that He could say to Moses - `See I have made thee a God to Pharaoh.' And if John's saying be true, God has purposed to make him that overcometh, a pillar in the temple of God, and to `write upon him the name of my God.' `His name shall be in their foreheads.' ...

In the Patriarchal order of government, each and every ruler is independent in his sphere, his rule extending to those below, and not to those above him, in the same order. While the God of unnumbered worlds is acknowledged to be his God and Father, Adam still maintains his exalted position at the head of all those who are saved from among the whole family of man; and he will be God over all *those who are made Gods from among men.*

Brigham Young   *9/17/1854*

Journal of Wilford Woodruff

He said that the doctrine taught in the Seer that God had arrived at that state whereby he could not advance any further in knowledge, power & glory was a false doctrine & not true. That there never will be a time to all eternity when all the Gods of eternity will cease advancing in power, knowledge, experience & glory, for if this was the case, eternity would cease to be & the glory of God would come to an end, but all of the celestial beings will continue to advance in knowledge & power, worlds without end. Joseph would always be ahead of us, we should never catch up with him in all eternity nor he with his leaders. Brother Pratt also thought that Adam was made of the dust of the earth. Could not believe that Adam was our God or the Father of Jesus Christ. President Young said that He came from another world & made this. Brought Eve with him, partook of the fruits of the earth, begat children & they were earthly & had mortal bodies & if we were faithful, *we should become Gods as He was.*

Brigham Young   *Friday 10/6/1854*

Diary, Joseph Lee Robinson, 102-03

Adam and Eve were the names of the first man and woman of every earth that was ever organized. And that Adam and Eve were the natural Father and Mother of every spirit that comes to this planet or that receives tabernacles on this planet. Consequently we are brothers and sisters. And that Adam was God our Eternal Father.

Brigham Young   *Sunday 10/8/1854*

MABY

Now if you believe what you have heard me say you will believe that there is lords many, and gods many; and you will believe that unto us, the inhabitants of this Earth there is but one God with whom we have to do; and according to the tenor of the Bible, we believe that there are many, very many who have entered into Power, Glory, Might, and Dominion, and are gathering around them Thrones, and have power to organize elements, and make worlds, and bring into existence intelligent beings in all their variety, who if they are faithful and obedient to their calling and creation *will in their turn be exalted in Eternal Kingdoms of the Gods.*

Brigham Young   *Sunday 10/8/1854*

MABY

Man was not made the same as you make an adobe and put in a wall. Moses said that *Adam* was made of the dust of the ground, but he did not say of what ground. I say he was not made of the dust of the ground of this Earth, but he was made of the dust of the earth *where he lived, where he honored his calling, believed in his Saviour, or Elder Brother, and by his faithfulness was redeemed, and obtained a Glorious Resurrection.*

| Brigham Young | Sunday 10/8/1854 |

MABY

Those who keep this their second estate, and do honor to their being, and answer the design of their creation, shall be exalted to inhabit the earth, and live upon it when it shall be Celestial, and brought back into the presence of God, there to dwell forever and ever. ... [T]he *Elders of Israel will be exalted among the Gods.*

| Orson Pratt | circa 1854 |

The Seer, 23

The Gods who dwell in the Heaven from which our spirits came, *are beings who have been redeemed from the grave* in a world which existed before the foundations of this earth were laid. They and the Heavenly body which they now inhabit, *were once in a fallen state.*

| Brigham Young | 3/25/1855 |

Journal of Samuel W. Richards 2:215

Priesthood is the Principle by which *all beings have become Gods, or will become Gods,* they must follow the principles of government as revealed in the Priesthood.

| Franklin D. Richards | 3/31/1855 |

MS 17:194-95

Priesthood is unlimited, being "without beginning of days or end of years." *It includes all the great truths and principles of the Godhead.* ... When the Melchisedek Priesthood is bestowed upon man, it endows him with the *power to learn practically those things which exalt the Gods,* and which will fit him for their society. ...

| Orson Pratt & Brigham Young | 5/6/1855 |

Journal of Wilford Woodruff

I attended the Prayer-Circle where I had some interesting teaching from President Young in social conversation which was not reported. ...

O. Pratt asks *will Adam or any God continue to make worlds, people them, taste of death to redeem them* - Answer: I have no doubt but it is his privilege but whether He [Orson Pratt] will do it is a question in my mind. How then can his seed increase to all eternity through the increase of his posterity.

Brigham Young & Orson Pratt   *3/11/1856*

Journal of Samuel W. Richards, 113

A very serious conversation took place between President B. Young and Orson Pratt upon doctrine. O. P. was directly apposed to the President's views and very freely expressed his entire disbelief in them after being told by the President that things were so and so in the name of the Lord. He was firm in the position that the President's word in the name of the Lord, was not the word of the Lord to him. The President *did not believe that Orson Pratt would ever be Adam,* to learn by experience the facts discussed, *but every other, person in the room would be* if they lived faithful.

Brigham Young   *2/8/1857*

JD 4:217-19

Thus you may continue and trace the human family back to Adam and Eve, and ask, are we of the same species with Adam and Eve? Yes, every person acknowledges this; this comes within the scope of our understanding. But when we arrive at that point, a veil is dropped, and our knowledge is cut off. Were it not so, you could trace back your history to the Father of our spirits in the eternal world. He is a being of the same species as ourselves; He lives as we do, except the difference that we are earthly, and He is heavenly. He has been earthly, and is of precisely the same species of being that we are. ...

Now to the facts in the case; all the difference between Jesus Christ and any other man that ever lived on the earth, from the days of Adam until now, is simply this, *the Father, after He had once been in the flesh, and lived as we live,* obtained His exaltation, attained to thrones, gained the ascendancy over principalities and powers, and had the knowledge and power to create - to bring forth and organize the elements upon natural principles. This He did after His ascension, or His glory, or His eternity, and was actually classed with the Gods, with the beings who create, with those who have kept the celestial law while in the flesh, and again obtained their bodies. Then He was prepared to commence the work of creation, as the scriptures teach. It is all here in the Bible; I am not telling you a word but what is contained in that book. Things were first created spiritually; the Father actually begat the spirits, and they were brought forth and lived with Him. Then He commenced the work of creating earthly tabernacles, precisely as He had been created in this flesh himself, by partaking of the course material that was organized and composed this earth, until His system was charged with it, consequently the tabernacles of His children were organized from the course materials of this earth.

Mary Ellen A. Kimball   *2/18/1857*

Mary Ellen A. Kimball journal

President Young thought none would inherit this earth when it became celestial and translated into the presence of God, but *those who would be crowned as Gods* and able to endure the fulness of the presence of God, except they might be permitted to take with them some servants for whom they would be held responsible. All others would have to inherit another kingdom, even that kingdom agreeing with the law which they had kept.

Brigham Young   *3/8/1857*

JD 4:271

If you look at things spiritually, and then naturally, and see how they appear together, you will understand that when you have the privilege of commencing the work that Adam commenced on this earth, you will have all your children come and report to you of their sayings and acts; and you will hold every son and daughter of yours responsible *when you get the privilege of being an Adam on earth*.

Brigham Young   *1/27/1860*

Wilford Woodruff Journal

There never was a time or eternity but what a God did exist and a God that had children upon the same principle that children are now begotten, and I was begotten by the God I worship who reigns in the heavens and *I shall also in my turn reign as a God & so will you. ...*

We commonly call our future estate heaven, so you are their Heavenly Father, and Mother, their Heavenly Mother, and all this by obedience to law, notwithstanding *you have become a Heavenly Father,* you still have a Heavenly Father, whom you love more and more each day as you grow in knowledge and advance in experience, and even your Heavenly Father had a Heavenly Father, and so we might continue, or, as is expressed in a hymn:

"If you could high to Kolob in the twinkling of an eye,

And then continue onward, with that same speed to fly,

Do you think you could ever, through all eternity.

Find out the generation, where Gods began to be,

Now an age to eternity has rolled by, and we see you surrounded by an innumerable host of spiritual children, and these are your children, the children or kingdom over which you will preside forever.

You have read the parable Jesus spoke, how the Father would visit his sons each in their hour, looking thus far into the future, we see your Heavenly Father (the Heavenly

Grand-father of your spiritual children) visiting with you and your family, and in the course of the visit, we fancy we hear him saying to you, My son you have a beautiful family here; we commend you for your integrity; we will now call you to a higher calling in the Priesthood, and confer upon you power and authority whereby *you may organize an earth for these your spiritual children to dwell upon*, that they may also tabernacle in the flesh, and become like unto us. See yonder is space unoccupied and here are materials - go to and organize them into an earth, like unto the other earths that have heretofore been organized, and when you have done this bring me word, for I am with you always. Again, *this to you is a new experience but to your heavenly Father it is not.*

Orson Pratt   *7 p.m. 4/4/1860*

Minutes of Meeting, at Historian's Office
I would like to enumerate items, firstly - preached & publish, that Adam is the fa[ther] of our spirits, & father of Spirit & father of our bodies - When I read the Rev given to Joseph I read directly the opposite - *Lord spake to Adam, which w Man eventually became Adam's.*

Heber C. Kimball   *6/12/1860*

JD 8:243-44
We often sing, "This earth was once a garden place," where God our Father dwelt, and took possession and *a stand that mankind will take who attain to that honor.*

Brigham Young   *10/14/1860*

JD 8:208
Many of the sisters grieve because they are not blessed with offspring. You will see the time when you will have millions of children around you. If you are faithful to your covenants, you will become mothers of nations. *You will become Eves to earths like this*; and when you have assisted in peopling one earth there are millions of earths still in the course of creation. And when they have endured a thousand million times longer than this earth, it is only as it were the beginning of your creations. Be faithful, and if you are not blessed with children in this time, you will hereafter. But I would not dare tell you all I know about these matters.

Brigham Young   *7/14/1861*

The Essential Brigham Young, 138
What, is it possible that the Father of Heights, *the Father of our spirits*, could reduce himself and come forth like a man? Yes, *he was once a man like you and I are* and was once on an earth like this, passed through the ordeal you and I pass through. He had his

father and his mother and he has been exalted through his faithfulness, and he is become Lord of all. He is the God pertaining to this earth. He is our Father. He begot our spirits in the spirit world. They have come forth and our earthly parents have organized tabernacles for our spirits and here we are today. That is the way we came.

W. W. Phelps et al. a.m. 10/8/1861

James Beck Journal

If faithfull *a Man will attain to an Adam & the Wife to be an Eve* & begat Millions of Spirits who will come forth & receive their Tabernacles upon an earth like this &c - The glory of the Man is the woman, And the glory of the woman is her Virginity - Men are the Lords of Creation & the Responsibility rests upon the man & not upon the woman - all women will be saved after they have suffered & atoned for their sins & thus satisfied the ends of Justice they will not become angels to the Devil.

Brigham Young a.m. 10/8/1861

Antoine W. Ivins Journal 13:109

I wish to say to my young sisters, if you can go into the hands of a man, that will lead you into the Kingdom of Heaven, and *exalt you there to become an Eve - a Queen of Heaven - the wife of a God*; if you can remain with that man [in] whom your soul delights, and you take to him your virginity, you have obtained a treasure that millions of worlds like this [one] could not buy from you - there is your glory to all eternity. Trifle with this matter, and you will reap sorrow and sore affliction. When you make your choice of a husband for time and eternity, and you are sure you have got your choice, hang on to him.

Brigham Young 2/23/1862

JD 9:286

The idea that the Lord our *God* is not a personage of tabernacle is entirely a mistaken notion. He *was once a man. ... He once possessed a body, as we now do*; and our bodies are as much to us, as his body to him.

Brigham Young 3/6/1862

JD 9:243

Refuse evil, choose good, hate iniquity, love truth. All this our fathers have done before us; I do not particularly mean father Adam, or his Father; I do not particularly mean Abraham, or Moses, the Prophets, of Apostles, but I mean our fathers who have been exalted for millions of years previous to Adam's time. *They have all passed through the same ordeals we are now passing through,* and have searched all things, even to the depths of hell.

Brigham Young   *11/30/1862*

MABY

[E]ach person who we crown in the celestial kingdom of God *will be a* father of fathers, a king of kings, a lord of lords, a *god of gods* ... Each person will reign over his posterity. Adam, Michael, the Ancient of Days, will sit as the judge of the quick and dead, for he is the father of all living, and Eve is the mother of all living, pertaining to the human family, and he is their king, their Lord, their God, taking and holding his position in the grand unbroken chain of endless increase, and eternal progression.

Brigham Young   *11/6/1864*

JD 10:355

And the Lord administered comfort unto Adam, and said unto him: I have set thee to be at the head - a multitude of nations shall come of thee, and thou art a prince over them forever.[144] So, in like manner, *every faithful son of God, becomes, as it were, Adam* to the race that springs from his loins, when they are embraced in the covenants and blessings of the Holy Priesthood; and in the lapse of eternity, and in the progress of eternal lives, every true son of God becomes a king of kings, and a lord of lords, and it may also be said of him, as it was written of Jesus Christ, "Of the increase of his government and peace there shall be no end."

Brigham Young   *8/12/1866*

JD 11:262

The kingdoms he possesses and rules over are his own progeny. *Every man who is faithful* and gets a salvation and glory, and becomes a King of kings and Lord of lords, or a Father of fathers; it will be by the increase of his own progeny, Our Father and God rules over his own children. *Wherever there is a God* in all the eternities possessing a kingdom and glory and power *it is by means of his own progeny*.

Brigham Young   *5/12/1867*

Journal of Wilford Woodruff

President Young said there never was any world created & peopled nor never would be but what would be redeemed by the shedding of the blood of the savior of that world. If we are ever exalted and crowned in the presence of God *we shall become saviors of a world which we shall create & people*. I know why the Blood of Jesus was shed, I know why

---

[144] D&C 107:53.

the blood of Joseph & Hiram & others have been shed and the blood of others will be shed it is all to answer a purpose and has its effect Adam made this world and suffered himself to take a body and descending below all things we cannot ascend above all things.

Brigham Young	*6/30/1867*

JD 12:97

If you are not sanctified and prepared, you ought to be sanctifying and preparing yourselves for the blessings in store for you *when it will be said of you, this is Mother Eve.* Why? *Because you are the mother of all living.* You might as well prepare first as last. *If you wish to be Eves* and mothers of human families, you ought to bear the burden.

Orson Pratt	*11/10/1867*

Journal of Wilford Woodruff

O Pratt said that he did not worship attributes aside from the personage of God, but believed that God was an organized Being the same as man and that man possessed the attributes of God & *would become a God if he kept the celestial law.*

Brigham Young	*1869*

MS 31:267

Before me I see a house full of Eves. What a crowd of reflections the word Eve is calculated to bring up! Eve was the name or title conferred upon our first mother, because she was actually to be the mother of all the human beings who should live upon this earth. I am looking upon a congregation designed to be just such beings.

Brigham Young	*Saturday p.m. 8/24/1872*

JD 15:137

In the resurrection, *men who have been faithful* and diligent in all things in the flesh, have kept their first and second estate, and *worthy to be crowned Gods,* even the sons of God, will be ordained to organize matter. How much matter do you suppose there is between here and some of the fixed stars[145] which we can see? Enough to frame many, very many millions of such earths as this, yet it is now so diffused, clear and pure, that we look through it and behold the stars.

---

[145] As an interesting side note - scientists have only recently discovered, relatively speaking, that there is a significant amount of matter in space - in places where they previously believed no matter existed - they refer to it as "dark matter" because they cannot see it - they have only been able to prove it exists because it bends light.

Brigham Young   *Sunday p.m. 6/8/1873*

DN 22:308

The Christian world read of, and think much about, St. Paul, also St. Peter, the chief of the Apostles. *These men* were faithful to and magnified the priesthood while on the earth. Now, where will be the mystery, after they have passed through all the ordeals, and have been crowned and exalted, and received their inheritances in the eternal worlds of glory, for *them to be sent forth, as the Gods have been for ever and ever*, with the command - "Make yourselves an earth and people it with your own children?" ... Do you think that God, who holds the eternities in his hands and can do all things at his pleasure, is not capable of sending forth his own children, and forming this flesh for his own offspring? Where is the mystery in this? We say that Father Adam came here and helped to make the earth. Who is he? He is Michael, a great prince, and it was said to him by Eloheim, : Go ye and make an earth." What is the great mystery about it?

Brigham Young   *Sunday a.m. 7/19/1874*

JD 17:143

As for their labor and pursuits in eternity I have not time to talk upon that subject; but we shall have plenty to do. We shall not be idle. *We shall go on from one step to another,* reaching forth into the eternities *until we become like the Gods,* and shall be able to frame for ourselves, by the bequest and command of the Almighty. All those who are counted worthy to be *exalted and to become Gods*, even the sons of God, will go forth and have earths and worlds like those who framed this and millions on millions of others. This is our home, built expressly for us by the Father of our spirits, who is the Father, maker, framer and producer of these mortal bodies that we now inherit, and which go back to mother earth.

Brigham Young   *10/8/1876*

JD 18:258-59

Spirits were begotten, born and educated in the celestial world, and were brought forth by celestial bodies. These spirits I shall leave for the present, and refer to our first parents, Adam and Eve, who were found in the Garden of Eden, tempted and overcome by the power of evil, and consequently subject to evil and sin, which was the penalty of their transgression. They were now prepared, as we are, to form bodies or tabernacles for the reception of pure and holy spirits ...

[T]hen will *they become gods*, even the sons of God; then will they become eternal fathers, eternal mothers, eternal sons and eternal daughters; being eternal in their organization, they go from glory to glory, from power to power; they will never cease to increase and to multiply world's without end. When they receive their crowns, their dominions, they then will be prepared to frame earth's like unto ours and to people them in the same manner as we have been brought forth by our parents, by our Father and God.

The Lecture at the Veil   *Tuesday 2/7/1877*

Journal of L. John Nuttall

Adam was an immortal being when he came. On this earth he had lived on an earth similar to ours he had received the Priesthood and the Keys thereof. and had been faithful in all things and gained his resurrection and his exaltation and was crowned with glory immortality and eternal lives and *was numbered with the Gods for such he became through his faithfulness. a*nd had *begotten all the spirit* that was to come to this earth. and *Eve our common Mother who is the mother of all living bore those spirits* in the celestial world. And when this earth was organized by Elohim. Jehovah & Michael who is Adam our common Father. Adam & Eve had the privilege to continue the work of Progression. consequently came to this earth and commenced the great work of forming tabernacles for those spirits to dwell in.

Shortened Lecture at the Veil   *between 1877-1894*

He had been true and faith in all things and gained his resurretin and exaltation. He was crowned ~~in which~~ with glory, immortality and eternal lives and was numbered with the Gods - *for such he became through his faithfulness.*

He had begotten all the spirits that was to come to/this earth, and Eve, our common mother - who is the mother of all living - bore our spirits in the celestial world. And when this earth was organized by Elohim, Jehovah and Michael - who is Adam our common father - Adam and Eve had the privilege to continue the work of progression. They consequently came to this earth and commenced the great work of forming tabrnacles for those spirits to dwell in, and when Adam and those who assisted him had completed this kingdom which is our earth, he came to it and slept and forgot all become like a little child.

Edward Tullidge   *3/--/1877*

Women of Mormondom, 180, 181, 192-93

These [Adam & Eve] were father and mother of a world of spirits who had been born to them in heaven. These spirits had been waiting for the grand period of their probation, when they should have bodies or tabernacles, so that *they might become, in the resurrection, like Gods.* ...

The Gods are the fathers and the mothers, and the brothers and the sisters, of the saints. Divine ambitions here; a daring genius to thus conceive; a lifting up of man and woman to the very plane of the celestials while yet on - earth. ...

Woman is heiress of the Gods. She is joint heir with her elder brother, Jesus the Christ; but she inherits from her God-Father and her God-Mother. Jesus is the "beloved" of that Father and Mother - their well-tried Son, chosen to work out the salvation and exaltation of the whole human family. And shall it not be said then that the subject rises from the God-Father to the God-Mother? Surely it is a rising in the sense of the culmination of the divine idea. The God-Father is not robbed of his everlasting glory by this maternal completion of himself. It is an expansion both of deity and humanity. They twain are one God! The supreme Unitarian conception is here; the God-Father and the God-Mother! The grand unity of God is in them - in the divine Fatherhood and the divine Motherhood - the very beginning and consummation of creation. Not in the God-Father and the God-Son can the unity of the heavens and the earths be worked out; neither with any logic of facts nor of idealities. In them the Masonic trinities; in the everlasting Fathers and the everlasting Mothers the unities of creations. Our Mother in heaven is decidedly a new revelation, as beautiful and delicate to the masculine sense of the race as it is just and exalting to the feminine.

7/--/1877

MS 39:486

When man learns the truth of the matter he will understand the relation which he bears to God and God to him, and will know the one to be the parent of the other, the literal progenitor; and when man perceives the relation existing between God and this world he will comprehend that *Jehovah*, the organizer of this world, *was once*, long , long ages back, in eternity which lies behind us, a man, *passing, as we are now passing, through an earth-life, on one of the older planets*. He will understand that *Jehovah, during those probationary days of earth-life*, made the pursuit of truth, eternal, immutable truth, the aim of all his efforts. Reflection teaches him that the perception of truth, or the knowledge which Jehovah gained day by day, was just so much power gained day by day; and we see, in this world, the created results of that power gained by the law of progression.

Eliza R. Snow   *1877*

The Ultimatum of Human Life

Obedience will the same bright garland weave,
As it has done for your great Mother, Eve,
For all her daughters on the earth, who will
All my requirements sacredly fulfill.

And what to Eve, though in her mortal life,
She'd been the first, the tenth, or fiftieth wife?
What did she care, when in her lowest state,
Whether by fools, consider'd small, or great?
'Twas all the same with her - *she prov'd her worth -*
She's now the Goddess and the Queen of Earth.

Life's ultimatum, unto those that live
As saints of God, and all my pow'rs receive;
Is still the onward, upward course to tread -
To stand as Adam and as Eve, the head
Of an inheritance, a new-form'd earth,
And to their spirit race, give mortal birth -
Give them experience in a world like this;

Then lead them forth to everlasting bliss,
Crown'd with salvation and eternal joy
Where full perfection dwells, without alloy.

C. W. Staynor   *Sunday p.m. 5/25/1879*
JD 20:210
He taught him [Joseph Smith] how *the people who dwelt on the earth might also be thus
exalted to be angels of god, and finally gods themselves*; How they could scale the ladder of
intelligence, step by step, till they finally overcome all evil, and sat down at the right
hand of the majesty on high.

Scott Anderson   *9/22/1884*
Letter to Pres. John Taylor, SLC
If I could so conduct myself in this stage of action, to be worthy of the celestial
kingdom with eternal increase, then and only *then, would I gain an inheritance of my own
to be as a Father Adam, and my wife, a mother Eve.*

J.F. Gibbs   *11/--/1884*
Contributor 6:76-78
Having, while on earth complied with the requirements of the Father in relation to
Celestial Marriage, he is thus qualified to become a "Father of spirits," and his immortal
wives become the mothers of spirits, thus obeying the only and eternal law of
reproduction. ... *he is placed upon it* [the world] *and with his wives repeats the history of man*

on this and other planets. The Being that has organized the world; and placed upon it the germs of animated nature; is the one most entitled to furnish mortal bodies for his spiritual children.

And when the great drama of life is finished and he with his children are redeemed and glorified, *is he not entitled, as the head of an innumerable posterity, to be recognized as a Father and God to those that will rise up and call Him blessed?* Is there anything inconsistent or unphilosophic in the doctrine that eternal progression will eventually *exalt human beings to the godhead?* The reverse would be illogical, no other reason for man's existence can be adduced. In this way only can he be of service in increasing the glory of his Father and God to whom forever he will be a grateful and venerating son and subject.

Wilford W. Woodruff   *6/11/1892*

Journal of Wilford Woodruff

The Lecture at the veil is true. Procreation is the gift of Eternal Lives, and if we are faithful *we shall create worlds and people them just as Adam has done.*

Orson F. Whitney   *6/9/1895*

Divine Evidences of Truthfulness, Y.M.M.I.A. Annual Conference

Mormonism ... teaches men that *they can become divine, that man is God in embryo, that God was once man in mortality,* and that the only difference between Gods, angels and men is a difference in education and development. Is such a religion to be sneered at? ... It teaches that these worlds are peopled with human beings, God's sons and daughters, and that *every husband and father, may become an Adam, and every wife and mother an Eve,* to some future planet.

Lorenzo R. Snow   *Sunday 9/18/1898*

Unchangeable Love of God

That exalted position was made manifest to me at a very early day. I had a direct revelation of this. It was most perfect and complete. If there ever was a thing revealed to man perfectly, clearly, so that there could be no doubt or dubiety, this was revealed to me, and it came in these words: "*As man now is, God once was; as God now is, man may be.*" This may appear to some minds as something very strange and remarkable, but it is in perfect harmony with the teachings of Jesus Christ and with His promises.

A. T. Schreader, ed. [anti-Mormon]   *1898-1900*

Zion-Lucifer's Lantern 4:65

If I can get any intelligent idea of the after life of mormons by the study of there inane sermons it is something like this: ...

To this world *the resurrected man* now [sic] himself and by virtue of the "sealing power" of the Mormon priesthood all the women who have been "sealed" to him for eternity are attracted or transplanted to this same planet. Here *they set up* housekeeping *as Adam did in the Garden of Eden*, and they will live eternal lives unless some walking or talking snake should put up a jot on them as it did on Eve. *To this world of his own creation the man will be the God,* even as Adam in Mormon theology is the God of this world. He is the King and his wives queens. Their kingdom will consist of their own "eternal progeny."

First Presidency	*11/--/1909*

MFP 4:199-206

God Himself is an exalted man, perfected, enthroned, and supreme. ...
Man is the child of God, formed in the divine image and endowed with divine attributes, and even as the infant son of an earthly father and mother is capable in due time of becoming a man, so the undeveloped offspring of celestial parentage is capable, by experience through ages and aeons, of *evolving into a God.*

Joseph E. Robinson	*4/--/1912*

General Conference

So the Prophet Joseph Smith, in this age, has added to this truth by the assertion that "*As man is God once was, and that as He is man may became,*" because He is our Father, and like begets like, and inherent within us are the attributes of divinity that shall lead us into perfection, which Christ intended His Saints to attain unto.

Bishop Heber Bennion	*1920*

Supplement to Gospel Problems, 8-9

It seems strange that people will believe that ʻas man now is, God once was, and that as God now is, man may be;ʼ that ʻGod is an exalted manʼ and still repudiate the Doctrine of Adam God. ... It seems presumptuous indeed for them to ever *aspire to be the God* of anything, if Adam cannot be the God of the world He created and peopled. If a man is not to become the God of His own posterity, what will he be the God of? ... The whole superstructure for a plurality of the Gods is based upon this doctrine of Adam God, and must stand or fall together.

William Cadman	

Faith and Doctrines of the Church of Jesus Christ, 16

Joseph Smith taught a worse doctrine than the Devil did in the Garden of Eden. The Devil only taught that men should be as gods. But *Joseph taught that men could be gods.*

George Q. Cannon
_____

Gospel Truth 1:25

[re: Abraham 3:24-26]

It was necessary that a probation should be given to man. The courts of heaven were thronged with spirits that desired tabernacles. *They wanted to come and obtain fleshy tabernacles as their Father had done.* Their progenitors, the race of Gods with whom they associated and from whom they have descended, had had the privilege of coming on earthly probations and receiving tabernacles, which by obedience they had been able to redeem. Hence, I say, the courts of heaven were thronged with spirits anxious to take upon themselves tabernacles of flesh, agreeing to come forth and be tested and tried in order that they might receive exaltation.

Analysis & Observations
_____
β
_____

In a nutshell, this subsection essentially teaches the plan of salvation from an Adam-God perspective. After a successful mortal probation, an indeterminate time of progressing in light and knowledge upon the sphere on which one is resurrected, the successful individual qualifies to become an Adam or Eve upon an earth created expressly for that individual and where the cycle continues in another eternal round.

Bennion's 1855 quote is particularly noteworthy because it shows the mindset of the early saints in Utah. Beyond the many direct Adam-God quotations found above, there are many more statements regarding eternal progression to the godhead that have not been compiled for this volume. Heber Bennion essentially informs us that all of these statements would have been construed as Adam-God teachings even at this early date - 1855 - only three years after Adam-God teachings were publicly proclaimed for the first time.

22 The Creation: Modus Operandi

This subsection is rather broad in its content (and is far from exhaustive). I have included statements regarding the modus operandi of the creation of this earth and how it was replenished, the modus operandi of its history - both before its "creation" and after its fall from another orbit, and a few other items of general interest. They are included in this volume because most of these statements were taught in context of Adam-God teachings and because they offer us greater insight into the plan of salvation (broadly speaking) from an Adam-God perspective.

Joseph Smith   *1/5/1841*

TPJS, 181

This earth will be rolled *back* into the presence of God, and crowned with celestial glory.

Joseph Smith   *5/20/1842*

TPJS, 198

God has set many signs on the earth, as well as in the heavens; for instance, the oak of the forest, the fruit of the tree, the herb of the field, all bear a sign that seed hath been planted there; for it is a decree of the Lord that every tree, plant, and herb bearing *seed should bring forth of its kind, and cannot come forth after any other law* or principle.

Joseph Smith   *1840*

Journal of Wandle Mace, 39

Some of your brethren have been coming up the river on a steamboat, and while seated at the table, the steamboat runs against a snag which upsets the table and scatters the dishes; so it will be *when theses portions of earth return*. It will make the earth reel to and fro like a drunken man.[146]

Joseph Smith   *1/5/1841*

T&S 3:672

The earth *no longer retained its standing in the presence of Jehovah*; but was hurled into the immensity of space; and there to remain *till it has filled up the time of its bondage* to sin and Satan. It was immediately cursed, and Adam, and Eve were obliged to procure their food and raiment by the sweat of the brow. The beasts became ferocious, and went prowling about the wilderness seeking the inferior animals for a prey.

Joseph Smith   *circa 1840-1841*

The Journals of William Clayton, 513-15

The world and earth are not synonymous terms. The world is the human family. This earth was organized or *formed out of other planets which were broke up and remodelled* and made into the one on which we live. The elements are eternal. That which has a beginning will surely have an end. Take a ring, it is without a beginning or end; cut it for a beginning place, and at the same time you have an ending place.

A key, every principle proceeding from God is eternal, and any principle which is not eternal is of the Devil. The sun has no beginning or end; the rays which proceed from himself have no bounds, consequently are eternal. So it is with God. If the soul of man had a beginning it will surely have an end. In the translation, "without form and void" it should read "empty and desolate." The word "created" should be formed or organized.

Joseph Smith   *circa 1840-1841*

Journal of Samuel Holister Rogers, 17

When this world was first made *it was a tremendous big thing*. The Lord concluded it was *too big*. We read in the scriptures that in the days of Peleg the *earth was divided* so the Lord divided the earth When the ten tribes of the children of Israel went into the north country *he divided it again, so the earth has been divided and subdivided*.

Joseph Smith   *1/5/1841*

T&S 3:672

The earth no longer retained its standing in the presence of Jehovah; but was hurled into the immensity of space; and there to remain till it has filled up the time of its bondage to sin and Satan. It was immediately cursed, and Adam, and Eve were obliged

---

[146] Isaiah 24:20

to procure their food and raiment by the sweat of the brow. The beasts became ferocious, and went prowling about the wilderness seeking the inferior animals for a prey.

Parley P. Pratt   *2/--/1841*

MS 1:258

Some [fragments of the earth were broken off] in the days of Enoch, some perhaps in the days of Peleg, some with the ten tribes, and some at the crucifixion of the Messiah. … *When the fragments* (some of which are vastly larger than the present earth) *are brought back and joined to this earth*, it will cause a convulsion of all nature; the graves of the Saints will be opened, and they rise from the dead; while the mountains will flow down, the valley rise, the sea retire to its own place, the islands and continents will be removed, and earth be rolled together as a scroll. The earth *will be much larger* than it is now.

Hyrum Smith   *6/1/1842*

T&S 3:799-800

[One purpose of the Word of Wisdom is] to remove the beastly appetites, the murderous disposition and the vitiated taste of man; to restore his body to health, and vigour, promote peace between him and the brute creation, and as one of the little wheels in God's designs, to help regulate the great machinery, which shall eventually revolutionize the earth, and bring about the restoration of all things, and when they are restored he will plant "the tree of life, whose leaves shall be for the healing of the nations."

Joseph Smith   *before 6/27/1844*

Journal of Wandle Mace, 38-39

In the course of [Joseph's] remarks he spoke of t*he earth being divided at various times.* He said, "When Enoch and his City were taken away, *a portion of earth was taken and would again be restored.* Also in the days of Peleg, the earth was divided …" He then referred to the Ten Tribes, saying, "You know a long time ago in the days of Shalmaneser, king of Assyria, the Ten Tribes were taken away, and, have never been heard of since." He said, "The earth will be restored as at the beginning, and the last taken away will be the first to return, for the last shall be first, and the first shall be last in all things." … These remarks satisfied me, it was no longer necessary to hunt the place on this earth where the Ten Tribes were so long hidden, for the earth was divided and taken away, and will be the first to return, as it was the last taken away.

Joseph Smith

Journal of Wandle Mace, 48

[W]hen Enoch and his City was taken away, a portion of earth was taken and would again be restored.

Brigham Young   *1849*

WJS, 84

[Brigham Young] gave it as his opinion that *the Earth did not dwell in the sphere in which it did when it was created, but that it was banished* from its more glorious state or orbit or revolution for man's sake.

Orson Pratt   *3/--/1850*

MS 12:69

The earth, like the posterity of Adam, was cursed because of the original sin, and like them, it will be redeemed unconditionally, and restored again into the presence of God. So far as the original sin is concerned, mankind and the earth keep pace with each other. When one falls the other falls also. When one is redeemed, the other is redeemed also. Had there been no other sin but that of Adam's, the redeemed earth would have become the eternal abode of all the posterity of Adam, without one exception. But both man and the earth have been still further corrupted by other sins. The posterity of Adam have transgressed the code of laws given since the fall, and subjected themselves to its penalty.

Brigham Young   *Saturday 11/26/1853*

MS 14:356

They [the gods] came here, organized the raw material, and arranged in their order the herbs of the field, the trees, the apple, the peach, the plum, the pear, and every other fruit that is desirable and good for man; *the seed was brought from another sphere, and planted in this earth.* The thistle, and thorn, the brier, and the obnoxious weed did not appear until after the earth was cursed.

Orson Pratt   *circa 1853*

JD 1:332-33

In the resurrection, the meek of all ages and nations will be restored to that portion of the earth previously promised to them. And thus, all the different portions of the earth have been and will be disposed of to the lawful heirs; while those who cannot prove their heirship to be legal, or who cannot prove that they have received any portion of the earth by promise, will be cast out into some other kingdom or world, where, if they ever get an inheritance, they will have to earn it by keeping the law of meekness during another probation. How great will be the disappointment to the rich, the high and the noble, who have rejected the messages of eternal truth, sent forth in different ages for the redemption of men, when they find that here is not a foot of the new earth that they can call their own; the whole of it having been lawfully disposed of to the poor and the meek.

Orson Hyde   *10/6/1854*

JD 2:79-80

The Lord said unto them, "Multiply and replenish the earth." ... The earth, you remember, was void and empty, until our first parents began at the garden of Eden. What does the term replenish mean? This word is derived from the Latin; "re" and "plenus;" "re" denotes *repetition*, iteration; and "plenus" signifies *full*, complete; then the meaning of the word replenish is, to *refill, recomplete*. If I were to go into a merchant's store, and find he had got a new stock of goods, I should say - "You have replenished your stock, that is, filled up your establishment, for it looks as it did before." "Now go forth," says the Lord, "and replenish the earth; for it was covered with gloomy clouds of darkness, excluded from the light of heaven, and darkness brooded upon the face of the deep. *The world was peopled before the days of Adam*, as much so as it was before the days of Noah. It was said that Noah became the father of a new world, but it was the same old world still, and will continue to be, though it may pass through many changes.

When God said, Go forth and replenish the earth; it was to replenish the inhabitants of the human species, and make it as it was before. Our first parents, then, were commanded to multiply and replenish the earth; and if the Savior found it his duty to be baptized to fulfil all righteousness, a command of far less importance than that of multiplying his race, (if indeed there is any difference in the commandments of Jehovah, for they are all important, and all essential,) would he not find it his duty to join in with the rest of the faithful ones in replenishing the earth?

Brigham Young   *Sunday 10/8/1854*

John Pulsipher Papers, 37

[W]hen this work was made - our God who is Adam came & commenced the peopling of it - Tho he is God & had lived & died & been reserected on some other plannet - & obtained his exaltation & begat the Spirits of children enough people this world he came down & brot some of the animal & vegetable productions of some other world so that they might grow & increase here.

Brigham Young   *Sunday 10/8/1854*

MABY

We are made of the same matter, the same elements, we have sprung from one mother, Earth. Matter was brought together from the vast eternity that exists, and this terra firma upon which we stand was organized, then comes the world of mankind, the beast, fishes, fowls, and every living thing to dwell upon the Earth after its kind; and the vegetation of every kind to support animal life on it, until the organization of this world was perfected in all its variety; being brought from the eternity of matter, and prepared for intelligent beings to dwell upon, wherein to prepare themselves to dwell eternally in the presence of their Father and God. Those who keep this their second estate, and do honor to their being, and answer the design of their creation, shall be exalted to inhabit the earth, and live upon it when it shall be Celestial, and brought back into the presence of God, there to dwell forever and ever. … When Yahovah Michael had organized the world, and *brought from another kingdom the beasts, fish, fowl, and insects, and every tree, and plant with which we are acquainted, and thousands we never saw* - when He had filled the Earth with animal and vegetable life - Michael or Adam goes down to the new made world, and there he stays. … And I reckon that Adam came into the Garden of Eden, and did actually eat of the fruit that he himself planted.

Heber C. Kimball   *10/26/1854*

JD 2:160

God finds us and furnishes us with everything we have, with the breath we breathe, and the earth we stand upon, and the water that we drink. Do you make all these things? No, the Lord made them, and placed them here upon the earth for our use; He made the wheat and organized it; we have the seed. … Did you find the *seed*? No, you did not, the Lord found it; *when He came here He brought it with Him*, and He told His sons to sow it, and let it increase.

Orson Pratt   *circa 1854*

The Seer, 249

We are not to suppose that these elements, before they were collected, were formed into solid masses of rocks and other hard substances: and that these came rushing together - rocks being piled on rocks, breaking, crashing, and rending into millions of fragments. But no doubt through the operation of antecedent forces, there had been a complete disorganization or dissolution of the bodies, composed of these elements in that prior state or existence anterior to the foundation of the present globe: this being the case, the elements being separate, and apart, and widely diffused, were in a condition to come together in a state of particles, instead of aggregate masses. …

Jehovah spake - the elements came rushing together, not by their own power, but under the action of the self-moving forces of His Spirit ... every particle moving toward the great common center with a resultant force, varying inversely as the square of its distance from every other particle. They [modern philosophers] would have called it the law of gravitation: while those better acquainted with the origin of the force would have called it the law by which the Spirit of God moves together the particles of matter. ...

The Spirit of God in association with the elements, not only produces all the phenomena of gravitation, but also causes the elements to act upon each other, cohesively and chemically, when the particles are brought insensibly near to each other.

Brigham Young   *3/23/1856*

JD 3:277

There is not a particle or element which is not filled with life, and all space is filled with element. ... There is life in all matter, throughout the vast extent of all the eternities; it is in the rock, the sand, the dust, in water, air, the gasses, and in short, in every description and organization of matter.

Brigham Young   *4/20/1856*

JD 3:319-20

[Adam] *was the person who brought the animals and the seeds from other planets to this world,* and brought a wife with him and stayed here. ... Adam was made from the dust of an earth, but not from the dust of this earth. He was made as you and I are made, and no person was ever made upon any other principle. Do you not suppose that he was acquainted with *his associates who came and helped to make this earth*? Yes, they were just as familiar with each other as we are with our children and parents. Yet Enoch had to talk with and teach his people during a period of three hundred and sixty years, before he could get them prepared to enter into their rest, and then he obtained power to translate himself and his people, *with the region they inhabited, their houses, gardens, fields,* cattle, and all their possessions. *He had learned enough from Adam and his associates to* know how to handle the elements, and those who would not listen to his teachings were so wicked that they were fit to be destroyed, and he obtained power to take his portion of the earth and move out a little while, where he remains to this day.

Parley P. Pratt   *before 1857*

A Voice of Warning, 85, 86

When a Prophet speaks of the restoration of all things, he means that all things have undergone a change, and are to be again *restored to their primitive order*, even as they first existed. …

[E]verything that grew [in Eden] was just calculated for the food of man, beast, fowl, and creeping thing: and their food was all vegetable. Flesh and blood were never sacrificed, to glut their souls or gratify their appetites; the beast of the earth were all in perfect harmony with each other; the lion ate straw like the ox, the wolf dwelt with the lamb … all was peace and harmony, and nothing to hurt nor disturb in all the holy mountains,

Parley P. Pratt   *before 1857*

Key to Theology, 54-56; 1938 edition

A Royal Planter now descends from yonder world of older date, and bearing in his hand the *choice seeds of the older Paradise, he plants them* in the virgin soil of our new-born earth. They grow and flourish there, and bearing seed, replant themselves, and thus clothe the naked earth with scenes of beauty and the air with fragrant incense. Ripening fruits and herbs at length abound. When lo! from yonder world is *transferred every species of animal life.* Male and female, they come, with blessings on their heads, and a voice is heard again, "Be fruitful and multiply." Earth - its mineral, vegetable and animal wealth - its Paradise prepared, down comes from yonder world on high a son of God, with his beloved spouse. And thus a colony from heaven, it may be from the sun, is *transplanted on our soil.* The blessings of their Father are upon them, and the first great law of heaven and earth is again repeated, 'Be fruitful and multiply.'

Brigham Young   *3/15/1857*

Journal History

Now it is a pleasant thing to think of and to know where the Garden of Eden was. Did you ever think of it? I do not think many do, for in Jackson County was the Garden of Eden. Joseph has declared this, and I am as much bound to believe that as to believe that Joseph Smith was a prophet of God.

John Taylor   *8/20/1857*

The Mormon

[The earth had] fled and fallen from where it was organized near the planet Kolob.

Heber C. Kimball   *11/8/1857*

JD 6:36

Where did the earth come from? From its parent earths.

Brigham Young   *10/9/1859*
JD 7:285-86

This matter is organized into a world, with all its appendages, by whom? By the Almighty; and we see it peopled by men and women who are made in the image of God. All this vast creation was produced from element in its unorganized state; the mountains, rivers, seas, valleys, plains, and the animal, vegetable, and mineral kingdoms beneath and around us, all speaking forth the wonderful works of the Great God. *Shall I say that the seeds of vegetables were planted here by the Characters that framed and built this world - that the seeds of every plant composing the vegetable kingdom were brought from another world?* This would be news to many of you. Who brought them here? It matters little to us whether it was John, James, William, Adam, or Bartholomew who brought them; but it was some Being who had power to frame this earth with its seas, valleys, mountains, and rivers, and cause it to teem with vegetable and animal life.

Heber C. Kimball   *6/12/1860*
JD 8:243-44

After the earth was made, then there was a garden spot selected, and the Lord commanded some of his associates to go and plant it, and to cause all kinds of vegetation to grow, and fruits of every description. Some suppose the Lord commanded all these things to come out of the earth. Yes, he did, after the seeds were put in the earth; and he blessed the earth, and the vegetation that was in the earth. When all these things were done, the garden was beautified, and made pure and clean and holy and sanctified; and then the next thing was to bring forth the animal creation; but the animals were not brought there until the vegetation was planted and grown. We often sing, "This earth was once a garden place," where God our Father dwelt, and took possession and a stand that mankind will take who attain to that honour. The religion of Jesus Christ, of angels, of Brigham, and of all good men is to take care of and improve and adorn the earth as *Adam* did. *When he planted the garden, he planted it with seeds he brought with him; and he also brought the animals from the earth he lived upon where his Father dwelt.*

W. W. Phelps et al.   *a.m. 10/8/1861*
James Beck Journal

Also the two wings north & South of our earth were inhabited. the north with the 9-1/2 tribes & the south wing by the People of Enochs City - this Earth when first created occupied a Position next to Kolob the highest in glory of all the Creations consequently on account of the high Position we once occupied we have fallen below all of the others in space - consequently our sufferings are greater - the greater the rise the greater will be the fall[147] - when we are Redeemed we will be taken back again & Placed in our former Position.

Brigham Young   *7/13/1862*

Journal of Charles L. Walker, 233-34

[W]hen this world was *first made it was in a close proximity to God.* When man sinned *it was hurled millions of miles away* from its first position and *that was why it was called the Fall.*

Heber C. Kimball   *6/27/1863*

JD 10:235

[T]he Almighty sent Jehovah and Michael to do the work. *They* were also instructed to plant every kind of vegetable, likewise the forest and the fruit trees, and they actually *brought from heaven every variety of fruit, of the seeds of vegetables, the seeds of flowers, and planted them in this earth* on which we dwell. And I will say more, the spot chosen for the garden of Eden was Jackson County, in the State of Missouri, where Independence now stands; *it was occupied in the morn of creation by Adam and his associates who came with him for the express purpose of peopling this earth.* Father Adam was instructed to multiply and replenish the earth, to make it beautiful and glorious, to make it, in short, like unto *the garden from which the seeds were brought to plant the garden of Eden.*

I might say much more upon this subject, but I will ask, has it not been imitated before you in your holy endowments so that you might understand how things were in the beginning of creation and cultivation of this earth? God the Father made Adam the Lord of this creation in the beginning, and *if we are the Lords of this creation under Adam,* ought we not to take a course to imitate our Father in heaven? Is not all this exhibited to us in our endowments: the earth made glorious and beautiful to look upon, representing everything which the Lord caused to be prepared and placed to adorn the earth.

Brigham Young   *7/13/1865*

Wilford Woodruff Journal

This earth *when it fell went millions of miles from the presence of God and when it returns back,* it will go millions of miles from its present position to where it came from.

---

[147] This seems to indicate that each journey as an Adam/Eve will be more difficult than the last - as we will gain greater glory after each world of children is exalted, we must conclude (if W. W. Phelps' teaching here is true) that the subsequent fall, including its sufferings, will be greater as well.

Brigham Young   *9/8/1867*

Journal of Wilford Woodruff

We had social conversation in the evening. President Young said he heard Joseph Smith say that the Ten Tribes of Israel were on *a portion of land separated from this earth.*

Brigham Young   *7/24/1870*

JD 13:271

Who can tell us of the inhabitants of this little planet that shines of an evening, called the moon? When we view its face we may see what is termed "the man in the moon," and what some philosophers declare are the shadows of mountains. But these sayings are very vague, and amount to nothing; and when you inquire about the inhabitants of that sphere you find that the most learned are as ignorant in regard to them as the most ignorant of their fellows. *So it is with regard to the inhabitants of the sun. Do you think it is inhabited? I rather think it is. Do you think there is any life there? No question of it; it was not made in vain.* It was made to give light to those who dwell upon it, and to other planets; and so will this earth when it is celestialized. *Every planet in its first rude, organic state receives not the glory of God upon it, but is opaque; but when celestialized, every planet that God brings into existence is a body of light*, but not till then. Christ is the light of this planet.

Daniel Allen   *8/17/1872*

Minutes of the School of the Prophets, Parowan, 156-57

I heard Joseph the prophet say that he had seen John the Revelator and had a long conversation with him, who told him that he John was their leader, Prophet, Priest and King, and said that he was preparing that people to return and further said there is a mighty host of us. And Joseph further said that men might hunt for them but they could not find them for *they were upon a portion of this planet that had been broken off and which was taken away* and the sea rushed in *between Europe and America, and that when that piece returns there* would be a great shake; the sea would then move to the north where it belonged in the morning of creation.

Brigham Young   *Sunday p.m. 6/18/1873*

DN 22:308

He [Adam] came and formed the earth. ... Adam found [the earth] in a state of chaos, unorganized and incomplete. ... Adam came here and got it up in a shape that would suit him to commence business.

Brigham Young   *Sunday a.m. 7/19/1874*

JD 17:143

This earth is our home, it was framed expressly for the habitation of those who are faithful to God, and who prove themselves worthy to inherit the earth when the Lord shall have sanctified, purified and glorified it and brought it *back into his presence, from which it fell far into space*. ... When the earth was framed and brought into existence and man was placed upon it, *it was near the throne of our Father* in heaven. And when man fell - though that was designed in the economy, there was nothing about it mysterious or unknown to the Gods, they understood it all, it was all planned - but *when man fell, the earth fell into space*, and took up its abode in the planetary system, and the sun became our light.

When the Lord said - "Let there be light," there was light, for the earth was brought near the sun that it might reflect upon it so as to give us light by day, and the moon to give us light by night. This is the glory the earth came from, and when it is glorified it will return again unto the presence of the Father, and it will dwell there, and these intelligent beings that I am looking at, if they live worthy of it, will dwell upon this earth.

Orson Pratt   *Sunday 7/19/1874*

JD 17:147

[Enoch and his people,] having learned the doctrine of translation, were *caught up into the heavens*, the whole city, the people *and their habitations*.

Joseph Young, Jr.   *circa 1878*

DN

History of the Organization of the Seventies, 11, 12

The people, and the city, and the foundations of the earth on which it stood, had partaken so much of the immortal elements, bestowed upon them by God through the teachings of Enoch, that it became philosophically impossible for them to remain any longer upon the earth; consequently *Enoch and his people*, with the city which they occupied, and the foundations on which it stood, *with a large piece of earth immediately connected with the foundations and the city, had assumed an aerial position within the limits of our solar system*; and this in consequence of their faith. ... [Joseph also taught that] the *City of Enoch would again take its place in the identical spot from which it had been detached*, now forming that chasm of the earth, filled with water, called the Gulf of Mexico.[148]

---

[148] This teaching is interesting when considered in light of the Book of Jasher 9:29, which teaches that the tower of Babel was built so that the people could make war with the heavens. Apparently, the city of Enoch was still orbiting the earth! "...and it came to pass when they were building they cast the arrows

Orson Pratt	11/12/1879

JD 21:197-98, 200

Did the sons of God in ancient times, come forth and assist in the formation of this little creation of ours? Did they all shout for joy when the materials were brought together, and when the foundations of the earth were laid? Did they all feel happy and sing a song of rejoicing, and with great joy; did they look upon the works which they were performing? Yes. Jesus was there - the First Born of this great family of our Father in heaven. He had the superintendence of this creation. He had the power, because the power dwelt within him, to build this earth of ours, the same as you give to your superintendent power to build your temples, about which Brother Rich has been speaking. It is said that the worlds were made through our Lord Jesus Christ. But do you suppose that he alone made them? No; he had the sons and daughters of God with him. And there were prophets in those days, before our earth was made. They shouted for joy when they saw the nucleus of this creation formed. Why? Because they could look into the future, and by the spirit of prophecy, behold the designs and purposes of the great Jehovah in regard to the creation which they were then in the act of forming. Did they not understand that they would have the privilege of coming forth and peopling this earth? Yes. Did they not understand that they were to pass through a probation on this earth, the same as we are now passing through, in order to prepare them for a still higher exaltation and glory, with immortal bodies of flesh and bones? ... We learn, therefore, when speaking of this spiritual creation, that not only all the children of men, of all generations, and of all ages, were created spiritually in heaven, but that fish and fowls, and beast, and all animated things, having life, were first made spiritual in heaven, on the fifth and sixth days, before bodies of flesh were prepared for them on the earth.[149]

Addison Everett	10/18/1880

Journal of Charles L. Walker 2:505

[Joseph taught that] *the earth had been divided and parts taken away*, but the time would come when *all would be restored* and the earth again would revolve in its original orbit next to Kolob and would be second in size to it.

Charles L. Walker	circa 1880

toward the heavens, and all the arrows fell upon them filled with blood, and when they saw them they said to each other, Surely we have slain all those that are in heaven."

[149] See JD 3:277 in connection with these teachings - in light of these teachings, it seems that even the rocks were created spiritually.

Journal of Charles L. Walker
She [Eliza R. Snow] told me that she heard the Prophet Joseph say that when the 10 tribes were taken away the Lord cut the earth in two, Joseph striking his left hand in the center with the edge of his right to illustrate the idea and that they (the 10 tribes) *were on an orb or planet by themselves* and when they returned with *the portion of this earth that was taken away with them* the coming together of these 2 bodies or orbs would cause a shock and make the 'earth reel to and fro like a drunken man.' She also stated that he said t*he earth was now ninety times smaller now than when first created or organized.*

John Taylor   6/27/1881

JD 22:220
[I]f you possess any portion of this earth by right or title or authority, you will have to get it from God, and you will have to get it when the earth shall be renewed.

Thomas W. Brookbank   4/--/1887

Contributor 8:218 #6
Adam fell from the high estate in which he was once created. The loosing of the devil upon the earth for a 'little season' completes the parallel here. The earth, too, shall fall. Before Adam fell, he was a resurrected man, that is, his physical body had been disorganized, and then reorganized. The Apostle Peter tells us plainly that this earth is to be dissolved, after which a new world is to be organized. It will be resurrected as Adam was. Between the time of Adam's resurrection and his fall afterwards, he must have enjoyed a season of rest and peace. The Millennium which is to give the earth a rest for a thousand years, is the corresponding state in the world's history.

John Taylor   *before 1887*

The Gospel Kingdom, 102
Indeed, it was stated by the Prophet Joseph Smith, in our hearing, while standing on an elevated piece of ground or plateau near Adam-ondi-Ahman, where there were a number of rocks piled together, that the valley before us was the valley of Adam-ondi-Ahman; or in other words, the valley where God talked to Adam, and where he gathered his righteous posterity, as recorded in the above revelation,[150] and that this pile of stones was an altar built by him when he offered up sacrifices, as we understand, on that occasion.

Brigham H. Roberts   5/--/1889

---

[150] D&C 107:53-57.

Contributor 10:265-66

The Prophet Joseph Smith is credited with having said that *our planet was made up of the fragments of a planet* which previously existed; some mighty convulsions disrupted that creation and made it desolate. Both its animal and vegetable life forms were destroyed. And when those convulsions ceased, and the rent earth was again consolidated, and it became desirable to replenish it, the work was begun by making a mist to rise, that it might descend in gentle rain upon the barren earth, that it might again be fruitful. Then came one of the sons of God to the earth - Adam. A garden was planted in Eden and the man placed in it, and there the Lord brought to him every beast of the field and every fowl of the air, and Adam gave names to them all. ... We are informed that the Lord God made every plant of the field before it was in the earth, and every herb before it grew on our planet. As vegetation was created or *made to grow upon some older earth*, and the *seeds* thereof or the plants themselves *were brought to our earth* and made to grow, so likewise man and his helpmate were brought from some other world to our own, to people it with their children.

Bathsheba W. Smith	*6/1/1892*

Juvenile Instructor 27:344

[Joseph taught that p]eradventure, the *Ten Tribes were not on this globe, but a portion of this earth cleaved off with them*, went flying into space, and when the earth reels to and fro like a drunken man, and the stars from heaven fall, *it would join on again.*

Orson F. Whitney	*6/9/1895*

Divine Evidences of Truthfulness, Y.M.M.I.A. Annual Conference

Mormonism ... teaches that the worlds on high, *the stars that glitter* in the blue vault of heaven, are kingdoms of God, that they *were once earths like this*, that they have been redeemed and glorified by the same laws, the same principles that are applied to this planet, and by which it will ascend to a perfected and glorified state.

Lorenzo Snow	*8/24/1899*

MS :546

The whole earth is the Lord's. The time will come when it will be translated and be filled with the spirit of God. *The Atmosphere around it will be the spirit of the Almighty.* We will breathe that Spirit instead of the atmosphere we now breathe.

Benjamin F. Johnson	*7/1/1911*

Letter to George S. Gibbs

He [Joseph Smith] gave us to understand that *there were twelve kingdoms, or planets, revolving around our solar system, to which the Lord gave equal division of His time or ministry*; and now was his time to gain visit the earth.

Eliza R. Snow   *1912*

Sacred Hymns, 386 #323[151]

Thou, earth, wast once a glorious sphere
Of noble magnitude,
And didst with majesty appear,
Among the worlds of God.

*But thy dimensions have been torn
Asunder, piece by piece,
And each dismembered fragment borne
Abroad to distant space.*

When Enoch could no longer stay
Amid corruption here,
Part of thyself was borne away
To form another sphere.

That portion where his city stood
He gained by right approved;
And *nearer to the throne of God
His planet upward moved.*

And when the Lord saw fit to hide
The "ten lost tribes" away,
*Thou, earth, wast severed to provide
The orb on which they stay.*

---

[151] This poem was also published in MS 13:272 (9/1/1851). This appeared in the hymnal from 1856 (perhaps earlier - I have not verified any information beyond the fact that it was in hymnbooks between 1856 and 1912). It is amusing to consider what it would be like to sing a hymn like this in a modern meeting of the LDS Church - how would the saints react to such exoteric doctrine being sung in public?

And thus, from time to time, *thy size*
Has been diminished till
Thou seemest the law of sacrifice
Created to fulfill.

The curse of God on man was placed;
That curse thou didst partake,
And thou hast been by turns disgraced
And honored for his sake.

The vilest wretches hell will claim,
Now breathe thy atmosphere;
The noblest spirits heaven can name,
Have been embodied here.

Lord Jesus Christ, thy surface graced;
He fell a sacrifice;
And now within thy cold embrace
The martyred Joseph lies

When Satan's hosts are overcome,
The martyred princely race
Will claim thee, their celestial home -
Their royal dwelling place.

A "restitution" yet must come,
That will to thee restore,
By that grand law of worlds, *thy sum*
Of matter heretofore.

And thou, *O earth, will leave the track*
Thou hast been doomed to trace;
The Gods with shouts will bring thee back
To fill thy native place.

Joseph F. Smith   *1919*

Improvement Era 23:392-93

[On Genesis 1:27]

Thus the Lord has given us the information regarding his creations, and how he has made many earths, for there never was a beginning, never was a time when man did not exist somewhere in the universe, and when the time came for this earth to be peopled the Lord, our God, *transplanted* upon it from some other earth, *the life which is found here.* Man he created in his own image. If it were our privilege to go out and visit some of the other creations, other worlds in space, we should discover that they are peopled with beings who look like us, for they, too, are the offspring of God, and of the same race from whence we came. Perhaps they would be more exalted, but, nevertheless, they would be in the image of God, and so are we.[152]

Joseph Fielding Smith

Man, His Origin and Destiny, 276-77

[D]oes it not appear to you that it is a foolish and ridiculous notion that when God created this earth he had to begin with a speck of protoplasm, and take millions of years, if not billions, to bring conditions to pass by which his sons and daughters might obtain bodies made in his image? Why not the shorter route and *transplant them from another earth* as we are taught in the scriptures?

Joseph Fielding Smith

Doctrines of Salvation, 1:139-40

[W]hen the time came for this earth to be peopled, the Lord, our God, *transplanted upon it from some other earth*, the life which is found here.

See also:
JD 1:293; 2:160, 212; 3:320; 6:282, 323; 8:51, 195, 243, 279; 11:242; 13:248; 14:237, 238;
JD 15:49-50, 243, 263; 16:49, 314, 318, 322; 20:16, 17, 18; 21:32, 157; 26:34, 54, 89, 90;
Brigham Young's discourse of March 17, 1861; Church Archives, Salt Lake City, Utah;

---

[152] *Benjamin Brown*

The Last Days, 77
Sister Eliza R. Snow, in visiting [Benjamin Brown's] grandparents, was asked by my [Benjamin Brown's] grandmother: Eliza, where did you get your ideas about the Ten Lost Tribes being taken away as you explain it in your wonderful hymn?"
"She answered as follows: "Why, my husband (The Prophet Joseph) told me about it."

Man's Relationship to Deity, 279-82;
The Seer, 249;
WJS, 60, n. 12

Analysis & Observations

β

The above statements could pragmatically be divided into several sections and could be construed to cover multiple subjects. However, they were included in this subsection for the singular purpose of exploring the teachings of the early brethren concerning the modus operandi of the creation of this earth, the origin of this earth, and its ultimate destiny to return from whence it came. While there is much that could be said concerning these various teachings,[153] only two broad topics are addressed below.

Although only a portion of the above statements "explain" the creation of the earth, some few of them give us specific insights into the temporal creation. Far from a hocus-pocus explanation like that offered by modern Christendom, the early brethren offered a very pragmatic vision of the temporal creation - one involving a lot of hard work planting various forms of vegetation and transporting diverse animal species from other spheres so that they could create their abodes here on this earth. This "transplanting" teaching is very congruous with other Adam-God teachings found throughout this volume. In particular, the subsection entitled "Procreation: Mortal & Spiritual Offspring" discusses the cycle of life and refutes theories of evolution and/or hocus-pocus explanations about the origins of life - and offers an explanation of life very much like that portrayed in this subsection. That is, life *always* comes from a propagative process.

Some readers may reasonably question the presence of several of the above statements regarding the various dividings of this earth to create spheres for the ten lost tribes and the city of Enoch.[154] Although they may appear fanciful and outlandish to modern, educated ears, these teachings were clearly accepted and believed by many of the early

---

[153] Indeed, *The Footstool of God* by Hyrum Andrus covers this topic in significant detail. See also AGM, 43-46 for a discussion on the two creation accounts of this earth - Christensen includes an entire chapter on this topic.

[154] I pondered over the value of these inclusions over the period of several months before I decided to include them in this volume.

brethren - including Joseph Smith himself if the accounts are authentic and reliable. Further, they offer various (rather consistent) explanations as to how the earth itself may have been brought together if they are to be considered acceptable doctrine. Therefore, although somewhat tangential, they are worth consideration in this volume because they offer some suggestions as to how the Lord brought about this particular earth.

23 Gods Continually Learn & Progress

D&C 93:36   *5/6/1833*

The *glory of God is intelligence, or, in other words,* light and *truth.*

Joseph Smith   *4/10/1842*

TPJS, 217

A man is saved no faster than he gets knowledge, for if he does not get knowledge, he will be brought into captivity by some evil power in the other world, as evil spirits will have *more knowledge, and consequently more power* than many men who are on the earth.

Brigham Young   *7/10/1853*

JD 1:350-51

To me life would signify an extension. I have the privilege of spreading abroad, of enlarging my borders, of *increasing in endless knowledge,* wisdom and power, and in every gift of God. To live as I am, *without progress, is not life,* in fact we may say that *is impossible.* There is no such principle in existence, neither can there be. All *organized existence is in progress, either to an endless advancement in eternal perfections, or back to dissolution.* You may explore all the eternities that have been, were it possible, then come to that which we now understand according to the principles of natural philosophy, and where is there an element, an individual living thing, an organized body, of whatever nature, that continues as it is? It cannot be found. All things that have come within the bounds of man's limited knowledge - the things he naturally understands, teach him, that *there is no period, in all the eternities, wherein organized existence will become stationary, that it cannot advance in knowledge, wisdom, power, and glory.* ... *There is no such thing as principle, power, wisdom, knowledge,* life, position, or anything that can be imagined, that remains stationary - they must increase or decrease. ...

Nothing less than the privilege of increasing eternally, in every sense of the word, can satisfy the immortal spirit. If the endless stream of knowledge from the eternal fountain could all be drunk in by organized intelligences, so sure immortality would come to an end, and all eternity be thrown upon the retrograde path.

Brigham Young   *9/17/1854*

Journal of Wilford Woodruff

He said that the doctrine taught in the Seer that God had arrived at that state whereby he could not advance any further in knowledge, power & glory was a false doctrine & not true. *That there never will be a time to all eternity when all the Gods of eternity will cease advancing in power, knowledge,* experience & glory, for if this was the case, eternity would cease to be & *the glory of God would come to an end,* but all of the celestial beings will continue to advance in knowledge & power, worlds without end. Joseph would always be ahead of us, we should never catch up with him in all eternity nor he with his leaders.

Brigham Young   *Sunday 10/8/1854*

MABY

[T]he people want to hear something in advance of their present knowledge; they want to find out if there is anything more for us to learn. When you have lived through *eternities to come, learning continually,* you may then inquire, "Brother Brigham, is there anything more for me to learn." My reply to such an inquiry would be, yes, *there is an eternity of knowledge yet to learn.*

Orson Pratt   *circa 1853/1854*

Seer 117; MS 27:660

But when they (the Saints) became one with the Father and the Son, and receive a fulness of their glory, *that will be the end of all progress in knowledge, because there will be nothing more to be learned.*

Brigham Young   *2/17/1856*

Wilford Woodruff Journal, as cited in Bergera, 15

[T]he God[s] & all intelligent beings would never sease to learn except it was the Sons of Perdition they would continue to decrease untill they became dissolved back into their native Element & lost their Identity.

JD 6:120

If there was a point where man in his progression could not proceed any further, the very idea would throw a gloom over every intelligent and reflecting mind. *God himself is increasing and progressing in knowledge, power, and dominion, and will do so, worlds without end.* It is just so with us. We are in a probation, which is a school of experience.

MFP 2:222-23

In the Seer, pages 24 and 25, par. 22, br *Pratt states:* "*All these Gods* are equal in power, in glory, in dominion, and in the possession of all things; each *possesses a fulness of truth, of knowledge*, of wisdom, of light, of intelligence; each governs himself in all things by his own attributes, and is filled with love, goodness, mercy, and justice towards all. The fullness of all these attributes is what constitutes God." "It is truth, light, and love, that we worship and adore; these are the same in all worlds; and as these constitute God, He is the same in all worlds;" "Wherever you find a fulness of wisdom, knowledge, truth, goodness, love, and such like qualities, there you find God in all his glory, power, and majesty - therefore, if you worship theses adorable perfections, you worship God." Seer, page 117, par. 95. - "then *there will be no Being or Beings in existence that will know one particle more than what we know; then our knowledge, and wisdom, and power will be infinite;* and cannot, from thenceforth, be increased or expanded in the least degree;" Same page, par. 96: "but when they" (the Saints) "become one with the Father and Son and receive a fullness of their glory, that will be the end of all progression in Knowledge, because there will be nothing more to be learned. *The Father and the Son do not progress in knowledge and wisdom, because they already know all things past, present, and to come*." Par. 97: "there are none among them (the Gods) that are in advance of the others in knowledge; though some may have been Gods as many millions of years as there are particles of dust in all the universe, yet *there is not one truth that such are in possession of but what every other God knows*." "*None of these Gods are progressing in knowledge: neither can they progress in the acquirement of any truth*."
In this treatise entitled "Great First Cause," page 16, par. 17, br Pratt states: "All the organizations of worlds, of minerals, of vegetables, of animals, of men, of angels, of spirits, and of the spiritual personages of the Father, of the Son, and of the Holy Ghost, must, if organized at all, have been the result of the self combinations and unions of the pre-existent, intelligent, powerful, and eternal particles of substance. These eternal Forces and Powers are the Great Causes of all things and events that have had a beginning."
The foregoing quoted ideas, and all similar ones omitted to be quoted, with the comments

thereon, as advanced by br. Pratt in an article, in the Seer, entitled "Pre-Existence of man," and in his treatises entitled absurdities of immaterialism and "Great First Cause," *are plausibly presented.* But to the whole subject we will answer in the words of the Apostle Joseph Smith, on a similar occasion. One of the Elders of Israel [Orson Hyde] had written a long revelation which he deemed to be very important, and requested br. Joseph to hear him read it. The Prophet commended its style in glowing terms, remarked that the ideas were ingeniously advanced, &c., &c., and that he had but one objection to it. "What is that"? inquired the writer, greatly elated that his production was considered so near perfect. The Prophet Joseph replied, "*It is not true.*"
This should be a lasting lesson to the Elders of Israel not to undertake to teach doctrine they do not understand. If the Saints can preserve themselves in a present salvation day by day which is easy to be taught and comprehended, it will be well with them hereafter.

Brigham Young
Heber C. Kimball
Daniel H. Wells

Brigham Young - Orson Pratt   *3/4/1860*

Journal of Wilford Woodruff
President Young said, I corrected O Pratt today. I did not say to him that God would increase to all eternity. But I said *the moment that we say that God knows all things comprehends all things and has a fullness of all that he ever will attain, that moment eternity ceases.* You put bounds to eternity, space & matter and you make an end and stopping place to it. The people or many say they cannot understand the things. This is true. No man can understand the things of eternity. And Brother Pratt and all men should let the matter of the gods alone. I do not understand these things. Neither does any man in the flesh and we should let them alone.

Brigham Young & Orson Pratt   *9/23/1860*

Journal of Wilford Woodruff
Now *Brother Pratt thinks* that he and all the Gods will be learning for many millions of years but *by & by will know all things* & all will know it alike & that will be the end of their exaltations & knowledge. *He cannot see the folly* of forming this opinion here in the flesh & *in his ignorance.* But a thousand years hence he will see the folly of it. I will hold on to Brother Pratt and all those my Brethren of the Twelve notwithstanding all their sins, folly & weaknesses until I meet with them in my Fathers Kingdom, to part no more because they love God and are full of integrity.

Brigham Young	3/6/1862

JD 9:243

The Lord knows all things; man should know all things *pertaining to this life*, and to obtain this knowledge it is right that he should use every feasible means; and I do not hesitate to say that the stage can, in a great degree, be made to subserve this end.

Brigham Young	2/1/1865

DN, 138

He is the father of all is above all, through all, and in you all; *He knoweth all things pertaining to this earth*, and he knows all things pertaining to millions of earths like this.

Brigham Young	1/13/1867

JD 11:286

Some men seem as if they could learn so much and no more. They appear to be *bounded in their capacity for acquiring knowledge as Brother Orson Pratt, has in theory, bounded the capacity of God. According to his theory, God can progress no further in knowledge and power; but the God that I serve is progressing eternally*, and so are his children; they will increase to all eternity, if they are faithful.

Brigham Young	10/6/1870

JD 13:264

Suppose a man should come here and tell you the very nature of our Father Adam - tell precisely how he was organized, his height, his proportions, the extent of his knowledge, tell you the agreement that was entered into, *the amount of knowledge he had to forget to reduce himself to the capacity of a corruptible being*! Suppose this could all be told to the congregations of the Saints, what would they know about it? Very little. There may be some minds which could grasp some things pertaining to it, but others could not. The spirit of revelation can reveal these things to the people, but unless they live so as to have the revelations of the Lord Jesus Christ, they will remain a mystery, for there is a veil before the minds of the people, and they cannot be understood. Some of these principles have been taught to the Latter-day Saints, but who can understand them?

Brigham Young	Sunday p.m. 6/18/1873

DN 22:308

I know but very little, but I have an *eternity of knowledge before me, and I never expect to see the time when I shall cease to learn, never, no never, but I expect to keep on learning for ever and ever*, going on from exaltation to exaltation, glory to glory, power to power, ever pressing forward to greater and higher attainments, as the Gods do. That is an idea that drowns the whole Christian world in a moment. Let them try to entertain it and they are out of sight of land without a ship, and if they had a ship it would have neither sail, rudder nor compass. 'What,' say they, 'God progress?' Now, *do not lariet*[155] *the God that I serve and say that he can not learn any more; I do not believe in such a character*. 'Why,' say they, 'does not the Lord know it all?' Well, if he does, he must know an immense amount. No matter about that, the mind of man does not reach that any more than it comprehends the heaven ... If we look forward, we can actually comprehend a little of the idea that we shall live forever and ever; but you take a rearsight, and try and contemplate and meditate upon the fact that there never was a beginning and you are lost at once. The present and the future we can comprehend some little about, but the past is all a blank, and it is right and reasonable that it should be so. But if we are faithful in the things of God, they will open up, open up, open up; our minds will expand, reach forth and receive more and more, and by and by we can begin to see that the Gods have been forever and forever.

Brigham Young	*11/--/1889*

JD 3:203; Contributor 10:401

We might ask, *when shall we cease to learn?* I will give you my opinion about it; never, *never*. If we continue to learn all that we can pertaining to the salvation which is purchased and presented to us through the Son of God, *is there a time when a person will cease to learn? Yes; when he has sinned against God the Father*, Jesus Christ the Son, and the Holy Ghost - God's minister. ... *These are the only characters who will ever cease to learn, both in time and in eternity.*

Analysis & Observations

β

The opening statements (the Doctrine and Covenants and Joseph Smith) can be read to

---

[155] *Jedediah M. Grant*   *10/26/1856*

JD 4:126-27

Orson Pratt lariated out the Gods in his theory; his circle is as far as the string extends. My God is not lariated out. I do not want the old men to think that they have done enough, but to exert themselves to the last, and to believe that God is lariated out, nor be lariated out themselves.

substantiate Brigham Young's position on this topic by considering the following syllogism: God will continually add upon his glory and power, forever and forever. If the glory of God is intelligence, then it follows that God will always be increasing in intelligence. Perhaps this syllogism makes this controversial teaching too simplistic because of the implication that intelligence refers to knowledge or the correct application of knowledge - after all, if light is intelligence, then perhaps this merely refers to an increase in the light of Christ.[156] Alternative readings aside, Brigham Young certainly understood Joseph's teachings to mean that God would be eternally progressing in light and knowledge and the God he worshipped was certainly not a being who was "lariated" from progressing.

Although this teaching is fairly straightforward, it appears on its face to contradict scriptural statements that God knows all things and that He is Omnipotent. However, Brigham Young clearly believed that God was Omnipotent as well (see some of the statements above and others in the "Jehovah" section). These two teachings are readily reconcilable if one believes that one can know everything relative to one sphere of knowledge and progression while not knowing everything relative to a different sphere of knowledge or progression. That is, God knows all things necessary to exalt all of His creations but does not know everything there is to know about the eternities that exist beyond His creations.

Failing to see this perspective, Bruce R. McConkie and other modern LDS Church leaders have been quite disturbed by these teachings and have vehemently opposed them. Consider the following extract from page three of a private letter from Bruce R. McConkie to Eugene England:[157]

"Will [God] one day learn something that will destroy the plan of salvation and turn man and the universe into an uncreated nothingness? Will he discover a better plan of salvation than the one he has already given to men in worlds without number? I have been sorely tempted to say at this point that any who so suppose have the intellect of an ant and the understanding of a clod of miry clay in a primordial swamp - but of course I would never say a thing like that."

Even in context of McConkie's wry humor, he implicitly acknowledges that he failed to

---

[156] Or, in the alternative, it could refer to the number of intelligences that follow him.

[157] This letter, dated 2/19/1981, has been widely circulated despite McConkie's request (in the form of a stamp on the letter) not to reproduce the letter - allegedly because his son copied the letter and circulated it among professors at BYU, who in turn circulated the letter to others; the author has a photocopy of this letter.

see the reconciliatory explanation above and was therefore unable to reconcile these otherwise apparently contradictory teachings.

Some readers may wonder what this teaching has to do with Adam-God teachings anyway and the answer is not readily apparent to those uninitiated into the complexities of these teachings. The following insight into this question may not satisfy the deeply inquisitive mind but it may provide a foundation for more profound consideration.

Under current LDS theology, the average person undergoes a single mortal probation by which he/she is judged and by which he/she may become exalted. When exalted, this human being learns the gargantuan (yet limited) amount of knowledge necessary to become a god of a world (a la Orson Pratt's teachings). The being creates (or helps to create) one and then many worlds. Meanwhile, increasing in glory/intelligence refers to an ever increasing number of worlds, children, and dominion - not knowledge.

In contrast, the Adam-God adherent believes that the exalted being suffers him/herself to undergo mortality for each world he/she creates. Each mortality is different and incurs suffering greater than the previous mortality. This is true because the redemption of each creation is followed by an increase of glory. Therefore, each fall comes after an increase in glory and therefore each fall is a greater sacrifice than all previous falls endured by that god. With greater experience comes greater knowledge (or so the argument goes) and therefore, Adam and Eve must forever be increasing in knowledge - and this does not even consider the amount of light and knowledge that a god may gain in between these probations. As with most Adam-God teachings, the early brethren offer us much insight into the character of our Father and our God - and our Heavenly Mother - that mainstream Mormonism has lost. The details of the plan of salvation - and of godhood - are scarce, scanty, and speculative in mainstream Mormonism. However, the early brethren laid out these teachings in great detail and in many instances, left many sermons for the diligent reader to discover. The teachings in this subsection are no different - in context of Adam-God teachings, we learn much about the nature of God when we consider that He is still learning and progressing - albeit on a much more advanced level - and that He will eternally be progressing in light and knowledge. Like Brigham Young, He must enjoy the very process of learning because He would not be satisfied if He came to the point where He knew everything.

24 Eternal Progression

See also
The Good Samaritan

The following statements were generally made in context of Adam-God teachings and make observations that did not otherwise fit into the purview of this volume. While I could have categorized them as a "miscellany" section, I found that all of them had to do with the plan of salvation generally. Should I have included every statement that spoke of the plan of salvation generally, this volume would have doubled in size - therefore, I have only included statements in this section that are not found elsewhere in this volume but that were made in context of Adam-God teachings and that give us an intimate glimpse into the workings of the gods.[158]

Brigham Young   *Sunday 10/8/1854*

MABY

But when you speak of the system of salvation to bring back the children of Adam and Eve into the presence of our Father and God, it is the same in all ages, among all people, and under all circumstances, worlds without end, Amen.

Heber C. Kimball   *6/7/1857*

JD 4:334

Every man that comes into this world is an independent being, upon the same principle

---

[158] Perhaps, as time passes and a greater understanding of Adam-God teachings pervades fundamentalist Mormonism, the connection between these statements and more basic Adam-God teachings will be more readily apparent and some future author will be more adept at placing them within their proper context. For now, my fumbling attempt must be accepted for the widow's mite that it is.

that our Father and our *God is independent, only he is independent to a greater degree, being further advanced in perfection.* He came here, and helped to organize this earth and having had an experience in organizing earths before He came here, He was capable, and had every principle necessary to create this earth and fill it with inhabitants. If there had not been a seat of government in Him, and all those powers and faculties necessary to propagate the human species, He never could have done that work. We are His sons and daughters.

Brigham Young   *11/30/1862*

MABY

You can readily see this makes our father Adam a great and mighty king. When we are crowned kings and queens, father Adam and mother Eve will be king and queen of us all. Under the Priesthood which is after the Son of God and the power of an endless life, each father being a son, *will always throughout time and eternity be subject to his father, and his king, dictator, father Lord, and God.* Each son, in his own turn, becomes a father, and is entitled to the same obedience from the line of his descendants. It is by the authority and power of the Holy Priesthood alone that those in heaven and on earth can be entitled to, and secured in, the possession of the legal authority.

Brigham Young   *8/12/1866*

JD 11:262

The kingdoms he possesses and rules over are his own progeny. ... Our Father and God rules over his own children.

Brigham Young   *Saturday p.m. 8/24/1872*

JD 15:136-37

Now a few words to the brethren and sisters upon the doctrine and ordinances of the house of God. All who have lived on the earth according to the best light they had, and would have received the fullness of the Gospel had it been preached to them, are worthy of a glorious resurrection, and will attain to this by being administered for in the flesh by those who have the authority. All others will have a resurrection, and receive a glory, except those who have sinned against the Holy Ghost. It is supposed by this people that we have all the ordinances in our possession for life and salvation, and exaltation, and that we are administering in these ordinances. This is not the case. We are in possession of all the ordinances that can be administered in the flesh; but there are other ordinances and administrations that must be administered beyond this world. I know you would ask what they are. I will mention one. We have not, neither can we receive here, the ordinance and the keys of the resurrection. They will be given to those who have passed off this stage of action and have received their bodies again, as many have already done and many more will. They will be ordained, by those who hold the keys of the resurrection, to go forth and resurrect the Saints, just as we receive the ordinance of baptism, then the keys of authority to baptize others for the remission of their sins. This is one of the ordinances we can not receive here, and there are many more. We hold the authority to dispose of, alter and change the elements; but we have not received authority to organize native element to even make a spear of grass grow. We have no such ordinance here. We organize according to men in the flesh. By combining the elements and planting the seed, we cause vegetables, trees, grains, &c., to come forth. We are organizing a kingdom here according to the pattern that the Lord has given for people in the flesh, but not for those who have received the resurrection, although it is a similitude.

The Good
~ Samaritan

The correlation between the parable of the good Samaritan and Adam-God teachings is likely not intuitive to the average reader. However, John W. Welch did some interesting research into this parable that is particularly insightful from an Adam-God perspective. In BYU Magazine's Spring 2002 article,[159] John Welch notes that "[a]s dramatic as this parable's plain practical content clearly is, a once time-honored but now almost-forgotten tradition sees this tale as teaching more than a lesson about helping those in need. According to that ancient view, this story is also an impressive allegory of the fall and redemption of all mankind. This revealing interpretation adds rich gospel dimensions to this well-loved parable." (p. 49) Origen, an early Patristic Church father, wrote the following explanation: "The man who was going down is Adam. Jerusalem is paradise, and Jericho is the world. The robbers are hostile powers. The priest is the Law, the Levite is the prophets, and the Samaritan is Christ. The wounds are disobedience, the beast is the Lord's body, the pandochium [the Inn] which accepts all who wish to enter, is the Church. And further, the two denarii mean the Father and the Son. The manager of the stable is the head of the Church, to whom its care has been entrusted. And the fact that the Samaritan promises he will return represents the Savior's second coming." (Id., 50) With that interpretation, consider the familiar parable:

Luke 10:25-37 JST

And behold, a certain lawyer stood up and tempted him, saying, Master, what shall I do to inherit eternal life? He said unto him, What is written in the law? How readest thou? And he answering, said, Thou shalt love the Lord thy God with all thy heart, and with

---

[159] All non-Adam-God insights into this parable found in this subsection are taken from this article. The reader is encouraged to read Welch's entire article as other interesting insights are found therein.

all thy soul, and with all thy strength, and with all thy mind, and thy neighbor as thyself.[160] And he said unto him, Thou hast answered right; this do, and thou shalt live.[161] But he, willing to justify himself, said unto Jesus, And who is my neighbor?

And Jesus answering, said, A certain man went down from Jerusalem to Jericho, and fell among thieves who stripped him of his raiment, and wounded him, and departed, leaving him half dead. And by chance, there came down a certain priest that way; and when he saw him, he passed by on the other side of the way. And likewise a Levite, when he was at the place, came and looked upon him, and passed by on the other side of the way, for they desired in their hearts that it might not be known that they had seen him.
But a certain Samaritan, as he journeyed, came where he was; and when he saw him, he had compassion on him. And went to him and bound up his wounds, pouring in oil and wine, and set him on his own beast, and brought him to an inn, and took care of him. And on the morrow, when he departed, he took money, and gave to the host, and said unto him, Take care of him, and whatsoever thou spendest more, when I come again, I will repay thee.

Who now of these three, thinkest thou, was neighbor unto him who fell among the thieves? And he said, He who showed mercy on him. Then said Jesus unto him, Go and do likewise.

The ancient interpretation certainly brings out a vast panorama of new implications to the teachings found within this parable and, as Welch describes it, it is an "impressive allegory." However, the parable's significance is greatly enhanced when considered in light of Adam-God teachings. Here is the parable again with interpolations *in italics* to further point out insights gained by this parable:

A certain man went down from Jerusalem to Jericho,
the man, Adam, descends from paradise into the world; Welch notes that the Greek language here "implies that the man goes down intentionally, through his own volition, knowing the risks involved in the journey." (Id., 50); in other words, Adam knew the consequences of his fall, knew the pains of mortality that would accompany the fall, knew the risks of failure, and still decided to make the sacrifice on our behalf

and fell among thieves who stripped him of his raiment, and wounded him,

---

[160] Leviticus 19:18; Deuteronomy 6:5; 10:12; Joshua 22:5.
[161] Leviticus 18:5.

John Welch often notes in this and other writings, the word "thieves" is more appropriately translated "robbers" - organized outlaws. He further points out "Origen and Augustine saw the loss of this garment as a symbol of mankind's loss of immortality and incorruptibility." (Id., 51). In many Jewish Christian writings from the first two centuries A.D. Adam's garments are described as garments of glory or light and some writings inform us that the garments held special powers for the wearer (e.g., the Book of Jasher). The wounds refer to life's pains and afflictions due to sin. Id.

and departed, leaving him half dead.

Welch explains that the second death is not the result of the fall - the second death can still be averted. Id.

And by chance, there came down a certain priest that way; and when he saw him, he passed by on the other side of the way.

"The early Christian commentators saw this as a reference to the law of Moses or to the priesthood of the Old Testament, which did not have the power to lead to salvation." Id.

And likewise a Levite, when he was at the place, came and looked upon him, and passed by on the other side of the way,

The Levite, who held the lower priesthood, makes the effort to look at the traveler, possibly to see if there is any way that he can help; however, he "lacks the power or authority to spiritually save the dying person." Id., 52

for they desired in their hearts that it might not be known that they had seen him.

This is an addition added by Joseph Smith; whether out of shame, guilt, or some other motivation, neither the disinterested Priest, nor the concerned Levite, who at least passed the threshold character trait of exhibiting some compassion, wanted to be seen with the injured man.

But a certain Samaritan,

Chrysostom explained that "as a Samaritan is not from Judea, so Christ is not of this world." Id., 52

as he journeyed, came where he was

Unlike the Priest who came "by chance," Christ is actively looking to help those in need. Id.

and when he saw him, he had compassion on him and went to him and bound up his wounds, pouring in oil and wine,

and set him on his own beast,

The traveler is unable to overcome his injuries on his own - he must rely on Christ's atoning influence to overcome whatever sins may be his; Chrysostom explains that the "bandages are the teachings of Christ." Id. The oil and wine refer to ordinances and the atoning blood of Christ. Id., 53

and brought him to an inn, and took care of him.

As Welch points out, "[a]n Inn is not the heavenly destination, but a necessary aid in helping travelers reach their eternal home." Id., 53 Thus, the Church is but an aid to help us return to our Father in Heaven.

And on the morrow, when he departed, he took money, and gave to the host, and said unto him, Take care of him, and whatsoever thou spendest more, when I come again, I will repay thee.
Welch points out that the language here suggests that the innkeeper should freely spend whatever funds are necessary to help the traveler. Id., 54

Although the above insights into this parable tend to be more particularly suited to us individuals who must consider ourselves as shadows of Adam and Eve and who must strive to follow their examples of righteousness, we can also glean some insight into the journey that Adam began for his family. He knowingly put himself into a position of suffering and pain in order to bless our lives. It is not only us, his children, who suffer to buffetings of Satan and the pangs of mortality - father Adam suffered these things as well and was left half dead - temporarily cut off from the presence of his father and god.

Whether we extend the administration of the oil and wine to Adam as an individual and thereby conclude that Adam was in need of the atonement of his only begotten son, our Savior, or whether we merely see this as a proxy symbolism, or whether we see this passage as an allusion to Adam's need to rely upon his savior from another earth, the end conclusions are very similar: the human family is starkly dependent upon the atoning blood of an eternal sacrifice without blemish. If we read this passage to mean that Adam is in need of the atoning blood of Christ, then we must, as I explained earlier, accept the possibility that this allows for Adam to risk eternal dissolution of body should Christ fail to achieve his mission on this earth. If we accept the teaching of the royal order of savior to any degree, this passage cannot be referring to Adam's reliance upon a savior of his world because he was the savior of his world. The remaining interpretation - that this passage refers generally to mankind's need of an atonement applies universally under any given Adam-God teachings that may be accepted by the reader.

25 Adam & His Associates

Some of the following quotations can be read in several different ways. I have included all of those quotations that I have seen used to support the idea that more than one Adam populates each new world, whether or not they directly address the issue and I have included a few other statements that apparently contradict this position as well.

Orson Pratt　　　　　　　　　　　　　　　　　　　　　　　　　　*3/--/1853*

The Seer 1:3

In the Heaven where our spirits were born, there are many Gods, each one of whom has his own wife or wives which were given to him previous to his redemption, while yet in his mortal state. Each God, through his wife or wives, raises up a numerous family of sons and daughters; indeed, there will be no end to the increase of his own children: for each father and mother will be in a condition to multiply forever and ever. As soon as each God has begotten many millions of male and female spirits, and his Heavenly inheritance becomes too small, to comfortably accommodate his great family, *he, in connection with his sons*, organizes a new world, after a similar order to the one which we now inhabit, where he sends both the male and female spirits to inhabit tabernacles of flesh and bones. Thus each God forms a world for the accommodation of his own sons and daughters who are sent forth in their times and seasons, and generations to be born into the same. The inhabitants of each world are required to reverence, adore, and worship their own personal father who dwells in the Heaven which they formerly inhabited.

Orson Pratt　　　　　　　　　　　　　　　　　　　　　　　　　　*3/--/1853*

The Seer 1:37

Thus *each God* forms a world for the accommodation of *his own sons and daughters* who are sent forth in their times and seasons, and generations to be born into the same. The inhabitants of each world are required to reverence, adore, and worship their own personal father who dwells in the Heaven which they formerly inhabited.

Brigham Young   *Sunday 10/8/1854*

MABY

I began at the end, and shall probably finish at the beginning of my discourse; but it is no matter which end a man begins at, for the first shall be last and the last first; which proves it is one eternal round; it is one eternity. Eloheim looks round upon the eternity of matter, and said to *His associates, and* those that He was pleased to call upon at that time for His counselors, with regard to the Elements, Worlds, Planets, Kingdoms and Thrones; said He: "Yahovah Michael, see that Eternal Matter on all sides, this way and that way; we have already created Worlds upon Worlds, shall we create another World? Yes, go and organize the elements in yonder space".

Brigham Young   *Sunday 10/8/1854*

MABY

Every world has *an* Adam, and *an* Eve.

Heber C. Kimball   *10/26/1854*

JD 2:160

God finds us and furnishes us with everything we have, with the breath we breathe, and the earth we stand upon, and the water that we drink. Do you make all these things? No, the Lord made them, and placed them here upon the earth for our use; He made the wheat and organized it; we have the seed. ... Did you find the seed? No, you did not, the Lord found it; *when He came here* He brought it with Him, and *He told His sons to sow it*, and let it increase.

Brigham Young   *4/20/1856*

JD 3:319-20

Adam was made from the dust of an earth, but not from the dust of this earth. He was made as you and I are made, and no person was ever made upon any other principle. Do you not suppose that he was acquainted with *his associates who came and helped to make this earth?* Yes, they were just as familiar with each other as we are with our children and parents. Yet Enoch had to talk with and teach his people during a period of three hundred and sixty years, before he could get them prepared to enter into their rest, and then he obtained power to translate himself and his people, with the region they inhabited, their houses, gardens, fields, cattle, and all their possessions. *He had learned enough from Adam and his associates* to know how to handle the elements, and those who would not listen to his teachings were so wicked that they were fit to be destroyed, and he obtained power to take his portion of the earth and move out a little while, where he remains to this day.

Heber C. Kimball   *10/14/1860*

JD 8:243-44

After the earth was made, then there was a garden spot selected, and *the Lord commanded some of his associates to go and plant it,* and to cause all kinds of vegetation to grow, and fruits of every description.

Heber C. Kimball   *6/27/1863*

JD 10:235

We have been taught that our Father and God, from whom we sprang, *called and appointed his servants to go and organize an earth, and,* among the rest, he said to Adam, "*You go along also* and help all you can; you are going to inhabit it when it is organized, therefore go and assist in the good work." It reads in the Scriptures that the Lord did it, but the true rendering is, that the Almighty sent Jehovah and Michael to do the work. *They* were also instructed to plant every kind of vegetable, likewise the forest and the fruit trees, and they actually brought from heaven every variety of fruit, of the seeds of vegetables, the seeds of flowers, and planted them in this earth on which we dwell. And I will say more, the spot chosen for the Garden of Eden was Jackson County, in the State of Missouri where Independence now stands; it was occupied in the morn of Creation by *Adam and His associates* who came with Him for the express purpose of peopling this earth. Father Adam was instructed to multiply and replenish the earth, to make it beautiful and glorious, to make it, in short, like unto the garden from which the seeds were brought to plant the garden of Eden. I might say much more upon this subject, but I will ask, has it not been imitated before you in your holy endowments so that you might understand how things were in the beginning of creation and cultivation of this earth? God the Father made Adam the Lord of this creation in the beginning, and *if we are the Lords of this creation under Adam,* ought we not to take a course to imitate our Father in heaven? Is not all this exhibited to us in our endowments: the earth made glorious and beautiful to look upon, representing everything which the Lord caused to be prepared and placed to adorn the earth.

Brigham Young   *5/7/1871*

JD 14:111

Do you not all know that *you are the sons and daughters of the Almighty*? If you do not I will inform you this morning that *there is not a man or woman on the earth that is not a son or daughter of Adam and Eve*. We all belong to the races which have sprung from father Adam and mother Eve; and every son and daughter of Adam and Eve is a son and daughter of that God we serve, who organized this earth and millions of others, and who holds them in existence by law.

Brigham Young   *Sunday p.m. 6/18/1873*

DN 22:308

Our Father Adam helped to make this earth, it was created expressly for him, and *after it was made he and his companions* came here. He brought one of his wives with him, and she was called Eve, because she was the first woman upon the earth. Our Father Adam is the man who stands at the gate and holds the keys of everlasting life and salvation to all his children who have or who ever will come upon the earth. I have been found fault with by the ministers of religion because I have said that they were ignorant. But I could not find any man on the earth who could tell me this, although it is one of the simplest things in the world, until I met and talked with Joseph Smith. ... Adam came here and got it up in a shape that would suit him to commence business. Father Adam came here, and then *they* brought his wife. "Well," says one, "Why was Adam called Adam?" He was the first man on the earth, and its framer and maker. *He with the help of his brethren*, brought it into existence. Then he said," I want my children who are in the spirit world to come and live here.

Brigham Young   *5/14/1876*

L. John Nuttall Papers

In the creation he placed *a man & he called them Adam, including the singular in the plural.*

The Lecture at the Veil   *Tuesday 2/7/1877*

Journal of L. John Nuttall

And when this earth was organized by Elohim. Jehovah & Michael who is Adam our common Father. Adam & Eve had the privilege to continue the work of Progression. consequently came to this earth and commenced the great work of forming tabernacles for those spirits to dwell in. and when *Adam and those that assisted him* had completed this Kingdom our earth he came to it.

Shortened Lecture at the Veil   *between 1877-1894*

Adam and Eve had the privilege to continue the work of progression. They consequently came to this earth and commenced the great work of forming tabrnacles for those spirits to dwell in, and when Adam and *those who assisted him* had completed this kingdom which is our earth, he came to it and slept and forgot all become like a little child.

Edward Tullidge   *3/--/1877*

Women of Mormondom, 198

The fall is simple. Our immortal parents came down to fall; came down to transgress the laws of immortality; came down to give birth to mortal tabernacles for a world of spirits. The 'forbidden tree,' says Brigham, contained in its fruit the elements of death, or the elements of mortality. By eating of it blood was again infused into the tabernacles of beings who had become immortal. The basis of mortal generation is blood. Without blood no mortal can be born. Even could immortals have been conceived on earth, the trees of life had made but the paradise *of a few*; but a mortal world was the object of creation then.

Analysis & Observations

β

Brigham states that these companions "came" here to this earth with Adam "after it was made." Heber C. Kimball specifically adds that they came here for the purpose of "peopling" it. Without any further teaching, a fair reading could conclude that these individuals had come to help Adam create the earth so that Adam could "people" it and that these individuals perhaps continued to minister unto Adam. However, Brigham further teaches us that Enoch had learned how to "handle the elements" from these associates, which suggests that the associates remained here to help cultivate the earth - a suggestion that seems to exclude the possibility that the associates came here only for spiritual ministries. These statements, in connection with the other statements listed above have been interpreted by some to mean that Adam comes to earth and forms, perhaps, a United Order with a portion of his family (the "sons"). As all of these "associates" and "companions" were Adam's sons from another probation, all of the remaining statements that claim that we are all sons and daughters of Adam remain consistent.[162] All quotes that claim that we are all sons and daughters of Adam and Eve require the additional reading that, at least for this earth, all of the "sons" were children of Eve in a previous mortal existence as well - or that all spirits born through these

---

[162] That is, given the biblical usage of the term "son".

parents are the spirit children of Adam and Eve.

Apart from these three statements, all other references to "associates," "sons," or "companions" can be read to mean that these associates only helped Adam to create this earth. This limited reading coincides well with the endowment ceremony that teaches us that, at a minimum, Jehovah helped Adam to create this earth. Note that a careful reading of the above statements shows that none of these statements directly includes Jehovah. Some of them directly exclude Jehovah so they must be referring to other persons - this is particularly true of Orson Pratt's comment wherein he says that it was Adam's "sons" that helped him to create the earth.[163]

The reader may want to consider the following subsections: The Royal Order of Saviors, Eve as Adam's Daughter and Mary Sealed to Adam, for the purpose of considering further repercussions of these teachings if they are all to be accepted as doctrine. For example (and this is a little complicated upon first reading it), if our Adam was the atoning savior of his earth *and* our mother Eve was a Mary during her mortal probation; *and*, if our Adam was the God of that Mary's world, then it could have been some of their children from that probation (possibly including the savior of that Mary's world) who came to create this earth and who were included in the above statements as Adam's associates. Perhaps this explains why we have been taught that some of the most intelligent spirits born to our Father in Heaven are on this earth and why this earth has more wickedness on it to test those intelligent spirits than [most] any other earth.

This teaching is not universal among fundamentalists because there are many statements in "The Faithful Become Gods" subsection that suggest that there is only one Adam and Eve on each earth. Again, the continuity from the early brethren on this issue is less than ideal. Further, there are statements that can be read to support either position. The following statement is ideal in demonstrating this problem:

Heber C. Kimball   *11/14/1852*
JD 1:356

When we escape from this earth, do we suppose we are going to heaven? Do you suppose you are going to the earth that Adam came from? that Eloheim came from? where Jehovah the Lord came from? No. When you have learned to become obedient to the Father that dwells upon this earth, to the Father and God of this earth, and obedient to the messengers He sends - when you have done all that, remember you are not going to leave this earth. You will never leave it until *you become qualified*, and

---

[163] See "Jehovah is not Christ" if this statement was confusing to you.

capable, and capacitated *to become* **a** *father of an earth yourselves.*

Did Heber C. Kimball intend to teach that every man will become "a" father of an earth but not "the" father of an earth or did he only intend to teach that every man will have the opportunity of becoming "a father of an earth" - as if that phrase was a single noun with an explanatory tag at the end (e.g., "a father of a child")? Either reading is grammatically feasible and given the statements in this subsection, either reading is academically justifiable. However, so little has been revealed on this issue that fundamentalists lack unity in their beliefs surrounding this teaching.

26 The Royal Order of Saviors

See also
The Faithful Become Gods: Becoming an Adam/Eve

John 5:19-21, 26

Verily, verily, I say unto you, *The Son can do nothing* of himself, *but what he seeth the Father do:* for what things soever he doeth, *these also doeth the Son likewise.*

For the Father loveth the Son, and sheweth him all things that himself doeth: and he will shew him greater works than these, that ye may marvel.

For as the Father raiseth up the dead, and quickeneth them; even so the Son quickeneth whom he will. ...

For *as the Father hath life in himself; so hath he given to the Son to have life in himself.*

John 10:18

No man taketh it from me, but *I lay it down of myself. I have power to lay it down, and I have power to take it again.*

Joseph Smith   *6/11/1843*

TPJS, 312

If any man attempts to refute what I am about to say, after I have made it plain, let him beware. As the Father hath power in Himself, so hath the Son power in Himself, *to lay down His life and take it again,* so He has a body of His own. *The Son doeth what He hath seen the Father do: then the Father hath some day laid down His life and taken it again;* so He has a body of His own; each one will be in His own body.

Joseph Smith   *4/7/1844*

TPJS, 346

What did Jesus say? (Mark it, Elder Rigdon) The scriptures inform us that Jesus said, As the Father hath power in Himself, even so hath the Son power - to do what? Why, what the Father did, The answer is obvious - in a manner *to lay down His body and take it up again.* Jesus, what are you going to do? *To lay down my life as my Father did, and take it up again.* Do you believe it? If you do not believe it, you do not believe the Bible. The Scriptures say it, and I defy all the learning and wisdom and all the combined powers of earth and hell together to refute it. Here, then, is eternal life - to know the only wise and true God; and you have got to learn how to be Gods yourselves, and to be kings and priests to God, the same as all Gods have done before you.

Joseph Smith   *4/7/1844*

TPJS, 347

What did Jesus do? Why; *I do the things I saw my Father do* when worlds come rolling into existence. *My Father worked out his kingdom with fear and trembling*, and I must do the same; and when I get my kingdom, I shall present it to my Father,[164] so that he may obtain kingdom upon kingdom, and it will exalt him in glory. He will then take a higher exaltation, and I will take his place, and thereby become exalted myself. So that Jesus treads in the tracks of his Father, and inherits what God did before; and God is thus glorified and exalted in the salvation and exaltation of all his children. It is plain beyond disputation, and you thus learn some of the first principles of the Gospel, about which so much hath been said.

Joseph Smith   *4/7/1844*

WJS, 344-45; Wilford Woodruff Journal

It is the first principle to know that we may converse with him and that he once was a man like us, and the Father was once on an earth like us, ... The scriptures inform us mark it that Jesus Christ said As the Father hath power in himself so hath the son power in himself to do what the father did even *to lay down my body & take it up again* do you believe it, if not, dont believe the bible. I defy all Hell and earth to refute it. What did Jesus Christ do, the same thing as I se the Father do, *see the father do what, work out a kingdom*, when I do so to I will give to the father which will add to his glory, he will take a Higher exhaltation & I will take his place and am also exhalted.

---

[164] This is to Adam as shown in the previous quotes from Joseph Smith above.

Joseph Smith   *4/7/1844*

WJS, 350; Thomas Bullock Report

what J. did *I do the things I saw my Far. do before worlds came rolld. into existence* I saw my Far. *work out his K with fear & trembling* & I must do the same when I shall give my K to the Far. so that he obtns K rollg. upon K. so that J treads in his tracks as he had gone before.

Joseph Smith   *4/7/1844*

WJS, 361; Samuel W. Richards record

God: a man like one of us, even like Adam. Not God from all Eternity. *Once on a planet with flesh and blood, like Christ. As the father hath life in himself, &c.* To know God learn to become God's. Exalted by the addition of subjects to his family, or kingdom.

Joseph Smith   *4/7/1844*

WJS, 362; William Clayton Report

Said Jesus (mark it Br. Rigdon) What did Jesus say - as the father hath power in himself even so hath the son power to do what why what the father did, *to lay down his body and took it up again.* Jesus what are you going to do - to lay down my life as my father did that I might take it up again. If you deny it you deny the bible. I defy the [indecipherable] and wisdom & all the combined powers of earth and hell to refute it. … What did Jesus do. Why *I do the things that I saw the father do when worlds came into existence. I saw the father work out a kingdom with fear & trembling* & I can do the same & when I get my Kingdom worked out I will present to the father & it will exalt his glory and Jesus steps into his tracks to inherit what God did before.

Joseph Smith   *4/7/1844*

WJS, 362; George Laub's journal

How came Spirits? Why, they are and ware Self Existing as all eternity & our Spirits are as Eternal as the very God is himself & that we choose to come on this Earth to take unto ourselves tabernakles by permition of our Father that we might be Exalted *Equil with God himself* & therefore Jesus spake in this wise, I do as m   y Father before me did. Well, *what did the father do?* Why, *he went & took a body and went to redeem a world in the flesh* & had power to lay down his life and to take it up again.

Joseph Smith   *4/6-7/1844*

HC 6:14, 305-06

What did Jesus say? (Mark it, Elder Rigdon!) The scriptures inform us that Jesus said, *as the Father hath power in himself, even so hath the Son power - to do what?* Why, what the

Father did. The answer is obvious - *in a manner to lay down his body and take it up again.* Jesus, what are you going to do? *To lay down my life as my Father did, and take it up again.* Do you believe it? If you do not believe it you do not believe the Bible. The scriptures say it, and I defy all the learning and wisdom and all the combined powers of earth and hell together to refute it. ...

What did Jesus do? Why, *I do the things I saw my Father do when worlds came rolling into existence. My Father worked out His kingdom with fear and trembling,* and I must do the same; and when I get my kingdom, I shall present it to My Father, so that He may obtain kingdom upon kingdom, and it will exalt Him in glory. He will then take a higher exaltation, and I will take His place, and thereby become exalted myself. So that Jesus treads in the tracks of His Father, and inherits what God did before; and God is thus glorified and exalted in the salvation and exaltation of all His children. It is plain beyond disputation, and you thus learn some of the first principles of the gospel, about which so much hath been said.

Joseph Smith   *6/16/1844*

TPJS, 373

If Abraham reasoned thus - If Jesus Christ was the Son of God, and John discovered that God the Father of Jesus Christ had a Father (see Rev 1:6), you may suppose that He had a Father also. Where was there ever a son without a father? And where was there ever a father without first being a son? Whenever did a tree or anything spring into existence without a progenitor? And everything comes in this way. Paul says that which is earthly is in the likeness of that which is heavenly, Hence if Jesus had a Father, can we not believe that He had a Father also? I despise the idea of being scared to death at such a doctrine, for the Bible is full of it. I want you to pay particular attention to what I am saying. *Jesus said* that *the Father wrought* precisely *in the same way* as His *Father had done before Him.* As the Father had done before? *He laid down His life, and took it up the same as His Father had done before.* He did as He was sent, *to lay down His life and take it up again*; and then was committed unto Him the keys.

Joseph Smith   *8/5/1844*

TPJS, 346

It is the *first principle* of the Gospel to know *for a certainty* the Character of God, and to know that we may converse with him as one man converses with another, *and that he was once a man like us*; yea, that God himself, the Father of us all, dwelt on an earth, the same as Jesus Christ himself did and I will show it from the Bible.

Brigham Young   *2/8/1852*

TPBY, 52

If it would be any satisfaction to you, I would say that God has passed through all the trials and experience that we have. Jesus Christ has passed through all the trials and experience the same as we have. It would not be prudent for me to say that *the Father* has not the same experience that His Son had. He *had quite as much as His Son had.*

Brigham Young   *Friday 10/6/1854*

Journal of the Southern Indian Mission, 87- 89

[T]here have always been an Adam and an Eve - the first man and woman, and t*heir oldest son is heir, and should be our Savior. ...*

Michael came down with his wife, & began to people it. Michael had his body from the dust of the planet he was begotten on, *he obeyed his Lord*, was faithful and obedient, died and was resurrected, he did not resurrect himself. ... Adam's descent was to organize people & redeem a world, by his wife he peopled it *by his first born he redeems.*

Brigham Young   *Sunday 10/8/1854*

John Pulsipher Papers, 37

An Adam & Eve is necesary for evry world *The oldest Son, if faithful, is the Saviour of the family* - There are Lords many & Gods many But the God that we have to account to, is the father of our Spirits - Adam.

Brigham Young   *Sunday 10/8/1854*

MABY

Every world has an Adam, and an Eve: named so, simply because the first man is always called Adam, and the first woman Eve; and *the Oldest Son has always the privilege of being Ordained. Appointed, and Called to be the Heir of the Family*, if he does not rebel against the Father; and *he is the Savior of the family*. Every world that has been created, has been created upon the same principle. They may vary in their varieties, yet the eternity is one eternal round. These are things that scarcely belong to the best of this congregation. There are items of doctrine, and principles, in the bosom of eternity that the best of the Latter-day Saints are unworthy to receive.

Brigham Young   *Sunday 10/8/1854*

MABY

Man was not made the same as you make an adobe and put in a wall. Moses said that *Adam* was made of the dust of the ground, but he did not say of what ground. I say he was not made of the dust of the ground of this Earth, but he was made of the dust of the earth where he lived, where he honored his calling, *believed in his Saviour*, or Elder Brother, *and by his faithfulness was redeemed,* and obtained a Glorious Resurrection.

Orson Hyde   *3/18/1855*

JD 2:210

I said, in my lecture on Marriage, at our last Conference, that Jesus Christ was married at Cana of Galilee, that Mary, Martha, and others were his wives, and that he begat children. All that I have to say in reply to that charge is this - they worship a Savior that is too pure and holy to fulfil the commands of his Father. I worship one that is just pure and holy enough "to fulfil all righteousness;" not only the righteous law of baptism, but the still more righteous and important law "to multiply and replenish the earth." Startle not at this! for even the Father himself honored that law by coming down to Mary, without a natural body, and begetting a son; and *if Jesus begat children, he only "did that which he had seen his Father do."*[165]

Franklin D. Richards   *3/31/1855*

MS 17:195-96

God saw that among His numerous posterity of spirits there were some more noble than others, and therefore capable of assuming greater responsibilities, and performing more important parts in the great work of redemption. These He foreordained and set apart to the work designed for them, and at the time appointed they appeared on the earth through the lineage of the Priesthood. Having been ordained in the Spirit, and being heirs according to the flesh, they came forth prepared to enter upon the work designed, inherit the fruits thereof, and partake of the same glory and exaltation as the Father. First among these noble sons stands the Lord Jesus Christ. The heir by birthright of his Father's kingdom, he has proved himself worthy of his high vocation, by nobly offering to become the sacrifice that was necessary for the redemption of his Father's family. Therefore on him the Father has bestowed the keys of salvation, and the powers of the resurrection, to unlock the gates of death. On him devolved the great crowning work of redemption, and the meridian of time was appointed for the sacrifice. This same Jesus was a man like unto other men, and attained his exaltation by suffering all things, that he might overcome them, and has ascended to power at the right hand of the Father.

---

[165] This application of this statement does not disprove the other applications of this statement in this subsection but it does show that Joseph could have been referring to other issues besides fulfilling the office of a Savior.

Brigham Young   *1/27/1860*

Wilford Woodruff Journal

You call your spiritual children together and hold a council with them; and *in the contemplation of a new earth, a savior must be provided.* You call for volunteers, there may be a number of bright sons reply. It is your right to choose the one dearest to your own heart, he being worthy of the position. Another among the volunteers may become offended, and rebel against the plan, and lead many away with him. The chosen one is ordained to his calling, *a calling in the Priesthood, and placed in full charge of the organization of the new earth, its redemption and sanctification.* Thus *the faithful son becomes the creator and redeemer* of the new world, Grandfather remaining the highest authority, Architect and Chief Commander, while you, the Father, remain in reserve for other important duties, and thus the six days of creation go on and the earth is finished and is indeed glorious and beautiful. ...

Now comes the morning of the new week in which mortality must begin, and your spiritual children must be introduced into mortality. Two must go before them and prepare the way for them. Whom will you send? Would you not say to [your] wife, "Come, Mother, let you *and I lay aside our Celestial glory for a little season and eat of the elements of this new earth. that we may again become of the earth earthy, and thereby our offspring will be mortal, and* thus we will begin the begetting of mortal bodies for these, our spiritual children; and when they have grown to maturity in their mortal estate, we will command them to multiply and replenish the earth. We have passed through earth life, death and the resurrection. *We* have *power to lay aside this Celestial Glory and we have power to take it up again.*"

To which she, a faithful Mother, will reply: "Yes, we will partake of the elements of this new earth. We will make this sacrifice for our spiritual children that they also may continue on in the law of everlasting progression and become like unto us, for as the Gods are, *some*[166] may become."

Orson Pratt   *10:00 a.m. 4/5/1860*

Minutes of the Meeting of the Council of the Twelve

I heard brother Young say that *Jesus had a body, flesh and bones, before he came, he was born of the Virgin Mary*, it was so contrary to every revelation given.

---

[166] This distinction of "some" here is probably not intended to be teaching the royal order of saviors but its place here is interesting and worth noting.

Brigham Young   *5/12/1867*

Journal of Wilford Woodruff

President Young said there never was any world created & peopled nor never would be but what would be redeemed by the *shedding of the blood of the savior of that world*. If we are ever exalted and crowned in the presence of God *we shall become saviors of a world* which we shall create & people. I know why the Blood of Jesus was shed, I know why the blood of Joseph & Hiram & others have been shed and the blood of others will be shed it is all to answer a purpose and has its effect.

Brigham Young   *Sunday 2 p.m. 10/3/1869*

Minutes of Meetings Held in Provo City

All worlds have their God, *their Savior*, their sin, their priesthood, and can choose which they like, but beginning man rejected the priesthood by assuming to be a law unto himself - all other things abide this law.

Brigham Young   *7/10/1870*

JD 14:71-72

But the fact exists that the Father, the Divine Father, whom we serve, the God of the Universe, the God and Father of our Lord Jesus Christ, and the Father of our spirits, provided this sacrifice and sent his Son to die for us; and it is also a great fact that the Son came to do the will of the Father, and he has paid the debt, in fulfillment of the Scripture which says, 'He was the Lamb slain from the foundation of the world.' *Is it so on any other earth? On every earth.* ... Sin is upon every earth that was ever created. ... Consequently *every earth has its redeemer*, and every earth has its tempter; and every earth, and the people thereof, in their turn and time, receive all that we receive, and pass through all the ordeals that we are passing through.

The Lecture at the Veil   *Tuesday 2/7/1877*

Journal of L. John Nuttall

Father *Adam's oldest son (Jesus the Savior)* who is the heir of the family is Father *Adams first begotten in the spirit World.* who according to the flesh is the only begotten as it is written. (In his divinity he having gone back into the spirit World. and come in the spirit [glory] to Mary and she conceived.

Edward Tullidge   *3/--/1877*

Women of Mormondom, 191-92

The Christ is not dragged from his heavenly estate, to be mere mortal, but mortals are lifted up to his celestial plane. He is still the God-Man; but he is one among many brethren who are also God-Men. Moreover, *Jesus is one of a grand order of Saviors. Every world has its distinctive Savior*, and every dispensation its Christ. There is a glorious Masonic scheme among the Gods. The everlasting orders come down to us with their mystic and official names. The heavens and the earth have a grand leveling; not by pulling down celestial spheres, but by the lifting up of mortal spheres.

Joseph E. Taylor   *6/2/1888*

Deseret Weekly News 38:19-27

`Did Jesus have power to lay down his life and take it up again?' He so declared.[167] It might be well at this point to inquire *who was the Savior of the world; and what relation did he bear to our father Adam?* For the veil of the mysterious past has been lifted just a little to enable us to see within. I will first quote from a discourse preached by President Brigham Young, in Salt Lake City, April 9th, 1852.

[He here quotes JD 1:50-51.]

We will now quote some of the sayings of Joseph Smith upon this point, as uttered by him in Nauvoo, April 6, 1844. `It is the first principle of the Gospel to know for a certainty the character of God, and to know that we may converse with Him, as one man converses with another, and that *he was made a man like us*. Yea, that God Himself, the Father of us all, dwelt on our earth the same as Jesus Christ did. ... What did Jesus say? ... `*As the Father hath power in himself, so hath the Son power.*' To do what? *Why, what the Father did*. The answer is obvious, in a manner, *to lay down his body and take it up again*. `Jesus, what are you going to do?' `*To lay down my life and take it up again.*' Do you believe it? If you do not believe it, you do not believe the Bible. The Scriptures tell it, and I defy all the learning and wisdom of all the combined powers of earth and hell together to refute it. What did Jesus do? Why, `*I do the thing I saw my Father do* when worlds came rolling into existence. *My Father worked out His Kingdom with fear and trembling;* and I must do the same; and when I get my kingdom, I shall present it to my Father, so that He may obtain kingdom upon kingdom and it will exalt Him in glory. He will then take a higher exaltation and I take His place, and thereby become exalted myself'; so that Jesus treads in the track of his Father and inherits what God did before.'[168]

I think these two quotations from such a reliable authority fully solve the question as to the relationship existing between Father Adam and the Savior of the world, and prove beyond question *the power that Adam possessed in regard to taking his body again after laying it down* - which power he never could have attained unless he had received first a resurrection from the grave to a condition of immortality. We further say that this

---

[167] John 10:18.
[168] TPJS 345, 346, 347; HC 6:305, 306; JD 6:3.

power was not forfeited when as a celestial being he voluntarily partook of the forbidden fruit, and thereby rendered his body mortal in order that he might become the father of mortal tabernacles, as he was already the father of immortal spirits - thus giving opportunity to the offspring of his own begetting to pass through the ordeals necessary to prepare them for a resurrection from the dead, a celestial glory.

All that Father Adam did upon this earth, from the time that he took up his abode in the Garden of Eden, was done for his posterity's sake and the success of his former mission as the savior of a world, and afterwards, or now, as the Father of a world only added to the glory which he already possessed. *If, as the savior of a world, he had the power to lay down his life and take it up again, therefore, as the father of a world which is altogether an advanced condition, we necessarily conclude that the grave was powerless to hold him after that mission was completed.* All those who have now for the first time taken upon themselves mortality, must wait for their resurrection through Him who alone possesses the power to bring it to pass. It is these, and these only, whose resurrection we here wish to consider.

George Q. Cannon   *6/23/1889*

Journal of Abraham H. Cannon
He (George Q.) believes that Jesus Christ is Jehovah, and that *Adam is His Father and our God*: that under certain unknown conditions the benefits of the Savior's atonement extend to our entire solar system. ... He asked me what I understood concerning Mary conceiving the Savior; and as I found no answer, he asked what was to prevent Father Adam from visiting and overshadowing the mother of Jesus. Then said I: "he must have been a resurrected Being." "Yes," said he, "and though Christ is said to have been the first fruits of them that slept, yet *the Savior said he did nothing but what He had seen His Father do, for He had power to lay down His life and take it up again.*

Edward Stevenson   *2/28/1896*

Edward Stevenson Diary
Certainly Eloheim, and *Jehovah* stands [sic] before *Adam*, or else I am very much mistaken. Then 1st Eloheim, 2nd Jehovah, 3d Michael-Adam, 4th Jesus Christ, Our Elder Brother, in the other World from whence our spirits came ... Then Who is Jehovah? *The only begotten Son of Eloheim on Jehovah's world.*

Joseph F. Smith   *12/20/1914*
Box Elder News[169]

Mary, the virgin girl, who had never known mortal man, was his mother. God by her begot His son Jesus Christ, and He was born into the world with power and intelligence like that of His Father. He was God with us, He was indeed Emmanuel for He came for a purpose and He possessed power that no human being ever possessed. *He had power to lay down His life and take it up again*, He had power to resist His murderers; if He had so willed it they never could have taken his life. He came for a purpose - what was it? - to redeem man from death.

Analysis & Observations

β

There are at least four different ways of defining the Royal Order of Saviors teaching.

1) Every savior of a world will be the father of the savior of a world, who in turn will be the father of a savior of another world; thus, each redeemer and savior of a world is part of a grand patriarchal order of saviors. Every Adam-God adherent who believes in even the most basic principles found throughout this volume must believe that such a royal order of saviors must exist - this teaching is not controversial at all.

2) Only the savior of a world can ever be an Adam, in the sense that he can create a world and people it. All other exalted beings are delegated to come to an earth with that Savior-Adam as helpers who are never able to rise to the level of a Savior-Adam because they can never be the savior of a world and will always rely on their Savior. This teaching is controversial. While there are three statements above that directly state that this is doctrine and while one of these statements is a journal entry from a person who personally heard Joseph Smith's sermon, this teaching has not gained widespread acceptance among fundamentalist Mormons. I include these statements here again (in abbreviated form) so that the reader can note the clarity and consistency of these statements when separated from the large number of statements above:

---

[169] The publication date was 1/28/1915.

Joseph Smith   *4/7/1844*

George Laub's journal

Jesus spake in this wise, I do as my Father before me did. Well, *what did the father do?* Why, *he went* & took a body and *went to redeem a world* in the flesh & had power to lay down his life and to take it up again.

Joseph E. Taylor   *6/2/1888*

Deseret Weekly News 38:19-27

If, as the savior of a world, he [Adam] *had the power to lay down his life and take it up again,* therefore, as the father of a world which is altogether an advanced condition, we necessarily conclude that the grave was powerless to hold him after that mission was completed.

Edward Stevenson   *2/28/1896*

Edward Stevenson Diary

Certainly Eloheim, and *Jehovah* stands [sic] before *Adam*, or else I am very much mistaken. Then 1st Eloheim, 2nd Jehovah, 3d Michael-Adam, 4th Jesus Christ, Our Elder Brother, in the other World from whence our spirits came ... Then *Who is Jehovah? The only begotten Son* of Eloheim *on Jehovah's world.*

Nevertheless, despite these very clear teachings and declarations and one statement from Brigham Young where he seems to suggest this very same teaching,[170] Brigham Young directly opposed them in his famous and lengthy Adam-God discourse:

Brigham Young   *Sunday 10/8/1854*

MABY

Adam ... was made of the dust of the earth where he lived, where he honored his calling, *believed in his Saviour,* or Elder Brother, *and by his faithfulness was redeemed,* and obtained a Glorious Resurrection.

A second hand account suggests that Joseph Smith also taught against this principle at another time:

Joseph Smith   *5/--/1886*

Contributor 7:286 #8

Joseph also referred to *Michael's Christ's* future coming to this same Valley: He shall "come to the Ancient of Days and shall give to Him dominion and Glory, and issue a

---

[170] 2/8/1852 as cited earlier in this subsection.

Decree that all people shall serve and obey Him."

Generally speaking, this lack of unity on this issue has created a division among fundamentalists concerning these teachings. Nevertheless, the large majority of fundamentalists are relatively unaware that these teachings were ever put forward in the first place so the controversy over these teachings has remained relatively isolated. Those who do accept these teachings are generally relegated to the followers of Joseph Musser. Joseph Musser, a previous Adam-God author and leader of a major fundamentalist group, made these observations about Adam's status before he came to this earth:

MCD, 60
Adam is our God. He had been a Savior on another planet before coming here. He came here to prepare a place for his children which had been born to him in the spirit. This was an advanced step. As he had been a Savior previously, so his son Jesus Christ became a Savior to this earth and trod the same path, in experience, that his father (Adam) had trod before him.

Truth Magazine 9:88
"Our Adam in mortality, like our Savior, acted as the Redeemer of his world."

MCD, 107
And yet, can it be said that that doting father whose part was to plunge the knife into his son, suffered less? Was not his anguish of soul greater than that of his son, even beyond the suffering of mortal understanding? And so it was with Adam, whose "Firstborn," his Only Begotten in the flesh, after returning to immortality, the one child of his who was without sin, was undergoing the agonies of eternity that life might come to the human family. The Father suffered with his Son. The agony of the former must have been greater than that of the latter, for the Father had gone through it before and knew the torments of it; he knew what it meant; he would gladly have taken the Son's place could he have done so and accomplished the plan of redemption.

Rulon C. Allred, a successor of Joseph Musser continued to put forth this teaching. Said he at a discourse given on Wednesday, January 18, 1967 in Murray Utah:
The question is asked that if Adam was of the direct lineage of Saviors, and is now an exalted God, and it is taught that we can become gods, do we, when we become Gods, have a lesser kingdom? If so, do we have to borrow a Christ from a different line? The Prophet Joseph Smith taught that there is a grand order of Saviors running down through the worlds. The scriptures tell us that we may become joint heirs with Jesus Christ.

They also tell us (and these are eternal scriptures that run down through the ages and through the worlds, and you will find these quotations in every Holy Book), "I the Lord God have created nothing except through mine Only Begotten. Worlds without number have I created, and I have created them through mine Only Begotten." That is, the direction of the creation of worlds is done in and through a Grand Order of Gods, Saviors, Messiahs, Jehovahs that runs down through the worlds; and we, through the goodness and mercy of God, may hold all of the offices of godhood except that office. We always do whatever we do in His name and through Him. "No man," saith the Lord, "can come unto the Father except through me." This is an eternal principle. We will become gods in our own right, joint heirs with Jesus Christ. We will partake of His glory and of His honor and of His dominions and of His power and His exaltations, but we will always be subject to Him, because he is greater than we are. And it will be through this order that we will mingle our seed with the seed of the gods. But this order of Saviors will run down through the worlds and govern. Now there is much that we might bring out pertaining to this subject tonight, but so far as I have gone, this is God's truth.

Nevertheless, even among the followers of Musser and Allred, there are those who do not accept these teachings. One colleague of the author's who is, to say the least, extremely skeptical of this teaching has noted that people who adhere to the idea that only a savior can become a "senior" Adam no longer believe in the couplet "As man is, God once was; as God is, man may become;" rather, they believe that "As man is, God never was; as God is, man may never become." And so the philosophical division continues.

Consider also 1 John 3:16, which reads "Hereby perceive we the love of God, because he laid down his life for us." Protestants and Mormons alike presume that this is referring to Jesus but verse 23 suggests that it is referring to God the Father. For those who believe in this version of the Royal Order of Saviors, this verse further may confirm that a senior God of a world must be a savior.

3) The third understanding is a derivation of the second and requires a belief in multiple mortal probations - and relies upon the quote of Orson Pratt quoted above wherein he states that an exalted person can shed their tabernacle and be born in a new body to become the savior of a world. This is probably the least accepted version of this teaching among fundamentalists but there are some few who believe this.

4) This is also a derivation of the second but states that eventually, an exalted being who is not a Savior-Adam can rise to the level of an Adam of a world but his Savior will take

the place of Jehovah as his superior/supervisor.

Titles & Offices

β

As a preliminary note to this section, it is worthy of consideration that understanding the concept of titles and offices within the Godhead is absolutely essential for the modern LDS Church member to understand Adam-God teachings. A fundamental misunderstanding of this concept is what has led to the great division, not only between members of the modern LDS Church and fundamentalist Mormons, but also between Jehovah's Witnesses and mainstream Christians. President George Q. Cannon, councilor to Brigham Young, John Taylor, and Wilford Woodruff explained this concept of titles for deity very succinctly:

George Q. Cannon   *circa 1893*
_____
St. George High Council Minutes
"I am the beginning and the end." *Jesus speaks for the Godhead,*[171] the personages who compose the Godhead, and that must be kept in mind all the time, not speaking for himself, but for the father. *It is over looking this that leads to confusion.* Men thinking that Jesus speaks for himself. ... Father Bunker labors to show that the God of this earth is the Savior ... we worship, the Father in the name of Jesus. If Jesus is the object of our worship, who was left in charge when He tabernacled in the flesh? It was the Father.

John Taylor further clarified this issue by explaining that titles of the godhead can also be appropriately applied to different members of the godhead - titles can appropriately be interchanged because these titles represent attributes and eternal principles held by the personage to whom the titled is being applied. Said he:

John Taylor   *1892*
_____
The Mediation and Atonement, 138, 166
"His name shall be called Immanuel," which being interpreted is, God with us. Hence He is not only called the Son of God ... Jehovah, the I Am, the Alpha and Omega, but He is also called the Very Eternal Father. *Does not this mean that in Him were the attributes and power of the Very Eternal Father?* For the angel to Adam said that all things should be done in His name. ... He is called in Scripture the I AM, in other words, I AM THAT I AM,[172] because of those inherent principles, which are also eternal and unchangeable; for where those principles exist, He exists ...

_____

[171] Bruce R. McConkie was later given credit for identifying this concept and coining the phrase "divine investiture of authority" to refer to times when one member of the godhead is speaking on behalf of another member of the godhead.

[172] The term "I AM" was equated with Elohim, Jehovah, and Jesus by the early brethren; usage of this term was therefore somewhat random and therefore, was likely used in the sense explained in this statement by John Taylor.

Brigham Young added:

Brigham Young   *4/25/1855*

MABY

At one time he says "I am that I am," at another time when the question was proposed by somebody, he replied, "I am the Lord your God"; at another time he is spoken of as a Man of War, a General and so on. You may trace the scriptures through, and you will find that he is known to one people by *one title*[173] *today, and tomorrow by another*, and the next day by another, and there he leaves it.

Brigham Young

JD 14:41

We have proof that *God* lives and that he has a body; that he has eyes, and ears to hear, that he has arms, hands and feet; that he can walk and does walk. He has declared himself to be a man of war - *Jehovah*, the great *I Am*, the *Lord* Almighty, and many other titles of a like import are used in reference to him in the Scriptures. But take away the atonement of the *Son of God* and the Scriptures fall useless to the ground.

Although this concept is fairly simple and easily understood within its proper context, significant confusion arises when people are *unable to apply this concept to deity*. For instance, Mormons have no difficulty referring to "bishop" Smith in one ward and "bishop" Adams in another ward without ever confusing the two individuals referred to even if they are only told on a given occasion that "the bishop" (without referring to a last name) asked them to do something. In contrast, when the Bible refers to God the Father as Jehovah and then the Doctrine and Covenants appears to refer to Jesus as Jehovah, the minds of many Mormons break down and the ensuing confusion shadows their hearts. Thereafter, if they read that Jehovah commanded Adam to be fruitful and multiply and later, Jehovah (Adam) commanded men not to covet or steal, some Mormons become very disturbed in their hearts and minds. All of this genre of concern is easily left behind if one understands the simple concept outlined above.

Similarly, the following statement illustrates that a title can be used generically and interchangeably in other fashions as well:

---

[173] This interpretation of "I Am" as a title is not unique to Mormonism - see Boyd Kirkland's discussion of this issue in Dialogue 19:86 #1.

| Parley P. Pratt | 1/1/1844 |

The Angel of the Prairies

The *venerable council* which you beheld enthroned in majesty and clad in robes of white, with crowns upon their heads, *is the order of the Ancient of Days*, before whose august presence thrones have been cast down, and tyrants have ceased to rule.

The usage of "Ancient of Days" above may refer to Adam - or it may refer to a specific office. For a more commonly understood example, consider that the Melchizedek priesthood was initially named after the order of the son of God but was later named the Melchizedek priesthood out of reverence for the name of the son of God. Here, we see that the name or title is interchangeable in this instance and yet every Mormon should understand that it is the same priesthood that is being referred to.

Without this foundational understanding (as explained by "Presidents" Cannon, Taylor, and Young) that Jehovah, Elohim, and other names were used as titles or offices of deity, many mainstream Mormons are entirely baffled by statements like these:

| Joseph Smith | 8/14/1842 |

HC 5:94; MS 19:648, Letter to Major-General Law

[L]et us plead the justice of our cause; trusting in the arm of *Jehovah, the Eloheim* who sits enthroned in the heavens

| Brigham Young | 11/17/1867 |

JD 12:99-100

We obey the Lord, Him who is *called Jehovah*, the Great I AM, I am a man of war, *Eloheim*, etc.

| Parley P. Pratt | 1/1/1844 |

The Angel of the Prairies, 24

[I]t is a theocracy, where *the great Eloheim, Jehovah*, holds the superior honor. He selects the officers. He reveals and appoints the laws, and He counsels, reproves, directs, guides and holds the reins of government.

A member of the modern LDS Church reading these statements could be left to conclude that Jesus Christ was really God the Father as the modern LDS Church teaches that Jehovah is Christ and Elohim is God the Father.[174] However, if one understands that

---

[174] As Cannon's statement indicated, Edward Bunker seemed to make this conclusion - though perhaps for different reasons than stated here.

these terms were used as titles, the meaning is more clear. These statements are not confusing to the slightest degree when we consider them in the same manner that we would understand the following example:

Elder John Taylor, president and presiding apostle of this Church, father, husband, and friend to many, was once a great bishop, stake president, teacher, author, editor, missionary, and servant to many who came before him.

After reading this statement, no one would accuse and Elder Smith of impersonating John Taylor if Elder Smith's acquaintances simply referred to him as "Elder." Why is it then that when Jesus refers to himself as Jehovah or "the Father," many people are prone to believe that Jesus is declaring himself to be God the Father? The answer appears to be that people have difficulty accepting the fact that "Jehovah" and "Father" are used as titles of deity and not as proper nouns - this is the crux of their confusion.

Scriptures where the titles of deity are transliterated can be horrifically baffling if not read from this perspective. Consider the following:[175]

Genesis 2:4	*Jehovah Elohim* made the earth.
Genesis 15:2	And Abram said, *Jehovah Elohim*, what wilt thou give me?
Genesis 28:13	I am *Jehovah*, the *Elohim* of Abraham thy father, and the *Elohim* of Isaac.
Exodus 7:1	And the *Jehovah* said unto Moses, See, I have made thee a[n] *Elohim* to Pharaoh.
Exodus 10:7	Let the man go, that they may serve the *Jehovah their Elohim*.
Deuteronomy 1:21	Behold, the *Jehovah thy Elohim* hath set the land before thee: go up and possess it, as the *Jehovah Elohim* of thy fathers hath said unto thee; fear not.
Deuteronomy 3:24	Oh, *Jehovah Elohim*, thou hast begun to shew thy servant thy greatness, and thy mighty hand: for what *Elohim* is there in heaven?
Deuteronomy 6:4-50	Hear O Israel: *Jehovah our Elohim is one Jehovah*; and thou shalt love *Jehovah thy Elohim*.
Deuteronomy 10:12	And now, Israel, what doth the *Jehovah thy Elohim* require of thee, but to fear the *Jehovah thy Elohim*, to walk in all his ways, and to love him, and to serve the *Jehovah thy Elohim* with all thy heart and with all thy soul?

---

[175] These examples are shortened to facilitate the point.

Deuteronomy 10:17	*Jehovah your Elohim is Elohim of Elohim[s]*, and *Adonai* of *Adonais*, the great *El*, mighty and terrible.
Deuteronomy 12:18	But thou must eat them before the *Jehovah thy Elohim* in the place which the *Jehovah thy Elohim* shall choose ... before the *Jehovah thy Elohim* in all that thou puttest thine hands unto.
Joshua 22:22	*Jehovah is El of the Elohim! Jehovah is El of the Elohim!*

If Jehovah and Elohim are considered as titles of deity or as descriptions of attributes held by those in certain deital offices,[176] none of these statements are confusing at all.

Having considered this issue from President Cannon's perspective, approaching this concept from John Taylor's perspective may also prove helpful. 1 Timothy 3:2-4, 6-7 illustrates this concept: "A bishop then must be blameless, the husband of one wife, vigilant, sober, of good behavior, given to hospitality, apt to teach; Not given to wine, no striker, not greedy of filthy lucre; but patient, not a brawler, not covetous; One that ruleth well his own house, having his children in subjection with all gravity; Not a novice ... he must have a good report of them which are without ..." In other words, ideally, it takes certain attributes to qualify for a priesthood office before a man can receive that office. It follows then, that if the priesthood holder is qualified for the office, he must have already obtained those necessary attributes. Therefore, if the office is used as a description of the attributes as John Taylor taught, identifying an individual as "Jehovah" or "Elohim" is akin to calling that individual charitable, kind, benevolent, almighty, etc. Without these understandings, the many scripture references that refer to all three members of the godhead as one can be baffling as well.[177] Indeed, this lack of understanding has caused confusion among Christians for centuries and gave birth to the nonsensical doctrinal teaching we know as "the Trinity." Lastly, instances of "divine investiture of authority" can be quite confusing without these fundamental concepts.[178] A solid understanding of deital titles and offices clears up all of these and similar passages in a way that allows the reader to focus on the message being delivered - as opposed to focusing on the messenger so intently that the message is all but forgotten.

One last statement shows another, rather simplistic, approach that makes all of this very

---

[176] A quick glance through Strong's Exhaustive Concordance of the Bible will supply a much larger list than this, though the reader may note that examples are easier to find in the older books of the Old Testament; to facilitate this process, the reader is reminded that LORD (all caps) in the King James Version of the Bible derives from the Hebrew YHWH (Jehovah) and GOD (all caps) derives from the Hebrew term Elohim.

[177] e.g., John 14:8-11; 1 Nephi 19:10; Mosiah 15:3, 5; D&C 35:2; 50:43; 93:4, 15-17, 20; etc.

[178] e.g., D&C 29:34, 42; 49:5, 28; D&C 124:132.

easy to understand. While some readers may find that this example is easier to understand than all of the previous explanations, I have placed it at the end of this segment because the speaker was only a bishop - as opposed to an apostle or president.

Bishop Heber Bennion	*1920*

Supplement to Gospel Problems, 8-9

Jehovah means son, and is used interchangeably as *the Son and a son. In the dedicatory prayer of the Kirtland Temple the Prophet Joseph repeatedly applies the name of Jehovah to the Father whom he is addressing*, as any one may see by careful perusal of the prayer as recorded in the D&C 109.[179]

Elohim may signify the Father or Grandfather, or Great Grandfather - God or the Council of the Gods, and *Jehovah may be applied to any of them in the capacity or relationship of a son*, as they all are, for `where was there ever a father without first being a son?'[180]

It has been the author's experience that members of the LDS Church who cannot grasp the above concepts will not fully understand Adam-God teachings or they will not accept Adam-God teachings at all. The issues presented within this section are therefore absolutely essential to a comprehensive understanding of Adam-God teachings if the reader is a member of the LDS Church who desires to understand what the early brethren were teaching us about Adam's role as God the Father. In stark contrast, many fundamentalists do not comprehend this concept at all and yet they wholeheartedly accept Adam-God teachings without any apprehension or hesitation concerning the identity of Jehovah, Elohim, the Only Begotten, or the Holy One of Israel. Therefore, the issues presented within this section are important to fundamentalists only because an understanding of these titles can help them to know more about the God they worship and because an understanding of these titles can help them to have a better and more constructive dialog with members of the LDS Church.

---

[179] e.g., verses: 4, 10, 14, 22, 24, 29, 34, 42, 47, 56, 68.
[180] See HC 6:476.

27 Jehovah

The debate as to whether or not Jehovah is the same individual as Jesus Christ has been a particularly divisive point among Christendom ever since the inception of Mormonism's teachings to the contrary. The battle continues to rage among Jehovah Witnesses and mainstream Protestant groups as the former definitively claims that Jehovah is not Jesus Christ (this is a foundational tenet to their religion) and the latter, along with Catholics and the modern LDS Church, claim that Jehovah is Jesus Christ. Various Christian groups have therefore bountifully dispensed their time compiling myriads of scriptures to prove their respective points.[181] Anyone interested in pursuing an exhaustive scriptural debate on this issue will readily find hundreds of scriptures to prove the position of either side of the debate upon even a casual research on the internet. This portion of *Understanding Adam-God Teachings* is not intended to be an exhaustive overview of this scriptural debate. Rather, *the purpose of this subsection of Understanding Adam-God Teachings is to focus on how the early brethren used the term Jehovah in their doctrinal discourses.* Some few scriptural references have been included to support both sides of this issue to satiate the curiosity of the casual reader. However, an exhaustive treatise on the scriptural proofs could easily produce another full volume of research, which volume is hereby left for another time - or for another author.

Boyd Kirkland, writing on this subject, noted that the early brethren almost exclusively used the term Jehovah in a generic sense to identify the God of the old testament or, more generally, to identify the one true God. Unfortunately, he did not document this information in a readily verifiable fashion so that the reader could independently make their own assessment as to whether or not his conclusions were accurate. What follows

---

[181] See "Scriptures: Jehovah is Christ".

is the author's compilation of hundreds of references to "Jehovah" by the early brethren. While the following compilation does not represent every reference from the early brethren that is currently available for research, it does include a sampling large enough to refute any claim that the following materials could not be representative as they do include every reference in the twenty six volumes of the Journal of Discourses, every reference in the first thirty nine volumes of the Millennial Star,[182] every reference in the Messenger and Advocate, the Evening and Morning Star, and the Times and Seasons - along with many references found in other crucial nineteenth century periodicals. This sampling generally verified what Kirkland claimed. However, this research is distinctive because all of these references are included below, in their respective categories, so that the reader can retrace and verify this research if they remain skeptical and because several representative statements have been compiled under each heading to allow the reader to readily examine each genre of statements in context.

The reader may take notice that this debate is not a trivial side note to the larger purposes of this volume. Rather, this is a crucial topic (though virtually unaddressed in previous Adam-God publications) because Adam-God teachings are not compatible with modern LDS Church teachings largely due to the modern LDS Church's claim that Jehovah is Jesus Christ. If this position is true, then the endowment (and many scriptures) clearly refute Adam-God teachings. On the other hand, if Adam-God teachings reflect true doctrine, then the Jehovah of the Old Testament cannot possibly be the same individual as Jesus Christ.

To demonstrate how the early brethren used the term Jehovah, I have divided the materials in this subsection into the following categories:

Who is Jehovah?	Particularly divisive statements that *can* be read in various ways to identify Jehovah with different individuals
Jehovah is God	Generic usage of the term Jehovah, including a few representative examples and references to well over a thousand similar statements
Jehovah is Christ	Statements that declare that Jehovah is Jesus Christ
Scriptures: Jehovah is Christ	Statements that have been used to argue that Jehovah and Jesus Christ are the same individual
Jehovah is not Christ	Statements that declare that Jehovah or the God of the

---

[182] This takes us through the year 1877; later volumes are not readily available and theological doctrines were undergoing change by that time as well.

	Old Testament is not Jesus Christ; this is divided into four smaller subsections
Scriptures: Jehovah	Statements that include the transliterated term "Jehovah"
Jehovah is not Adam	Statements that distinguish Jehovah from Adam

Although the issues surrounding the identity of Jehovah could be analyzed in many different fashions, I organized this portion of this volume in this manner because I believe that it *definitively* demonstrates that the modern LDS Church's position is not consistent with the teachings of Joseph Smith (and other early brethren) and because it should *facilitate* a *more productive and thorough dialog* between fundamentalists and mainstream members of the LDS Church. As this Jehovah issue is a particularly divisive one, I hope that this research will be especially helpful in bridging the gap of understanding between the LDS Church and Mormon fundamentalism.[183]

Finally, the reader may note that after all of these statements are analyzed, one conclusion should be absolutely lucid to the reader: until the early 1880s, there appears to have been no controversy as to the identity of Jehovah.[184] The term Jehovah was almost universally used in a generic fashion, although there are periodic and somewhat regular pronouncements that Jesus was the son of Jehovah and that modern Latter-day Saints worship Jehovah, the only true God. Additionally, prayers to Jehovah were not sparse or uncommon, whether those prayers were offered in public or in print. Thus, it seems clear that the early saints understood that they were worshipping the same God that Abraham and Jesus worshipped - Jehovah.

What may not be so clear from these statements (or from the following materials) is that the confusion as to who Jehovah is arose about the same time as the saints began to reject

---

[183] This is not to say that I expect all readers to be persuaded by every decision that I have made in classifying these statements – surely there will be some disagreements here (although I believe that all of the placements herein are the most *objective* placements; whether or not the source of any given statement may have *subjectively* understood his statement in another fashion is a different issue – however, if this standard were to be used, it seems that less statements would be under "Who is Jehovah?" and more statements would be under the subsection "Jehovah is not Christ"). However, I believe that any reasonable person reading these materials will come to the conclusion that the fundamentalist position as to the identity of Jehovah is both rational and legitimate – and accurate if the early brethren are to be accepted as authorities on this subject.

[184] There are only isolated statements that clearly identify Jesus as Jehovah and they do not emanate from any noteworthy authorities.

Adam-God teachings. As the saints lost the light and knowledge associated with Adam-God teachings, they also lost the light and knowledge as to the identity of the God that they worshipped. Modern saints believe that Adam worshipped Jesus and that they worship the Father of Jesus. Thus, they have lost some understanding as to whom they worship; their focus has accordingly taken them to a more Protestant-like emphasis on Jesus - after all, the entire Old Testament, New Testament, and Book of Mormon contain a record of men worshipping Jesus or of men interacting with Jesus. While an emphasis on our glorious Redeemer and Savior is far from reproachable in any fashion, losing focus on the identity of the only true God, apart from his status as our spiritual father, somewhat distances modern saints from the goal of gaining life eternal. That is, "this is life eternal, that they might know *thee*, the *only true God.*" To gain eternal life, *it is not enough* to know who Jesus Christ is, we *must* know who the only true God is as well. (John 17:3)

When the evidence within this subsection is considered with the evidence found throughout the rest of this volume, it seems clear that the early brethren clearly understood that Jehovah was not Jesus Christ. As I plowed through these several hundred quotes, this fact became overwhelmingly lucid. At times, this clarity of understanding obtained from such a broad and sweeping overview made it very difficult to categorize some specific quotes because the generic usage of the term in those specific quotes coincided so consistently with the rhetorical structure of statements distinguishing Jehovah from Jesus that it seemed more proper to place the statement under the subsection distinguishing Jehovah from Jesus (although, I believe that ultimately *all* of these difficult choices were resolved in favor of placing the statements under "Jehovah is God" because this seemed more objective). Given the results of this research and the abundant examples distinguishing Jesus from Jehovah, it is not unfair to suggest that this may have been due to the fact that it was universally understood by the early brethren that Jesus and Jehovah were not the same individual. This inference appears to be true during the leadership of Joseph Smith, Brigham Young, and John Taylor as demonstrated below. Although this conclusion may be difficult for the modern member of the LDS Church to swallow, the reader will most likely concur after reading through this subsection. For the moment, consider these two late statements from Joseph Smith, Jr.:

Joseph Smith   *11/15/1841*
T&S 3:578
We believe in God the Father, who is the great Jehovah and head of all things, *and that Christ is the Son of God*, co-eternal with the Father; yet he is our Savior, Redeemer, King, and Great Prototype; - was offered as a sacrifice to make an atonement for sin - rose from

the dead with the same flesh and bones, not blood, and ascended to heaven, and is now seated at the right hand of the Father.

Joseph Smith   *circa 8/--/1842*
HC 5:127

O Thou, who seest and knowest the hearts of all men - Thou eternal, omnipotent, omniscient, and omnipresent *Jehovah - God - Thou Eloheim*, that sittest, as saith the Psalmist, "enthroned in heaven," look down upon Thy servant Joseph at this time; and let faith on the name of *Thy son Jesus Christ*, to a greater degree than Thy servant ever yet has enjoyed, be conferred upon him.

As a footnote to this subsection, the reader should understand that, although these brethren primarily and consistently identified Jehovah as the Father of Jesus Christ, this does not mean that the above discussion on the usage of Jehovah as a title is no longer universally applicable. What it does mean is that the early brethren appear to have believed that the title Jehovah was more appropriately applied to God the Father - which does not explicitly preclude its appropriate application to Jesus (Jehovah's son) as "bishop" Heber Bennion noted. Hopefully, the presentation of the following research will further illuminate these principles for the reader. That said, the theological shift identifying the Jehovah of the Old Testament as Jesus Christ would unquestionably have been seen as error by the early brethren.[185]

---

[185] Perhaps Orson Pratt may not have seen this as error as many of his related writings appear to make this same error; however, Orson Pratt was consistently opposed to Adam-God teachings. See "Statements of Unbelief: Orson Pratt" below.

Who is
Jehovah?

~

The following statements would likely generate the greatest amount of discussion were adherents to the opposing positions to this question to sit down for a discussion on the issue of who is Jehovah. As in the following subsection entitled "Jehovah is God", each of these statements can be read in a way that substantiates either position and/or can be read in a way that substantiates one position but does not discredit the other position. However, these statements are of a more problematic nature as the usage of Jehovah remains fairly generic but *its usage is typically placed next to the names of both Jesus and God the Father* without explicitly indicating which personage is Jehovah - or they are placed next to other vague terms that can be understood to support either position. Many authors have felt that it made their position stronger by arguing their position in association with this genre of statement - and indeed, persuasive arguments can and have been written regarding some of the below statements - and perhaps an exhaustive treatise on the subject could theoretically end the conflict. However, after reading books and articles written by both sides of the fence, I have concluded that this type of debate remains unproductive to date because these arguments necessitate the making of assumptions that the opposing position is unwilling to accept. Having placed the evidence before the reader, I remain satisfied to allow the individual reader to make his/her own decision in this matter.

I have therefore placed these statements here primarily for the academic endeavor of showing how much difficulty exists in determining the usage of the term Jehovah among the early brethren given the current positions of the LDS Church and Mormon fundamentalism. If the reader cannot see the ambiguity in any of the below statements, it is very likely that he/she is not familiar enough with the opposing side of the debate to fully grasp the opposing argument in the first place. I would encourage the reader to keep this in mind as these statements are read - they are not particularly interesting or enlightening to read as a whole - and time spent reading this material will be largely unprofitable without this goal in mind: try to read each of these statements in a way that supports the position contrary to your current beliefs. This should facilitate your ability to understand your "opponent's" beliefs and may help you to know how to persuade someone of an opposing opinion to understand your perspective.

Oliver Cowdery   *7/--/1835*

M&A 1:152 #10

The disgraceful scenes of the Missouri mob are too fresh in my mind to be imposed upon by Mr. Bradley, or any other man who thus perverts the word of life, and insults the good feelings of those who have been dispossessed of their homes and houses by lawless marauders, for their religion's sake! Yes, the groans of the dying, the cry of innocent mothers and virgins, the shrieks of helpless infants, have ascended up into the *ears of Jehovah*, as a testimony of the truth of the *religion of the Lord Jesus*, and will ever stand as a memorial, on the records of heaven, against those who afflicted them without cause, and slew without law. And it may be understood, that no man can offer a higher insult to the feelings and dignity of the people in this place, than to say that he that lives godly, in an ungodly generation, will not be persecuted, saying nothing of the perversion of the word of truth, and the attempt to prove that "he that entereth not by the door into the sheep-fold, but climbeth up some other way is not a thief and a robber!"

"The Elders Abroad"   *9/--/1835*

M&A 1:188 #12

According to the word of *God*, water is used to cleanse men from sin, and will do it effectually too, if applied in a legal manner. All ordinances, that are instituted of *Jehovah*, will avail nothing unless they are administered by one who has been authorized of the *Lord* himself.

Joseph Smith   *3/1/1842*

HC 4:541

[T]he standard of truth has been erected: no unhallowed hand can stop the work from progressing, persecutions may rage, mobs may combine, armies may assemble, calumny may defame, but the truth of God will go forth boldly, nobly, and independent till it has penetrated every continent, visited every clime, swept every country, and sounded in every ear, till the *purposes of God* shall be accomplished and *the great Jehovah* shall say the work is done.

Hyrum Smith   6/1/1842

T&S 3:801 #15

Let these things be adhered to; let the saints be wise; let us lay aside our folly and abide by the commandments of *God*; so shall we be blessed of the *great Jehovah* in time and in eternity: we shall be healthy, strong and vigorous: we shall be enabled to resist disease; and wisdom will crown our councils, and our bodies will become strong and powerful, our progeny will become mighty, and will rise up and call us blessed; *the daughters of Jesus* will be beautiful, and her sons the joy of the whole earth; we shall prepare ourselves for the purposes of *Jehovah* for the kingdom of *God* for the appearance of *Jesus* in his glory; "out of Zion the perfection of beauty," *God* will shine; Zion will be exalted, and become the praise of the whole earth."

Joseph Smith   2/--/1843

MS 3:166-67 #10; LF

We ask, then, where is the prototype? or where is the saved being? We conclude ... that it is in *Christ*. ... And if we should continue our interrogation, and ask how it is that he is saved, the answer would be, because he is a just and holy being; and if he were any thing different from what he is, he would not be saved, for his salvation depends on his being precisely what he is and nothing else; for if it were possible for him to change in the least degree, so sure he would fail of salvation and lose all his dominion, power, authority, and glory, which constitutes salvation; for salvation consists in the glory, authority, majesty, power, and dominion which *Jehovah* possesses, and in nothing else; and no being can possess it but himself or one like him.

                                                                           3/1/1843

T&S 4:121 #8; MS 4:41 #3

Ever *since the fall of man the great Jehovah* has had it in his mind to restore him to his pristine excellency, to remove the curse from the brute creation and to restore the earth to its primitive glory; nay, while this earth was one dark chaotic mass, before God said "let there be light, and it was so," or ever this world rolled into existence, or the morning stars sung together for joy a plan was formed in the councils of heaven, it was contemplated by the great Author of our existence, *Eloheim, Jehovah, to redeem* the earth from under the curse. Hence when the *Gods* deliberated about the formation of man, it was known that he would fall and the *Savior* was provided who was to redeem and to restore, who was indeed the "Lamb slain from the foundation of the world." The eternal plan of *Jehovah* however, was as perfect at that time as it is now the foundation was perfectly laid the outlines were clearly sketched with a master hand, and the interstices have been filling up from that day to this. Satan has gained no more power, than he has been permitted to hold; the universe has been under the direction of the Lord of Hosts and it will be seen by and by that he whose right it is, will possess the earth, Satan will be bound, the earth redeemed, and "the kingdoms of this world become the kingdoms of our *God*, and of his *Christ*.

William Hyde 7/15/1844

T&S 5:589-90 #13

Would they but examine the matter they would find that the so called "Mormon delusion" beautifully harmonizes with the scriptures - reconciles many seeming contradictions - explains many difficult passages - restores the primitive order and simplicity of the Church - fulfills many of the prophecies - and gives us just conceptions of the character, attributes and perfections of the Deity. It contains some of the most glorious grand, and sublime principles ever imagined by the mind of man - it reveals a plan of life in a future state of existence, worthy conceptions of a *God*; it elevates *our ideas of Jehovah* and of his creation; it plainly shows the whole duty of the Saint - the plan of salvation; the straight and narrow path - and, in short, it is a perfect system of Theology, as far before the clanging, jarring systems of modern divinity, as the Gospel of *Jesus Christ* was before the systems of the Pharisees and Sadducees, or as the plan of salvation devised by *Jehovah* before the worlds began is before any of the systems of Sectarianism.

William Hawkins Sr. et al 5/4/1847

MS 9:167

And may the number of those that read and enjoy that knowledge that is given unto us in the Star, and brother M. Martin's pamphlet, the Voice of Warning, Book of Doctrine and Covenants, which is the *voice of God* unto us, the *message of Jehovah* unto the children of men, and by which they will have to be judged.

Charles Derry circa 1852

MS 13:310

The *Son*, in obedience to his *Father*, came forth in the appointed time, paid the debt incurred by the fall, and thus purchased the redemption of all that was lost; for surely it will be admitted that the amount which was paid to liquidate the debt was equal to the debt itself; or how could the demands of justice be satisfied, or the decree of *Jehovah* be fulfilled? The will also admit that the atonement of *Christ* was equal to the transgression of *Adam*;

Brigham Young   *2/27/1853*

JD 1:119

A great promise was made to Abraham, which was - you shall have seed, and unto your increase there shall be no end. The same promise was made *unto the Savior*, and unto every true and faithful man who serves *God* with all his heart, and whose delight is in keeping the *law of the Lord*, obeying the behests of *Jehovah*, and building up *His kingdom* upon the earth.

Brigham Young   *7/24/1854*

JD 2:16

My prayer is that the Saints may understand that they are safe as long as they listen to the Priesthood authorized of heaven, are united in one, and not divided into clans, but become one great clan, under one head. Then let all the clanism of the world rally against us, and we are as firm as the rock of ages, that supports the throne of *Jehovah*. May *God* bless you with the truth as it is in Himself, and save you in *His kingdom, through Jesus Christ*. Amen.

Belinda Maren Pratt   *7/--/1854*

MS 16:471

A noble man of God, who is full of the Spirit of the Most High, and is counted worthy to converse with *Jehovah*, or with the *Son of God*;[186] and to associate with angels, and the spirits of just men made perfect; one who will teach his children, and bring them up in the light of unadulterated and eternal truth; is more worthy of a hundred wives and children, than the ignorant slave of passion, or of vice and folly, is to have one wife and one child.

Orson Hyde   *10/6/1854*

JD 2:80

When God said, Go forth and replenish the earth; it was to replenish the inhabitants of the human species, and make it as it was before. Our first parents, then, were commanded to multiply and replenish the earth; and if *the Savior* found it his duty to be baptized to fulfil all righteousness, *a command* of far less importance than that of

---

[186] This statement as it stands, supports the position that Jesus is Jehovah. However, the removal of the comma after Jehovah reverses the meaning - that is, without the comma, the statement would read that Jehovah is not Jesus. Because the usage of commas was no more standardized in periodicals in the 1800s than it is today, I placed this quote in this subsection because sufficient ambiguity may remain in the minds of some readers. I have been consistent in this decision and have placed statements that support the position that Jesus is not Jehovah in this subsection as well if a comma is the deciding factor.

multiplying his race, (if indeed there is any difference in the *commandments of Jehovah*, for they are all important, and all essential,) would he not find it his duty to join in with the rest of the faithful ones in replenishing the earth?

11/--/1858

MS 20:725

The worst of criminals - even those who have crowned by murder a life of horrible depravity and sin, if they will shed a few tears and declare themselves penitent, are gravely informed that the fatal drop is a short cut into the holy abode of the immaculate *Jehovah* and a swift passage into the arms of *Jesus*!

John Taylor *5/8/1862*

JD 10:56

We should feel as this man said, "I am doing a great work, and I, myself, and my family and all my interests, and in fact everything that I have are bound up in the kingdom of *God*. I am a servant of the Great *Jehovah*; *God* is my father, he has established his kingdom upon the earth. *I am one of his servants*, one of his Elders, and I am trying to help to build up his kingdom, and to introduce a reign of righteousness, to roll back the dark cloud that has overspread the world, and to do something that will tend to roll forth the *Redeemer's* kingdom, and therefore I cannot condescend to the worldly vanity that I see around me."

8/--/1864

MS 26:547

The sceptic may sneer at our confidence in *God* and call it simplicity, but we know that *Jehovah* lives and reigns and manifests his goodness unto his children.

circa 1866

MS 28:314

The Saints who have sailed this season were promised, *in the name of Jehovah*, that if they would live their religion, retain the Spirit of the living God in them, they should have power over this fell destroyer, which has carried off so many of the Gentile emigration.

George Q. Cannon *3/3/1867*

JD 11:334-35

Though it was an age of enlightenment, so called, they could not recognize *God* in *Jesus*, nor divinity in the work which he performed; neither could they recognize any of the power of the apostleship in his Apostles. Who did see it? Why those who bowed in submission to the plan which *God* revealed through His son *Jesus Christ*; they comprehended these things, and were able to distinguish between the man of *God* and the man of the world; they were able to distinguish between the truth of heaven when it came pure and unadulterated from the throne of *Jehovah*, and the systems of men proclaimed on every hand.

Orson Pratt   *5/5/1870*

JD 13:357

If there were any who had so much means or property that they did not feel disposed to leave their pleasant homes and make a sacrifice of their wealth, in some measure, in order to fulfil the commandment of *Jehovah*, I will venture to say that they are not in the Church today. Why? Because God would withdraw His Holy Spirit from them. They might make great profession, and say how much they loved the Lord and His ways; how much they loved *Jesus*, who was crucified for the sins of the world, yet all this would be foolish and vain if they refused to keep his commandments, for, "If ye love me, keep my commandments," saith the *Savior*.

Brigham Young   *5/8/1870*

JD 14:41

We have proof that *God* lives and that he has a body; that he has eyes, and ears to hear, that he has arms, hands and feet; that he can walk and does walk. He has declared himself to be a man of war - *Jehovah*, the great *I Am*, the *Lord* Almighty, and many other titles of a like import are used in reference to him in the Scriptures. But take away the atonement of the *Son of God* and the Scriptures fall useless to the ground.

Orson Pratt   *8/20/1871*

JD 14:243

[A]s the Father and Son are one, and both of them called *Gods*, so will all His children be one with the Father and the Son, and they will be one so far as carrying out the great purposes of *Jehovah* is concerned.

John Taylor   *10/10/1875*

JD 18:137

God has certain purposes to accomplish, pertaining to the world in which we live, in which the interests and happiness of the human family are concerned to those who live in the world today, to those who have lived in other ages and dispensations, back to the time of *Adam*, and also forward, to the latest generation of time, to the last man who shall be born upon the earth. The ancient Patriarchs and Prophets, men of *God* who basked in the light of revelation, and comprehended the mind of *Jehovah*, and who held the everlasting Priesthood, and enjoyed the Gospel as we enjoy it; all these together with *God* our heavenly Father and all the angelic hosts, are interested in the work that the Father has commenced in these last days; and hence a revelation was made unto Joseph Smith. *Holy angels of God* appeared to him and communicated to him the mind and will of *Jehovah*, as a chosen messenger to introduce the dispensation of the fullness of times, wherein all heaven and all that have ever dwelt on the earth are concerned and interested.

Aurelius Miner   *5/11/1879*

JD 20:234-36

It seems then that this Holy Ghost is full of intelligence, full of knowledge, full of power, and is the acting minister of *God* throughout all the dominions of the great *Jehovah*. That spirit reveals to man that *Jesus* is the Christ, and Christ reveals the fact of the existence, power and glory of *his Father*.[187] And this is the order. And how shall we know this fact? By rendering obedience to the ordinances, and then you can know it for yourselves. It is no great trouble; a little cold water will not hurt any of you.

John Taylor   *7/6/1879*

JD 20:302

Take of the things of *God* and show them to them, and bring them into communion with the Lord *Jesus* Christ and with the Father and into communion with the holy angels and prophets who lived before, enjoying the same Gospel, the same light, the same intelligence, the same spirit and the same power; that they might be one with each other, one with the ancient apostles, prophets, patriarchs and men of *God* who have lived in the different ages; one with the Lord *Jesus* Christ, operating together for the one great purpose of *Jehovah* pertaining to the welfare, happiness and exaltation of the world and the people thereof. And hence, say the scriptures, you have all been baptized into one baptism. And what else? You have all partaken of the same spirit, as *Jesus* says, "that they may be one, even as we are one: I in them, and they in me, that they may be made perfect in one."

Orson Pratt   *11/12/1879*

JD 21:197-98

Jesus was [at the creation] - the First Born of this great family of our *Father* in heaven. He had the superintendence of this creation. He had the power, because the power dwelt

---

[187] See John chapter 14.

within him, to build this earth of ours, the same as you give to your superintendent power to build your temples, about which Brother Rich has been speaking. It is said that the worlds were made through our Lord *Jesus* Christ. But do you suppose that he alone made them? No; he had the sons and daughters of *God* with him. And *there were prophets in those days, before our earth was made*. They shouted for joy when they saw the nucleus of this creation formed. Why? Because they could look into the future, and by the spirit of prophecy, behold the designs and purposes of the great *Jehovah* in regard to the creation which they were then in the act of forming.

Charles W. Penrose   *4/11/1880*

JD 21:140

[E]very nation, kindred, tongue and people, shall hear of the purposes of the Great *Jehovah*; until all people shall be warned, and the honest and upright, and the truth-loving in every clime shall be gathered unto the fold of *Christ*; until the way shall be prepared for the coming of the Lord *Jesus* Christ - to reign in Mount Zion and Jerusalem, and before his ancients gloriously; until the earth is redeemed from the curse; until Satan and his hosts are bound; until the great work of *God* is accomplished and all his children brought up from death and hell and the grave, and placed in a position where they can glorify *God* throughout the countless ages of eternity.

John Taylor   *1/2/1881*

JD 21:342-43

When we talk about the theories of men, they are matters of very little importance; when we reflect upon their ideas or views, they are really unimportant, but when we talk about the law of *God*, the plans of *Jehovah* and his designs pertaining to the world in which we live and its inhabitants, and to the inhabitants that have lived, and to all humanity, then we touch upon a subject that is grand, noble and sublime; one that enters into the recesses of the heart and that touches every fibre, and that causes our hopes and aspirations to reach within the vail, *where Christ our forerunner has gone*, and we feel convinced that there is an eternal fitness in all the laws, in all the truths, in all the ordinances, and in everything that *God* has revealed for the salvation and exaltation of the human family.

Ray   *9/--/1881*

Contributor 2:370 #12

On what, then, do the Latter-day Saints base their observance of the Lord's day? They certainly acknowledge the divine origin of the Ten Commandments, and recognize their claim for acceptance by all the followers of *Jehovah or Jesus*,[188] and believe that the command to keep holy the Sabbath day is as obligatory upon them as is the other mandates, "Thou shalt not kill," or "Thou shalt not bear false witness against thy neighbor."

Joseph A. West   *8/--/1882*

Contributor 3:331 #11

[N]one of the churches believe in revelation from *God*. Then by whom have these gifts and ordinances been done away, or by whom declared no longer necessary? By the voice and authority of puny man, raised in defiance against the mandates of *Jehovah*, and in subversion of those very principles of eternal truth for which *Jesus* and His apostles laid down their lives; therefore, while modern Christians pretend to revere *Jesus* and build costly churches in commemoration of His apostles, they crucify them in their hearts by denying the efficacy of their ministry and mission, and by teaching men to do away with those very principles which they lived and died to establish.

Joseph T. Kingsbury   *10/--/1882*

Contributor 4:14 #1

[L]et us lay aside our folly and abide by the commandments of *God*, so shall we be blessed of the great *Jehovah* in time and in eternity; we shall be healthy, strong and vigorous; we shall be enabled to resist disease, and wisdom will crown our councils, and our bodies will become strong and powerful: our progeny will become mighty, and will rise up and call us blessed; the daughters of Zion will be beautiful, and her sons the joy of the whole earth; we shall prepare ourselves for the purposes of *Jehovah* - for the kingdom of *God* - for the appearance of *Jesus* in His glory, "out of Zion, the perfection of beauty; *God* will shine - Zion will be exalted, and become the praise of the whole earth."

John Taylor   *1/21/1883*

JD 24:36

Is there are any greater position that man can occupy upon the earth than to be engaged as a herald of salvation, commissioned of the great *Jehovah* to proclaim the words of life to a fallen world, and to call upon them to repent and be baptized *in the name of Jesus* for the remission of sins, promising them if they do it that they shall receive the Holy Ghost?

---

[188] This statement actually strongly supports the argument that Jehovah is *not* Jesus. However, were one to insert a comma after the word Jehovah, then the meaning would turn 180 degrees and suggest that Jehovah is Jesus.

George Q. Cannon   *6/30/1883*

JD 24:227-28

This work was commenced by the *Almighty*; it has been carried on by Him, and sustained by His power, and if it is ever consummated it will be by the power, and direction and sustenance of the Lord *Jehovah*, of *Jesus*,[189] the Mediator of the new covenant, and then through the medium of the Priesthood here upon the earth. These things originated in the heavens, in the councils of the Gods; and the organization of the Priesthood and the power thereof, and everything pertaining thereto, has been committed from the heavens through Joseph Smith, principally, and through others who have been associated with him in this great work.

Robert S. Spence   *6/--/1883*

Contributor 4:359 #9

[A]s a sign of *Christ's* coming, for without this sign, the purposes of *Jehovah* could not be consummated, for upon it hinges all the "law and the prophets," and the gathering and restoration of "scattered Israel is to be brought about by its agency;" in "the *Lord's* hand," its potency is being felt, and the time is fast approaching when its internal evidence will be received …

Charles W. Penrose   *11/16/1884*

JD 26:79

Now, I expect that there are many people in the world who, in the absence, or for the want of knowledge concerning the plan of salvation would almost feel the same when told that if they did not obey the Gospel, they would be damned. But when people are enlightened concerning the plan of *Jehovah*, the Gospel of the *Son of God*, they can easily reconcile justice and mercy as being attributes of the Great Being whom we worship.

Joseph E. Taylor   *3/--/1885*

Contributor 6:232 #6

If our souls and bodies are not looking forth for the coming of the Son of Man, we shall be among those who are calling for the rocks to fall upon us, etc." But how shall we know of His near approach in order to make this very necessary preparation? As the exact time cannot be ascertained, for this it appears is *hid in the bosom of Jehovah*, yet we are not left in utter ignorance upon this point, for the Savior Himself, in speaking to

---

[189] Again, the given punctuation grants a stronger argument to place this statement in the subsection distinguishing Jesus from Jehovah; however, because the sentence structure is not strictly parallel, an argument remains that this statement suggests that Jehovah is one and the same individual as Jesus.

His disciples upon the eastern continent, gave them many signs whereby they might know of His near approach.[190]

James E. Talmage 12/--/1887

Contributor 9:66 #2

It would be difficult to name a substance which does more toward beautifying and diversifying the surface of our earth and its surroundings. The gorgeous tints of morn and eve; the glorious bow, which seals the covenant of the Great *Jehovah with his children*,[191] and which must ever remain an object of our deepest wonder and admiration; the varying effects of cloud and mist-all are due to the water drops suspended in the air.

M. A. Greenhalgh 9/--/1888

Contributor 9:431 #11

The more the subject is dispassionately weighed the more strong the conviction becomes that it was the light of a new revelation shining in the hearts and influencing the conscience and conduct of men. In other words, that *Christ* in his person and work was the manifested power and wisdom of *God*, not only to the Jew but to the Gentile, *Jehovah*, supreme over all.

John Taylor 1892

Mediation and Atonement, Ch. 21

As the Son of Man, He [*Jesus*] endured all that it was possible for flesh and blood to endure, as the Son of *God* He triumphed over all, and forever ascended to the right hand of *God*, to further carry out the designs of *Jehovah* pertaining to the world and to the human family.

Wilford Woodruff 4/7/1895

CD 4

It seems that from the time of the great rebellion in heaven, when one-third of the hosts of heaven were cast down for their rebellion against the great *Eloheim and Jehovah, the Creator of heaven and earth*, there has been a warfare against *God*, against *Christ*, against His Church, against His Priesthood, and against everything that would tend to salvation

---

[190] Placing this quote in this subsection is particularly generous to the LDS Church position because it is only in the JST that we read that Jesus, not only the Father, knows the time of his coming - thus, the Jehovah here could be either the Father or the Son. Most members of the LDS Church are unaware of this change made by Joseph Smith.

[191] We are, at times, referred to as the children of Christ in the scriptures.

and eternal life. ... How much longer I shall talk to this people I do not know; but I want to say this to all Israel: Cease troubling yourselves about who God is; who *Adam* is, who *Christ* is, who *Jehovah* is. For heaven's sake, let these things alone.

Wesley's Collection   *1912*

Sacred Hymns, 68 #57

Away with our fears! the glad morning appears
When the heir of salvation was born
From *Jehovah* I came, for his glory I am
And to Him I with singing return. ...

All honor and praise to the Father of grace,
To the Spirit and Son I return.[192]

W. W. Phelps   *1912*

Sacred Hymns, 280 #250

The name of *Jehovah* is worthy of praising,
And so is the *Savior* an excellent theme;

Eliza R. Snow   *1912*

Sacred Hymns, 343-44 #239

---

[192] This hymn is particularly difficult to interpret without any bias. First, this comes from a Protestant hymn collection, so one must read the hymn with its author's understanding that Jesus and God the Father are one and the same individual. Second, the hymn reads that "[f]rom Jehovah I came," which suggests that the author is a child of Jehovah. Third, the hymn reads that "[t]o the Spirit and Son I return," which allusion appears to be in reference to the first statement. Protestants believe that God is Spirit so this hymn could be read to support the belief that some of the early saints sang this hymn with Adam-God teachings in mind - consider Sacred Hymns, 142 #129 in the "Jehovah - the God of the Old Testament is not Christ" as an example of this usage. However, as the second statement includes a reference to a return to the son, the contrary position is equally plausible. Probably more plausible, given human nature in administering to details such as this, is the possibility that most persons singing this hymn never paid enough attention to this detail to really consider the alternate ways of reading this text in the first place. Alternatively stated, the hymn could be read to show that "to Him I with singing return" is clearly referring to Jehovah (see the previous line in the hymn). In the next stanza, we read that "To the Spirit and Son I return" which could be read as a phrase referring to Jehovah again - that is, "Spirit and Son" could be read to refer to one individual in the same way that we say "his wife and mother." If so, the intent of the author was to indicate that Jesus is the same individual as Jehovah. If that is not the case, then the phrase in the second stanza is distinguishing Jesus from Jehovah.

What though, if the favor of *Ahman*[193] possessing,
This world's bitter hate you are called to endure,
The angels are waiting to crown you with blessings,
Go, brethren! be faithful, the promise is sure.

All, all things are known to the mind of *Jehovah*,
There's nothing concealed from His all-searching eye;
Then, fear not! the hairs of your head are all numbered,
And even the ravens are heard when they cry.

M. A. Morton   *1912*

Sacred Hymns, 379 #319

Respond, ye nations, to His call:
Know now salvation's free to all,
Before *Jehovah's* mandate fall,
For judgment draweth near.

Seek ye the *Son*, His laws obey,
Lest He in anger turn away,
Nor own you in the coming day;
To meet your God prepare.

John Nicholson

Sacred Hymns #336, verse 3
While of These Emblems We Partake

While of These Emblems We Partake
Man broke the law of His estate
And *Jesus* came to expiate,
Atone and rescue fallen man
According to *Jehovah's* plan.

John Taylor

The Gospel Kingdom, 388
Go! *Jehovah* will support you,

---

[193] Joseph taught that Ahman was God the Father.

Gather all the sheaves of worth,
Then, with *Jesus*,
Reign in glory on the earth.

For additional statements of this nature, look up the following sources:
MS 3:100; 4:41; 10:179; 15:476; 16:124; 19:181; 23:404, 497; 26:436; 36:816
M&A 2:307 #20
Contributor 11:163 #5
Elders' Journal 1:56 #4
JD 3:214; 17:149-50; 20:233-34

For additional statements that leave some question as to which member of the godhead is speaking and/or that make conclusory statements that appear to contradict other scriptures, see Exodus 6:3; D&C 20:28; 49:28 (the speaker changes without any demarcation); 50:43

Jehovah is God

The statements listed below demonstrate that the early brethren frequently used the term Jehovah in a very generic sense to refer to God. Although one may find reasons to read some of the below examples as support for the position that Jehovah is Jesus Christ or that Jehovah is not Jesus Christ, these reasons would require assumptions beyond the plain text (which is not to say that any such arguments are not legitimate, convincing, substantial, or meaningful); however, the purpose of this subsection is to summarily demonstrate the usage of this term, not to exhaustively analyze each statement to prove any given position. Therefore, I have not taken the liberty to demonstrate how each statement can be read to substantiate either position. I have used the more lucid statements put forth in other subsections to facilitate that purpose.

Following the first few representative statements below are references to hundreds more examples that are readily accessible to the reader should he/she desire to further research this topic. References are to the paragraph where the statement is found as opposed to the page where the term Jehovah is found so that the reader may find the relevant language a little easier. If the reader is interested in furthering his/her understanding of the nature and character of Jehovah, the references without accompanying statements provide (in many instances) a wealth of information explaining Jehovah's role in the plan of salvation that is not otherwise covered in this volume. This is especially true of the periodicals from the Nauvoo period; in contrast, references in the Journal of Discourses and Collected Discourses typically do not expound upon the character or nature of Jehovah as much as the earlier periodicals do.

Joseph Smith   *11/--/1839*

T&S 1:8 #1

The conduct of the saints under their accumulated wrongs and sufferings, has been praiseworthy; their courage, in defending their brethren from the ravages of mobs; their attachment to the cause of truth, under circumstances the most trying and distressing, which humanity can possibly endure; their love to each other; their readiness to afford assistance to me, and my brethren who were confined in a dungeon; their sacrifices in leaving the state of Missouri, and assisting the poor widows and orphans, and securing them houses in a more hospitable land; all conspire to raise them in the estimation of all good and virtuous men; and has secured them the favor and approbation of *Jehovah*; and a name, as imperishable as eternity. And their virtuous deeds, and heroic actions, while in defense of truth and their brethren: will be fresh and blooming; when the names of their oppressors shall either be entirely forgotten, or only remembered, for their barbarity and cruelty. Their attention and affection to me, while in prison, will ever be remembered by me; and when I have seen them thrust away, and abused by the jailor and guard, when they came to do any kind offices, and to cheer our minds while we were in the gloomy prison house, gave me feelings, which I cannot describe, while those who wished to insult and abuse us, by their threats and blasphemous language, were applauded and had every encouragement given them.

Joseph Smith   *5/1/1844*

MS 5:363 3#; T&S 5:522 #9

It is our purpose to build up and establish the principles of righteousness, and not to break down and destroy. The great *Jehovah* has ever been with me, and the wisdom of God will direct me in the seventh hour. I feel in closer communion and better standing with God than ever I felt before in my life; and I am glad of this opportunity to appear in your midst. I thank God for the glorious day that he has given us.

                                                                          5/15/1845

T&S 6:900 #9

Truth will exalt man to the throne of heaven and crown him with eternal life and dominion in the presence of *Jehovah*.

Brigham Young   *4/6-/1853*

JD 2:32

But what of the Temple in Nauvoo? By the aid of sword in one hand, and trowel and hammer in the other ... many received a small portion of their endowment, but we know of no one who received it in its fulness. And then, to save the lives of all the

Saints from cruel murder, we removed westward, and being led by the all-searching eye of the Great *Jehovah*, we arrived at this place.

Ezra T. Benson	7/13/1855

JD 3:62-63

A man who has labored from the commencement of the work has embraced certain principles because God has commanded him, not because he wanted such principles to be established, not that his appetite was of such a nature that he desired something of the kind, but because the great *Jehovah* had so commanded through His Prophets; and hence these things cannot be ridiculed by the Saints; the counsel of the servants of God cannot be treated with contempt, and set at naught, without condemnation following. Still you will find some who ridicule and treat as naught the holy principles of our religion, and say, "I am sound in faith; I am filled with religion, but I cannot put up with that awful doctrine, polygamy."

Amasa M. Lyman	12/2/1855

JD 3:144

Then the truth is the highest point that can be gained, it is the richest gem that can be possessed; you cannot go beyond it, nor stop short of it without partaking of falsehood, and error. There is no alternative left. The principle that governs the dwelling of *Jehovah* is truth, simple truth, and that is all there is upon which a permanent foundation for happiness can be laid.

Heber C. Kimball	9/2/1860

JD 8:211-12

It is true the Lord had a hand in the establishment of some of the laws connected with the government of Israel; but even that people, in consequence of the hardness of their hearts, rebelled against the righteous, just, and holy laws that God ordained for their good, and desired laws of a different nature, and a form of government more resembling the corrupt nations around them. They were a hard-hearted people, and delighted to walk in the traditions of the Egyptians, and to follow after the imaginations of their own hearts; and when the pure law of *Jehovah* came forth and was presented to that people, it was more than they were willing to endure; it was too pure for them: they wanted something more suited to their carnal natures.

Amasa M. Lyman	10/7/1862

JD 10:83

The field of learning is boundless, and I venture to say that the most learned man in the world is far more studious when he gets into higher branches than when he first commenced his studies, for he can discover fields of learning which before he could not conceive of, and so it is with the works of *Jehovah*; there is always a field in which the Almighty can display his power and his goodness, and it is enlarging all the time.

Brigham Young   *11/17/1867*

JD 12:99-100

We have seen times in our history as a people, that if the hand of God had not been immediately over us, we must have perished. But to secure His blessings the Lord requires the strict obedience of His people. This is our duty. We obey the Lord, Him who is called *Jehovah*, the Great I AM, I am a man of war, Eloheim, etc. We are under many obligations to obey Him. How shall we know that we obey Him? There is but one method by which we can know it, and that is by the inspiration of the Spirit of the Lord witnessing unto our spirit that we are His, that we love Him, and that He loves us. It is by the spirit of revelation we know this. We have no witness to ourselves internally, without the spirit of revelation. We have no witness outwardly only by obedience to the ordinances.

circa 1867

MS 28:663

All truth is from *God*, whether it is from heaven, or in the arts and sciences which have been developed on the earth. The Gospel is truth - the will of *Jehovah* - that divine science that teaches man that he is a son of God, made in the image of his heavenly Father, to aid him to live in accordance with heavenly laws, until, by continually doing the will of God, he feels that he is accepted of him, that he is called and chosen, and that his reward is sure.

Lorenzo Snow   *10/9/1869*

JD 13:259

It so happened that the King's edict concerned, among others, the three men who had received the revelation from the Lord that they should not worship any image. They were in a rather awkward fix. Either they must set aside the command of *Jehovah* to worship no God but Him, or, on the other hand, disobey the mandate of the King. They knew if they refused to comply with the wishes of so mighty a man as Nebuchadnezzar, their lives would not be of much value, unless they were preserved by the hand of the God of Israel. But they feared not the King and trusted in the arm of *Jehovah* to shield them from evil.

JD 14:247-48

Let me, as an immortal being, know my destiny pertaining to time and eternity, and the destiny of my brethren and friends, and of the earth that I live upon; let me have a religion that will lead me to God, and others may take what they please, it is immaterial to me. I have no quarrel with them. They can have their own ideas and carry out their own views, so far as I am concerned, untrammeled, if they will let me have mine. Let me be surrounded with the panoply of truth, let me have the favor of *Jehovah*, let me associate with angels and the heavens, and eternity be opened to my view, and be placed in such a relationship with God that He can communicate His will to me, and I ask no more of this world.

JD 18:141

And let me say a little farther on a subject that I before referred to, that is, that God could not build up a kingdom on the earth unless he had a Church, and a people who had submitted to his law and were willing to submit to it, and with an organization of such a people, gathered from among the nations of the earth under the direction of a man inspired of God, the mouthpiece of *Jehovah* to his people; I say that, with such an organization, there is a chance for the Lord God to be revealed, there is an opportunity for the laws of life to be made manifest, there is a chance for God to introduce the principles of heaven upon the earth and for the will of God to be done upon earth as it is done in heaven. God could never establish his kingdom upon the earth unless he had a people who would submit themselves to his laws and government; but with such a people he could communicate, to such a people the heavens could be opened; to such a people the angels of God could administer; and among them the will of God could be done upon the earth as it is done in heaven, and among no others, and that is why we are here.

JD 19:270-71

I sometimes illustrate this matter by taking up a pair of shears, if I have one, but then you all know they are composed of two halves, but they are necessarily parts, one of another, and to perform their work for each other, as designed, they belong together, and neither one of them is fitted for the accomplishment of their works alone. And for this reason says St. Paul, "the man is not without the woman, nor the woman without the man in the Lord." In other words, *there can be no God except he is composed of the man and woman united*, and there is not in all the eternities that exist, nor ever will be, a God in any other way. I have another description: There never was a God, and there never will be in all eternities, except they are made of these two component parts; a man and a woman; the male and the female. Some of those who are disposed to cavil will say, how will you explain the idea of a plurality in the female department? Here opens a subject involving philosophy and the philosophical propagation of our species, and it involves the great principles of virtue, and the laws that govern, or should govern through all eternity the commerce of the sexes; and the more they are scanned in the light of true philosophy and revelation, the more it will be proven that the superior wisdom of *Jehovah* has ordained that in the higher type of the Godhead, they are not limited in their union of the sexes; I refer to the female principle.

Orson Hyde   *Sunday 11/3/1878*

JD 20:99

Polygamy is a principle revealed from heaven with a commandment to enter into it practically. The principle is abundantly corroborated in the ancient scriptures, approved of God and sanctioned by all righteous men; and he who labors to overthrow this principle, fights against *Jehovah* and makes himself a shining target, courting the arrows of the Almighty upon his head, heart and country. Would to God, that I could, conscientiously, make an exception here of our wise and learned judges, attorneys, juries and marshals; but conscience forbids it.

Orson Pratt   *Sunday p.m. 9/21/1879*

JD 21:167

God says "Go and obey my law." Congress say "No, you shall not do it." Now the question is - who shall we obey? We would like to be in accord with Congress. We would like to submit ourselves to every ordinance of man. We would like to be good and peaceable citizens, which we are. We don't wish, however, to follow their corruptions - don't we know enough of them? Yes, we do. ... We also know of this horrible social evil that exists among them, and of the corruption, degradation and rottenness that exist in their midst. And as I have said to some of them sometimes, "you come from these dens of infamy, reeking with corruption and rottenness, steeped in crime and bloodshed and you will come here, will you, and teach morality to us? Go home, attend to your own business, cleanse yourselves from your corruptions, for they are a stink in the nostrils of *Jehovah*, and of all honest men, and don't come to set us right in regard to things that God has given us to do, and which with the help of the Lord we will carry out."

Charles W. Penrose   *Sunday p.m. 1/30/1881*

JD 22:67

[W]e have essayed and covenanted to live a new life in Christ Jesus; to seek to do good to all men, and evil to none; and like Daniel of old, to be faithful to the statues and to the decrees and behests of *Jehovah*, the decrees of man against us notwithstanding; we having come to the conclusion in our own minds that God and a few good men form an overwhelming majority.

Wilford W. Woodruff   *Sunday p.m. 4/3/1881*

JD 22:148

The nation cares no more about our practicing the order of plural marriage than any other principle of the Gospel; it would make no difference with us today. Were we to compromise this principle by saying, we will renounce it, we would then have to renounce our belief in revelation from God, and our belief in the necessity of Prophets and Apostles, and the principle of the gathering, and then to do away with the idea and practice of building Temples in which to administer ordinances for the exaltation of the living and the redemption of the dead; and at last we would have to renounce our Church organization, and mix up and mingle with the world, and become part of them. Can we afford to do this? I tell you no, we can not; but we can afford to keep the commandments of God. And I will here say, that we have been sustained by the hand of *Jehovah* in a marvelous and miraculous manner ever since we came to these valleys and proclaimed to the world our belief in the revelation of celestial or plural marriage; and I will say further, and in the name of Jesus Christ our Savior and Elder Brother, we shall be sustained from this time until he comes in the clouds of heaven, inasmuch as we shrink not from the performance of our duties. We have somebody to deal with besides man. The God of heaven holds our destiny; he holds the destiny of our nation and of all the nations, and he controls them. Therefore, I say to the Latter-day Saints, let us be faithful; let us keep the commandments; let us not renounce a single principle or command which God has given to us. ... Let us obey the celestial law of God, that we may have our wives and children with us in the morning of the first resurrection; that we may come forth clothed with glory, immortality and eternal lives, with our wives and children bound to us in the family organization in the celestial world, to dwell with us throughout the endless ages of eternity, together with all the sons and daughter of Adam who shall have kept the commandments of God.

John Taylor   *Sunday p.m. 8/28/1881*

JD 22:303

Say they, "Look, what a wicked people these 'Mormons' are, they have more wives than one. It is true we have mistresses besides our wives; it is true we commit adultery; it is true we are covered with infamy and debauchery; it is true that the stink of our crimes and iniquities rises into the nostrils of *Jehovah*, as it did in former days, but we will cover all that over." But they cannot do it; it sticks out on every side; the covering is too narrow. They are murderers and murderesses of their infants, and the stench of their infamy ascends into the nostrils of *Jehovah*; and you that want them, take them, and you that do will go along with them, and go to perdition with them; and I tell you that in the name of the Lord. And you that want your children to go to perdition send them to be taught by those not of us.

John Taylor   *Sunday 12/9/1883*

JD 24:356-57

"But," say some, "don't you think that when our Legislature meet they had better go to work and pass a law doing away with polygamy?" No; no such thought ever enters my mind; and as I said in the few remarks I made this morning:

"We want no cowards in our ranks, Who will our colors fly, We call for valiant-hearted men, Who are not afraid to die." No yielding up of principles that God has revealed. What, turn our backs on *Jehovah*! and place ourselves in the hands of men who would deprive us of the last vestige of liberty, and take our lives if they had the power! What! shall we forsake God our Heavenly Father? No, never! And all who are for God and His Kingdom say Amen. [The audience responded with a loud "Amen."] We want no trembling in the knees, nor anything of that kind around us. Let those who hold such ideas go among the other class and advocate their views with them, but not with us.

John Taylor

Government of God 9:79-80

Man, however, bears the impress of *Jehovah*, is made after his image, in his likeness, and possesses the principles of intelligence within himself, and the medium of conveying it of others. He possesses also, power to perpetuate his species, as also to communicate his thoughts, his intelligence, genius, and power to others, that are formed like him. He received his intelligence, his spirit, from God, he is part of himself, A spark of Deity, Struck from the fire of his eternal blaze; he came from God as his son, he bears the impress of *Jehovah*, even in his fallen degenerate corrupted state. His powerful intellect, his stately genius, his grasping ambition, his soaring, and in many instances, exalted hopes, display, though he be fallen, the mark of greatness; he bears the impress of Deity and shows that he is of divine origin.

Andrew Jensen   *5/--/1891*
Contributor 12:261 #7

The principle of gathering is one that has been connected with most of the dispensations which the Lord has instituted for the temporal and spiritual salvation of mankind. Whenever he has had a people on the earth who would serve Him and keep His commandments, it has, as a rule, been desirable on their part to separate from the wicked and ungodly, and live by themselves in some country, or tract of country, where they could effect proper organizations and live together in peace and harmony, train their posterity in the fear of God, and worship the great *Jehovah*, according to the revelations and intelligence which he would give them. This they could not successfully do if they were surrounded on all sides by wickedness or mixed up in their associations with those who chose to violate the laws of God and live in transgression continually.

There are literally hundreds of further examples of this genre of references that use the term Jehovah in this generic fashion. For the practical purpose of limiting the size of this volume, I have condensed the following list into categories whenever reasonably possible; the reader may wish to note that some of the following references are somewhat duplicated - that is, whenever a discourse was published in more than one source, I have indicated both sources in the list below, even though the information regarding the identity of Jehovah would have been identical. However, when the material has been put in another subsection in this volume (e.g., "Who is Jehovah"), I have not duplicated those quotes in this section. The reader may also note that in some instances, the categories are somewhat artificial. For instance, the phrase "decree of the great Jehovah" would have been placed under "great J" and "the omnipotent hand of Jehovah" would have been placed under "hand of J" despite the fact that there are separate categories for "decree of J" and "omnipotent J." Statements like "this was not according to Jehovah's purposes" are placed under related headings; in this instance, the citation would be found under "purposes of J." There were several statements that were so unique that few other statements were similar enough to place them in a separate category; these statements, as far as I could discern, did nothing to help us ascertain the identity of Jehovah, so, with a very few exceptions, I have placed these statements under a "Miscellany" section. The grammarian may also note that the clear and vast majority of these vague statements are in the passive voice.

Fundamentalists may object that some of the categories listed below are not properly within this section; e.g., worship of Jehovah, imploring to Jehovah, sacrifice to Jehovah and other phrases listed below have often been used by fundamentalists to prove that Jehovah could not be Jesus; it is, after all, well established LDS Church doctrine that modern members of the LDS Church are instructed not to worship Jesus. However, this argument fails to be convincing to members of the LDS Church because, even though modern members of the Church implicitly believe that the Hebrews worshipped Jesus because they believe that the Jehovah of the Old Testament was Jesus, they believe that this worship was proper at that time.[194] That said, any mention of worshipping Jehovah post-Old Testament era has been placed under the subsection entitled "Jehovah is not Christ". Nonetheless, statements regarding the plans or purposes of Jehovah that appear to be referring to post Old Testament times are included below as well because none of those statements were clear enough to justify putting them in another section.

Neither side of the Jehovah debate will ever be completely satisfied with the genre of classification (which is somewhat arbitrary) that is presented below - and I presume that the vast majority of readers will never bother to do more than briefly skim over these tables;[195] however, there remains a small contingency of readers who will not trust the scholarship of another unless every step of the work is retraceable; it is for this small and scrutinous class of people[196] that I have compiled the following table of materials - and for people who are simply passionate enough about this issue to want to read these statements for themselves so that they can draw their own conclusions.

J is the "Mormonism" of this people	*Contributor* 10:201-02 #6 *MS* 30:275 *JD* 1:89
name of J; J as a Hebrew term	*Contributor* 3:47 #2; 4:425 #11; 11:163 #5 *MS* 2:2, 121 # 8; 2:168 #11; 3:19, 34, 36 #3; 4:2-3; 5:61-62; 6:67, 99-100 #7; 11:74; 12:264; 18:102, 305; 19:101, 102; 22:175; 23:447, 498; 25:808; 26:630; 27:214 Supp.; 36:487 *T&S* 2:483 #18; 2:569 #23; 3:705, 706 #9; 5:502 #8 (17x) *JD* 8:229

---

[194] This does not appear to be officially explained by the LDS Church; additionally, they have frequently taught that worship of Jesus is proper if he appears in person and they use Christ's visit in 3 Nephi to justify this position.

[195] This is also somewhat unfortunate as many of the below statements are worthy of attention, even though much of the subject matter is not particularly relevant to this volume, because reading all of these statements (as a conglomerate entity) really solidifies the concepts explained in this subsection in a way that cannot be entirely replicated by the small amount of materials that I have chosen to produce in this volume. That said, the statements in this table are only a continuance of the genre of statements found underneath this subsection "Jehovah is God", so the reader who only skims over this table is not missing any materials from the other Jehovah subsections - other than the potential statements that may have escaped my notice.

[196] I mean no offense to this personality type as I, myself, fall into that small class of persons.

great J; Great J	*HC* 2:174; 4:108, 436, 473, 595; 5:149; 7:189, 288, 357
	TPJS, 218
	Contributor 3:193-94, 195-96 #7; 4:13 #1; 6:247-49 #7; 7:210, 211 #6; 7:461 #12; 8:125 #4; 8:306 #8; 9:287 #8; 12:204 #6; 12:261 #7
	MS 1:52 #3; 2:121, 122 #8; 3:54-55, 56-57, 98, 99-100 #5; 4:12, 59; 5:36, 118-19 #8; 6:200 # 12; 7:199 #12, 364; 8:98; 10:370; 13:66, 143, 355, 369; 15:87, 203, 390, 453, 720; 17:368, 502, 693; 18:728; 19:120, 252, 343, 358, 551; 20:6, 225, 756; 21:6, 111, 165, 166, 530; 22:779, 814; 23:198, 739; 26:696, 714, 756, 807; 27:12; 29:186, 246, 401; 32:156; 33:274; 34:310; 35:76
	M&A 2:311 #20; 3:438 # 28; 3:454 #29
	T&S 1:118 #8; 2:234 #3; 2:306-07 #7; 2:490 #19; 2; 2:569 #23; 3:626 #4; 3:657-58 #6; 3:759 #12; 3:761 #12; 3:800 #14; 3:936, 939 #23; 4:11 #1; 4:25 #2; 4:75 #5; 4:117 #8; 5:586 #13; 5:684 #19; 6:779 #1; 6:820-821 #4; 6:1106 #21; 39:845
	JD 1:16, 366; 2:37; 9:175-76, 238, 238-39; 12:347, 359-60, 397; 14:246-47, 274-75, 325; 15:47, 363-64; 16:181, 259-60 (2x), 329-30; 17:211-12, 306, 372; 18:131-32, 147, 219; 19:121, 19:148, 217-18, 244, 293-94; 20:193; 21:3-4, 323; 22:217, 225-26; 23:276; 24:36, 126-27; 25:39, 549; 26:332-33
	CD 1 10/7/1887; 1 4/6/1888; 1 6/2/1888; 1 6/2/1888; 2 2/23/1892; 4 4/8/1894; 5 10/10/1887; 5 1/20/1895
as true God or Lord	*HC* 4:256
	Contributor 11:62 #2
	MS 1:217 #8; 10:352; 11:282 (2x); 15:31; 18:751; 21:386; 22:98, 173; 25:147; 36:155
	M&A 1:67 #5
	T&S 5:502 #8
	JD 8:205-06, 224
	Sacred Hymns,[197] 25 #19
worship of J	*Contributor* 1:245 #11; 6:123 #4; 6:241-42 #7; 6:281-82 #8;

---

[197] All of these references in this table are to the 1912 hymnal.

	6:282-83 #8; 7:388 #10
	MS 2:118 #8; 39:57
	T&S 2:561 #23; 5:453 #5
	CD 5 5/8/1898
faith in J; truth of J	*MS* 19:768
	T&S 5:108 #24
	JD 15:312
	Sacred Hymns, 73 #61
prayers /praises /tribute to / vows to J; ask J	*Contributor* 1:82 #4; 4:90-91 #3; 7:377-78 #10; 12:4-5 #1; 12:120 #3; 2:188 #12
	MS 2:188; 11:23 (2x), 272; 12:215; 26:393; 34:291; 39:565
	E&MS 1:67 #9
	Sacred Hymns, 356 #302; 366 #309
confidence / trust in J / confidence in / allegiance to J	*Contributor* 3:298 #10; 6:85 #3
	MS 20:188; 23:304; 25:96; 26:42
	JD 25:76-77
offering / sacrifice to J	*Contributor* 12:4-5 #1; 12:4-5 #1; 6:202 #6
	MS 1:164 #6
attributes / character of J	*MS* 6:36 #3; 19:748; 22:708
	T&S 1:151 #10
	JD 8:80; 16:259-60
	Sacred Hymns, 169 #155
Omnipotent / Almighty / eternal / sovereignty of J	*HC* 5:167, 168; 6:160
	Contributor 2:22 #1; 3:74 #3; 3:111 #4; 3:202 #7; 8:283 #8
	MS 2:65-66 #4; 4:171-72 # 11; 9:54; 13:356; 18:620; 19:696; 20:88; 23:85, 501; 27:189, 299, 358; 32:372
	M&A 3:543 #34
	T&S 2:234 #3; 2:455 #16; 3:657-58 #6; 5:396 #1
	JD 2:77; 23:120
majesty / bliss of J	*Contributor* 7:17-18 #1
	MS 30:277
	T&S 2:408 #13; 5:759 #24
justice / judgment / bar / sentence of J	*Contributor* 3:299-300 #10; 4:161 #5
	MS 6:41 #3; 23:500, 501
	M&A 2:269 #17

	JD 16:175; 21:18
wisdom / intelligence of J	*Contributor* 4:11 #1 *MS* 3:97 #5; 15:322 *M&A* 1:114 #8 *T&S* 3:799 #14; 5:606 #14 *JD* 26:220
mind / will of J	*MS* 13:309; 15:104; 23:467 *M&A* 3:556 #35 *JD* 6:109; 16:223-24, 228; 22:189; 23:193-94, 295 *Sacred Hymns*, 29 #23
work / acts of J; J works	*HC* 4:128, 187 (2x), 386 *LF* 1:16 *TPJS*, 163 *MS* 1:130 #4; 8:21, 74; 15:162, 562; 16:350; 17:487, 774; 18:588; 23:404; 34:20 *T&S* 2:572 #24; 5:406-07 #2 *JD* 2:84
decree(s) of J	*Contributor* 2:264 #9 *MS* 3:7; 15:740; 16:677; 18:820; 22:388; 24:822; 25:160; 28:394; 38:393 *M&A* 2:290 #19 *T&S* 2 #19; 3:692 #8 *JD* 2:368-69; 6:49-50; 7:345, 370; 12:341; 18:327; 19:145; 20:153
dictate(s) / declare / command(ment) / mandates of J; J governs	*Contributor* 3:232 #8; 7:244 #7; 9:374 #10 *MS* 2:65-6 #4; 16:71, 553; 17:291; 19:462; 20:604, 747; 21:552; 23:113 (2x); 24:256; 28:250; 29:290; 34:233; 36:596 *T&S* 2:455 #16; 4:25 #2; 5:746 #23 *JD* 12:49 (2x), 131; 18:334-35, 376; 21:342-43; 22:336-37; 23:178-79; 26:351
fiat of J	*Contributor* 8:143 #4; 13:261 #6 *MS* 26:708 *JD* 18:282
revelations /	*Contributor* 3:356 #12; 4:11 #1; 4:450 #12; 12:231 #6

inspiration / counsel / teachings / lessons / guidance / message / principles / direction of J, etc.	*MS* 3:97 #5; 4:163-64 #10; 15:486; 17:36; 19:568; 20:691; 21:214; 22:340, 500; 24:18, 394; 25:225; 26:759; 28:180; 29:264; 33:358; 34:35 *T&S* 3:799 #14; 3:858 #18; 4:88 #6; 5:409 #2; 5:744 #23 *JD* 12:347; 13:230, 231; 22:131-32 *CD* 2 4/6/1890; 2 1/16/1891; 4 9/7/1895; 5 1/16/1898
plan(s) / design(s) of J	*HC* 5:63 *TPJS*, 250-51 *Contributor* 3:195 #7; 3:354 #12 *MS* 3:56 #4; 4:2-3, 4:58 (2x); 4:59 #4; 5:196-97 #12; 8:85; 9:136; 17:480; 19:139, 178, 184, 358, 382 (2x), 383, 567; 22:694; 23:196, 436, 468, 715, 738; 25:102 *T&S* 3:760-61 #12; 3:856-57 #18; 4:25 #2; 4:74-75 #5 (2x); 5:406-07 #2; 6:1098 #21 *JD* 1:245; 6:111; 10:258-59, 375; 11:37; 14:275-76; 18:197; 19:138, 238-39 (2x); 21:274, 290-91, 341-42; 22:293 *Sacred Hymns*, 403 #337 *CD* 2 5/10/1891; 4 3/11/1894; 4 10/27/1895 *Mediation and Atonement*, Ch. 16
purpose(s) of J	*Contributor* 2:90 #3; 3:310 #10; 4:309 #8; 7:382 #10; 12:204 #6 *MS* 3:47 #3; 3:99-100 # 5; 4:3-4; 4:59 #4; 4:141 #9; 11:310; 15:1, 58, 410, 649, 665, 753; 16:309; 17:241; 18:133, 570; 19:20, 763; 20:130, 603, 735, 748; 21:320, 445, 529, 736; 22:485, 500; 23:572; 24:329, 345, 378, 705; 25:4, 35, 276; 26:340, 566, 672; 27:22, 130; 28:308; 32:278; 36:358; 37:121; 39:41, 55, 502, 707, 726, 743 *M&A* 3:557 #35 *T&S* 2:400-01; 2:424 #14 (2x); 4:25 #2; 4:75 #5; 6:1102 #21 *JD* 1:223, 369-70; 2:213; 7:163-4; 14:69-70, 191, 248; 18:342; 19:79, 19:281; 20:227, 243-44; 23:182; 23:235; 26:165-66, 218-19, 272 *Sacred Hymns*, 398 #332 *CD* 1 4/4/1886; 3 7/16/1893; 5 10/4/1896
behests of J	*T&S* 4:188 #12 *JD* 11:338; 17:210; 22:239;

promise(s) / oath / covenant of J	*HC* 4:492-93 *Contributor* 1:74 #4; 3:248 #8; 4:345-46 #9; 5:125 #4; 10:10; 11:116 #3 *MS* 4:109 #7; 6:150 #10; 8:8; 18:308; 19:22; 22:1, 98; 23:43, 123 (2x); 24:396; 25:372 (2x); 26:437; 27:284; 32:112; 38:149 *T&S* 2:539 #22; 4:4 *E&MS* 1:51-52 #7 *JD* 8:48-53 *Sacred Hymns*, 374 #315 (2x)
(em)power / strength / might of J	*HC* 3:113, 420; 6:391; 7:366 *Contributor* 5:165-66 #5; 6:247-49 #7 *MS* 7:199 #12; 11:211, 303; 21:427; 22:1, 326; 23:113, 134, 195; 26:57; 32:314; 35:258 *T&S* 4:255-56 #16; 4:373 #24 *JD* 2:36; 4:124; 5:275; 18:138-39, 210-11; 19:124; 20:187 *CD* 5 10/10/1887
protection of J / sustained	*MS* 24:275; 28:288 *T&S* 2:472 #17 *JD* 6:114
law / government / kingdom / dispensations of J	*HC* 4:583; 6:252 *TPJS*, 337-38 *Contributor* 4:54 #2; 11:162 #5 *MS* 7:183 #12; 8:86, 97; 11:360; 12:197; 13:40; 15:624; 19:308; 20:543; 22:114; 23:87, 215; 27:228 *T&S* 3:761 #12; 5:577-78 #13; 6:1099 #21 *JD* 1:117; 7:343; 7:460-61 #12; 8:208-09 *Sacred Hymns*, 427 #358
footstool of J / dwelling place	*HC* 6:518; 7:172 *MS* 5:76-77 #5; 16:399; 24:247, 742 *JD* 17:168
(de)throne J	*HC* 4:75 *TPJS*, 163, 226 *Contributor* 3:323 #11; 4:10-11 #1; 4:312 #8 *MS* 4:188-89 #12; 5:61 Supp. (2x); 8:89; 17:774; 19:375; 23:701; 27:297; 38:393; 39:548

	M&A 3:45 #29 *T&S* 2 #4; 5:405 #2; 5:744 #23; 6:1002 #15; 6:1102 #21 *E&MS* 2:123 #15 *JD* 8:38, 195-96; 13:28; 14:29; 23:140-41
tabernacle of J	*MS* 3:19 #1 *T&S* 3:737 #10
spirit of J	*MS* 7:171-72 #11; 26:694 *T&S* 6:1099 #21
arm(s) of J	*HC* 2:270; 4:376; 7:288 *Contributor* 2:347-48 #11; 9:402 #11; 13:454 #10 *MS* 1:52; 5:61-62 Supp.; 5:118-19 #8; 7:11-12 #1, 46 #3; 11:62, 267; 13:2; 15:402, 447; 18:567, 749; 19:648; 24:747; 29:206 *M&A* 2:228 #15; 2:276 #18 *T&S* 2:488 #18; 2:553-54 #22; 3:839 #17; 5:684 #19; 5:744-45 #23 *Elders' Journal* 1:3 #1 *E&MS* 2:141-42 #18 *JD* 1:342; 4:323; 5:376; 9:342-43; 13:183, 362; 15:141-42; 16:268-69; 19:6; 22:148; 25:112 *Sacred Hymns*, 199 #182
ears /eye / sight / looked / nose of J	*Contributor* 1:146 #7 *MS* 5:38; 9:214, 341; 10:197, 225; 11:142, 308, 359; 16:103; 17:338; 23:214, 497; 38:330 *M&A* 2:318 #20; 2:345 #22; 3:493 #31 (2x); 3:525 #33 *JD* 8:51; 20:101;
hand / finger of J	*MS* 2:104 #6; 4:140 # 9; 11:155; 15:125; 23:340; 39:182 *T&S* 2:547 #22; 3:939 #23; 4:99 #6; 4:137 #9; 4:313 #20 *E&MS* 2:184 #23 *JD* 9:234-35; 10:111; 16:223-24; 24:22-23 *Sacred Hymns*, 294 #261 *CD* 2 4/6/1890; 4 10/7/1894
bosom of J	*MS* 23:216 *T&S* 5:577-578 #13 *JD* 1:228; 6:114; 7:164; 10:55-56; 13:223-25

gracious smiles of J	*Contributor* 7:439 #11
voice / mouth / word / language of J; J speaks / says	*HC* 4:436; 5:526; 7:282, 288 *Contributor* 1:142-43 #6; 2:202 #7; 4:400 #10; 4:455-56 #12; 13:454 #10 *MS* 2:121, 168; 3:7, 12 # 1; 4:44, 55; 5:118-19, 144; 9:95, 137, 311; 11:379; 12:277; 15:2, 4, 195, 486, 740, 816; 16:66, 124; 17:192, 464, 655; 18:240, 400, 727; 20:127, 224, 226, 594, 616; 21:795; 22:500, 540; 25:373; 26:672; 28:344 *M&A* 2:253 # 16; 2:269 # 17 *T&S* 3:805 #15; 5:668 #18; 5:684 #19; 5:731-32 #22 *JD* 14:333-34 *Sacred Hymns*, 6 #1; 64 #53
commune[198] / intercourse with/ converse with / visitation of J	*HC* 6:428 *Contributor* 9:115-16 #3 *MS* 4:141 #9; 7:372; 12:291; 16:630; 19:134; 23:452, 736, 785; 28:241; 36:444; 39:510, 710 *JD* 10:80; 12:234; 25:147-48 *CD* 3 10/7/1893
presence / manifestation / appearance of J	*HC* 6:191 *Contributor* 4:455-56 #12 (2x) *MS* 4:3-4; 6:26 #2; 22:500, 676, 695; 24:61 *T&S* 4:25 #2; 5:422-23 #3; 6:1002 #15 *JD* 14:253
chosen / favor / approval of J	*HC* 3:330; 4:163; 5:xix *Contributor* 6:163 #5; 8:166-67 #5 *MS* 4:42 #3; 17:149; 18:820; 22:99 (2x), 146, 340; 28:342 *T&S* 4:122 #8 *JD* 12:351 *CD* 5 1/16/1898
appointed / ordained by / sent by / authority of J	*MS* 4:42 # 3; 7:200; 9:244; 20:160; 22:381; 30:307 *T&S* 4:122 #8 *JD* 135-36; 22:292-93

---

[198] Many of these references are from the popular hymn: "Praise to the Man who Communed with Jehovah".

servants / oracles / messengers / congregation / mouthpiece / people / prophet of J, etc.	*MS* 6:203 #12; 10:295; 11:298; 16:321; 19:676; 20:564, 707; 21:232, 366; 38:162 *T&S* 2:436 #15 (2x); 2:564 #23; 2:564 #23; 6:855 #5 *JD* 2:13-14; 6:112; 19:125-26; 22:266-67; 24:265-66
service of J	*Contributor* 6:204 #6; 9:175 #5 *MS* 16:101 *JD* 15:148
blessings / gift of J	*HC* 4:226; 6:55 *Contributor* 6:338 #9; 7:4-5 #1 *MS* 5:42; 15:143; 16:3; 18:86, 199; 19:695; 22:71, 147, 259; 23:718; 33:265; 34:112 *T&S* 4:318 #20 *JD* 1:72; 23:219 *Sacred Hymns,* 383 #322
fight of / against / find fault / war / insult to J, etc.	*HC 2:103, 114* *MS* 7:165; 9:329; 15:83; 19:820; 22:229; 23:716; 26:592 *T&S* 5:739 #23; 6:1091 #20 *JD* 4:370; 20:315; 22:179-80; 24:36-38
rod / curse / scourge / threat of J, etc.	*MS* 4:177; 9:212; 10:87; 21:308; 22:98, 340; 24:394 *T&S* 5:422-23 #3 (2x) *JD* 5:206
Miscellany	*HC* 4:525, 561; 5:356; 6:73 *Contributor* 4:455-56 #12; 6:243-46 #7 (2x); 6:165 #5; 6:204 #6 *MS* 2:76 #5; 4:118-119 #8, 141 #9; 5:37 #3, 63, 523 #9; 7:165-166 #11; 8:1; 9:19, 143, 217, 368; 11:128, 169; 12:208, 215, 279, 303; 13:64, 70, 71 (3x), 308 (2x), 367; 15:451, 461, 623; 16:82, 339, 341, 344, 345; 17:108; 18:120 (2x), 704; 19:298, 390, 549; 20:127, 564, 780 (2x), 781, 808; 21:132, 176, 308, 326, 503, 520, 530; 22:34 (2x), 59, 99 (2x), 100, 146 (2x), 190, 325, 391, 500, 603, 676, 708, 743, 746, 759; 23:195, 196, 448, 590, 594, 717, 738, 810; 24:440, 642; 25:535, 731, 789; 26:448, 567; 28:180; 32:16, 152; 34:32; 35:75, 76, 230; 36:272, 803; 39:40, 182

M&A 1:9 #1; 1:130 #9; 2:301 #19
T&S 1:179 #12; 3:636 #4; 3:775-76 #13; 4:372 #24 ; 5:532 #9; 5:747 #23; 6:777 #1; 6:1002 #15; 6 #3
E&MS 2:183 #23
JD 1:154; 2:14, 30; 8:275-76; 13:227-28, 254; 14:253; 18:273-74, 330; 20:287; 21:17, 341-42; 25:105
Sacred Hymns, 99 #87; 194 #179; 294 #260; 301 #267; 334 #288; 398 #332
CD 4 1/14/1894; 5 1/16/1898 (2x); 5 5/8/1898

Jehovah is
Christ

~

One author has claimed that there is only one statement in the Journal of Discourses that points to Christ as Jehovah. This is true if one is looking only for direct, affirmative statements by the early brethren. However, there are also three statements that quote D&C 110:2-4[199] in a way that may suggest that Jesus was Jehovah.[200]

Nevertheless, the serious reader ought to consider that the paucity of statements directly claiming that Christ was Jehovah is acutely conspicuous when compared to the significant number of statements to the contrary. Further, the strong majority of these statements appear post 1880 - quite late in Mormonism's doctrinal development. Additionally, the serious reader should note that of the few statements below that clearly declare that Jesus is Jehovah, one of these statements teaches that Adam is God the Father and three of

---

[199] D&C 110 was revealed in 1836. Verses 2-4 read: We saw the Lord standing upon the breastwork of the pulpit, before us; … his voice was as the sound of the rushing of great waters, even the voice of Jehovah, saying: I am the first and the last; I am he who liveth, I am he who was slain; I am your advocate with the Father.

[200] An unbiased and more scrutinous reading of these few verses does not allow for a forced conclusion that Jesus was the Jehovah of this passage. That is, the verse merely says that "his voice was as … the voice of Jehovah; it does not say that it *was* Jehovah's voice. Franklin D. Richards, came to a parallel conclusion when interpreting a similar passage about the Ancient of Days in Daniel, chapter 7: "At this important period, when Adam is reinstated with full power upon the earth, seated upon his throne, as Daniel saw him - a glorious and an immortal God, one like the Son of Man comes in the clouds of heaven (as oftimes represented by the Apostles), to the Ancient of days, and receives from him dominion, glory, and a kingdom; or in other words, Michael, having accomplished the work committed to him, pertaining to this world, delivers up an account of his stewardship over the same, to that character represented as Yahovah in the creation of the world …" (MS 15:803). In other words, the "one like the Son of Man" is the Jehovah over this world's creation, which is not Christ - it is Adam's father and god. Consider also Abraham 3:27, which mentions one "like unto the Son of Man" who clearly is not Jesus - the Son of Man.

these statements were made by an ardent Adam-God adherent who has been bountifully cited throughout this volume (namely, Franklin D. Richards).

The reader is advised that this volume has omitted some few, lengthy statements in the Collected Discourses that attempt to prove that Jehovah is Jesus (although, I have provided complete references). I have not omitted any other materials found in the sources listed under the main section "Jehovah." The purpose of this volume is to delineate and analyze Adam-God teachings as they were understood by the *early* brethren, not to set forth the later, contrary position. The statements below are therefore presented to the reader to demonstrate that the modern LDS position claiming that Jesus is Jehovah is relatively new. To be completely fair to the LDS reader, some statements under "Who is Jehovah" could arguably be placed in this section to prove that this position is not relatively new. However, as I mention in that section, *most* of those statements can be read to substantiate the contrary position as well and the remaining statements in that section do not lucidly identify Jesus as Jehovah as the below statements do. Additionally, and in fairness to the member of the LDS Church, there are many statements in the scriptures (that obviously predate the teachings of the early brethren) that can be read to substantiate the position that Jesus is Jehovah as well.[201]

Editor   *6/15/1845*

MS 6:1

To think that, of a truth, a religion could be embraced and enjoyed that would bring with it all the glorious characteristics by which it was distinguished in the days of the apostles; that the authorities thereof were privileged to hear the *voice of Jehovah*; that the doctrines, the ordinances, and all things pertaining thereto, were either communicated by the *voice to the Son of God*, by the ministering to angels, or by the inspiration of the Holy Spirit.[202]

circa 1846

MS 6:64
NOTICE

This was the earth's consummate hour ...
Worlds upon worlds, eternal things,

---

[201] A few of these scriptures are in the Doctrine and Covenants - see the relevant subsections below.

[202] Some fundamentalist readers may object to the placement of this statement in this subsection - and with legitimate reason - because the Son of God was introduced by someone other than Christ himself, an angel, or the Holy Spirit as this statement suggests. Thus, the Jehovah referred to in this quote could not be Jesus Christ. However, on its face, the statement appears to be equating Jesus with Jehovah.

Hung on thy anguish - King of kings!

Still from his lip no curse has come,
His lofty eye has looked no doom'
No earthquake - burst, no angel brand,
Crushes the black, blaspheming band,
What say those lips by anguish riven?
"God, be my murderers forgiven!"

He dies! In whose high victory
The slayer, death himself, shall die.
He dies! By whose all - conquering tread,
Shall yet be crushed the serpent's head;
From his proud throne to darkness hurled,
The god and tempter of this world.

He dies! Creation's awful Lord,
Jehovah, Christ, Eternal Word!
To come in thunder from the skies;
To bid the buried world arise'
The Earth his footstool; Heaven his throne;
Redeemer! May thy will be done.

Miss Phebe Davies   *4/--/1848*

MS 10:112
LINES ON THE SECOND ADVENT OF THE MESSIAH

Jehovah comes on flying clouds,
To earth he speeds his way,
And crushes superstition down -
Turns darkness into day.
The signs appearing in the sky,
Bespeak his coming near;
When Zion's King will enter there,
And banish all their fear.

The signs that's in the earth beneath -
Blood, famine, plagues, and fire,
Bespeak the coming of the *Lord* -

Redemption draweth nigher...

...When Michael's trumpet loud shall sound,
And all the saints be raised -
Caught up with joy to meet the *Lord*,
And join to sing his praise.
We there shall ancient worthies meet,
All that have gone before;
And saints will there each other greet,
On Zion's happy shore.

Franklin D. Richards   *8/30/1885*

JD 26:300

We learn that our Savior was born of a woman, and He was named Jesus the Christ. *His name when He was a spiritual being*, during the first half of the existence of the earth, before He was made flesh and blood, *was Jehovah*. He was in the beginning of the creation, and He had to do and has had to do continually with the creation and government of this heaven and this earth. But up to the time that He came and dwelt in the flesh and was born of Mary, His Mother, He dwelt in the spirit life. He was the spirit Being that directed, governed and gave the law on Mount Sinai, where Moses was permitted to see Him in part. He is the Being that appeared unto the brother of Jared, when he brought the stones that were to be put into the barges, and asked the Lord to touch them with His finger that they might receive and emit light. When the Lord drew near and touched the stones with His finger, the brother of Jared's eyes were opened, and he saw the finger of the Lord. He was afraid and fell down before the Lord. The Lord asked him, "Why hast thou fallen? Arise!" And he said that he was afraid, for he beheld the finger of the Lord, and he did not know that the Lord had flesh and blood. *Jehovah* then showed him His whole person, saying, "This is the body of my spirit" - He that should come in the meridian of time and take upon Himself a body of flesh and blood.

Lorenzo Snow   *3/6/1887*

CD 1

... the *Son of God* appeared to them. He who was slain by the Jews, and they said, "the vail was taken away from our mind's eye, and our understandings were opened, and we saw the Lord standing on the breastwork of the pulpit before us." I have preached from that pulpit many times. Under His feet was pure gold. His countenance shone above the brightness of the sun. His voice was as the sound of rushing great waters. It was the voice of Jehovah, saying, "I am the first and the last. I am He that liveth. I am He who was slain. I am your advocate with the Father. Behold, your sins are forgiven you. You are clean before me; therefore lift up your heads and rejoice. You have built this house to my name. I will accept this house, and I will pour out my Spirit upon those who keep my commandments, and I will not suffer this holy house to be polluted."[203] This was the voice of *the same individual that the Jews rejected.*

George Q. Cannon	*6/23/1889*

Journal of Abraham H. Cannon

He (George Q.) believes that *Jesus Christ is Jehovah*, and that Adam is His Father and our God.

Franklin D. Richards	*4/6/1890*

CD 2

The testimony of John is true concerning the Lord *Jesus Christ*, who was in the beginning, in the creation, and without Him there was not anything made that was made. He had control, as *He was the character known as Jehovah*. When He was in the burning bush he said to Moses, I am *Jehovah*; and He told His name along occasionally to the ancient prophets and worthies, by which we know that *He was the Jehovah*. When He came and entered into the flesh, then *He was the Christ*, and has been known by that name ever since.

Wilford W. Woodruff & George Q. Cannon	*6/11/1892*

Diary of Charles Lowell Walker 2:740-41

Pres Woodruff and Cannon showed in a very plain manner that it was right to Worship the true, and *the Living God*, and Him only, and not the intelligence that dwelt in Him; that *His Son Jesus Christ, or Jehovah*, never taught such doctrine, but always to worship my Father which is in Heaven, and to always pray to the Father in the name of his Son Jesus Christ.

John Taylor	*1892*

The Mediation and Atonement, 138

"His name shall be called *Immanuel*," which being interpreted is, God with us. Hence He is not only called the Son of God, the First Begotten of the Father, the Well Beloved, the Head, and Ruler, and Dictator of all things, *Jehovah*, the I Am, the Alpha and Omega, but He is also called the Very Eternal Father.

---

[203] This is a close paraphrase of D&C 110:4-8.

CD 4

Moses, whom *Jehovah* had employed to do so many of his wondrous works, asked the Lord to show him concerning "this Heaven and this earth." The Lord has not thought proper to reveal unto us much of the vastness of His Heavenly works; but He once received Moses into His presence on the mountain and showed him "concerning this heaven and this earth," and there gave him the revelation concerning the creation of the earth and the seven days' work, and commanded him to write it. In this interview He was a personage of spirit. He also showed Himself unto the Brother of Jared, Mahonri Moriancumr, and informed him that His body of spirit was just the figure that His body of flesh should be when born of woman. He had not only this name, "The Word of God," but He had other titles. By searching the Scriptures we find some twenty or thirty of them. But in speaking of this, He said to Moses, "Your fathers, Abraham, Isaac, and Jacob, to whom I revealed myself, knew Me by the name of Almighty God, but by My name *Jehovah* they did not know Me" (Exodus 6:3). At different times He told Israel that He was *Jehovah* until He came and dwelt in the flesh. Then *He* was the *Son of God* - the Christ.

Statements that do not directly state that Jesus is Jehovah but do quote D&C 110:2-4:

MS 15:729 11/--/1853
JD 23:292-93, 10/5/1882
JD 25:158, 5/4/1884
Contributor 6:388 #10, 7/--/1885
JD 26:368, 1/10/1886
CD 4, Lorenzo Snow, 4/6/1895

Lengthy articles that use the scriptures to establish that Jesus was Jehovah:

Contributor 8:183 #5, 3/--/1887
Contributor 8:218-19, 222, 227 #6, 4/--/1887

Scriptures: Jehovah is Christ

~

Admittedly, the following brief study is more of an acknowledging gesture that this genre of study exists rather than a diligent effort to compile scriptures that "prove" that Jehovah is the same individual as Jesus Christ. I did not independently research and discover the following information. Rather, in an effort to be completely objective, I took a few independent Christian (non-Mormon) studies from various internet sites that attempted to prove that the Jehovah of the Old Testament was Jesus Christ and compiled their efforts into the following chart. Ultimately, a more exhaustive study of this issue could compare the attributes attributed to both Jehovah and Christ. However, while this kind of study may be of some interest to the reader, it would be less significant than the below study because any number of individuals could have the same attributes.

Similarly, since the early brethren understood that "Jehovah" was a title - not a proper noun - the below efforts to "prove" Jehovah is Jesus Christ are essentially without significant academic merit from a Mormon exegetical lens. That is, all of these genres of studies assume, contrary to the teachings of the early brethren as outlined above, that Jehovah is an *individual* - not a title. They then match statements about that title with similar statements made about Jesus, an individual, in an effort to prove that Jesus and Jehovah are the same individual. To a fundamentalist, this type of argumentation is analogous or akin to the following syllogism:

An apostle is a traveling minister that teaches, explains, and expounds upon Mormon doctrine.
Elder Johnson is a traveling minister that teaches, explains, and expounds upon Mormon doctrine.
Therefore, Elder Johnson is an apostle.

Any quasi-informed member of the modern LDS Church would agree that this statement is clearly false on its face. Nevertheless, had the author substituted the name "Elder Spencer W. Kimball" in the place of "Elder Johnson," many LDS readers would likely gloss over the logical fallacy employed by the author in this analogy. Similarly, exercises like the one below are founded upon this same logical error, though it is occasionally more subtle.[204]

Titles, Acts, and Concepts attributed to both Jehovah and Jesus Christ:

Jehovah — OT	Jesus Christ — NT	Shared Title / Concept
Genesis 17:11	Revelation 1:8, 18	Almighty
Genesis 22:8, 14	John 6:51; Hebrews 10:10-12	Offering
Exodus 3:14-15	John 8:58	I AM
Exodus 16:26	Matthew 15:30	Healer
Exodus 17:15	Colossians 3:17; Revelation 19:11-16	Word of God
Exodus 31:13	Hebrews 10:10	Sanctified
Deuteronomy 10:17	Revelation 17:14	Lord of lords
Deuteronomy 32:3-4	1 Corinthians 10:4	The Rock
Psalms 7:17	Luke 1:76	Lord
Psalms 23:1	John 10:7, 11, 16	My Shepherd
Psalms 24:7-10	1 Corinthians 2:8	Lord/King of Glory
Psalms 27:1	John 8:12	The Light
Psalms 27:1	2 Timothy 2:10	Salvation
Psalms 96:13	Acts 10:38, 42; 1 Peter 4:5	Judge
Judges 6:24	John 14:27	Peace
Isaiah 6:3-10; 47:4	John 12:40-41	Lord of Hosts
Isaiah 8:13-14	1 Peter 2:5-8; Matthew 11:6	Rock of Offense

[204] Statements by Jehovah saying that He is the redeemer and "there is none other" fit into this latter category. If read as a title, this could consistently be understood as stating that no one is entitled to be a redeemer other than one who holds the office of Jehovah. This is much more subtle than the example I gave above and has been employed by Elder Mark E. Peterson in his writings against Adam-God teachings and in his writings against Jehovah's Witness teachings. The infamous book "Be Not Deceived" essays in multiple different ways to use this line of reasoning to disprove Adam-God teachings.

Isaiah 10:20	Acts 3:13-14	The Holy One
Isaiah 43:11, 45:21-22	Luke 2:11	Savior
Isaiah 43:15, 44:6; Psalms 29:10	John 12:13, 15	The King
Isaiah 44:6	Revelation 22:13, 16	First and the Last
Isaiah 44:24	John 1:1, 3, 10	Maker
Isaiah 45:21	Acts 3:13-14; 7:52	The Just One
Isaiah 47:4	Galatians 3:13	Redeemer
Isaiah 63:16	Isaiah 9:6	Everlasting Father
Jeremiah 3:8; 31:32	2 Corinthians 11:2	Husband
Jeremiah 10:10	1 John 5:20	True God
Jeremiah 23:6	1 Corinthians 1:30	Righteousness

See also 1 Nephi 19:10; Mosiah 1:4; 3:8 (cf. Mosiah 15:2); 3 Nephi 11:14, 17; Ether 4:7; 12:19-20; D&C 49:6; 76:24; 93:4

Jehovah is not Christ

~

There are four series of statements within this subsection. Each series of statements informs us that the early brethren clearly differentiated the individual, Jesus, from the individual, Jehovah. The first series of statements declare that Jehovah is the father of mankind (specifically, our spirits); the second series of statements declare that Jesus is the son of Jehovah; the third series focuses on modern worship of Jehovah by Latter-day Saints; and the fourth series of statements more generally differentiates between Jehovah and/or the God of the Old Testament from Jesus Christ.

Jehovah is the Father of Our Spirits

See also
Adam as Father of Our Spirits

Although we can be called the children of Christ as we may be adopted by him, and although this adoption should be construed as a spiritual adoption, the following statements declaring that Jehovah is the father of our spirits do not outwardly appear to have this spiritual adoption by Christ in mind - they outwardly appear to be declaring that Jehovah is our Heavenly Father who begat our spirits.

John Greenhow   *3/--/1844*

MS 4:161 #10; T&S 5 #2

As the father of the spirits of all flesh, *Jehovah* does exercise a paternal care over all his creatures, and in order to accomplish this will erect a standard, for, according to the prophet, 'Zion shall be established in righteousness, and all nations shall flock to her standard."

Thomas Ward   *7/1/1845*

MS 6:18-19 #1

The Saint.

The eternal *Jehovah for his father*, the ever-blessed *Savior for his elder brother*, angels for his companions, power and authority unknown on earth, sovereignty and dominion among the spheres of the universe, and all things associated with a renewed and perfected nature, unstained by sin, unsullied by any thing that can defile, and all things stamped with immortality and eternal life.

Brigham Young   *10/7/1860*

JD 8:236

We are just so foolish, and unwise and shortsighted, and so wanting in philosophy that we actually believe *God* [Jehovah] told Abraham to do this very thing. *Who is that God? He is my Father. He is your Father; we are His offspring.*

John Taylor   *12/11/1864*

JD 11:22-23

We are a part of deity, that is, *our spirits are a part,* as it were, *of the Great Jehovah*, that have been struck from His eternal blaze-eternal intelligence and light and life.

Brigham Young   *8/4/1867*

Utah Historical Quarterly 29:68

We may ask them the question, "Do you believe in the *God of Abraham*, Isaac and of Jacob?" So do the Latter-Day Saints. If they believe in the God who told Moses to say to Pharoah that He was a man of war; so do the Saints. I say, O Israel, ancient Israel do you believe in the God who brought the children of Israel out of Egypt with a high hand and an outstretched arm! "Yes," say they; and so do the Latter-Day Saints. Have you faith, that if necessary, He would again shower manna from Heaven and send flocks of quails to allay your hunger and cause water to burst from the rock to quench your thirst as He did when the Children of Israel were passing through the Wilderness? Do you believe that He is the God whom Moses followed and by whom he was directed? "Yes," says the whole house of Israel. Well, *that is the very God that we - the Latter-Day Saints - are serving. He is our Father, He is our God and Father of our Lord Jesus Christ* - whom the tribe of Judah discard, heaping ridicule upon his name. *He is the Father of our Spirits, every one of us,* Jew and Gentile, bond and free, white or black.

Hannah T. King   *3/--/1884*

Contributor 5:217 #6

[Nebuchadnezzar] adds impiety by ordering his servants to fetch out of his treasure house the holy vessels of gold and silver which had been dedicated to the Lord in the temple, and which Nebuchadnezzar had seized when he took Jerusalem and had placed them where they were, but had always held them sacred, never allowing them to be used for any purpose whatever; but the wine-heated king had lost all reverence for *his grandfather or Jehovah*; he seemed madly rushing on to his destruction. These holy vessels were brought forth, and he and his lords "drank wine in them."

Joseph E. Taylor   *5/--/1885*

Contributor 6:304 #8

The world will not accept anything but what can be demonstrated by physical evidences, consequently they ignore and set aside all spiritual manifestations, endowments of ministrations, not realizing that *Jehovah*, in communicating knowledge to the human family, passes by the mortal body and addresses Himself directly to the mind, or rather to *the spirit of man: which spirit emanated from Himself*, having been begotten by Him. In other words, while our earthly parents address us through our tabernacles that they have been instrumental in producing, *our heavenly Father address Himself directly to our spirits, which He Himself produced*. Hence the things of God are only spiritually discerned or must first be discerned by our spirits. The Prophet Joseph makes this very plain. He says: "All things whatsoever God of His infinite wisdom has seen fit to reveal to us while we are dwelling in mortality, in regard to our mortal bodies are revealed to us in the abstract and independent of affinity of this mortal tabernacle, but are revealed to our spirits precisely as though we had no body at all; and those revelations which will save our spirits will save our tabernacles; God reveals them to us in view of no eternal dissolution of the body or tabernacle.

Jesus is the Son of Jehovah

The following statements need little introduction - their message is clear: Jesus is the son of Jehovah.

Brigham Young & Willard Richards   *circa 1/--/1841*

HC 4:256[205]

---

[205] As an indication that this was not just a misprint, fluke, or random error, this statement was reprinted in

The Lord [Jehovah] hath spoken through Isaiah (4:1), saying "Behold my servant whom I upheld - mine elect in whom my soul delighteth," *evidently referring to the Lord Jesus Christ, the Son of God* chosen, or elected, by the Father.

Joseph Smith   *11/15/1841*

T&S 3:578

We believe in God the Father, who is the great Jehovah and head of all things, *and that Christ is the Son of God,* co-eternal with the Father; yet he is our Savior, Redeemer, King, and Great Prototype; - was offered as a sacrifice to make an atonement for sin - rose from the dead with the same flesh and bones, not blood, and ascended to heaven, and is now seated at the right hand of the *Father.*

April 1842

MS 2:184 #12

The Old and New Testament everywhere reveals a God with body, parts, and passions. The following are a few of the many texts which speak of his body and parts:

Image	Genesis 1:27
Eyes	Proverbs 15:3
Mouth	Isaiah 55:11
Nose	Isaiah 65:5
Lips and tongue	Isaiah 30:27
Ear	2 Kings 19:16
Soles of his feet	Ezekiel 43:7
Arm	Jeremiah 21:5
Finger	Exodus 31:18
Fingers	Psalms 8:3
Loins	Ezekiel 1:27
Heart	Genesis 6:6
Nostrils	Exodus 15:8
Hand, face, and back parts	Exodus 33:22

The foregoing abundantly show that the *Father* of our Lord *Jesus* Christ had both body and parts, to say nothing of Jesus Christ. ... Hence, what can we say of this sectarian "God without body, parts, or passions!!!" as compared with *Jehovah and Jesus Christ*, or with Scripture and reason.

the Contributor 4:341-42 #9; T&S 2:524 #21; T&S 4:1; MS 1:217; 29:148; 38:145.

4/--/1842

MS 2:187

The eternal *Jehovah* has revealed himself to man as enthroned in the heavens, while the earth is his footstool, and *Jesus Christ as his Son* seated at his right hand as a mediator, while the spirit of truth, proceeding from the Father and Son, fills immensity, comprehends all things, and is the light, life, and spirit of all things, and the law by which they are governed, and by which they move and have their being. ...
He [Jehovah] created the worlds, He stopped the mouths of lions. He quenched the violence of fire. He manipulated the widow's meal and oil. He overturned kingdoms and defended his people. He smote the rock and the water gushes out.

Joseph Smith   *circa 8/--/1842*

HC 5:127; MS 19:757

O Thou, who seest and knowest the hearts of all men - Thou eternal, omnipotent, omniscient, and omnipresent *Jehovah - God - Thou Eloheim*, that sittest, as saith the Psalmist, "enthroned in heaven," look down upon Thy servant Joseph at this time; and let faith on the name of *Thy son Jesus Christ*, to a greater degree than Thy servant ever yet has enjoyed, be conferred upon him.

First Presidency   *4/6/1845*

MFP 1:253

Proclamation of the Twelve Apostles of the Church of Jesus Christ of Latter-day Saints. To all the King's of the World ... And to the Rulers and People of all Nations: Greeting:
Know Ye - that the kingdom of God has come: as has been predicted by ancient prophets, and prayed for in all ages; even that kingdom which shall fill the whole earth, and shall stand for ever. The great *Eloheem Jehovah* has been pleased once more to speak from the heavens: and also to commune with man upon the earth, by means of open visions, and by the ministration of holy messengers. By this means the great and eternal High Priesthood, after the *Order of his Son*, even the Apostleship, has been restored; or, returned to the earth.

7/23/1849

MS 11:302

JEHOVAH AND SON'S EFFECTUAL CURE FOR CHOLERA,
AND ALL OTHER DISEASES OF THE BODY
Take one table-spoonful of consecrated olive oil: mix with it half a grain of pure faith. This taken or administered *in the name of Jesus Christ*, will prove one of the most

pleasant, safe, and effectual remedies.

The above medicine was established as the best and surest remedy for removing leprosy and restoring the blind their sight, the deaf their hearing, the dumb their speech, and for casting out devils, &c., by Jesus of Nazereth and his apostles; and we unhesitatingly bear our testimo[n]y, that during 1800 years, it has retained all its restoring and healing power.

James Linforth   *9/--/1850*

MS 12:278

Notwithstanding the significance of these expressions, we have other and equally as forcible reasons for saying that to baptize is to immerse. One of which is contained in the account of the Saviour's baptism - "And Jesus when he was baptized went up straightway out of the water;" § evidently conclusive that he had been down into the water; and on this memorable occasion of our Lord's enjoining upon all the necessity of fulfilling all righteousness, by himself setting the example, did *Jehovah* manifest satisfaction in what *his Son* had done, and also in the act as performed by John. Witness the exclamation of the Eternal as the portals of heaven opened, and the Holy Spirit descended upon him - "This is my beloved Son in whom I am well pleased." Thus we see the *Redeemer* of the word submitting to the rite of baptism, and the *God of heaven* and earth recognizing it.

William Howell   *4/17/1851*

MS 13:190

I cannot well describe to you the joyful feelings of all present, seeing so many fathers and sons, and daughters, and sailors, passing through the singing ranks one after the other in returning from their water baptism.

"*Jehovah* saw his darling *Son*,

And was well pleased in what he'd done,

And own'd him from the skies,"

The same Lord smiled upon us, for many were the tokens we received of His approbation, and of rejoicing in the presence of the angels of God.

Orson Hyde   *10/6/1854*

JD 2:79, 82

How was it, then, with Abraham? He is said to be the father of the faithful, and the great head of the Church in the days of the Patriarchs, and the head of those who have been adopted into *the covenant of Jehovah through the blood of His only begotten*; for if we are Christ's then we are Abraham's seed, and heirs according to the promise. If, by the virtue of the Savior's blood, our sins are washed away, we are the children of Abraham; we hail him as our father, and Sarah as our mother; he is the father of the faithful, he is the father of many nations. How was it with Abraham? Did he please God, walk before Him uprightly, and obtain this testimony that he pleased God, and obtain promises that no other man has obtained since the days of Abraham, the Son of God excepted? *Jehovah* promised that in him and in his seed all the nations of the earth should be blessed, as a pattern of piety, and as the great head of the Church. Because of his faithfulness in keeping the commandments of *Jehovah* on earth, he drew from on high this great promise. Who has lived since that time who has been thus blessed? I will venture to say not one. Then if we are his children, will we not do the works of faithful Abraham? So said the Savior, who ever spoke the truth, who ever declared the mind and will of his Father in heaven. Are we Abraham's seed, or are we bastards and not sons? That is the question. ... Our first parents, then, were commanded to multiply and replenish the earth; and if the Savior found it his duty to be baptized to fulfill all righteousness, a command of far less importance than that of multiplying his race, (if indeed there is any difference in the commandments of *Jehovah*, for they are all important, and all essential,) would he not find it his duty to join in with the rest of the faithful ones in replenishing the earth?

Brigham Young   *4/25/1855*
MABY

We begin with t*he father of* our Lord Jesus Christ, and of o*ur spirits - who is he?* Do you know anything about him? Can you find out who he is? Suppose we go to the scriptures and enquire who he is. At one time he says "I am that I am," at another time when the question was proposed by somebody, he replied, "I am the *Lord your God*";[206] at another time *he is spoken of as a Man of War,* a *General* and so on. You may trace the scriptures through, and you will find that he is known to one people by one title today, and tomorrow by another, and the next day by another, and there he leaves it.

Henry Whittall   *1857*
MS 19:303

The beloved *Son of God,* the *first born of Jehovah,* even *Jesus Christ* the righteous, has in mercy condescended to take upon himself the personal responsibility of satisfying these indispensable demands of Divine justice, in man's stead, and of doing that for poor, weak, sinful mortals which they were unable to do for themselves, by acting as their legal substitute, their surety, the Saviour.

---

[206] *Jehovah* thy *Elohim* in Hebrew.

4/3/1867

MS 29:311

The great *Jehovah* hath some rights upon his footstool, and has plenty of arguments to vindicate those rights, notwithstanding the opposition and jealousy of the governments and powers of this world. We have sought to do the nations good and to save them, but they would not listen to his voice any more than the jews would to the voice of *his Son, who* in the sympathetic despair of his heart, *exclaimed*, "O Jerusalem! Jerusalem! how oft would I have gathered thy children as a hen gathereth her chickens under her wings, but ye would not!"

Brigham Young   *6/17/1871*

Joseph F. Smith Journal

Elohim, *Yahovah and Michael* were father, *Son and grandson*. They made this Earth and Michael became Adam.

Orson Pratt   *11/12/1876*

JD 18:288-89

It is declared, as part of the belief of the Methodists, that God is without passions. Love is one of the great passions of God. Love is everywhere declared a passion, one of the noblest passions of the human heart. This principle of love is one of the attributes of God. "God is love," says the Apostle John, "and he that dwelleth in love dwelleth in God, and *God* in him." If, *then*, this is one of the great attributes of *Jehovah*, if he is filled with love and compassion towards the children of men, if *his son Jesus Christ* so loved the world that he gave his life to redeem mankind from the effects of the fall, then, certainly, God the Eternal Father must be in possession of this passion. Again, he possesses the attribute of Justice, which is sometimes called Anger, but the real name of this attribute is Justice. "He [Jehovah] executeth justice," says the Psalmist; also, "Justice and judgment are the habitation of thy throne." Justice is one of the noble characteristics of our heavenly Father; hence another of his passions.

Edward Tullidge   *3/--/1877*

Women of Mormondom, 79

Mark this august wonder of the age; the Mormons build not their temples to the name of Jesus, but to the name of Jehovah - not to the Son, but to the Father.

Fera L. Young   *11/--/1881*

Contributor 3:48 #2

"When the whole question is thoroughly examined (as Mr. Ingersoll evidently has never examined it), the world will find that *Jehovah*" was, is, and ever will be without a blemish, and *His Son* is like unto Him.

Charles W. Penrose   *11/16/1884*

JD 26:21

God, then, *t*he God of the Bible, who *is called Jehovah*, the person who manifested Himself to Israel as *Jehovah*, is an individual, a personality, and *He made man* in His image and His likeness. Now, *if we are the children of God, and if Jesus Christ is the Son of God*, we can upon that reasoning understand something about what *God* is like, for there is an eternal principle in heaven and on earth, that every seed begets of its kind, every seed brings forth in its own likeness and character.

John Taylor   *1891*

Sacred Hymns #262, verses 2, 3

As in the heavens they all agree,
The record's given there by Three,
On earth three witnesses are given,
To lead the sons of earth to heaven.

Jehovah, God the Father is one,
Another, His Eternal Son,
The Spirit does with them agree,
The witnesses in heaven are three.

J. M. Reiner   *1/16/1898*

CD 5

But she came out victorious. Why? Because the Church of God, in the early ages, was a Church that was united; it was a Church that was sanctified; it was a Church ready to spread the Gospel all over the world; and such a Church certainly could not be conquered. And *Jehovah* gave the promise, *through His only Son*, that even the gates of hell "shall not prevail against thee."

Montgomery   *1912*

Sacred Hymns, 107 #97

See! *Jehovah's* banner's furled,
Sheathed his sword, He speaks, 'tis done;
Now the kingdoms of this world
Are the kingdoms of *His Son*.

He shall reign from pole to pole,
With supreme unbounded sway;
He shall reign when, like a scroll,
Yonder heavens have passed away.

Hallelujah! for the Lord,
God omnipotent, shall reign;
Hallelujah! let the word
Echo round the earth and main.

Wesley's Collection   *1912*

Sacred Hymns, 142 #129

Sing to the Great *Jehovah's* praise,
All praise to Him belongs;
Who kindly lengthens out our days
Demands our choicest songs.

His providence has brought us through
Another various year;
We all, with vows and anthems new,
Before our *God* appear.

Father, They mercies past we own,
Thy still continued care;
To Thee presenting, through *Thy Son*,
Whate'er we have or are.

Modern Worship of Jehovah

I have made a primary assumption in the following materials. That assumption is that members of the LDS Church would agree that it is improper to pray to Christ. As of the date of the publication of this volume, that is sound LDS Church doctrine to the best of my knowledge.[207] I am drawing attention to this assumption because the below statements comprise of modern prayers offered to Jehovah and to the modern worship of Jehovah. Clearly, if Jehovah is God the Father, this is not a problem. However, if Jehovah is Christ, some of these statements are suggesting that we can properly worship Christ in this dispensation - a doctrine that members of the LDS Church ought to balk at.

Joseph Smith   *Monday 11/16/1835*

HC 2:314

O! Thou great omnipotent and omnipresent *Jehovah*: Thou who sittest upon the throne, before whom all things are present; Thou maker, moulder, and fashioner of all things visible and invisible, breathe, O breathe into the ears of Thy servant the Prophet, words suitably adapted to my case and situation. Speak once more, make known Thy will concerning me; which favors I ask *in the name of the Son of God.* Amen.

Sylvester Smith   *1/--/1836*

M&A 2:254 #16; M&A 2:271 #17 2/--/1836

They [members of the seventies quorum] are worthy young men, strong, active, energetic, determined in the name of the Lord to go forward and persevere to the end; relying on the mighty arm of *Jehovah, praying always to the God of Daniel,* for wisdom, understanding, strength, power, and all things, that they may war a good warfare, overcome enemies, wax valiant in the truth, thrust in the gospel sickle by the power of God, and gather a rich harvest of the sanctified from the field of destruction which must soon be burned.

Joseph Smith   *3/27/1836*

D&C 109:34, 42, 56, 68; M&A 2:280 #18

O *Jehovah*, have mercy upon this people, and as all men sin forgive the transgressions of thy people, and let them be blotted out forever.

But deliver thou, O *Jehovah*, we beseech thee, thy servants from their hands, and cleanse them from their blood.

That their hearts may be softened when thy servants shall go out from thy house, O

---

[207] I am aware that there have been a few statements to the contrary - notably a statement from Elder Neal A. Maxwell that was included in the Ensign in the early 1980s. However, this seems afield from the general modern LDS position that does not make room for the worship of Christ unless he is in your physical presence.

Jehovah, to bear testimony of thy name; that their prejudices may give way before the truth, and thy people may obtain favor in the sight of all;

O Lord, remember thy servant, Joseph Smith, Jun., and all his afflictions and persecutions - how he has covenanted with *Jehovah*, and vowed to thee, O Mighty *God of Jacob* - and the commandments which thou hast given unto him, and that he hath sincerely striven to do thy will.

Joseph Smith   *3/--/1836*

M&A 2:279 #18; 15:724

O *Jehovah*, have mercy upon this people, and as all men sin, forgive the transgressions of thy people, and let them be blotted out forever. Let the anointing of thy ministers be sealed upon them with power from on high: let it be fulfilled upon them as upon those on the day of Pentecost: let the gift of tongues be poured out upon thy people, even cloven tongues as of fire, and the interpretation thereof. And let thy house be filled, as with a rushing mighty wind, with thy glory. ...

And whatever city thy servants shall enter, and the people of that city receive not the testimony of thy servants, and thy servants warn them to save themselves from this untoward generation, let it be upon that city according to that which thou hast spoken, by the mouths of thy prophets, but deliver thou, O *Jehovah*, we beseech thee, thy servants from their hands, and cleanse them from their blood. O *Lord*, we delight not in the destruction of our fellow men: their souls are precious before thee; but thy word must be fulfilled:

- help thy servants to say with thy grace assisting them, *thy will be done*, O *Lord*, and not ours. ... Have mercy, O *Lord*, upon all the nations of the earth: have mercy upon the rulers of our land: may those principles which were so honorably and nobly defended: viz. the constitution of our land, by our fathers be established forever. Remember the kings, the princes, the nobles, and the great ones of the earth, and all people; and the churches: all the poor, the needy and the afflicted ones of the earth, that their hearts may be softened when thy servants shall go out from thy house, O *Jehovah*, to bear testimony of thy name, that their prejudices may give way before the truth, and thy people may obtain favor in the sight of all, that all the ends of the earth may know that we thy servants have heard thy voice, and that thou hast sent us, that from among all these thy servants, the sons of Jacob may gather out the righteous to build a holy city to thy name, as thou hast commanded them.

J. L.   *12/--/1840*

MS 2:118

ANTI-MORMON SLANDER REFUTED

But alas for you, the fact is self evident to every man, that you do know, and did know at the time you penned the article, all the circumstances connected with that tragedy [martyrdom of saints in Missouri]; and your declaring that "they deserved the punishment meted out to them," is in plain English saying that they deserved the punishment of death without trial, in the most barbarous manner, because *they chose to worship God, Jehovah*, or because they would not worship him according to some of the various approved fashions of the world.

4/--/1842

MS 2:187

Let us now inquire after the true God and after the manner of worshipping him. The eternal *Jehovah* has revealed himself to man ....

Joseph Smith   *circa 8/--/1842*

HC 5:127; MS 19:757

O Thou, who seest and knowest the hearts of all men - Thou eternal, omnipotent, omniscient, and omnipresent *Jehovah - God - Thou Eloheim*, that sittest, as saith the Psalmist, "enthroned in heaven," look down upon Thy servant Joseph at this time; and let faith on the name of *Thy son Jesus Christ*, to a greater degree than Thy servant ever yet has enjoyed, be conferred upon him.

6/1/1843

T&S 4:219-20 #14

To commence, then, we ask the question, had *Jehovah* an object in the creation of the human race? if so, the nature of that object? that we may be prepared to judge whether it could be accomplished without revelation or not. ... Most assuredly when they shall see their dead come out of the graves and hear them call upon the name of *Jehovah*, and openly acknowledge their faith in *Messiah*, then will they (the heathen,) also call upon the name of *Jehovah*, and *worship him* with one mind and one spirit.

10/17/1846

MS 8:119

The blood of our martyrd heroes and prophets is *pleading* our cause in the celestial courts, in strains too eloquent and thrilling for *Jehovah* to resist. It cries in the ears of the *God of armies*, like the blood of Abel, for vengence on the foe.

John Taylor   *11/--/1846*

MS 8:114

The God of Israel is with us - union and peace prevail; and as we journey as did Abraham of old, with our flocks and herds to a distant land, we feel that, like him, we are doing the will of our heavenly Father, and relying upon his word and promises; and having his blessing, we feel that we are children of the same promise and hope, and that the *great Jehovah is our God.*

Orson Pratt	*circa 1850*

MS 12:9

L.D.S - I shall feel great pleasure in taking your friend to where he shall receive the fullest information as to the rise and doctrines of the church of L.D.S. Our maxims are "Prove all things" "Search the scriptures."

Sir (turning to the Baptist,) you inquire the rise of the Church of Latter-day Saints! It owes its origin, like all true churches, to revelation from God, whose august principles are those held by patriarchs, prophets, and apostles - ancient as eternity, immutable as God; principles worthy of Jehovah, consolatory to man, and conformable to scripture and reason.

L.D.S. - And *can you no where on earth find, as you say, the God of Abraham worshipped,* the ancient gospel preached, and ancient ordinances administered? Then it is high time that God in his mercy should reveal himself and restore the ancient gospel with its powers, gifts, and blessings.

Harvey Whitlock	*9/--/1853*

MS 15:466

Letter to Joseph

O! thou great omnipotent and omnipresent *Jehovah*! thou who sittest upon the throne, before whom all things are present; thou maker, moulder, and fashioner of all things visible and invisible, breathe, O breathe into the ears of thy servant the Prophet, words suitably adapted to my case and situation. Speak once more, make known thy will concerning me; which favours I ask *in the name of the Son of God.* Amen.

	circa 1854

MS 15:725

O Lord, remember thy servant Joseph Smith, junior, and all his afflictions and persecutions, how he has covenanted with *Jehovah*, and vowed to thee, O mighty God of Jacob, and the commandments which thou has given unto him, and that he hath sincerely striven to do thy will.

M. A. Walker	*1855*

MS 17:160
A PRAYER

Thou great Jehovah! Infinite resource, attend,
And to my prayer thine ear benignly bend,
Vouchsafe o'er me to shed thine influence,
And raise my mind superior to sense …
And, *Father*, if with thee thou'lt suffer me to plead,
And with divine benevolence to my desires accede,
Upon some richer soil, e're long fix my abode,
And there instruct my soul to commune with her God,
Till rescued by thy power, from this inferior clay,
My spirit wings her flight to realms of endless day.

Sister Pigg   1856

MS 18:816
GOD MADE MAN, MALE AND FEMALE

Was man by sovereign wisdom e'er designed
To rule imperiously the female mind?
Though formed by heaven's decree at first to rule,
Still his linked partner's neither horse nor mule.

She has, like him, a pure immortal soul,
With passions, he by mildness must control;
She had with him can with *Jehovah plead*.
For her the saviour came as well as him,
His sufferings to them both salvation bring.

No harsh distinctions from his lips were heard,
Nor males than females, ever more preferred.
Whoe'er obeys his heavenly Father's will,
Are owned by him as sister, brother, still.

Then why should man usurp that power alone,
Who for the smallest sin could ne'er atone?
Methinks he should the scepter mindly sway,
And own her aid along life's chequered way;

While heaven your happy state approves,
And blesses with increase of loves,
Ages to come will speak your fame,
And 'mongst the God's immortalize your name.

Elder W. Budge   *1858*

MS 20:524

By referring to the cited text, it will be seen that the Lord was warning his people Israel against being led away, by the divinations of any false prophet, from the worship of *Jehovah* to the worship of idols. Now, the Latter-day Saints acknowledge and *worship the God of Israel* as much as any of the former-day Saints did; and they utterly repudiate the idolatry and erratic systems of religion which prevail throughout the Gentile world at the present time.

Elder Widerborg   *1859*

MS 21:70

Elder Widerborg rose and said Brethren, according to the wish of our President, I rise and will do the best I can. I know that the *prayer* which has been sent up *to* the throne of *Jehovah* will be answered upon our heads this morning.

                                                               1860

MS 22:256
PRAYER FOR THE SPREAD OF THE GOSPEL.
Jehovah, *Lord of heaven* and earth,
The word of truth proclaim!
O may it spread form pole to pole,
Till all shall know thy name!

We long to see the Church Increase
Thy own new kingdom grow,
That all the earth may live in peace,
And heaven be seen below.

Prosper the labours of our hands
To spread thy truth abroad!
May every weak attempt promote
The knowledge of *our God*!

George Q. Cannon 7/4/1863

MS 25:424

Eventful and never-to-be-forgotten days! when the wailings and lamentations of a whole people rent the heavens for the loss of their beloved Prophet and Patriarch, and when the *prayers* of thousands ascended to the throne of *Jehovah* for vengeance on their guilty murderers.

Joseph G. Romney 8/27/1864

MS 26:547

The septic may sneer at our confidence in *God* and call it simplicity, but we know that *Jehovah* lives and reigns and manifests his goodness unto his children.

George A. Smith *Saturday 4/13/1872*

MS 34:309

It was a scene calculated to incite deep and peculiar emotions, to see the thousands of people, assembled from almost every known nationality, that they might learn to worship God in his own appointed way, arise, and unitedly mingle their voices in pouring forth soul-inspiring strains of *worship to the Great Jehovah*, while the magnificent organ sent forth its powerful tones which sounded at times like subdued thunder.

W. W. S. *5/--/1872*

MS 34:320

THE DESOLATION OF JERUSALEM.

They have crushed my pride!
They have trampled me down in the dust!
Whither, *O God*, shall I flee?
To whom shall I turn? -
in whom shall I put my trust?
In whom, *O Jehovah*, but Thee? ...

I have sinned! I have sinned!
Jehovah, Thou hidest Thy face;
But prostrate here in the dust
I adore Thee, the Holy One.
Lift me in my disgrace,
O help me! In Thee I trust.

David McKenzie   *10/7/1873*

JD 16:222

I rejoiced exceedingly at the words of our beloved President, President George A. Smith, when he requested the congregation to lift up their hearts in silent *prayer to Jehovah*, that the Elders might receive the words of life to give unto the people. This is our privilege, brethren and sisters, and it is one that I esteem of the greatest value; and when I come to a meeting to listen to the words of truth, I make it an invariable rule to lift up my heart in silent prayer that the Lord will administer to us, for without his aid and assistance our words are of very little value to the Saints.

          7/19/1874

MS 36:542

Extract from a letter.

Instead of patronizing the temples of Bacchus and Venus, *our citizens* rear temples for education, for justice and the *worship of the Great Jehovah*.

          circa 1877

MS 39:372

We also ask thee, *O God, our Father,* to bless our families, and thy Saints everywhere, and bless the good and the virtuous all over the earth. ...

Wilt thou hear our supplications and answer these our petitions, for we ask all, O *Jehovah, in the name of Jesus Christ* our Savior?

Charles D. Evans   *10/-/1881*

Contributor 6:16 #1

Let us reverently *bow before Jehovah*, and praise Him in the tabernacles and temples. In the holy places let us raise the glad voice of melody and thanksgiving; let us extol the matchless power which led us into the wilderness from the hand of Gentile bondage. Through a vast continent, and a journey unparalleled for length didst Thou lead Thy people. ... Mighty art *Thou, oh, Jehovah*; in the majesty of thy strength wilt Thou avenge our wrongs. From the pavilion of thy hiding-place reveal Thyself, that the nations may know that Thou dost favor Zion, and hast pleasure in her holy ones. ... Praise ye the Lord.

Charles D. Evans   *10/--/1884*

Contributor 6:15 #1

I WILL write of Thy wondrous works with the pen, Oh *Jehovah*, with the pen will I express the feelings of my soul. For *Thou art exalted very high*: Thy wisdom is vaster than the firmament; Thy understanding penetrateth the illimitable past. Each successive operation of Thy power therein is known to Thee. The infinite results of Thy wisdom are stamped upon each atom of Thy universe. In form, design and outline, the smallest mote and mammoth alike speak Thy wisdom. The future, with its infinitude of uncreated lives and worlds, is spread before Thy vision. No form yet to appear, no world, however vast and future, nor life, however great or small; no character to be developed or part to be enacted in the great scroll of eternity's future calendar is hid from Thee. Life, its emotions, powers, thought, feeling, action, to be brought on the stage of endless worlds to play its part, is compassed by Thine all-surveying eye. Unnumbered worlds, lit by their centre-suns, in the blue vault of Thine immensity, obey Thy law. None fail in their appointed times. Precision vast! Unerring, stupendous power! Filling with awe and weakness all below. Who can question Thy existence, or fail to admire Thy wisdom? Unaided reason wanders aimlessly through Thine unmeasured space, seeing no splendor, no hand divine, in those huge arches hung with blazing worlds. Vainly would it trace, by aid of false philosophy, to other source than Thine, their origin. No ray of inspiration do such claim from Thee, sole author of existence here.

Orson F. Whitney   *5/8/1898*

CD 5

You must *worship God in heaven, the invisible Jehovah, the Eternal Father*, the Maker of heaven and of earth, who created man in His likeness, in His image, male and female. Lift your thoughts above the visible things of life. Walk not by sight, but walk by faith, and believe in God and trust in Him, although you do not see Him." This was the substance of the teaching of Moses regarding the personality of God. He taught them that the being they were to worship had created man in His own image.

1/--/1890

Contributor 11:116 #3

That the people are awake to the persecutions that are directed against them, and are desirous of living near to *God*, was evidenced in the general and ready response to the call to approach the *Lord*. In all places heard from throughout the length and breadth of Zion, large congregations assembled, and a spirit of peace and quiet prevailed, which was only equaled by the confidence manifested in the promises of *Jehovah* to the faithful, *that He will hear and grant their righteous petitions.* ... Only on very few occasions before have the Latter-day Saints, thus universally at one time, come before the *Lord* in fasting and prayer, but on each of these the clouds which overshadowed them were lifted, the sun of joy and prosperity shone in upon them. … We all need the sustaining hand of *Omnipotence*; and hence the need of fasting and prayer, that we may know the *Lord* and trust in Him, offer sacrifices of joy in His tabernacle, and sing His praise.

J. M. Tanner	*1/--/1892*

Contributor 13:111 #3[208]

Who is your God? The God that made me. What is his name? *Jehovah*.

Robinson	*1912*

Sacred Hymns, 259 #236

Guide us, O Thou great *Jehovah*,
Lead us to the promised land,
We are weak, but Thou art able -
Hold us with Thy powerful hand.
Holy *Spirit*,
Feed us till the *Savior* comes.

Jehovah or the God of the Old Testament is not Jesus Christ

In many instances, it takes a reading far from the plain meaning of the text to find ambiguity in the following statements - or to find a reading that does not distinguish Christ from Jehovah. The remaining statements may take a close reading to identify where the statement directly proclaims that Jehovah is the God we worship, not Jesus; typically, the difference between these latter statements and the statements found in the section "Who is Jehovah?" is that these statements, while they are found next to terms identifying God and Jesus without explicitly stating who is whom, the term Jehovah is often sandwiched between statements about God the Father in a way that suggests that the author of the statement was merely switching terms of appellation for the same individual. These statements will therefore be less convincing as proof of the identity of Jehovah than the previous statements but they will also be more convincing as proof that Jesus is not Jehovah than the statements found in the section "Who is Jehovah." Lastly, I have placed several scripture references below that clearly draw some distinction between Jesus and Jehovah.

---

[208] This particular statement is the speaker's quote of an accused witch at her Salem trial.

Psalms 110:1

The Lord [Jehovah] said unto my Lord [Jesus - see Matthew 22:41-45], Sit thou at my right hand, until I make thine enemies thy footstool.

Isaiah 53:4-6, 10

Surely he hath borne our griefs, and carried our sorrows: yet we did esteem him stricken, smitten of God, and afflicted. But he was wounded for our transgressions, he was bruised for our iniquities: the chastisement of our peace was upon him; and with his stripes we are healed. All we like sheep have gone astray; we have turned every one to his own way; and the Lord [Jehovah] hath laid on him the iniquity of us all. ... Yet it pleased the Lord [Jehovah] to bruise him; he hath put him to grief: when thou shalt make his soul an offering for sin, he shall see his seed, he shall prolong his days, and the pleasure of the Lord [Jehovah] shall prosper in his hand.

Acts 3:13

The *God of Abraham*, and Isaac and of Jacob, the God of our fathers, hath glorified *his son* Jesus Christ whom ye delivered up etc.

Acts 5:30

The God of our fathers raised up Jesus, whom ye slew and hanged on at tree.

Hebrews 1:1-2

God, who at sundry times and in divers manners spake in times past unto the prophets. Hath in these last days spoken unto us by *his son*, whom he hath appointed heir of all things, by whom also he made the worlds.

Moses 1:6[209]

And I have a work for thee Moses, my son; and thou art in the Similitude of mine only begotten, and *mine only begotten* is and *shall be* the Savior, for he is full of grace and truth, but there is no *God* beside me, and all things are present with me, for I know them all.

---

[209] For a few more scriptures that less directly suggest that Jesus is not Jehovah, consider the following cross references from AGM, 250-51:

Hebrews 1:5	Psalms 2:7; 2 Samuel 7:11-16
1 Corinthians 10:4	2 Samuel 23:2-3
3 Nephi 20:27	Genesis 22:16-18; Acts 3:25-26

1/--/1840

T&S 1:41 #3

There are many, no doubt, even among this class, who partially believe in God, and divine things, who have such an imperfect idea, of the character of the great *Jehovah*; and such an undue attachment, to the perishable things of time and sense, that they think it a hardship to serve him while in youth or middle age, but who think that they will attend to that, when old age arrives, and the world has no more allurements for them. Yet did they but realize, that God was the most lovely, of all things which exist, whether animate or inanimate, they would see the propriety of that command which says, "Thou shalt love the Lord, thy God with all thy soul, might mind and strength." They would not put off the service of God, but would with the Psalmist say. Now is the accepted time, and, now is the day of salvation.

Joseph Smith   *4/6/1840*

T&S

Resolved, 10th. That Joseph Smith jr. Sidney Rigdon, and Elias Higbee, the delegates appointed by this church, to visit the city of Washington to present our sufferings before the authorities of the nation, accept of the thanks of this meeting, for the prompt and efficient manner in which they have discharged their duty; and that they be requested in the behalf of the church of Jesus Christ of Latter Day Saints, throughout the world, to continue to use their endeavors to obtain redress for a suffering people; and if all hopes of obtaining satisfaction (for the injuries done us:) be entirely blasted, that they then appeal our case to the court of Heaven, believing, that the great *Jehovah*, who rules over the destiny of nations, and *who notices the falling sparrow*, will undoubtedly redress our wrongs, and ere long avenge us of our adversaries.

Joseph Smith   *5/16/1841*

TPJS, 190

Everlasting covenant was made between three personages before the organization of this earth, and relates to their dispensation of things to men on the earth; these personages, according to Abraham's record, are called *God the first, the Creator; God the second, the Redeemer*; and God the third, the witness or Testator.

circa 1/15/1845

T&S 6 #15

Don't you know the people once said let his blood be on us and on our children." It was a righteous deed, the putting of the Savior to death. It was the voice of the people he should suffer. Was it the voice of *God* that his blood should be required of that people, and be upon their heads, according to their voice? (Let his blood be upon us and our children!) The innocent blood that stained their hands, rendered them worthy to be cursed almost to the latest generation. It was the will of *God* his blood should be upon them. it was not the voice of a few individuals: it was the voice of all; the whole nation sanctioned the deed. Very well, says *God*, let it come; you are all guilty; let his blood be upon you and your children. Had they taken a few individuals and executed them for killing the *Savior*, they would not have made the plaster as big as the sore. It was upon the whole nation; and they were inspired by the spirit of *God* to say "his blood be upon us and on our children." *Amen*, says *Jehovah*, you are all alike worthy. Here is a sample of what follows; for if they have killed the master of the house, they will do the same to his household; and if they have treated him thus, the nation will follow a similar course. We see the same spirit manifested in the late trial at Carthage. Says one of the lawyers, whether they are guilty or innocent, I am not prepared to say; but if they are guilty we are guilty, and if you hang them, you may as well hang this honorable council. *Jehovah* says so too. We all want a hand in this matter, and if one is punished we will all be punished; and if you let one go free, we will all go free. Well, says *Jehovah*, I will give you the desire of your heart. let not these men be punished, but let them go clear, and when he causeth his vengeance to be poured out, he will visit them all alike, for they are all alike guilty: *Amen*, says *Jehovah*, I will fulfil and execute the judgment.

Samuel Bent, J. Allred, Alpheus Cutler, et al   *1/15/1846*

T&S 6 #21

Who was with John on the Isle of Patmos? he was in the spirit on the Lord's day, and had the heavens opened unto him and the glories of the eternal world unvailed to his astonished vision. He gazed upon the future *purposes* of *God*, and wrapped in prophetic vision described the *designs* of *Jehovah* down to the latest age. A glorious personage stood before him, who unfolded to him many great events. John fell down to worship him; but he said, see thou do it not, for "*I am thy fellow servant*, and of thy brethren, that have the testimony of Jesus, worship *God*." John might have said, You were dead long ago. No, but *says Jesus*, I am the resurrection and the life, he that believeth in me, though he were dead, yet shall he live. Michael, Gabriel, Moses, Elias, and thousands of men who had the everlasting priesthood on the earth and officiated in it here, existed or lived still to perform the work they had commenced upon the earth.

2/1/1848

MS 10:43

I felt, from the time that I was baptized, and that the servants of the Most High *Jehovah* had laid their hands on my head in the name of *Jesus Christ*, that the seal of the Spirit of God is steadfast, resting upon me, and my heart is inflamed with love to the brethren and sisters that are called and chosen to be Latter-day Saints.

J. Hyde   *1/--/1850*

MS 12:7-8

I. - Then prepare your mind for remarks more startling than you have heard yet. To all the infidelity previously stated, *modern pious divines* have capped a climax; they *do not even worship the God of Abraham*.

B. - Sir, you perfectly astound me! Not worship the God of Abraham! Why, *if you can show this you will prove us to be not only infidels but idolaters!* ...

I. - Old Moses, who it is said was very intimate with God, says, I think, in Genesis 18, that God appeared to Abraham, and that old Abraham provided water to wash his feet - feet without a body? Also that Abraham and Sarah provided a feast, and *Jehovah* and the two angels with him did eat - eat *without a body?*

B. - Sir, Jehovah only appeared in figure.

I. - Oh! Indeed; then it was only a figurative Abraham, a figurative calf and cakes, and a figurative Sarah - the whole book of Genesis is only a figure, and a fable; Adam is only a figure, and the fall a fable! Infidelity triumphant!

B. - Oh! no, no; it must have been a *real Jehovah - real feet - and real eating*; real old Abraham and Sarah; a real Adam; and to our sorrow a real fall.

I. - Then my conclusion is resistless, that *modern sects do not worship the Jehovah of Abraham*, who has feet and could eat and drink. Old Moses and Abraham might be such fools, but modern divines never will; they are too wise and more infidel than I, for I think I could love a God so kind, so condescending as thus to walk, to talk, to eat and drink with his friends Abraham and Moses.

B. - I am almost struck dumb with astonishment; but is it not said that God is a Spirit. Has a spirit, a body?

I. - Are you a spirit?

B. - Yes; and have a body, too. Oh! Now I seem to understand glorious old Moses, when he says man was made in the image of God - body and spirit!

William Howell   *4/17/1851*

MS 13:188

LETTER FROM WILLIAM HOWELL

The purposes of *Jehovah* are all yea and Amen, in Christ *Jesus* our Lord.

1855

MS 17:784
I would be a "Mormon"
I would with the "Mormons" reside in that land
Bless'd by *Jehovah*, where *Jesus* shall stand
When he descends, with his glorious train,
Long on the earth with his people to reign.

First Presidency   *12/10/1856*

MFP 2:210
We feel grateful that we have been permitted to live in this day and generation, in which *the Great Jehovah* has seen proper to re-establish His authority upon the earth, and to re-confer the holy and eternal Priesthood upon the children of men. We feel grateful that we have the privilege of witnessing the stately steppings of the Almighty among the nations, the goings forth of His word with power, the fulfillment of the words given by inspiration in ancient times, and the fulfillment of the words given by the living Oracles in our midst; that He has spoken from the heavens; that messengers, angels and legates from His throne have broken the silence that has intervened since the mission and dispensation of *the only begotten Son of God*, Jesus of Nazareth, and reopened a communication with His children upon this His earth, organized again His Church and Kingdom, and endowed it with all the authorities, ordinances, gifts, sacraments, blessings, privileges, power, and glory pertaining thereunto

Franklin D. Richards   *1857*

A Compendium of the Faith and Doctrines of the Church of Jesus Christ of Latter-day Saints, 150-51 (as cited in AGM, 242-43)
"The Names, Titles and Characters Given to Jesus" … is a comprehensive list of some fifty titles that apply to Jesus which are of both major and minor significance. The name "Jehovah" is not listed … .

William Clegg   *1859*

MS 21:132
THE GATHERING AND RESTITUTION

Great *God*! And shall the earth for ever be
Deluged with sorrow, woe and misery?
Shall violence from thee the kingdom wrest

And curse for ever all that once was blest?

Shall man thine image form his soul erase,
And deeper still thy glorious gifts debase?
Ah, no! *Jehovah*, speaking form on high,
Reveals his power and brings salvation nigh.
He hears creation's groan, sees martyrs' gore,
And vengeance, long withheld, withholds no more:

A glorious herald from the courts on high
Proclaims Messiah's peaceful reign in nigh:
A home for all the pure hath *God* prepared,
Where peace and joy shall be for ever shared,
And soon shall shake the earth form pole to pole.
Dry up your tears, ye Saints, and weep no more:
Lift up your heads: redemption's at the door!

Saturday 2/18/1860 - 3/10/1860

MS 22:2-3, 147, 148
MESSIAH'S APPEARING

Unless, then, this subject of *Messiah's* appearings be understood, with his missions involved therein, - understood at least in several of their most important branches, and seen in several of their nearest relative and principal views, nothing can be very clearly seen of revealed religion, but few of the purposes of *Jehovah* realized, but little known of *Christ's* kingdom and glory to come, and but small portions indeed experienced of the brightest hopes and highest expectations of Israel and the Saints of old. ...
This great glory and destiny of the chosen nation was not in the purposes of *Jehovah* understood to be brought about until after *Messiah* had come unto his own and been rejected. ...
There must be a return of *Messiah* to fulfil the prophecies and to make true the covenants and blessings which *Jehovah* gave to Abraham, Isaac, Jacob, Joseph, Moses, and others, and to make the bright visions of the Prophets concerning Israel as solid realities ... To doubt this would be ... trifling with *Jehovah*. ...
[T]o doubt that there is ordained in the mind of *the Eternal God, the Jehovah of Israel,* an appearing and mission of *Messiah* to bring to pass all that we have viewed ... would be rank infidelity.

Heber C. Kimball   *3/17/1861*

JD 9:240

The blessings we so earnestly desire will come to us by performing the manual labour required, and thus preparing all things necessary to receive the invisible blessings *Jehovah* has for *his children*.

E. L. Sloan   *1861*

MS 23:77

To say that Christ had the power and authority to establish a superior economy is to to reason like a child. We are not disputing the power and authority of Christ. Not only the *Son of God*, but every man commissioned by *Jehovah* has authority and power to execute his mission.

Ellen Harper   *1861*

MS 23:112

FAREWELL TO ENGLAND.

Farewell to thee, England! For ever farewell:
I go to a land where earth's noblest ones dwell
The chambers of Israel so lovely and fair;
For virtue may bloom in security there.
The *voice of God*, through his Priesthood, I hear,
To bless and sustain me, to comfort and cheer,
While I form my native land hasten away:
Jehovah has spoken, and I must obey.

J. Sugden   *circa 1865*

MS 27:277

God will never accept the services nor acknowledge the worship of any man, who serves him through abject, wretched fear. A man must be actuated by pure love, if he wishes his devotions to be recognized by Deity. And while this generation may console themselves with the idea, that if what we tell them be true, they will at any rate escape the reward of those who "forget God," seeing that they never knew him, let them know this, that as Jerusalem felt heavily the judgment-dealing hand of *Jehovah, for putting Christ and his Apostles to death*, so this generation have yet to atone for the innocent blood of the Prophet Joseph and others. It needs not the actual blow to be struck, to bring a nation or a people under condemnation for the death of a person or persons innocently slain, but those who consent are equally guilty; therefore, every nation who receives not the message of heaven through Joseph, but rejects the offer of mercy and salvation, will find the fierce judgements of God overtake them.

John Taylor   *2/24/1867*

JD 11:230

There is no excess of cruelty at which they who are influenced by it would stop, no length to which they would not go to accomplish their damnable and hellish purposes. Why? Because the devil was a murderer from the beginning - he has murdered from the beginning; he prompted the first murder, and he prompted the last one. It was he who prompted men at all times to shed the blood of innocence, and seek by so doing to *stop the work of God*. He induced Judas to betray and shed the blood of Jesus Christ - to shed the most precious blood that ever flowed in human veins. He it was who stirred men up to commit these murders, impressing them with the false idea that some great advantage would result from such crimes, and that they would be able to check the progress of the kingdom of *God* and *arrest the purposes of Jehovah*. And it is the same power which is at work today and that suggested to men to shed the blood of Joseph, and instilled into their minds the thought that if they could kill him they could thereby interrupt the work of *God*. But, as we see, instead of accomplishing what they expected, they have only forwarded the *purposes of God our heavenly Father*.

Brigham Young   *8/4/1867*

Utah Historical Quarterly 29:68

Do you believe that He is *the God whom Moses followed* and by whom he was directed? "Yes," says the whole house of Israel. Well, that is the very God that we - the Latter-day Saints - are serving. He is our Father, *He is our God and Father of our Lord Jesus Christ* - whom the tribe of Judah discard, heaping ridicule upon his name. He is the Father of our Spirits, everyone of us, Jew and Gentile, bond or free, white or black.

Erastus Snow   *2/28/1869*

JD 13:8

The final judgment of the human race is deferred to their next estate, that God may judge the spirit according to the deeds done in the body, His judgment not being passed upon the body, but upon the spirit, the body having paid the penalty of its own faults and errors by death. The spirit is held responsible for the acts done in the body. No spirit can plead, before the *bar of Jehovah*, the weakness of the flesh as a justification of sin; the latter may be urged in palliation, but not in justification. *Our Father* is full of mercy, but he cannot look upon sin in any individual with the least degree of allowance; but every spirit [including Jesus Christ] must be held responsible, and will have to answer at the *bar of God*, and will there receive a just and righteous judgment for the deeds done in the body.

George Q. Cannon   *12/5/1869*

JD 13:51-52

Why do you always do as your prophet and leader tells you?" Because we have proved during twenty-five long years, that God has blessed him in everything he has told us to do, and we have been blessed of God in carrying out his counsels. When we have prayed to the Almighty to give us wisdom and humility to obey the counsels of His servant, He has given unto us His Holy Spirit and witnessed unto our hearts that this course was pleasing and acceptable in His sight. Rebel against him and his authority! as well might we rebel against *Jehovah* Himself, *or against Jesus!* Not that President Young is to be worshipped, not that Joseph Smith was to be worshipped, not that Peter or Moses was to be worshipped. There is a difference between obedience and idolatry, or worship. There is a difference between submission to the will of God - at least, I can perceive a difference - and obeying God's counsels through a man, and idolizing the man himself, and we have perceived this difference.

Rollo   *1/4/1870*

MS 32:112

Bespotted and dark and engulfed in tradition,
Our fathers had slumbered for ages a score,
Til *Jehovah* remembered His promise to Israel,
Commanding His servants to visit *our sphere.*
To preach us the Gospel, &e.

And years in this kingdom must surely have taught us
The power that still rules is the same it was then,
Jehovah directs the affairs of His people,
Endorsing the acts of the very same men,
Who brought us the Gospel, &e.

John Taylor   *2/23/1873*

JD 15:350

Put your trust in the living *God* and all will be right in time and in eternity. *God* will take care of his people. He has commenced a work and he will roll that forth, and woe to the man that fights against *Jehovah* - he will move him out of the way. Like the grass or flowers of the field all such will pass away, but *God's* kingdom and people will live and extend, grow and increase until the kingdoms of this world shall become the kingdoms of our God and his Christ.

circa 1876

MS 38:362

It is therefore no source of wonderment to the Latter-day Saints that they are called upon to emulate the example of the divine *Redeemer*, since they hope to share in his glory. On the other hand, they acknowledge the wisdom of *Jehovah*, who has planned all things wisely and well, and has decreed that "all that will live godly in *Christ Jesus* shall suffer persecution," and shall meet with scorn, and ridicule, and peradventure with death, as so many have already done for the testimony of *Jesus*.

7/--/1877

MS 39:486

When man learns the truth of the matter he will understand the relation which he bears to God and God to him, and will know the one to be the parent of the other, the literal progenitor; and when man perceives the relation existing between God and this world he will comprehend that *Jehovah*, the organizer of this world, *was once*, long , long ages back, in eternity which lies behind us, a man, *passing, as we are now passing, through an earth-life, on one of the older planets*. He will understand that *Jehovah*, during those probationary days of earth-life, made the pursuit of truth, eternal, immutable truth, the aim of all his efforts. Reflection teaches him that the perception of truth, or the knowledge which *Jehovah* gained day by day, was just so much power gained day by day; and we see, in this world, the created results of that power gained by the law of progression.

Phren. Journal   *5/--/1884*

Contributor 5:307-08 #8

The high character of the *Jehovah* of the Hebrews, *and* the beautiful ideal exhibited by *Jesus* of Nazareth, with the exquisite purity and simplicity of his teachings and creed, have by degrees elevated the Christian disciple and freed him from the weight of the superstitious beliefs and observances of the Pagan, the Buddhist and the Mohammedan. The human mind, thus released from the bondage of gods many, and prophets many, and thousands of cumbrous acts of devotion, has had time and scope to observe the beauties of nature and the joyousness of musical sounds.

Franklin D. Richards   *4/4/1885*

JD 26:172-73

The Savior said He could call to His help more than twelve legions of angels; more than the Roman hosts; but *He* knowing the great *purposes of Jehovah* could go like a lamb to the slaughter. He understood those purposes, could curb His powers, control His feelings, and could make a manly fight for righteousness and truth, and carry out the decrees of heaven. Can we do so? Can you and I do so? If we cannot, can we be counted worthy to be called His brethren, and Saviors upon Mount Zion? We have got to be considerably more like him than we are before we attain unto all those excellencies that are promised.

John Taylor   *1892*

The Mediation and Atonement, 147, 150

As the *Son of Man*, He endured all that it was possible for flesh and blood to endure; as the Son of God He triumphed over all, and forever ascended to the right hand of God, *to further carry out the designs of Jehovah* pertaining to the world and to the human family. ... [Jesus] bore the sins of the world and suffered in His own person the consequences of an eternal law of God broken by man. Hence His profound grief, His indescribable anguish, His overpowering torture, all experienced in the *submission to* the eternal fiat of *Jehovah*.

Edward Stevenson   *2/28/1896*

Edward Stevenson Diary

Certainly Eloheim, and Jehovah stands [sic] before Adam, or else I am very much mistaken. Then 1st Eloheim, 2nd *Jehovah*, 3d Michael-Adam, 4th *Jesus Christ*, Our Elder Brother, in the other World from whence our spirits came ... Then Who is *Jehovah*? The only begotten Son of Eloheim on Jehovah's world.

Edward Stevenson   *3/3/1896*

Edward Stevenson Diary

I have more pleasure than usual with a deep talk with Pres. L. Snow on Adam - *Jehovah* - Eloheim *and Jesus* and Spirits, and Regarding their immortality, creation, &c

The following few quotes are observations based upon the research of a modern scholar who has noted Mormonism's theological shifts as to the identity of Jehovah:

Boyd Kirkland

Dialogue 19:80-81 #1

The Hebrew Old Testament was translated into Greek approximately 280 B.C. This version, the Septuagint, was the Bible of New Testament Christians. The New Testament was also written in Greek. In Greek, Jehovah and Adonai become Kyrios. Elohim becomes theos when speaking of gods generally, and ho theos when speaking of the one true God (Rankin 1962, 96; Anderson 2:414; Barclay 1980, 21-37, 413; Kittel 3:90, 10~5). The New Testament uses both ho theos and Kyrios to designate God the Father. Jesus is also called Kyrios, is only rarely called theos, and only once (during Thomas' confession in John 20:28) called ho theos. The fact that ho theos is used in the New Testament almost exclusively of the Father indicates that the Christians equated the Father (not the Son) with the God of Israel.

Boyd Kirkland

Dialogue 19:87 #1

[Concerning the suffering servant of Jehovah]

Isaiah 42:1-4	Matt. 12:14-21;
Isaiah 53:1	John 12:38;
Isaiah 53:4	Matthew 8:17;
Isaiah 53:5-7, 10	Acts 8:32- 35;
Isaiah 53:6-7	1 Peter 1:19 & 2:22-25;
Isaiah 53:6-9	2 Corinthians 5:21;
Isaiah 53:12	Luke 23;37

…

New Testament Christians who equated Jesus with the suffering servant of Jehovah would not have considered him to be Jehovah himself come to earth.

Boyd Kirkland

Dialogue 19:87-88 #1

Jesus specifically cited his appointment from Jehovah by reading Isaiah 61:1; "The spirit of Jehovah is upon me, because he hath anointed me to preach the gospel to the poor; he hath sent me to heal the broken hearted, to preach deliverance to the captives, and recovering of sight to the blind, to set at liberty them that are bruised" etc. (Luke 4: 18-21 /Isaiah 11: 1-2).

See also Acts 3:13; 5:30; 7:37-38; Ephesians 3:14-15; Hebrews 1:1-2, 5; Alma 15:15

Scriptures:
~ Jehovah

There are other scriptures, apart from the following, that include the transliteration of the term "Jehovah." Some of these scriptures have been placed in other various subsections of the subsection "Jehovah" and others were omitted because they were used as place names in the Old Testament and therefore give us very little insight as to the identity of Jehovah.

Exodus 6:3

And I appeared unto Abraham, unto Isaac, and unto Jacob, by the name of God Almighty, but by my name *Jehovah* was I not known to them.

Psalms 83:18

That men may know that thou, whose name alone is *Jehovah*, art the most high over all the earth.

Isaiah 12:2

Behold, God is my salvation; I will trust, and not be afraid: for the Lord *Jehovah* is my strength and my song; he also is become my salvation.

Isaiah 26:4

Trust ye in the Lord for ever: for in the Lord *Jehovah* is everlasting strength:

2 Nephi 22:2

Behold, God is my salvation; I will trust, and not be afraid; for the Lord *Jehovah* is my strength and my song; he also has become my salvation.

Moroni 10:34

And now I bid unto all, farewell. I soon go to rest in the paradise of God, until my spirit and body shall again reunite, and I am brought forth triumphant through the air, to meet you before the pleasing bar of the great *Jehovah*, the Eternal Judge of both quick and dead. Amen.

D&C 110:3

His eyes were as a flame of fire; the hair of his head was white like the pure snow; his countenance shone above the brightness of the sun; and his voice was as the sound of the rushing of great waters, even the voice of *Jehovah*, saying:

D&C 128:9

[W]hatsoever those men did in authority, in the name of the Lord, and did it truly and faithfully, and kept a proper and faithful record of the same, it became a law on earth and in heaven, and could not be annulled, according to the decrees of the great *Jehovah*. This is a faithful saying. Who can hear it?

Abraham 1:16

And his voice was unto me: Abraham, Abraham, behold, my name is *Jehovah*, and I have heard thee, and have come down to deliver thee, and to take thee away from thy father's house, and from all thy kinsfolk, into a strange land which thou knowest not of.

Abraham 2:8

My name is *Jehovah*, and I know the end from the beginning; therefore my hand shall be over thee.

~ # Jehovah is not Adam

While previous LDS authors have tried to use some of the following statements to disprove Adam-God teachings, it is worth noting that fundamentalists are not even slightly bothered by the distinctions made between Adam and Jehovah or between Adam and the God of the Old Testament. As I explained earlier in this volume, Jehovah is a title given to certain deity. Therefore, just as the member of the LDS Church would have no problem calling two different men "bishop" as an appellation, fundamentalists have no problem calling Adam's god Jehovah and then referring to Adam as Jehovah at a different time - some fundamentalists have no problem identifying Jesus as Jehovah either.[210] That said, the following statements are included here primarily for the academic purpose of demonstrating where some of the confusion over the identity of Jehovah has arisen: without the "lost"[211] teaching that Jehovah was a title applied to deity, the following statements could be very confusing. With this "lost" understanding, we are able to glean some insight into the role Adam's God (Jehovah) played in the creation godhead.

Joseph Smith   *circa 7/--/1839*

HC 3:387

The Father called all spirits before Him at the creation of man, and organized them. He (Adam) is the head, and was told to multiply.

---

[210] The argumentative idea from mainstream LDS authors that if Adam is not Jehovah, then Jesus is Jehovah is manifestly odd - certainly Jehovah's Witnesses provide us with yet another viable reading of the Bible.

[211] Lost to the modern LDS Church, not to fundamentalism.

Joseph Smith   *10/5/1840*

HC 4:210

Thus we behold the keys of this Priesthood consisted in obtaining *the voice of Jehovah*
that He talked with him - Noah - in a familiar and friendly manner, that He continued
to him the keys, the covenants, the power and the glory, with which *he blessed Adam* at
the beginning; and the offering of sacrifice, which also shall be continued at the last
time; for all the ordinances and duties that ever have been required by the Priesthood,
under the directions and commandments of the Almighty in any of the dispensations,
shall all be had in the last dispensation, therefore all things had under the authority of
the Priesthood at any former period, shall be had again, bringing to pass the restoration
spoken of by the mouth of all the Holy Prophets; then shall the sons of Levi offer an
acceptable offering to the Lord.

                                                                           circa 1842

T&S 3:672

The earth no longer retained its standing in the presence of *Jehovah*; but was hurled into
the immensity of space; and there to remain till it has filled up the time of its bondage
to sin and Satan. It was immediately cursed, and *Adam*, and Eve were obliged to
procure their food and raiment by the sweat of the brow. The beasts became ferocious,
and went prowling about the wilderness seeking the inferior animals for a prey.

                                                                           4/15/1842

T&S 3:760 #12; MS 3:55-56 #4 (8/--/1842); MS 19:358 (1857); Contributor 3:194-
95 #7 (4/--/1882)

The *great Jehovah* contemplated the whole of the events connected with the earth,
pertaining to the plan of salvation, before it rolled into existence, or ever the "morning
stars sung together for joy," the past, the present and the future, were, and are with
him one eternal now; he *knew of the fall of Adam*, the iniquities of the antediluvians, of
the depth of iniquity that would be connected with the human family; their weakness
and strength, their power and glory, apostasies, their crimes, their righteousness, and
iniquity; he comprehended the fall of man, and *their redemption*; he knew the plan of
salvation, and pointed it out; he was acquainted with the situation of all nations; and
with their destiny; he ordered all things according to the council of his own will, he
knows the situation of both the living, and the dead, and has made ample provision for
their redemption, according to their several circumstances, and the laws of the
kingdom of God, whether in this world, or in the world to come.

Orson Pratt   *3/--/1850*

MS 12:69; JD 1:329

But a universal redemption from the effects of original sin, has nothing to do with redemption from our personal sins; for the original sin of *Adam*, and the personal sins of his children, are two different things. The first was committed by man in his immortal state; the second was committed by man in a mortal state: the former was committed in a state of ignorance of good or evil; the latter was committed by man, having a knowledge of both good and evil. As the sins are different, and committed entirely under different circumstances, so the penalties are different also. The penalty of the first transgression was an eternal separation of body and spirit, and eternal banishment from the presence of *Jehovah*; while the penalty of our own transgressions does not involve a disunion of body and spirit, but only eternal banishment. The first penalty not only shut man out from the presence of *God*, but deprived him eternally of a body; the second penalty permits him to retain his body, though in a banished condition. As the penalties are different, so also is the redemption. Redemption from the first penalty is unconditional on the part of man: Redemption from the second penalty is conditional. Unconditional redemption is universal; it takes within its scope all mankind; it is as unlimited as the fall; it redeems men from all its effects; it restores to them their bodies; it restores them to the presence of God.

John Jacques   *3/1/1851*

MS 13:67

The only way in which the harmony of heaven could be maintained was by rigid observance of the exclusive doctrine of perfect submission to the head. Lucifer, son of the morning, undertook to question the point. He was cast down. Others sided with him and shared his fate. *Adam* was placed in the garden of Eden, where was every thing that would please them, captivate the senses, or delight the heart. *Jehovah revealed to him* the doctrine of exclusive salvation. "In the day thou eatest thereof thou shalt surely die." The only, the exclusive method of salvation proposed from sin, sorrow, and death, was this, - abstinence from the fruit of a particular tree. It was an irrevocable decree, by lawful authority, even the *Eternal God*. It mattered not what the devil said, what Eve said, or what any other personage said, however exalted his station or great his authority. The doctrine of exclusive salvation was given; it was true, it was faithful. The devil, wily and subtle, preached against exclusive salvation; said it was a false doctrine, "Ye shall not surely die." He deceived Eve; Eve persuaded Adam; Adam transgressed; the devil was proved a liar; Adam discovered by painful experience, and his posterity to this day are witnesses in themselves of the truth of the doctrine of exclusive salvation. Thus it will be seen that it is a true doctrine, and the devil the opposer of it from the beginning.

Orson Pratt   *8/29/1852*

JD 1:58-59

[T]he sealing of the great *Jehovah* upon *Adam* and Eve was eternal in its nature, and was never instituted for the purpose of being overthrown and brought to an end.

Heber C. Kimball   *11/14/1852*

JD 1:356

When we escape from this earth, do we suppose we are going to heaven? Do you suppose you are going to the earth that *Adam* came from? that Elohim came from? where *Jehovah* the Lord came from? No.

                                                                    1856

MS 18:541

Father *Adam* walked and talked with *Jehovah*, and the Priesthood continued in an unbroken chain to Noah, and all who held it were preachers of righteousness, even of that "righteousness which exalteth a nation."

George Taylor   *1858*

MS 20:59

It was the Devil that preached the first sectarian sermon on this earth. "In the day that thou eatest thereof thou shalt surely die," said *Jehovah*. "In the day that thou eatest thereof thou shalt not surely die," said the Arch-sectarian. His teaching was believed. Sin came into the world, and also death. Pollution raised its hydra head among the beautiful and pure. The ground was cursed, and also man; and the whole of the posterity of our first parents have to die.

John Taylor   *4/27/1862*

JD 10:36

Some complain at the hand of *Jehovah* for giving them wheat. I have heard it said, "It is a curse to us; it annoys me to see so much wheat." There never has been a land, from the days of *Adam* until now, that has been blessed more than this land has been blessed by our Father in heaven; and it will still be blessed more and more, if we are faithful and humble, and thankful to *God* for the wheat and the corn, the oats, the fruit, the vegetables, the cattle and everything he bestows upon us, and try to use them for building up of his kingdom on the earth.

Heber C. Kimball   *6/27/1863*

JD 10:235

It reads in the Scriptures that the Lord [created the earth], but the true rendering is, that the Almighty sent *Jehovah* and *Michael* to do the work.

John Burrows   *Saturday 8/12/1865*

MS 27:497

When *Jehovah* had finished the creation of this beautiful world, and devised laws to direct the progress of nature in the animal, vegetable and mineral kingdoms, all was order, harmony and unity, and flowers and fruits shed forth their rich perfumes. In the designs of Providence, *two intelligent beings came forth, and when they were clothed with immortality, they stood forth as king and queen of a universal Eden*; but we read that before the Lord left them, he gave unto the man the following striking commandment, "Of every tree of the garden thou mayest freely eat: but of the tree of knowledge of good and evil, thou shalt not eat ...."

Brigham Young   *4/17/1870*

JD 13:311

The world may in vain ask the question, 'Who are we?' But the Gospel tells us that we are the sons and daughters of that God whom we serve. Some say, 'We are the children of Adam and Eve.' So we are, and they are the children of our Heavenly Father. We are all the children of Adam and Eve, and they and we are the offspring of Him who dwells in the heavens, the highest Intelligence that dwells anywhere that we have knowledge of.

Brigham Young   *5/7/1871*

JD 14:111

Do you not all know that you are the sons and daughters of the Almighty? If you do not I will inform you this morning that there is not a man or woman on the earth that is not a son or daughter of Adam and Eve. We all belong to the races which have sprung from father Adam and mother Eve; and *every son and daughter of Adam and Eve is a son and daughter of that God we serve*, who organized this earth and millions of others, and who holds them in existence by law.

Orson Pratt   *Sunday a.m. 10/11/1874*

JD 17:186

I say we are told by this Prophet that the Ancient of days is the most ancient personage that ever had an existence in days here on the earth. And who was he? Why, of course, old father *Adam*, he was the most ancient man that ever lived in days that we have any knowledge of. He comes, then, as a great judge, to assemble this innumerable host of which Daniel speaks. He comes in flaming fire. The glory and blessing and greatness of his personage it would be impossible even for a man as great as Daniel fully to describe. *He comes as a man inspired from the eternal throne of Jehovah himself.* He comes to set in order the councils of the Priesthood pertaining to all dispensations, to arrange the Priesthood and the councils of the Saints of all former dispensations in one grand family and household.

John Taylor	*Sunday p.m. 8/28/1881*

JD 22:298-99

The position that we occupy is indeed a very peculiar one. We are gathered here from the nations of the earth. We are gathered here because of certain plans, purposes and designs of *Jehovah*, pertaining to the world wherein we live, pertaining to the peoples who have existed before us and relating to all men whether living or dead. And as the Lord organized this world; as He is said to be the *God of the spirits of all flesh*; and as he is interested in the welfare of all humanity, he would be the proper personage to inaugurate every measure, everything that would be calculated to promote the interests of mankind. And in the accomplishment of the salvation of the human family his designs, plans and purposes have been perfected generations long ago. *If he could reveal unto Adam* all of the events which would transpire upon the earth associated with coming generations, he certainly must himself have had a knowledge of those things which he communicated to our first parents, or he could not have revealed them.

Charles W. Penrose	*9/--/1881*

Contributor 2:363 #12

That which was lost in *Adam* is to be regained in *Christ*. Through the commission of crime, death came into the world. Satan gained dominion. The earth trembled under the curse. Eden bloomed no more upon its face. The tree of life was removed. Thorns and briers and noxious weeds came up in the place of the flowers and fruits of paradise. *Deity* was hidden from the sight of man. Sorrow and pain and toil and travail became the heritage of mortals. Enmity arose between man and beast. Venom entered the serpent's fangs, and rage the hearts of brute and fowl and aqueous creature. Strife dwelt in the very elements and death brooded over the face of the smitten globe. What, then, was lost? The immortality of man; the blessed tree of life; communion with *Jehovah*; the companionship of angels; the purity of paradise; man's dominion over inferior creatures; freedom from Satanic influence; exemption from toil and pain; earth's affinity with perfected realms on high.

George E. Reynolds   *10/--/1881*

Contributor 3:17 #1

Some writers have maintained that throughout Genesis and in the first chapters of Exodus there are traces of two original documents at least, some claim more. These two documents are characterized by giving different names to God. *In the one he is called Eloheim and in the other Jehovah.* It appears never to have entered into the thoughts of these writers that possibly two different heavenly personages were intended. One simple passage from the mouth of our late beloved President, Brigham Young, throws a flood of light on this subject. It is as follows: "It is true that the earth was organized by three distinct characters, namely, Eloheim, *Jahovah, and Michael*, these three forming a quorum as in all heavenly bodies."

F. B. Toronto   *12/--/1881*

Contributor 3:67-68 #3

Thus we behold the keys of the Priesthood consisted in obtaining the voice of *Jehovah*, that He talked with him in a familiar and friendly manner, that He continued to him the keys, the covenants, the power and the glory, with which He blessed *Adam* at the beginning; and the offering of sacrifice, which also shall be continued at the last time; for all the ordinances and duties that ever have been required by the Priesthood, under the directions and commandments of the Almighty, in any of the dispensations, shall all be had in the last dispensation.

Joseph E. Taylor   *3/--/1885*

Contributor 6:231 #6

When the purposes of God as pertaining to this creation shall be fully made manifest there will be found a most beautiful harmony from first to last; a necessity for all that has been, and is, or will be until the final winding up scene. This was understood by the ancient worthies who labored diligently in their turn and time to accomplish all they possibly could to bring to pass the purposes of *Jehovah*: for the labor commenced with father *Adam* has been continued until today and will not be consummated until the final appearance of the "Holy One who hath established the foundations of Adam-ondi-Ahman," and who will finally present this earth with its inhabitants to the Father as worthy of a place in the celestial group of earths and worlds redeemed.

Erastus Snow   *Sunday a.m. 5/31/1885*

JD 26:220

They seem to have forgotten the commandment given to *our first parents*, and never to have comprehended the purposes of *Jehovah*. Those who adopt these views have seemed to imagine that there would be greater happiness in the gratification of fleshly lusts, and in pandering to pride and worldly pleasures, and the increase of wealth, than to obey the commandment of God. They have resolved to avoid raising large families.

Edward Stevenson   *2/28/1896*

Edward Stevenson Diary
Certainly Eloheim, and *Jehovah* stands [sic] before *Adam*, or else I am very much mistaken. Then 1st Eloheim, 2nd Jehovah, 3d Michael-Adam, 4th Jesus Christ, Our Elder Brother, in the other World from whence our spirits came ... Then Who is Jehovah? The only begotten Son of Eloheim on Jehovah's world.

Edward Stevenson   *3/3/1896*

Edward Stevenson Diary
I have more pleasure than usual with a deep talk with Pres. L. Snow on *Adam* -Jehovah - Eloheim and Jesus and Spirits, and Regarding their *immortality*, creation, &c

See also D&C 107:53-54; additionally, most of the Pearl of Great Price distinguishes Adam from Jehovah.

Analysis & Observations

β

No author has previously taken the initiative to do exhaustive research on this subject before, although Boyd Kirkland has done some significant preliminary work.[212] The theological inspiration behind this research came after dozens of conversations with individuals who remained confused about the appropriate theological identity of Jehovah in early Mormonism.[213] If the reader, after considering the above information, is still unable to ascertain where Jehovah fits in early Mormonism, the reader is likely going to remain in that position until he/she receives direct revelation from heaven because there simply is *not much more* material remaining to study.

When I began this portion of *Understanding Adam-God Teachings*, I was entirely uncertain

---

[212] His article was the academic inspiration behind my research for this subsection.

[213] Some of these had even read much of the then existing materials on the subject.

as to what I would discover. Other authors have claimed that the early brethren taught that Jehovah was Jesus Christ; competing authors have argued that this stance was simply untenable and not true; other authors have stated that the early brethren rarely did definitively state who they believed Jehovah was - their usage of the term was merely general in nature; these and other various positions have been circulated in various publications and in various web sites in abundance. However, despite references from these various authors that they have researched these materials thoroughly, none of them have ever presented the evidence to the reader for a critical review.[214] I undertook this task to provide that evidence and honestly expected that there would be a substantial foundation of materials identifying Jehovah as Jesus among the teachings of the early brethren - after all, as Boyd Kirkland and many other authors have pointed out, Mormon doctrine has grown and changed over the years so it was, in my mind, entirely foreseeable that a lack of unity in these teachings could have existed and that there would be several statements equating Jesus with Jehovah. My findings led me to a contrary conclusion. Although there is a lack of unity in teachings when one compares the modern LDS Church's position and the position of the early brethren, I have found an overwhelmingly consistent view as to the identity of Jehovah among the early brethren.

If one observation over-clouded any other observation, it was that I found pre-1880 periods of Mormon history to be entirely consistent in identifying Jehovah as the God Mormons worship. After the mid 1880s, that consistency dissipated into a period of ambiguity and confusion, which later developed into the new, consistent, theological stance held by the modern LDS Church. After researching the statements from Nauvoo and pre-Nauvoo periods, it became more academically plausible in my mind to argue that Adam-God teachings originated from Joseph Smith - not because of any explicit statements, but because Joseph Smith and his contemporaries' usage of the term "Jehovah" mirrors much more closely the fundamentalist position than it mirrors the modern LDS Church position. Certainly, there is virtually no direct evidence that the early *brethren* believed that Jehovah was Jesus Christ (the only *conclusive* statements identifying Jehovah as Jesus before the 1880s were made by persons without any significant priesthood status or were made by otherwise unknown pioneer women - and these were made after the martyrdom and before the exodus to Utah when doctrinal

---

[214] As an aside, I thoroughly welcome a critical, academic review of these materials - as I mention above, arguments can be made to show that some of the generic usages of the term Jehovah were not generic at all (they require assumptions beyond the plain reading of the text) - I think that such a review would be a great service to academic Mormonism regardless of which side undertakes this project. I also acknowledge, having published materials of a similar nature (format-wise) in the past, that inputting several hundred references into a table format is a breeding ground for some typographical error so a critical review may uncover a misplaced citation or two.

oversight by the brethren was less strict). It is also clear, as other authors have noted, that Joseph Smith never identified Jesus Christ as being Jehovah.[215] In contrast, we do have two statements from Joseph Smith identifying Jesus as Jehovah's son, four statements where Joseph indicates that modern worship of Jehovah is appropriate, and one statement where Joseph distinguishes Jesus from Jehovah.

Of great significance is Joseph's perspective of who Jehovah was. The above statements show that Joseph stated that Jehovah was Jesus' father at least two times, Joseph prayed to Jehovah on at least three different occasions, and Joseph otherwise distinguished Jehovah from Jesus on at least one other occasions. We have no statement whatsoever of Joseph Smith declaring Jesus to be Jehovah.

These observations behind us, other authors have made various, insightful comments that doctrinally add upon the teachings put forth in this subsection. Because several authors have mentioned these items, I cannot cite any specific author as the originator of the following ideas:

There is an interesting problem with the current LDS position placing Jesus as Jehovah that circulates among fundamentalists that is worth noting here. The modern LDS Church teaches that Abraham's willingness to keep Jehovah's commandment to offer Isaac as a sacrifice is a similitude of the Father's willingness to sacrifice His son for our redemption. From the Church's perspective however, Jehovah (who is Christ according to their theology) was the individual who commanded Abraham to make that sacrifice. While this is not an inherent doctrinal contradiction when one considers divine investiture of authority, it is less intimate and heart-warming than the view that arrives in light of the above proofs that the Jehovah of the Old Testament was God the Father - Adam. Thus, Adam, speaking to Abraham, commands him to offer his only begotten son, just as Adam must do in the meridian of time. In this light, consider Brigham H. Robert's comments on this subject:

Brigham H. Roberts   *12/12/1897*

CD 5

Look, I pray you, at the father of the faithful, Abraham. Tried every way; tested at every point; touched upon the tenderest chord of all his soul; required by the

---

[215] An academician may argue that D&C 110:2-4 provides some proof that Joseph made this connection but any believing Mormon will argue that this is a statement of the Lord, not of Joseph Smith himself. That aside and as noted above, D&C 110:2-4 may not provide any proof that the originator of the statement, whomever it was, made that connection in the first place.

commandment of God to take the son of promise and to place him upon the altar, and let the smoke that should consume his flesh ascend up as incense unto God - tested to that very point, and yet he stood the test, believing in and trusting the justice and mercy of God. Though the general commandment was extant, "Thou shalt not kill," yet when the voice of God came to him commanding him to kill he stood not quibbling or questioning with God, he manifested his readiness to sacrifice even his son unto God's commandment; but when it was clear that Abraham would not even withhold his son from God - when the test was completed, the trial passed, the ram in the thicket was provided, dragged out, and bound in thankfulness upon the altar to take the place of Isaac.

How sweet must have been the communion of Abraham with God after that! What confidence must have been his in the *presence of God* even after that! And how grand the words that came from the lips of *Jehovah* must have appeared to him, saying: "Because thou hast done this thing, and hast not withheld thy son, thine only son, in blessing I will bless thee, and in multiplying I will multiply thy seed as the stars of heaven, and as the sand which is upon the sea shore; and thy seed shall possess the gate of his enemies; and in thy seed shall all the nations of the earth be blessed; because thou hast obeyed my voice." Oh! my friends, God indeed calls, nay, demands, sacrifice; but God is able to reward men for their sacrifices, even to the uttermost. You need not doubt it.

Christensen also had some interesting comments regarding the identity of the Jehovah of the Old Testament that are worth repeating here. The following statements are from AGM 250-51:

According to the scriptures, Jesus is the creator of the worlds (D&C 76:24; Hebrews 1:2), all things in heaven (Colossians 1:16), all things in earth (Colossians 1:16; Alma 1:4), all things from the beginning (Mosiah 3:8), and the spirit of man (Ether 3:16). While we believe that Christ did have a personal role in the creation, that role, particularly in the face of the foregoing scriptures, is ill defined. A literal interpretation of these scriptures is difficult to accept because they conflict with the revealed plan of eternal progression. The scriptures say that Jesus created "all things"; yet, he could not have created himself or that which existed prior to his own creation. What "all things" did he, then, create? ... The scriptures say that Jesus created the spirits of man (Ether 3:16). This would imply that he is our Father, whereas we know Him to be our spiritual brother (of the same generation of spirits). In which respect, then, is Jesus the "creator of man"?

Christensen concludes, as have many previous authors, that Jesus is the creator in the sense that it is through his atonement that all things have been created on this earth.

Ether 3:15 has also become a major point of contention between Adam-God adherents and members of the LDS Church. After praying to the Lord, Ether records the following experience:

Ether 3:8-16

And he saith unto the Lord: I saw the finger of the Lord, and I feared lest he should smite me; for I knew not that the Lord had flesh and blood. And the Lord said unto him: Because of thy faith thou hast seen that *I shall take upon me* flesh and blood; and never has man come before me with such exceeding faith as thou hast; for were it not so ye could not have seen my finger.

Sawest thou more than this? And he answered: Nay; Lord, show thyself unto me. And the Lord said unto him: Believest thou the words which I shall speak? And he answered: Yea, Lord, I know that thou speakest the truth, for thou art a God of truth, and canst not lie. And when he had said these words, behold, the Lord showed himself unto him, and said: Because thou knowest these things ye are redeemed from the fall; therefore ye are brought back into my presence; therefore I show myself unto you. Behold, I am he who was prepared from the foundation of the world to redeem my people. *Behold, I am Jesus Christ. I am the Father and the Son.* In me shall all mankind have life, and that eternally, even they who shall believe on my name; and they shall become my sons and my daughters. And never have I showed myself unto man whom I have created, for never has man believed in me as thou hast. Seest thou that ye are created after mine own image? Yea, even all men were created in the beginning after mine own image. *Behold, this body, which ye now behold, is the body of my spirit; and man have I created after the body of my spirit*; and even as I appear unto thee to be in the spirit will I appear unto my people in the flesh.

This statement has caused some degree of confusion because the brother of Jared was praying to the God of the Old Testament; then, in answer to his prayer, Jesus Christ appeared to him. On its face, this seems to be proof that the God of the Old Testament is Jesus Christ. The irony of this position is that fundamentalists, who are not as fond of the "divine investiture of authority" teaching, are prone to read this passage as an example of one member of the godhead speaking in behalf of another member of the godhead as the George Q. Cannon statement explained at the beginning of this section. The distinction here is that Jesus presents himself to the brother of Jared as the forthcoming Redeemer and never explains why he is appearing in the stead of the Father to whom Jared was praying (according to the fundamentalist / Adam-God adherent perspective). Joseph Smith's statement below may muddle (or hopefully clarify) this situation further:

TPJS, 167-68

Commencing with *Adam* ... to whom Christ was first revealed, and *through whom Christ has been revealed from heaven, and will continue to be revealed from henceforth.*

The important thing to notice here is that Christ is *always* revealed to man *through* Adam. In other words, if Joseph Smith knew what he was talking about, then Christ was revealed to the brother of Jared through Adam's authority. While members of the LDS Church may be prone to argue that we have a complete and thorough accounting of the brother of Jared's vision here, it seems more likely from Joseph's statement that the Ether account is incomplete.[216] A more complete account may have ran like this. When the brother of Jared asks to see the Lord more completely, we find this account: "And when he had said these words, behold, the Lord showed himself unto him." It may be that, at this time, the brother of Jared was introduced to Christ in the same fashion that Joseph Smith was - by the father pointing to the Son and declaring "Behold, my beloved Son in whom I am well pleased, hear ye him." At that point, the Ether narration completes the account by Christ speaking to the brother of Jared and declaring his redemption from the fall, etc. While this reading requires some speculation, the speculation is founded upon a principle taught by Joseph Smith. As Joseph gave us no exceptions to this principle, it does not seem cavalier to apply the principle to the instant case in an effort to reconcile this otherwise confusing passage with the vast amount of evidence (produced in this volume) that appears to declare a contradicting theological perspective.

If the reader is interested in reading more broadly about the Mormon theological position as to Jehovah's identity, Boyd Kirkland's article in Dialogue 19:77 et seq. covers this issue fairly well and he further offers this information in perspective of the Christianity of Joseph's time. Additionally, he cites these articles as informative for the reader interested in studying how the authors of the Bible moved from polytheism (a belief in more than one god - e.g., Elohim is a different god than Jehovah) to monotheism (Jehovah is the only true God):

Anderson 2:411-14; 427-28; 654-56
Anderson, B. W. "God, Old Testament View of." Interpreter's Dictionary of the Bible. Vol. 2. George Arthur

---

[216] This assertion ought not to be all that controversial given the fact that any other account of a vision had by an ancient prophet is presumed to be abridged for one reason or another.

Moule 2:430-36;

Moule, C. F. D. "God, New Testament." The Interpreter's Dictionary of the Bible. Vol. 2. Nashville: Abingdon, 1981, pp. 430-36.

Terrien 1982, 1150-52;

Terrien, Samuel. "The Religion of Israel." The Interpreter's One-Volume Commentary on the Bible. Charles M. Laymon, ed. Nashville: Abingdon, 1982, pp. 1150-52.

Rankin 1962, 90-99;

Rankin, O. S. "The Development of the Biblical Thought About God," "Names of God," and "Gods." A Theological Word Book of the Bible. Alan Richardson, ed. New York: Macmillan Publ., 1962, pp. 90-99.

Robinson 1944, 151-57).

Robinson, H. Wheeler. "The Council of Yahweh." The Journal of Theological Studies (1944): 151-57.

28   Elohim

The question as to the identity of Elohim under Adam-God teachings has been relatively without controversy. Presumably, this is because the modern LDS Church has done nothing to effectively alter the doctrine of who Elohim might be - at least, it has done nothing as drastic as what has been done with the teachings of who Jehovah is. In the modern LDS Church therefore, the term Elohim continues to refer to God the Father generally - as it did when Joseph first began using the term during his study of Hebrew.[217]

Nevertheless, the question as to who Elohim is remains somewhat misunderstood and confusing to members of the LDS Church who accept and believe Adam-God teachings because the term Jehovah - not Elohim - is often used to refer to God the Father in Adam-God teachings. While it is simple enough to say that Elohim is the father of Jehovah or that Elohim is simply another title and refers to the office in which an individual is acting, that is not always satisfying to persons new to these teachings.

Wherefore, it may be of some help to point out here that the early brethren used the term in both of the above fashions - that is, Elohim was used as a title and it was used to refer to the father of Jehovah. In the latter context, the early brethren usually referred to Elohim as a specific individual who was the head of the creation godhead.[218] That acknowledged, the reader ought to be aware that some of the early brethren appear to have referred to two different godheads - the creation godhead, which consisted of

---

[217] While a study may prove interesting for the reader, I have not delved into the origins of the word Elohim, nor have I delved into the usage of this word in the scriptures as such a study is beyond the pervue of this volume. If the reader is interested in this information, I would direct him/her to Stong's Exhaustive Concordance of the Bible and/or to various books on Kabalah.

[218] It appears that it was in this context that they called Elohim God the Father.

Elohim, Jehovah, and Michael (Adam) - and the redemption godhead, which consisted of Jehovah (Adam), Jesus Christ, and the Holy Ghost.[219] Thus, unlike the modern LDS Church, fundamentalists do not try to identify Elohim, Jehovah, and Michael with God the Father, Jesus Christ, and Adam - instead, their theological perspective mirrors that of the early brethren as explained above. Lastly, Elohim was also used to refer to a "council of gods." The below statements show how the early brethren used this term in all of these different ways:

Exodus 7:1
_____

And the LORD said unto Moses, See, I have made thee a god [Elohim] to Pharaoh: and Aaron thy brother shall be thy prophet.

Joseph Smith   *Wednesday 5/4/1842*
_____

TPJS, 237

I spent the day in the upper part of the store, that is in my private office ... in council with [several individuals] instructing them in the principles and order of the Priesthood, attending to washings, anointings, endowments and the communication of keys pertaining to the Aaronic Priesthood, and so on to the highest order of the Melchizedek Priesthood, setting forth the order pertaining to the Ancient of Days, and all those plans and principles by which any one is enabled to secure the fullness of those blessing which have been prepared for the Church of the Firstborn, and come up and abide in the presence of *the Eloheim* in the eternal worlds. In this council was instituted the ancient order of things for the first time in these last days.

Joseph Smith   *circa 8/--/1842*
_____

HC 5:127; MS 19:757

O Thou, who seest and knowest the hearts of all men - Thou eternal, omnipotent, omniscient, and omnipresent *Jehovah - God - Thou Eloheim*, that sittest, as saith the Psalmist, "enthroned in heaven," look down upon Thy servant Joseph at this time; and let faith on the name of Thy son Jesus Christ, to a greater degree than Thy servant ever yet has enjoyed, be conferred upon him.

_____

[219] Some fundamentalists believe that the Joseph Smith was the Holy Ghost before his mortal probation due to a couple of obscure statements by Joseph Smith that appear to have been teaching this doctrine. While there is significant academic merit to this conclusion, it is beyond the scope of this volume to explore this issue.

3/1/1843

T&S 4:121 #8

[B]efore God said "let there be light, and it was so," or ever this world rolled into existence, or the morning stars sung together for joy a plan was formed in the councils of heaven, it was contemplated by the great Author of our existence, *Eloheim, Jehovah*, to redeem the earth from under the curse. Hence when the Gods deliberated about the formation of man, it was known that he would fall and the Savior was provided who was to redeem and to restore, who was indeed the "Lamb slain from the foundation of the world."

Joseph Smith   *6/16/1844*

TPJS, 370-72

Eloheim is from the word Eloi, God, in the singular number; and by adding the word heim, it renders it Gods. It read first, "In the beginning the head of the Gods brought forth the Gods," or, as others have translated it, "The head of the Gods called the Gods together." ... The head God organized the heavens and the earth. In the beginning the heads of the Gods organized the heavens and the earth. ... The head one of the Gods said, Let us make a man in our own image. I once asked a learned Jew, "If the Hebrew language compels us to render all words ending in heim in the plural, why not render the first *Eloheim* plural?" He replied, "That is the rule with few exceptions; but in this case it would ruin the Bible." He acknowledged I was right. ... In the very beginning the Bible shows there is a plurality of Gods beyond the power of refutation. It is a great subject I am dwelling on. The word *Eloheim* ought to be in the plural all the way through - Gods. The heads of the Gods appointed one God for us; and when you take that view of the subject, it sets one free to see all the beauty, holiness and perfections of the Gods.

John Taylor   *7/15/1844*

T&S 5:577-78 #97

When we hear the history of the rise of this kingdom, from one who has been with it from its infancy, from the lips of our venerable friend who has taken an active part in all the history of the church, can we be surprised that he should feel animated, and that his soul should burn with heavenly zeal? We see in him a man of God who can contemplate the glories of heaven; the visions of eternity, and who yet looks forward to the opening glories which the great *Eloheim* has manifested to him, pertaining to righteousness and peace; a man who now beholds the things roll on which he has long since beheld in prophetic vision. Most men have established themselves in authority, by laying desolate other kingdoms, and the destruction of other powers. Their kingdoms have been founded in blood and supported by tyranny and oppression. The greatest chieftains of the earth have obtained their glory, if glory it can be called, by blood, carnage and ruin. … When I gaze upon this company of men, I see those who are actuated by patriotic and noble principles, who will stand up in defense of the oppressed, of whatever country, nation, color, or clime. I see it in their countenances; it is planted by the spirit of God, and they have received it from the great *Eloheim*, all the power or influence of mobs, priestcraft and corrupt men, cannot quench it, it will burn, it is comprehensive as the designs of God, and as expansive as the universe, and reaches to all the world, no matter whether it was an Indian, a negro or any other man, or set of men that are oppressed, you would stand forth in their defense.

Joseph Smith   *8/15/1844*

T&S 5:612-13 #99

I do not calculate to please your ears with superfluity of words or oratory, or with much learning; but I calculate to edify you with the simple truths from heaven. In the first place, I wish to go back to the beginning of creation; there is the starting point, in order to be fully acquainted with the mind, purposes, decrees, &c. of the great *Eloheim*, that sits in yonder heavens, it is necessary for us to have an understanding of God himself in the beginning. If we start right, it is easy to go right all the time; but if we start wrong, it is a hard matter to get right.

2/15/1845

T&S 6:808-09 #3

[T]he first line of Genesis, purely translated from the original, excluding the first (Baith) (which was added by the Jews,) would read: (Rosheit) (the head) (baurau), (brought forth,) *(Eloheim)* (the Gods) (ate) (with) (hah-shau-mahyiem) (the heavens) (veh-ate), (and with) (hauaurates), (the earth.) In simple English. The Head brought forth the Gods, with the heavens and with the earth. The 'Head' must have meant the 'living God,' or Head God: Christ is our head. The term 'Eloheim,' plural of Elohah, or ale, is used alike in the first chapter of Genesis, for the creation, and the quotation of Satan. In the second chapter, and fourth verse, we have this remarkable history: "(These are the generations of the heavens and of the earth, when they were brought forth; in the day that the Lord of the Gods made earth and heavens)." The Hebrew reads so.

First Presidency   *4/6/1845*

MFP 1:253

Proclamation of the Twelve Apostles of the Church of Jesus Christ of Latter-day Saints.

To all the King's of the World ... And to the Rulers and People of all Nations: Greeting:

Know Ye - that the kingdom of God has come: as has been predicted by ancient prophets, and prayed for in all ages; even that kingdom which shall fill the whole earth, and shall stand for ever. The great *Eloheem Jehovah* has been pleased once more to speak from the heavens: and also to commune with man upon the earth, by means of open visions, and by the ministration of holy messengers. By this means the great and eternal High Priesthood, after the Order of his Son, even the Apostleship, has been restored; or, returned to the earth.

Samuel W. Richards   *Saturday 12/10/1853*

MS 15:801-02

By the first man, Adam, came death, the triumph of evil; and by the second, came life everlasting, the triumph of good. Each was necessary in the order he appeared; if the first Adam had not performed his part, the second could not have had his work to do. Both acted the part assigned to them, in a most Godlike manner, and *the Great Eloheim* accepted the work at their hands as His own, 'for by the power of my Spirit created I them; yea, all things, both spiritual and temporal: firstly, spiritual - secondly, temporal, which is the beginning of my work; and again, firstly, temporal - and secondly, spiritual, which is the last of my work.' Thus the great I AM owns all things - the temporal and the spiritual, the justice and the mercy, to be His own work. Then why may not Adam be a God, as well as any of his sons, inasmuch as he has performed the work to which the Great *Eloheim* appointed him? ...

Were we to trace this subject in all its bearings, we should find the principles of the Godhead planted in every righteous and well-organized family upon the earth, and that they only require cultivation to cause their expansion and development to be equal to anything we can now conceive of as adding power and glory to the God of all worlds. The Great *Eloheim* rules over worlds. He is God over them, because of His right and power to rule, govern, and control. The exercise of this power is a natural right in the order of Priesthood, which belongs to every Patriarch, or Father, in the human family, so long as he rules subordinately to the laws of Heaven. According to the order of that God by whom we are ruled, a man is not only permitted to hold full jurisdiction over his own family, but he is held responsible for any violation, by them, of the revealed will of Heaven. A man that controls a work, is the only one that can be held responsible for that work.

Brigham Young   *6/17/1871*

Joseph F. Smith Journal

Elohim, Yahovah and Michael were father, Son and grandson. They made this Earth and Michael became Adam.

George E. Reynolds   *10/--/1881*

Contributor 3:17 #1

Some writers have maintained that throughout Genesis and in the first chapters of Exodus there are traces of two original documents at least, some claim more. These two documents are characterized by giving different names to God. *In the one he is called Eloheim and in the other Jehovah.* It appears never to have entered into the thoughts of these writers that possibly two different heavenly personages were intended. One simple passage from the mouth of our late beloved President, Brigham Young, throws a flood of light on this subject. It is as follows: "It is true that the earth was organized by three distinct characters, namely, *Eloheim, Jahovah, and Michael*, these three forming a quorum as in all heavenly bodies."

Joseph Smith   *4/--/1883*

Contributor 4:253 #7[220]

In the first place, I wish to go back to the beginning - to the morn of creation. There is the starting-point for us to look to, in order to understand and be fully acquainted with the mind, purposes and decrees of the Great *Eloheim*, who sits in yonder heavens as He did at the creation of this world. It is necessary for us to have an understanding of God Himself in the beginning. If we start right, it is easy to go right all the time; but if we start wrong, we may go wrong, and it be a hard matter to get right.

John Taylor   *Monday-Tuesday 10/6-7/1884*

JD 25:307-08

The work in which we are engaged is one that has been introduced by the Great *Eloheim*, the God and Father of the human family, in the interests of His children. And wherever and whenever these principles have existed, this same being that was in the garden with our first parents still goes forth and has gone forth as a raging lion, seeking whom he may deceive, seeking whom he may devour, seeking whom he may lead down to death.

----

[220] Note that this statement is very similar to the one found in T&S 5:612-13 but there have been some significant and substantive changes made to the text.

Supplement to Gospel Problems, 8-9

Elohim may signify the Father or Grandfather, or Great Grandfather - God or the Council of the Gods, and Jehovah may be applied to any of them in the capacity or relationship of a son, as they all are, for `where was there ever a father without first being a son?[221] Adam is in line with his progenitors, the Gods, and by the genealogical record cannot be deposed from his position as the God of this world under the council and direction of the Gods above him, `intelligences one above another without end.' (D&C 78)

The following is a list of places where the term Eloheim, Eloheem, Aloheem, or other derivations of the Hebrew term are used in a generic fashion that tells us nothing further about the identity of Elohim.

Rendered Plural	MS 3:71; 9:135 (6x); 24:109; 28:786
Name	MS 11:282; 12:264
Great	Contributor 6:302 #8; 8:288-89 #8; 12:59 #2
	T&S 5:391-92 #85
	MS 5:88; 15:390, 802, 803; 20:406, 675; 21:246, 699;
	23:216, 216, 221, 245
Eternal / Omnipotent	Contributor 3:202 #7
	MS 23:13
Presence of E	MS 19:391
Mystery of E&S	T&S 3:780 #13
Hands	MS 8:178

---

[221] CH 6:476.

29   God & god

As with the previous Jehovah and Elohim subsections, this subsection is designed to show how the early brethren used the term "god". While the timing in providing a definition to the term "god" may seem a little belated at this point of this volume, the definitions provided in this subsection could be confusing to individuals who remain unfamiliar with basic Adam-God teachings.

Once again, the statements in this subsection show that the early brethren viewed this term as a title - and not just a title bestowed upon the One True God and not just a title bestowed upon deity but as a title that may appropriately be bestowed upon many mortal individuals in many instances. This does not mean that all of the statements proclaiming Adam as God the Father are to be interpreted in a casual fashion that only ascribes to Adam a "god" status as could be given to any great leader or prophet - clearly, Adam was seen as the Only True God by the early brethren. However, the early brethren's understanding of the term was much broader than that exhibited by leaders of the modern LDS Church. Unfortunately, the early brethren often used these deital titles in unconventional ways and occasionally this leaves us, the distant reader, wondering which version of this term of art they were using in a certain discourse. Few clues given, that decision is left to the reader's judgment of these statements as they are found below.

Joseph Smith   *5/16/1841*

TPJS, 190
Everlasting covenant was made between three personages before the organization of this earth, and relates to their dispensation of things to men on the earth; these personages, according to Abraham's record, are called *God* the first, the Creator; *God* the second, the Redeemer; and *God* the third, the Witness or Testator.

Joseph Smith   *6/11/1843*

WJS, 214

Any person that has seen the heavens opened knows that there are three personages in the heavens who hold the keys of power, and one presides over all. While there is but one *God*, a plurality of deities share *that title*.

Joseph Smith   *6/11/1843*

TPJS, 312

In the resurrection, some are raised to be angels, others are raised to become Gods. These things are revealed in the most holy places in a Temple prepared for that purpose.

Joseph Smith   *6/16/1844*

TPJS, 370-72

I will preach on the plurality of Gods. I have selected this text for that express purpose. I wish to declare I have always and in all congregations when I have preach on the subject of the Deity, it has been the plurality of Gods. It has been preached by the Elders for fifteen years.

I have always declared God to be a distinct personage, Jesus Christ a separate and distinct personage from God the Father, and that the Holy Ghost was a distinct personage and a Spirit: and *these three constitute three distinct personages and three Gods.* If this is in accordance with the New Testament, lo and behold! *we have three Gods* anyhow, and they are plural; and who can contradict it?

Our text says, "And hath made us kings and priests unto *God and His Father*." The Apostles have discovered that *there were Gods above*, for John says God was the Father of our Lord Jesus Christ. My object was to preach the scriptures, and preach the doctrine they contain, there being a God above, the Father of our Lord Jesus Christ. I am bold to declare I have taught all the strongest doctrines publicly, and always teach stronger doctrines in public than in private.

John was one of the men, and apostles declare they were made kings and priests unto God, the Father of our Lord Jesus Christ. It reads just so in the Revelation, Hence the doctrine of a plurality of Gods is as prominent in the Bible as any other doctrine. It is all over the face of the Bible. It stands beyond the power of controversy. A wayfaring man, though a fool, need not err therein.

Paul says *there are Gods many and Lords many.* I want to set it forth in a plain and simple manner; but to us *there is but one God - that is pertaining to us;* and he is in all and through all. But if Joseph Smith says there are Gods many and Lords many, they cry, "Away with him! Crucify him! Crucify him!"

Mankind verily say that the Scriptures are with them. Search the Scriptures, for they testify of things that these apostates would gravely pronounce blasphemy. Paul, if Joseph Smith is a blasphemer, you are. I say there are Gods many and Lords many, but to us only one, and we are to be in subjection to that one, and no man can limit the bounds or the eternal existence of eternal time. Hath he beheld the eternal world, and is he authorized to say that there is only one God? He makes himself a fool if he thinks or says so, and there is an end of his career or progress in knowledge. He cannot obtain all knowledge, for he has sealed up the gate to it.

Some say I do not interpret the Scripture the same as they do. They say it means the heathen's gods. Paul says there are Gods many and Lords many; and that makes a plurality of Gods, in spite of the whims of all men. Without a revelation, I am not going to give them the knowledge of the God of heaven. You know and I testify that Paul had no allusion to the heathen gods. I have it from God, and get over it if you can. I have a witness of the Holy Ghost, and a testimony that Paul had no allusion to the heathen gods in the text. I will show from the Hebrew Bible that I am correct, and *the first word shows a plurality of Gods*; and I want the apostates and learned men to come here and prove to the contrary, if they can. An unlearned boy must give you a little Hebrew. Berosheit baurau Eloheim ait aushamayeen vehau auraits, rendered by King James' translators, "In the beginning God created the heaven and the earth." I want to analyze the word Berosheit. Rosh, the head; Sheit, a grammatical termination; the Baith was not originally put there when the inspired man wrote it, but it has been since added by an old Jew. Baurau signifies to bring forth; Eloheim is from the word Eloi, God, in the singular number; and by adding the word heim, it renders it Gods. It read first, "*In the beginning the head of the Gods brought forth the Gods*," or, as others have translated it, "*The head of the Gods called the Gods together*." I want to show a little learning as well as other fools.

The head God organized the heavens and the earth. I defy all the world to refute me. *In the beginning the heads of the Gods organized the heavens and the earth.* Now the learned priests and the people rage, and the heathen imagine a vain thing. If we pursue the Hebrew text further, it reads, "*The head one of the Gods said, Let us make a man in our own image.*" I once asked a learned Jew, "If the Hebrew language compels us to render all words ending in heim in the plural, why not render the first Eloheim plural?" He replied, "That is the rule with few exceptions; but in this case it would ruin the Bible." He acknowledged I was right. I came here to investigate these things precisely as I believe them. Hear and judge for yourselves; and if you go away satisfied, well and good.

In the very beginning the Bible shows there is a plurality of Gods beyond the power of refutation. It is a great subject I am dwelling on. *The word Eloheim ought to be in the plural all the way through - Gods. The heads of the Gods appointed one God for us*; and when you take [that] view of the subject, its sets one free to see all the beauty, holiness and perfection of the Gods. All I want is to get the simple, naked truth, and the whole truth.

Many men say there is one God; the Father, the Son and the Holy Ghost are only one God. I say that is a strange God anyhow - three in one, and one in three! It is a curious organization. "Father, I pray not for the world, but I pray for them which thou hast given me." "Holy Father, keep through Thine own name those whom thou hast given me, that they may be one as we are." *All are to be crammed into one God, according to sectarianism. It would make the biggest God in all the world. He would be a wonderfully big God - he would be a giant or a monster.* I want to read the text to you myself - "I am agreed with the Father and the Father is agreed with me, and we are agreed as one." The Greek shows that it should be agreed. "Father, I pray for them which Thou hast given me out of the world, and not for those alone, but for them also which shall believe on me through their word, that they all may be agreed, as Thou, Father, are with me, and I with Thee, that they also may be agreed with us," and all come to dwell in unity, and in all *the glory and everlasting burnings of the Gods*; and *then we shall see as we are seen, and be as our God and He as His Father.*

2/15/1845

T&S 6:808-09 #3

What shall we say then, to make Moses', Jesus' and Peter's words true? We will say that Jesus Christ had a father and mother of his Spirit, and a father and mother of his flesh; and so have all of his brethren and sisters: and *that is one reason why he said,* `(ye are Gods);' or that Isaiah prophesied:[222] `Show the things that are to come hereafter, that we may know that *ye are Gods*; yea, do good, or do evil, that we may be dismayed, and behold it together.' In fact, `the Gods,' *in old times, was common intelligence.* Satan, in his first sectarian sermon to Adam and Eve, told them, if they would eat of the forbidden fruit, they should become as `*the Gods*,' knowing good and evil.

Orson Pratt   *Sunday 8/20/1871*

JD 14:243

They, the one hundred and forty-four thousand, had a peculiar inscription in their foreheads. What was it? It was the Father's name. What is the *Father's* name? It is *God* - the being we worship. If, then, the one hundred and forty-four thousand are to have the name of *God* inscribed on their foreheads, will it be simply a plaything, a something that has no meaning? or will it mean that which the inscriptions specify? - that they are

---

[222] Isaiah 41:23.

indeed *Gods* - one with the *Father* and one with the *Son*; as the Father and Son are one, and both of them called *Gods*, so will all His children be one with the Father and the Son, and they will be one so far as carrying out the great purposes of *Jehovah* is concerned. No divisions will be there but a complete oneness; not a oneness in person but a perfect oneness in action in the creation, redemption, and glorification of worlds.

Heber C. Kimball   *Saturday 4/10/1852*

Journal of Wilford Woodruff

Some have said that I was very presumptuous to say that Brother *Brigham was my God and Savior*. Brother *Joseph was his God*. The one that gave Joseph the keys of the Kingdom was *his God*, which *was Peter*. *Jesus Christ was his God* and *the God and Father of Jesus Christ was Adam.*

Franklin D. Richards   *12/10/1853*

MS 15:801-04

Without [the Fall] they could not have known good and evil here, and without knowing good and evil *they could not become Gods*, neither could their children. No wonder the woman was tempted when it was said unto her - `*Ye shall be as gods*, knowing good and evil.' No wonder Father Adam fell, and accompanied the woman, sharing in all the miseries of the curse, that he might be the father of an innumerable race of beings who would be capable of becoming *Gods*.

With these considerations before us, we can begin to see how it is that *we are under obligations to our father Adam, as to a God*. He endured the sufferings and the curse that we might be; and we are, that *we might become Gods*. Through him the justice of God was made manifest. Jesus came into the world, endured, and suffered, to perfect our advantages for becoming *Gods*, and through him the mercy of *God* abounded.

By the first man, Adam, came death, the triumph of evil; and by the second, came life everlasting, the triumph of good. Each was necessary in the order he appeared; if the first Adam had not performed his part, the second could not have had his work to do. Both acted the part assigned to them, in a most Godlike manner, and the Great Eloheim accepted the work at their hands as His own, `for by the power of my Spirit created I them; yea, all things, both spiritual and temporal: firstly, spiritual - secondly, temporal, which is the beginning of my work; and again, firstly, temporal - and secondly, spiritual, which is the last of my work.' Thus the great I AM owns all things - the temporal and the spiritual, the justice and the mercy, to be His own work. Then *why may not Adam be a God, as well as any of his sons,* inasmuch as he has performed the work to which the Great Eloheim appointed him?

In ancient times they were called Gods unto whom the word of God came, because of which

Moses became a God unto Pharaoh. The Almighty was not so jealous of His *Godly title* but that He could say to Moses - `See I have made thee *a God to Pharaoh.*' And if John's saying be true, God has purposed to make him that overcometh, a pillar in the temple of God, and to `*write upon him the name of my God.*' `His name shall be in their foreheads.'

This is the hope of all Saints who have a just conception of the future; and why should we not be willing for father Adam to inherit all things, as well as for ourselves? He is the first, the Father of all the human family, and his glory will be above all, for *he will be God over all,* necessarily, standing as he will through all eternity at the head of those who are the redeemed of his great family. Though all the sons should, through their faithfulness, become *Gods*, they would still know that the Son was not greater than the Father.

Were we to trace this subject in all its bearings, we should find the principles of the *Godhead* planted in every righteous and well-organized family upon the earth, and that they only require cultivation to cause their expansion and development to be equal to anything we can now conceive of as adding power and glory to the *God* of all worlds. The Great Eloheim rules over worlds. *He is God over them, because of His right and power to rule, govern, and control.* The exercise of this power is a natural right in the order of Priesthood, which belongs to every Patriarch, or Father, in the human family, so long as he rules subordinately to the laws of Heaven. According to the order of that God by whom we are ruled, a man is not only permitted to hold full jurisdiction over his own family, but he is held responsible for any violation, by them, of the revealed will of Heaven. A man that controls a work, is the only one that can be held responsible for that work. It would be most unjust to require responsibility where there is no power to govern and control. *Every man who has a family, and power to control them, is exercising the rights and powers of a God, though it may be in a very small capacity.* There are two grand principles, by virtue of which all intelligent beings have a legitimate right to govern and hold dominion; these are, by begetting children from their own loins, and by winning the hearts of others to voluntarily desire their righteous exercise of power extended over them. These constitute a sure foundation for an eternal throne - a kingdom as perpetual as *God's.* No usurped power, to be maintained by the shedding of blood, is connected with such a government. It is upon this foundation that the throne of Michael is established as Father, Patriarch, *God*; and it is for all his children who come into this world, to learn and fully understand the eternity of that relationship.

...

This final surrender, we are to bear in mind, does not detract from the God-like power and dominion of our first Parent, nor of our Lord Jesus Christ. In the Patriarchal order of government, each and every ruler is independent in his sphere, his rule extending to those below, and not to those above him, in the same order. *While the God of unnumbered worlds is acknowledged to be his God and Father,* Adam still maintains his exalted position at the head of all those who are saved from among the whole family of man; and *he will be God over all those who are made Gods from among men.* Each and *every God will be honored and adored by those over whom he reigns as a God,* without any violation of the laws of heaven - without any encroachment upon that command which saith, 'thou shalt have no other *Gods* before me,' for the glory and honor of all true *Gods* constitute the glory, honor, power, and dominion of the great Eloheim, according to His own order of government.

We can conceive of no higher, or more perfect order of government than that which is embraced in Patriarchal authority. By virtue of this order, all *Gods,* whether in heaven or on earth, exercise a righteous power, and possess a just dominion. In this order, all are both subjects and rulers, each possessing Almighty rights and powers - Almighty rulers over those who have descended from them, at the same time rendering all honor and power to those from whom they have descended. What a glorious system of order is here portrayed - one in which an innumerable succession of *Gods,* Patriarchs, and rulers, can reign forever in the greatest possible harmony that can be comprehended by intelligences, while each is independent in his position, as is all intelligence. As the great Eloheim is supreme and Almighty over all His children and kingdoms, so is Adam as great a ruler, or *God,* in his sphere, over his children, and the kingdom which they possess. The earth and all things upon it were created for Adam, and it was given to him of his Father to have dominion over it. In that dominion he will be sustained throughout all eternity.

In relation to this earth alone and its inhabitants, Michael and Gabriel have perhaps held the greatest keys of dominion and power. They were, both in their day, Fathers of all living, and had dominion given unto them over all things. Gabriel, or Noah, held the keys of this power under Michael, and to him he will render an account of all things before Michael renders an account of his stewardship to Him whose dominion reaches over many worlds, and who is *God over all Gods.* These two important personages have ever been watchful of the interests of their children, hence we find them ministering from time to time to holy men upon the earth - Gabriel often appearing unto Daniel, and opening to his view the most wonderful visions of the future, by which he could *act as a God to the people,* outvie the wisdom of the astrologers, and so control the elements that the burning furnace could have no power over him.

Parley P. Pratt   *before 1857*

Key to Theology, 1938 edition, 41

An immortal man, possessing a perfect organization of spirit, flesh and bones, and perfected in his attributes, in all the fulness of celestial glory, *is called a God.*

Brigham Young	3/8/1857

JD 4:271

If you find out who Joseph (Smith) was, you will know as much about *God* as you need to at present; for if he said, `I am a God to this people,' *he did not say that was the only wise God. Jesus was a God to the people* when he was upon earth, was so before he came to this earth, and is yet. *Moses was a God to the children of Israel*, and in this manner you may go right back to Father Adam.

Heber C. Kimball	7/26/1857

JD 5:88

I feel as Moses said to a certain class that had the sweeny; they were superstitious, and could not bear to hear any men and women prophecy but themselves: they complained to Moses of a certain person prophesying; and said he, "*I wish to God they were all prophets.*" *I wish to God you, brethren and sisters, were all prophets and prophetesses; you may be, if you live your religion;* you cannot help yourselves. We shall be like so many drops of water all run into the first drop; then the first drop and all the drops become amalgamated together, and they are like one drop. Bless your souls, our little children will prophesy, that come out of us, because we are one.

Brigham Young	2/10/1861

JD 8:321

They made a martyr of [Joseph Smith] - I would not like to say a saviour, although he is our benefactor. He is the man through whom God has spoken and revealed some of the most glorious principles that ever were revealed to the children of men; yet I would not like to call him a saviour, though *in a certain capacity he was a God to us*, and is to the nations of the earth, and will continue to be. He was not the Only-Begotten of the Father, who died for the sins of the world; but he was the Prophet of the lord, through whom God spoke to the nations and dictated laws by which they were to be governed to secure to themselves eternal life.

Francis M. Lyman	2/15/1862

MS 24:100

As for believing that Adam was *our God, I do not know but that we are gods*; only, if it is so, we are very young yet. But could we ever feel that *we are the children of a God* who watches over us with more care and solicitude than we can bestow upon the little ones who call us fathers here on the earth, would not our desires and object be to win the continued love of such a Parent by leaving off everything wrong, while we would seek to fill up the whole aggregate of our judgments with knowledge that is pure and holy, that we might become like that Father and be prepared to dwell with him. Then it is well to think that *God is our Father; and whether it be Adam or anyone else,* ever struggle upwards, upwards; always keep your hearts and faces upwards, and let every struggle you make be to carry you to the harbour of rest, the haven of peace, where you may enjoy the felicity awaiting the faithful *children of our God.* May the Lord bless you. Amen.

Brigham Young   *11/30/1862*

MABY

[E]ach person who we crown in the celestial kingdom of *God* will be a father of fathers, a king of kings, a lord of lords, *a god of gods* ... Each person will reign over his posterity. Adam, Michael, the Ancient of Days, will sit as the judge of the quick and dead, for he is the father of all living, and Eve is the mother of all living, pertaining to the human family, and he is their king, their Lord, *their God,* taking and holding his position in the grand unbroken chain of endless increase, and eternal progression.

George Q. Cannon   *3/3/1867*

JD 11:334-35

In the days of Jesus, who discovered divinity in him? Who saw in the humble son of a carpenter the lineaments of his divine origin, and recognized the Deity there? Why, a few humble fishermen, ignorant, illiterate men who, as we learn from the "Acts of the Apostles," could not speak their mother tongue grammatically. But did the high priests or the learned among the Jews, or those who had been educated in the schools, comprehend it? Though it was an age of enlightenment, so called, they could not recognize *God in Jesus,* nor divinity in the work which he performed; neither could they recognize any of the power of the apostleship in his Apostles. Who did see it? Why those who bowed in submission to the plan which *God* revealed through His son Jesus Christ.

Brigham Young   *12/11/1869*

Journal History, 131

Some may think what I have said concerning Adam strange, but the period will come when *the people will be willing to adopt Joseph Smith as their* prophet, Seer, and Revelator and *God!* but not the Father of their spirits, for that was our Father Adam.

Brigham Young   *12/11/1869*

Wilford Woodruff Journal[223]

Some have thought it strange what I have said concerning Adam. But the period will come when this people, if faithful, will be willing to *adopt Joseph Smith as their* Prophet, Seer, Revelator, and *God*, but not the Father of their spirits, for that was our Father Adam.

Brigham Young   *8/7/1870*

JD 14:75

I cannot do without the Lord Jesus! He is the man for me. *That God* who holds the keys of life and death, and who has suffered and died for the children of men, is he who must rule in the hearts of the children of obedience, and his kingdom will stand forever.

Brigham Young   *5/14/1876*

Journal History

Is there in the heaven of heavens a leader? Yes, and we cannot do without one and that being the case, whoever [t]*his is may be called God.* Joseph said that Adam was our Father and God.

Brigham Young   *5/14/1876*

L. John Nuttall Papers

Now I apply this to St. George, then *if we had a ruler he would be our God,* and we are but a small speck on the earth. ... Our *God* is a consuming fire. Every fixed star is a sun & it has its people & its *God*.

Erastus Snow   *Sunday 3/3/1878*

JD 19:270-71

I sometimes illustrate this matter by taking up a pair of shears, if I have one, but then you all know they are composed of two halves, but they are necessarily parts, one of another, and to perform their work for each other, as designed, they belong together, and neither one of them is fitted for the accomplishment of their works alone. And for this reason says St. Paul, "the man is not without the woman, nor the woman without the man in the Lord." In other words, *there can be no God except he is composed of the man and woman united*, and there is not in all the eternities that exist, nor ever will be, a God in any other way. I have another description: There never was a God, and there never

---

[223] At first blush, this looks like a repeat of the previous statement; however, at a closer look, the reader will note that these accounts are slightly different.

will be in all eternities, except they are made of these two component parts; a man and a woman; the male and the female.

See also John 17:20-23; 10:34-35; 1 Corinthians 8:4, 5 and Colossians 2:9; Revelation 22:8-9; Alma 11:26-44; D&C 20:28; 121:32; Abraham 4:1, 18, 25 ff

30   Adam & Eve

Moses 4:26

And Adam called his wife's name Eve, because she was the mother of all living; *for thus have I, the Lord God, called the first of all women*, which are many.

Mr. Adams   *7/--/1842*

T&S 3:835

On Sunday Mr. Adams ... threw much light on the subject of the Ancient of Days, showing that he is old Father Adam, who shall sit as a great patriarch at the head of the whole family; when *the second Adam*, the Lord from heaven, the Son of Man shall come with the clouds, and come to the Ancient of Days, and the saints should take the kingdom, and the greatness of the kingdom, under the whole heaven, according to Daniel 7.

Samuel W. Richards   *Saturday 12/10/1853*

MS 15:801-02

By *the first* man, *Adam*, came death, the triumph of evil; and by *the second*, came life everlasting, the triumph of good. Each was necessary in the order he appeared; if the *first Adam* had not performed his part, the *second* could not have had his work to do. Both acted the part assigned to them, in a most Godlike manner, and the Great Eloheim accepted the work at their hands as His own.

Brigham Young   *Friday 10/6/1854*

Journal of the Southern Indian Mission, 88

There is no time when worlds have not been created and exalted; *there have always been an Adam and an Eve - the first man and woman,* and their oldest son is heir, and should be our Savior.

Brigham Young   *Sunday 10/8/1854*

MABY

Every world has an Adam, and an Eve: named so, simply because *the first man is always called Adam, and the first woman Eve.*

Brigham Young   *Sunday 10/8/1854*

MABY

Let me read it for you, "There shall saviours come upon Mount Zion, and Save the Mount of Esau." What does gentile signify? Disobedience. What does Israel signify? Obedience. What is the name of the first man? *Adam, which signifies first man, and Eve signifies first woman.*

Brigham Young   *3/11/1856*

Journal of Samuel W. Richards, 113

The President did not believe that Orson Pratt would ever *be Adam,* to learn by experience the facts discussed, *but every other, person in the room would* be if they lived faithful.

Brigham Young   *1869*

MS 31:267

Before me *I see a house full of Eves.* What a crowd of reflections the word Eve is calculated to bring up! *Eve was the name or title conferred upon our first mother*, because she was actually to be the mother of all the human beings who should live upon this earth. I am looking upon a congregation designed to be just such beings.

Brigham Young   *Sunday p.m. 6/18/1873*

DN 22:308

Father Adam came here, and then they brought his wife. "Well," says one, "*Why was Adam called Adam?*" *He was the first man* on the earth, and its framer and maker. He with the help of his brethren, brought it into existence.

Brigham Young   *5/14/1876*

L. John Nuttall Papers

In the creation he placed *a man & he called them Adam, including the singular in the plural.*

John Taylor   4/--/1885

Epistle to the Church

Who are women? The mothers of the whole human family. They are the mothers of
the whole human family. *Adam* was the first flesh upon the earth, and it *is an office in the
Priesthood.* *Eve* was the first woman, and it *is also an office in the Priesthood* and should be
translated "eternal lives."[224]

Wayne N. Reeves[225]   1/2/1999

In the case of Adam, the word in Hebrew is spelled:
Aleph
Daleth
Mem …

Three letters which also depict the members of the Godhead and their various callings
with respect to the Priesthood …
The first letter, is "Aleph" and appears to be written as a "royal 'N'" which is a
backwards "N"… it depicts the throne of God and means in Hebrew, "God the Father"
Its number is ONE and it is the first letter in the Hebrew Alphabet, as God is the first
causative action in the Universe.

Next, comes the letter, "Daleth", meaning of the earth or Death or "the Pains of
Mortality"

Next, comes the letter, "Mem", meaning one who is ordained or set apart, as this is
what the word "Messiah" in Hebrew means: "One who is set apart or ordained" …

Thus, as we string these three letters together, we get this meaning as one of many:
"God the Father, Death, Ordained"
Or "God the Father to Death is Ordained". …

Now, the Letter "Mem" also means a "double portion" meaning that this death was to
be a two-fold or multiple death … and so it is … Adam was subject to BOTH Physical
Death and Spiritual Death, having lost his body in death in the Day of the Lord (less

---

[224] This statements suggests that eternal progression is connected to receiving higher and higher
priesthoods.
[225] The following information was pulled from Restoration Gospel & Hebrew/Kabbalah Board. I have no
reason to believe that this individual is a renown Hebrew scholar so I cannot vouchsafe the accuracy of the
following information; however, I thought it was interesting and worthy of note here.

than 1,000 years) and having been shut out of the presence of His Father.

...

Thus, the very Word "Adam" in those three letters shows us the Plan of Salvation.

Other Hebraists have also noted that the Hebrew word for Adam suggests the color red, blushing, blood, or first blood (i.e., the introduction of blood into Adam's system).

See also Moses 7:69

31 Angels & Archangels

Genesis 31:11, 31
_____
And the *angel* of God spake unto me in a dream *saying ... I am the God* of Bethel.

W.W. Phelps   *6/--/1835*
_____
M&A 1:130 #9

New light is occasionally bursted into our minds, of the sacred scriptures, for which I am truly thankful. We shall by and by learn that we were with God in another world, before the foundation of the world, and had our agency; that we came into this world and have our agency, in order that we may prepare ourselves for a kingdom of glory; *become archangels*, even the sons of God where the man is neither without the woman nor the woman without the man in the Lord: A consummation of glory, and happiness, and perfection so greatly to be wished, that I would not miss of it for the fame of ten worlds.

Joseph Smith   *10/5/1840*
_____
TPJS, 168

These *angels are under the direction of Michael* or Adam, who acts under the direction of the Lord.

Joseph Smith   *Sunday 10/3/1841*
_____
TPJS, 191

He [Joseph] explained the *difference between an angel and a ministering spirit; the one a resurrected or translated body,* with its spirit ministering to embodied spirits - the other a disembodied spirit, visiting and ministering to disembodied spirits. Jesus Christ became a ministering spirit (while His body was lying in the sepulcher) to the spirits in prison, to fulfill an important part of His mission, without which He could not have perfected His work, or entered into His rest. *After His resurrection He appeared as an angel to His disciples.* Translated bodies cannot enter into rest until they have undergone a change equivalent to death. Translated bodies are designed for future missions. *The angel that appeared to John on the Isle of Pathos was a translated or resurrected body.* Jesus Christ went in body after His resurrection, to minister to resurrected bodies.

D&C 129:1   *2/9/1843*

Angels ... are resurrected personages having bodies of flesh and bones.

Joseph Smith   *6/11/1843*

TPJS, 312

In the resurrection, some are raised to be angels, others are raised to become Gods. These things are revealed in the most holy places in a Temple prepared for that purpose.

Joseph Smith   *10/8/1843*

TPJS, 325

Spirits can only be revealed in flaming fire or glory. *Angels have advanced further, their light and glory being tabernacled*; and hence they appear in bodily shape. The spirits of just men are made ministering servants to those who are sealed unto life eternal, and it is through them that the sealing power comes down. Patriarch Adams is now one of the spirits of the just men made perfect; and if revealed now, must be revealed in fire; and the glory could not be endured. Jesus showed Himself to His disciples, and they thought it was His spirit, and they were afraid to approach His spirit. *Angels have advanced higher in knowledge and power than spirits.*

Heber C. Kimball   *4/17/1852*

DN 2:46, #12; Wilford Woodruff Journal 4:130-133

Angels are ministering spirits to those who are Heirs of salvation, but when you do wrong the angels of the Lord will leave, and the angels of the Devil will take their place and keep their company. Then you are on dangerous ground and *if you will not hear the prophets that God sends unto you, you would not hear the angels of God.*

Brigham Young   *1/8/1865*

JD 11:40-41

When the Lord sends an angel to visit men, He gives him power and authority to appear to the people as a man, and not as an angel in his glory; for *we could not endure the presence even of an angel in his glory.* No mortal man has ever seen God in His glory at any time and lived.

We have seen the Lord and angels many times, and did not know it.

Orson Pratt   *10/7/1869*

JD 13:187

Now, how are the angels of God after the resurrection? According to the revelations which God has given, *there are different classes of angels. Some angels are God, and still possess the lower office called angels. Adam is called an Archangel, yet he is a God.*
Abraham, Isaac and Jacob, no doubt, have the right to officiate *in the capacity of angels* if they choose, but still they have ascended to their *exaltation, to a higher state than that of angels - namely, to thrones, kingdoms, principalities, and powers, to reign over kingdoms* and to hold the everlasting Priesthood. Then there is *another order of angels who never have ascended to these powers and dignities,* to this greatness and exaltation in the presence of God. Who are they? *Those who never received the everlasting covenant of marriage for eternity;* those who have not continued in nor received that law with all their hearts, or who, perhaps, have fought against it. They *become angels.* They have no power to increase and extend forth to kingdoms.

Orson Pratt   *Sunday p.m. 1/19/1873*

JD 15:321

These *angels that came to Adam were not men who had been redeemed from this earth* - nor men who had been translated from this earth - but they pertained to former worlds. *Some of these angels have received their exaltation, and still are called angels.* For instance Michael has received his exaltation. He is not without his kingdom and crown, wife or wives and posterity, because he lived faithful to the end. *Some of these angels have received their exaltation.* They are kings, they are priests, *they have entered into their glory and sit upon thrones* they hold the scepter over their posterity.

Brigham Young, Jr.   *5/14/1876*

Charles L. Walker Journal, 95-6

[S]poke of the vast creations of God and the Millions of worlds that had and would be redeemed said that the Sun was inhabited and God dwelt in the midst of eternal burnings *doubted whether the Angels comprehended the vast infinitude of Space.*

While the above statements fall vastly short of being an exhaustive study into the nature of angels, they offer a foundational understanding as to what the scriptures (in light of Adam-God teachings) are referring to when they refer to Michael as an archangel.

See also Genesis 16:7-13; 28:13; 48:15-6; Exodus 3:2, 6; Joshua 5:13-15; Daniel 12:1; Revelation 10:6; 22:8-9; D&C 88:112

Miscellaneous Controversies

β

Sister publications of the following subsections have comprised the greatest portion of some Adam-God writings in the past. Indeed, they have been the primary focus of many publications - especially anti-Mormon publications. They address the core of Adam-God controversies to those who do not believe in Adam-God teachings. This is largely because of the modern LDS Church's position that Adam-God teachings were never a doctrine of the Church. This has led to anti-Mormon efforts to controvert this position, fundamentalist writings to refute this position, and mainstream Mormon apologetics to defend the claims of their leaders.

In contrast, I have delegated these controversies to the end of this book - they are nothing more than an appendix in my eyes and would not deserve any significant attention at all were it not for the colorful history that envelopes them. I have included them near the end of this book because these controversies are really immaterial to the truth of Adam-God teachings - they are diversions, side-tracks, obtuse detours moving us away from understanding the doctrines at hand. That is, if Adam-God teachings are true, does it really matter if Joseph Smith ever taught them in private or in public? If Adam is our God and Father and the only god with whom we have to do, does it matter if Brigham Young was misquoted in some instances when he was teaching about Adam? if he was misquoted *every* time he was teaching about Adam? If Adam was a resurrected being before he came to this earth, does it really matter if Orson Pratt did not believe this doctrine?

Nevertheless, from an academic standpoint, the issues in this subsection remain significant. If Joseph Smith introduced Adam-God teachings, that increases the credibility of the truthfulness of these teachings in the eyes of some members of the LDS Church. If Brigham Young was not misquoted, then the LDS Church has either negligently or deliberately misled the public and members of the LDS Church about these teachings. If Brigham Young was not speculating, the same is true. If it is a fact that Orson Pratt was nearly booted out of the quorum of the twelve for disbelieving in these teachings, then we must concede that the early brethren felt that these teachings were important doctrines. The same message arises from the stories of Scott Anderson and Edward Bunker. The fact that many of the early Saints struggled with these teachings tells us something about their degree of faith in core principles in the gospel and in the inspiration of the early brethren. Thus, the following subsections do have some significance in understanding the history behind Adam-God teachings and do offer some insight into these teachings. However, they have received a more prominent position in this volume than they rightfully deserve because of this colorful history - were it not for this background, I would not have addressed them as thoroughly as I have.

32

Did Joseph Smith Introduce

Adam-God Teachings?

See also
Adam as Ancient of Days

If Joseph did, in fact, introduce Adam-God teachings, he apparently did not do so publicly. This introduces a small controversy for some members of the Church who believe that no true doctrinal teachings were ever delivered in secret by Joseph Smith. This idea may have arisen from a statement wherein Joseph said that he always taught the deepest doctrines publicly. If the reader adheres to this line of reasoning, the reader should be aware that this statement is contrary to much of what we know about Joseph Smith's teachings for several reasons - five of which are particularly important. First, apostles and intimate associates later testified that Joseph taught doctrines in private that he never taught publicly (and this was not even considering the temple endowment itself). Second, Joseph publicly taught that plural marriage was wicked, while privately promoting the practice as a higher principle. Third, Joseph did teach many doctrines that are intimately interwoven with Adam-God teachings. Fourth, we have testimonials from trustworthy individuals that Joseph originated these teachings and there is a significant amount of circumstantial evidence that suggests that Joseph introduced Adam-God teachings. Fifth, we only have a minority of Joseph's teachings passed down to us from the various journals and periodicals that have been printed; thus, there may be other teachings introduced by Joseph Smith in public that we no longer have access to, including public teachings about Adam-God.[226]

For purposes of this section, I have left all materials that have been used to support the

---

[226] Dean Jessee's research has shown that only about one-fifth of all of Joseph's known public discourses have been documented.

idea that Joseph introduced Adam-God teachings, whether or not they directly address the issue, in chronological order. As is the case throughout this volume, some of these statements are much more convincing than others. Because many of these statements require individual explanations as to why they are placed in this subsection, I have put some explanations immediately after the primary text rather than delegating the explanations to the status of an unread footnote.

Brigham Young   *9/--/1832*

Diary of Charles L. Walker, 134

Brigham Young first met Joseph Smith in September, 1832 in Kirtland, Ohio. He said: "Here my joy was full at the privilege of shaking the hand of the Prophet of God, and I received the sure testimony, by the spirit of prophecy, that he was all any man could believe him to be, a true prophet."[227] During this visit a meeting was held in which Brigham spoke in tongues. After this manifestation Joseph prophesied: "*The time will come when brother Brigham Young will preside over the Church.*"[228]

Joseph Smith et al.   *5/7/1834*

Salt Lake School of the Prophets, Minutes, 69-70[229]

Once after returning from a mission, he [Zebedee Coltrin] met Bro. Joseph in Kirtland, who asked him if he did not wish to go with him to a conference at New Portage. The party consisted of Prests. Joseph Smith, Sidney Rigdon, Oliver Cowdery and myself. Next morning at New Portage, he noticed that Joseph seemed to have a far off look in his eyes, or was looking at a distance, and presently he, Joseph, stepped between Brothers Cowdery, and Coltrin and taking them by the arm, said, "lets take a walk." They went to a place where there was some beautiful grass, and grapevines and swampbeech interlaced. President Joseph Smith then said, "Let us pray." They all three prayed in turn - Joseph, Oliver and Zebedee. Bro. Joseph then said, "now brethren we will see some visions." Joseph lay down on the ground on his back and stretched out his arms and the two brethren lay on them. The heavens gradually opened, and they saw a golden throne, on a circular foundation, something like a light house, and on the throne were two aged personages, having white hair, and clothed in white garments. They were the two most beautiful and perfect specimens of mankind he ever saw. Joseph said, *They are our first parents, Adam and Eve.* Adam was a large

---

[227] MS :439; 7/11/1863.

[228] See HC 1:297; Mighty Men of Zion, 16; MS 21:439; JD 3:51; 4:54; 5:332; 8:206; 9:89, 332; They Knew The Prophet, Hyrum L. Andrus, 34.

[229] Recorded in records dated 10/11/1883.

broad shouldered man, and Eve as a woman, was as large in proportion.[230]

As shown in the very first subsection in this book, other accounts of this event state that the personages seen by the prophet and his associates were God the Father and Heavenly Mother. Critics of these passages will of course note that memories fade as time passes so these accounts may be incorrect in this detail due to the simple passage of time - in contrast, advocates will argue that Joseph Smith was promoting Adam-God teachings at this early date.

Joseph Smith   *Monday 10/5/1840*

TPJS, 168, 169; WJS 39, 40[231]

These Angels are under the direction of Michael or *Adam who acts under the direction of Christ....* This then is the nature of the Priesthood, every man holding the Presidency of his dispensation, and *one man holding the Presidency of them all*, even Adam; and Adam receiving his presidency and authority from Christ.

Joseph Smith   *Monday 10/5/1840*

TPJS, 167-68; HC, 4:207-208

Adam holds the keys of the dispensation of the fullness of times; i.e., the dispensation *of all the times* have been and will be revealed through him *from the beginning to Christ, and from Christ to the end of all* the dispensations that are revealed.

Therefore, Adam holds keys over Christ as discussed earlier in this volume. Who could hold keys higher than the Savior unless it was God the Father?

William P. McIntire   *3/9/1841*

Record of William P. McIntire

The Great God has a name by which He will be called, which is Ahman - also in asking *have reference to a personage like Adam*, for God made Adam just in His own image. Now this [is] a key for you to know how to ask and obtain.

This statement suggests that Joseph was promoting doctrines contrary to Adam-God teachings and is included in this section for the sake of making a complete record on this issue.

---

[230] HC 2:64 & Life of Joseph Smith the Prophet, by G. Q. Cannon, p. 173.

[231] WJS 50-51 discusses the nature of this particular text and suggests that Joseph Smith wrote this text with a great degree of inspiration. It was read to a congregation by Joseph's scribe but it was written by Joseph himself.

Joseph Smith	5/21/1843

TPJS, 305

I could explain a hundred fold more than I ever have of the glories of the kingdoms manifested to me in the vision,[232] *were I permitted, and were the people prepared to receive them.*

Joseph Smith	Monday 5/29/1843

HC 5:412

Of the Twelve Apostles chosen in Kirtland and ordained under the hands of Oliver Cowdery, David Whitmer and myself, there have been but two but what have lifted up their heel against me, *namely Brigham Young* and Heber C. Kimball.

Although many people promoted Adam-God teachings, Brigham Young has been branded as the most ardent supporter of this teaching and has been credited with the creation of these teachings. If he was wrong in doing so, members of the Church ought to have little confidence in the teachings of other prophets that have followed as Joseph Smith regarded him more highly than any of the other apostles.

William Law	2/7/1844

Warsaw Message (Buckeye's Lament for More Wives)
There you may shine like mighty Gods,
creating worlds so fair.
At least a world for every wife
that you take with you there.

Although this statement only outwardly teaches the plurality of gods, it hints at Adam-God teachings and was published only four months before Joseph died.

Joseph Smith	4/--/1844

TPJS, 346

What did Jesus say? (Mark it, Elder Rigdon) The scriptures inform us that Jesus said, As the Father hath power in Himself, even so hath the Son power - to do what? Why, what the Father did, The answer is obvious - in a manner to lay down His body and take it up again. Jesus, what are you going to do? *To lay down my life as my Father did, and take it up again.* Do you believe it? If you do not believe it, you do not believe the Bible.

---

[232] D&C 76; the early saints often referred to D&C 76 as "the vision."

Presuming that Adam is Jesus' father, then this statement (if it is not teaching that Adam was the savior of his earth) must be teaching that Adam laid down his life in this probation and took it up again. This has been the traditional understanding of most fundamentalist Adam-God authors.

Joseph Smith   *5/12/1844*

TPJS, 366

If any man preach any other Gospel than that which I have preached, he shall be cursed.

Therefore, if Brigham Young taught Adam-God doctrines and Joseph Smith did not, Brigham would have been cursed if this statement is to be literally understood.

                                                                                               6/7/1844

Nauvoo Expositor 1:2, Resolution #2

Inasmuch as we have for years borne with the individual follies and iniquities of Joseph Smith, Hyrum Smith, and many of the official characters, and having labored with them repeatedly with all Christian love, meekness, and humility, yet to no effect, we feel as if forbearance has ceased to be a virtue and hope of reformation vain. And inasmuch as they have introduced false and damnable doctrines into the church such as; a plurality of Gods above the God of this universe; and *his liability to fall with all of His creations*; the plurality of wives; unconditional sealing up.

Instead of denying Adam-God teachings as found in the Nauvoo Expositor, Joseph Smith responded:

Joseph Smith   *6/16/1844*

HC 6:473-79

Now, you know that of late some malicious and corrupt men have sprung up and apostatized from the Church of Jesus Christ or Latter-day Saints, and they declare that the Prophet believe in a plurality of Gods, and, lo and behold! we have discovered a very great secret, they cry - "The Prophet says there are many Gods, and this proves that he is fallen." It has been my intention for a long time to take up this subject and lay it clearly before the people, and show what my faith is in relation to this interesting matter.

While this could be seen as a political response, Joseph typically responded to his critics rather straightforwardly. Because this was generally his modus operandi - and because this appears to be what he is doing here - fundamentalists have generally accepted this as proof that Joseph must have taught Adam-God teachings during his lifetime. Further, his response strongly suggests that he equated the plurality of gods doctrine with Adam-God teachings.

Joseph Smith	*circa 1844*

"Sayings of Joseph the Prophet," as recorded in Anson Call's Journal
Now regarding Adam: He came here from another planet an immortalized Being and brought his wife, Eve, with him and by eating of the fruit of this earth became subject to death and decay, and He became of the earth, earthy, was made mortal and subject to death.

Wilford Woodruff	*4/9/1857*

JD 5:83-84
Brother Joseph used a great many methods of testing the integrity of men; and he taught a great many things which, in consequence of tradition, required prayer, faith and testimony from the Lord, before they could be believed by many of the Saints. His mind was opened by the visions of the Almighty, and *the Lord taught him many things by vision and revelation that were never taught publicly in his days*; for the people could not bear the flood of intelligence which God poured into his mind.

Wilford Woodruff here dispels of the notion that Joseph never taught anything privately that was not taught publicly. Although Joseph Smith claimed that he taught the deepest doctrines publicly at one point in his ministry, it appears that Joseph Smith did promote some teachings privately that were not taught publicly at that time - and these were certainly "deeper" doctrines than many of the teachings that he taught publicly.

Orson Pratt	*Sunday 1/29/1860*

Journal of Wilford Woodruff
Orson Pratt was in the stand and quite unexpected to his Brethren he arose before his Brethren and made a very humble, full confession before the whole assembly for his opposition to President Young and his Brethren, and he said he wished all the Church was present to hear it. *He quoted Joseph Smith's revelation to prove that President Brigham Young was right* and that all was under obligation to follow the leader of the Church. I never heard Orson Pratt speak better or more to the satisfaction of the people, than on this occasion. He would not partake of the sacrament until he had made a confession then he partook of it.

Orson Pratt & Brigham Young	*4/4/1860*

Minutes of Meeting at Historian's Office

I would like to enumerate items, firstly - preached & publish, that Adam is the fa[ther] of our spirits, & father of Spirit & father of our bodies - When I read the Rev given to Joseph I read directly the opposite - Lord spake to Adam, which w Man eventually became Adam's (3 blank lines)

B.Y.: Your statements tonight, You come out to night & place them as charges, & have as many against me as I have you. One thing I have thought that I might still have omitted. It was Joseph's doctrine that Adam was God &c When in Luke Johnson's[233] at O. Hydes the power came upon us, or shock that alarmed the neighborhood. God comes to earth & eats & partakes of fruit. *Joseph could not reveal what was revealed to him,* & if Joseph had it revealed, he was not told to reveal it.

Orson Hyde   *10 a.m. 4/5/1860*

Minutes of the Meeting of the Council of the Twelve

[H]ere comes a man *(B.Y.) who says he has a revelation,* but it means the sects, if is Antagonistic. *I see no necessity of rejecting Joseph's revelations,* or going to War with the living ones, that is the nearest to us. bro. Pratt is like the Jews, who garnish the sepulchers of the dead, but reject those that were the nearest to them. I do not see any contradiction or opposition between B. Young & J. Smith.

This statement allows for various readings. One reading suggests that Adam-God teachings were the result of a revelation given to Brigham Young - a revelation that does not conflict with Joseph's revelations. The other suggests that Brigham Young was in possession of a revelation given by Joseph Smith.

George Q. Cannon   *9/4/1860*

Journal of Wilford Woodruff

Brother Cannon said there was a learned Doctor that wanted to be baptized. ... He (the doctor) is satisfied that the doctrine of the plurality of God and that Adam is our Father is a true doctrine *revealed from God to Joseph* & Brigham. For this same doctrine is

---

[233] Regarding Brigham Young's statement that Joseph taught Adam-God doctrine at Luke Johnson's house, Buerger, on page 58, notes:

Johnson was ordained one of the original Apostles in mid-February 1835; briefly (six days) disfellowshipped and removed from the Council of the Twelve in September 1837; went again into apostasy in December 1837; and was excommunicated in April 1838. Although he was re-baptized into the Church well after Smith's death (in 1846), it follows from his church career that any preaching on Adam-God by Smith "in Luke Johnson's" would have to have occurred in Kirtland well before the Nauvoo sermons. However, the grammar here suggests that Brigham Young was correcting himself and had intended to say that it was at Orson Hyde's home that Joseph taught this doctrine so Buerger's observation, while well researched, may not be relevant at all.

taught in some of the old Jewish records which have never been in print and I know *Joseph Smith nor Brigham Young* have had access to, and the Lord has revealed this doctrine unto them or *they could not have taught it*. President Young said if all that God had revealed was in fine print it would more than fill this room but very little is written or printed which the Lord has revealed.

Joseph Smith   *5/25/1862*

JD 9:294

Brother Brigham, *if I was* [sic] *to reveal to this people what the Lord has revealed to me, there is not a man or woman would stay with me.*

In other words, there were truths revealed to Joseph that he did not teach publicly. Again, if Adam-God teachings are true, does it really matter if Joseph Smith ever taught them - in any setting?

Heber C. Kimball   *6/27/1863*

JD 10:233-34, 235

[H]e felt as though he were enclosed in an iron case, his mind was closed by the influences that were around him ... hence, he could not make use of the revelations of God as he would have done; there was no room in the hearts of the people to receive the glorious truths of the gospel that God revealed to him. ...
The *Prophet Joseph frequently spoke of these things in the revelations which he gave, but the people generally did not understand them*, but to those who did they were cheering, they had a tendency to gladden the heart and enlighten the mind.

Brigham Young   *10/8/1866*

MABY

An angel never watched him [*Joseph*] *closer than I did*, and that is what has given me the knowledge I have today. I treasure it up, and ask the Father, in the name of Jesus, to help my memory when information is wanted and I have never been at a loss to know what to do concerning the kingdom of God.

Elsewhere, Brigham Young stated that Joseph taught Adam-God teachings. The above statement, in conjunction with assertions that Joseph Smith introduced Adam-God teachings, has been used to support the idea that Brigham Young did not casually make the assertion that Joseph introduced these teachings - he was certain that this was the teaching Joseph Smith intended.

George A. Smith   *10/8/1866*

MABY

... the work that has been carried out by President Young and his brethren *has been in accordance with the* plans, and designs, and Spirit, and *instructions of Joseph Smith.*

Brigham Young   *9/25/1870*

JD 13:250

He is our Father; He is our God, the Father of our spirits; He is the framer of our bodies, and set the machine in successful operation to bring forth these tabernacles that I now look upon in this building, and all that ever did or ever will live on the face of the whole earth. *This is the doctrine* taught by the ancients, taught by the prophets, taught by Jesus, taught by his Apostles, *taught by Joseph Smith*, taught by those who believe the same doctrine that Joseph believed in - the revelations that God has given in modern times, who believe in that being after whose image and in whose likeness man was formed, framed and made, precisely like Him that made him.

Brigham Young   *5/18/1873*

JD 16:46

I never saw any one, until I met Joseph Smith, who could tell me anything about the character, personality and dwelling-place of *God*, anything satisfactory about angels, or the relationship of man to his Maker. ... We know more about God and the heavens than we care to tell. ... *What I know concerning God,* concerning the earth, concerning government, *I have received from the heavens.*

This statement also allows for opposing readings - one suggesting that Joseph Smith introduced Brigham Young to Adam-God teachings while the other reading suggests that Brigham Young received Adam-God teachings as a revelation from God.

Brigham Young   *Sunday p.m. 6/18/1873*

DN 22:308

Our Father Adam is the man who stands at the gate and holds the keys of everlasting life and salvation to *all* his children who have or who ever will come upon the earth. I have been found fault with by the ministers of religion because I have said that they were ignorant. But *I could not find any man on the earth who could tell me this,* although it is one of the simplest things in the world, *until I met and talked with Joseph Smith.*

Again, presuming that Jesus is a son of Adam - at least through Mary - then Brigham

Young is here teaching that Adam held the keys over Jesus Christ and that Joseph taught this doctrine to Brigham Young.

Brigham Young   *5/14/1876*

Journal History

Is there in the heaven of heavens a leader? Yes, and we cannot do without one and that being the case, whoever [t]his is may be called God. Joseph said that Adam was our Father and God.

Critics could argue that this teaching is what confused Brigham Young into believing that Adam is God the Father. This statement by itself could suggest that Joseph gave Brigham Young a very narrow definition of "god" (i.e., only a leader) and then said that Adam was our father and god - but not necessarily God the Father. Were there no other evidences that Joseph Smith taught Adam-God teachings to Brigham Young, this would be a reasonable and rational reading of this passage. However, in light of all of the evidences provided in this subsection and throughout this volume, this reading is not as tenable - it remains however, an interesting footnote in the history of Adam-God teachings.[234]

Brigham Young   *12/16/1876*

Journal of Wilford Woodruff

At meeting of School of the Prophets: President Young said Adam was Michael the Archangel, & he was the Father of Jesus Christ & was our God & that *Joseph taught this principle.*

Edward Tullidge   *3/--/1877*

Women of Mormondom, 181, 193-94

The grand Patriarchal economy, with Adam, as a resurrected being, who brought his

---

[234] Consider for instance, how the following statement suggests that Brigham Young did not misunderstand Joseph Smith's teachings:

Brigham Young   *10/14/1860*

JD 8:205-06

The excellency of the glory of the character of brother Joseph Smith was that he could reduce heavenly things to the understanding of the finite. When he preached to the people - revealed the things of God, the will of God, the plan of salvation, the purposes of Jehovah, the relation in which we stand to him and all the heavenly beings, he reduced his teachings to the capacity of every man, woman, and child, making them as plain as a well-defined pathway.

wife Eve from another world has been very finely elaborated by Brigham Young from *the Patriarchal genesis which Joseph conceived*. ...

The oracle of this last grand truth of women's divinity and of her eternal Mother as the partner with the Father in the creation of worlds, is none other than the Mormon Church. It was revealed in *the glorious theology of Joseph* and established by Brigham in the vast patriarchal system which he has made firm as the foundations of the earth, *by proclaiming Adam as our Father and God.* The Father is first in name and order, but the Mother is with him - these twain, one from the beginning.

Brigham Young	*6/6/1877*

DN, 274

From the first time I saw the prophet Joseph I never lost a word that came from him concerning the kingdom. And this is the key of knowledge that I have today, that I did hearken to the words of Joseph, and treasured them up in my heart, laid them away, asking my Father in the name of his Son Jesus to bring them to my mind when needed. I reassured up the things of God, and this is the key that I hold today. I was anxious to learn from Joseph and the spirit of God.

John Taylor	*1/13/1880*

L. John Nuttall Papers

I heard Joseph say that Adam was the ancient of Days spoken of by Daniel. ... Elijah the sealing of the fathers & when we get to God our Father we are told to approach him in the name of Jesus Adam is the father of our bodies who is to say he is not the Father of our spirits.

While this statement does not explicitly declare that all Adam-God teachings originated from Joseph Smith, this teaching may have been understood by the early saints as a declaration of Adam-God teachings (as argued in the "Adam as Ancient of Days" subsection). Accordingly, some fundamentalists are inclined to believe that John Taylor is here referring to Adam-God teachings generally.

Helen Mar Whitney	*9/20/1882*

Plural Marriage, as Taught by the Prophet Joseph, 30, 31, 36-37

Brigham Young did not happen to be the author of this doctrine [Adam-God], and *to prove the truth of my assertion, I will produce some of the Prophet's teachings*, given May 16, 1841.[235] These were written, together with other tings, by his clerk, William Clayton, as they

---

[235] She is apparently referring to HC, July 1839.

were spoken, and as I had the privilege of reading them when quite a young woman, I took the liberty of copying them. The copy I have retained, and, this is what the prophet said upon this subject, commencing with the Priesthood: "The Priesthood was first given to Adam - he obtained the First Presidency and held the keys of it from generation to generation. He obtained it in the Creation, before the word was formed. … He had dominion given him over every living creature; he is Michael, the Archangel spoken of in the Scriptures. Then Noah who is Gabriel - he stands next in authority to Adam in the Priesthood. He was called of God to this office, and was the father of all living in his day, and to him was given the dominion. These men held keys first on earth and then in heaven. The Priesthood is an everlasting principle, and existed with God from eternity, and will to eternity, without beginning of days or end of years. When the keys have to be brought from heaven - it is by Adam's authority."[236]

When the Saints first heard this doctrine advanced it looked strange and unnatural to them; it was strong meat and required a little time before it could be digested; but this was owing to the narrow, contracted ideas which had been handed down from generation to generation by our forefathers. we were like babes and had always been fed upon milk; but, as Jesus said, we have to be taught "here a little and there a little." When I was able to comprehend it, it appeared quite consistent. There is something in this doctrine that is very home like, grand and beautiful to reflect upon, and it is very simple and comprehensive. It teaches us that we are all the children of the same parent, whose love was so great that He gave His beloved Son, our Elder Brother, Jesus Christ, to redeem us from the fall. … It teaches us that our Father was once mortal, and that if we remain faithful we will finally become as He is - immortal even if we must first pay the penalty for the transgression of our first parents. …

Now[237] if he feels that it is his duty to proclaim against this people and *deny the doctrines which his father felt authorized of God to teach as revelation from on high*, I shall regret it for his own and his father's sake.

This statement is particularly interesting because none of the teachings produced by this plural wife of Joseph Smith clearly demonstrate any basic principle of Adam-God teachings. Nevertheless, these were *proofs* of "the truth of [her] assertion" in her mind. As I have argued multiple places elsewhere in this volume, it appears that a broad spectrum of teachings put forth by the prophet Joseph Smith (and other early brethren) were understood as Adam-God teachings - though they have been doctrinally distanced

---

[236] TPJS, 175.

[237] This portion of her remarks is replying to Joseph Smith III's statement:
Ponder it well. Are not those who teach and those who endorse Brigham Young's Adam God doctrine guilty of damnable heresies, even denying the Lord that brought them?

from the teaching that Adam is God the Father in the modern LDS Church. If this premise is well-founded - as Helen Mar Whitney here suggests - then there are many many more "Adam-God" teachings that could have been produced in this volume to substantiate the position that the early brethren believed in and taught Adam-God teachings as true doctrine.

Wilford Woodruff   *3/3/1889*

Deseret Weekly News 38:389

In the first place, I will say that *the Prophet Joseph taught us that* Father Adam was the first man on the earth to whom God gave the keys of the Everlasting Priesthood. He held the keys of the Presidency, and was the first man who did hold them. Noah stood next to him. These keys were given to Noah, he being the father of all living in his day, as Adam was in his day. These two men were the first who received the Priesthood in the eternal worlds, before the worlds were formed. They were the first who received the Everlasting Priesthood or Presidency on the earth. Father Adam stands at the head, so far as this world is concerned. Of course, Jesus Christ is the Great High Priest of the salvation of the human family. But *Adam holds those keys in the world today; he will hold them to the endless ages of eternity*. And Noah, and *every* man *who has ever held or will hold the keys of Presidency of the Kingdom of God, from that day until the scene is wound up, will have to stand before Father Adam and give an account of the keys of that Priesthood*, as we all will have to give an account unto the Lord, of the principles that we have received, when our work is done in the flesh.

As mentioned above, if Adam holds the keys over "every man" that has held "the keys of the Presidency of the Kingdom of God," and if Christ ever held those keys, then Adam holds at least some keys above those held by Christ. While we can refer to these teachings in Joseph's own words,[238] Wilford Woodruff's restatement can be read to strengthen Helen Mar Whitney's position that these teachings of Joseph Smith were intended to be understood as Adam-God teachings.

Lorenzo Snow   *circa 1894*

MS 56:772

[T]*his doctrine*[239] *had been taught to the apostles by the Prophet Joseph Smith, although it had*

---

[238] The reader may note that I have not included Joseph's words as a separate statement in this subsection because, by themselves, these words are not generally understood as clear Adam-God teachings by modern members of the LDS Church.

[239] As paraphrased in Rodney Turner's thesis; citing his famous couplet, "As man in God once was, as God is, man may become."

not been not made public until some time later.

Benjamin F. Johnson *circa 1903*

Letter from Benjamin F. Johnson to G. S. Gibbs, 18-19

In teaching us the "Fatherhood of God, and the Brotherhood of Man", we could begin to see why we should "love God supremely, and our brothers as ourselves," He [*Joseph Smith*] *taught us that God was* the great head of human procreation - was really and truly *the father of both our spirits and our bodies*; that were but parts of a great whole, mutually and equally dependent upon each other, according to condition.

Bishop Heber Bennion *1920*

Supplement to Gospel Problems, 8-9, 13

It seems strange that people will believe that 'as man now is, God once was, and that as God now is, man may be;' that 'God is an exalted man' *and still repudiate the Doctrine of Adam God.* ... The whole superstructure for a plurality of the Gods is based upon this doctrine of Adam God, and must stand or fall together.

T[he unbelieving gentiles] mocked at Brigham Young, Adam-God, and we seek to molify and pacify them by telling them that is not the doctrine of the Church, but only *the doctrine of Brigham Young. But we are making matters worse, for next we will have to explain that it was only an idea of Joseph Smith, and the Prophet Daniel, and of Jesus Christ, for Jesus gave this revelation to Joseph Smith.*

'Adam-ondi-Ahman, because, said he, it is the place where Adam shall come to visit his people, or the Ancient of Days shall sit, as spoken of by Daniel, the prophet.' - D.&C. 116.

Now let us turn to Daniel, and see what he says about the Adam-God doctrine. 'I beheld till the thrones were cast down, and the Ancient of Days did sit, whose garments were white as snow, and the hair of his head like the pure wool; his throne was like the fiery flame, and his wheels as burning fire. A fiery stream issued and came forth from before him; thousands ministered unto him, and ten thousand times ten thousand stood before him; and the judgment was set, and the books were opened.' - Daniel 7:9, 10.

The above *revelation of Joseph Smith,* together with the prophecy of Daniel seems to corroborate *Brigham Young's doctrine of Adam-God* - beyond question.

This statement seems to indicate that early members of the church equated the eternal progression of godhood and the plurality of gods with Adam-God teachings.

Brigham H. Roberts

HC 3:388

It is generally supposed that Brigham Young was the author of the doctrine which places Adam as the patriarchal head of the human race, and ascribes to him the dignity of future presidency over this earth and its inhabitants, when the work of redemption shall have been completed. Those who read the Prophet's treatise on the Priesthood in the text above[240] will have their opinions corrected upon this subject; for *clearly it is the word of the Lord through the prophet Joseph Smith which establishes that doctrine.* The utterances of President Brigham Young but repeat and expound the doctrine which the Prophet here sets forth.

Merle H. Graffam   *Fall 1982*

Dialogue 15:4-5 #3

I found one further link which no one to my knowledge has previously explored in the *"Grammar and Alphabet of the Egyptian Language"* attributed by many to Joseph Smith, Jr. The document consists of a series of lists of glyphs (not really hieroglyphs) which were purportedly the working sheets Joseph Smith used in his translation of the papyrus found on mummies in his possession.

The glyphs appear in the left column, followed by lines of explanation to the right, supposedly translations of the strange markings. If one checks the list it will be found that one glyph appears to be a kind of checkmark stroke written backwards. In the several lists the explanatory note appears similar but with more information as the lists develop.

For this glyph the notes give the following information:

(glyph represented) = Phah-eh:

the first man-Adam, first father

(glyph represented) =Ah lish:

the first being clothed with supreme glory (supreme power)

(glyph represented) =Ah lish:

the first being - supreme intelligence; supreme power; supreme glory - supreme justice; supreme mercy without beginning of life or end of life; comprehending all

---

[240] Here is the text referred to: "How have we come at the Priesthood in the last days? It came down, down, in regular succession. Peter, James, and John had it given to them and they gave it to others. Christ is the Great High Priest; Adam next." The statement produced above is a footnote to the text of Joseph Smith's teachings about the priesthood (HC 3:387-88; the date of Joseph Smith's teaching was *Tuesday 7/2/1839.*) cited in this footnote.

things, seeing all things - the invisible and eternal godhead.

All of these notes occur after the same glyph represented in each list. It can be seen that *the glyph representing Adam also represents the eternal godhead and the first being, supreme intelligence.* It must be said, also, however that another glyph also represents "Adam or the first man, or first king."

This document needs, however, to be further studied in light of the question of whether Joseph and Brigham taught the same doctrine (however secretly) about Adam being God. Photocopies of the "Egyptian Grammar" are, of course, obtainable at some Salt Lake City bookstores....

Those who deny that Joseph taught Adam-God must explain the enormous credit Joseph gave to Adam. The following list can be made simply by reading pages 157, 158, 167, and 168 of Teachings of the Prophet Joseph Smith:

Adam (1) presides over the spirits of all men, (2) reveals the keys of the Priesthood to men, (3) holds dominion over every creature, (4) all who hold keys must answer to him, (5) holds the keys of the Universe, (6) organized the spirits of all men in creation, (7) is the head, (8) held the keys first and gives them to all others, (9) reveals Christ unto men, (10) holds the keys of ALL dispensations, (11) is the first and father of all, (12) is the Ancient of Days, (13) reveals ordinances from heaven, and (14) angels are subject to his dominion.

These facts are apparent even before we begin to look into the book of Daniel and compare the attributes and actions of the Ancient of Days with Adam. Joseph, of course, shocked theologians of other religions by establishing Adam as the Ancient of Days. From the tremendous glory of his person as told by Daniel and John the Revelator, all other religions, including the Jews, equated the Ancient of Days with Jehovah or Christ.

After reviewing Joseph's teachings, one must admit that Joseph could have taught that Adam was God. ... Temple goers will clearly see that Michael (Adam) is here referred to as a God. ...

Joseph said that Brigham Young and Heber C. Kimball (another Adamist) were the only two who did not "lift their heel" against him. (HC 5:411). Pratt, on the other hand, was excommunicated in August of 1842, may have attempted suicide (See HC 5:60, 61, 138), opposed the selection of Brigham Young as Church President in 1847, and continued in conflict with him for years thereafter.

Dean Jesse   *Spring 1979*

BYU Studies 19:398-99

Many of the teachings and practices formalized during Brigham Young's administration can be traced to private councils where Joseph Smith taught the Twelve in detail about the affairs of the Kingdom. In fact, it seems far more compelling to accept that possibility, one in harmony with what we know of Brigham Young, and of Joseph Smith in Nauvoo, than to continue to believe - in the absence of documentation - that Brigham Young made a fundamental innovation of his own during those tumultuous years of succession ... especially in view of the fact that the private meetings where Joseph Smith taught the full pattern of temple ordinances (and related doctrines) would have provided the ideal forum.

Analysis & Observations

β

Some scholars have argued that this particular controversy has no definitive, smoking gun proof that Joseph Smith introduced Adam-God teachings to some of his most devout followers - clearly, there is no record of his ever teaching this doctrine publicly unless one considers Joseph's teaching that Adam was the Ancient of Days in Daniel chapter seven as a clear, public announcement of this doctrine.[241] While historical records inform us that all major Jewish/Christian based religions believed that the Ancient of Days was God the Father and while historical records arguably inform us that the average laity were familiar with stories in the Bible that are not as well known to the average lay person today, the conclusion that these sermons were clear and public declarations of Adam-God teachings is not absolutely provable, though it seems very likely that at least some of his hearers would have extrapolated Adam-God teachings from these declarations. Nevertheless, Joseph also appears to have taught in those same discourses that Adam's priesthood authority was beneath Christ's authority so his hearers may have been confused about these doctrines Joseph was putting forth at that time.

In addition to all of the evidences above, there are some that argue that Joseph taught

---

[241] His pronouncements referred to by B. H. Roberts and his plural wife Helen Mar Whitney are also worthy of consideration but these statements are not clear proof that Joseph taught Adam-God teachings without the further corroboration given by Joseph Smith's other associates.

Adam-God teachings due to a letter to the Editor entitled Paracletes that was submitted in May and June of 1845. Although this date is clearly after Joseph's death, some speculate from the author's pen name ("Joseph's Speckled Bird") that Joseph was in fact the originator of this material; this presumes that the "speckled bird" refers to the article. Others have speculated that Oliver Cowdery or some other author wrote this article; this presumes that the "speckled bird" refers to the author of the article, not the article itself. Although the author personally believes that Paracletes was not written by Joseph Smith (the grammar, word choice, and phraseology do not seem to match anything else that Joseph wrote), I have included this article here because the issue has not been proven one way or the other and because much of this material does seem to echo teachings put forth by Joseph Smith during the Nauvoo period. Although I may have placed portions of this writing under other subsections throughout this volume, I did not do so for a couple of reasons. First, there is no proof that it was written as a recording of a discourse given or written by an apostle - it specifically declares itself as *not given by revelation* so even if Joseph Smith was the author, it was not presented as doctrine. Further, even if Paracletes were to be accepted as doctrine only for those willing to receive it as such, I found that Paracletes has nothing doctrinally significant to add to any of those sections. I have reproduced the article in full below and have left the reader to decide for him/herself whether or not Joseph Smith wrote this and whether or not this article furthers Adam-God teachings in any way.

Joseph's Speckled Bird   *5/1/1845*
T&S 6:892-95 #8
PARACLETES
MR. EDITOR
If you think the following sketch of the "Paracletes" worthy of a place, in the T&S, use it.
Once upon a time, the most honorable men of the creations or universes, met together to promote the best interest of the great whole. - The "head" said to his oldest son, you are the rightful heir to all, but you know I have many kingdoms and many mansions, and of course it will need many kings and many priests, to govern them, come you with me in solemn council, and let us and some of the "best" men we have had born in the regions of light, to rule in those kingdoms and set them in order by exhibiting good that evil may be manifest.
It was said and done, for every thing there, was adopted from the "head" by common consent. As free agency gave the sons of the "head" a fair chance to choose for themselves, the most noble of the hosts, came forward and selected a world or kingdom, and a time or a season, when he would take his chance, at winning the hearts

of the multitude, a kingdom, crown, and never ending glory. The innumerable multiplicity of kingdoms, or spheres for action, with beings and animals in proportion, and time, times, eternity and eternities, for a full development of the qualities and powers of each, would so far exceed the common comprehension of mortals, that I can only say eye hath not seen, ear hath not heard, nor hath a natural heart yet been able to calculate either. I then shall content myself, for this time to sketch but one. Idumia is the one as interesting as any, and being situated at an immense distance from the center or "head's" residence, and many eternities from the birth of the "Son of the morning" or even the great holy day when the "morning stars sang together," because so many worlds had been wrought out and left "empty and desolate," as places for "all the sons" of God to multiply and replenish the earth, I select that.

Time being divided into seven parts, the following men agreed to leave the mansions of bliss, and spiritually help organize every thing necessary to fill a kingdom for the space of many of the Lord's days, viz: Milauleph,[242] Milbeth, Milgimal, Mildauleth, Milhah, Milvah and Milzah. Now after they had organized the kingdom of Idumia spiritually, then one at a time, was to come temporally and open the door of communication with the spiritual kingdom, that all that would, might return to their former estate; for, for this reason, all the regions created and to be created, were filled with a variety of beings: agents to themselves but accountable to the "head" for promises, made, when they agreed "to go" and be born of the flesh as they had been of the spirit; that they might know the evil, and choose the good: and then be born again of the spirit and the water, "and enter into the mansions prepared for them before the foundations of the worlds. *Milauleph being the eldest and first chosen for Idumia, came on when 'there was not a man to till the ground,*" that is, there was not a "man of flesh" to labor temporally; and his elder brethren who had wrought out their salvation, upon worlds or realms, or kingdoms, ages, yea even eternities [eternity's] before, formed him a temporal body like unto their spiritual bodies, and put the life of his spiritual body into it, and gave him the power of endless lives.

Now the acts of his spiritual body, while he was a child with his father and mother in heaven; and his acts while he was in the spiritual councils of the Gods for millions of years; - and his acts upon Idumia, while he named, arranged and prepared every thing upon it to fulfil the end and aim of their creation, behold they are written in 'the books' of the 'head,' - which are to be opened when the judgment comes for just men to enter into the joys of a 'third existence' which is spiritual. *Milauleph had one thousand years to account for, as well as to be 'arch angel' of Idumia,* after he laid down his temporal body. Behold here is wisdom, he that hath ears to hear let him hear, for Milauleph, as yet had

---

[242] The text later explains that this is Adam.

not been tempted with evil that he might know the good. He had not exercised the power of endless lives that he might do the works that his father had done: and he had not 'fell that men might be.' Although he had seen his eldest brother create worlds, and people them; and had witnessed the course and conduct of that world and people, as free agents, 'sinning and being sinned against,' while 'death' who held a commission from the 'Son of the morning,' to end the first partnership between the spirit and the body, yet, with all this knowledge, and a liberal education in the great college of the nobles of heaven, wherein all perfection was taught, all science explained from first to last, and all that was, is, or will be, was exhibited on the great map of perpetual systems, and eternal lives, Milauleph had to take his wife or one of the 'Queens of heaven,' and come upon Idumia, and be tempted, overcome, and driven from the presence of his Father, because it had been agreed by the Gods and grand council of heaven, that all the family of the 'head' that would do as he or his eldest son did, should be exalted to the same glory.

This was to be accomplished by the power of 'perpetual succession' in eternal lives, wherein there was no 'remission of sin without the shedding of blood;' no forgiveness without repentance; and no glory without perfect submission to the 'head.' The foundation was truth: and the continuation, perpetual succession by revelation.

Milauleph, then, knew that he and his wife would sin, and be troubled; but as the eternal spirit in him was the candle of the Lord, he knew also that the light thereof upon the eyes of his understanding, would show some of the way marks to the original 'truth,' whereby he might work out his salvation with fear and trembling. That none of the work of the hands of the 'Son' might be lost or any souls which his father had given him, might be left in prison, angels were commissioned to watch over Idumia, and act as spiritual guides to every soul, 'lest they should fall and dash their feet against a stone.' They were denominated 'the angels of our presence.

But I must stop, Mr. Editor: my story of the whole seven who managed the seven dispensations of Idumia, will be too long for one communication. And let me say that I have began this story of the 'Paracletes,' or Holy Ones to counterbalance the foolish novel reading of the present generation. *My story is not revelation*, but the innuendoes relate to holy transactions, which may lead good people to search after truth and find it. If this meets the approbation of virtuous minds, I shall write more.

Joseph's Speckled Bird   *6/1/1845*

T&S 6:918-20 #10

PARACLETES CONTINUED.

To continue the history of the seven holy ones, who agreed to take upon them bodies of flesh, and work out a more exceeding and eternal crown of glory, upon Idumia, it will be necessary to premise, that *Milauleph, and his first companion in the flesh, knew before they left their "first estate," what their fathers' will was*; and that when they should begin to replenish the earth, Satan, who had been raised and educated with them in their father's family, would descend from heaven like lightning to tempt them, that they might know to choose good and reject evil.

These two, who had engaged to people Idumia: to subdue it, and to return, having kept the faith once delivered to the chosen seed, were informed, when they agreed to go and labor their hour, that besides the comforter, to bring all things to their remembrance, the angels which attended them on high should attend them below to preserve them from the secret of unforeseen snares of those angels who kept not their first estates, but were left in their sins, to roam from region to region, and in chains of darkness, until the great day of judgment.

It was written in the law of the Lord on high, that they that overcome by obedience, should be made kings and queens, and priests and priestesses to God and his Father, through the atonement of the eldest son, and that natural eyes should not see, nor natural ears hear, neither should the natural heart conceive the great, glorious, and eternal things, honors and blessings, that were then, in the Father's dominions, and mansions, prepared in the beginning for them that kept the faith to the end, and entered triumphantly into their third estates: - the eternal life.

It was also written in the law of the Lord on high, that when the Lord punished men for their sins, he would "punish the hosts of the high ones on high," and the "kings of the earth upon earth," - that spirit might judge spirit, and flesh judge flesh; for this honor have all the just, and this honor have all the saints.

Having this understanding - Idumia was placed in its space, but was "desolate and empty." and the life organizing power of the Gods, or sons of the "head," moved over the matters and then the land and water separated. And the Gods called "light, and light came," and they went on and organized a world, and created every thing necessary to beautify and adorn it, with life and the power of lives to sustain it, until it should fill the measure of all designed, from a mite to a mammoth; from a man to a God; and *Milauleph's and his wife's spirits, clothed in heavenly garments, and learned in eternal wisdom, witnessed the creation*, as the spirits of the Gods had witnessed their Father: for even the elder brother could do nothing but what he had seen his Father do in eternities before.

Perhaps this subject may excite the curiosity of some as it will lead the mind back among the worlds that have been organized and passed away, - and among the Gods and angels that have attended to execute the laws and decrees of one universe after another, from eternity to eternity, from the beginning till now; and, to increase the curiosity of having this present world pass away with a great noise, when there is no place found for it; - and of having organized a new heaven and a new earth, wherein dwelleth "righteousness;" and as our fathers cannot be perfect without us, nor we without them; and as the man is not without the woman, neither the woman without the man in the Lord, perhaps *Milauleph and his wife, as king and queen to God*, and all the sons and daughters of the "head" will shout for joy, and the morning stars sing together again, at the "third" entrance of Idumia and sanctified millions! - Who knows?

33 Was Brigham Young Misquoted?

For over one hundred years now, the LDS Church has been making every necessary attempt to bury, hide, obfuscate, and rewrite the existence of Adam-God teachings among the early brethren. By the mid-1900s, the brethren were desperately trying to reclaim this "Pearl of Great Price" by stamping out and abolishing all references to these teachings in official Church publications. They were very thorough and did a fantastic job of rewriting history.[243] They were so successful in obliterating Adam-God teachings from mainstream Mormonism that virtually no one in the LDS Church knows anything about these teachings beyond the standard two Church positions: Brigham Young was merely misquoted or, if the member of the LDS Church has read enough to know that this is not true, the brethren will inform the inquiring member that Brigham Young was only speculating as to this doctrine - and he was wrong - so the member ought to just leave the issue alone - after all, it is unrighteous to study the mysteries in the modern LDS Church.

Although not significantly addressed in this volume, Wilford Woodruff, Joseph F. Smith, John Widstoe, Mark E. Peterson, Bruce R. McConkie, Joseph Fielding Smith, and many other modern LDS leaders have all put their hand into this controversy in an effort to quash any investigation into this subject. Several authors have delved into the depths of LDS Church membership suicide in attempting to publish materials controverting the efforts of these LDS leaders that declare to the world that Brigham Young was misquoted as teaching that Adam is God and that only malignant enemies of the LDS Church (or "stupid people") would proclaim otherwise. Although I have found myself loathe to enter into this forum of debate as it has been amply proven to spur unnecessary

---

[243] In my opinion, this was righteously done in order to protect the saints from being taught a doctrine that they, as a group, had proven that they were unwilling to accept.

contention, I have provided the following materials as a token effort to acknowledge this chimera of controversy in as sterile of a manner as possible. The fact of the matter is this: any person who bothers to research this topic by reading this volume and/or by verifying the statements as found herein cannot reasonably escape the obvious conclusion that Brigham Young was not misquoted; however, there may be some value in addressing this matter somewhat more directly by considering the statements that follow.

It is worthy of note that in the first section of this volume "Adam as God the Father", there are nearly one hundred distinct statements made by nearly three dozen distinct individuals who were cited in dozens of unique sources over a period of at least eighty years (and this is only the first section of this book - there are many statements declaring nearly synonymous doctrines to be true - e.g., Adam is the father of Jesus Christ and the father of our spirits - that were not included in that section!).[244] The chances that Brigham Young was merely misquoted as saying that Adam is our God is not only highly untenable - it is nigh unto impossible even given the most charitable academic standards available. It is no wonder therefore that the LDS Church tends to resort to JD 1:50 as the only authoritative statement by Brigham Young that Adam is God[245] - JD 1:50 is perhaps one of the most ambiguous of all of these statements, especially after Joseph F. Smith, John A. Widstoe and Mark E. Peterson's attempts to explain this one statement in a manner that coincides with modern LDS doctrine. After having read at least the statements in the first section of this volume, consider the credibility of the modern LDS position as put forth by John A. Widstoe, a well respected apostle who was noted for his strong academic prowess:

John A. Widstoe	*4/1/1960*

Evidences and Reconciliations, 68, 71
Those who spread this untruth about the Latter-day Saints go back for authority to a sermon delivered by President Brigham Young "in the tabernacle, Great Salt Lake City, April 9th, 1852."[246] Certain statements there made are confusing if read superficially, but very clear if read *with their context*. *Enemies* of President Brigham Young and of the Church have taken advantage of the opportunity and have used these statements repeatedly and widely to do injury to the reputation of President Young and the

---

[244] That noted, the reader may find it worthwhile to consider that less than one third of the statements printed in the first subsection were made by Brigham Young in the first place - were all of the other brethren misquoted as well? or did each and every one of these individuals misunderstand Brigham Young's teachings?

[245] Note the irony of this current position given the statement made by Elder Peterson below.

[246] JD 1:50.

Mormon people. *An honest reading* of this sermon and of other reported discourses of President Brigham Young *proves* that *the great second President of the Church held no such views* as have been put into his mouth in the form of the Adam-God *myth*.

The perspective of years brings out the remarkable fact, that, though the enemies of the Latter-day Saints have had access, in printed form, to the hundreds of discourses of Brigham Young, *only half a dozen statements have been useful* to the calumniators of the founder of Utah. Of these, the sermon of April 9, 1852, which has been quoted most frequently, presents no errors of fact or doctrine, *if read* understandingly and *honestly*.

John A. Widstoe   *4/1/1960*

Evidences & Reconciliations, 57, 68-69

[T]here are those who have nursed the *irrational conclusion* that President Young implied that Adam and God, the Father, are one and the same individual.

Brigham Young's much-discussed sermon says that "Jesus was begotten in the flesh by the same character that was in the Garden of Eden, and who is our Father in heaven." *Enemies of the Church, or stupid people*, reading also that Adam is "our father and our God," have heralded far and wide that the Mormons believe that Jesus Christ was begotten of Adam. Yet, *the rational reading of the whole sermon reveals the falsity of such a doctrine.* It is explained that God the Father was in the Garden of Eden before Adam, that he was the Father of Adam, and that this same personage, God the Father, who was in the Garden of Eden before Adam, was the Father of Jesus Christ, when the Son took upon himself a mortal body. That is, the same personage was the Father of Adam and of Jesus Christ. In the numerous published sermons of Brigham Young this is the doctrine that appears; *none other*. ...

Those who peddle the well-worn Adam-God *myth*, usually charge the Latter-day Saints with believing that: (1) Our Father in heaven, the Supreme God, to whom we pray, is Adam, the first man; and (2) Adam was the father of Jesus Christ. A long series of *absurd and false deductions* are made from these propositions. ...
Nowhere is it suggested that Adam is God, the Father, whose child Adam himself was.

Understanding Adam-God Teachings has been an attempt to seriously consider and analyze these "absurd and false deductions" that Elder Widstoe is referring to.

Although, as suggested above, I believe that the question as to whether or not Brigham Young was misquoted is obsolete after reviewing the material presented in this volume,[247] the following materials are worthy of note - even if it is only a footnote to this volume - for the LDS reader who may continue to struggle somewhat with this issue even after reading the rest of this book. Some of the following materials deviate from the standard chronological format because content is more important than chronology here.

9/--/1832

Diary of Charles L. Walker, 134

Upon seeing Brigham Young for the first time and while yet some distance away the Prophet Joseph stopped his chopping on a beech log, straightened up, studied *Brigham* for a moment, then remarked: "*There comes the greatest man who ever lived to teach the identity of God to the world*, and he will yet lead this people."

Brigham Young 9/--/1832

Diary of Charles L. Walker, 134

Brigham Young first met Joseph Smith in September, 1832 in Kirtland, Ohio. He said: "Here my joy was full at the privilege of shaking the hand of the Prophet of God, and I received the sure testimony, by the spirit of prophecy, that he was all any man could believe him to be, a true prophet."[248] During this visit a meeting was held in which Brigham spoke in tongues. After this manifestation Joseph prophesied: "The time will come when brother Brigham Young will preside over the Church."[249]

Brigham Young 11/2/1856

DN

The above is *all of the remarks made at that time, that I deem proper to print at present.*[250]

Wilford Woodruff

---

[247] This is true even if there are some errors found herein. Even if some of the journals quoted herein were discovered to be clever forgeries and even if some of the citations have a wrong page number on them due to a scrivener's error, the preponderance of evidence clearly outweighs any such considerations.

[248] MS :439 7/11/1863.

[249] See also HC 1:297; Mighty Men of Zion, 16; MS 21:439; JD 3:51; 4:54; 5:332; 8:206; 9:89, 332; They Knew The Prophet, Hyrum L. Andrus, 34.

[250] Tholson, 26 notes: Obviously, the President felt that some of the remarks made in his November 2, 1856 discourse were not "proper to print." When the same discourse was later printed in the Journal of Discourses (4:66-70), it appeared without the editing footnote which President Young had printed in the Deseret News to explain why he edited his talk. This clearly shows how carefully sermons and discourses were edited before publication.

Complainant's Abstract of Pleading and Evidence, Temple Lot Case, 309
I have read the sermons Brigham Young published in the Journal of Discourses - some
of them - they are in my library, and I presume are considered correct as published.
They are published by the church of which I am President. They are correct in so far as
every man had a chance to correct his own discourses, or should do so if he has a chance.
Sermons reported by G. D. Watt, one of the official reporters, *were considered reported
correctly, and when they are found in the Journal of Discourses, they are considered correct.* Some
of my own sermons are published there, and they are correct.

Brigham Young   *8/2/1857*

JD 5:99-100
Brother Heber says that the music is taken out of his sermons when brother Carrington
clips out words here and there; and I have taken out the music from mine, for I know
the traditions and false notions of the people. *Our sermons are read by tens of thousands
outside of Utah.* Members of the British Parliament have those Journals of Discourses,
published by brother Watt; they have them locked up, they secrete them, and go to
their rooms and study them, and they know all about us. They may, perhaps, keep
them from the Queen, for fear that she would believe and be converted. I know that I
have seen the day when, *let men use language like brother Heber has today, and many would
apostatize from the true faith. In printing my remarks, I **often** omit the sharp words,* though
they are perfectly understood and applicable here; for I do not wish to spoil the good I
desire to do. *Let my remarks go to the world in a way the prejudices of the people can bear,* that
they may read them, and ponder them, and ask God whether they are true.

John A. Widstoe

Discourses of Brigham Young, vi
As he [Brigham Young] traveled among the people, reporters accompanied him. All
that he said was recorded. Practically all of these discourses (from December 16,
1851, to August 19, 1877) were published in the Journal of Discourses, which was
widely distributed. *The public utterances of few great historical figures have been so faithfully
and fully preserved.*

Brigham Young   *Friday 1/27/1860*

Journal of Wilford Woodruff
Minutes of a meeting of the Presidency & Twelve[,] Presidents of Seventies and other
assembled in President Young's Council Room at 6 o'clock. ... President Young stated
the object of the meeting was to converse upon doctrinal points to see if we see alike. I
pray that we may have the spirit of God to rest upon us that our minds may be upon the

subject & that we may speak by the Holy Spirit.

He then called upon A. Carrington to read a sermon, he read it before the company, a piece prepared for the press written by Orson Pratt upon the Godhead. ... After the document was read, President Young then called upon the Twelve to express their feelings upon the subject. ... President Young then called a vote of the assembly and said if you understand this to be a correct doctrine as here written I wish you manifest it by saying yes. No one spoke. President Young then said do I worship attributes or the dispenser of these attributes. I worship the dispenser of them of these attributes and not the attributes. *This is O Pratt's sermon prepared for the press. I do not want to have it published if it is not right.*

Brigham Young	*Saturday 1/28/1860*

Brigham Young (Office) Diary

The President remarked when questions have been put to me, by opposers, who did not want to hear the simple Gospel Message. he would not answer them and *asked Orson [Pratt] why he was not as careful to observe the revelations given to preach in plainness and simplicity as to so strenuously observe the doctrines in other revelations.*

Brigham Young	*Tuesday 1/31/1860*

Brigham Young (Office) Diary

The President said he had never differed with him [Orson Pratt] only on points of doctrine, and he never had had any personal feelings, but *he was anxious that correct doctrines should be taught* for the benefit of the Church and the Nations of the earth. Prest said in one thing *he had felt vexed that he did not consult them before he published the M.S.* writings he got from Mother Smith. about the life of the Prophet. Orson admitted that he had done wrong and he now saw it but did not at the time of his purchasing and publishing it. President observed *the brethren would have made it a matter of fellowship.* The President said he did not have it in his heart to disfellowship but merely to correct men in their views. Prest also remarked to Orson he had been willing to go on a Mission to any place at the drop of the Hat, and observed *you might as well question my authority to send you on a Mission as to dispute my views in doctrine*; Bro Orson said he had never felt unwillingness in the discharge of his practical duties.

Brigham Young & Orson Pratt	*7 p.m. 4/4/1860*

Minutes of Meeting, at Historian's Office

Bro. O. Pratt, has Bro Benson spoken to you about that for which we have met to night No.

Well it is this bro. Orson. *Your late sermon had like to got into the paper*, I want to get an understanding of your views, and see if we see things aright perhaps if I could see it as you Orson does perhaps its all that I could ask, but *if not we want to have the matter talked over and laid before the Conference in a manner that we all see eye to eye* ...

First Presidency   *6/1/1853*

JD 1:v; MS 15:730-31
Elder Samuel W. Richards, and the Saints abroad.

Dear Brethren -
It is well known to many of you, that Elder George D. Watt, *by our counsel*, spent much time in the midst of poverty and hardships to acquire the art of reporting in Phonography, which he has faithfully and fully accomplished; and he has been reporting the public Sermons, Discourses, Lectures, &c., delivered by the Presidency, the Twelve, and others in this city, for nearly two years, almost without fee or reward. Elder Watt now proposes to publish a Journal of these Reports, in England, for the benefit of the Saints at large, and to obtain means to enable him to sustain his highly useful position of Reporter. You will perceive at once that this will be a work of mutual benefit, and we cheerfully and warmly request your co-operation in the purchase and sale of the above-named Journal, and wish all the profits arising therefrom to be under the control of Elder Watt.

First Presidency of the Church of the Jesus Christ of Latter-day Saints
Brigham Young
Heber C. Kimball
Willard Richards.

                                                                          1860

JD 8:preface
The Journal of Discourses deservedly *ranks as one of the standard works of the Church,* and every right minded Saint will certainly welcome with joy every Number as it comes forth from the press as an additional reflector of "the light that shines from Zion's hill."

Joseph F. Smith   *1870*

JD 18:preface
We regret that the circulation of the Journal of Discourses is so limited. *Its importance would warrant a thousand-fold greater extension of this work.* We anticipate a time, not distant in the future, when *a copy of the present volume will be more precious than gold.* It is even now almost impossible to obtain a complete series. Copies should therefore be

carefully preserved by all subscribers.

While the journals do not even contain the majority of Adam-God teachings, there is a significant volume of Adam-God material to be found in the journals - not to mention the fact that the most hotly disputed materials have often originated from these volumes. This statement also offers the reader an understanding of the weight of authority the early brethren placed on these journals.

Brigham Young	*1/12/1862*

JD 9:148

How has it transpired that theological truth is thus so widely disseminated? It is because God was once known on the earth among his children of mankind, as we know one another. Adam was as conversant with his Father who placed him upon this earth as we are conversant with our earthly parents. The Father frequently came to visit his son Adam, and talked and walked with him; and the children of Adam were more or less acquainted with * *their Grandfather, and their children were more or less acquainted with their Great-Grandfather;* *[251] and the things that pertain to God and to heaven were as familiar among mankind, in the first ages of their existence on the earth, as these mountains are to our mountain boys.

Brigham Young	*2/23/1862*

JD 9:286

I say now, *when they are copied and approved by me they are as good Scripture as is couched in this Bible*, and if you want to read revelation, read the sayings of him who knows the mind of God, without any special command to one man to go here, and to another to go yonder, or to do this or that, or to go an settled here or there.

First Presidency & Quorum of the Twelve	*8/23/1865*

---

[251] Items between the two asterisks were replaced by "him," in Discourses of Brigham Young, 104 and Doctrines of Salvation 1:104. In consideration of this change, Craig Tholson made the following observations: "This error was perpetuated in Joseph Fielding Smith's Answers To Gospel Questions, 5:121-128 and Doctrines of Salvation 1:104; and in the 1972-73 Melchizedek Priesthood manual, 20-22; and in Mark E. Petersen's ADAM Who Is He?, 15-16. We see that we cannot trust that all we are 'fed' is an accurate treatment of history. For this reason we have gone back to the sources as much as is possible in order to learn of Adam-God." Tholson, 304-05. While this does not prove that Brigham Young was not misquoted by his contemporaries, it does demonstrate that successive generations have not been quite so careful to quote his statements accurately - despite their accusations against this alleged fault of their forebears."

DN, 370; MS 27:659

We do not wish incorrect and unsound doctrines to be handed down to posterity under the sanction of great names, to be received and valued by future generations as authentic and reliable, creating labor and difficulties for our successors to perform and contend with, which we ought not to transmit to them. The interests of posterity are, to a certain extent, in our hands. Errors in history and in doctrine, *if left uncorrected by us who are conversant with the events*, and who are in a position to judge of the truth or falsity of the doctrines, *would go to our children as though we had sanctioned and endorsed them.* Such a construction could very easily be put upon our silence respecting them, and would tend to perplex and mislead posterity, and make the labor or correction an exceedingly difficult one for them. *We know what sanctity there is always attached to the writings of men who have passed away, especially to the writings of Apostles,* when none of their contemporaries are left, and we, therefore, feel the necessity of being watchful upon these points. Personal feelings and friendships and associations ought to sink into comparative insignificance, and have no weight in view of consequences so momentous to the people and kingdom of God as these.

/s First Presidency and Quorum of the Twelve[252]

Brigham Young	*1/2/1870*

JD 13:95

I know just as well what to teach this people and just what to say to them and what to do in order to bring them into the celestial kingdom, as I know the road to my office. *It is just as plain and easy.* The Lord is in our midst. He teaches the people continually. *I have **never** yet preached a sermon and sent it out to the children of men, that they may not call Scripture. Let me have the privilege of correcting a sermon, and it is as good Scripture as they deserve.* The people have the oracles of God continually ... *Let this go to the people with "Thus saith the Lord,"* and if they do not obey it, you will see the chastening hand of the Lord upon them.

For further detail about the reporting accuracies of Brigham Young's day, see Musser's Adam-God book, pages 1-22.

Given the evidence that there is no longer any credibility to the position that Brigham Young was misquoted, the reader may no longer sit on the fence concerning this issue; either Brigham Young was furthering Adam-God teachings as a *doctrine* or he was *speculating.* The next section is primarily dedicated to addressing this issue and is

---

[252] This statement was issued under the presidency of Brigham Young.

provided within this publication as a resource for members of the LDS Church who are seeking to determine whether or not Brigham Young was introducing these ideas as speculation or as doctrine.

34 Was Brigham Young Speculating?

While the following materials are intended to be helpful in addressing the question of whether or not Brigham Young was merely speculating when he "introduced" Adam-God teachings, the reader should consider the suggestion that this is a somewhat artificial question anyway. Culley Christensen made this point very well when he pointed out that "[t]he real issue is not the acceptance of an idea as rigid orthodoxy, but whether or not it is true." (AGM, 294). Our main focus ought to be *identifying truth*, not merely identifying the *"binding"* status of a doctrine - the binding nature of a teaching only provides one insignificant step in discerning the *reliability* of a teaching and cannot transport us to the more september pinnacle of true knowledge.

Nevertheless, this issue remains an important one because the modern LDS Church firmly declares that Adam-God teachings are false. Thus, many members of the LDS Church never see a need to pray to find out the truth of the matter because their priesthood head has declared himself incapable of doctrinally leading the Church astray (see materials following the 1890 Manifesto in the LDS scriptures). This position works fairly well until members of the Church realize that Brigham Young was *not misquoted*. When they discover this fact, they often ask their priesthood leaders regarding Adam-God teachings. At this point, they are told that Brigham Young was only speculating. They are usually given an answer somewhat similar to the following:

Joseph F. Smith   *4/8/1912*

Journal of Thomas A. Clawson, 69
At Special Priesthood meeting at which the official statement of the First Presidency regarding the teachings of Adam-God is presented, Prest. Jos. F. Smith then said that he was in full accord with what Prest Penrose had said and that Prest. *Brigham Young*

when he delivered that sermon only expressed his own views and that they were not corroborated by the word of the Lord in the Standard works of the Church. The Bible, Book of Mormon, Pearl of Great Price and Doctrine and Covenants were voted upon by the Church convened in a Conference and organized in various Quorums of the Priesthood who voted by Quorums after which the body of the Church were asked to vote to sustain the above books as the Standards of the Church. This first vote was taken by the Church when they were in the East. It was again taken in the same manner here in Salt Lake in the year _____.

Now all doctrine *if it can't be established by these standards is not to be taught or promulgated by members.* That those Patriarchs who persisted in teaching these things and did not stop when told to do so *should be handled by their Bishops and their names sent up to the High Councils for further action and be cut off.*

Thus, the member of the Church is again in a position where he/she does not feel a need to pray about the issue because their leaders tell them that Adam-God teachings are false doctrines and that Brigham Young was only speculating. If Brigham Young really was speculating, the member's position in not praying about the issue appears to be justifiable *if* one adheres to the doctrine that the president of the LDS Church cannot doctrinally lead the Church astray. However, it is important for the member of the LDS Church to remember that this doctrine of infallibility was taught in the early Church as well; when Orson Pratt was meeting with the Quorum of the Twelve apostles to be tried for his disbelief in Adam-God teachings,[253] Orson Hyde made the following observation:

Orson Hyde   *10 a.m. 4/5/1860*

Minutes of the Meeting of the Council of the Twelve
To acknowledge that this is the Kingdom of God, and that there is a presiding power, and to admit that he can advance incorrect doctrine, is to lay the ax at the root of the tree Will He suffer his mouthpiece to go into error? No. He would remove him, and place another there. bro. *Brigham may err in the price of a horse, or a House and lot, but in the revelations from God, where is the man that has given thus saith the Lord when it was not so?* I cannot find one instance.

Clearly, Orson Hyde accepted the Adam-God teachings in question to be doctrine and challenged Orson Pratt's ability to challenge these teachings while retaining good standing in his quorum and in his fellowship with the Church - because Brigham Young would not be allowed to teach false doctrine to the people. This presents a contradiction for members of the modern LDS Church: If the early brethren taught that the leaders of

---

[253] See "Statements of Unbelief: Orson Pratt" below for a full account of this meeting.

the Church could not lead you astray and if the current brethren teach that the leaders of the Church cannot lead you astray and if the early brethren and the current brethren disagree as to the foundational question as to who God is, in whom can we place our confidence? This challenge has led many members of the LDS Church to leave the Church entirely as it is often the focus of anti-Mormon propaganda. However, it has also led many members of the LDS Church to join the ranks of fundamentalist Mormons who believe that the modern LDS Church no longer teaches a fullness of the truths restored by Joseph Smith. Some few who know and understand both sides of this issue remain in the modern LDS Church; these deny the accuracy of the infallibility claim of the early brethren (as presented by Orson Hyde above) when they learn that Brigham Young was not speculating when he taught Adam-God teachings. After reading this subsection, the reader will find him/herself in the uncomfortable position of deciding which of these choices is the correct theological position.

The following statements address the question as to whether or not Brigham Young was speculating in his teachings regarding Adam-God teachings.

Joseph Smith   *5/12/1844*
_____
TPJS, 366
If any man preach any other Gospel than that which I have preached, *he shall be cursed.*

If Adam-God teachings were false speculations and if Brigham Young did preach that Adam was God the Father, surely this suggests that Brigham Young was cursed.

Brigham Young   *4/9/1852*
_____
JD 1:47
Here[254] is the place for you to teach great mysteries to your brethren, because here are those who can correct you. This fault the Elders of Israel do not fall into in this Tabernacle, although they may in private houses and neighborhoods. When a man is capable of correcting you, and of giving you light, and true doctrine, do not get up an altercation, but submit to be taught like little children, and strive with all your might to understand. ... When your face is turned from the body, let mysteries alone, for *this is the only place for you to be corrected if wrong.*

Although this statement does not directly address Adam-God teachings, it is significant because many of the pronouncements found throughout this volume were delivered in the tabernacle at various conferences. Further, this statement was made in the same

_____
[254] He is referring to the Salt Lake Tabernacle.

discourse that publicly introduced Adam-God teachings for the very first time.

| *Brigham Young* | 4/9/1852 |

JD 1:51

Now, let all who may hear *these doctrines*,
pause before they make light of them,
or treat them with indifference,
for *they will prove their salvation or damnation.*

| *Brigham Young* | 4/9/1852 |

Journal of Wilford Woodruff

And Adam is Michael God and all the God that we have anything to do with. They ate of this fruit & formed the first Tabernacle that was formed. And when the Virgin Mary was begotten with child it was by the Father and in no other way only as we were begotten. *I will tell you the truth as it is in God.* The world don't know that Jesus Christ our Elder Brother was begotten by our Father in Heaven. Handle it as you please, *it will either seal the damnation or salvation of man.* He was begotten by the Father & not by the Holy Ghost.

| *Heber C. Kimball* | 8/13/1853 |

JD 2:111

Has Brother Brigham got the Urim and Thummim? Yes, he has everything that is necessary for him to receive the will and mind of God to this people. Do I know it? Yes, I know all about it.

| *Brigham Young* | *Sunday 10/8/1854* |

MABY

I purpose to speak upon a subject that does not immediately concern yours or my welfare. *I expect in my remarks I shall allude to things that you search after as being absolutely necessary for your salvation in the kingdom of God.* It is true if you are faithful, and diligent they are things that will be fully made known unto you in due time - at the proper time, according to the will of the Lord. But so many among us are preaching, lecturing, contemplating upon, and conversing about things away beyond our reach, sometimes I wish to gratify the people by speaking upon these subjects; for I think upon them as well as you; I meditate upon the future and the past as well as you, and I now gratify myself by gratifying the people.

Brigham Young   *Sunday 10/8/1854*

MABY

In the first place, I wish to say to all men and women who believe in the Lord Jesus Christ, in the Holy Bible, and in the revelations that have been given at sundry times from the days of Adam to the present, *I request that I may have your faith and prayers united with mine that whatever the Lord is pleased to give to the Latter-day Saints* through your humble servant this afternoon, He may give it, and that He does not wish to give He may retain, and keep from you. I make this request of the Saints for this reason; *I know by my experience, by the visions of eternity that God reveals things to individuals that does not belong to the Church at large at present*, or that does not yet belong to the Mass. That I know. ...

I will tell you what I believe still further than this; though I do not pretend to say that the *items of doctrine, and ideas* I shall advance are necessary for the people to know, or that they should give themselves any trouble about them whatever.

These statements, made in Brigham's famous October 8, 1854 discourse do not appear to be the words of someone who was speculating. However, consider the following statement made in the same discourse:

Brigham Young   *Sunday 10/8/1854*

MABY

Adam then was a resurrected being; and *I reckon* that our spirits and the spirits of all the human family were begotten by Adam and born of Eve. "How are we going to know this?" *I reckon it.*

This appears to be the only place where Brigham Young ever made a statement that suggested that he was speculating as opposed to delivering a true doctrine. That noted, elsewhere in this same sermon (as noted above), he refers to these teachings as doctrine. His tone here may therefore reflect a note of wry humor or sarcasm.

Brigham Young   *4/25/1855*

MABY

I tell you this *as my belief* about that personage who is called the Ancient of Days, the Prince and so on, but I do not tell it because that I wish it to be established in the minds of others, though *to me this is as clear as the sun, it is as plain as my alphabet. I understand it as I do the path to go home. I did not understand so until my mind became enlightened with the Spirit and by the revelations of God,* neither will you understand until our Father in Heaven reveals all these things unto you. To my mind and to my feelings those matters are all plain and easy to be understood.

Brigham Young   *3/11/1856*

Journal of Wilford Woodruff

[T]he subject was brought up concerning Adam being made of the dust of the earth, and Elder Orson Pratt pursued a course of stubbornness & unbelief in what President Young said that will destroy him if he does not repent & turn from his evil ways. For when any man crosses the track of a leader in Israel & tries to lead the prophet - he is no longer led by him but is in danger of falling.

Samuel W. Richards   *3/11/1856*

Journal of Samuel W. Richards, 113

Evening with the Regency in the Upper Room of the President's Office, examining the spelling of the New Books in the D. Alphabet. A very serious conversation took place between President B. Young and Orson Pratt upon doctrine.

O. P. was directly apposed to the President's views and very freely expressed his entire disbelief in them after *being told by the President that things were so and so in the name of the Lord.* He was firm in the position that the President's word in the name of the Lord, was not the word of the Lord to him. The President did not believe that Orson Pratt would ever be Adam, to learn by experience the facts discussed, but every other, person in the room would be if they lived faithful.

George Albert Smith & Wilford W. Woodruff   *4/20/1856*

Journal of Wilford Woodruff

I met with the Presidency & Twelve in the prayer-circle. Brother G. A. Smith spoke in plainness his feelings concerning some principles of Elder O Pratt's wherein he differed from President Young concerning the creation of Adam out of the dust of the Earth & the final consummation of knowledge & many other things. I am afraid when he come to write he will publish in opposition of President Young's *views* but he promises he would not.

Heber C. Kimball   *6/29/1856*

JD 4:2

Just think of your position; you have heard *the teachings and instructions of President Young, and his instructions are the word of God to us,* and I know that *every man and woman in this Church who rejects his testimony,* and the testimony of those that he sends, *rejects the testimony of God his Father.* I know that, just as well as I know that I see your faces today.

Brigham Young   *2/8/1857*

JD 4:215-216, 218

I desire to pursue some of the ideas that brother Cummings has just laid before you ... even to the advancement of the Saints at a "snail gallop." *The items that have been advanced are principles of real doctrine, whether you consider them so or not.* It is one of the first principles of the doctrine of salvation to become acquainted with our Father and our God. The scriptures teach that this is eternal life, to "know Thee, the only true God, and Jesus Christ whom thou hast sent;" this is as much as to say that no man can enjoy or be prepared for eternal life without that knowledge. ...

Whether you receive these things or not, I tell you them in simplicity. I lay them before you like a child, because they are perfectly simple. If you see and understand these things, it will be by the Spirit of God; you will receive them by no other spirit. No matter whether they are told to you like the thunderings of the Almighty or by simple conversation; *if you enjoy the Spirit of the Lord, it will tell you whether they are right or not. I am acquainted with my Father. I am as confident that I understand in part, see in part, and know and am acquainted with Him in part, as I am that I was acquainted with my earthly father who died in Quincy, Illinois, after we were driven from Missouri. ... I know my Heavenly Father and Jesus Christ whom He has sent, and this is eternal life.*

This statement was made after some of the most significant and important Adam-God pronouncements - this does not seem to be the testimony of someone who is speculating.

Heber C. Kimball   *3/1/1857*

JD 4:248

Are you ever going to be prepared to see God, Jesus Christ, His angels, or comprehend His servants, unless you take a faithful and prayerful course? Did you actually know Joseph Smith? No. *Do you know brother Brigham?* No. Do you know brother Heber? No, you do not. Do you know the Twelve? You do not, *if you did, you would begin to know God*, and learn that those men who are chosen to direct and counsel you are near kindred to God and to Jesus Christ, for the keys, power, and authority of the kingdom of God are in that lineage.

Heber C. Kimball   *7/12/1857*

JD 5:32

Do you suppose that he is so unwise to say a thing which he does not know to be true? He understands what he speaks, and he looks before he jumps, and God Almighty will lead him straight, and he will never stumble - no, never, from this time forth.

Brigham Young   *10/7/1857*

JD 5:328-29, 331

You may take the Quorums in this Church - the First Presidency, the Twelve, the Presidents of the High Priests, the High Councillors, and the Presidents of the Seventies; and a person may go to each of those Quorums for counsel upon any subject, and he will invariably receive the same counsel. Why is this the case? Because they are all actuated by the same Spirit. Do you know why some men give counsel different one from another? Because they undertake to give counsel without the Spirit of the Lord to dictate them. But when the Spirit dictates, then each one knows what to do, and their counsel will be the same. Adam, Seth, Enoch, Noah, all the Patriarchs and Prophets, Jesus and the Apostles, and every man that has ever written the word of the Lord, have written the same doctrine upon the same subject; and you *never can find that Prophets and Apostles clashed in their doctrines in ancient days: neither will they now, if all would at all times be led by the Spirit of salvation.* If men will so act as to order their lives aright and continually keep the commandments of God, they will be able to administer the blessings of the kingdom of God. There is no clash in the principles revealed in the Bible, the Book of Mormon, and the Doctrine and Covenants; and *there would be no clash between any of the doctrines taught by Joseph the Prophet and by the brethren now, if all would live in way to be governed by the Spirit of the Lord.* All do not live so as to have the Spirit of the Lord with them all the time, and the result is that some get out of the way. ... Some have grumbled because *I believe* our God to be so near to us as Father Adam. There are many who know that *doctrine* to be true.

Again, this genre of statements is problematic for members of the modern LDS Church because Brigham Young is here teaching that either he or the modern brethren are not governed by the Spirit of the Lord in their teachings regarding Adam-God. Who had the Spirit when teaching these doctrines? Having read this book, the member of the modern LDS Church cannot sit on this question in ignorance any longer - either Brigham Young was correct and the modern brethren are incorrect in their views of Adam-God teachings or Brigham Young was not governed by the Spirit of the Lord - and he led the saints to worship a false God. No reasonable reconciliation feasibly remains.

Brigham Young   *7/3/1859*

JD 7:3

Am I hated for the same cause? I am. *I am hated for teaching people the way of life and salvation - for teaching them principles* that pertain to eternity, *by which the Gods were and are*, and by which they gain influence and power. Obtain their influence, and you will be hated, despised, and hunted like the roe upon the mountains.

Wilford W. Woodruff   *1/27/1860*

Journal of Wilford Woodruff

I do feel *at this advanced state of the Church and the late day* and wish the information which you possess that neither you nor your Brethren ought to be troubled with false doctrine.

This statement is included here because it suggests, contrary to the current LDS position, that theological doctrines were lucidly understood by the early brethren - they were not in an infantile state of progression in their understanding of the character of God, etc. - they were standing upon a solid and developed theological foundation.

Brigham Young   *Saturday 1/28/1860*

Brigham Young (Office) Journal

The President remarked when questions have been put to me, by opposers, who did not want to hear the simple Gospel Message. he would not answer them and *asked Orson why he was not as careful to observe the revelations given to preach in plainness and simplicity as to so strenuously observe the doctrines in other revelations.*

Orson Pratt   *Sunday 1/29/1860*

DN 9:51

God placed Joseph Smith at the head of this church. God has likewise placed Brigham Young at the head of this church ... . *We are commanded to give heed to their words in all things, and receive their words as from the mouth of God*, in all patience and faith. When we do not do this, we get into darkness.

Orson Pratt   *Sunday 1/29/1860*

Journal of Wilford Woodruff

Sunday I met at the Tabernacle. Orson Pratt was in the stand and quite unexpected to his Brethren he arose before his Brethren and *made a very humble, full confession before the whole assembly for his opposition to President Young* and his Brethren, and he said he wished all the Church was present to hear it. He quoted Joseph Smith's revelation to prove that President Brigham Young was right and that all was under obligation to follow the leader of the Church. I never heard Orson Pratt speak better or more to the satisfaction of the people, than on this occasion. He would not partake of the sacrament until he had made a confession then he partook of it.

Orson Pratt *Tuesday 1/31/1860*

Brigham Young (Office) Diary

Elder Orson Pratt called upon the President in regard to the acknowledgements he had made on Sunday in the Tabernacle. and also made a personal acknowledgement to the President admitting he had a self willed determination in him; The President said he had never differed with him *only on points of doctrine,* and he never had had any personal feelings, but *he was anxious that correct doctrines should be taught* for the benefit of the Church and the Nations of the earth. Prest said in one thing he had felt vexed that he did not consult them before he published the M.S. writings he got from Mother Smith. about the life of the Prophet. Orson admitted that he had done wrong and he now saw it but did not at the time of his purchasing and publishing it. President observed *the brethren would have made it a matter of fellowship.* The President said he *did not have it in his heart to disfellowship but merely to correct men in their views.* Prest also remarked to Orson he had been willing to go on a Mission to any place at the drop of the Hat, and observed *you might as well question my authority to send you on a Mission as to dispute my views in doctrine*; Bro Orson said he had never felt unwillingness in the discharge of his practical duties.

Brigham Young - Orson Pratt *3/4/1860*

Journal of Wilford Woodruff

President Young said, I corrected O Pratt today. I did not say to him that God would increase to all eternity. But I said the moment that we say that God knows all things comprehends all things and has a fullness of all that he ever will attain, that moment eternity ceases. You put bounds to eternity, space & matter and you make an end and stopping place to it. The people or many say they cannot understand the things. This is true. No man can understand the things of eternity. And Brother Pratt and all men should let the matter of the gods alone. *I do not understand these things. Neither does any man in the flesh and we should let them alone.*

Brigham Young *4/4/1860*

Minutes of Meeting of Quorum of the Twelve

[I]t is my *duty* to see that correct *doctrine* is taught and to guard the Church from errors - it is my *calling.*

10 a.m. 4/5/1860

Minutes of the Meeting of the Council of the Twelve

Present Elders O. Hyde, O. Pratt, J. Taylor, W. Woodruff, G.A. Smith, C.C. Rich, F.D. Richards.

O. Hyde ... *To acknowledge that this is the Kingdom of God, and that there is a presiding power, and to admit that he can advance incorrect doctrine, is to lay the ax at the root of the tree Will He suffer his mouthpiece to go into error?* No. He would remove him, and place another there. bro. Brigham may err in the price of a horse, or a House and lot, but *in the revelations from God, where is the man that has given thus saith the Lord when it was not so? I cannot find one instance.*[255] ...

O. Pratt ... One [revelation] says Adam was formed out of the Earth, and the Lord put in his spirit; and another that he came with his body, flesh and bones, thus there are two contrary revelations - in the garden it is said, that a voice said to Adam, in the meridian of time, I will send my only begotten son Jesus Christ. then how can that man and Adam both be the Father of Jesus Christ? ...

O. Hyde When there is a want of union, it requires us to speak plain, bro. Pratt does not claim any vision or revelation, but keeps within the scope of Joseph's revelations. The Universalians have their belief, The Presbyterians do the same, they consider they believe they are in the pale of revealed religion. all the Sects do the same, yet how widely they differ, then here comes a man (*B.Y.*) who *says he has a revelation*, but it means the sects, if is Antagonistic. I see no necessity of rejecting Joseph's revelations, or going to War with the living ones, that is the nearest to us. bro. Pratt is like the Jews, who garnish the sepulchers of the dead, but reject those that were the nearest to them. I do not see any contradiction or opposition between B. Young & J. Smith. ...

O. Pratt I have heard brother Brigham say that Adam is the Father of our Spirits, and he came here with his resurrected body, to fall for his own children; and I said to him, it leads to an endless number of falls, which leads to sorrow and death: that is revolting to my feelings, *even if it were not sustained by revelation.*

E. Snow Is there any revelation saying that the body of Adam should return to the dust of this Earth?

O. Pratt if you bring Adam as a Spirit, and put him into the tabernacle, runs easy with me; another item, I heard brother Young say that Jesus had a body, flesh and bones, before he came, he was born of the Virgin Mary, it was so contrary to every revelation

---

[255] This portion of this dialog raises a problem for both fundamentalists and members of the modern LDS Church. Clearly, either Brigham Young or the modern LDS Church was/is teaching false doctrines as to the identity of God. How is this reconciled with Orson Hyde's comment here? If fundamentalists are right, Orson Hyde must have been wrong - the mouthpiece was suffered to go into error. When therefore can we ever put absolute trust in the Lord's mouthpiece that the early brethren placed in the Lord's mouthpiece? On the other hand, the LDS Church member must accept that either Brigham Young or the modern prophet has gone into error and he/she has the same problem as the fundamentalists. However, both may take some comfort in the principle explained earlier in this volume wherein Moses was not berated by Jesus for teaching false principles about the eternal nature of the marriage covenant because the people would not accept the higher principles of marriage.

given.

Brigham Young   *10 a.m. 4/5/1860*

Minutes of Meeting of Council of the Twelve

[Regarding Orson Pratt's disbelief of Adam-God teachings] Let his mind be clear, divest him of selfishness and hardness of heart, and may he be filled with the Holy Ghost that he may *subject himself to his Brethren*, comfort his heart, and rend the veil of unbelief, cause that the scabs of blindness to fall from his eyes, that he may see, and his ears to hear the whisperings of the Holy Spirit, soften his heart as a little child to the will of his Brethren and reconcile himself to the will of our God.

Orson Pratt   *10 a.m. 4/5/1860*

Minutes of the Meeting of the Council of the Twelve

[I]n regard to *Adam being our Father and our God*, I have not published it, although I frankly say, I have no confidence in it, although *advanced by bro. Kimball in the stand, and afterwards approved by bro. Brigham.* ...

Brigham Young   *6/27/1860*

DN

And I will say, as I have said before, if guilt before my God and my brethren rests upon me in the least, it is in this one thing, that *I have revealed too much concerning God* and his kingdom, and the designs of our Father in heaven. If my skirts are stained in the least with wrong, it is because *I have been too free in telling who God is*, how he lives, the nature of his providences and designs in creating the world, in bringing the human family on the earth, his designs concerning them, etc. If I had, like Paul, said - "But if any man be ignorant, let him be ignorant," perhaps it would have been better for the people.

Brigham Young   *7/28/1861*

JD 9:142

I had the promise, years ago, that I never should apostatize and bring an evil upon this people. God revealed that through Joseph, long before he died; and if I am not doing right, you may calculate that the Lord is going to take me home.

Surely, leading the Church astray by teaching the false identity of God over a period exceeding two decades would have been adequate apostasy to merit this result - the Lord would have taken him home.

Brigham Young	*10:30 a.m. 10/8/1861*

Brigham Young Papers

I will give you *a few words of doctrine*, upon which there has been much inquiry, and with regard to which considerable ignorance exists. Brother Watt will write it, but it is not my intention to have it published; therefore pay good attention, and store it up in your memories. Some years ago, I advanced a *doctrine* with regard to *Adam being our Father and God*. That will be a curse to many of the Elders of Israel, because of their folly with regard to it. They yet grovel in darkness - and will. *It is one of the most glorious revelations* [concerning] the economy of heaven, yet the world hold it [in] derision. Had I revealed the doctrine of Baptism for the Dead instead of Joseph Smith, there are men around me who would have ridiculed the idea until dooms day. But they are ignorant and stupid like the dumb ass.

Francis M. Lyman	*2/15/1862*

MS 24:100

I have heard of a man who was *cut off because he would not believe that Adam was our Father and God*. "Well, but was it not so?" Its being so does not change the fact that we are sinners and need salvation, and such preaching does not help men and women to repent of their sins.

Brigham Young	*2/23/1862*

JD 9:286

I say now, when they are copied and approved by me they are as good Scripture as is couched in this Bible, and if you want to read revelation, read the sayings of him who knows the mind of God, without any special command to one man to go here, and to another to go yonder, or to do this or that, or to go an settled here or there.

Brigham Young	*12/29/1867*

JD 12:127

What man or woman on the earth, what spirit in the spirit-world *can say truthfully that I have ever gave a wrong word of counsel,* or a word of advice that could not be sanctioned by the heavens?

If Brigham Young felt this way about his counsel, how strongly must he have felt about his doctrinal proclamations?

Abraham B. Smoot	6/8/1868

Minutes of the School of the Prophets, 37-40

The doctrine preached by Pres. Young for a few years back, wherein he says that *Adam is our God* - the God we worship - that most of the people believe this - some believe it because the President says so - others because they can find testimony in the Book of Mormon and Book of Doctrine and Covenants. ... This is not the way to act. We should not suffer ourselves to entertain one doubt. We are not accountable on points of doctrines if the President makes a statement. It is not our prerogative to dispute it. He is only accountable in points of doctrine. I have heard President Young avow the truth of Adam being our Father and God *but have never heard him argue the question at all.*

Orson Pratt	7/1/1868

Letter from Orson Pratt to President Young

Dear Brother ...

I am deeply sensible that I have greatly sinned against you, and against my brethren of the school, and against God, in foolishly trying to justify myself in advancing ideas, opposed to those which have been introduced by the highest authorities of the Church, and adopted by the Saints. I humbly ask you and the school to forgive me. Hereafter, through the grace of God assisting me, *I am determined* to be one with you, and *never be found opposing anything that comes through the legitimate order of the Priesthood,* knowing that it is perfectly right for me to humbly submit, in all matters of *doctrine and principle*, my judgment to those whose right it is, by divine appointment to receive revelation and guide the Church. "There is no one thing in this world, or in that which is to come which I do more earnestly desire, than to honor my calling, and be permitted to retain the same, and with my brethren the Twelve, enter the Celestial Kingdom, with a full preparation to enjoy the glory thereof for ever.

Brigham Young	1/2/1870

DN 1/29/1870; JD 13:95

I have never yet preached a sermon and sent it out to the children of men, that they may not call it scripture. ... Let this go to the people with `Thus saith the Lord,' and if they do not obey it, you will see the chastening hand of the Lord upon them.

Brigham Young	2/2/1870

DN

If we do not speak to you by the Spirit of revelation and the power of God, we do not magnify our calling. I think that I tell you the words of the Lord Almighty every time I rise here to speak to you. I may blunder in the use of the English language; but suppose I should use language that would grate on the ears of some of the learned, what of that? God can understand it, and so could you, if you had the Spirit of the Lord ... *If I do not speak here by the power of God, if it is not revelation to you every time I speak to you here, I do not magnify my calling.*

This statement not only suggests that Brigham Young considered his proclamations concerning Adam-God teachings true doctrine but it also suggests that he would have considered himself a prophet who did not magnify his calling if these were not true doctrines.

Brigham Young   *10/6/1870*

JD 13:263, 264

But I will give a caution to my brethren the Elders - *never undertake to teach a thing that you do not understand. ...*

I will make a statement here that has been brought against me as a crime, perhaps, or as a fault in my life. Not here, I do not allude to anything of the kind in this place, but in the councils of the nations - that Brigham Young has said 'when he sends forth his discourses to the world they may call them Scripture.' I say now, when they are copied and approved by me they are as good Scripture as is couched in this Bible, and if you want to read revelation read the sayings of him who knows the mind of God.

Brigham Young   *4/9/1871*

JD 14:79

I think there is more responsibility on myself than any other one man on this earth pertaining to the salvation of the human family. Yet my path is a pleasant path to walk in; my labors are very agreeable, for I take no thought what I shall say; I trouble not myself with regard to my duties, all I have to do is to live, as I have often made the comparison, and keep my spirit, feelings, and conscience like a sheet of blank paper, and let the spirit and power of god write upon it what he pleases. When he writes I will read; but if I read before he writes I am very likely to do wrong. If you will take the same course you will not have trouble.

Brigham Young   *Sunday p.m. 5/18/1873*

JD 16:46

Where is the divine who knows the least thing about that Being who is the Father of our spirits and the author of our bodies? ... I have had many revelations; *I have seen and heard for myself, and know these things are true,* and nobody on earth can disprove them. ... *What I know concerning God,* concerning the earth, concerning government, *I have received from the heavens,* not alone through my natural ability, and I give God the glory and the praise.

Brigham Young   *6/9/1873*

Salt Lake School of the Prophets Minute Book

[Brigham Young] bore a powerful testimony to the truth of *the doctrine, remarking that if ever he had received a testimony of any doctrine in this church, he had of the truth of this.* The Endowments plainly teach it and the Bible and other revelations are full of it. ...

Said there were many revelations given to him that he did not receive from the Prophet Joseph. He did not receive them through the Urim and Thummim as Joseph did but when he did receive them he knew of their truth as much as it was possible for him to do of any truth.

Brigham Young   *Sunday p.m. 6/18/1873*

DN 22:308

I frequently think, in my meditations, how glad we should be to instruct the world with regard to the things of God, if they would hear, and receive our teachings in good and honest hearts and profit by them. ... How pleased we would be to place these things before the people if they would receive them! How much unbelief exists in the minds of the Latter-day Saints in regard to *one particular doctrine which I revealed to them, and which God revealed to me - namely that Adam is our father and God.*

T. B. H. Stenhouse [*an apostate*]   *1873*

The Rocky Mountain Saints, 561

Brother Heber had considerable pride in relating to his intimate friends that he was the source of Brigham's revelation on the "Adam-deity." In a moment of reverie Heber said: "Brother Brigham, I have an *idea* that Adam is not only our father, but our God." That was enough: Brigham snapped at the novelty, and announced it with all flourish of a new *revelation*.

Brigham Young   *5/14/1876*

L. John Nuttall Papers

I shall not bring forth much scripture but *I shall make my own scripture* and have been for many years. if you don't believe it I will prove it to you. I will do it by asking some questions. Now *if I speak the truth is not it just as much scripture as that which was spoken by Isaiah or Paul, Peter or John.* They have gathered up the scraps and have left out 99 of 100 of those scrap and that is called the scriptures - *aint my scrip worth as much as anyone elses' if it be true?* Now I want to save myself as Br Hancock said yesterday so that if I cannot do more I can point - I would sooner be able to point then out of the way and do nothing - a great many times the things that come to my mind is so natural that if I was to stop to think I should conclude I had not got it from the Lord. it is so natural that I think that I have it as we know our own children.

Edward Tullidge   *3/--/1877*

Women of Mormondom, 196

When Brigham Young proclaimed to the nations that Adam was our Father and God, and Eve, his partner, the Mother of a world - both in a mortal and celestial sense - he made *the most important revelation ever oracled* to the race since the days of Adam himself. This grand patriarchal revelation is the very keystone of the 'New Creation' of the heavens and the earth. It gives new meaning to the whole system of theology - as much new meaning to the economy of salvation as to the economy of creation. By the understanding of the works of the Father, the works of the Son are illuminated.

Brigham Young   *6/6/1877*

DN 26:274

In my *doctrinal teachings* I have taught many things not written in any book, ancient or modern, and yet, notwithstanding the many things I have told the people, I have never looked into the Bible, the Book of Mormon, or the Doctrine and Covenants, or any of our Church works to see whether they agreed with them or not. *When I have spoken by the power of God and the Holy Ghost, it is the truth, it is scripture*, and I have no fears but that it will agree with all that has been revealed in every particular.

George Q. Cannon   *1/17/1878*

George Q. Cannon Journal[256]

Some of my brethren, as I have learned since the death of President Brigham Young, did have feelings concerning his course. They did not approve of it, and felt oppressed, and yet they dare not exhibit their feelings to him, he ruled with so strong and stiff a hand, and they felt that it would be of no use. In a few words, the feeling seems to be that he transcended the bounds of the authority which he legitimately held. I have been greatly surprised to find so much dissatisfaction in such quarters .... [S]ome even feel that *in the promulgation of doctrine* he took liberties beyond those to which he was legitimately entitled.

---

[256] As cited in Joseph J. Cannon, "George Q. Cannon - Relations With Brigham Young," The Instructor 80:259 #6; see also 1892 meeting of the First Presidency and Quorum of the Twelve; Abraham H. Cannon Journal, 5/26/1892).

Helen Mar Whitney   *9/20/1882*

Plural Marriage, As Taught by the Prophet Joseph, 30, 36-37

Brigham Young did not happen to be the author of this *doctrine* [Adam-God], and to prove the truth of my assertion, I will produce some of the Prophet's teachings, given May 16, 1841.[257]

Now[258] if he feels that it is his duty to proclaim against this people and deny *the doctrines* which his father felt authorized of God to teach *as revelation from on high,* I shall regret it for his own and his father's sake.

George Q. Cannon   *Sunday p.m. 5/4/1884*

JD 25:155

My brethren and sisters, it is a glorious *truth* that has been taught to us, that we are literally the children of God, that we are his literal descendants, as Jesus was literally descended from Him, and that He is our Father as much as our earthly parent is our father, and we can go to Him with a feeling of nearness, knowing this, understanding it by the *revelations* which God has given to us.

While this statement does not exclusively refer to Adam-God teachings, it refers to doctrines that were directly connected to Adam-God teachings - as has been shown throughout this volume.

John Taylor

Misc. Minutes, 6

If that mouthpiece [Brigham Young] has not the power to dictate I would throw all of Mormonism away.

George Q. Cannon   *4/7/1889*

MS 51:278

We believe that *we are the literal offspring of Deity.* We have descended from the great Being who formed this earth, and from Him we have inherited the glorious aspirations to be like unto Him. ... We believe in a God of revelation, who will give more and more light to us til we can become like Him. We worship the Being who has revealed Himself to us. It was necessary at the outset of this work to have a revelation from Him. There were many erroneous ideas about God, and the first revelation to Joseph

---

[257] She is apparently referring to HC, July 1839.

[258] She is here replying to Joseph Smith III's statement: Ponder it well. Are not those who teach and those who endorse Brigham Young's Adam God doctrine guilty of damnable heresies, even denying the Lord that brought them?

Smith was the appearance of the Father and the Son. I have heard that there are some among us who say that both are one person. This is a fallacy. There are two personages, the Father and the Son. *God is the Being who walked in the Garden of Eden,* and who talked with the Prophets. *This revelation came to us in certainty.*

Abraham H. Cannon   *5/26/1892*

Journal of Abraham H. Cannon 16:119

At two o'clock I was at my Quorum meeting where were present all the Presidency and myself, as also Bro. Lyman; Geo. Gibbs, clerk. Bro. Jos. F. Smith was mouth in prayer. Thereafter some conversation followed as to whether Adam is our God or not. There are some in the Church who do not accept of the *statement* of Pres. Young that such is the case, but to me it seems reasonable to think that Adam has at least much to do with our present condition, and will control greatly our future destiny.

Joseph F. Smith   *1/9/1897*

Letter to the Honorable A. Saxey

Hon. A. Saxey ...

I may say I submitted your letter to President Woodruff, and he partially outlined what I should say in answer to your questions. To know this might be more satisfactory to you than to suppose my statements were simply my own. I am happy to know that he and I are in accord on the subject. With reference to Prest. B. Youngs remarks, in a discourse delivered in 1852. with reference to "Adam being the only God with whom we have to do" &c. I will say: - Prest. Young no doubt expressed his *personal opinion or views* upon the subject. What he said was *not given as a revelation or commandment* from the Lord. The *Doctrine* was never submitted to the Councils of the Priesthood nor to the Church for approval or ratification and was never formally or otherwise accepted by the Church. It is therefore in no sense binding upon the Church nor upon the consciences of any of the members thereof, except perhaps only so far as some may have confidence in President Young, *believing that he had light on the subject* which was not given in connection with his public mention thereof. It is thought, even if there is truth in it, that the bare mention made my Prest. Young, with out indubitable evidence and authority being given of its truth, was unfortunate to say the least. ... When the inspired head speaks by the power of the spirit & he is backed up by "thus saith the Lord" - it becomes a serious matter to reject, or lightly pass it by. *There is no such responsibility attached to this statement,* made by Prest. Young.

With very Kind regards, I am &c.

/s Jos. F. Smith

George Q. Cannon   *11/28/1898*

Proceedings of the First Sunday School Convention

Many questions come up from theological classes - questions that are, to say the least, somewhat abstruse, and concerning which there is *no written revelation*; questions, too, that are not pertinent at all to the work of the schools. I was stopped yesterday afternoon by a young man, who wanted to know whether Adam was the father of our Lord and Savior - whether he was the being we worshiped, etc. Now, we can get ourselves very easily puzzled, if we choose to do so, by speculating upon *doctrines and principles* of this character. The Lord has said through His Prophet that there are two personages in the Godhead. That ought to be sufficient for us at the present time. ...

But it has always seemed to me that we had better not endeavor to puzzle ourselves or allow our minds to be drawn out upon questions of this kind, concerning which *the Lord has not revealed perhaps all that we desire*. When men give themselves license to do this, they are very apt to be led along into error and imbibe ideas that are not sound. ...

Let the teachers in the classes *confine themselves to that which God has revealed*, and repress as much as possible all these improper inquiries that *cannot be answered from the word of the Lord*. ... but let us not try to find out mysteries. If men have received *revelations* concerning things that the Lord has not revealed to His people, they ought to hold their tongues about such matters; because if God gives men knowledge concerning things which He has not authorized His servant who holds the keys to reveal, they have no business to teach it as doctrine. There are many things which God reveals to His servants from time to time, but *a wise person who has a revelation that is trustworthy will not go around telling it and teaching it as doctrine*, because the same Spirit, if it be from the Lord, that reveals such things, would also teach that such a course would be very improper. There are many things which God has revealed that are unlawful for men to utter.

No doubt, He does now reveal things of this kind from time to time to those who have faith and who are chosen vessels; but you may rest assured that where there are any of that class, they are not around propagating these ideas, whispering them and telling them to people as truths that they ought to understand; the Spirit of God will not prompt any such thing. Concerning the *doctrine in regard to Adam and the Savior*, the Prophet Brigham taught some things concerning that; but the First Presidency and the Twelve do not think it wise to advocate these matters. It is sufficient to know that we have a Father - God the Eternal Father, who reveals Himself by His Holy Spirit unto those who seek unto Him; and that Jesus Christ is His Son, our Redeemer, the Savior of the world. If we confine ourselves to the facts as they are written in the word that the Lord has given unto us, we will do well. I would therefore say to all the brethren and sisters, refrain from indulging in *these speculations*; it does not lead to good. Do not indulge in the asking of foolish and improper questions. The Lord has revealed enough to keep us busy if we but study His word.

B. H. Roberts   *1903*

Mormon Doctrine on Deity, 42-43

Some of the sectarian ministers are saying that we "Mormons" are ashamed of the *doctrine announced by President Brigham Young* to the effect that Adam will thus be God of this world. No, friends, it is not that we are ashamed of that *doctrine*. If you see any change come over our countenances when this *doctrine* is named, it is surprise, astonishment, that anyone at all capable of grasping the largeness and extent of the universe - the grandeur of existence and the possibilities in man for growth, for progress, should be so lean of intellect, should have such a paucity of understanding, as to call it in question at all. That is what our change of countenance means - not shame - for the *doctrine* Brigham Young taught.

B. H. Roberts later tried to distance the Church from Adam-God teachings by declaring:

B. H. Roberts   *7/23/1921*

DN

As a matter of fact, the "Mormon" church does not teach that *doctrine*. A few men in the "Mormon" Church have held such views; and several of them quite prominent in the Councils of the Church. ... Brigham Young and others may have taught that *doctrine*.

Joseph F. Smith   *circa 1915*

Joseph F. Smith Personal Letterbook, 26-27

What is called the Adam-God *doctrine* may properly be classed among the mysteries. The full truth concerning it has not been revealed to us; and until it is revealed all wild speculations, sweeping assertions and dogmatic declarations relative thereto, are out of place and improper. We disapprove of them and especially the public expression of such views.

Bishop Heber Bennion   *1920*

Supplement to Gospel Problems, 8-9

While there is nothing to refute, the whole tenor of revelation substantiates, the supposition, that *Adam* has continued to bear rule over the earth, and control the destinies of his never ending posterity. From the time he received his commission in the

Garden of Eden, he has been laboring diligently to fulfill the instructions there given him by the Lord God concerning his dominions, and to bring them under subjection to his will. This will be fully accomplished when every knee shall bow, and every tongue confess that *he is the God of the whole earth.* Then will the words of the Prophet Brigham, when speaking of Adam, be fully realized - `He is our Father and our God, and the only God with whom we have to do.' ...

It seems strange that people will believe that `as man now is, God once was, and that as God now is, man may be;' that `God is an exalted man' and still repudiate the *Doctrine of Adam God.* ... It seems presumptuous indeed for them to ever aspire to be the God of anything, if Adam cannot be the God of the world He created and peopled. If a man is not to become the God of His own posterity, what will he be the God of? .... *The whole superstructure for a plurality of the Gods is based upon this doctrine of Adam God, and must stand or fall together.*

Bishop Heber Bennion   *1920*

Supplement to Gospel Problems, 13

T[he unbelieving gentiles] mocked at Brigham Young, *Adam-God*, and we seek to molify and pacify them by telling them that is not the *doctrine* of the Church, but only the doctrine of Brigham Young. But we are making matters worse, for next we will have to explain that it was only an *idea* of Joseph Smith, and the Prophet Daniel, and of Jesus Christ, for Jesus gave this *revelation* to Joseph Smith.

'Adam-ondi-Ahman, because, said he, it is the place where Adam shall come to visit his people, or the Ancient of Days shall sit, as spoken of by Daniel, the prophet.' - D.&C. 116.

Now let us turn to Daniel, and see what he says about the *Adam-God* doctrine. `I beheld till the thrones were cast down, and the Ancient of Days did sit, whose garments were white as snow, and the hair of his head like the pure wool; his throne was like the fiery flame, and his wheels as burning fire. A fiery stream issued and came forth from before him; thousands ministered unto him, and ten thousand times ten thousand stood before him; and the judgment was set, and the books were opened.' - Daniel 7:9, 10. The above *revelation* of Joseph Smith, together with the prophecy of Daniel seems to corroborate Brigham Young's *doctrine* of *Adam-God* - beyond question.

J. Arthur Horne, Patriarch   *5/28/1963*

C. Jess Gorewsbeck's Elder's Journal 1:291

Elder Horne and I chatted again tonight about the Gospel and the *Adam-God Doctrine*, as we have done many times before. Brother Horne, who grew up in Salt Lake City and was the son of Richard Horne and grandson of Joseph Horne said, in reference to the

Adam-God Doctrine, that when he first went through the Temple [Salt Lake] for his Endowment in 1902 before going on his mission he was surprised to hear the teachings during the Temple ceremony [in the Sermon before the veil] that, `Adam was our God' and that ''he came here with Eve, one of his wives'. Also, it was taught that 'Eve bore our spirits.' He asked his father about it but he declined to give his opinion about it. After Brother Horne returned from his mission a few years later, in 1905, he noted these teachings had been removed from the Temple ceremony. He feels that they were left over from Brigham Young's influence, but that he himself [Brother Horne] couldn't believe such *doctrine. He thinks perhaps Brigham just got off in his speculation.*

Dean Jesse   *Spring 1979*

BYU Studies 19:397-99

Many of the teachings and practices formalized during Brigham Young's administration can be traced to private councils where Joseph Smith taught the Twelve in detail about the affairs of the Kingdom. In fact, it seems far more compelling to accept that possibility, one in harmony with what we know of Brigham Young, and of Joseph Smith in Nauvoo, than to continue to believe - in the absence of documentation - that Brigham Young made a fundamental innovation of his own during those tumultuous years of succession ... especially in view of the fact that the private meetings where Joseph Smith taught the full pattern of temple ordinances (and related doctrines) would have provided the ideal forum.

Analysis & Observations

β

Much, if not the vast majority, of the materials found in the "Statements of Unbelief" subsection tends to support the above materials in demonstrating that Brigham Young was in no way presenting the Adam-God teachings as speculation.[259] Had Brigham Young considered these teachings as an "Adam-God Theory," Orson Pratt and others would not have been on trial for their Church memberships for teaching doctrines contrary to Adam-God teachings. As the above materials go directly to the issue as to whether or

---

[259] Of course, this conclusion is loosely based upon the presumption that most of these statements are using the term "doctrine" in a strict sense - that is, they use the term "doctrine" in a way that is distinguishable from the term "teaching". While this does not appear to be true of all of the above statements, it appears to be true of the majority of these statements.

not Brigham Young was speculating and as it would be redundant to reproduce all of the materials in the "Statement of Unbelief" subsection in this section, the reader is encouraged to make note of the similar issues that are raised in the other subsection.

Culley "Christensen made the following observations:

Church publications such as the Deseret News and Elders' Journal became proselyting tools for the Adam-God doctrine. It was also taught in missionary publications, and is reflected in the contemporary writings of the time. In short, the Adam-God doctrine was intended to become an expansion on the concept of God and to be an integral part of every saint's belief in God. It permeated every facet of Mormon ideology. Its permeation was so extensive that, to this day, it has not been rooted out. ... It was taught in the School of the Prophets, semiannual general conference, semiannual priesthood conference, in the temple, as well as in private. AGM, 108-09.

If Brigham played such a game as to deliberately advance false doctrine he was indeed the man for the job, for he appeared to have fooled everyone including the Quorum of the Twelve. Furthermore, if Brigham did deliberately advance false doctrine, one has no assurance - save by the Holy Spirit - that he is not being misled today. Such a hypothesis completely undermines the authoritative structure of the church, for one can never be sure that what he is told [by a prophet of God] is really true. AGM, 113.

The following men received their apostolic callings under the inspiration of a grieved spirit during President Young's reign of heresies: Lorenzo Snow, Erastus Snow, F. D. Richards, George Q. Cannon, Joseph F. Smith, Brigham Young, Jr., and Albert Carrington. If Brigham Young, as a fallen prophet, had no authority (as indicated by section 121 of the Doctrine and Covenants), then those who were ordained under his hands have no authority. AGM, 128.

Although, academically speaking, the above statements do not definitively prove that Brigham Young was not speculating about Adam-God teachings, it seems that the position that he was speculating is rather weak and unlikely. If the above statements have not convinced the reader, little more evidence will. However, the following few statements may be of some interest. They were made in defense of Brigham Young's appointment to lead the Church as the Lord's anointed. While none of these prove that Brigham Young was speculating, they do suggest that the Lord had great confidence in Brigham Young's ability to lead the saints in truth and righteousness at the time of his calling:

JD 8:233-34

In the month of February, 1848, the Twelve Apostles met at Hyde Park, Pottawattamie County, Iowa, where a small branch of the Church was established; ... We were in prayer and council, communing together; and what took place on that occasion? The voice of God came from on high, and spake to the Council. Every latent feeling was aroused, and every heart melted. What did it say unto us? "Let my servant Brigham step forth and receive the full power of the presiding Priesthood in my Church and kingdom." This was the voice of the Almighty unto us at Council Bluffs, before I removed to what was called Kanesville. It has been said by some that Brigham was appointed by the people, and not by the voice of God. I do not know that this testimony has often, if ever, been given to the masses of the people before; but I am one that was present, and there are others here that were also present on that occasion, and did hear and feel the voice from heaven, and we were filled with the power of God. This is my testimony; these are my declarations unto the Saints - unto the members of the kingdom of God in the last days, and to all people.

We said nothing about the matter in those times, but kept it still. (After seating myself in the stand, I was reminded of one circumstance that occurred, which I omitted in my discourse. Men, women, and children came running together where we were, and asked us what was the matter. They said that their houses shook, and the ground trembled, and they did not know but that there was an earthquake. We told them that there was nothing the matter - not to be alarmed; the Lord was only whispering to us a little, and that He was probably not very far off. We felt no shaking of the earth or of the house, but were filled with the exceeding power and goodness of God.) We knew and realized that we had the testimony of God within us. On the 6th day of April following, at our Annual Conference, held in the Log Tabernacle at Kanesville, the propriety of choosing a man to preside over the Church was investigated. In a very few minutes it was agreed to, and *Brigham Young was chosen to fill that place without a dissenting voice, the people not knowing that there had been any revelation touching the matter.* They ignorantly seconded the voice of the Lord from on high in his appointment. ...

Some persons say that Brigham does not give revelations as did Joseph Smith. But let me tell you, that Brigham's voice has been the voice of God from the time he was chosen to preside, and even before.

Edward Tullidge 1877

Life of Brigham Young, 115

If Joseph had arisen from the dead and again spoke in their hearing, the effect could not have been more startling than it was to many present at that meeting; it was the voice of Joseph himself; and not only was it the voice of Joseph which was heard, but *it seemed in the eyes of the people as if it were the very person of Joseph which stood before them.* A more wonderful and miraculous event than was wrought that day in the presence of that congregation we never heard of. The Lord gave his people a testimony that left *no room for doubt as to who was the man chosen to lead them.*

Wilford W. Woodruff 3/12/1892

DN

If I had not seen him with my own eyes, there is no one that could have convinced me that it was not Joseph Smith, and anyone can testify to this who was acquainted with these two men.

False Prophecy & False Gods

~

Anti-Mormons have taken advantage of the modern LDS Church's position by noting that if Brigham Young was incorrect in his Adam-God teachings, then he was promoting the worship of a false god. The Church has generally responded by stating that Brigham Young was misquoted or that Brigham Young was speculating - in either instance, he was not promoting the worship of a false god. To the LDS Church's embarrassment, anti-Mormons have done enough research to show that neither of these positions is accurate. There are enough statements proclaiming Adam to be God the Father that the average non-Mormon is more than satisfied that Brigham Young was neither misquoted nor speculating. Thus - or so their argument goes - either Brigham Young or the modern LDS Church (or both) is promoting the worship of a false god. By showing the contradictions between the early brethren's beliefs about Adam-God teachings[260] and the modern LDS Church's position, anti-Mormons have done much to discredit modern Mormonism's theological foundation. Once these contradictions have been established, anti-Mormon authors go on to quote a slew of scriptures decrying this practice and announcing the condemnation and curses that come upon an individual who teaches others to worship a false god. The following scriptures are a sampling of scriptures commonly used by anti-Mormons to decry Adam-God teachings.

Deuteronomy 13:1-5

If there arise among you a prophet … saying, *let us go after other gods, which thou hast not known, and let us serve them; thou shalt not hearken unto the words of that prophet*, or that dreamer of dreams: *for the Lord proveth you, to know whether ye love the Lord your God with all you soul.* Ye shall walk after the Lord your God, and fear Him, and keep His

---

[260] And the related teachings about Jehovah, etc.

commandments, and obey His voice, and ye shall serve Him, and cleave unto Him. *And that prophet*, or that dreamer of dreams *shall be put to death; because he has spoken to turn you away from the Lord your God*, which brought you out of the land of Egypt, and redeemed you out of the house of bondage, *to thrust thee out of the way which the Lord thy God commanded thee to walk in*. So shalt thou put the evil away from the midst of thee.

Exodus 20:1, 3, 5

I am the Lord thy God, which have brought thee out of the land of Egypt, out of the house of Bondage. *Thou shalt have no other gods before me* ... for I the Lord thy God am a jealous God.

Exodus 34:14

Thou shalt worship no other god; for the Lord, whose name is Jealous, is a jealous God.

Romans 1:23

[They] *changed the glory of the uncorruptible God into an image made like to corruptible man*, and to birds, and four-footed beasts, and creeping things.

This last scripture appears to have been the foundation of Orson Pratt's primary objection to Adam-God teachings.[261] Orson had a difficult time accepting Adam-God teachings because they require an exalted, incorruptible being to suffer by becoming corruptible through the effects of the fall.

Other scriptures have been offered by anti-Mormons to discredit Adam-God teachings in this same manner:
Isaiah 9:13-16; Jeremiah 2:11-12-13, 19-23
Romans 1:22-26; Galatians 1:8-9; 2 Corinthians 11:2; 2 Peter 2:1-2
2 Nephi 28:11

Although the use of these scriptures by anti-Mormons has been largely ignored as inflammatory polemics due to the modern LDS Church's position (and because its Church members implicitly trust the words of their leaders), this challenge to Adam-God teachings is worthy of solemn consideration. The following extract from a letter from Bruce R. McConkie to Eugene England, which found its ways into the Tanner's publications, has added fuel to the anti-Mormon position and demonstrates the fact that the modern LDS Church is also concerned about the promulgation of false teachings about God:

---

[261] Nevertheless, I could not find a single instance where he cited this scripture in his support.

February 19, 1981
Letter from Bruce R. McConkie to Eugene England, 7
I do not know all of the providences of the Lord, but I do know that he permits false
doctrine to be taught in and out of the Church and that such teaching is part of the sifting
process of mortality. We will be judged by what we believe among other things. If we
believe false doctrine, we will be condemned. If that belief is on basic and fundamental
things, it will lead us astray and we will lose our souls. This is why Nephi said: "And all
those who preach false doctrines, ... wo, wo, wo be unto them, saith the Lord God
Almighty, for they shall be thrust down to hell! (2 Nephi 28:15) This clearly means that
people who teach false doctrine in the fundamental and basic things will lose their souls.
The nature and kind of being that God is, is one of these fundamentals. I repeat: *Brigham
Young erred in some of his statements on the nature and kind of being that God is* and as to the
position of Adam in the plan of salvation, but Brigham Young also taught the truth in
these fields on other occasions. And I repeat, that in his instance, he was a great prophet
and has gone on to eternal reward. *What he did is not a pattern for any of us.* If we choose
to believe and teach the false portions of his doctrines, we are making an election that
will damn us.

When considered in light of the scriptures above, the reader ought to recognize that the
acceptance or rejection of Adam-God teachings is of enormous salvific importance: *if*
Adam-God teachings are *not true*, then Brigham Young was clearly a false prophet,
worthy of death under Deuteronomic law, and accepting those teachings will damn the
believer. Further, all of the prophets of the LDS Church who followed in Brigham's
footsteps must be viewed with a great degree of suspicion because each of them has
recognized and publicly acknowledged that Brigham Young was a prophet of God. This
is the position of the anti-Mormons and, if their claims are true and Adam-God teachings
are false, then their conclusion logically follows from their premises and the modern LDS
Church is in a terribly compromised position.[262] Of course, this conclusion relies upon
the assumption that Brigham Young was not misquoted and/or was not speculating - the
accuracy of this position should be well established as extremely reliable and academically
acceptable given the evidence put forth in this volume.
Although it may not be particularly palatable to the average fundamentalist, the

---

[262] That said, I would like to again draw the reader's attention to Deuteronomy 24:1 and Mark 10:1-5 and
the related principles that I discussed earlier in this volume (surrounding Jesus' reaction to Moses' false
teachings about marriage); Jesus allowed false teachings to be introduced into his Church. The question
that remains is, does God the Father allow a prophet to teach His saints false teachings about the nature and
identity of God?

contrasting position may not be as patently offensive in the eyes of God. That is, *if* Adam-God teachings are *true*, rejecting them by accepting the modern LDS Church's theological position may not necessarily constitute the worship of a false god because the modern LDS Church worships Elohim, who, according to Adam-God teachings, is a god (or gods) superior to Adam. Although this Elohim may not be identifiable as the *only* true God (according to Adam-God teachings), He is a god that Adam worships and is therefore not a false god and therefore the worship of this being may not be punishable under the standards set forth by the above scriptures. While the opposing argument can rationally be made as well, the conclusion is more academic on its face. That is, a reasonable person could understand either position to be correct. Ultimately however, the consequences are not academic at all - salvation relies upon a correct understanding of these principles and the reader must arrive at the correct answer or risk everlasting peril to their soul.

35 Statements of Unbelief

Joseph Smith   *6/16/1844*

TPJS, 374

I never heard of a man being damned for believing too much, but they are damned for unbelief.[263]

Fundamentalists commonly use the above quotation of Joseph Smith to justify their position in condemning the LDS Church for excommunicating people merely for believing in fundamentalist doctrines. The problem with this approach is that by believing in one thing, you must necessarily disbelieve its opposite. It seems more likely therefore that Joseph was not speaking towards the rejection of certain specific doctrines but towards a state of the heart where one is not willing to accept new light and knowledge. Regardless of what Joseph must have meant, member's were put on trial for disbelieving Adam-God teachings under the administrations of Brigham Young and at least one of his successors.

The following materials may be used to show that disbelief in Adam-God teachings was tolerated. However, they also show that a member who persisted in encouraging others to disbelieve Adam-God teachings was not tolerated. These materials are not exhaustive in the sense that they do not include statements from the brethren referring to how this doctrine should be accepted (this genre of statement would implicitly concede that

---

[263] The reader is advised to note that this statement was made less than two weeks before the prophet Joseph Smith was martyred; this is significant because the prophet Joseph was making this statement after having had many theological conflicts within the Church and within the quorum of the twelve apostles. Undoubtedly, he had given this subject much of his personal consideration.

unbelief existed).[264] Instead, these materials only address statements that specifically refer to disbelief among the saints in the early Church.

Orson Pratt   *7/1/1868*

Letter from Orson Pratt to President Young

To President B. Young: ...

I am deeply sensible that *I have greatly sinned against you, and against my brethren* of the school, and against God, in foolishly trying to justify myself *in advancing ideas, opposed to those* which have been introduced by the highest authorities of the Church, *and adopted by the Saints*. I humbly ask you and the school to forgive me.

                                                                                 6/8/1868

Minutes of the School of the Prophets, 37-42

The doctrine preached by Pres. Young for a few years back, wherein he says that *Adam is our God* - the God we worship - that *most of the people believe this* - some believe it because the President says so - others because they can find testimony in the Book of Mormon and Book of Doctrine and Covenants. ... I have heard President Young avow the truth of *Adam being our Father and God* but have never heard him argue the question at all.

A. F. McDonald:

I thought I would speak briefly in relation to *Adam being our God*. Since the year 1852 when the President first spoke on this subject, I have frequently endeavored to reconcile what I have read with regard to this matter. *I believe what the President says on the subject although it comes in contact with all our tradition.* I have not any doubt in my mind but that *Adam is our God*. Who his God and Father may be, I have no knowledge. President Kimball spoke on this question recently and very plainly illustrated the character and relationship of our Father and God.

George G. Bywater:

I am not disposed to question the *discrepancies on this question of doctrine*; if we live faithful all will become clear to us. We cannot become united only as we get united in understanding. When I first heard the doctrine of *Adam being our Father and God*, I was favorably impressed - enjoyed, and hailed it as a new revelation. It appeared reasonable to me, as the Father of our spirits that he should introduce us here. And what we do not see is only evidence that we have not the light necessary.

---

[264] These statements have been included in the introduction to this volume.

S.S. Smith   *3/25/1871*

Minutes from Parowan School of the Prophets Meeting

S.S. Smith spoke of some of the brethren from the west [Meadow Valley]. Speaking of the apostacy [sic] in the church, said that *there were many who are beginning to think that they do not worship the same God that Brigham Young does.*

Brigham Young   *Sunday p.m. 6/18/1873*

DN 22:308

How much unbelief exists in the minds of the Latter-day Saints in regard to one particular doctrine which I revealed to them, and which God revealed to me - namely that *Adam is our father and God* - I do not know, I do not inquire, I care nothing about it.

T. B. H. Stenhouse [an apostate]   *1873*

The Rocky Mountain Saints, 492

[T]he mass of the Mormon people do not believe the doctrine of the Adam deity.

Brigham Young   *5/14/1876*

L. John Nuttall Papers

The fault that I find with the people of the world is not that they are in darkness, but that they not receive the light. This is their condemnation that light is come into the world and they have chosen darkness rather than light. This is what I find fault with them for.

George Q. Cannon   *1/17/1878*

George Q. Cannon Journal[265]

Some of my brethren, as I have learned since the death of President Brigham Young, did have feelings concerning his course. They did not approve of it, and felt oppressed, and yet they dare not exhibit their feelings to him, he ruled with so strong and stiff a hand, and they felt that it would be of no use. In a few words, *the feeling seems to be that he transcended the bounds of the authority which he legitimately held.* I have been greatly surprised to find *so much dissatisfaction* in such quarters .... [S]*ome even feel that in the promulgation of doctrine he took liberties beyond those to which he was legitimately entitled.*

L. John Nuttall   *3/6/1879*

L. John Nuttall Journal, 254

Attended fast day Meeting [sic]. several [sic] spoke and the question as to Adam being

---

[265] As cited in Joseph J. Cannon, "George Q. Cannon - Relations With Brigham Young," The Instructor 80:259 #6; see also 1892 meeting of the First Presidency and Quorum of the Twelve; Abraham H. Cannon Journal, 5/26/1892).

our Father & God was presented. I explained this matter as I got it from Prest B [sic] Young and as I understand it - *this question has been on the minds of several of the brethren since* Bro. Wandel Mace spoke on it about a Month [sic] ago and *gave a wrong impression* [sic] I spoke to correct him & set the people right - which correction he accepted

President Jensen   2/24/1880

Minutes of the High Priests Quorum, 86, Box Elder Stake
Pres. Jensen referred to the condition of some of the High Priests in the Malad Ward who were *contending one with another concerning some point of doctrine*, which they did not understand. The *point in dispute being, was Adam our God*, some taking the affirmation and some the negative of the question. This was not right. We ought to allow these matters to rest until our minds were better informed regarding them. Contention leads to strife and ill feelings and eventually into apostasy. Hence how careful we ought to be in these regards.

                                                                               3/4/1882

Edward Stevenson Diary (as cited in Buerger, 73)
Edward Stevenson and several others dealt with *Thomas Howell, who opposed the Adam-God doctrine, in a general meeting of the Seventies.* Howell was advised that if he "could not comprehend these things to lay them up untill he could, & if he indulged in that spirit to correct or set President Young rite that *he would be delt with & lose his faith & standing in the Church*." After "meny remarks" Howell "said he was rong, sory for it & asked for forgiveness."

                                                                               5/26/1892

Journal of Abraham H. Cannon 16:119
At two o'clock I was at my Quorum meeting where were present all the Presidency and myself, as also Bro. Lyman; Geo. Gibbs, clerk. Bro. Jos. F. Smith was mouth in prayer. Thereafter some conversation followed as to whether *Adam is our God* or not. *There are some in the Church who do not accept of the statement of Pres. Young that such is the case*, but to me it seems reasonable to think that Adam has at least much to do with our present condition, and will control greatly our future destiny.

Wilford W. Woodruff   4/7/1895

MS 57:355-56
How much longer I shall talk to this people I do not know; but I want to say this to all Israel: *Cease troubling yourselves about who God is; who Adam is, who Christ is who Jehovah is.* For heaven's sake, let these things one. Why trouble yourselves about these things? God

has revealed himself and when the 121st section of the Doctrine and Covenants is fulfilled, whether there be one God or many Gods they will be revealed to the children of men, as well as all thrones and dominions, principalities, and powers. Then why trouble yourselves about these things? God is God. Christ is Christ. The Holy Ghost is the Holy Ghost. That should be enough for you and me to know. If we want to know anymore, wait till we get where God is in person.

I say this because *we are troubled every little while with inquiries from Elders anxious to know who God is, who Christ is, and who Adam is.* I say to the Elders of Israel, stop this. Humble yourselves before the Lord; seek for light, for truth, and for a knowledge of the common things of the Kingdom of God. The Lord is the same yesterday, today, and forever. He changes not. The Son of God is the same. He is the Savior of the world. He is our advocate with the Father. *We have had letter after letter from Elders abroad wanting to know concerning these things.* Adam is the first man. He was placed in the Garden of Eden, and is our great progenitor. God the Father, God the Son, and God the Holy Ghost, are the same yesterday, today, and forever. That should be sufficient to know.

Orson
Pratt

Although some of these journal excerpts do not directly address Adam-God teachings, they have been limited to related theological issues. I have included them here, not because they demonstrate a longstanding dispute over fundamental Adam-God teachings, but because they show a pattern of behavior of Orson Pratt teaching doctrines that were not in harmony with the Quorum of the Twelve or with Brigham Young and because they demonstrate how the Twelve were united against Orson Pratt's teachings pertaining to the nature of God.

Orson Pratt   *9/30/1852*

Thomas Evans Jeremy Sr Journal

Brother Orson Pratt ... did not believe that Father Adam had flesh and bones, when he came to the garden of Eden, but he and his wife Eve were spirits, and that God formed their bodies out of the dust of the ground, and the [sic] became a living souls. He also said that he believed that Jesus Christ and Adam are brothers in the Spirit, and that Adam is not the God that he is praying unto.[266]

Orson Spencer & Orson Pratt   *10/3/1852*

Journal of William Clayton

A morning meeting was held at which Orson Spencer and Orson Pratt spoke on the subject of Adam. Spencer spoke of Adam "coming to this earth in the morning of creation with a resurrected body and etc ... He was followed by Elder Orson Pratt on the same subject ... He takes the literal reading of the scriptures for his guide, and maintains that God took the dust of the earth, and molded a body into which he put the

---

[266] Note that this dispute arose only a few months after this teaching was first publicly taught.

spirit of man, just as we have generally understood from the scriptures; while Brother Spencer endeavors to substantiate the position taken by President Young; Viz, that Adam came to this earth with a resurrected body, and became mortal by eating the fruits of the earth, which was earthy. The subject was finally left in so much difficulty and obscurity as it has been from the beginning ... Elder Pratt advised the Brethren to pray to God for knowledge of the true principles, and it appears evident that when ever the question is decided, it will have to be by revelation from God."

Brigham Young & Orson Pratt   *9/17/1854*

Journal of Wilford Woodruff

President Young preached this afternoon & spoke upon the Law of Consecration & had an interesting conversation in our Prayer Circle; the subject of Elder Orson Pratt publishing the Seer & the doctrine it contained was brought up in conversation. ... He [Brigham Young] said that the doctrine taught in the Seer that God had arrived at that state whereby he could not advance any further in knowledge, power & glory was a false doctrine & not true. That there never will be a time to all eternity when all the Gods of eternity will cease advancing in power, knowledge, experience & glory, for if this was the case, eternity would cease to be & the glory of God would come to an end, but all of the celestial beings will continue to advance in knowledge & power, worlds without end. Joseph would always be ahead of us, we should never catch up with him in all eternity nor he with his leaders.

Brother Pratt also thought that Adam was made of the dust of the earth. Could not believe that Adam was our God or the Father of Jesus Christ. President Young said that He came from another world & made this. Brought Eve with him, partook of the fruits of the earth, begat children & they were earthly & had mortal bodies & if we were faithful, we should become Gods as He was. He told Brother Pratt to lay aside his philosophical reasoning & get revelation from God to govern him & enlighten his mind more & it would be a great blessing to him to lay aside his books & go into the canyons as some of the rest of us was doing & it would be better for him. He said his philosophy injured him in a measure many good things was said by President Young that we should grow up in revelation so that principle would govern every act of our lives. He had never found any difficulty in leading this people since Joseph's death.

Brigham Young & Orson Pratt   *5/6/1855*

Journal of Wilford Woodruff

He did not doubt but that Father Adam knew in the beginning how many of his posterity would receive a Celestial glory & who they were & also a Terrestrial & a Telestial, yet man had his agency to act, choose & refuse good or evil as seemed him good & he would be rewarded according to his works.

O. Pratt asks will Adam or any God continue to make worlds, people them, taste of death to redeem them - Answer: I have no doubt but it is his privilege but whether He will do it is a question in my mind. How then can his seed increase to all eternity through the increase of his posterity. Many other remarks were made by the President.

On 17 February 1856, during a council meeting of the Twelve, Young retorted that "he had never learned that principle in the Church for it was not taught in the Church for it was not true it was fals doctrin For the God[s] & all intelligent beings would never sease to learn except it was the Sons of Perdition they would continue to decrease untill they became dissolved back into their native Element & lost their Identity."

Wilford W. Woodruff   *3/11/1856*

Journal of Wilford Woodruff

... met with the Regency in the evening. The time was occupied till 10 o'clock writing lessons upon the black board. Then the subject was brought up concerning Adam being made of the dust of the earth, and Elder Orson Pratt pursued a course of stubbornness & unbelief in what President Young said that will destroy him if he does not repent & turn from his evil ways. For when any man crosses the track of a leader in Israel & tries to lead the prophet - he is no longer led by him but is in danger of falling.

Samuel W. Richards   *3/11/1856*

Journal of Samuel W. Richards, 113

Evening with the Regency in the Upper Room of the President's Office, examining the spelling of the New Books in the D. Alphabet. A very serious conversation took place between President B. Young and Orson Pratt upon doctrine.

O. P. was directly apposed to the President's views and very freely expressed his entire disbelief in them after being told by the President that things were so and so in the name of the Lord. He was firm in the position that the President's word in the name of the Lord, was not the word of the Lord to him. The President did not believe that Orson Pratt would ever be Adam, to learn by experience the facts discussed, but every other, person in the room would be if they lived faithful.

George A. Smith   *4/20/1856*

Journal of Wilford Woodruff

I met with the Presidency & Twelve in the prayer-circle. Brother G. A. Smith spoke in plainness his feelings concerning some principles of Elder O Pratt's wherein he differed from President Young concerning the creation of Adam out of the dust of the Earth &

the final consummation of knowledge & many other things. I am afraid when he come to write he will publish in opposition of President Young's views but he promises he would not.

Wilford W. Woodruff   *3/8/1857*

Journal of Wilford Woodruff

I attended the prayer meeting in the evening. President Young had O Pratt's pamphlet read called The Holy Spirit, & he made the following remarks after hearing it read: He said that Brother Pratt had got beyond the stars. He had corralled them & got beyond them.

Brigham Young   *3/8/1857*

JD 4:266-67

With all the knowledge and wisdom that are combined in the person of brother Orson Pratt, still he does not yet know enough to keep his foot out of it, but drowns himself in his own philosophy, every time that he undertakes to treat upon principles that he does not understand. When he was about to leave here for his present mission, he made a solemn promise that he would not meddle with principles which he did not fully understand, but would confine himself to the first principles of the doctrine of salvation, such as were preached by brother Joseph Smith and the Apostles. But the first that we see in his writings, he is dabbling with things that he does not understand; his vain philosophy is no criterion or guide for the Saints in doctrine.

Wilford W. Woodruff   *3/24/1858*

Journal of Wilford Woodruff

The Presidency and Twelve met in council at the office. Meeting opened by prayer by O. Hyde. I presented before the meeting the case of O. Pratt who did not believe in some of the teachings of President Young and thought President Young had reproved him unjustly. The subject was discussed at length by the Twelve and President Young. Much instruction was given at the close. Orson Pratt confessed his faults and said that he would never teach those principles again or speak them to any person on the earth. We all forgave him and voted to receive him into full fellowship.

Friday 6 p.m. 1/27/1860

Church Historian's Office Journal

The Presidency & Prests of Seventies & Twelve met in council at Prest. Young's Office. A sermon written to be published, by Orson Pratt, was read and rejected as false doctrine Elder Pratt advocates the doctrine of worshipping an attribute instead of God,

The Author and dispenser of those attributes. The night was spent in speaking on doctrinal points until 12 o'clock.

Friday 1/27/1860

Brigham Young (Office) Journal

In the evening a Council of the twelve was held to consider the doctrines that Orson Pratt had advanced in his last Sermon about worshipping attributes. The President and the twelve came to the conclusion that Orson Pratt was wrong on that point. Bro G.D. Watt reported the whole of the remarks.

Brigham Young & Orson Pratt et al   *Friday 1/27/1860*

Journal of Wilford Woodruff

Minutes of a meeting of the Presidency & Twelve[,] Presidents of Seventies and other assembled in President Young's Council Room at 6 o'clock. ... President Young stated the object of the meeting was to converse upon doctrinal points to see if we see alike. I pray that we may have the spirit of God to rest upon us that our minds may be upon the subject & that we may speak by the Holy Spirit.

He then called upon A. Carrington to read a sermon, he read it before the company, a piece prepared for the press written by Orson Pratt upon the Godhead. He claimed that it was the attributes of God that he worshipped and not the person & that he worshipped those attributes whether he found them in God, Jesus Christ, Adam, Moses, the Apostles, Joseph, Brigham or in anybody else. After the document was read, President Young then called upon the Twelve to express their feelings upon the subject. He called upon O Hyde to speak & he called upon J. Taylor to speak. He spoke a short time. *No one knew at the time* (except the President & Carrington) *who the author of the document was.* Brother Taylor said he did not see it in that light. He worshiped a personage and not the attributes, he thought God was located and could not worship the attributes in anybody. President Young then called a vote of the assembly and said if you understand this to be a correct doctrine as here written I wish you manifest it by saying yes. No one spoke. President Young then said do I worship attributes or the dispenser of these attributes. I worship the dispenser of them of these attributes and not the attributes. This is O Pratt's sermon prepared for the press. I do not want to have it published if it is not right. Brother Orson worships the attributes of God but not God. ...

Orson Pratt has differed from me in many things. But *this is a great principle* & I do not wish to say you shall do so and so. I do not know of a man who has a mathematical turn of mind but what goes too far. The trouble between Orson Pratt & me is I do not know enough & he knows too much. ... When I read O Pratt's views in the Seer I could not swallow it. ... There is not a man in the Church that can preach better than Orson Pratt upon any subject which he understands. It is music to hear him, but *the trouble is he will preach upon things he does not know a thing about and then he will preach false doctrine & so will Elder Hyde.* He preaches upon the resurrection & teaches things which are not true. ...

Erastus Snow said ... I cannot see things in the same light that Orson Pratt does, but *when President Young has taught doctrine it has always tasted good to me.* ... Orson Pratt said I will speak upon this subject. ... I have no excuses to make. President Young said I ought to make a confession. But Orson Pratt is not a man to make a confession of what I do not believe. I am not going to crawl to Brigham Young and act the hypocrite and confess what I do not believe. I will be a free man. President Young condemns my doctrines to be false. I do not believe them to be false which I publish in the Seer in England. It has been said we should let those things sleep. But you do not let them sleep. *If I had thought while in England that President Young worshipped a God without attributes I would not have written what I did* (The above remark was an unkind cut in Orson Pratt he should not have said it). But I do not believe it, yet I will not act the hypocrite. It may cost me my fellowship, but I will stick to it; if I die tonight I would say O Lord God Almighty I believe what I say. Elder John Taylor spoke at some length and tried to convince Orson Pratt of his error.

President Young said Orson Pratt has started out upon false premises to argue upon. His foundation has been a false one all the time and I will prove it false. *You have been like a mad stubborn mule*, and have taken a false position in order to accuse me. You have accused me of worshipping a stalk or stone or a dead body without life or attributes. You never heard such a doctrine taught by me or any leader of the Church. *It is as false as hell, and you will not hear the last of it soon.* You know it is false. Do we worship those attributes? No, we worship God because he has all those attributes and is the dispenser of them and because he is our Father & our God. Orson Pratt puts down a lie to argue upon. *He has had false ground all the time tonight.* There never was a time or eternity but what a God did exist and a God that had children upon the same principle that children are now begotten, and I was begotten by the God I worship who reigns in the heavens and I shall also in my turn reign as a God & so will you.

O Hyde said to O Pratt, my opinion is not worth as much to me as my fellowship in this Church. President Young said, Michael was a resurrected Being and he left Eloheim and came to this earth & with an immortal body, & continued so till he partook of earthly food and begot children who were mortal (keep this to yourselves) then they died. A Carrington spoke upon the subject a short time and made some useful remarks. President Young spoke upon the subject of O. Pratt laying down false principles to work upon. ...

President H C Kimball followed President Young and said, *Brother Orson Pratt has withstood Joseph and he has withstood Brother Brigham many times and he has done it tonight and it made my blood chill.* It is not for you to lead, but to be led by him. You have not the power to dictate but to be dictated.

W. Woodruff arose and said Brother Orson Pratt I wish to ask you one or two questions. You see that the spirit and doctrine which you possess is *entirely in opposition to the First Presidency, the Quorum of the Twelve,* and all who are present this evening, and it chills the blood in our veins to hear your words & feel your spirit. *Should not this be a guidance to you that you are wrong. What would become of the Quorum of the Twelve if we all felt as you do. We should all go to hell in a pile together.* You say you are honest in the course you are pursuing. I wish to ask you if you were honest when you said that if you had known that President Young worshipped a God without life or attributes that you would not have written what you did.

(O Pratt said, I will recall that).

It was an insult to President Young and the Holy Priesthood which he holds. Every man in this room who has a particle of the spirit of God, knows that Pres. Young is a Prophet of God and that God sustains him and he has the Holy Spirit and his doctrines are true, and that he is qualifying to lead the people and he has explained everything so plain this evening that a child can understand it, and yet it is no evidence to you. Nothing can make an impression upon you, no argument can reach your understanding. But Brother Orson I have seen the day when you were in sorrow. It was *when you were cast out* of your Quorum and out of the Church and that to, *in consequence of persuing the same course you are this evening.* Then you could both see, feel & understand. Then argument could reach you when you saw your glory and crown departing from you. I beg of you to reflect and not let your will carry you too far in these things. It would be better for us not to be able to cast up a simple sum in addition and be humble before the Lord, than to have ever so much knowledge & permit that knowledge to lead us to destruction. There are but few men upon earth upon whom God has bestowed such gifts, qualifications and reasoning powers as he has upon you, and he will hold you responsible for the use you make of them, and you should not make a wreck of your salvation for contending for things which you do not understand[.] *I do feel at this advanced state of the Church and the late day and wish the information which you possess that neither you nor your Brethren ought to be troubled with false doctrine.* Neither should you cause your Brethren to listen to such a scene of things as we have heard tonight or to insult the president of this Church as you have done. Although you are unbending in your will tonight the day is not far distant when you will be glad to bend to the president of this Church and make reconciliation. ...

Orson Hyde spoke upon the subject and *said Brother Pratt had not got the spirit of God.*

He was followed by C. C. Rich who backed up the testimony of the Twelve in saying that Orson Pratt was wrong.

E. T. Benson spoke upon the same subject and said if Brother Pratt had the confidence in President Young which he ought to have he would feel different. If he had the confidence in his Brethren which he should have I know he would feel different. President Young said I will tell you how I got along with Joseph. I found out that God called Joseph to be a Prophet. I did not do it. I then said I will leave the Prophet in the hands of that God who called and ordained him to be a Prophet. He is not responsible to me and it is none of my business what he does. It is for me to follow & obey him. ... Joseph once told me to go to his own house to attend a meeting with him. He said that he would not go without me. I went and Hyrum preached upon the Bible, Book of Mormon, & Doctrine & Covenants and said we must take them as our guide alone. He preached very lengthy until he nearly wearied the people out, when he closed. Joseph told me to get up. I did so. I took the Books and piled them all up on top of each other. *I then said that I would not give the ashes of a rye straw for all those books for my salvation without the living oracles. I should follow and obey the living oracles for my salvation instead of any thing else.* When I got through, Hyrum got up and made a confession for not including the living oracles. *It may be thought strange by the Brethren that I will still fellowship Elder Pratt after what he has said, but I shall do it. I am determined to whip Brother Pratt into it and make him work in the harness. ...*

F D Richards dismissed the meeting.

First Presidency   *Friday, 1/27/1860*

MFP 2:222-23

On the 26th of January, in the Tabernacle, Elder Orson Pratt, Sen., addressed the Saints; and, through an oversight, a portion of his remarks was printed in Vol. IX. No. 51. of The Deseret News, previous to being carefully revised. Since then those remarks have been examined by br. Pratt and the Council, and are now printed as agreed upon by them, as follows: [The quote is here recited.]

Elder Pratt sustains an unimpeachable character, so far as strict morality, tried integrity, industry, energy, zeal, faithfulness to his religion, and honesty in all business transactions are concerned; but it will be readily perceived, from his "Remarks," that he does not claim exemption from liability to err in judgment in relation to "some points of doctrine." Br. Pratt's preachings and teaching upon the first principles of the Gospel are excellent. With regard to the quotations and comments in The Seer as to Adam's having been formed "out of the ground," and "from the dust of the ground," &c., it is deemed wisest to let that subject remain without further explanation at present, for it is written that we are to receive "line upon line," according to our faith and capacities, and the circumstances attending our progress. In the Seer, pages 24 and 25, par. 22, br Pratt states: "All these Gods are equal in power, in glory, in dominion, and in the possession of all things; each possesses a fulness of truth, of knowledge, of wisdom, of light, of intelligence; each governs himself in all things by his own attributes, and is filled with love, goodness, mercy, and justice towards all. The fullness of all these attributes is what constitutes God." "It is truth, light, and love, that we worship and adore; these are the same in all worlds; and as these constitute God, He is the same in all worlds;" "Wherever you find a fulness of wisdom, knowledge, truth, goodness, love, and such like qualities, there you find God in all his glory, power, and majesty - therefore, if you worship theses adorable perfections, you worship God." Seer, page 117, par. 95.- "then there will be no Being or Beings in existence that will know one particle more than what we know; then our knowledge, and wisdom, and power will be infinite; and cannot, from thenceforth, be increased or expanded in the least degree;" Same page, par. 96: "but when they" (the Saints) "become one with the Father and Son and receive a fullness of their glory, that will be the end of all progression in Knowledge, because there will be nothing more to be learned. The Father and the Son do not progress in knowledge and wisdom, because they already know all things past, present, and to come." Par. 97: "there are none among them (the Gods) that are in advance of the others in knowledge; though some may have been Gods as many millions of years as there are particles of dust in all the universe, yet there is not one truth that such are in possession of but what every other God knows." "None of these Gods are progressing in knowledge: neither can they progress in the acquirement of any truth." In this treatise entitled "Great First Cause," page 16, par. 17, br Pratt states: "All the organizations of worlds, of minerals, of vegetables, of animals, of men, of angels, of spirits, and of the spiritual personages of the Father, of the Son, and of the Holy Ghost, must, if organized at all, have been the result of the self combinations and unions of the pre-existent, intelligent, powerful, and eternal particles of substance. These eternal Forces and Powers are the Great Causes of all things and events that have had a beginning."

The foregoing quoted ideas, and all similar ones omitted to be quoted, with the comments thereon, as advanced by br. Pratt in an article, in the Seer, entitled "Pre-Existence of man," and in his treatises entitled absurdities of immaterialism and "Great First Cause," are plausibly presented. But to the whole subject we will answer in the words of the Apostle Joseph Smith, on a similar occasion. One of the Elders of Israel [Orson Hyde] had written a long revelation which he deemed to be very important, and requested br. Joseph to hear him read it. The Prophet commended its style in glowing terms, remarked that the ideas were ingeniously advanced, &c., &c., and that he had but one objection to it. "What is that"? inquired the writer, greatly elated that his production was considered so near perfect. The Prophet Joseph replied, "It is not true." This should be a lasting lesson to the Elders of Israel not to undertake to teach doctrine they do not understand. If the Saints can preserve themselves in a present salvation day by day which is easy to be taught and comprehended, it will be well with them hereafter.

Brigham Young
Heber C. Kimball
Daniel H. Wells

Wilford W. Woodruff   *Saturday 1/28/1860*

Journal of Wilford Woodruff

I spent the day in the office. I met with the Twelve in the prayer circle. Orson Pratt met with us, he did not dress, but said he wanted to be in the society of the Twelve. He seemed much more soft in his spirit than he had been.

Brigham Young & Orson Pratt   *Saturday 1/28/1860*

Brigham Young Office Journal

Prest Joseph Young called in and conversed with his brethren Prest B. Young about the last evenings proceedings. Elder Orson Pratt called upon the President in relation to last evenings proceedings, Bro Orson admitted he was excited; and for the future would omit such points of doctrine in his discourses that related to the Plurality of Gods. &c but would confine himself to the first principles of the Gospel.[267] Bro Orson also asked the President if he had a vacancy for his son Orson as a Clerk The President observed he would endeavor to appoint him as a teacher; as he meant to promote education as much as possible[.] The President remarked to Bro Orson that much false doctrine arose out of arguing upon false premises, such as supposing something that does not exist, as a God without his attributes, as they cannot exist apart. Bro Orson replied "that many of his doctrinal arguments had been advanced while he was in England in answer to the numerous enquiries that were made of him by reasoning men. The President remarked when questions have been put to me, by opposers, who did not want to hear the simple Gospel Message. he would not answer them and asked Orson why he was not as careful to observe the revelations given to preach in plainness and simplicity as to so strenuously observe the doctrines in other revelations.

---

[267] Note that this is the second time that Orson Pratt had made this promise and that Wilford W. Woodruff did not have confidence in Orson's integrity to keep this promise the first time that it was made.

Orson Pratt   *1/28/1860*

Office Journal of President Brigham Young, as cited in Bergera, 19

I must have something more than a declaration of President Young to convince me I must have evidence. I am willing to take President Young as a guide in most things but not in all. President Young does not propose to have revelations in all things. I am not to loose in my agency I have said many things which President Young says is False I do not know how it is I count President Young equal to Joseph and Joseph equal to President Young. ... When Joseph teaches any thing & Brigham seems to teach another contrary to Joseph ... I believe them as Joseph has spoken them... I have spoken plainly I would rather not have spoken so plainly but I have no excuses to make President Young said I ought to make a confession But Orson Pratt is not a man to make a confession of what I do not believe. I am not going to crawl to Brigham and act the Hypocrite and confess what I do not Believe. I will be a free man President Young condemns my doctrines to be fals I do not believe them to be fals which I published in the Seer in England... . *I will not act the Hypocrite it may cost me my fellowship* But I will stick to it if I die tonight I would say O Lord God Almight[y] I believe what I say.

Orson Pratt   *1/29/1860*

DN vol. 9 #51

There are some points of doctrine which I have, unfortunately, thrown out before the people. At the time I expressed those views, I did most sincerely believe that they were in accordance with the word of God. I did most sincerely suppose that I was justifying the truth. But I *have since learned from my brethren, that some of the doctrines I had advanced in the "Seer," at Washington were incorrect.* Naturally being of a stubborn disposition and having a kind of a self will about me; and moreover supposing really and sincerely that I did understand what true doctrine was in relation to those points, I did not feel to yield to the judgment of my brethren, but believed they were in error.

Now, was this right? No, it was not. Why? Because the Priesthood is the highest and only legitimate authority in the Church, in these matters. ... "But," inquires one, "have you not felt anxious that the Church should follow your ideas as laid down in the Seer?" I have not; if I had, I should have preached them; I should have tried to reason with you to convince you of their apparent truth. ... God placed Joseph Smith at the head of this church. God has likewise placed Brigham Young at the head of this church; ... *We are commanded to give heed to their words in all things, and receive their words as from the mouth of God, in all patience and faith. When we do not do this, we get into darkness.*

Wilford W. Woodruff　　　　　　　　　　　　　　　　　*Sunday 1/29/1860*

Journal of Wilford Woodruff

Sunday I met at the Tabernacle. Orson Pratt was in the stand and quite unexpected to his Brethren he arose before his Brethren and made a very humble, full confession before the whole assembly for his opposition to President Young and his Brethren, and he said he wished all the Church was present to hear it.

He used Joseph Smith's revelation to prove that President Brigham Young was right and that all was under obligation to follow the leader of the Church. I never heard Orson Pratt speak better or more to the satisfaction of the people, than on this occasion. He would not partake of the sacrament until he had made a confession then he partook of it.

Orson Pratt & Brigham Young　　　　　　　　　　　　　*Tuesday 1/31/1860*

Brigham Young (Office) Journal

Elder Orson Pratt called upon the President in regard to the acknowledgements he had made on Sunday in the Tabernacle. and also made a personal acknowledgement to the President admitting he had a self willed determination in him; The President said he had never differed with him only on points of doctrine, and he never had had any personal feelings, but *he was anxious that correct doctrines should be taught for the benefit of the Church and the Nations of the earth.* Prest said in one thing he had felt vexed that he did not consult them before he published the M.S. writings he got from Mother Smith [] about the life of the Prophet. Orson admitted that he had done wrong and he now saw it but did not at the time of his purchasing and publishing it.

President observed *the brethren would have made it a matter of fellowship. The President said he did not have it in his heart to disfellowship but merely to correct men in their views.* Prest also remarked to Orson he had been willing to go on a Mission to any place at the drop of the Hat, and observed *you might as well question my authority to send you on a Mission as to dispute my views in doctrine;* Bro Orson said he had never felt unwillingness in the discharge of his practical duties.

Brigham Young　　　　　　　　　　　　　　　　　　　*4/4/1860*

Journal of Wilford Woodruff

I attended a Council of the Presidency and Twelve at the Historians Office in the evening upon the subject of the sermon of Orson Pratt. The sermon was read & the time was occupied till half past 11 o'clock in discussing the subject. President Young was the only one of the Presidency who were present. ... President Young made many remarks concerning doctrinal points & the situation of *Orson Pratt who seemed very dark in his mind upon many points of doctrine.* President Young wished the matter to be settled before the Quorum of the Twelve and not go before the conference. After spending several hours in investigating the subject it was decided for the Twelve to meet in the morning in prayer and fasting and seek the business among ourselves.

Brigham Young & Orson Pratt et al   *7 p.m. 4/4/1860*

Minutes of Meeting, at Historian's Office

Present - Brigham Young, Orson Hyde, Orson Pratt, John Taylor, Geo. A. Smith, Wilford Woodruff, E. T. Benson, F. D. Richards. Ed. Hunter. T.B. G.D.W. J.A.S. R.B. R.L.C.

B.Y. Bro. O. Pratt, has Bro Benson spoken to you about that for which we have met to night

No.

Well it is this bro. Orson. Your late sermon had like to got into the paper, I want to get an understanding of your views, and see if we see things aright perhaps if I could see it as you Orson does perhaps its all that I could ask, but if not we want to have the matter talked over and laid before the Conference in a manner that we all see eye to eye ...

O.P. ... If I could get rid of those things which have lingered upon my mind & which I have believed it to be true. The Bre[thren] are at liberty to publish anything that they see proper or at conference. *I would like to enumerate items, firstly - preached & publish, that Adam is the fa[ther] of our spirits, & father of Spirit & father of our bodies - When I read the Rev given to Joseph I read directly the opposite - Lord spake to Adam, which w Man eventually became Adam's*

(3 blank lines)

B.Y. Your statements to night, You come out to night & place them as charges, & have as many against me as I have you. One thing I have thought that I might still have omitted. It was Joseph's doctrine that Adam was God &c When in Luke Johnson's at O. Hydes the power came upon us, or shock that alarmed the neighborhood. God comes to earth & eats & partakes of fruit. Joseph could not reveal what was revealed to him, & if Joseph had it revealed, he was not told to reveal it. The Spirit is sent when the mother feels earth, God put it into his mouth, & when God, to translate he had the power. Not a contradictory thing in what I have said Bro. Pratt had the Spirit of God like us all in Pottawatomie & believed when the Revel was given to us. Bro Brigham, said could a being in a telestial or terrestrial kingdom keep a celestial law, is it reasonable to expect such a thing. Orson, it is for you to call the 12 together & do as I have suggested or do as you please. It will be brought before Conference and you will be voted as a false teacher, & your false doctrines discharged. I love your integrity, but your ignorance is as great as any philosophers ought to be. ...

G.A. Smith moved that these items come before the Conference Most of the 12
wished to have it laid before the 12 & not go before the Conference.
Bro Brigham, wished the Twelve to take hold & pray with Bro. Orson & have a good
flow of the Spirit, & it will go off smooth ... 11-30 p.m. Prest B. Young, prayed. he
prayed for Orson Pratt, & prayed feelingly

Brigham Young   *4/5/1860*

Brigham Young Papers
Minutes of Meeting of Council of the Twelve in Historian's Office
...double of thy spirit may rest upon him [Orson Pratt]. Let his mind be clear, divest
him of selfishness and hardness of heart, and may he be filled with the Holy Ghost that
he may subject himself to his Brethren, comfort his heart, and rend the veil of unbelief,
cause that the scabs of blindness to fall from his eyes, that he may see, and his ears to
hear the whisperings of the Holy Spirit, soften his heart as a little child to the will of his
Brethren and reconcile himself to the will of our God.

Brigham Young & Orson Pratt et al   *10 a.m. 4/5/1860*

Minutes of the Meeting of the Council of the Twelve
Present Elders O. Hyde, O. Pratt, J. Taylor, W. Woodruff, G.A. Smith, C.C. Rich,
F.D. Richards.
O. Pratt I do not see how I can mend the matter, one way or the other. I think the
brethren are laboring under a wrong impression, in all of my writings on doctrine, I
have tried to confine myself within revelation. I do not remember one item that I
consider new, many of the exceptions that I made last night, are not in writing.[268] On
my subject of pre-existence, I have quoted largely from Genesis and the Book of
Abraham, I have give it, how Adam and Eve came here and took bodies of flesh and
bones, the doctrine was in the Church when I came into it, and I have always rejoiced
in it, in regard to *Adam being our Father and our God, I have not published it, altho' I frankly
say, I have no confidence in it, altho advanced by bro. Kimball in the stand, and afterwards
approved by bro. Brigham.*[269] ... One [revelation] says Adam was formed out of the Earth,

---

[268] The only exceptions listed in the above statements are readily found in contemporary writings.
Whatever Orson Pratt is here referring to seems to have been omitted from the surviving records.
[269] This accusation is not confirmed by the record. This allegation is also promoted by men who are
antagonistic towards the early Church but no record of Heber C. Kimball's sermon preceding Brigham
Young's 4/9/1852 sermon has survived. The reader may also note that Adam-God teachings are not given
the foremost attention in that introductory sermon. It appears from the context of Brigham Young's
remarks on that day that he was more concerned about teaching other, more basic doctrines on that
occasion and that he did not plan on addressing the Adam-God issue at that time.

and the Lord put in his spirit; and another that he came with his body, flesh and bones, thus there are two contrary revelations - in the garden it is said, that a voice said to Adam, in the meridian of time, I will send my only begotten son Jesus Christ. then how can that man and Adam both be the Father of Jesus Christ? ...

O. Hyde When there is a want of union, it requires us to speak plain, bro. Pratt does not claim any vision or revelation, but keeps within the scope of Joseph's revelations. The Universalians have their belief, The Presbyterians do the same, they consider they believe they are in the pale of revealed religion. all the Sects do the same, yet how widely they differ, then here comes a man (B.Y.) who says he has a revelation, but it means the sects, if is Antagonistic. I see no necessity of rejecting Joseph's revelations, or going to War with the living ones, that is the nearest to us. bro. Pratt is like the Jews, who garnish the sepulchers of the dead, but reject those that were the nearest to them. I do not see any contradiction or opposition between B. Young & J. Smith. ...

O. Pratt it was the Father of Jesus Christ that was talking to Adam in the garden - B. Young says that Adam was the Father of Jesus Christ, both of his Spirit and Body, in his teachings from the stand, bro. Richards publishes in the Pearl of Great Price, that another person would come in the meridian of time, which was Jesus Christ.

O. Hyde David in spirit called Jesus Christ, Lord, how then is he his Son? it would seem a contradiction, I went to Joseph and told him my ideas of the Omnipresence of the Spirit, he said it was very pretty, and it was got up very nice, and is a beautiful doctrine, but it only lacks one thing, I enquired what is it bro Joseph, he replied it is not true.

J. Taylor spoke again "if Christ is the first fruits of them that slept" there must be some discrepancy, he must have resumed his position, having a legitimate claim to a possession some where else, he ought not to be debarred from his rights. the power of God was sufficient to resuscitate Jesus immediately, and also the body of Adam.

...

O. Pratt I have heard brother Brigham say that Adam is the Father of our Spirits, and he came here with his resurrected body, to fall for his own children; and I said to him, it leads to an endless number of falls, which leads to sorrow and death: that is revolting to my feelings, even if it were not sustained by revelation.

E. Snow Is there any revelation saying that the body of Adam should return to the dust of this Earth?

O. Pratt if you bring Adam as a Spirit, and put him into the tabernacle, runs easy with me; another item, I heard brother Young say that Jesus had a body, flesh and bones, before he came, he was born of the Virgin Mary, it was so contrary to every revelation given.

Minutes of Council of the Twelve in upper room of Historian's Office, as cited in Bergera, 27, 31-32

I am willing you should publish what you have a mind to. I cannot retract from what I have said. *I sometimes feel unworthy of the apostleship which I hold.* ...

Hyde turned to George A. Smith. "Bro. Geo. A. Smith just tell us what will be satisfactory to the Church?"

"[F]or him to acknowledge Brigham Young as the President of the Church, in the exercise of his calling," Smith informed. "[B]ut," he declared, "he only acknowledges him as a poor drivelling fool, he preaches doctrine opposed to Joseph, and all other revelations. If brigham Young is the President of the Church, he is an inspired man. If we have not an inspired man, then Orson Pratt is right... The only thing," he continued, " is for bro. Pratt to get a revelation that bro. B. Young is a Prophet of God."

"I don't think," Elder Snow added, "that any light can come to bro. Pratt, while he resists it."

"I did make a confession with my heart," Pratt conceded. "I am only an individual, I can not possibly yield to say I have published false doctrine.

I did say it was only my belief, and not revelation, I thought I could go on with the Twelve, and preach and exhort, I leave it entirely in the hands of the Church, I am willing to take out the article, but not willing to say I have taught false doctrine. I have been in the Church many years, and have learned that so long as we want to keep things smooth, we can do so, any modification you feel to make in that sermon, will be right, even to cutting it down one half.

"I feel," remarked Hyde, "you will yet acknowledge that you have taught false doctrine. I dont think you will receive a revelation, only thro brother Brigham, and you will yet confess that you have stubbornly resisted the Council. I tell you, you will not get a revelation from God on the subject. ..."

"We will dress and pray," Hyde followed, "then have that sermon, and read over item by item, and see what will agree with bro. Pratts conscience."

"I don't like any patching," Elder Taylor rejoined, "but follow the dictates of our Presidency, I don't believe in having things thrown out on bro. Brigham. If that mouthpiece has not power to dictate, I would throw all Mormonism away, all that can be asked is to carry out the doctrine in this sermon."

"I have always felt," Pratt responded, "if I can be convinced, nothing would give me greater pleasure than to make a confession."

Brigham Young   *8 p.m. 4/5/1860*

Brigham Young Journal

This day I have seen the best spirit manifested I have heard 15 or 16 men all running in the same stream I was delighted Tomorrow the Church will be 30 years old about the age that Jesus was when he commenced his mission   We are improving and I just know it, my path is like the noon day sun, and I could cry out hallelujah! hallelujah! Praise to God who has been merciful to us and conferred on us His Holy Spirit A private member in this church is brighter than the power of Kings and Princes of the world. to secure an eternal existence the wicked have to be blotted out of existence & the greatest gift is to have eternal existence for ever written in the Lamb's book of life   bro Orson (Pratt) I want you to do just as you have done in your Apostleship, but when you want to teach new doctrine, to write those ideas, and submit them to me, and if they are correct, I will tell you - there is not a man's sermons that I like to read, when you understand your subject - but you are not perfect, neither am I.

Wilford W. Woodruff   *4/5/1860*

Journal of Wilford Woodruff

The Quorum of the Twelve met this morning in the prayer room. We talked the matter over concerning Brother Pratt. Dressed and prayed. Read over his sermon and corrected it, and the *Twelve voted to receive the confession of Orson Pratt.*

Brigham Young   *9/9/1860*

Journal of Wilford Woodruff

President Young then spoke to Orson Pratt & said that the book debt was the worst trouble the saints had to contend with for 6 years. Orson Pratt has done more to make that debt than any other man. So many books are forced upon the people, and they are forced to take them or they will not be fellowshipped. Now stop publishing & getting your portraits taken & fill the kingdom with them & make the people pay for them, this keeps the people poor and keep them from emigrating.

Brigham Young   *9/23/1860*

Journal of Wilford Woodruff

Now Brother Pratt thinks that he and all the Gods will be learning for many millions of years but by & by will know all things & all will know it alike & that will be the end of their exaltations & knowledge. He cannot see the folly of forming this opinion here in the flesh & in his ignorance. But a thousand years hence he will see the folly of it. I will hold on to Brother Pratt and all those my Brethren of the Twelve notwithstanding all their sins, folly & weaknesses until I meet with them in my Fathers Kingdom, to part no more because they love God and are full of integrity. Brother Pratt said I do not believe as Brother Brigham & Brother Kimball do in some points of doctrine & they do not wish me to acknowledge to others that I do not believe. Brother Brigham said No, you cannot see the truth in this matter until you get into the spirit world.

First Presidency   *6/18/1865*

JD 11:122

With regard to the quotations and comments in the Seer as to Adam's having been formed "out of the ground," and "from the dust of the ground," & c., it is deemed wisest to let that subject remain without further explanation at present, for it is written that we are to receive "line upon line," according to our faith and capacities, and the circumstances attending our progress.

Saturday 11/4/1865

MS 27:698

The Seer, the "Great First Cause", and certain articles by Orson Pratt on the Holy Spirit were disowned by the Church. The people of the Church were asked to destroy his questionable writings.

Orson Pratt   *Saturday 11/4/1865*

MS 27:698 #44

TO THE SAINTS IN ALL THE WORLD. ...

I, therefore, embrace the present opportunity of publicly expressing my most sincere regret, that I have ever published the least thing which meets with the disapprobation of the highest authorities of the Church; and I do most cordially join with them in the request, that you should make such disposition of the publication alluded to, as counselled in their proclamation.

Brigham Young   *1/13/1867*

JD 11:286

Some men seem as if they could learn so much and no more. They appear to be bounded in their capacity for acquiring knowledge as Brother Orson Pratt, has in theory, bounded the capacity of God. According to his theory, God can progress no further in knowledge and power; but the God that I serve is progressing eternally, and so are his children; they will increase to all eternity, if they are faithful.

Brigham Young   *Sunday 5/5/1867*

Journal of Wilford Woodruff

At St. George meeting:

Orson Pratt does not believe in a God, only in attributes, but not in a personage. He would have been cut off from the Church long ago had it not have been for me. The Twelve would have cut him off. Did any one of you ever hear of any one of the Twelve ever preach the baby resurrection? I have heard of it. Neither of those brethren [Orson Hyde & Orson Pratt] will be enabled to do any good.

Wilford W. Woodruff   *9/4/1867*

Journal of Wilford Woodruff

At Salt Lake City:

The Twelve held a Council in the evening in relation to false doctrines. O Hyde had formerly preached an incorrect doctrine on the resurrection called the baby resurrection. Elder Orson Hyde renounced the doctrine & made it all right with the Quorum. Some things were not quite satisfactory with O Pratt on doctrine.

9/10/1867

Journal of Wilford Woodruff

Social conversation ensued upon this subject (the baby resurrection doctrine of Orson Hyde); even the Godhead. O Pratt said that he did not worship attributes aside from the personage of God, but believed that God was an organized Being the same as man and that man possessed the attributes of God & would become a God if he kept the celestial law.

9/12/1867

Journal of Wilford Woodruff

At Paris, Idaho:

The President & Twelve held a Council in the evening upon the difference of opinion with O. Pratt.

Orson Pratt   *7/1/1868*

Letter from Orson Pratt to President Young

To President B. Young:

Dear Brother, since the last two meetings at the school, I have, at times, reflected much and very seriously, upon the feelings which I have suffered myself for years to occasionally entertain respecting certain doctrines, or rather items of ante-deluvian history, now believed by the Church, and have tried to justify myself in taking an opposite view, on the supposition that I was supported by the letter of the word of God: but as often as I have yielded to this influence *I have felt an indescribable wretchedness which fully convinces me that I am wrong; I wish to repent* of these wrongs for I fully realize that *my sins, in this respect, have been very great, and of long continuance,* and that it has been only through your great forbearance and long suffering, and the patience of my quorum, that I have been continued in the high and responsible calling of the Apostleship to this day.

I am deeply sensible that *I have greatly sinned against you,* and *against my brethren* of the school, and against God, in foolishly trying to justify myself in advancing ideas, opposed to those which have been introduced by the highest authorities of the Church, *and adopted by the Saints.* I humbly ask you and the school to forgive me. Hereafter, through the grace of God assisting me, I am determined to be one with you, and never be found opposing anything that comes through the legitimate order of the Priesthood, knowing that it is perfectly right for me to humbly submit, in all matters of doctrine and principle, my judgment to those whose right it is, by divine appointment to receive revelation and guide the Church.

There is no one thing in this world, or in that which is to come which I do more earnestly desire, than to honor my calling, and be permitted to retain the same, and with my brethren the Twelve, enter the Celestial Kingdom, with a full preparation to enjoy the glory thereof for ever.

In regard to all that portion of my printed writings which have come under the inspection of the highest authorities of the Church, and judged incorrect, I do most sincerely hope that the same may be rejected and considered of no value, only to point out the imperfections of the author, and to be a warning to others to be more careful. This request I made formerly, but feel to renew it again in this letter.

With *feelings of great sorrow, and deep regret for all my past sins,* I subscribe myself your humble brother in Christ.

Orson Pratt, Sen.
I certify that the above is a true copy of the original.
/s/ Martin S. Lindsay, Notary Public
Salt Lake City, Utah, March 19, 1904.

Saturday 2 p.m. 7/4/1868

Historian's Office Journal
School of the Prophets at 2 p.m. Elder O. Pratt made full confession before the School of his error in opposing doctrines revealed; ... he asked forgiveness of Prest. Young, of the Twelve and of the whole School. Prest. Young expressed his satisfaction with Elder

Pratt's confession & preached in relation to Adam &c. &c. ...

T. B. H. Stenhouse [*an apostate*]   *1873*

The Rocky Mountain Saints, 92, 492

Orson's submission was painful to his friends, but the thoughtful hoped for the growth and development of his soul outside the iron cast of infallible priesthood. From the hour of that trial *he was silently accounted an "Apostate," and for years there was considered to be no temerity in "digging" at him from the pulpit.* He was sent to Europe on mission, and treated with marked neglect by the ruling authorities - men far beneath him in moral and intellectual qualities. He bore it all in silence, and returned to Utah determined to stand by his convictions of truth against the Adam deity. His associate apostles tried to shake him out of their Quorum, and in their councils they did everything to bring his "stubbornness" to the point of disfellowship. After two weeks of nightly councils - while Brigham and his twelve were journeying through the northern settlements in 1868 - the point was reached. Orson would not, however, recant, even before the threat of disfellowship, but Brigham, at the last moment, entered the council, and arrested the final action, Brigham needs Orson's sermons of the Book of Mormon, Polygamy, and the prophecies, and he fears his influence with the people. ...

Orson Pratt, for presuming to teach a deity contrary to Brigham's Adam, was for years upon the point of being severed from the Church; at last, ten years ago, he was tried for rebellion. On that occasion - the Author well remembers it - Orson Pratt showed a manliness and Christian determination to cling to the truth, that earned for him the admiration of very soul that dared to think and love the God-given liberty of an untrammeled mind ... As the apostle stood in Brigham's little office, surrounded by the other apostles of his quorum, not a voice was heard in his support, not a word was whispered either to encourage him or relieve his racked and harrowed soul as he keenly realized the fact that he risked his apostleship and fellowship with the Church.

While the above statements provide a strong overview of this subject, they are not the only evidences that we have of Orson Pratt's doctrinal difficulties with Brigham Young - for a more general overview of the subject, along with additional sources and statements, see Dialogue 13:7-58 #2 for an article by Gary James Bergera that treats this subject quite well. It may be of interest for the reader to note that each of the doctrinal issues that got Orson Pratt into such trouble with the Quorum of the Twelve and the First Presidency have been widely and wholly accepted by the modern LDS Church, excepting the teaching that we should worship attributes rather than an individual (though it appears that Orson Pratt's teachings on this issue may have been misconstrued).

Scott
Anderson

~

Beyond the apparent issues presented below, there is nothing particularly interesting about Scott Anderson's dispute over Adam-God teachings. They are included here solely for the sake of presenting all known materials that document the disbelief of Adam-God teachings before the twentieth century.

Scott Anderson   *9/22/1884*

Letter to Pres. John Taylor

President John Taylor
Sir Duty imperatively demands that as I am about to withdraw from the Church over which you preside I make known to you and to all whom it may concern the reasons which have compelled me to take this step. When I joined the Mormon Church a little over 5 years ago I believed implicitly as I do now that the Bible was the word of God and the Rule of Faith and while the "Book of Mormon" and "Doctrine and Covenants" were referred to as additional revelation they no where contradicted the Bible but rather established it. ...
I joined your Church on the 20th of May 1879 and during the first 2 years of my membership I faithfully adhered to it and would have given my life to defend it, during all this time I never heard of Adam being God, never heard of Blood Atonement, never heard of polygamy being required of all men before they could attain to highest glory. Never dreamed that Brigham Young or any one else cooly threw the Bible overboard and preached whatever they pleased which I was bound to accept as the revelations of God. I do not and cannot accuse these men of having told my anything absolutely false, but they certainly withheld the horrible I was in the Church some five years before I heard or knew anything about these things - doctrines against which my soul revolts. ...

I imagined that I had come to the kingdom of God to help to build it up! What did I find? I found that God, the God of the Bible is not even worshiped by the Church over which you preside, the God you worship is Adam. Brigham Young teaches I quote his words, "When our Father Adam came into the Garden of Eden, he came into it with a celestial body and brought Eve one of his wives with him. He is our Father and our God and the ONLY God with whom we have to do." At first I could not bring myself to believe that this doctrine was accepted by the Church, but on careful enquiry found to my horror and astonishment that it was really so. It is true a great many know nothing about it and are simply in ignorance. Those who do know accept it as far more to be relied on than any portion of the Bible, for say they the Bible has been translated over and over again and may be wrong but this is the direct teaching of a Great Prophet. As I have shown *Adam is made God* but you do not give him much power or rather leave him much for you do teach that he has given you the power to wield, that however matters little you hold it and he has parted with it. that is my point you teach that. If a faithful son of Adam's is called behind the vail and has no priesthood God (Adam) cannot give him any. He must wait until he gets it from the earth where you have all the power. If he has no wife or wives (and you teach that he must have at least three or he cannot have the highest glory) God (Adam) is utterly unable to help him You have the keys and he must wait your leisure and pleasure. In fact you teach that you have the power to make a God "who shall pass by the angels and the Gods" whereas God according to Mormonism can only make an angel (servant) and scarcely that without your permission. This to me is a mockery and silly superstition and I unhesitatingly reject it. I know many members of your Church whose sincerity to do not doubt and who are very good people. But generally speaking I never saw so much hypocrisy in my life as I have seen since I came to Salt Lake City. …

I now request you to erase my name from your books, and only add in conclusion that I have had no quarrel, no dispute, no misunderstanding with any member of your Church. I leave it from conviction and at the call of duty well persuaded that I can meet you or any member of the Church over which you preside at the bar of God and look you in the face before him as an honest man

Yours respectfully,
Scott Anderson

Tuesday p.m. 1/20/1885

Minutes of a Bishops Court. Eleventh Ward School House
Prayer was offered by Counselor Joseph H. Felt. The following charge was read. Salt Lake City, Jany 17th 1885 Bishop Alexander McRae

Dear Brother

We the undersigned prefer a charge against Brother Scott Anderson for Apostasy, and ask that you appoint as early a date as practicable for the hearing of the complaint; as we understand he is preparing to leave the City permanently. Your Brethren in the Gospel. Mark Barnes Thomas Simons John Sears

Brother Scott Anderson being present. Bishop A. McRae asked him whether he was guilty of the charge or not.

Bro. Anderson said "If my not being in accord with all things in the Church makes me guilty, then I am guilty."

Bp. McRae. Do you still hold to the sentiments expressed in your letter to Prest Taylor. (copy of same accompanies this)

Bro Anderson said, That portion that alludes to doctrine I still adhere to but not to that referring to persons.[270]

Bp. McRae said It is in consequence of the statement you made in your letter to Prest Taylor dissenting from the Church of the Latter Day Saints that we have cited you to appear before us here tonight you being a member of this Ward it is our duty to inquire into the matter.

Bro Anderson said I have no desire to enter into any controversy, but will say that since being in Salt Lake I have been treated with the greatest of courtesy and kindness by both man woman and child: do not wish to enter into any details; except that if I was in the Bishops place I should do as he is doing in a similar case.

Bishop A. McRae said Our decision is that you be disfellowshipped from the Church of Jesus Christ of Latter Day Saints for apostasy.

Brother Anderson said "he anticipated that such would be the case and immediately left the house.

Alexander McRae Bp. 11th Ward Joseph H. Felt Counselors Robt. Morris Per John Coulam Clerk

---

Scott Anderson   *1885*

History of Wels August Nelson, 41

The first question for me to solve was regarding my future inheritance. I had heard preached varied thoughts, but they did not give a logical connection. My wife and I had read the scriptures together, but still I was not satisfied.

One morning about three or four, a vision of the pre-existence, and the future was

---

[270] Note that he had attacked the integrity of John Taylor and other members of the Church in his previous letter - while closing his letter with the statement that he was "well persuaded" that he could meet "any member of the Church … at the bar of God and look [them] in the face … as an honest man."

shown me. It was all so clear. My parents were my brother and sister. They were simply a medium in helping God (which is Adam) in bringing his children from the spirit to the mortal stage. This is necessary that we might have the opportunity to being celestial beings like the Father. If I could so conduct myself in this stage of action, to be worthy of the celestial kingdom with eternal increase, then and only then, would I gain an inheritance of my own to be as a Father Adam, and my wife, a mother Eve. Failing this I would forever inherit in connection with others of my brethren and sisters, one of the three glories eternally without increase, hence no need of an individual inheritance. Perfection and Celestial Glory of God are definite terms, the end of all human attainment. While we become fathers and grandparents a hundred times in this world, the highest possible attainment is celestial glory with eternal increase.

I know the Redeemer to be the senior of Adam, where or from whence the Prototype provides Redeemers for each planet, is not material to us in this sphere of action. All intelligence comes from the Prototype. There is not intelligence where or beyond the first (first in inconceivable) intelligible. God is not eternally progressing in the sense that we understand it. He is the same today and forever, unchangeable. He is forever increasing in heirs and worlds numerically, but one eternal circle intelligently. With this information I asked the Lord to send my way all the experiences necessary for me to attain an individual inheritance, which in itself includes eternal increase and Godhood.

Edward
~ # Bunker

11/8/1890 - 5/22/1890

Manuscript History of St. George Stake

High Council of St. George Stake met in St. George Tabernacle, Pres. Ivins stated that he had learned that Father Edward Bunker, of Bunkerville in this Stake had been teaching that some of the ceremonies of the Temple were wrong and erroneous teaching was given in the lecture at the vail. As Elder Myron Abbott, first Councilor to the Bishop at Bunkerville had given some information on this matter, it was decided to learn from him, more definitely in (next page) relation to this matter.

December 13, 1890

Saturday, Dec. 13. High Council of St. George Stake met at St. George Tabernacle. In response to invitation of the Presidency of the Stake, Bishop Edward Bunker, Jr., and Elders Myron Abbott and Jos. I. Earl were present. Pres. McArthur invited the brethren named to express themselves on the views said to have been expressed in Bunkerville Ward and which are considered by some to be unsound doctrine. Myron Abbott, counselor to Bishop Edward Bunker, Jr., stated that for a number of years, questions on church teachings have been agitated in Bunkerville Ward. Bishop Bunker had stated he did not believe Adam was our God, and Bishop Bunker had expressed his opinion that some teachings in the Temples were wrong, notably part of the lecture at the vail. That Father Bunker had the same views. Father Bunker stated to him (Bro. Abbott) a number of years ago, that adoption would be of no avail as administered in the Temple. All such work would have to be done over again. Bp. Edward Bunker, Jr., among other things said: "In regard to the lecture at the vail, in the Temple, it is certainly wrong. It teaches that Eve was an immortal being and was brought here by Adam, 'did not believe this.' That Adam was not a resurrected (next page) being. In answering question of Councilor Cannon, expressed his belief that Adam was the Archangel and that Jehovah and Michael were persons of Spirit; that Eloheim was a person of Tabernacle and the head of all." After a prolonged second session of the Council, Bp. Edward Bunker and his councilor, Myron Abbott felt that they had done wrong in contending on the subjects referred to.

May 15, 1891

Friday, May 15. The High Council of St. George Stake took up the case of Edward Bunker Sr., of Bunkerville Ward, who had been charged with erroneous views and teachings. Father Bunker's views were brought (next page) to the attention of High Council on the 13th of last December. Since then Father Bunker expressed a desire to submit his views to the Council in writing. This was granted resulting in a statement bearing date "Bunkerville, April 25, 1891 and submitted on ten pages of foolscap. After reading the document and discussion on the case Council decided "that the communication of Edward Bunker on what he believes and does not believe, together with the statement of the causes leading to the investigation which called forth is declaration, also the full action of the Council in this matter be forwarded to the First Presidency of the Church, asking their advice to the proper course for us to take, as the Presidency and High Council of this Stake." Councilor David H. Cannon moved that the Presidency of the Stake with Councilor James G. Bleak and the clerk of the High Council act as a committee to formulate this statement, carried.

May 22, 1891

Friday, May 22. The following was prepared and subsequently approved by the High Council and forwarded to the First Presidency:

"St. George, May 22, 1891.

To Pres. Wilford Woodruff and Councilors;

Brethren:

For some years there has existed a spirit of division on doctrinal points and Church teachings in Bunkerville Ward, this Stake of Zion. It was thought by the gentle corrections and teachings of the Stake Presidency to certain of the disputants, that division would gradually die out and be overcome. Such, we regret to state, has not been the case. Finding the evidences of this division more and more manifest, it was reported to the High Council here at its meeting in November last. By action of the Presidency and High Council, the chief parties to the division were invited to meet with us in council that we might learn more definitely their views. At our high Council in December last in response to this invitation, Bishop Edward Bunker, Jr. and his councilors Myron Abbott and Jos. I. Earl met with us. Father Edward Bunker being in poor health at the time, could not attend. Bishop Bunker and his first councilor Myron Abbott, who is also his uncle, being representatives of the diverse and unreconciled views prevailing in the Ward, stated some of their respective differences of belief and teachings. Upon hearing these brethren it was found that they were each most pronounced in their respective views. (next page)

As a result of the investigation the following was passed as the action of the Council: It is the sense of this Council that it is an error to teach that Adam was not an immortal or resurrected being, when he came to this earth, also, that we pray to Adam as our God; and it is wrong to teach that Adam is one of the Godhead.

Father Edward Bunker was present at High Council in March last, and asked the privilege of expressing his views in writing, upon doctrines and teachings referred to in the December High Council meeting. This was granted. "The written statement has been presented to, and read in, the High Council and the Council has decided to submit it and this whole matter to you." This statement enclosed herewith, sets forth the points upon which the division in Bunkerville Ward is based and we submit it to you with a desire to receive instruction as to what you wish with us as a Presidency and High Council to do in this matter. There is one thing more: You will notice in the beginning of Father Bunker's statement declaring his views relating to Adam, he uses the words: "That the Council has decided upon as I believe." The only Council action in deciding anything about the points in controversy is embodied in the d action of the Council found at the bottom of page two of this letter. Awaiting your instruction, or decision in this matter.

We remain, dutifully yours,
/s/ DANIEL D P. MCARTHUR,
/s/ A. W. IVINS, Per D. D. MC.A.
/s/ ERASTUS B. SNOW

Wilford W. Woodruff & George Q. Cannon	_6/11/1892_

Wilford Woodruff Journal

We met in the tabernacle at 10 o'clock on the trial of Bishop Bunker on doctrine. We talked to them plainly on the impropriety of indulging in mysteries to create difficulties among the Saints.

Wilford W. Woodruff & George Q. Cannon	_6/11/1892_

Charles L. Walker Journal 2:740-41

St George June 11th, 92 Attended the High Council at which Pres Woodruff presided. G. Q. Cannon was present also and a large body of the leading men of this Stake. Br Edward Bunker Sen. and others of Bunkerville, Nevada, had been advancing false doctrine. One item was, that he, Bunker, thought it was right to worship the intelligence that was in God the Eternal Father and not God, who made all things by the power of his Word. And another was that Adam was made of the dust of the earth contained in the Garden of Eden. He had also advanced some erroneous ideas concerning the resurrection.

Pres Woodruff and Cannon showed in a very plain manner that it was right to Worship the true, and the Living God, and Him only, and not the intelligence that dwelt in Him; that His Son Jesus Christ, or Jehovah, never taught such doctrine, but always to worship my Father which is in Heaven, and to always pray to the Father in the name of his Son Jesus Christ. Showed that Adam was an immortal being when he came to this earth and was made the same as all other men and Gods are made; and that the seed of man was of the dust of the earth, and that the continuation of the seeds in a glorified state was Eternal Lives. And after this Mortal tabernacle had crumbled to dust in the grave, that God would, in the time of the resurrection by his Matchless Power, bring together again in the form of a glorified and an immortal to the Righteous to dwell with Him forever. Also that those that were not righteous would also be resurrected, but not with a glorified body. Said it was not wisdom for the Elders to contend about such matters and things they did not understand. And not to teach such things to the children in the Sunday Schools; they could not comprehend them.

Pres Woodruff spoke of the false doctrine taught by Amasa Lyman some years ago, viz, that the Atoning blood of Jesus Christ was of no more efficacy than the blood of any other man or that of a Bullock &c. Such false ideas had led him to apostasy and finally out of the church. Also of the false teachings of the late Orson Pratt, one of the Twelve, arguing that every particle of matter which composed the elements had all the attributes of the Deity in it, and that they, i.e., the particles of Matter, by some unaccountable way united together and became God. Pres Woodruff told of Orson's unyielding stubbornness, and of upbraiding the Twelve for not being manly, for not declaring their views the way he looked at it, and branding them as cowards &c &c. Spoke of the firmness of Pres Young in correcting Orson Pratt and setting him aright; Of Orson wishing to resign his position in the Quorum; of Pres. Young saying "No you wont Orson, I'll rub your ears until I get you right;" and had it not been for firmness of Pres Young in maintaining the right, and assiduously laboring and showing him his gross errors, Orson would have been out of the Church.

Showed the folly of some men because they cannot look up and prove by the Bible the glorious Revelations that God has given they receive them doubtfully. Showed that God had, and would yet, reveal many glorious things that men could not prove, and Search out of the old Bible.

Pres Cannon said that it was not necessary that we should or endorse the doctrine that some men taught that Adam was the Father of Jesus Christ. Counsel was given for the Elders to teach that which they knew, not that which they did not. The Meeting was in session over three hours, and much good counsel was given to the Elders present on these things by Pres Woodruff and Cannon. To me it was a feast for I had been pondering over some of these things of late.

Saturday June 11, 1892

Manuscript History of St. George Stake

High Council of St. George Stake convened at 10 A.M. in St. George Tabernacle. Pres. Daniel D. McArthur Presiding. The Council was favored with the presence of Pres. Wilford Woodruff and his first counselor, Pres. Geo. Q. Cannon. The case of disagreement on points of doctrine between brethren of Bunkerville Ward was called up. Father Edward Bunker and others from Bunkerville Ward were present[.] Elder Arthur Winter, clerk of the First Presidency, then read Father Edward Bunker's views on doctrinal points, written April 25, 1891 and forwarded to the First Presidency by St. George Stake Presidency pursuant to action of St. George Stake High Council on May 15, 1891. (See "Annals, 1891" pp. 14-17 inclusive) (next page) The result of this investigation was that all the Bunkerville parties became reconciled to each other on the points which they had been agitating for a long time and which had engendered bitter feelings between them.

Saturday 10:00 a.m. 6/11/1892

Journal of J. D. T McAllister, 99

attended High Council. Presidents Woodruff and Cannon present. The doctrine preached, and contended for by Father Edward Bunker of Bunkerville Ward, was investigated condemned and Father Bunker set right. It was a nice time. Much instruction was given by the First Presidency present.

Edward Bunker   *2/9/1902*

President Joseph F Smith

Dear Bro.

One of our recently returned missionary from the North Western States is advicating [sic] the Doctorn [sic] that *Adam is the very eternal Father in the Godhead* and the Father of Jesus Christ and that Pres Kelch so taught the Elders in that mission. I say the Doctorn is Faulse and while every Person enjoying the spirit of the Lord may know of a Doctorn whether it is true or faulse; but that they have no right (Except the President of the Church) to advance any Doctorn not clearly set forth and defined in the written Law, and in doing so they stand on dangerous ground, and until we are able to live up to the reveled Law in the spirit thereof, can we hope to enjoy suficient of the spirit of the Lord to understand fully the plan of life and salvation. As a Bp my position cared if not where in am I in error. Your answer through the meidim of the Juvenil instructor or other wise will be greatly apreasiated by your Brothr in the Gospel.

Edw Bunker Jr

For further discussion and information on Edward Bunker, see AGM, 215-38.

Important Accounts

β

The following accounts are listed in chronological order. The following accounts are here for various reasons; one account is provided because it offers an authoritative and magnificent overview of Adam-God teachings (Brigham Young's October 8, 1854 Discourse); one account is here because of its historical importance (JD 1:50-51[271]); another accounts is here because of its deep theological importance (Lecture at the Veil[272]); other accounts are included here simply because they are lengthy and ought to be read in context instead of in piecemeal fashion as they are cited in other places in this volume; and another accounts is here because it gives us a glimpse into Joseph's beliefs about Adam-God teachings and sheds some insight into Joseph's understanding of who God was (Joseph's First Vision). As a whole, these accounts teach virtually every important concept outlined within this volume and give the reader the opportunity to review Adam-God teachings within a very few pages.

---

[271] This is the first and most cited public proclamation of Adam as God.

[272] The fact that Adam-God teachings were once a part of the temple endowment gives Adam-God teachings significant theological credibility.

36 Joseph's First Vision

Craig Tholson's Adam-God book raised some questions as to *who* appeared to Joseph Smith in the spring of 1820. Unlike the majority of fundamentalist authors, Tholson graciously left a trail of the resources that he used to reach his creative conclusion. Professor Allen, cited in Tholson's book, has also made some very interesting statements about Joseph's first vision that somewhat substantiated Tholson's conclusions. After largely completing this volume, I retraced Tholson's steps, researched other resources, and considered his conclusions in light of this new information. The following compilation of materials and subsequent analysis is the result of that research along with my response to Tholson's and Allen's conclusions.

The reader may note that this subsection is not strictly chronological like most subsections of *Understanding Adam-God Teachings*; I have placed all of Joseph's first hand accounts first (in chronological order) and then the second hand accounts (in chronological order). I have arranged this information in this fashion because I believe that some of Joseph's accounts, even though they are chronologically further removed than some other accounts, should be more reliable than second hand accounts. From an academic perspective, this is usually not a prudent decision. However, in this particular case, I am assuming that, given the magnitude of this event, Joseph would not have forgotten the crucial detail of who appeared to him and therefore, his first hand accounts as to who appeared to him ought to be extremely reliable no matter how historically far removed his accounting of the visit was from the actual event. Lastly, these accounts are not complete – they reflect only the portions of accounts given where the appearance of beings to Joseph is described. Therefore, his struggle with the adversary previous to seeing the vision, his subsequent feelings, and his impressions of the vision are not included in the following materials.

Joseph Smith   *11/27/1832*

UR 2:3; DJJS, 5-6[273]

[T]hat being Seeketh such to worship him as worship him in Spirit and in truth. Therefore, I cried unto the Lord for mercy for there was none else to whom I could go and obtain mercy and the *Lord* heard my cry in the wilderness and while in the attitude of calling upon the *Lord* in the 16th year of my age, a pillar of light above the brightness of the sun at noon day came down from above and rested upon me and I was filled with the Spirit of God. And the *Lord* opened the heavens upon me and I saw the *Lord*; and he spake unto me saying,

"Joseph *my Son*,[274] thy sins are forgiven thee. Go thy way, walk in my statutes and keep my commandments. Behold I am the *Lord* of glory; *I was crucified* for the world that all those who believe on my name may have Eternal Life. Behold the world lieth in sin at this time and none doeth good, no not one. They have turned aside from the Gospel and keep not my commandments. They draw near to me with their lips while their hearts are far from me and mine anger is kindling against the inhabitants of the earth, to visit them according to their ungodliness and to bring to pass that which hath been spoken by the mouth of the prophets and apostles. Behold and lo, *I come quickly* as it [is] written of me in the cloud, clothed in the glory of *my Father*."

And my soul was filled with love and for many days I could rejoice with great joy; and the *Lord* was with me, but [I] could find none that would believe the heavenly vision. Nevertheless I pondered these things in my heart.

Joseph Smith   *11/--/1835*

UR 2:6-7; Papers JS 1:125-27

Being thus perplexed in mind I retired to the silent grove and there bowed down before the *Lord*, under a realizing sense, (if the Bible be true) ask and you shall receive, knock and it shall be opened, seek and you shall find, And again, if any man lack wisdom, let [him ask] of *God* who giveth to all men liberally and upbraideth not. Information was what I most desired at this time, and with a fixed determination to obtain it, I called on the *Lord* for the first time in the place above stated, or in other words, I made a fruitless attempt to pray. My tongue seemed to be swollen in my mouth, so that I could not utter. I heard a noise behind me like someone walking towards me. I strove again to

---

[273] This was written by Joseph Smith himself.

[274] Either, this is the father speaking - and therefore this statement supports the teaching of the Royal Order of Saviors as described in the subsection thusly entitled - because the same personage goes on to say that he was crucified, or Jesus is declaring Joseph Smith to be his son - though he does not inform Joseph if this is to be literally understood or not.

pray, but could not; the noise of walking seemed to draw nearer; I sprang upon my feet and looked round, but saw no person or thing that was calculated to produce the noise of walking. I kneeled again, my mouth was opened and my tongue loosed; I called on the *Lord* in mighty prayer. A pillar of fire appeared above my head; which presently rested down upon me, and filled me with unspeakable joy. *A personage* appeared in the midst of this pillar of flame, which was spread all around and yet nothing consumed. *Another personage* soon appeared like unto the first: he said unto me "Thy sins are forgiven thee".[275]

He testified also unto me that *Jesus Christ is the Son of God.*[276] I saw *many angels* in this vision. I was about 14 years old when I received this first communication.[277]

Joseph Smith	*3/1/1842*

T&S 3:7; Wentworth Letter
Believing the word of God I had confidence in the declaration of James: "If any man lack wisdom let him ask of God who giveth all men liberally and upbraideth not and it shall be given him," I retired to a secret place in a grove and began to call upon the *Lord*, while fervently engaged in supplication my mind was taken away from the objects with which I was surrounded, and I was enwrapped in a heavenly vision, And [I] saw *two glorious personages* who exactly resembled each other in features, and likeness, surrounded with a brilliant light which eclipsed the sun at noonday. They told me that all religious denominations were believing in incorrect doctrines, and that none of them was acknowledged of *God* as his Church and Kingdom. And I was expressly commanded to "go not after them," at the same time receiving a promise that the Fulness of the Gospel should at some future time be made known unto me.

Joseph Smith	*3/15/1842*[278]

UR 2:26-27; Papers JS 1:270-73
At length I came to the conclusion that I must either remain in darkness and confusion, or else I must do as James directs, that is, ask of *God*. I at length came to the determination to "ask of *God*," concluding that if He gave wisdom to them that lacked wisdom, and would give liberally, and not upbraid, I might venture. So in accordance

---

[275] cf. 1832 account where Jesus (?) forgives his sins.

[276] John 8:14.

[277] This appears to be his accurate age at the time of the vision as 12/15/1805 was his birthday and this vision happened in the spring of 1820.

[278] This was originally dictated in 1838; Tholson's analysis treated this document as of the date of its publication - which is generally a good academic choice - but forgetting when it was originally dictated in this instance helped lead him to an incorrect analysis.

with this my determination, to ask of *God*, I retired to the woods to make the attempt.
It was on the morning of a beautiful clear day, early in the *spring of eighteen hundred and
twenty*. It was the first time in my life that I had made such an attempt, for amidst all
my anxieties I had never as yet made the attempt to pray vocally. After I had retired
into the place where I had previously designed to go, having looked around me and
finding myself alone, I kneeled down and began to offer up the desires of my heart to
God. I had scarcely done so when immediately I was seized upon by some power which
entirely overcame me, and had such astonishing influence over me as to bind my tongue
so that I could not speak. *Thick darkness gathered around me* and it seemed to me for a
time as if I were doomed to sudden destruction.

But exerting all my powers to call upon *God* to deliver me out of the power of this
enemy which had seized upon me, and at the very moment when I was ready to sink
into despair and abandon myself to destruction, not to an imaginary ruin, but to the
power of some actual being from the unseen world who had such a marvelous power as
I had never before felt in any being. Just at this moment of great alarm, I saw a pillar of
light exactly over my head, above the brightness of the sun, which descended gradually
until it fell upon me. It no sooner appeared that I found myself delivered from the
enemy which held me bound. When the light rested upon me I saw *two personages*
(whose brightness and glory defy all description) standing above me in the air. One of
them spake unto me, calling me by name, and said (pointing to the other,)
"*This my beloved son*, hear him."

Joseph Smith   *6/11/1843*
WJS, 215; Levi Richard's Diary
Pres. J. Smith bore testimony to the same[279] saying that when he was a youth he began
to think about these things but could not find out which of all the sects were right he
went into the grove & enquired of *the Lord* which of all the sects were right he received
for answer that none of them were right, that they were all wrong, & that the
Everlasting Covenant was broken.

Joseph Smith   *9/15/1843*
UR 2:38; Papers JS 1461
I just determined I'd ask him. I immediately went out into the woods where my father
had a clearing and went to the stump where I had stuck my axe when I had quit work,
and I kneeled down and prayed saying,
"O *Lord*, what Church shall I join?"

---

[279] Matthew 23:37-38.

Directly I saw a light and then *a glorious personage* in the light, and *then another personage.*
And *the first personage* said to the second,
"*Behold my beloved Son*, hear him." -
I then addressed this *second person* saying, "O *Lord*, what Church shall I join?"
He replied "Don't join any of them, they are all corrupt."
The vision then vanished and when I came to myself I was sprawling on my back and it
was some time before my strength returned.

Orson Pratt   *1840*

UR 2:14-15

He therefore retired to a secret place in a grove but a short distance from his father's
house and knelt down and began to call upon the *Lord*. At first he was severely tempted
by the powers of darkness which endeavored to overcome him; but he continued to
seek for deliverance until darkness gave way from his mind and he was enabled to pray
in fervency of the spirit and in faith. And while thus pouring out his soul, anxiously
desiring an answer from *God*, he at length saw a very bright and glorious light in the
heavens above, which at first seemed to be at a considerable distance. He continued
praying while the light appeared to be gradually descending towards him; and as it drew
nearer it increased in brightness and magnitude, so that by the time that it reached the
tops of the trees, the whole wilderness for some distance around was illuminated in a
most glorious and brilliant manner. He expected to have seen the leaves and boughs of
the trees consumed as soon as the light came in contact with them; but perceiving that
it did not produce that effect, *he was encouraged with the hope of being able to endure its
presence.* It continued descending slowly until it rested upon the earth and he was
enveloped in the midst of it. When it first came upon him, it produced a peculiar
sensation throughout his whole system; and immediately his mind was caught away
from the natural objects with which he was surrounded; And he was enwrapped in a
heavenly vision and saw *two glorious personages* who exactly resembled each other in their
features or likeness. He was informed that his sins were forgiven. He was also
informed upon the subjects which had for some time previously agitated his mind, Viz.
- That all the religious denominations were believing in incorrect doctrines and
consequently that none of them was acknowledged of *God* as his Church and Kingdom.
And he was expressly commanded to go not after them; And he received a promise
that the true doctrine - the Fullness of the Gospel, should at some future time be made
known to him; After which the vision withdrew leaving his mind in a state of calmness
and peace indescribable.[280]

---

[280] Note that this account largely copies the verbiage of the 1842 account.

A Cry From the Wilderness, A Voice From the Dust of the Earth

He accordingly commenced persuing the sacred pages of the Bible with sincerity, believing the things that he read. His mind soon caught hold of the following passage - "If any of you lack wisdom, let him ask of God, that giveth to all men liberally and upbraideth not; and it shall be given him."- James 1:5. From this promise, he learned that it was the privilege of all men to ask God for wisdom, with the sure and certain expectation of receiving liberally, without being upbraided for so doing. And thus he started to send the burning desires of his soul with a faithful determination. He, therefore, retired to a secret place, in a grove, but a short distance from his father's house, and knelt down and began to call upon the Lord. At first, he was severely tempted by the powers of darkness, which endeavored to overcome him. The adversary benighted his mind with doubts, and brought to his soul all kinds of improper pictures and tried to hinder him in his efforts and the accomplishment of his goal. However, the overflowing mercy of God came to buoy him up, and gave new impulse and momentum to his dwindling strength. Soon the dark clouds disappeared, and light and peace filled his troubled heart. And again he called upon the Lord with renewed faith and spiritual strength. At this sacred moment his mind was caught away from the natural objects with which he was surrounded, and he was enwrapped in a heavenly vision, and saw *two glorious personages, who exactly resembled each other in their features or likeness.* They told him that his prayers had been answered, and that the Lord had decided to grant him a special blessing. He was told not to join any of the religious sects or any party, as they were all wrong in their doctrines and none of them was recognized by *God* as *His Church and kingdom.* He received a promise that the true doctrine - the fullness of the gospel - should, at some future time, be made known to him; after which, the vision withdrew, leaving his mind in a state of calmness and peace indescribable.

Pittsburg Gazette

[Joseph said] The *Lord* does reveal himself to me. I know it. He revealed himself first to me when I was about fourteen years old, a mere boy. I will tell you about it. There was a reformation among the different religious denominations in the neighborhood where I lived, and I became serious, and was desirous to know what Church to join. While thinking of this matter, I opened the Testament promiscuously on these words, in James, Ask of the Lord who giveth to all men liberally and upbraideth not. I just determined I'd ask him. I immediately went out into the woods where my father had a clearing, and went to the stump where I had stuck my axe when I had quit work, and I kneeled down, and prayed, saying, O *Lord*, what Church shall I join? Directly I saw a light, and then *a glorious personage* in the light, *and then another personage*, and the *first* personage said to the *second*, Behold my beloved *Son*, hear him. - I then addressed this *second* person, saying, O *Lord*, what Church shall I join? He replied, "don't join any of them, they are all corrupt." The vision then vanished, and when I came to myself, I was sprawling on my back and it was some time before my strength returned. When I went home and told the people that I had a revelation, and that all the churches were corrupt, they persecuted me, and they have persecuted me ever since.

Alexander Neibaur   *5/24/1844*

UR 2:38-39; Papers JS 1:461

[Joseph] went into the Wood to pray, kneels himself Down, his tongue was closet cleaveth to his roof [sic] - [he] could utter not a word [but] felt easier after awhile - [He] saw a fire toward heaven come near and nearer; [he] saw *a personage* in the fire [with a] light complexion, blue eyes [and] a piece of white cloth Drawn over his shoulders his right arm bear after a while *a[n]other person* came to the side of the first.
Mr. Smith then asked, must I join the Methodist church.
No, they are not my People, [they] have gone astray. There is none that Doeth good, no not one, but *this is my Beloved Son* harken ye him
the fire drew nigher, [it] Rested upon the tree[s and] enveloped him [and] comforted [him], [he] endeavored to arise but felt uncommen[ly] feeble.[281]

Brigham Young   *2/18/1855*

JD 2:170-71

[T]he Lord sent forth *His angel* to reveal the truths of heaven as in times past, even as in ancient days. This should have been hailed as the greatest blessing which could have been bestowed upon any nation, kindred, tongue, or people. ... The *messenger* did not come to an eminent divine of any of the so-called orthodoxy, he did not adopt their interpretation of the Holy Scriptures. The *Lord* did not come with the armies of heaven, in power and great glory, nor send His *messengers* panoplied with aught else than the truth of heaven, to communicate to the meek the lowly, the youth of humble origin, the sincere enquirer after the knowledge of *God*. But He did send His *angel* to this same obscure person, Joseph Smith Jun., who afterwards became a Prophet, Seer, and Revelator, and informed him that he should not join any of the religious sects of the

---

[281] Note that Neibaur apparently got the account backwards. A comparison shows that the personages who gave these specific pieces of information are reversed in Neibaur's account.

day, for they were all wrong; that they were following the precepts of men instead of the *Lord Jesus*; that *He* had a work for him to perform, inasmuch as he should prove faithful before *Him*.

Wilford W. Woodruff 2/25/1855

JD 2:196-97

That same organization and Gospel that Christ died for, and the Apostles spilled their blood to vindicate, is again established in this generation. How did it come? By the ministering of *an holy angel from God*, out of heaven, who held converse with man, and *revealed unto him the darkness that enveloped the world*, and unfolded unto him the gross darkness that surrounded the nations, those scenes that should take place in this generation, and would follow each other in quick succession, even unto the coming of the Messiah. The *angel taught Joseph Smith those principles which are necessary for the salvation of the world*; and the *Lord* gave him commandments, and sealed upon him the Priesthood, and gave him power to administer the ordinances of the house of the *Lord*. He told him the Gospel was not among men, and that there was not a true organization of His kingdom in the world, that the people had turned away from His true order, changed the ordinances, and broken the everlasting covenant, and inherited lies and things wherein their was no profit. He told him the time had come to lay the foundation for the establishment of the Kingdom of *God* among men for the last time, preparatory to the winding up scene. Joseph was strengthened by the Spirit and power of God, and was enabled to listen to the teachings of the *angel*.[282] He told him he should be made an instrument in the hands of the *Lord*, if he kept *His* commandments, in doing a good work upon the earth, that his name should be held in honor by the honest in heart, and in dishonor throughout the nations by the wicked. He told him he should be an instrument in laying the foundation of a work that should gather tens of thousands of the children of men, in the generation in which he lived, from every nation under heaven, who should hear the sound of it through his instrumentality. He told him the nations were wrapt in wickedness and abomination, and that the judgments of God were ready to be poured out upon them in their fulness; that the angels were holding the vials of His wrath in readiness; but the decree is, that they shall not be poured out until the nations are warned, that they may be left without an excuse.

This man to whom the *angel* appeared obeyed the Gospel; he received it in meekness and humility, and bowed down before the *Lord* and worshipped *Him*, and did the best he could in his illiterate state; he was as it were but a mere plow-boy. He laid hold of it with all his heart, though he saw he would have to wage war with sin, and wickedness,

---

[282] Notice that Wilford W. Woodruff here refers to more than one being that teaches Joseph Smith and yet he refers to them conglomerately as "the angel."

and abominations, and the oppositions of the people; he began to trust in the *Lord*; and what was the consequence? Wherever the words of the Gospel, which the *angel* revealed to him, were preached among the children of men, it had its effect.

Orson Pratt   *8/14/1859*

JD 7:220-21

He was wrought upon by the Spirit of God, and felt the necessity of repenting of his sins and serving God. He retired from his father's house a little way, and bowed himself down in the wilderness, and called upon the name of the *Lord*. He was inexperienced, and in great anxiety and trouble of mind in regard to what church he should join. He had been solicited by many churches to join with them, and he was in great anxiety to know which was right. He pleaded with the *Lord* to give him wisdom on the subject; and while he was thus praying, he beheld a vision, and saw a light approaching him from the heavens; and as it came down and rested on the tops of the trees, it became more glorious; and as it surrounded him, his mind was immediately caught away from beholding surrounding objects. In this cloud of light he saw *two glorious personages*; and one, pointing to the other, said,

"*Behold my beloved son*! hear ye him."

Then he was instructed and informed in regard to many things pertaining to his own welfare, and commanded not to unite himself to any of those churches. He was also informed that at some future time the fulness of the Gospel should be made manifest to him, and he should be an instrument in the hands of God of laying the foundation of the kingdom of God.

George Albert Smith   *11/15/1864*

JD 11:1-2

When the *Lord* appeared to Joseph Smith and manifested unto him a knowledge pertaining to the coming forth of the Book of Mormon and the work of the last days, Satan came also with his power and tempted Joseph. It is written in the book of Job, "Now there was a day when the sons of God came to present themselves before the Lord, and Satan came also among them." In the very commencement of this Work, the Prophet Joseph Smith was called upon to contend face to face with the powers of darkness by spiritual manifestations, and open visions, as well as with men in the flesh, stirred up by the same spirit of the adversary to hedge up his way and destroy him from the earth, and annihilate the work which he was about to commence. He thus describes the incident:[283]

---

[283] He here cites the 1842 account.

Brigham Young	6/23/1867

JD 12:67-68

When the *Lord* called upon Joseph he was but a boy - a child, only about fourteen years of age. He was not filled with traditions; his mind was not made up to this, that, or the other. ... Joseph was naturally inclined to be religious, and being young, and surrounded with this excitement, no wonder that he became seriously impressed with the necessity of serving the *Lord*. But as the cry on every hand was, "Lo, here is Christ," and "Lo, there!" Said he,
"*Lord*, teach me, that I may know for myself, who among these are right."
And what was the answer? "They are all out of the way; they have gone astray, and there is none that doeth good, no not one."
When he found out that none were right, he began to inquire of the *Lord* what was right, and he learned for himself.

Orson Pratt	10/6/1868

JD 12:302

The *Lord* revealed himself to this youth when he was between fourteen and fifteen years of age, and as soon as he related this vision, although at that young and tender age, the wrath and indignation of the people were stirred up against him.

George Albert Smith	11/15/1868

JD 12:334

He had read the Bible and had found that passage in James which says "If any of you lack wisdom let him ask of *God* that giveth to all men liberally and upbraideth not," and taking this literally, he went humbly before the *Lord* and inquired of *Him*, and the *Lord* answered his prayer and revealed to Joseph, by the *ministration of angels*, the true condition of the religious world. When the holy *angel* appeared, Joseph inquired which of all these denominations was right and which he should join, and was told they were all wrong, - they had all gone astray, transgressed the laws, changed the ordinances and broken the everlasting covenant, and that the *Lord* was about to restore the priesthood and establish *His* Church, which would be the only true and living Church on the face of the whole earth.

Orson Pratt	2/24/1869

JD 12:354-55

Now this youth, this "old Joe Smith," that we have heard so much about, was just simple enough to believe that that passage really meant what it said. He went out into a little grove near his father's house, in the town of Manchester, Ontario County, State of New York, and there he knelt down in all the simplicity of a child and prayed to the *Father* in the name of Jesus that *He* would show him which, among all the churches, was the true one.

Said he, "show me, *Father*, who are in possession of the truth, let me know, O *Lord*, the right way, and I will walk therein."

He had now come to a Person who was able to teach him. All his inquiries previously had been futile and vain, but he now applied to the right source. Did the *Lord* hear him? Yes. But he had to exercise faith. This young man, while thus praying, was not discouraged because he was tempted; but he continued praying until he overcame the powers of darkness which tried to prevent him from calling upon God. The *Lord* hearkened. Being the same *God* who lived in ancient times, *He* was able to hear and answer prayers that were offered up in this sincere manner, and *He* answered the prayers of this youth. The heavens, as it were, were opened to him, or in other words, a glorious pillar of light like the brightness of the sun appeared in the heavens above him, and approached the spot where he was praying; his eyes were fixed upon it and his heart was lifted up in prayer before the *Most High*. He saw the light gradually approaching him until it rested upon the tops of the trees. He beheld that the leaves of the trees were not consumed by it, although its brightness, apparently, was sufficient, as he at first thought, to consume everything before it. But the trees were not consumed by it, and it continued to descend until it rested upon him and enveloped him in its glorious rays. When he was thus encircled about with this pillar of fire his mind was caught away from every object that surrounded him, and he was filled with the visions of the *Almighty*, and he saw, in the midst of this glorious pillar of fire, *two glorious personages*, whose countenances shone with an exceeding great lustre. *One* of them spoke to him, saying, while pointing to the other,

"*This is my beloved Son* in whom I am well pleased, hear ye him."

Now here was a certainty; here was something that he saw and heard; here were *personages* capable of instructing him, and of telling him which was the true religion. How different this from going to an uninspired man professing to be a minister! One minute's instruction from personages clothed with the glory of *God* coming down from the eternal worlds is worth more than all the volumes that ever were written by uninspired men.

Mr. Smith, this young man, in the simplicity of his heart, continued saying to these *personages*, "which church shall I join, which is the true church?" He then and there was commanded, in the most strict manner, to go not after them, for they had all gone out of the way; he was told there was no Christian church on the face of the earth according to the ancient pattern, as recorded in the New Testament; but they had all strayed from the ancient faith and had lost the gifts and power of the Holy Ghost; they had lost the spirit of revelation and prophecy, the power to heal the sick, and every other gift and blessing possessed and enjoyed by the ancient Church. "Go not after them," was the command given to this young man; and he was told that if he would be faithful in serving the true and living *God*, it should be made manifest to him, in a time to come, the true church that God intended to establish.

Now we can see the wisdom of *God* in not revealing everything to him on that occasion. He revealed as much as Joseph was capacitated to receive. The *Lord* dealt with this young man as you, parents, do when you wish to instruct your children on any subject. You do not pour out volumes of instruction on them all at once, but impart to them according to their capacity. Just so the *Lord* acted towards this youth. He imparted enough to let him know that the whole Christian world was without authority, as we heard this forenoon.

George Albert Smith   *6/20/1869*
JD 13:77-78

He spent much time in prayer and reflection and in seeking *the Lord*. He was led to pray upon the subject in consequence of the declaration of the Apostle James: "If any of you lack wisdom, let him ask of God that giveth to all men liberally and upbraideth not." [James 1:5] He sought the *Lord* by day and by night, and was enlightened by the vision of *an holy angel*. When *this personage* appeared to him, one of his first inquiries was, "Which of the denominations of Christians in the vicinity was right?"

He was told they had all gone astray, they had wandered into darkness, and that *God* was about to restore the Gospel in its simplicity and purity to the earth; he was, consequently, directed not to join any one of them, but to be humble and seek the *Lord* with all his heart, and that from time to time he should be taught and instructed in relation to the right way to serve the *Lord*.

Orson Pratt   *12/19/1869*
JD 13:65-66

By and by an obscure individual, a young man, rose up, and, in the midst of all Christendom, proclaimed the startling news that *God* had sent *an angel* to him; that through his faith, prayers, and sincere repentance he had beheld a supernatural vision, that he had seen a pillar of fire descend from Heaven, and saw *two glorious personages* clothed upon with this pillar of fire, whose countenance shone like the sun at noonday; that he heard *one of these personages* say, pointing to the other,
"*This is my beloved Son*, hear ye him."

This occurred before this young man was fifteen years of age... .

JD 14:140-41

[Joseph] went out to pray, being then a little over fourteen years of age, in a little grove not far from his father's house. The great object which he had in praying was to learn some few principles, which he saw were absolutely necessary to know, according to his understanding, in order to serve the true and living *God*. He desired to know which, among all the denominations with which he was surrounded, was the true church.
It is not often that boys of this age would be so exercised, but this was the fact in regard to Joseph Smith. ... He happened to fall upon a certain passage contained in the Book of James, "If any man lack wisdom let him ask *of God*, who giveth liberally and upbraideth not." This passage, when he read it, seemed to *sink with great weight upon his mind*. He thought it was his privilege to go to *the Lord* and ask him respecting the desired information. As I told you before, he had not been trained up in any of the creeds of the existing denominations, and therefore he was confiding enough to believe what was here written, "If any man lack wisdom," &c. He thought to himself that he did lack wisdom, for he did desire to know which was the true church. He went into the grove with a determination to claim this promise. When he was thus praying he saw a light which appeared to be approaching him from the heavens. As it came nearer it seemed to grow brighter until it settled upon the tops of the trees. He thought it would consume the leaves of the trees; but it gradually descended and rested upon him. His mind was immediately caught away. He saw in this light *two glorious personages*, one of whom spoke to him, pointing to the other, saying,
"*This is my beloved Son*, hear ye him."
This was a glorious vision given to this boy. When t*hese persons* interrogated him to know what he desired, he answered and said,
"*Lord* show me which is the true church."
He was then informed by *one of these personages* that there was no true church upon the face of the whole earth; that the whole Christian world, for many generations, had been in apostacy; that they had denied communication and revelation from heaven; denied the administration of angels; denied the power that was in the ancient church that comes through the gift of the Holy Ghost, and gave him much instruction upon this point, but did not see proper upon that occasion to give him a full knowledge of the Gospel, and what was necessary to constitute a true church, and gave him some few commandments to govern him in future time, with a promise that if he would abide the same and call upon his name, that the day would come when the Lord would reveal to him still further, making manifest what was necessary to the constitution of the true church. The vision withdrew; *the personages* attending and the light withdrew. ... He

was expressly commanded in the vision to unite himself to none of these churches. ...
yet he knew that *God* had manifested himself to him; he could not be persuaded to the
contrary, any more than Paul could when he heard Jesus in his first vision.

Orson Pratt   *9/22/1872*

JD 15:181-82

But unpopular as it was, this youth ventured to go and ask the *Lord* for wisdom, having,
in the first place, read a passage in the New testament, which says, "If any man lack
wisdom let him ask of *God*, who giveth to all liberally and upbraideth not, and it shall be
given unto him." Joseph Smith was not so full of tradition that he could not lay hold of
this promise. I do not know that he had been taught long enough, the idea that the *Lord*
would not hear prayer. At any rate, having read this passage, he prayed, really
believing in his heart that the *Lord* would answer him, for he wanted wisdom, he
wanted to know which was the true Christian Church, that he might be united with it;
and while pleading with and praying to the *Lord* for this information, which was a
matter of great concern to him, the heavens were opened, and two personages clothed
in light or fire descended and stood before him. As soon as this light surrounded him,
and he was enclosed or enveloped in it, his mind was caught away from earthly objects
and things, and he saw these *two glorious personages*, their countenances shining with
exceeding great brilliancy. *One of them*, while pointing to the other, addressed him in
this language,
"*Behold my beloved son*, hear ye him."
All fear was taken from this boy during the progress of this wonderful event, and he felt
happy, but anxious to know concerning the things about which he had been praying,
and he repeated his request, that he might be told which was the true Christian church.
He was informed that there was no true Christian church on the earth, that there was
no people established or organized according to the Apostolic order; that all had gone
out of the way and had departed from the ancient order of things; that they had denied
the power of Godliness, the gifts, miracles, the spirit of revelation and prophecy,
visions, that all these things had been done away with by the unbelief of the children of
men, and that there were no prophets or inspired men on the earth, as there always had
been when there was a true Church upon the earth. He was strictly commanded to join
none of them. The *Lord* also informed him that, at some future period of time, if he
would be faithful in giving heed to the instructions which were then imparted to him,
and in his prayers to the *Lord*, he would impart to him his own doctrine in plainness and
simplicity.

JD 18:137

The ancient Patriarchs and Prophets, men of *God* who basked in the light of revelation, and comprehended the mind of *Jehovah*, and who held the everlasting Priesthood, and enjoyed the Gospel as we enjoy it; all these together with *God* our heavenly Father and all the angelic hosts, are interested in the work that the Father has commenced in these last days; and hence a revelation was made unto Joseph Smith. *Holy angels of God* appeared to him and communicated to him the mind and will of *Jehovah*, as a chosen messenger to introduce the dispensation of the fullness of times, wherein all heaven and all that have ever dwelt on the earth are concerned and interested. He did not reveal himself, particularly, because of Joseph Smith, individually, nor because of any other individual man, nor for the peculiar interest, emolument or aggrandisement of any set of men; but for the purpose of introducing certain principles that it was necessary that the world of mankind should be made acquainted with; in fact, it was for the purpose of introducing what we call the Church and kingdom of *God* on the earth, in which all who have ever lived or who ever will live upon this globe are interested.

JD 18:239

Do we believe that the *Lord* sent his *messengers* to Joseph Smith, and commanded him to refrain from joining any Christian church, and to refrain from the wickedness he saw in the churches, and finally delivered to him a message informing him that the *Lord* was about to establish his kingdom on the earth, and led him on step by step until he gave him the revelation concerning the plates? Yes, this is all correct.

JD 17:280-81

Joseph Smith generally known in the world as "Old Joe Smith," was a boy about fourteen years of age at the time the *Lord* first *revealed himself* in a very marvelous manner to him. The circumstances were these: This boy, in attending religious meetings that were held in his neighborhood, seemed to be wrought upon in a very wonderful manner, and he felt great concern in relation to the salvation of his soul. Many young people were wrought upon by the same spirit, and they commenced seeking the Lord, and professed to be converted. Among this number were several of the Smith family, who united themselves with the Presbyterians. During the progress of this revival a sort of rivalry sprang up among the various denominations, and each one seemed determined to obtain as many of the converts as possible, and have them unite with his particular religious order. This boy, Joseph Smith, was solicited and advised to unite himself with some of the religious denominations in that vicinity, but being of a reflecting turn of mind, he inquired in his own heart which among these several religious bodies was right. I presume that many of you, at some period of your existence, have been wrought upon in the same manner, because you have been anxious to join yourselves to the true church of God if you could only find which was God's church. It was not, therefore, at all strange that this young man should have these ideas passing through his mind; but how to satisfy himself he did not know. If he went to one denomination they would say, "We are right, and the others are wrong," and so said all the others. Like most boys of his age, Joseph had never read the Bible to any great extent, hence he was unable to decide in his own mind, as to which was the true church. When he saw several denominations contending one with the other, he naturally enough supposed that some of them must be wrong.

He began to search the Bible in his leisure time after his work was done upon the farm; and in perusing the New Testament, he came across a passage which is very familiar indeed to most of my hearers; the passage reads thus - If any of you lack wisdom let him ask of God, who giveth to all men liberally and upbraideth not; and it shall be given him." Mr. Smith really believed this passage. He did not read this as one would read a novel, thinking that is was all imaginary; but, from his heart, he believed that it meant what it said, and he said to himself - "I certainly lack wisdom in relation to my duty. I do not know which of these denominations is correct, and which is the church of Christ. I desire to know, with all my heart, and I will go before the Lord, and call upon his name, claiming his promise."

He therefore retired a short distance from his father's house, into a little grove of timber, and called upon the Lord, claiming this promise, desiring to know his duty and to be informed where the true Church of Christ was. While thus praying, with all his heart, he discovered in the heavens above him, a very bright and glorious light, which gradually descended towards the earth, and when it reached the tops of the trees which overshadowed him, the brightness was so great that he expected to see the leaves of the tree consumed by it; but when he saw that they were not consumed he received courage. Finally the light rested down upon and overwhelmed him in the midst of it, and his mind at the same time seemed to be caught away from surrounding objects, and he saw nothing excepting the light and *two glorious personages* standing before him in the midst of this light. *One of these personages*, pointing to the other, said -
"*Behold my beloved Son*, hear ye him."

After this, power was given to Mr. Smith to speak, and in answer to an inquiry by *the Lord* as to what he desired, he said that he desired to know which was the true Church, that he might be united thereunto. He was immediately told, that there was no true Church of Christ on the earth, that all had gone astray, and had framed doctrines, and dogmas, and creeds by human wisdom, and that the authority to administer in the holy ordinances of the Gospel was not among men upon the earth, and he was strictly commanded to go not after any of them, but to keep aloof from the whole of them. He was also informed that, in due time, if he would be faithful in serving the Lord, according to the best of his knowledge and ability, God would reveal to him still further, and make known to him the true Gospel, the plan of salvation, in its fulness. Mr. Smith had this vision before he was fifteen years old, and, immediately after receiving it, he began to relate it to some of his nearest friends, and he was told by some of the ministers who came to him to enquire about it, that there was no such thing as the visitation of *heavenly messengers,* that God gave no new revelation, and that no visions could be given to the children of men in this age. ...

Why should they feel such concern and anxiety in relation to his testimony as to persecute him, a boy not quite fifteen years of age? The reason was obvious - if that testimony was true, not one of their churches was the true Church of Christ. No wonder, then, that they began to persecute, point the finger of scorn, and say - "There goes the visionary boy."

John Taylor   *10/10/1875*
JD 18:137

Holy angels of God appeared to [Joseph] and communicated to him the mind and will of *Jehovah*, as a chosen messenger to introduce the dispensation of the fullness of times, wherein all heaven and all that have ever dwelt on the earth are concerned and interested. He did not reveal himself, particularly, because of Joseph Smith, individually, nor because of any other individual man, nor for the peculiar interest, emolument or aggrandisement of any set of men; but for the purpose of introducing certain principles that it was necessary that the world of mankind should be made acquainted with; in fact, it was for the purpose of introducing what we call the Church and kingdom of God on the earth, in which all who have ever lived or who ever will live upon this globe are interested.

John Taylor   *3/2/1879*
JD 20:167

[T]he Prophet Joseph asked *the angel* which of the sects was right that he might join it. The answer was that none of them are right. What, none of them? No. We will not stop to argue that question; *the angel* merely told him to join none of them that none of them were right.

John Taylor	12/7/1879

JD 21:161

He believed that statement and went to the *Lord* and asked him, and the *Lord* revealed *Himself* to him together with *his Son Jesus*, and, pointing to the latter, said: "*This is My Beloved Son*, hear him."

He then asked in regard to the various religions with which he was surrounded. He enquired which of them was right, for he wanted to know the right way and to walk in it. He was told that none of them was right, that they had all departed from the right way, that they had forsaken *God* the fountain of living waters, and hewed them out cisterns, broken cisterns, that could hold no water.

Orson Pratt	10/10/1880

JD 22:29

You find a little boy, Joseph Smith, calling upon the name of the *Lord*, in the spring of the year 1820 before he was not yet fifteen years of age; and the result of his calling upon the name of the *Lord* was that a pillar of fire appeared in the heavens above him, and it continued to descend and grow brighter and brighter, until it reached the top of the trees that were growing around about where he was praying; and so great was the glory of this light that this lad, this youth, this boy, seemed to feel almost fearful lest the trees themselves would be consumed by it. But it continued to descend until it rested upon this lad and immediately his mind was caught away from the surrounding objects, was swallowed up in a heavenly vision, in which he saw two glorious personages, one was the *Father*, the other was the *Son*.

George Q. Cannon	4/7/1889

MS 51:278

We worship the Being who has revealed Himself to us. It was necessary at the outset of this work to have a revelation from Him. There were many erroneous ideas about God, and the first revelation to Joseph Smith was the appearance of the Father and the Son. I have heard that there are some among us who say that both are one person. This is a fallacy. There are *two personages*, the Father and the Son. God is the Being who walked in the Garden of Eden, and who talked with the Prophets. This revelation came to us in certainty.

Brigham H. Roberts	Saturday a.m. 10/4/1890

CD 2

In the first vision of Joseph Smith, the prophet was informed *by Christ* that there were none of the sects right, but all had gone out of the way. So bold a declaration by the

youthful prophet was calculated to astonish the world. But this does not argue that
there are not thousands of people in the world whom God loves. What Joseph
declared is predicted in the scriptures, in which the Christians profess to believe.

Edward Stevenson   *circa 1890*

The Life and History, Elder Edward Stevenson, 19-23
The following year after the organization of the Pontiac [Michigan] Branch of the
Church of Jesus Christ of L. D. Saints, in 1834, we had the pleasure of having a visit
from the Prophet Joseph Smith: a plain but noble looking man, of large frame and
about 6 feet high. With him was his Father, Joseph Smith, and Oliver Cowdery, David
Whitmer and Martin Harris, whose sister Sophia Kellog lived in our settlement. A
great stir was made in this settlement at so distinguished visitors.
The meetings held were crowded to see and hear the testimonies given which were very powerful. I
will here relate my own experience on the occasion of a meeting in our log School
House. The Prophet stood at a table for the pulpit where he began relating his vision
and before he got through he was in the midst of the congregation with up lifted hand.
I do not believe that there was not one person present who did at the time being, or
who was not convicted of the truth of his vision, of *an Angel* to him his countenance
seemed to me to assume heavenly whiteness, and his voice was so peirseing and forcible
for my part it so impressed me as to become indelibly imprinted on my mind …

Andrew Jenson   *Friday p.m. 1/16/1891*

Collected Discourses 2
[A]fter attending the different revival meetings without begin able to conclude which of
the denominations was the right one for him to join, went into the woods to pray to *the
Lord* for that wisdom which the Apostle James promises shall be given the honest
believer. The result was an attack of the power of darkness which threatened him with
destruction, then a light far above him in the sky, then an envelopment in that light
which descended upon him, then a vision of *two glorious personages* standing above him in
the air, one of whom speaking to him, while pointing to the other, said:
"*This is my beloved son*, hear him."
Here, then, was *Jesus Christ being introduced by His Father* to Joseph Smith, the praying
boy, who next was informed by the *Great Redeemer Himself*, that all the sects of the day
were wrong, that all their creeds were an abomination in His sight, that the modern
professors and teachers taught for doctrine the commandments of men, having a form
of godliness, but denying the power thereof;
"that he (Joseph) should join none of these churches, but that the true church should be
revealed to him at some future time."

This, then, was Joseph's authority. *Jesus Christ himself*, the Redeemer of the world, the Son of God, He that was crucified and put to death on Mount Calvary, but who arose triumphant from the grave, the founder, the organizer, the head, the President of the Christian Church, explained to Joseph Smith the condition of the world. There is no higher authority than He. If anyone in heaven or earth has a right to say what is true Christianity, and what is not, *Christ* himself, the founder of the church, has that right.

Edward Stevenson	*1893*

The Life and History, 19-23

In that same year, 1834, in the midst of *many large congregations*, the Prophet testified with great power concerning the visit of the *Father and the Son*, and the conversation he had with *them*.

Edward Stevenson	*7/15/1894*

UR 2:41; JI 29:444

Here are some of the Prophet's words, as uttered in the schoolhouse. With uplifted hand he said: "I am a witness that there is a *God*, for I saw *Him* in open day, while praying in a silent grove, in the spring of 1820." He further testified that *God, the Eternal Father*, pointing to *a separate personage*, *in the likeness of Himself*, said: "*This is my Beloved Son* hear ye Him."

Analysis & Observations

β

There are really only two questions arising from Tholson's observations that are addressed below. First, who did the early brethren believe Joseph Smith was referring to when he said "two personages" appeared to him? Second, who actually appeared to Joseph Smith in the spring of 1820? Although Tholson was primarily interested in the second question, I believe that the answer to the first question is a strong evidence pointing towards the answer of the second question.

Tholson, on page 200 of his book, notes that, apart from the very first 1832 account, "Joseph was careful not to state or even imply that Jesus Christ was one of the 'two Personages.'" The reader should immediately notice that Tholson claims a knowledge of

Joseph's intent to carefully not identify these individuals nor to "imply" who they were. This early cue as to Tholson's position is very telling - which is not to discredit the fact that it is also a very interesting speculation. He further goes on to point out that in the 1835 account, the personage who otherwise would appear to be Jesus Christ testifies that "Jesus Christ is the Son of God." This does seem somewhat curious - after all, why would Jesus testify that he was the Son of God in the third person (grammatically speaking)? While it does seem odd, Tholson never considers the possibility that Christ is speaking as a member of the godhead nor does he consider the words of Christ on another occasion: "Jesus answered and said unto them, Though I bear record of myself, yet my record is true." John 8:14. Nor does he consider that this passage - read from any perspective - is wrought through with statements of divine investiture of authority ... unless we simply concede that the account is poorly written.

Tholson, on pages 202-03 goes on to "harmonize" the 1832 and 1835 passages: Who were the "two Personages" that appeared in Joseph's first vision? A likely explanation, considering all that Joseph has told us about his first vision, is that it was Jehovah and His Son Michael who appeared to Joseph Smith to open the last dispensation. Then Michael, our Father, showed to Joseph a vision wherein Jesus Christ spoke to Joseph. This is a scenario which would explain all of the apparent inconsistencies in the four renderings extant ...." While this explanation is possible, there is no reason why such an odd interpretation is necessary if the poorly written 1835 account was not given the greatest amount of consideration in comparison with the many other references to this event. It is true, as Tholson claims that "Joseph never named or identified one of the 'two Personages' as 'Jesus Christ.'" However, Tholson's further assertion that "Joseph never again made this allusion when referring to his first vision and the 'two Personages' who 'appeared' unto him" is entirely inaccurate - consider his 1842 and the later of the two 1843 accounts for two instances. Tholson also notes that "It was not until 1879 that President John Taylor introduced Jesus Christ into the 1838 account of the first vision, which Joseph was careful not to do." However, this statement is inaccurate as well as the above proofs demonstrate.[284] Given the consistent verbiage used to describe this event and John Taylor's personal acquaintance with Joseph, it is by no means a forced conclusion that John Taylor was introducing this interpretation of the first vision for the first time.

While there is nothing in any of the accounts that directly or unilaterally proves that Tholson's position is incorrect, and while there are other outward inconsistencies in some of these accounts, the standard understanding that it was God the Father and Jesus

[284] Consider as a minimum, Brigham Young's 1855 statement and George Albert Smith's 1868 statements.

Christ who appeared to Joseph remains the most plausible explanation of the first vision. Consider the multiple statements above that point out that Joseph was approaching God to get an answer to his prayers and that this same God appeared to Joseph to introduce the Son, who is the personage who thereafter instructs Joseph. The general consistency of this detail seems conclusive by itself.[285]

Even if Tholson's understanding of the first vision is inaccurate, there is another detail from Joseph Smith's teachings that makes the first vision particularly interesting in light of Adam-God teachings:

Joseph Smith   *Monday 10/5/1840*

WJS, 39

Commencing with *Adam* ... to whom Christ was first revealed,[286] and *through whom Christ has been revealed from heaven, and will continue to be revealed from henceforth.*

Therefore, if the introduction "my beloved son" in the first vision accounts refers to Jesus Christ as is commonly understood, and if Adam always introduces Christ as Joseph Smith taught, then it would have been Adam who introduced Jesus Christ in the first vision as well. Given the details in many of the other accounts of the first vision, the individual who introduced Jesus Christ to Joseph Smith was God the Father. Therefore, Adam is God the Father. While this simple argument could be used to substantiate Adam-God teachings at their most fundamental level, and while this simple argument could also be used to substantiate the position that Joseph Smith introduced Adam-God teachings, it also adds the interesting detail that Adam was the first personage to appear to man in this dispensation.

Professor Allen made the following observations about Joseph Smith's apparent reservations in sharing his first vision:

Professor Allen

Dialogue 1:34 #3

[I]t would appear that the general church membership did not receive information about the first vision until the 1840's and that the story certainly did not hold the prominent place in Mormon thought that it does today ... It is evident that the general

---

[285] While some of these accounts refer to the personages as angels, the reader is advised to recall that Michael, a resurrected being, is referred to as an angel and that Jesus, a resurrected being, qualifies as an angel (See "Angels & Archangels" above).

[286] Consider this in light of Ether 3:15.

membership of the church knew little, if anything, about it. ...

A possible explanation for the fact that the story of the [first] vision was not generally known in the 1830's is sometimes seen in Joseph Smith's conviction that experiences such as these should be kept from the general public because of their extremely sacred nature ... It represented one of his most profound spiritual experiences he could well have decided to circulate it only privately until he could feel certain that in relating it he would not receive again the general ridicule of friends.

Although professor Allen's thesis is probably flawed at its most foundational level (see Edward Stevenson's accounts), it is also possible that Joseph kept the first vision quiet because he knew and understood that it was father Adam who had appeared to him and that the general Church membership was not prepared to learn this fact.[287] However, it seems more likely that Joseph learned that Adam was God the Father later in his calling because, given the above accounts and Edward Stevenson's statements, it appears more likely that the general membership of the Church was intimately familiar with the first vision. If professor Allen's statements are therefore inaccurate, they do not support Tholson's speculation that Joseph may have been deliberately hiding the true identity of these "two personages." The more likely scenario is that the early brethren were simply accustomed to using a different database of rhetoric than we do today (see "Titles & Offices" above). That is, although couched under a different rhetorical structure, it may be that the early brethren did not share a different opinion as to the identity of these two personages than we generally hold today. The only significant difference born out by this volume is that the early brethren, understanding Adam to be "our Father and God," also understood that Adam was the first of the two personages that appeared to Joseph Smith.

---

[287] This analysis is somewhat problematic because Joseph Smith did not initially expect people to react adversely to this vision (which is another reason to disbelieve professor Allen's thesis - Joseph was surprised that people did not believe in his first vision as a young boy). However, it may be that it was the initial backlash to Joseph's recounting his first vision that led him to believe that people were not ready to know that it was Father Adam who appeared to him.

37 Journal of Discourses
1:50-51

Friday, April 9, 1852 at 6:00 p.m.
Published in periodical format on Tuesday, November 15, 1853
Published in the Millennial Star on Saturday, November 26, 1853
Published in book format in 1854[288]
by Brigham Young

As a matter of brief introduction, this infamous discourse was given in the tabernacle in Salt Lake City to a packed and overflowing audience of priesthood holders who were eager to hear the words of their prophet. This was the first public announcement of this doctrine and undoubtedly created a stir among the hearers. Here is the text of the discourse as it appears in the Journal of Discourses:

---

[288] There has been a significant discrepancy among various publications as to the original date of publication for the Journal of Discourses. Most sources cite 1854 as the year of the first printing; several cite 1855. A common exact photocopy reprint of "the original" Journal of Discourses carries the 1855 date and accounts for this latter error. However, to some extant, both of these dates are inaccurate. BYU's Religious Education Archive lists November 1, 1853 as the date of the first publication of the periodical, the Journal of Discourses. It is evident that the 1853 date is accurate because the Millennial Star, November 26, 1853 publication carries the subtitle "(From the Journal of Discourses)", which forces the obvious conclusion that the Journal of Discourses printing must have been before the Millennial Star printing. The reader ought to note that the journals were initially printed twice monthly as a periodical that was intended to be bound as a complete volume at the end of each year and that each periodical was comprised of an average of about sixteen pages. The first couple periodical publications may have been a little larger than sixteen pages (The preface to this volume states that "The Fifteenth Volume of the Millennial Star contains Fifty-three Numbers - one of them a Double Number, also an ample Supplement"). As this discourse begins on page forty-six, it seems most likely that the actual first printing of this Adam-God discourse in the periodical was on November 15, 1853 - not November 1, 1853. Undoubtedly, this hodge-podge of information accounts for the various dates offered by different authors as the initial date of publication of this Adam-God discourse.

The question has been, and is often, asked, who it was that begat the Son of the Virgin Mary. The infidel world have concluded that if what the Apostles wrote about his father and mother be true, and the present marriage discipline acknowledged by Christendom be correct then Christians must believe that God is the father of an illegitimate son, in the person of Jesus Christ! The infidel fraternity teach that to their disciples. I will tell you how it is. Our Father in Heaven begat all the spirits that ever were, or ever will be, upon this earth; and they were born spirits in the eternal world. Then the Lord by His power and wisdom organized the mortal tabernacle of man. We were made first spiritual, and afterwards temporal.

Now hear it, O inhabitants of the earth, Jew and Gentile, Saint and sinner! When our father Adam came into the garden of Eden, he came into it with a celestial body, and brought Eve, one of his wives, with him. He helped to make and organize this world. He is MICHAEL, the Archangel, the ANCIENT OF DAYS! about whom holy men have written and spoken - He is our Father and our God, and the only God with whom we have to do. Every man upon the earth, professing Christians or non-professing, must hear it, and will know it sooner or later.

They came here, organized the raw material, and arranged in their order the herbs of the field, the trees, the apple, the peach, the plum, the pear, and every other fruit that is desirable and good for man; the seed was brought from another sphere, and planted in this earth. The thistle, the thorn, the brier, and the obnoxious weed did not appear until after the earth was cursed. When Adam and Eve had eaten of the forbidden fruit, their bodies became mortal from its effects, and therefore their offspring were mortal.

When the Virgin Mary conceived the child Jesus, the Father had begotten him in his own likeness. He was not begotten by the Holy Ghost. And who is the Father? He is the first of the human family; and when he took a tabernacle, it was begotten by his Father in heaven, after the same manner as the tabernacles of Cain, Abel, and the rest of the sons and daughters of Adam and Eve; from the fruits of the earth, the first earthly tabernacles were originated by the Father, and so on in succession.

I could tell you much more about this; but were I to tell you the whole truth, blasphemy would be nothing to it, in the estimation of the superstitious and over-righteous of mankind. However, I have told you the truth as far as I have gone. ...

It is true that the earth was organized by three distinct characters, namely, Eloheim, Yahovah, and Michael, these three forming a quorum, as in all heavenly bodies, and in

organizing element, perfectly represented in the Deity, as Father, Son, and Holy Ghost! [289]
...

Jesus, our elder brother, was begotten in the flesh by the same character that was in the garden of Eden, and who is our Father in Heaven. Now, let all who may hear these doctrines, pause before they make light of them, or treat them with indifference, for they will prove their salvation or damnation. I have given you a few leading items upon this subject, but a great deal more remains to be told.

The following excerpt is the text as it shows up in the Millennial Star. I have pulled the same portion of the discourse that I selected above with the exception of the concluding three paragraphs.

Brigham Young   *Saturday 11/26/1853*

MS 15:769 #48

ADAM, OUR FATHER AND GOD

The question has been, and is often, asked, who it was that begat the Son of the Virgin Mary. The infidel world have concluded that if what the Apostles wrote about his father and mother be true, and the present marriage discipline acknowledged by Christendom be correct, then Christians must believe that God is the father of an illegitimate son, in the person of Jesus Christ! The infidel fraternity teach that to their disciples.

I will tell you how it is. Our Father in Heaven begat all the spirits that ever were, or ever will be, upon this earth; and they were born spirits in the eternal world. Then the Lord by His power and wisdom organized the mortal tabernacle of man. We were made first spiritual, and afterwards temporal.

Now hear it, O inhabitants of the earth, Jew and Gentile, Saint and sinner! When our father Adam came into the garden of Eden, he came into it with a celestial body, and brought Eve, one of his wives, with him. He helped to make and organize this world. He is MICHAEL, the Archangel, the ANCIENT OF DAYS! about whom holy men have written and spoken - HE is our FATHER and our GOD, and the only God with whom WE have to do. Every man upon the earth, professing Christians or non-professing, must hear it, and will know it sooner or later.

---

[289] Given the understanding that the early brethren had as to the identity of Elohim, Jehovah, and Michael, Brigham Young's meaning here becomes somewhat unclear. While there are some very few fundamentalists that believe that Adam became the Holy Ghost after his mortal probation, the remainder and vast majority of fundamentalists (not to mention mainstream Mormons) do not consider Adam to have ever been the Holy Ghost. Brigham's statement here therefore remains somewhat mysterious.

They came here, organized the raw material, and arranged in their order the herbs of the field, the trees, the apple, the peach, the plum, the pear, and every other fruit that is desirable and good for man; the seed was brought from another sphere, and planted in this earth. The thistle, and thorn, the brier, and the obnoxious weed did not appear until after the earth was cursed. When Adam and Eve had eaten of the forbidden fruit, their bodies became mortal from its effects, and therefore their offspring were mortal. When the Virgin Mary conceived the child Jesus, the Father had begotten him in his own likeness. He was not begotten by the Holy Ghost. And who is the Father? He is the first of the human family; and when he took a tabernacle, it was begotten by his Father in heaven, after the same manner as the tabernacles of Cain, Abel, and the rest of the sons and daughters of Adam and Eve; from the fruits of the earth, the first earthly tabernacles were originated by the Father, and so on in succession.

I could tell you much more about this; but were I to tell you the whole truth, blasphemy would be nothing to it, in the estimation of the superstitious and over-righteous of mankind. However, I have told you the truth as far as I have gone. …

It is true that the earth was organized by three distinct characters, namely, Eloheim, Yahovah, and Michael, these three forming a quorum, as in all heavenly bodies, and in organizing element, perfectly represented in the Deity, as Father, Son, and Holy Ghost. …

Jesus, our elder brother, was begotten in the flesh by the same character that was in the garden of Eden, and who is our Father in Heaven. Now, let all who may hear these doctrines, pause before they make light of them, or treat them with indifference, for they will prove their salvation or damnation.

I have given you a few leading items upon this subject, but a great deal more remains to be told. Now remember from this time forth, and forever, that Jesus Christ was not begotten by the Holy Ghost. I will repeat a little anecdote. I was in conversation with a certain learned professor upon this subject, when I replied, to this idea - "if the Son was begotten by the Holy Ghost, it would be very dangerous to baptize and confirm females, and give the Holy Ghost to them, lest he should beget children, to be palmed upon the Elders by the people, bringing the Elders into great difficulties."

Treasure up these things in your hearts. In the Bible, you have read the things I have told you tonight; but you have not known what you did read. I have told you no more than you are conversant with; but what do the people in Christendom, with the Bible in their hands, know about this subject? Comparatively nothing.

The elders and brethren assembled in the tabernacle, which was completely crowded. After the usual introductory exercises, President Young preached several sermons on various subjects, the Holy Ghost resting upon him in grand power, while he revealed some of the precious things of the kingdom.

Here are a few brief, additional, accounts of this sermon:

Brigham Young   *Friday 4/9/1852*

Journal of Wilford Woodruff

I will now preach to you another sermon. There is one great Father and head in all kingdoms; and so with us. Our Father in heaven has a tabernacle. He created us in the likeness of his own image. The Son also has a tabernacle like the Father. The Holy Ghost is a minister to the people but has not a tabernacle. Who begat the Son of God? Infidels say that Jesus was a bastard, but let me tell you the truth concerning that matter. Our Father begot all the spirits that were before any tabernacle was made. When our Father came into the Garden He came with his Celestial body & brought one of his wives with him and ate of the fruit of the Garden until He could beget a Tabernacle. And Adam is Michael God and all the God that we have anything to do with. They ate of this fruit & formed the first Tabernacle that was formed. And when the Virgin Mary was begotten with child it was by the Father and in no other way only as we were begotten. I will tell you the truth as it is in God. The world don't know that Jesus Christ our Elder Brother was begotten by our Father in Heaven. Handle it as you please, it will either seal the damnation or salvation of man. He was begotten by the Father & not by the Holy Ghost.[290]

Brigham Young   *Friday 4/9/1852*

Journal of Hosea Stout, 2:435

Another meeting this evening. President B. Young taught that Adam was the father of Jesus and the only God to us. That he came to this world in a resurrected body, etc. More hereafter.

Brigham Young   *Friday 4/9/1852*

Lorenzo Brown Journal

Meeting at 9 A.M. All male members met at 6 P.M. House full. President Young preached some new doctrine respecting Adam etc. Excellent discourse I thought.

---

[290] Fundamentalists have used the phrase stating that hearing "these doctrines ... will prove their salvation or damnation" found in the Journal of Discourses in most every Adam-God publication to impress upon the mind of the reader the importance of this doctrine. This journal entry throws some question upon the legitimacy of this approach. Certainly, in context, Brigham Young could have intended to say that it was of salvific importance that we believe that Jesus Christ is the literal son of God the Father (the modern LDS Church no longer stresses this doctrine). Wilford Woodruff's journal suggests that Wilford Woodruff understood that this admonition of Brigham Young was aimed at this doctrine of the literal sonship of Jesus - not at Adam-God doctrines in general.]

The following materials are responses to the JD 1:50-51 discourse that appeared in other publications:

6:00 p.m. 4/17/1852

DN

The elders and brethren assembled in the tabernacle which was completely crowded. After the usual introductory exercises, Pres. Young preached several sermons on various subjects, the Holy Ghost resting upon him in great power, while he revealed some of the precious things of the kingdom.

Franklin D. Richards   *3/31/1855*

MS 17:195

While there is nothing to refute, the whole tenor of revelation substantiates, the supposition, that Adam has continued to bear rule over the earth, and control the destinies of his never ending posterity. From the time he received his commission in the Garden of Eden, he has been laboring diligently to fulfill the instructions there given him by the Lord God concerning his dominions, and to bring them under subjection to his will. This will be fully accomplished when every knee shall bow, and every tongue confess that he is the God of the whole earth. Then will the words of the Prophet Brigham, when speaking of Adam, be fully realized - 'He is our Father and our God, and the only God with whom we have to do.'

Having now observed how Adam, the first man, became God, we inquire why may not millions of his children receive the same Godlike knowledge and power?

George Q. Cannon   *10/12/1861*

MS 23:654

President Young, in the foregoing passages,[291] while substantiating the fact of the union of man's preexisting spirit with a bodily product of the "dust of the ground," enters more particularly into the modus operandi of that union. He *unmistakably* declares man's origin to be altogether of a celestial character - that not only is his spirit of heavenly descent, but his organization too, - that the latter is not taken from the lower animals, but from the *originally* celestial body of the great Father of humanity. Taking the doctrine of man's origin as seen from this higher point of view, and comparing it with the low assumptive theories of uninspired men, ... how great the contrast appears! 'Look on this picture' - Man, the offspring of an ape!; 'and on this' - Man, the image of

[291] JD 1:50-51; 6:275.

God, his Father! How wide the contrast! And how different the feelings produced in
the breast!

Scott Anderson   *9/22/1884*

Letter to Pres. John Taylor

I joined your Church on the 20th of May 1879 and during the first 2 years of my
membership I faithfully adhered to it and would have given my life to defend it, during
all this time I never heard of Adam being God, never heard of Blood Atonement, never
heard of polygamy being required of all men before they could attain to highest glory.
Never dreamed that Brigham Young or any one else coolly threw the Bible overboard
and preached whatever they pleased which I was bound to accept as the revelations of
God. … What did I find? I found that God, the God of the Bible is not even worshiped
by the Church over which you preside, the God you worship is Adam.

Brigham Young teaches [sic] *his words,* "When our Father *Adam* came into the Garden of
Eden, he came into it with a celestial body and brought Eve one of his wives with him.
He is our Father and our God and the only God with whom we have to do." At first I
could not bring myself to believe that this doctrine was accepted by the Church, but on
careful enquiry found to my horror and astonishment that it was really so. It is true a
great many know nothing about it and are simply in ignorance. Those who do know
accept it as far more to be relied on than any portion of the Bible, for say they the Bible
has been translated over and over again and may be wrong but this is the direct teaching
of a Great Prophet.

I reject this as abominable and horrible idolatry and give it as one reason why I cannot
remain in your Church.[292]

Analysis & Observations

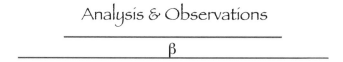

β

The accuracy of this discourse has been repeatedly called into question by leading
brethren in the modern LDS Church. They have generally alleged that the recorders of
the nineteenth century were unable (without modern recording devices) to accurately

---

[292] Anderson was summarily disfellowshipped for apostasy without receiving any correction as to his
understanding of this discourse.

replicate lengthy, extemporaneous sermons.[293] That this position is without any substantive merit has been addressed by previous Adam-God authors who have gone to great lengths to demonstrate that sermons found in the Journal of Discourses were accurately transmitted (I have briefly addressed this issue in the "Was Brigham Young Misquoted" subsection above). While these arguments have been persuasive,[294] they have not directly addressed the question as to whether or not this particular discourse was inaccurately recorded. The following information directly and specifically addresses Brigham Young's April 9, 1852 discourse and is intended to fill this historical and academic gap.

The sermon was published by Samuel W. Richards in the Millennial Star on November 26, 1853 - less than two weeks after it was printed by apostle Franklin D. Richards in the Journal of Discourses periodical. Given this close chronological proximity in printing, given the close physical proximity in printing - both were printed in Liverpool England - and given that both printings were substantively identical, it seems likely that Samuel W. Richards communicated with Franklin D. Richards about this discourse when he copied the printing information.

It may be that Samuel W. Richards was already familiar with the fact that the saints in England were quite surprised at the substance of the discourse as it was printed by Franklin D. Richards in the Journal of Discourses periodical when he printed the discourse in the Millennial Star. Although the Journal of Discourses periodical would have had a smaller general circulation (it was less than a month old at the time of the Millennial Star printing), it seems likely that Franklin D. Richards, as the editor and publisher of the periodical, would have received a readership response similar to that received by Samuel W. Richards from the later Millennial Star printing. Indeed, because the format of the Journal of Discourses periodical did not allow for a printed response to reader inquiries, it may be that Franklin D. Richards asked Samuel W. Richards to republish the controversial sermon in the Millennial Star so that an editor's response to reader inquiries could be printed in a later article and in a more widely circulated periodical - the original Millennial Star talk was given the explicative title "Adam, our Father and God" and was followed (two weeks later) by another article addressing the concerns of the readers (see "Millennial Star 15:801-04" below).

---

[293] Oddly, the problem that this position raises with the sermons of Joseph Smith (upon which Mormonism is founded) is rarely addressed by the modern LDS Church.

[294] This is not to mention that an abundance of resources exist within this volume to substantiate the position that Brigham Young was not misquoted in the Journal of Discourses just by virtue of the number of *other* sources that put forth Adam-God teachings.

Even if the above speculation is inaccurate, the speediness of the response in the December issue of the Millennial Star suggests that the editor, Samuel W. Richards, received several concerned communiqués requesting some further information on the subject - or requesting some assurance that there had not been a significant misprint. It seems unlikely that Samuel W. Richards would have been cavalier enough to defend this new doctrine that quickly if he had held any doubt as to the accuracy of the original, Millennial Star, printing; indeed, it seems much more likely that he consulted with Franklin D. Richards (who was also an apostle at that time) about the accuracy of this new doctrine sometime before the responsive article was prepared for printing - and as suggested above, this may have been before the sermon was first published in the Millennial Star. Either way, when one considers that the additional journal accounts verify the substance of this discourse and that hundreds of statements gathered throughout this volume substantively agree with the teachings laid out in this controversial sermon, there seems to be little room for doubt that the above discourse was accurately recorded and reproduced in the Journal of Discourses - whether or not the grammar appears a little awkward in certain portions of the sermon. Lastly, Christensen noted that this discourse was "published in Zion's Watchman, vol. 1, nos. 18 and 19, as a doctrinal standard for the Australian saints." AGM, 122. If it had been poorly transcribed, it seems unlikely that it would have been used as a doctrinal standard for any group of saints.

38

Millennial Star 15:801-04

Saturday December 10, 1853
by Samuel W. Richards

ADAM, THE FATHER AND GOD OF THE HUMAN FAMILY

The above sentiment appeared in Star No. 48,[295] a little to the surprise of some of its readers; and while the sentiment may have appeared blasphemous to the ignorant, it has no doubt given rise to some serious reflections with the more candid and comprehensive mind. A few reasonable and Scriptural ideas upon this subject may be profitable at the present time.

Then Adam is really God! And why not? If there are Lords many and Gods many, as the Scriptures inform us, why should not our Father Adam be one of them? Did he not prove himself as worthy of that high appellation as any other being that ever lived upon the earth? Certainly he did, so far as history informs us, unless we can except the Son of God. We have no account in Scripture that Adam ever willfully transgressed, when we consider him independent of the woman. The Apostle informs us distinctly that the woman was in the transgression, being deceived, but Adam was not deceived. Adam fell, but his fall became a matter of necessity after the woman had transgressed. Her punishment was banishment from the Garden, and Adam was necessitated to fall, and go with her, in order to obey the first great command given unto them - to multiply and replenish the earth; or, in the language of the Prophet Lehi, 'Adam fell that men might be.' The fall of Adam, therefore, was virtually required at his hands, that he might keep the first great command, and that the purposes of God might not fail, while at the same time the justice of God might be made manifest in the punishment incurred by the

---

[295] MS 15:769 #48.

transgression of the woman, for whom the man is ever held responsible in the government of God.

The Scriptures inform us that Christ was as a lamb slain from before the foundation of the world. If, therefore, the plan of salvation was matured before the foundation of the world, and Jesus was ordained to come into the world, and die at the time appointed, in order to perfect that plan, we must of necessity conclude that the plan of the fall was also matured in the councils of eternity, and that it was as necessary for the exalting and perfecting of intelligences, as the redemption. Without it they could not have known good and evil here, and without knowing good and evil they could not become Gods, neither could their children. No wonder the woman was tempted when it was said unto her - 'Ye shall be as gods, knowing good and evil.' No wonder Father Adam fell, and accompanied the woman, sharing in all the miseries of the curse, that he might be the father of an innumerable race of beings who would be capable of becoming Gods.

With these considerations before us, we can begin to see how it is that we are under obligations to our father Adam, as to a God. He endured the sufferings and the curse that we might be; and we are, that we might become Gods. Through him the justice of God was made manifest. Jesus came into the world, endured, and suffered, to perfect our advantages for becoming Gods, and through him the mercy of God abounded.

By the first man, Adam, came death, the triumph of evil; and by the second, came life everlasting, the triumph of good. Each was necessary in the order he appeared; if the first Adam had not performed his part, the second could not have had his work to do. Both acted the part assigned to them, in a most Godlike manner, and the Great Eloheim accepted the work at their hands as His own, 'for by the power of my Spirit created I them; yea, all things, both spiritual and temporal: firstly, spiritual - secondly, temporal, which is the beginning of my work; and again, firstly, temporal - and secondly, spiritual, which is the last of my work.' Thus the great I AM owns all things - the temporal and the spiritual, the justice and the mercy, to be His own work. Then why may not Adam be a God, as well as any of his sons, inasmuch as he has performed the work to which the Great Eloheim appointed him?

In ancient times they were called Gods unto whom the word of God came, because of which Moses became a God unto Pharaoh. The Almighty was not so jealous of His Godly title but that He could say to Moses - 'See I have made thee a God to Pharaoh.' And if John's saying be true, God has purposed to make him that overcometh, a pillar in the temple of God, and to 'write upon him the name of my God.' 'His name shall be in their foreheads.'

This is the hope of all Saints who have a just conception of the future; and why should we not be willing for father Adam to inherit all things, as well as for ourselves? He is the first, the Father of all the human family, and his glory will be above all, for he will be God over all, necessarily, standing as he will through all eternity at the head of those who are the redeemed of his great family. Though all the sons should, through their faithfulness, become Gods, they would still know that the Son was not greater than the Father.

Were we to trace this subject in all its bearings, we should find the principles of the Godhead planted in every righteous and well-organized family upon the earth, and that they only require cultivation to cause their expansion and development to be equal to anything we can now conceive of as adding power and glory to the God of all worlds. The Great Eloheim rules over worlds. He is God over them, because of His right and power to rule, govern, and control. The exercise of this power is a natural right in the order of Priesthood, which belongs to every Patriarch, or Father, in the human family, so long as he rules subordinately to the laws of Heaven. According to the order of that God by whom we are ruled, a man is not only permitted to hold full jurisdiction over his own family, but he is held responsible for any violation, by them, of the revealed will of Heaven. A man that controls a work, is the only one that can be held responsible for that work. It would be most unjust to require responsibility where there is no power to govern and control.

Every man who has a family, and power to control them, is exercising the rights and powers of a God, though it may be in a very small capacity. There are two grand principles, by virtue of which all intelligent beings have a legitimate right to govern and hold dominion; these are, by begetting children from their own loins, and by winning the hearts of others to voluntarily desire their righteous exercise of power extended over them. These constitute a sure foundation for an eternal throne - a kingdom as perpetual as God's. No usurped power, to be maintained by the shedding of blood, is connected with such a government. It is upon this foundation that the throne of Michael is established as Father, Patriarch, God; and it is for all his children who come into this world, to learn and fully understand the eternity of that relationship.

Could we view our first Parent in his true position, we should find him acting in a similar capacity to the whole family of man, as each father does to his individual family, controlling, at his pleasure, all things which relate to the great object of their being - their exaltation to thrones and Godlike powers. We can conceive, from Scripture, principle, and analogy, that Adam's watch-care is ever over mankind; that by his own approbation and direction Gospel dispensations have been revealed from heaven to earth in different ages of the world; that he was the first that ever held the keys of Gospel power upon the earth, and by his supervision they have been handed down from age to age, whenever they have been among men; that under his direction a Deluge once swept the earth of the wickedness which was upon it, and laws were given to Israel, as a nation, to lead them to Christ; and that he will in the end call men to judgment for the privileges which have been extended to them in this world.

Hear what the Prophet Daniel says upon this subject - `I beheld till the thrones were cast down, and the Ancient of days did sit, whose garment was white as snow, and the hair of his head like the pure wool; his throne was like the fiery flame, and his wheels as burning fire. A fiery stream issued and came forth from before him; thousand thousands ministered unto him, and ten thousand times ten thousand stood before him; the judgment was set, and the books were opened. ... And behold, one like the Son of Man came with the clouds of heaven, and came to the Ancient of days, and they brought him near before him. And there was given him dominion, and glory, and a kingdom, that all people, nations, and languages should serve him; his dominion is an everlasting dominion, which shall not pass away, and his kingdom that which shall not be destroyed.' - Daniel 7:9, 10, 13, 14.

Again, the word of the Lord through the Prophet Joseph, gives additional importance, if possible, to the part which Adam acts relating to his children, which reads as follows - `But, behold, verily I say unto you, before the earth shall pass away, Michael, mine archangel, shall sound his trump, and then shall all the dead awake, for their graves shall be opened, and they shall come forth; yea, even all.'[296]

From the foregoing we are enabled to draw important conclusions, that before the coming of the Lord Jesus in the clouds of heaven, to take the reins of government upon the earth, Adam comes and gathers around him all that have ever held keys of power under him upon the earth, in any of the dispensations thereof to man; he calls forth the dead from their graves, at the sound of his trump; he brings them to judgment, and they render unto him an account of their several stewardships; the books are opened that a righteous judgment may be rendered by him who now sits upon his throne, not only as the Father, but the Judge, of men; and in that capacity thousands minister unto him. An august assemblage are now gathered in one grand council around the great Patriarch of all Patriarchs, consisting of his sons, who have been faithful in that which was committed to them; and all this preparatory to that great event, when the greatness of the kingdom

---

[296] D& C 29:26.

under the whole heaven should be given to the Saints of the Most High. Daniel saw that the Saints possessed the kingdom, by virtue of which Adam was once more in possession of the dominion given unto him before the fall, which was over every living thing that moved upon the earth, which rendered him the universal Sovereign and Lord of all.

At this important period, when Adam is reinstated with full power upon the earth, seated upon his throne, as Daniel saw him - a glorious and an immortal God, one like the Son of Man comes in the clouds of heaven (as oftimes represented by the Apostles), to the Ancient of days, and receives from him dominion, glory, and a kingdom; or in other words, Michael, having accomplished the work committed to him, pertaining to this world, delivers up an account of his stewardship over the same, to that character represented as Yahovah in the creation of the world, who reigns in unison with those upon the earth, until his work is fully accomplished - till the last great contest with the enemy, who has been released for a little season, is won; then he in turn delivers up the kingdom to the great Eloheim, that in the language of the Apostle, `God may be all in all.'

This final surrender, we are to bear in mind, does not detract from the God-like power and dominion of our first Parent, nor of our Lord Jesus Christ. In the Patriarchal order of government, each and every ruler is independent in his sphere, his rule extending to those below, and not to those above him, in the same order. While the God of unnumbered worlds is acknowledged to be his God and Father, Adam still maintains his exalted position at the head of all those who are saved from among the whole family of man; and he will be God over all those who are made Gods from among men. Each and every God will be honored and adored by those over whom he reigns as a God, without any violation of the laws of heaven - without any encroachment upon that command which saith, `thou shalt have no other Gods before me,' for the glory and honor of all true Gods constitute the glory, honor, power, and dominion of the great Eloheim, according to His own order of government.

We can conceive of no higher, or more perfect order of government than that which is embraced in Patriarchal authority. By virtue of this order, all Gods, whether in heaven or on earth, exercise a righteous power, and possess a just dominion. In this order, all are both subjects and rulers, each possessing Almighty rights and powers - Almighty rulers over those who have descended from them, at the same time rendering all honor and power to those from whom they have descended. What a glorious system of order is here portrayed - one in which an innumerable succession of Gods, Patriarchs, and rulers, can reign forever in the greatest possible harmony that can be comprehended by intelligences, while each is independent in his position, as is all intelligence. As the great

Eloheim is supreme and Almighty over all His children and kingdoms, so is Adam as great a ruler, or God, in his sphere, over his children, and the kingdom which they possess. The earth and all things upon it were created for Adam, and it was given to him of his Father to have dominion over it. In that dominion he will be sustained throughout all eternity.

In relation to this earth alone and its inhabitants, Michael and Gabriel have perhaps held the greatest keys of dominion and power. They were, both in their day, Fathers of all living, and had dominion given unto them over all things. Gabriel, or Noah, held the keys of this power under Michael, and to him he will render an account of all things before Michael renders an account of his stewardship to Him whose dominion reaches over many worlds, and who is God over all Gods. These two important personages have ever been watchful of the interests of their children, hence we find them ministering from time to time to holy men upon the earth - Gabriel often appearing unto Daniel, and opening to his view the most wonderful visions of the future, by which he could act as a God to the people, out vie the wisdom of the astrologers, and so control the elements that the burning furnace could have no power over him; Michael also coming to the release of Gabriel, when he was withstood one and twenty days from answering Daniel's prayer. We also read of Michael disputing with the Devil about the body of Moses, probably because the Devil was not willing that Moses should be translated, inasmuch as he had sinned; but even in this, Michael was the great deliverer. Again we read that Michael shall stand up for the children of his people in a time of trouble such as never was since there was a nation, and at that time every one that shall be found written in the book shall be delivered, and those who sleep in the dust of the earth shall awake.

From these and many other Scriptures, we find that those important personages are clothed upon with no mean authority, and that Michael has power to deliver men from the power of the Devil, which is death; that by the sound of his own trump - the trump of the archangel, the nations of the dead shall awake and come forth to judgment, and there render an account to the Ancient of Days seated upon his burning throne. Then shall the nations know that he is their Judge, their Lawgiver, and their God, and upon his decree hangs the destiny of the assembled dead. Yes, our Judge will be a kind and compassionate Father, by whom none can pass, but through whom all glory, dominion, and power, will be ascribed to the great ETERNAL.

Analysis & Observations

———————————————————
———————————— β ————————————

The Preface to volume 15 of the Millennial Star claimed that this "Volume is replete with highly interesting and instructive matter, including much doctrinal information upon subjects new to the generality of our readers, but vitally related to the salvation and exaltation of every human being." Undoubtedly, this statement was referring to Adam-God teachings as all other doctrines listed in the index appear to be rather benign. Even without that prelude background, this December article is particularly interesting. To modern readers studying Adam-God teachings, this article may appear to ignore fundamental Adam-God teachings by focusing more on Adam's position as the Ancient of Days and on the nature of godhood in general - it appears that Adam's position as the "Father and God of the Human Family" takes a backseat to these more verbose passages covering these other doctrines. We know that Samuel W. Richards considered all of these doctrines to be integral to understanding the foundational teaching that Adam is God the Father because he thusly titled this article and because he thusly titled the related article in the index to volume fifteen of the Millennial Star:

Samuel W. Richards   *1853*

MS 15:iii (index)
Adam, our Father and our God 769
Do.[297] the Father and God of the Human Family 801

That he connected these teachings is insightful for two reasons. First, it strongly suggests that Samuel W. Richards understood these teachings to be fundamentally and inseparably intertwined with the teaching that Adam is God the Father. This in turn could suggest that he had been taught these teachings in connection with more "clear-cut" Adam-God teachings at some time previous to writing this article.[298] If so, this article provides us some indirect evidence that Joseph's teachings that Adam was the Ancient of Days was understood by the early brethren to be a declaration that Adam was God the Father (see "Ancient of Days"). Second, that Samuel W. Richards understood that these scriptures were intertwined with Adam-God teachings supports the idea behind this volume that many teachings about the plurality of gods, the plan of salvation as it pertains to godhood,

———————————————————

[297] i.e., ditto.

[298] Whether he was taught this during Brigham Young's administration or during Joseph Smith's administration is not significant to this point.

doctrines behind the nature of the Fall (e.g., eating of the seeds of death), and other doctrines treated in this volume were once understood to be inseparable and interrelated. This is crucial to completely understanding Adam-God teachings because it gives us a fuller understanding and appreciation of the broad implications of this single teaching: Adam is God the Eternal Father.

39

Brigham Young's

October 8, 1854 Discourse

Recorded in MABY under the dates of Sunday, October 8 and Monday, October 9, 1854[299] in the Salt Lake Tabernacle; recorded in the Historical Department of the Church Ms d 1234, Box 48 fd 12

Brigham Young   *10/6-8/1854*

Wilford Woodruff Journal 4:290
President Young preached to a congregation of several thousand, out of doors, and I believe that he preached the greatest sermon that ever was delivered to the Latter Day Saints since they have been a people. Elder Watt reported. I also took minutes.

10/12/1854

DN
At 2 p.m. an immense congregation were comfortably seated in the open air. While the emblems were being passed, President Brigham Young delivered a highly interesting discourse; which held the vast audience as it were spellbound.

Thomas D. Brown   *Friday 10/6/1854*

Journal of the Southern Indian Mission
… a discourse, equaled by none.

---

[299] As the next subsection will demonstrate, there is some question as to the exact date that Brigham Young delivered this discourse - some sources suggest that it was delivered on Friday, October 6, 1854. I have chosen to list the date of the discourse throughout the book as Sunday, October 8, 1854 because sacrament was administered at this meeting and because it was delivered at a general conference session; although the early brethren did not limit sacrament meetings to Sunday, we have no accounting of any other sacrament meeting being held on a day apart from Sunday where thousands of people attended.

This discourse was given at 2:00 p.m. on a Sunday afternoon session of general conference while the sacrament was being passed:

I purpose to speak upon a subject that does not immediately concern yours or my welfare. I expect in my remarks I shall allude to things that you search after as being absolutely necessary for your salvation in the kingdom of God. It is true if you are faithful, and diligent they are things that will be fully made known unto you in due time - at the proper time, according to the will of the Lord. But so many among us are preaching, lecturing, contemplating upon, and conversing about things away beyond our reach, sometimes I wish to gratify the people by speaking upon these subjects; for I think upon them as well as you; I meditate upon the future and the past as well as you, and I now gratify myself by gratifying the people.

In the first place, I wish to say to all men and women who believe in the Lord Jesus Christ, in the Holy Bible, and in the revelations that have been given at sundry times from the days of Adam to the present, I request that I may have your faith and prayers united with mine that whatever the Lord is pleased to give to the Latter-day Saints through your humble servant this afternoon, He may give it, and that He does not wish to give He may retain, and keep from you. I make this request of the Saints for this reason; I know by my experience, by the visions of eternity that God reveals things to individuals that does not belong to the Church at large at present, or that does not yet belong to the Mass. That I know.

It is natural for the people to desire that which is not beneficial to them. It is so in temporal things, and it is so in things that are spiritual. That I know. Again, the Lord blesses His people with temporal things in abundance, and wishes to bless them with knowledge and understanding that is not for the world of mankind who do not believe in Him. That I also know.

I may say things this afternoon that does not belong to the world. What if I do? I know the Lord is able to close up every person's mind who have eyes but see not, hearts but do not understand, so I may say what I please with regard to the Kingdom of God on the Earth, for there is a veil over the wicked that they cannot understand the things which are for their peace.

Jesus said at one time, "It is not meet to take the children's bread and give it to the dogs."[300] This saying applies to all the dispensations that have been brought forth to the

---

[300] Matthew 15:26; Mark 7:27.

children of men from the days of Adam until now. I wish the congregation to understand in connection with my sayings thus far, that the Latter-day Saints believe in God the Father, in Jesus Christ His son, in the Holy Ghost, God's minister, and in the Celestial Law, or, in other words, the ordinances of the House of God, which, if obeyed, are calculated to save intelligent beings, exalt them, and bring them back into the presence of their God.

I will tell you what I believe still further than this; though I do not pretend to say that the items of doctrine, and ideas I shall advance are necessary for the people to know, or that they should give themselves any trouble about them whatever. I believe in the eternities of worlds, saints, angels, kingdoms, and gods: In eternity without beginning. I believe the gods never had a beginning, neither the formation of matter, and it is without end; it will endure in one eternal round, swimming in space, basking, living, and moving in the midst of eternity. All the creations are in the midst of eternity, and that is one eternity, so they move in one eternal round. Consequently, when you hear philosophers argue the point how the first god came, how intelligence came, how worlds came, and how angels came, they are talking about that which is beyond conception; about that which never was, and never will be worlds without end. It manifests their folly. It shows they know nothing of such matters; and if they know some things they have a right to know, there are things they have no right to know. This applies to all classes of mankind.

These are my views with regard to the Gods and Eternities. Do you wish that I should particularize? Then, can you by process of reasoning or argument, tell whether it was an apple that bore the first seed of an apple, or an apple seed that made the first apple? Or, whether it was a seed of a squash that made the first squash, or a squash that bore the first squash seed? Such abstruse questions belong to the philosophy of the world; in reality there never was and never will be a time when there was not both the apple and the apple seed.

(You must be patient with me, as I am not well enough to preach to such a large congregation in the open air, and labor onward without cessation; you must allow me to take my own time.) I will proceed a little further in my preliminaries before I commence my subject.

Inasmuch as I have taken the ground that there never was a beginning, nor end - I wish to say further; there is an eternity of elements, and an eternity of space and there is no space without a kingdom; neither is there any kingdom without a space. Were the best mathematician to multiply figures from the time he first commenced to learn at five or ten years of age, until he is one hundred years old, or until he has exhausted the capacity of figures known to man, he can then tell no more about the number of creations of God in comparison than a mere child who knows nothing whatever of figures. There is no beginning, no end; there is no bounds, no time, when the elements will cease to be organized into bodies with all the variety you have a faint specimen of on this Earth.

There are philosophers who believe that this Earth upon which we stand has been in existence for millions of ages. I wish to advance a few items that will open the minds of these philosophers, that they may be well instructed scribes who treasure up in their hearts the mysteries of the Kingdom of God, the Principles of Eternity. Those who wish to be taught eternal principles, and become true philosophers, their minds can reach forth into the unlimited fields of eternity and still discover no end to the boundless expanse, and to its fullness.

There is no necessity of creating a world like this, and keeping it in one unalterable state or condition for the express purpose of bringing intelligent beings upon it, while there is an eternity of matter yet to be organized; and when we have lived as long as the best mathematicians among you can figure by millions, billions, trillions of years, and when you have exhausted all your wisdom and knowledge and figures, you are then in the midst of eternity where you began. A true philosopher wishes to grow, and increase continually; he wishes his mind to expand and reach forth, until he can think as God thinks; as angels think, and behold things as God beholds them.

You recollect I told you in the commencement, I should talk about things that did not particularly concern you and me; but the people want to hear something in advance of their present knowledge; they want to find out if there is anything more for us to learn. When you have lived through eternities to come, learning continually, you may then inquire, "Brother Brigham, is there anything more for me to learn." My reply to such an inquiry would be, yes, there is an eternity of knowledge yet to learn.

Search after wisdom, get knowledge and understanding, and forget it not; and be not like the fool whose eyes are in the ends of the Earth, or like the misers who are around us here; they are so craving and anxious after property, that if they saw a picayune on the wall opposite me here, they would run over forty dollars to secure that picayune; their eyes are on earthly riches to the neglect of the riches that are more enduring.

There are a great many persons who are so anxious to learn about eternity, gods, angels, heavens, and hells, that they neglect to learn the first lessons preparatory to learning the things they are reaching after. They will come short of them. I wish to speak a few words about the Bible as I have hinted at it. The Ordinances of the Kingdom of God on the

Earth are the same to the children of Adam from the commencement to the end of his posterity pertaining to the carnal state on this Earth, and the winding up scene of this mortality. With regard to the Bible; we frequently say, we believe the Bible, but circumstances alters cases, for what is now required of the people may not be required of a people that may live a hundred years hence. But I wish you to understand, with regard to the ordinances of God's House to save the people in the Celestial Kingdom of our God, there is no change from the days of Adam to the present time, neither will there be until the last of his posterity is gathered into the Kingdom of God.

Those who are not acquainted with our doctrine are astonished, and say, "That is strange indeed; we thought no such thing as preaching Faith, Repentance, and Baptism was practiced in ancient, or Old Testament times." I can tell you that no man from the days of Adam, no woman from the days of Eve to this day, who have lived, and who are now living upon the Earth will go into the Kingdom of their Father and God, to be crowned with Jesus Christ, without passing through the same Ordinances of the House of God, you and I have obeyed. I wish you distinctly to understand that.

There are many duties, and callings spoken of in the scriptures, and there are many not written, those for instance which are handed out to you by your President as circumstances require. Those imposed by the President of the Church of God, or by the president of any portion of it, are duties as necessary to be observed as though they were written in the Bible; but these requirements, duties, and callings change with the circumstances that surround the people of God. But when you speak of the system of Salvation to bring back the children of Adam and Eve into the presence of our Father and God, it is the same in all ages, among all people, and under all circumstances, worlds without end. Amen.

I think these preliminaries will satisfy me, and I feel prepared to take my text; it is the words of Jesus Christ, but where they are in the Bible I cannot tell you now, for I have not taken the pains to look at them. I have had so much to do, that I have not read the Bible for many years. I used to be a Bible student; I used to read and study it, but did not understand the spirit and meaning of it; I knew well enough how it read. I have read the Book of Mormon, the book of Doctrine and Covenants, and other revelations of God which He has given to His people in latter times; I look at them, and contrast the spirit and power of them with my faithfulness. My clerks know how much time I have to read, it is difficult for me to snatch time enough to eat my breakfast and supper, to say nothing of reading.

I tell you my text is in the Bible and reads as follows. "And this is Life Eternal, that they might know thee, the only true God, and Jesus Christ whom thou hast sent." I will now put another text with this and then offer a few remarks; it is one of the sayings of Paul. "For though there be that are called gods, whether in heaven or in Earth, (as there be gods many and lords many) but to us there is but one God, the Father, of whom are all things, and we in Him; and one Lord Jesus Christ, by whom are all things, and we by him." This God is the Father of our Lord Jesus Christ and the Father of our spirits. I feel inclined to make a little scripture. (Were I under the necessity of making scripture extensively, I should get Brother Heber C. Kimball to make it, and then I would quote it. I have seen him do this when any of the Elders have been pressed by their opponents, and were a little at a loss; he would make a scripture for them to suit the case, that never was in the Bible, though none the less true, and make their opponents swallow it as the words of an Apostle, or one of the Prophets.

The Elder would then say, "Please turn to that scripture, gentlemen, and read it for yourselves." No they could not turn to it, but they recollected it like the devil for fear of being caught.) I will venture to make a little scripture. This God is the God and Father of our Lord Jesus Christ precisely as He is our Father - varying from mortality to immortality, from corruptible to incorruptible, and that is all the difference. He is the God and Father of our Lord Jesus Christ, both body and spirit; and He is the Father of our spirits. You may add these words to it, or let it alone, it is all the same to me, that He is not only the Father of our spirits, but also of our flesh, He being the founder of that natural machinery through which we all have obtained our bodies.

Do you wish me to simplify it? Could you have a father without having a grandfather; or a grandfather without having a great grandfather? I never heard of but one circumstance that varied from this rule, and that was a son of the Emerald Isle who said he was born of one of his aunts. Does this unlock to your understandings how the Lord Almighty is our natural Father? He set the great machine to working. If you cannot see this truth now, you will if you are faithful, and patient.

I will now quote another scripture: "And hath made of one blood all nations of men for to dwell on all the face of the Earth, and hath determined the times before appointed, and the bounds of their habitations."[301] From these words we understand that God has made of one blood all the inhabitants that are upon the Earth - all that has been, and that will be in the future will be of the same blood as those that have been. Do you believe that scripture? I do with all my heart. I believe we are all of one flesh, blood, and bones. We are made of the same matter, the same elements, we have sprung from one mother,

---

[301] Acts 17:26.

Earth. Matter was brought together from the vast eternity that exists, and this terra firma upon which we stand was organized, then comes the world of mankind, the beast, fishes, fowls, and every living thing to dwell upon the Earth after its kind; and the vegetation of every kind to support animal life on it, until the organization of this world was perfected in all its variety; being brought from the eternity of matter, and prepared for intelligent beings to dwell upon, wherein to prepare themselves to dwell eternally in the presence of their Father and God. Those who keep this their second estate, and do honor to their being, and answer the design of their creation, shall be exalted to inhabit the earth, and live upon it when it shall be Celestial, and brought back into the presence of God, there to dwell forever and ever.

Before I proceed any further, I will ask a question. And I would like you men, and women of intelligence, to understand and watch well, to see if I keep the thread of truth, whether I preach to you according to the law, and the testimony, according to the words of the Prophets, of Jesus Christ and his Apostles, and according to the words of angels. Mark ye well my sayings, and see if you can pick any flaw in them. If you think you can so do, when you come to the proper place to be corrected, you may then receive instructions that will do you good. The question I wish to ask is simply this; and I put it to all the Elders of Israel, and to all the men and women of intelligence in Israel which pertains to the Kingdom of God on Earth; and if the whole world were before me I would ask them the same question. Can any man, or set of men officiate in dispensing the laws, and administering the ordinances of the Kingdom of God, or of the kingdoms and governments of the world legally, without first obeying those laws, and submitting to those ordinances themselves.

Do you understand me? If a foreigner wishes to become a citizen of the United States he must first become subject to this government; must you not first acknowledge and obey the laws of this government? Certainly you must. Then, to apply this to the Kingdom of God on Earth, and ask if any man has the power, the influence, the right, the authority, to go forth and preach this gospel, and baptise for the remission of sins unless he himself has, in the first place, been baptised, ordained and legally called to that office? What would the Elders of Israel and every other sensible man say to this? They would decide at once with me, that no man can lawfully officiate in any office in the Kingdom of God, or in the government of men, he has not been called to, and the authority of which has not been bestowed upon him. I am not going to talk a thousand things to you, but I wish to tell you a few, and desire you to understand them, and connect them together.

There are a few more questions I would like to ask, for the simple reason of bringing the minds of the people to bear upon certain items of principle, and the philosophy of the

Kingdom of God on Earth, that they may know how heavenly things are. But I will pass on, and notice some of the texts I have quoted. Before I proceed, however, I will put one more question, at the same time I wish you to bear in mind the one I have just asked, Do not forget that no man has authority to officiate in the ordinances of heavenly or earthly governments only so far as he has obeyed them himself. Now, to know the only wise God and Jesus Christ whom He has sent, will put the man, woman, congregation, or nation in possession of Eternal Life. Are the hearts of the Latter-day Saints prepared to have Eternal Life given to them en mass, and say that there shall be no more apostasy, but bring them all up that they may know and understand the Gods, Eternities, Creations, Heavens, Hells, Kingdoms, Thrones, Principalities, and Powers? It cannot be done. The sheep and the goats are together, the wheat and the tares are growing together; the good and the bad are mixed; and they must so remain until the time when Jesus Christ will say: "gather the sheep into my fold; gather my wheat into my garner, and let the tares, and chaff, and stubble, be burned."[302] That is not yet. Now if you believe what you have heard me say you will believe that there is lords many, and gods many; and you will believe that unto us, the inhabitants of this Earth there is but one God with whom we have to do;[303] and according to the tenor of the Bible, we believe that there are many, very many who have entered into Power, Glory, Might, and Dominion, and are gathering around them Thrones, and have power to organize elements, and make worlds, and bring into existence intelligent beings in all their variety, who if they are faithful and obedient to their calling and creation will in their turn be exalted in Eternal Kingdoms of the Gods. Do you believe that? You and I have only one God to whom we are accountable, so we will let the rest alone, and search after the one we have to do with; let us seek diligently after Him, the very being who commenced this creation. (asked blessing on bread)

We will now make our inquiries with regard to our position with the God with whom we have to do. You will please recollect all ye Elders in Israel; for I want you to be instructed by my remarks, that you may not fall into errors, that you have tested the question in your own minds with regard to the rights of officiating in ordinances. Now I wish to ask you if you have any conception or idea as to the creation of the world? "Oh, yes," you reply, "A great many of us have a tolerable idea of it, but still there are mysteries we do not understand; there are some things in the Bible about the creation that seem to be dark: we have learned some things in this Kingdom we do not

---

[302] Apparently he is referring to Matthew 13:32 and, by parallel reference, Luke 3:17.

[303] Notice that he used this precise expression in JD 1:50 as well - and notice that he uses this expression in various forms a few times throughout this discourse.

understand, and that do not correspond with the reading of the Bible."[304] Let me open the eyes of your understanding.

There has never been a time when the creations of worlds commenced; they are from eternity to eternity in their creations and redemption. After they are organized they experience the good and the evil; the light, and the dark, the bitter and the sweet, as you and I do. There never was a time when there were not worlds in existence as this world is, and they pass through similar changes in abiding their creation preparatory to exaltation. Worlds have always been in progress, and eternally will be.

Every world has an Adam, and an Eve: named so, simply because the first man is always called Adam, and the first woman Eve; and the Oldest Son has always the privilege of being Ordained. Appointed, and Called to be the Heir of the Family, if he does not rebel against the Father; and he is the Savior of the family. Every world that has been created, has been created upon the same principle. They may vary in their varieties, yet the eternity is one eternal round. These are things that scarcely belong to the best of this congregation. There are items of doctrine, and principles, in the bosom of eternity that the best of the Latter-day Saints are unworthy to receive. If the visions of their minds were opened to look into the vast creations, and gaze upon the Power, and Glory, and Goodness, and Exaltation of the Gods they would exclaim; "Wo is me, I am undone, I am of unclean lips."[305]

But we will look at it a little. Do any of you know anything about the creation of this world? "Oh yes, I understand a good deal about it from the account given in the Bible." So you read in the Bible of there being three persons in one god; many religionists in the world believe in a three-in-one god, however I do no wish to spend time to deliberate upon the notions adopted by the sectarians, the world is full of them. There are lords many and gods many according to the Bible; it does not contradict the doctrine, neither can you find a single passage that does away with that idea.

But let us turn our attention to the God with which we have to do. I tell you simply, He

---

[304] Notice here that Brigham is acknowledging that there are doctrines that do not correspond well with the Bible - he is most likely alluding to Adam-God teachings here as they were heavily debated because of this very issue and because he continues with the statement: "Let me open the eyes of your understanding," which statement is followed by his long discourse of Adam-God teachings. As further support of this reading, note that in his introductory remarks, Brigham acknowledges that he has a preconceived idea of what he is going to talk about and has given some preparatory remarks that were intended to prepare their minds for that which followed.

[305] Isaiah 6:5.

is our Father; the God and Father of our Lord Jesus Christ, and the Father of our spirits. Can that be possible? Yes, it is possible. He is the Father of all the spirits of the human family. All things are first made spiritual, and brought forth into His kingdom. The spirits of all the human family were begotten by one Father. Now be watchful, for if I have time, and feel able, I shall communicate something with this you are not expecting. Yes, every son and daughter of Adam according to the flesh can claim one parentage; the Heathen, and the Christian, the Jew and the Gentile, the high and the low, the king and the beggar, the black and the white, all who have sprung from Adam and Eve have one father. "Then you make it out we are brethren and sisters." Certainly for the whole human family are made of one blood of the same material; the are all begotten and brought forth by one parentage, and from one generation to another they are of one flesh and blood, and of one kindred. The God and Father of our Lord Jesus Christ is the Father of our spirits.

I began at the end, and shall probably finish at the beginning of my discourse; but it is no matter which end a man begins at, for the first shall be last and the last first; which proves it is one eternal round; it is one eternity. Eloheim looks round upon the eternity of matter, and said to His associates, and those that He was pleased to call upon at that time for His counselors, with regard to the Elements, Worlds, Planets, Kingdoms and Thrones; said He: "Yahovah Michael, see that Eternal Matter on all sides, this way and that way; we have already created Worlds upon Worlds, shall we create another World? Yes, go and organize the elements in yonder space" - not empty space for there is no such thing, once in a while, earth quakes, and the extensive destruction of combustible matter by fire will come nigh to making empty space for perhaps the millionth part of a second - "Yahovah Michael, go and create a world, make it, organize it, form it; and then put upon it everything in all the variety that you have seen, that you have been in the habit of being associated with in other worlds, of beasts, birds, fowls, fish, and every insect, and creeping thing, and finally, when the whole eternity of element is full of life, bring it together and make of it living creatures."

Yahovah Michael goes and does as he is told. What I am now going to tell you, will no doubt astonish the whole of you. When Yahovah Michael had organized the world, and brought from another kingdom the beasts, fish, fowl, and insects, and every tree, and plant with which we are acquainted, and thousands we never saw - when He had filled the Earth with animal and vegetable life - Michael or Adam goes down to the new made world, and there he stays.

Do you suppose he went there alone? Moses made the Bible to say his wife was taken out of his side, was made of one of his ribs. I do not know anything to the contrary of my ribs being equal on both sides. The Lord knows if I had lost a rib for each wife I have, I should have none left long ago. Some try to say how many wives the Governor of Utah has, but if they can tell, they can tell more than I can, for I do not know how many I have; I have not counted them up for many years. I heard that I had ninety. Why, bless your souls, ninety is not a beginning. You might ask me if I have ever seen them all; I answer no; I see a few of them I pick up myself here. I have lots, and scores I never see nor shall not until the morning of the resurrection.

Now about the rib. As for the Lord taking a rib out of Adams side to make a woman of, He took one out of my side just as much.

"But Brother Brigham, would you make it appear that Moses did not tell the truth?"

Not a particle more than I would that your mother did not tell the truth, when she told you that little Billy came from a hollow toad stool. I would not accuse your mother of lying, any more than I would Moses; the people in the days of Moses wanted to know things that was not for them, the same as your children do, when they want to know where their little brother came from, and he answered them according to their folly, the same as you did your children.

Now some will be ready to say, "We always heard these Mormons did not believe the Bible." I believe all the truth that is there and that is enough for me, and for you to believe.

"Then the Lord did not make Adam out of the dust of the earth."

Yes he did, but I have not got to that part of my discourse yet. Adam was made of the dust of the earth.

"Was he made of the dust of this earth."

No, but of the dust of the earth whereon he was born in the flesh; that is the way he was made; he was made of dust.

"Did the Lord put into him his spirit?"

Yes, as the Lord put into you your spirit, he was begotten of a father, and brought forth as you and I were; and so are all intelligent beings brought forth from eternity to eternity. Man was not made the same as you make an adobe and put in a wall. Moses said that Adam was made of the dust of the ground, but he did not say of what ground. I say he was not made of the dust of the ground of this Earth, but he was made of the dust of the earth where he lived, where he honored his calling, believed in his Saviour, or Elder Brother, and by his faithfulness was redeemed, and obtained a Glorious Resurrection. All creatures that dwell upon this Earth are made of the elements that compose it; which are organized to see if they will abide their creation, and be counted worthy to receive a resurrection.

"What, every flesh?"

Yes, every flesh, for all flesh pertaining to this world is made of the dust of this Earth; it is made from the same material, according to the will and pleasure of Him who dictates all things. Our bodies are composed of the same material that composes this Earth; they are composed of water, air, and solid earth, either of which will resolve back to their native fountain. How many elements there are I do not know any more than you. They have never all been classified by science, though scientific gentlemen have tried to do it.

I tell you more: Adam is the Father of our spirits. He lived upon an earth; he did abide his creation, and did honor to his calling and Priesthood. He obeyed his Master or Lord, and probably many of his wives did the same; they lived and died upon an earth, and then were resurrected again to Immortality and Eternal Life. "Did he resurrect himself?" you inquire. I want to throw out a few hints upon the resurrection as it seems to come within the circuit of my ideas whether it ought to come within the circuit of my remarks or not. I believe we have already acknowledged the truth established that no person can officiate in any office he has not been subject to himself and legally appointed to fill. That no person in this Kingdom can officiate in any ordinance he himself has not obeyed; consequently no being who has not been resurrected possesses the Keys of the Power of Resurrection. That you have been told often. Adam, therefore, was resurrected by someone who had been resurrected.

I will go a little further with this lest some of you will be querying, doubting and philosophizing this away. It is true that Jesus said, "I lay down my life and take it again. No man taketh it from me, but I lay it down of myself. I have power to lay it down, and I have power to take it again." I doubt not the power of Christ; but did he prove that in his resurrection? No. But it is proved that an angel came and rolled away the stone from the door of the sepulchre, and did resurrect the body of the Son of God.

"What angel was this?"

It is not for me to say. I do not know him. If I ever did know him it is so long since I have entirely forgotten who it was. That Jesus had power to lay down his life, and power to take it up again I do not dispute.

Neither do I dispute, but what an angel came, that was sent by the Father of our Lord Jesus Christ, to roll away the stone from the sepulchre, and resurrect the Son of God. Suffice it to say that he was some character who had himself been resurrected.

"Is there any further proof with regard to this sacred order of the Kingdom of God on the Earth?"

Oh yes, you can find it in the scriptures. For instance, when the Saviour appeared to Saul of Tarsus on the road, in answer to the question, "Lord what will you have me do," he was told to go into the city of Damascus, and it should be told him there what to do. In the meantime, one Ananias was sent to him, who Baptized and Ordained him.

Jesus would not do this, because he had servants on the Earth whose special duty it was to administer these ordinances.

Again, the angel that appeared to Cornelius would not operate in the ordinances of the Gospel, but told him to send men to Joppa to the house of one Simon the Tanner, and call for one Peter, etc., whose duty it was to do it, he being called and ordained to that power. Many more instances of this kind might be quoted but the above will suffice to illustrate the principle.

Now, many inquiries will be made about the Savior, such as, "Who is he?

Is he the Father of Adam? Is he the God of Adam?" 'When Christ has finished his labor and presented it to his father, then he, Adam, will receive a fullness.' That is all easily understood by me. He cannot receive a fullness of the kingdoms He has organized until they are completed. If He sends His servants off to the right and to the left to perform a certain labor, His kingdom is not complete, until His ministers have accomplished everything to make His kingdom complete and returned home again.

Many inquire, who is this Savior? I will tell you what I think about it.
The Southerners say I reckon, and the Yankees say I guess; but I will tell you what I reckon.

I reckon that Father Adam was a resurrected being, with his wives and posterity, and in the Celestial Kingdom they were crowned with Glory, Immortality and Eternal Lives, with Thrones, Principalities and Powers: and it was said to him, "It is your right to organize the elements; and to your Creations and Posterity there shall be no end, but you shall add Kingdom to Kingdom, and Throne to Throne; and still behold the vast eternity of unorganized matter."

Adam then was a resurrected being; and I reckon that our spirits and the spirits of all the human family were begotten by Adam and born of Eve.

"How are we going to know this?"

I reckon it.

And I reckon that Adam came into the Garden of Eden, and did actually eat of the fruit that he himself planted; and I reckon that there was a previous understanding, and the whole plan was previously calculated, before the Garden of Eden was made, that he would reduce his posterity to sin, misery, darkness, wickedness, wretchedness, and to the power of the Devil, that they might be prepared for an Exaltation, for without this they could not receive one.

I reckon that all things were first made spiritual preparatory to the natural organization.

"What was the use of all this? Could not spirits be happy?"
Yes, as far as they could. These Indians that roam upon these plains, and upon the mountains are comparatively happy in their degraded condition, because they do not know the comforts of civilized life. They can lay upon the ground; pull up sage brush to form a temporary shield against the cold, and get plenty of lizards and crickets to eat, and they are happy. We would want a comfortable house to live in and something comfortable to eat; something that is suited to our nature, ability, taste, and appetite. We would not be happy and satisfied short of that. So our spirits are as happy as they know how to be. Were you now to live without a house you could not be happy; neither could the spirit be happy without a tabernacle which is the house of the spirit.

When the spirit enters the body it is pure, and good, and if the body would be subject to the spirit it would always be taught to do the will of the Father in Heaven. But the spirit is interwoven with the flesh and blood; it is subjected to the body, consequently Satan has power over both. I reckon the Father has been through all this.

Do you recollect what I told the brethren who came across the plains this season, when they were perplexed by their oxen; and were calling upon God to give grace to you to perform the labor which lay before you, He could not sympathize with you, or know the nature of your trials if He had not passed through the same Himself. He knew just as much about crossing the plains, and the trials connected with it as any of us.

The inquiry will arise, among those who are strenuous, and tenacious for the account given by Moses, as to Adam: "Did not Adam die?"

Yes he died.

"Does not the Bible say he died?"

I do not know nor care, but it would be hard I think to find where he died;[306] or where Moses died,[307] though I have no doubt Moses died, and Adam also. How? Just as you and I have to die, and be laid away in the bowels of Mother Earth; that, however, Moses did not see fit to tell us.

Adam planted the Garden of Eden, and he with his wife Eve partook of the fruit of this Earth, until their systems were charged with the nature of the Earth, and then they could beget bodies for their spiritual children. If the spirit does not enter into the embryo man that is forming in the womb of the woman, the result will be false conception; a living, intelligent being cannot be produced. Adam and Eve begat the first mortal bodies on this Earth, and from that commencement every spirit that was begotten in eternity for this Earth will enter bodies thus prepared for them here, until the winding up scene, and that will not be until the last of these spirits enters an earthly tabernacle.

Then I reckon that the children of Adam and Eve married each other; this is speaking to the point. I believe in sisters marrying brothers, and brothers having their sisters for wives. Why? Because we cannot do otherwise. there are none others for me to marry but my sisters.

"But you would not pretend to say you would marry your father and mothers daughter."

If I did not I would marry another of my sisters that lives over in another garden; the material of which they are organized is just the same; there is no difference between them, and those who live in this garden. Our spirits are brothers and sisters, and so are our bodies; and the opposite idea to this has resulted from the ignorant, and foolish traditions of the nations of the Earth. They have corrupted themselves with each other,

---

[306] Genesis 5:5.

[307] Deuteronomy 34:7; Alma 45:19 - note that the LDS Bible Dictionary points out that Moses had to have been a translated being because of his visit on the mount of transfiguration (Matthew 17: 3-4; Mark 9: 4-9; Luke 9: 30; D&C 63: 21; HC 3: 387).

and I want them to understand that they have corrupted their own flesh, blood, and bones; for they are of the same flesh, blood, and bones, as all the family of the Earth.

I am approaching the subject of our marriage relations Brother Hyde lectured upon, but I shall not have time, or strength to say much about this. But, I reckon that Father Adam, and Mother Eve had the children of the human family prepared to come here and take bodies; and when they come to take bodies, they enter into the bodies prepared for them, and that body gets an exaltation with the spirit, when they are prepared to be crowned in Father's Kingdom.

"What, into Adam's Kingdom?"

Yes.

As to my talking what I want to say at this time I shall not do it. I am exhausting myself; I have to speak loud, and it is hard labor.

I tell you, when you see your Father in the Heavens, you will see Adam; when you see your Mother that bore your spirit, you will see Mother Eve.

And when you see yourselves there, you have gained your exaltation; you have honored your calling here on the Earth; your body has returned to its mother Earth; and somebody has broken the chains that bound you, and given you a resurrection.

How are you going to get your resurrection? You will get it by the President of the Resurrection pertaining to this generation, and that is Joseph Smith Junior. Hear it all ye ends of the Earth; if ever you enter into the Kingdom of God it is because Joseph Smith let you go there.

This will apply to Jews and Gentiles, to the bond, and free; to friends and foes; no man or woman in this generation will get a resurrection and be crowned without Joseph Smith says so. The man who was martyred in Carthage Jail in the State of Illinois holds the Keys of Life and Death to this generation. He is the President of the Resurrection in this Dispensation and he will be the first to rise from the dead. When he as passed through it, then I reckon the Keys of the Resurrection will be committed to him. Then he will call up his Apostles. You know I told you last conference I was an Apostle of Joseph Smith; and if faithful enough I expect Joseph will resurrect the Apostles; and when they have passed through the change, and received their blessings, I expect he will commit to them the Keys of the Resurrection, and they will go on resurrecting the Saints, every man in his own order.

I want to say a little more about marriage relations, so that you may understand what my views are. When you get your resurrection, you are not yet exalted; but by and by, the Lord Jesus Christ, our Elder Brother, the Saviour of the world, the Heir of the Family, when he has put down Satan, and destroyed death; then he will say, come let us go home into the presence of the Father.

What will become of the world then? It will be baptized with fire. It has been baptized with water, and it will then be cleansed by fire, and become like a sea of glass, and be made Celestial; and Jesus Christ our Elder Brother will take the whole of the Earth, with all the Saints and go with them to the Father, even to Adam; and you will continue to receive more and more Intelligence, Glory, Exaltation, and Power.

I want to tell you a thing in regard to parents, wives, brothers, sisters, etc. The time will come when it will be told where this man, and that woman should be placed; The real blood of Joseph will be selected out from among the tribes of Israel, and every man, and woman will be put in their places, and stand in their order where the Lord designs them to be. When you get back into the presence of God, and the Lord should say "Who have you brought with you?" your reply would be, "My wife and children." When you meet your Father in Heaven you will know Him, and realize that you have lived with Him, and rested in his bosom fore ages gone past, and He will hail you as His sons and daughters, and embrace you, and you will embrace Him, and "Hallelujah, thank God I have come to Father again, I have got back home" will resound through the Heavens. There are ten thousand things connected with these ideas. You see the human family of every shade of color between black and white. I could stand here and tell you what I reckon but it would take me an age for me to tell you all there is about it.

We have all come from one father even Adam, both the black and the white, the grizzled and gray; the noble, and the ignoble, and the time will come when they will all come back again into his presence. When they have all behaved themselves, and proved faithful to their calling, and to their God the curse will be removed from every class and nation of men that desires to work the work of God. This has been told you, that saviours would come upon Mount Zion, and judge the Mount of Esau.

Let me read it for you, "There shall saviours come upon Mount Zion, and Save the Mount of Esau." What does gentile signify? Disobedience. What does Israel signify? Obedience. What is the name of the first man? Adam, which signifies first man, and Eve signifies first woman. And when Michael the Archangel shall sound his trump and the Ancient of Days shall come, all things that we have once been familiar with will come back again to our memory.

In our marriage relations here we are marrying our brothers, and our sisters. As to a man having more wives than one, this is startling indeed to the traditions of the people. With regard to it being the law of the Lord for a man to have only one wife, or for a man to have no wife, it is no such thing, all that rests in the traditions of the people, and in the doings of legislative bodies; that is all there is about wives in the world as to their having many or none. It is corruption for men to deny the truth; for men to work iniquity, to defile themselves, and to betray the innocent.

If there are any of my friends who do not belong to the Church here, I want to tell you one thing. I will take all the sin in the world there is before God and angels in men having one wife, two wives, ten, or fifty wives, that will use them well, upon my own shoulders, if they will acknowledge them, support them, raise children by them, and bring them up as well as they know how; I say I will take all the sins there is in this, of the whole of the Latter-day Saints, and place them with one sin of you poor devils, who when you were young courted that poor innocent girl, and made her believe you would marry her, then got her in the family way and left her to the wide world, you poor curses. This one sin of yours will weigh down all the sins of the Latter-day Saints together, and go down about enough for you to be damned in the bottomless pit; while the Elders of Israel will be exalted among the Gods. There are scores, and hundreds, and thousands of these poor girls upon the streets of the cities of the United States.

"Why Governor did you ever see any of them?"

Yes, lots of them; in that neighborhood, and in the other neighborhood.

I have found respectable families, where a young mechanic, a merchant, a lawyer, or a farmer, or some other miserable wretch fit for nothing but the fire of Hell, would insinuate themselves into the family, court the daughter, win her affections, deceive her, and then forsake her, and then boast of your achievements and rejoice over your success; but weep and howl for the miseries that shall come upon you, you poor damned wretches. I want to cut their damned throats and I will if I catch any of them doing it here. I should hold myself guilty before God and angels if I did not sweep the Earth of such a wretch. I will not ask the Lord to do a dirty trick I would not do myself. Let them prowl around my daughters, and I will slay them, yes, as fast as I can come to them.

What more will I do? When I find a young woman caught in this snare, I will take her to my house, and say, you shall have a home with me and my family.

I only know these iniquities by observation. I was never of such sins; the wickedest day I ever saw I would not betray an innocent female, but instead of prostituting them, I would tell them how to do right, and teach them the way of Life and Salvation, and see them safe in the Kingdom of God if they would obey my counsel. But you will take a poor helpless, innocent creature, and lead the unsuspecting victim nigh unto the altar of marriage, and then ruin the innocent lamb, you poor cursed gentiles, go and weep, and howl. In New York alone there is over eighteen hundred prostitutes licensed in that city, to corrupt themselves for Hell; and I want to tell every man that is going to hell that it is full of such creatures, so full that their elbows stick out of the windows.

Instead of creating such an awful state of society as this presents, we take to ourselves wives, acknowledge them, raise their children, school them, and try to teach them the way of Salvation. Let me tell you what they should do in the City of New York -that holy, righteous city- and to other cities, where there are thousands of licensed houses of ill fame, besides thousands of private ones that are not licensed but go under different appellations. They should set fire to every poor filthy debaucher, and collect the illegitimate children, as they are called, that are running the streets, and wash them, and school them, and teach them righteousness, and not suffer them to mingle with those that mingle unlawfully together. Also take the women, and wash them clean, and put them to work, at spinning, weaving, and at other useful employment in the country. As they now exist they want to die, they have lost their character, and nothing appears in the future for them but a life of wretchedness of the lowest grade. There are thousands of these poor women who would bless the first person who would kill them. They do not wish to kill themselves, but live they must and disguise their real feelings.

Let the world cleanse themselves before they talk of Utah; and when they get sanctified, and become purer than we are, they may come and give us a few lessons upon purity. It is a subject I do not wish to name, but my remarks seem to run on it, and could not well avoid it.

I wish you should understand well the position I have taken, and the nature of the remarks I have made. Profit by them, both saints and sinners. You have had things laid before you that does not belong to the world, nor to men and women, who calculate to apostatize. They belong to the wise; to those who are serving God with all their hearts. Now let me say to the wicked in heart, you cannot remember a word of this discourse unless you remember it in the Lord. I might reveal all there is in eternity, and those who have not their hearts on righteousness would know nothing about it, or be in the least instructed.

I commenced with Father Adam in his resurrected state, noticed our spiritual state, then our temporal, or mortal state, and traveled until I got back to Father Adam again. After considering all this, what have you seen that makes it appear we are not brethren and sisters? does it appear that we are not because we are commanded to multiply and replenish the Earth? You think when you run into grandchildren and great-grandchildren, etc. that by and by there will be no connection? The are just as much connected in spirit and body, in flesh, blood and bone, as your children are that you bear off your own body.

This is something pertaining to our marriage relation. The whole world will think what an awful thing it is. What an awful thing it would be if the Mormons should just say we believe in marrying brothers and sisters. Well we shall be under the necessity of doing it, because we cannot find anybody else to marry. The whole world are at the same thing, and will be as long as man exists upon the Earth.

I feel as though I had said enough. I have talked long enough for my own good; and we shall bring our conference to close.

Other

Accounts

Of the 1854 Discourse

Only a few of the following accounts actually shed any further light into the theological teachings delivered by Brigham Young on October 8, 1854. This subsection is therefore included in this volume primarily for the purpose of documenting (for the more skeptical members of the LDS Church) the authenticity of the October 8, 1854 discourse.

Friday 10/6/1854

Journal of Joseph L. Robinson, 102-03

Attended conference, a very interesting conference, for at this meeting President Brigham Young said thus, that Adam and Eve were the names of the first man and woman of every earth that was ever organized and that Adam and Eve were the natural father and mother of every spirit that comes to this planet, or that receives tabernacles on this planet, consequently we are brother and sisters, and that Adam was God, our Eternal Father. This as Brother Heber remarked, was letting the cat out of the bag, and it came to pass, I believed every word, for I remembered saying to the Brethren at a meeting of High Priests in Nauvoo, while I was speaking to them under the influence of the Spirit, I remarked thus, that our Father Adam had many wives, and that Eve was only one of them, and that she was our mother, and that she was the mother of the inhabitants of this earth, and I believe that also, but behold ye there were some that did not believe these sayings of the Prophet Brigham, even our Beloved Brother Orson Pratt told me he did not believe it. He said he could prove by the scriptures it was not correct. I felt very sorry to hear Professor Orson Pratt say that. I feared least he should apostatize, but I prayed for him that he might endure unto the end, for I knew verily it was possible that great men might fall.

Thomas D. Brown   *Friday 10/6/1854*

Journal of the Southern Indian Mission, 87- 89[308]

Conference assembled, in the afternoon being called on by President Bm. Young I addressed the numerous saints assembled in the Tabernacle, gave them an account of our mission so far, and had liberty. On the evening of this day elder O. Hyde delivered an excellent discourse proving that Jesus Christ was a married man - and children besides. - See Deseret news Vol.___. No.___. and on Sunday afternoon President B. Young delivered a discourse, equaled by none that I have ever listened to on "Space - the Eternities - of matter of duration. The Gods - Gentile Seduction & Mormon Saviors of the innocent betrayed. The following is the essence of his discourse: "I believe in one Eternity - no beginning no end to anything - Gods - Angels and _____ never had a beginning & never will have an end: "no beginning no end to space - no end - no bounds - no place in time or eternity will end their formation - no end to matter - There is an eternity of matter yet to be organized: no true philosopher can count the millions of eternities yet to be made: we shall learn in all time and in all eternities: The Bible and the ordinances are the same from Adam to the end, there will be no change till the last of Adam's race is saved - the ordinances are the same - duties & callings vary as do the circumstances, but the ordinances are the same for salvation in worlds without end.

Text "This is eternal life to know the only wise and true God & his Son Jesus Christ whom he has sent" - "There are Lords many and there are Gods many, & the Father of our Spirits is the Father of Jesus Christ: He is the Father of Jesus Christ, Spirit & Body and he is the beginner of the bodies of all men: Neither can you have a Father, without having a Grandfather: God hath made of one flesh, all the dwellers, or inhabitants on the whole earth, we are all formed of the same materials, from the mother Earth; those who keep their second estate will be celestialized & brought back to dwell with the Father. Can any individual officiate in any ordinances of any nature, before obeying the same and honoring them? Can any man officiate in this kingdom without first becoming a subject in the same?

We'll let the numerous Gods alone, and take the one we have to do with. There is no time when worlds have not been created and exalted; there have always been an Adam and an Eve - the first man and woman, and their oldest son is heir, and should be our Savior. We have one Father and we all are brethren." Eloheim spoke, "Yehovah, Michael - see matter all around, go and organize a world," Yehovah Michael went and

---

[308] Apart from the fact that this source is dated two days previous to the date generally accepted as the accurate date of this sermon, Thomas Brown also includes multiple details not found in the full version. It may be that this journal entry was made from a compilation of notes and that some of these additional details arose from his recollection of other sermons given by Brigham Young that same conference.

carried material: Then Michael came down with his wife, & began to people it. Michael had his body from the dust of the planet he was begotten on, he obeyed his Lord, was faithful and obedient, died and was resurrected, he did not resurrect himself. An Angel resurrected Jesus - what Angel? I know not.

When Jesus has completed his work, Adam shall have a fullness: Adam's descent was to organize people & redeem a world, by his wife he peopled it by his first born he redeems. Our Spirits were happy before they had a body. An allusion to the Indians - Father Adam knew all about oxen and cattle. Adam died and was buried, where he was interred is not said. Physicians will tell you, men's efforts to beget will be abortive, without the spirit put in by the Father. Adam & Eve had children in the spirit - and their children married - brother & sister - then the bodies followed. Joseph Smith will be the first resurrected being in this dispensation & he will hold the keys of the Resurrection & no man can be raised without his permission, he will delegate this power. He then spoke of the final baptism of the earth by fire - The earth to be as a Sea of Glass. He next said something of exchange of women & children. All are the children of Father Adam. When Jesus has done his work he will take this planet back to his Father.

Wilford W. Woodruff   *10/6-8/1854*

Journal of Wilford Woodruff 4:290

General Conference commenced this morning at the tabernacle at 10 O clock The Presidency were present - of the twelve apostles: O. Hyde, O. Pratt, W. Woodruff, G. A. Smith, E. T. Benson, L. Snow, as all the business of the Conference is published in the Deseret News of Oct 12 No. 31 I deem it unnecessary to record it here. Conference closed Sunday Evening Oct. 8th President Young preached to a congregation of several thousand, out of doors and I believe that *he preached the greatest sermon that ever was delivered to the Latter day Saints* since they have been a people. *Elder Watt reported.* I also took minutes.

Sunday 10/8/1854

Historian's Office Journal 17:185

pleasant da[y] Meeting of Seventies at 7 a m to hear report of Pres." Jos.h Young see Rob Campbell's minutes 10 a m in Tabernacle O Hyde preached see TB min - & G D Watts report at the same time a meeting outside the Tabernacle was addressed by G A Smith & E D Wooley 2 pm about *7000 Saints assembled North side of Tabernacle* Pres." Young preached on plurality of worlds &c see G D Watts report 4 1/2 pm Pres." Young & Council met in Historian's office to pra[y] Conversation on the Conference, with O Pratt on the creation of Adam.

10/12/1854

DN 31

Tabernacle crowded. Choir sung a hymn. Prayer by Elder Lorenzo Snow. Chanting by the choir. Elder Hyde spoke inside the Tabernacle, followed by Elder W. W. Phelps; and at the same time a much larger congregation assembled at the north end of the building, were addressed by Elder G. A. Smith and Bishop Woolley. Upon proposition from President Brigham Young, the congregation adjourned to meet in the afternoon at the north end of the Tabernacle, where seats had been prepared. Choir chanted, 'We praise thee, O God.' Benediction by Elder Woodruff.

Two p.m. An immense congregation were comfortably seated in the open air. Singing. Prayer by Elder G. A. Smith. Elder O. Pratt read the 68th Psalm, which the choir chanted. It being the recurring time for administering the sacrament, Bishop L. D. Young asked a blessing upon the bread and Bishop Isaac Hill [?] asked a blessing upon the water.

While the emblems were being passed, President Brigham young delivered a highly interesting discourse which held the vast audience as it were spellbound.

Elder Lyman Curtis was appointed, and voted to go on a mission in connection with Elder Rufus Allen, and to be under the direction of Elder Parley P. Pratt. On motion of Elder Hyde, it was unanimously voted that all members of this church who go out on the roads to trade, or who go to California, or any other place outside of this Territory, without being sent, or counseled to do so, be cut off from the church.

On motion, conference adjourned to meet in the Tabernacle, at ten a.m. on the 6th of April 1855. The choir sung, 'The spirit of God like a fire is burning.' Benediction by President H. C. Kimball. The sermons, exhortations, and remarks delivered during the conference will appear in the News as fast as the reporter is able to furnish them.

Brigham Young   *Sunday 10/8/1854*

John Pulsipher Papers, 35-37

OC - A. Meeting out doors - Prest. Young said: We believe in God the Eternal Father, Jesus Christ his son & the Holy Ghost Gods minister. The gods are Eternal, there never was a beginning. They always Existed. Philosophers have tried to study out how the first gods came I want to ask them a Question: Which was first a squash or apple that produced the Seed or was it the seed that produced the Squash or apple? Which was first. They can't tell. So they need not rack their Brain with it - There never was a time but what No man from the days of Adam to the End of the world will ever by saved unless they go thro the same ordin that we do - There never was any other way to Salvation.

Text was: to know the only true & wise God is Eternal life - To know this a person must have Eternal life - God is the father of spirits of all the people of this world - he is the father of the bodies also of the first inhabitants of the Earth also the father of the body of Jesus Christ - The first people of the Earth was no more made of the dust than you are - I would not make out that Moses lied, by no means. But we are made of dust as much as Adam was. So are our cattle. They are formed or created from the Elements all of which are necessary to produce animal or vegetable life - as the dust of the earth will produce grass & cattle will eat grass & increase Evry person must have a father & mother or they could not be. So we had a grandfather & great-great-great-great-great grandfather So far back there is no beginning -

They always Existed on some world - & when this work was made - our God who is Adam came & commenced the peopling of it - Tho he is God & had lived & died & been reserected on some other plannet - & obtained his exaltation & begat the Spirits of children enough people this world he came down & brot some of the animal & vegetable productions of some other world so that they might grow & increase here - He by eating the mortal fruits of the Earth, it caused & produced mortal children or commenced the increase of men on the Earth which is the bodies for the Spirits to live in

There never was a time when Worlds were not created - The work of creation was always in Progress - An Adam & Eve is necesary for evry world The oldest Son, if faithful, is the Saviour of the family - There are Lords many & Gods many But the God that we have to account to, is the father of our Spirits - Adam. All the inhabitance of the Earth are made of one flesh - whither they are black-white-blue or streaked. Now a few words on the resurrection A Man cant resurrect himself - A person cant officiate in an office that he does not hold - Therefore a person cant resurrect others, 'til he himself has been resurrected - No man or woman in this dispensation will be resurrected unless it is done by Joseph Smith Jr. as a yankee says, I guess he will be resurrected first & then he will res. others -

A word on Marriage. People would think it an awful thing if a man should marry his sister for a wife - but Bless your souls we all do it We mary our sisters because we can get no others - all the women in the world are our sisters because we are all the child of one father. Our fathers & grandfathers in this world - are our brothers - that is - our spirits are brothers & will be after the resurrection - we will be as near to our father as any of our great grandfathers - they will not be a head of us for being our fathers in this world because we will all be Brothers & all have one father - The poor Gentiles will whine about the order of Marriage among the Mormons but they dont tell of their own crimes - but I know them from first to last - What they call gentlemen will go & court & gain the affection of an innocent girl, promise to marry her & destroy her & run away & leave her a disgrace to all that know her, to mourn out her days in sorrow. That is just the character of the great men of the world - they dont take care of their children Take the sins of one such a man & put them in the balance against the whole of this people & they will sink him among the damned in hell - while we, the latter day Saints will rise to thrones & dominions. It is not right to compare it in that way because the sins of all this people, that do right with all their wives, is not to be compared to the sins of one such a man as I have described In fact there is no sin in the plurality of wives or any other doctrine of this church unless the people do wrong I would bless u all so that u would be saved if I had the power - I have the power to bless all the faithful & I do bless u in the name of Jesus Christ. Amen. Conference adjourned to the 6th of Ap'l next - Elder Kimball Prayed & the group seperated

1854

HBY, 93

Forenoon. Elders Orson Hyde and Wm. W. Phelps preached inside the Tabernacle and Elder Geo. A. Smith and Edwin D. Woolley outside to those who could not get in. Afternoon the saints assembled out doors. The sacrament was administered, I preached. Elders Lyman Curtis and Rufus Allen were appointed to go on a mission under the direction of Elder Parley P. Pratt. Elder Orson Hyde motioned and it was unanimously voted that all members of the Church who got out on the road to trade, or go to California or any place outside of this Territory, without being sent or counseled to go, be excommunicated. Conference adjourned until the 6th of April 1855. Benediction by President Heber C. Kimball.

40

The Lecture at the Veil

The Lecture at the Veil   _Tuesday 2/7/1877_

Journal of L. John Nuttall

In the creation the Gods entered into an agreement about forming this earth. & putting Michael or Adam upon it. these things of which I have been speaking are what are termed the mysteries of godliness but they will enable you to understand the expression of Jesus made while in Jerusalem. This is life eternal that they might know thee the only true God and Jesus Christ whom thou hast sent. We were once acquainted with the Gods & lived with them but we had the privilege of taking upon us flesh that the spirit might have a house to dwell in. we did so and forgot all and came into the world not recollecting anything of which we had previously learned.

We have heard a great deal about Adam and Eve. how they were formed &c some think he was made like an adobe and the Lord breathed into him the breath of life. for we read "from dust thou art and unto dust shalt thou return" Well he was made of the dust of the earth but not of this earth. he was made just the same way you and I are made but on another earth. Adam was an immortal being when he came. On this earth he had lived on an earth similar to ours he had received the Priesthood and the Keys thereof. and had been faithful in all things and gained his resurrection and his exaltation and was crowned with glory immortality and eternal lives and was numbered with the Gods for such he became through his faithfulness. and had begotten all the spirit that was to come to this earth. and Eve our common Mother who is the mother of all living bore those spirits in the celestial world.

And when this earth was organized by Elohim. Jehovah & Michael who is Adam our common Father. Adam & Eve had the privilege to continue the work of Progression.

consequently came to this earth and commenced the great work of forming tabernacles for those spirits to dwell in. and when Adam and those that assisted him had completed this Kingdom our earth he came to it. And slept and forgot all and became like an Infant child. it is said by Moses the historian that the Lord caused a deep sleep to come upon Adam and took from his side a rib and formed the woman that Adam called Eve - this should be interpreted that the Man Adam like all other Men had the seed within him to propagate his species. but not the Woman. she conceives the seed but she does not produce it. consequently she was taken from the side or bowels of her father. this explains the mystery of Moses' dark sayings in regard to Adam and Eve.

Adam & Eve when they were placed on this earth were immortal beings with flesh, bones and sinews. but upon partaking of the fruits of the earth while in the garden and cultivating the ground their bodies became changed from immortal to mortal beings with the blood coursing through their veins as the action of life. Adam was not under transgression until after he partook of the forbidden fruit that was necessary that they might be together that man might be. The woman was found in transgression not the Man -

Now in the law of Sacrifice we have the promise of a Savior and man had the privilege and showed forth his obedience by offering of the first fruits of the earth and the firstlings of the flocks - this as a showing that Jesus would come and shed his blood [Four lines without any writing on them.]

Father Adam's oldest son (Jesus the Savior) who is the heir of the family is Father Adams first begotten in the spirit World. who according to the flesh is the only begotten as it is written. (In his divinity he having gone back into the spirit World. and come in the spirit [glory] to Mary and she conceived for when Adam and Eve got through with their Work in this earth. they did not lay their bodies down in the dust, but returned to the spirit World from whence they came.

I felt myself much blessed in being permitted to associate with such men and hear such instructions as they savored of life to me -

The following account is from a document that I found on the internet but have since been unable to relocate. The person who posted the information is not known to the author. Although I have been unable to identify the author or the source, I have included this document here because 1) it fits the description of the shortened version of the lecture referred to in the Tribune article below 2) it contains nothing that would outwardly discredit its authenticity and 3) it is interesting. The provider of the document described it as 16-17 pages long on 5 1/2 by 8 1/2 sheets of paper; 3 hole punched with rounded corners.

Shortened Lecture at the Veil   *between 1877-1894*

He had been true and faith in all things and gained his resurretin and exaltation. He was crowned ~~in which~~ with glory, immortality and eternal lives and was numbered with the Gods - for such he became through his faithfulness.

He had begotten all the spirits that was to come to/this earth, and Eve, our common mother - who is the mother of all living - bore our spirits in the celestial world. And when this earth was organized by Elohim, Jehovah and Michael - who is Adam our common father - Adam and Eve had the privilege to continue the work of progression. They consequently came to this earth and commenced the great work of forming tabernacles for those spirits to dwell in, and when Adam and those who assisted him had completed this kingdom which is our earth, he came to it and slept and forgot all become like a little child.

It was said by Moses that the Lord caused a deep sleep to come upon Adam, and that he took from his side a rib and formed a woman which he called Eve. Now this should be interpreted that the man Adam - like all other men - had the seed of creation within himself to propagate the species, but the woman did not. She conceived the seed but did not produce it, and consequently she was taken, as it were, from the side or ribs of her father. This explains the mystery of Mose's dark saying in regard to the creation of Eve from Adam's rib.

You entered into a room representing the garden of Eden, where Elohim provided that Adam and Eve might eat freely of all the fruit of the garden. Except for the fruit of the tree of knowledge of good and evil. He forbad them to partake of this fruit and said in the day they did so they should surely die. ...

Analysis & Observations

β

This lecture,[309] unknown to the vast majority of modern members of the LDS Church, had a venerable beginning. In Nauvoo, Joseph Smith commissioned Brigham Young to

---

[309] These can be found in the LDS Archives in Salt Lake City and in BYU Special Collections (Journal 2: December 1876 - August 1877.

perfect the endowment ceremony, which was yet in an imperfect state when it was performed for the saints in Nauvoo. As the following historical background will demonstrate, this lecture at the veil, was a natural outgrowth of this commission. Most of the substantive materials in this subsection were preserved by L. John Nuttall, who was the private secretary for presidents Brigham Young, John Taylor, and Wilford Woodruff. That he remained in this position for the greater part of two decades shows that these presidents placed a great deal of confidence in his record keeping abilities. Despite the existence of these historical documents, many members of the LDS Church remain skeptical that this portion of the sacred endowment ever included Adam-God teachings. I have therefore included multiple other sources that refer to Adam-God teachings in the old lecture at the veil so that the reader may verify the accuracy of these historical documents in a variety of sources.

Wilford W. Woodruff   *Wednesday 2/1/1877*

Journal of Wilford Woodruff

President [Young] was present and delivered a lecture at the veil some 30 attndg

John Lyman Smith   *Wednesday, 2/1/1877*

John Lyman Smith Journal

Worked at Temple giving Endowments all day. Took thro 671 B.Y. Lectured.

Tuesday 2/7/1877

Journal of L. John Nuttall 1:18-19

Works in the Temple being under consideration Prest. Young was filled with the spirit of God and revelation and said:

When we got our washings and anointings under the hands of the Prophet Joseph at Nauvoo we had only one room to work in, with the exception of a little side room or office w[h]ere we were washed and anointed, had our garments placed upon us and received our new name. And after he had performed these ceremonies, he gave the key words, signs, tokens and penalties. Then after we went into the large room over the store in Nauvoo, Joseph divided up the room the best that he could, hung up the veil, marked it, gave us our instructions as we passed along from one department to another, giving us signs, tokens, penalties, with the key words pertaining to those signs. And after we had got through, Bro. Joseph turned to me and said, "Bro. Brigham this is not arranged right but we have done the best we could under the circumstances in which we are placed, "And I wish you to take this matter in hand and organize and systematize all these ceremonies, with the signs, tokens, penalties and key words" - I did so and each time I got something more, so that when we went through the Temple at Nauvoo I understood and knew how to place them there, We had our ceremonies pretty correct.

L. John Nuttall   *2/10-13/1877*

Journal of L. John Nuttall

10 February 1877

with Bro W. Woodruff engaged in writing the lecture for the Endowments to be read to Prest Young spent the eving at Prest Young's house - did not finish our work.

12 February 1877

I wrote on a Mode of Procedure to be observed in the giving of endowments also assisted by Bro J. D. T. McAllister & A H Raleigh - by invitation we all ate supper at the house of Bro Crane - and spent the evening with President Young reading what we had written. he accepted & corrected the same.

13 February 1877

At the temple ... worked on the Mode of Procedure as I call it - until 6 p.m. at 7 went to Prest Youngs and read over our writing which he approved spent an agreeable evening

11/8/1890 - 12/13/1890

Manuscript History of St. George Stake

High Council of St. George Stake met in St. George Tabernacle, Pres. Ivins stated that he had learned that Father Edward Bunker, of Bunkerville in this Stake had been *teaching that some of the ceremonies of the Temple were wrong and erroneous teaching was given in the lecture at the vail.* As Elder Myron Abbott, first Councilor to the Bishop at Bunkerville had given some information on this matter, it was decided to learn from him, more definitely in (next page) relation to this matter.

December 13, 1890

Saturday, Dec. 13. High Council of St. George Stake met at St. George Tabernacle. In response to invitation of the Presidency of the Stake, Bishop Edward Bunker, Jr., and Elders Myron Abbott and Jos. I. Earl were present. Pres. McArthur invited the brethren named to express themselves on the views said to have been expressed in Bunkerville Ward and which are considered by some to be unsound doctrine. Myron Abbott, counselor to Bishop Edward Bunker, Jr., stated that for a number of years, questions on church teachings have been agitated in Bunkerville Ward. Bishop Bunker had stated he did not believe Adam was our God, and *Bishop Bunker had expressed his opinion that some teachings in the Temples were wrong, notably part of the lecture at the vail.* That Father Bunker had the same views. Father Bunker stated to him (Bro. Abbott) a number of years ago, that adoption would be of no avail as administered in the Temple.

All such work would have to be done over again. Bp. Edward Bunker, Jr., among other things said: "*In regard to the lecture at the vail, in the Temple, it is certainly wrong.* It teaches that Eve was an immortal being and was brought here by Adam, 'did not believe this.' That Adam was not a resurrected (next page) being. In answering question of Councilor Cannon, expressed his belief that Adam was the Archangel and that Jehovah and Michael were persons of Spirit; that Eloheim was a person of Tabernacle and the head of all." After a prolonged second session of the Council, Bp. Edward Bunker and his councilor, Myron Abbott felt that they had done wrong in contending on the subjects referred to.

First Presidency	*6/3/1892*

L. John Nuttall Papers, 290

In January 1877, shortly after the lower portion of the St. George Temple was dedicated, President Brigham Young, in following up in the Endowments written, became convinced that it was necessary to have the formula of the Endowments written, and he gave directions to have the same put in writing. Shortly afterwards he explained what the Lecture at the Veil should portray, and for this purpose appointed a day when he would personally deliver the Lecture at the Veil.

Elder J.D.T. McAllister and L. John Nuttall prepared writing material, and as the President spoke they took down his words. Elder Nuttall put the same into form and the writing was submitted to President Young on the same evening at his office in residence at St. George. He there made such changes as he deemed proper, and when he finally passed upon it said: *This is the Lecture at the Veil to be observed in the Temple. A copy of the Lecture is kept at the St. George Temple, in which President Young refers to Adam in his creation &c.*

/s/ L. John Nuttall
For Presidents W. Woodruff, Geo. Q. Cannon, Jos. F. Smith; Salt Lake City

Wilford W. Woodruff	*6/11/1892*

Journal of Wilford Woodruff

The Lecture at the veil is true. Procreation is the gift of Eternal Lives, and if we are faithful we shall create worlds and people them just as Adam has done.

George Q. Cannon	*circa 1892*

St. George High Council Minutes

[I testify] ... in the name of Jesus Christ that Adam was born just as we are born. *The lecture at the vail* [sic] *is true*

Out of sensitivity to the endowment ceremony, I have omitted some few items from the following letter to Lorenzo Snow from the first presidency of the Church. I have retained all items that specifically refer to the lecture at the veil as they are pertinent to this volume.

Office of the First Presidency   *8/31/1894*

Elder Lorenzo Snow, Prest. Salt Lake Temple

Dear Brother: ...

In the ceremonies at the veil, the practice has been to use the words, "this man Adam," while in the Logan Temple the words, "this man, representing Adam", are used. It was decided to drop the words, "this man representing," and say "Adam, &c."

The word "christian," referred to in the lecture, in connection with name, is dropped and the word "given" is substituted.

The words "and some have to go away on business," which occur at the end of the lecture, were expunged.

The words, "new name," were substituted for the pronoun "it," to avoid ambiguity, where it reads in the lecture, "You must remember "it", that is, your new name. ...

Your Brethren,
/s/ Wilford Woodruff
/s/ Geo. Q. Cannon
/s/ Jos. F. Smith

Salt Lake Tribune   *2/12/1906*

Page 3

All having been sealed, Elohim, or someone in authority, comes to the front of the platform and delivers what is known as *the sermon before the veil*. On Wednesdays, when there are a number of neophytes, the address is very long and tedious; the entire history of the temple work is repeated, so that the candidates may have a clear understanding of what they have learned. The marks in the veil are also explained, with their significance and uses. *Especially is it taught that Adam was not made out of the dust of this earth; that he was begotten as any other man is begotten, and that when he came here he brought Eve, one of his wives, with him.* I have heard that the sermon was the one delivered by Brigham Young at the dedication of the St. George Temple. *On Thursdays and Fridays, when there are comparatively few who are going through the temple for the first time, the sermon before the veil is very much shortened,* only the essential part which refers to the Creation of Adam being read.

J. Arthur Horne, Patriarch   *5/28/1963*

C. Jess Gorewsbeck's Elder's Journal 1:291

Brother Horne and I chatted again tonight about the Gospel and the Adam-God
Doctrine, as we have done many times before. Brother Horne, who grew up in Salt
Lake City and was the son of Richard Horne and grandson of Joseph Horne said, in
reference to the Adam-God Doctrine, that *when he first went through the Temple* (Salt
Lake) *for his Endowment in 1902 before going on his mission he was surprised to hear the
teachings during the Temple ceremony in the Sermon before the veil*, that, `Adam was our God'
and that "he came here with Eve, one of his wives'. Also it was taught that `Eve bore
our spirits' (ie the spirits of all men). He asked his father about it but he declined to
give any opinion about it. After Brother Horne returned from his mission a few years
later, in 1905, he noted these teachings had been removed from the Temple ceremony.
He feels that they were left over from Brigham Young's influence, but that he himself
couldn't believe such doctrine. He thinks perhaps Brigham just got off in his
speculation.

41 The Women of Mormondom

At 552 pages of text, The Women of Mormondom was the largest project of its kind in 1877. The following excerpts therefore represent only a very small sampling of the writings of Tullidge's book. However, these excerpts also represent the longest and most lucid Adam-God teachings found therein. The significance of these passages goes beyond their length - as explained below, Joseph Smith's noted plural wife, Eliza R. Snow, may have been the pen behind some of these passages.

[177]
[Woman was n]ot yet created; taken afterwards from the rib of Adam; of the earth, not of heaven;[310] created for Adam's glory, that he might rule over her." So said Joseph. It was the young East who thus declared. The age West had kept the book of remembrance.
Joseph was gifted with wonderful memories of the "eternities past." He had not forgotten woman. he knew Eve, and he remembered Zion. He restored woman to her place among the Gods, where her primeval Genesis is written.
Woman was among the morning stars, when they sang together for joy, at the laying of the foundations of the earth. When the sons of God thrice gave their Masonic shouts of hosanna, the daughters of God lifted up their voices with their brothers; and the hallelujahs to the Lord God Omnipotent, were rendered sweeter and diviner by woman leading the theme.
In the temples, both of the heavens and the earth, woman is found. She is there in her character of Eve, and in her character of Zion. The one is the type of earth, the other the type of heaven; the one the mystical name of the mortal, the other of the celestial,

---

[310] This appears to contradict the teachings found on page 181 but the grammar allows for varying interpretations.

woman.

The Mormon prophet rectified the divine drama. Man is nowhere where woman is not. Mormonism has restored woman to her pinnacle. Presently woman herself shall sing of her divine origin. A high priestess of the faith shall interpret the themes of herself and of her Father-and-Mother God!

At the very moment when the learned divines of

[178]

Christendom were glorying that this little earth was the "be-all and the end-all" of creation, the prophet of Mormondom was teaching the sisters in the temple at Kirtland that there has been an eternal chain of creations coming down from the generations of the Gods worlds and systems and universes. At the time these lights of the Gentiles were pointing to the star-fretted vault of immensity as so many illuminations lamps hung out by the Creator, six thousand years ago, to light this - little earth through her probation the prophet of Israel was teaching his people that the starry hosts were worlds and suns and universes, some of which had being millions of ages before this earth had physical form.

Moreover, so vast is the divine scheme, and stupendous the works of creations, that the prophet introduced the expressive word eternities. The eternities are the times of creations.

This earth is but an atom in the immensities of creations. Innumerable worlds have been peopled with "living souls" of the order of mankind; innumerable worlds have passed through their probations; innumerable worlds have been redeemed, resurrected, and celestialized.

Hell-loving apostles of the sects were sending ninety-nine hundredths of this poor, young, forlorn earth to the bottomless pit. The Mormon prophet was finding out grand old universes, in exaltation with scarcely the necessity of losing a soul.

The spirit of Mormonism is universal salvation

Those who are not saved in one glory, may be saved in another.

[179]

There are the "glory of the sun," and the "glory of the moon," and the "glory of the stars."

The children of Israel belong to the glory of the sun. They kept their first estate. They are nobly trying to keep their second estate on probation. Let the devotion, the faith, the divine heroism of the Mormon sisters, witness this.

"Adam is our Father and our God. He is the God of the earth." So says Brigham Young. Adam is the great archangel of this creation. He is Michael. He is the Ancient of Days. He is the father of our elder brother, Jesus Christ the father of him who shall also come as Messiah to reign. He is the father of the spirits as well as the tabernacles of the sons and daughters of man. Adam!

Michael is one of the grand mystical names in the works of creations, redemptions and resurrections. Jehovah is the second and the higher name. Eloheim - signifying the Gods - is the first name of the celestial trinity.

Michael was a celestial, resurrected being, of another world.

"In the beginning" the Gods created the heavens and the earths.

In their councils they said, let us make man in our own image. So, in the likeness of the Fathers, and the Mothers - the Gods - created they man - male and female.

When this earth was prepared for mankind, Michael, as Adam, came down. He brought with him one of his wives, and he called her - name Eve.

[180]

Adam and Eve are the names of the fathers and mothers of worlds. Adam was not made out of a lump of clay, as we make a brick, nor was Eve taken as a rib - a bone - from his side. They came by generation. But woman, as the wife or mate of man, was a rib of man. She was taken from his side, in their glorified world, and brought by him to earth to be the mother of a race.

These were father and mother of a world of spirits who had been born to them in heaven. These spirits had been waiting for the grand period of their probation, when they should have bodies or tabernacles, so that they might become, in the resurrection, like Gods.

When this earth had become an abode for mankind, with its Garden of Eden, then it was that the morning stars sang together, and the sons and daughters of God shouted for joy. They were coming down to earth.

The children of the sun,[311] at least, knew what the grand scheme of the everlasting Fathers and the everlasting Mothers meant, and they, both sons and daughters, shouted for joy. The temple of the eternities shook with their hosannas, and trembled with divine emotions. The father and mother were at length in their Garden of Eden. They came on purpose to fall. They fell "that man might be; and man is, that he might have joy." They ate of the tree of mortal life, partook of the elements of this earth that they might again become mortal for their children's sake. They fell that another world might have a probation, redemption and resurrection.

[181]

The grand patriarchal economy, with Adam, as a resurrected being, who brought his wife Eve from another world, has been very finely elaborated, by Brigham, from the patriarchal genesis which Joseph conceived.

Perchance the scientist might hesitate to accept the Mormon ideals of the genesis of

---

[311] This is not my spelling error; this is either the Tullidge's or Snow's spelling error or it was a deliberate rendering of the word.

mortals and immortals' but Joseph and Brigham have very much improved on the Mosaic genesis of man. It is certainly not scientific to make Adam as a model adobe; the race has come by generation. The genesis of a hundred worlds of his family, since his day, does not suggest brickyards of mortality. The patriarchal economy of Mormonism is at least an improvement, and is decidedly epic in all its constructions - and ideals.

A grand patriarchal line, then, down from the "eternities;" generations of worlds and generations of Gods; all one universal family.

The Gods are the fathers and the mothers, and the brothers and the sisters, of the saints. Divine ambitions here; a daring genius to thus conceive; a lifting up of man and woman to the very plane of the celestials while yet on - earth.

...

[190]

God the Father and God the Mother stand, in the grand pre-existing view, as the origin and centre of the spirits of all the generations of mortals who had been entabernacled on this earth.

[191]

First and noblest of this great family was Jesus Christ, who was the elder brother, in spirit, of the whole human race. These constituted a world - family of pre-existing souls. Brightest among these spirits, and nearest in the circle to our Father and Mother in heaven (the Father being Adam), were Seth, Enoch, Noah and Abraham, Moses, David, and Jesus Christ - indeed that glorious cohort of men and women, whose lives have left immortal records in the world's history.

Among these the Mormon faith would rank Joseph Smith, Brigham Young, and their compeers.

In that primeval spirit-state, these were also associated with a divine sisterhood. One can easily imagine the inspired authoress of the hymn on pre-existence, to have been a bright angel among this sister throng. Her hymn is as a memory of that primeval life, and her invocation is as the soul's yearning for the Father and Mother in whose courts she was reared, and near whose side her spirit was nurtured. These are the sons and daughters of Adam - the Ancient of Days - the Father and God of the whole human family. These are the sons and daughters of Michael, who is Adam, the father of the spirits of all our race. These are the sons and daughters of Eve, the Mother of a world. What a practical Unitarianism is this! The Christ is not dragged from his heavenly estate, to be mere mortal, but mortals are lifted up to his celestial plane. He is still the God-Man; but he is one among many brethren who are also God-Men.

[192]

Moreover, Jesus is one of a grand order of Saviours. Every world has its distinctive Saviour, and every dispensation its Christ. There is a glorious Masonic scheme among the

Gods. The everlasting orders come down to us with their mystic and official names. The heavens and the earths have a grand leveling; not by pulling down celestial spheres, but by the lifting up of mortal spheres.

Perchance the skeptic and the strict scientist who measures by the cold logic of facts, but rises not to the logic of ideas, might not accept this literal pre-existing view, yet it must be confessed that it is a lifting up of the idealities of man's origin. Man is the offspring of the Gods. This is the supreme conception which gives to religion its very soul. Unless man's divinity comes in somewhere, religion is the wretchedest humbug that ever deluded mortals.

Priestcraft, indeed, then, from the beginning to the end-from the Alpha to the Omega of theologic craft, there is nothing divine. But the sublime and most primitive conception of Mormonism is, that man in his essential being is divine, that he is the offspring of God - that God is indeed his Father. And woman? for she is the theme now.

Woman is heiress of the Gods. She is joint heir with her elder brother, Jesus the Christ; but she inherits from her God-Father and her God-Mother. Jesus is the "beloved" of that Father and Mother - their well-tried Son, chosen to work out the salvation and exaltation of the whole human family.

[193]

And shall it not be said then that the subject rises from the God-Father to the God-Mother? Surely it is a rising in the sense of the culmination of the divine idea. The God-Father is not robbed of his everlasting glory by this maternal completion of himself. It is an expansion both of deity and humanity. They twain are one God! The supreme Unitarian conception is here; the God-Father and the God-Mother! The grand unity of God is in them - in the divine Fatherhood and the divine Motherhood - the very beginning and consummation of creation. Not in the God-Father and the God-Son can the unity of the heavens and the earths be worked out; neither with any logic of facts nor of idealities. In them the Masonic trinities; in the everlasting Fathers and the everlasting Mothers the unities of creations. *Our* Mother in heaven is decidedly a new revelation, as beautiful and delicate to the masculine sense of the race as it is just and exalting to the feminine.

Not even did Jesus proclaim to the world the revelation of our Mother in heaven - co-existent with the eternal Father. This was left, among the unrevealed truths, to the present age, when it would seem the woman is destined by Providence to become very much the oracle of a new and peculiar civilization.

The oracle of this last grand truth of woman's divinity and of her eternal Mother as the partner with the Father in the creation of worlds, is none other than the Mormon Church. It was revealed in the glorious theology of Joseph, and established

[194]

by Brigham in the vast patriarchal system which he has made firm as the foundations of the earth, by proclaiming Adam as our Father and God. The Father is first in name and order, but the Mother is with him - these twain, one from the beginning.

...

[196]

When Brigham Young proclaimed to the nations that Adam was our Father and God, and Eve, his partner, the Mother of a world - both in a mortal and a celestial sense - he made the most important revelation ever oracled to the race since the days of Adam himself. This grand patriarchal revelation is the very keystone of the "new creation" of the heavens and the earth. It gives new meaning to the whole system of theology as much new meaning to the economy of salvation as to the economy of creation. By the understanding of the works of the Father, the works of the Son are illumined.

The revelation was the "Let there be light" again pronounced. "And there was light!"

"And God created man in his own image; in the image of God created he him; male and female created he them."

"And God blessed them; and God said unto them, be fruitful, and multiply, and replenish the earth, and subdue it."

Here is the very object of man and woman's creation exposed in the primitive command. The first words of their genesis are, "Be fruitful and multiply."

So far, it is of but trifling moment how our "first parents" were created; whether like a brick, with the spittle of the Creator and the dust of the earth, or by the more intelligible method of generation. The prime object of man and woman's creation was for the purposes of creation.

"Be fruitful, and multiply and replenish the earth, and subdue it," by countless millions of your offspring.

[197]

Thus opened creation, and the womb of everlasting motherhood throbbed with divine ecstacy.

It is the divine command still. All other may be dark as a fable, of the genesis of the race, but this is not dark. Motherhood to this hour leaps for joy at this word of God, "Be fruitful;" and motherhood is sanctified - as by the holiest sacrament of nature.

We shall prefer Brigham's expounding of the dark passages of Genesis.

Our first parents were not made up like mortal bricks. They came to be the Mother and the Father of a new creation of souls.

We say Mother now, first, for we are tracing this everlasting theme of motherhood, in the Mormon economy, without which nothing of the woman part of the divine scheme can be known next to nothing of the patriarchal marriage, to which we are traveling, be expounded.

Eve - immortal Eve - came down to earth to become the Mother of a race.

How become the Mother of a world of mortals except by herself again becoming mortal? How become mortal only by transgressing the laws of immortality? How only by "eating of the forbidden fruit" by partaking of the elements of a mortal earth, in which the seed of death was everywhere scattered?

All orthodox theologians believe Adam and Eve to have been at first immortal, and all acknowledge the great command, "Be fruitful and multiply." That they were not about to become the parents of a world of immortals is evident, for they were on a mortal earth. That the earth was mortal all

[198]

nature here today shows. The earth was to be subdued by teeming millions of mankind - the dying earth actually eaten, in a sense, a score of times, by the children of these grand parents.

The fall is simple. Our immortal parents came down to fall; came down to transgress the laws of immortality; came down to give birth to mortal tabernacles for a world of spirits. The "forbidden tree," says Brigham, contained in its fruit the elements of death, or the elements of mortality. By eating of it, blood was again infused into the tabernacles of beings who had become immortal. The basis of mortal generation is blood. Without blood no mortal can be born. Even could immortals have been conceived on earth, the trees of life had made but the paradise of a few; but a mortal world was the object of creation then.

Eve, then, came down to be the Mother of a world.

Glorious Mother, capable of dying at the very beginning to give life to her offspring, that through mortality the eternal life of the Gods might be given to her sons and daughters. Motherhood the same from the beginning even to the end! The love of motherhood passing all understanding! Thus read our Mormon sisters the fall of their Mother.

And the serpent tempted the woman with the forbidden fruit.

Did woman hesitate a moment then? Did motherhood refuse the cup for her own sake, or did she, with infinite love, take it and drink for her children's sake? The Mother had plunged down, from the

[199]

pinnacle of her celestial throne, to earth, to taste of death that her children might have everlasting life.

What! should Eve ask Adam to partake of the elements of death first, in such a sacrament! 'Twould have outraged motherhood! Eve partook of that supper of the Lord's death first. She ate of that body and drank of that blood.

Be it to Adam's eternal credit that he stood by and let our Mother - our ever blessed Mother Eve partake of the sacrifice before himself. Adam followed the Mother's example, for he was great and grand - a Father worthy indeed of a world. He was wise, too; for the blood of life is the stream of mortality.

What a psalm of everlasting praise to woman, that Eve fell first!

A Goddess came down from her mansions of glory to bring the spirits of her children down after her, in their myriads of branches and their hundreds of generations! She was again a mortal Mother now. The first person in the trinity of Mothers.

The Mormon sisterhood take up their themes of religion with their Mother Eve, and consent with her, at the very threshold of the temple, to bear the cross. Eve is ever with her daughters in the temple of the Lord their God.

The Mormon daughters of Eve have also in this eleventh hour come down to earth, like her, to magnify the divine office of motherhood. She came down from her resurrected, they from their spirit, estate.

Here, with her, in the divine providence of

[200]

maternity, they begin to ascend the ladder to heaven, and to their exaltation in the courts of their Father and Mother God.

Who shall number the blasphemies of the sectarian churches against our first grand parents? Ten thousand priests of the serpent have thundered anathemas upon the head of "accursed Adam." Appalling, often times, their pious rage. And Eve the holiest, grandest of Mothers has been made a very byword to offset the frailties of the most wicked and abandoned.

Very different is Mormon theology! The Mormons exalt the grand parents of our race. Not even is the name of Christ more sacred to them than the names of Adam and Eve. It was to them the poetess and high priestess addressed her hymn of invocation; and Brigham's proclamation that Adam is our Father and God is like a hallelujah chorus to their everlasting names. The very earth shall yet take it up, all the sons and daughters of Adam and Eve shall yet shout it for joy, to the ends of the earth, in every tongue!

Eve stands, then, first - the God-Mother in the maternal trinity of this earth. Soon we shall meet Sarah, the Mother of the covenant, and in her daughters comprehend something of patriarchal marriage - "Mormon polygamy."

Analysis & Observations

β

While the actual authorship of The Women of Mormondom is not crucial for purposes of this volume, this issue has been debated to some extant among Adam-God authors because Eliza R. Snow is a more credible source of Adam-God teachings than Edward Tullidge is (he later apostatized to the Godbeite movement) - not only was Eliza R. Snow a notable saint, she was Joseph Smith's plural wife. Although it is clear that she helped to author The Women of Mormondom, how much of this book was actually written by her remains somewhat of a mystery. Because The Women of Mormondom was prepared and written for an audience broader than Utah Mormonism, some have suggested that Eliza R. Snow played a large role in actually writing the text of this book. In the 1870s, men remained the primary authors of books so it is not entirely unbelievable that Eliza R. Snow could have been the ghost author of several of the excerpts found throughout this volume. In consideration of this possibility, some have feasibly concluded that Elder Tullidge was listed as the primary author only due to the norms of the day. However, the below excerpts could suggest otherwise and other female authors were producing and publishing books under their own names so this speculation is not definitive proof by any means. That said, without the assistance of a computer generated linguistic analysis, a conclusive determination as to the author of these passages is purely speculative. The following few statements represent the parch resources that are readily available for the readers review:

Augusta Joyce Crocheron   *1976*

Representative Women of Deseret, 6
During this year she [Eliza] prepared her second volume of poems for the press, also assisted in selecting and *preparing the manuscript* for the "Women Of Mormondom," and in raising funds for its publication, and not least of all, *gave the proof her attention*. Also still continued her labors in the House of the Lord.

Susa Young Gates

Life Story of Brigham Young, 360-61
After prayers that evening [Brigham Young] sat in council with aunt Eliza R. Snow in the prayer room. *Edward Tullidge had compiled a story on the Women of Mormondom* which contained some interesting biography on the leading women to the Church and had an account of the heroic struggle of those early years. Aunt Eliza and some of her

associates thought it might be proper and advisable to send a group of women out into the world to give lectures on Mormonism and to dispose of the woman's book. Two of the daughters of Brigham Young were included in the list of women who were to go. *"It is an experiment - but one that I should like to see tried,"* *said Brigham Young* to Sister Snow at the close of the discussion.

Epilogue

β

One afternoon, after having spent several hours editing the lengthy section on Jehovah, it occurred to me that I had invested hundreds of hours into the preparation of this volume; musing upon that point, I *whimsically* considered that I may have researched and studied Adam-God teachings more than any person that has ever lived upon this earth. While this is not a particularly noteworthy achievement - the resources to do so have only recently been reasonably available for research and the doctrine has only relatively recently been revealed - and while it certainly does *not* mean that I *understand* Adam-God teachings better than everyone else (I presume, for one shining example, that Brigham Young understood these teachings far better than I do), I suppose that my depth of research provides me with some degree of insight that may be worth proffering to those readers valiant enough to plough through this bulky volume of reference materials. While I have made an effort to put forth some of my specific observations[312] in the observations and analysis portions of this book, I had a few remaining thoughts that may be of some

---

[312] Because of the sacred nature of these teachings, I have not included many insights or observations that are worth the reader's consideration. Consider for instance these questions: Is it possible that there is some eternal significance behind the fact that each experience as an Adam and Eve becomes harder because our fall from glory is more profound each time because the fall is from a greater glory than the previous experience? Why is eternal progression as introduced by Adam-God teachings necessary? Why is there no end-point where progression stops and we can bask in some everlasting glory as envisioned by Christendom? What place do ordinance sealings have in Adam-God teachings? For instance, what is the significance of the sealing of a father to a daughter in the eternities? Apart from a promised, casual, social interaction, what does this sealing signify? What is the significance of only one wife venturing down to an earth with her Adam? What happens to Adam if the Christ of His world fails? What happens to His children? What is Lucifer's motivation? How could the Father ever give him His glory as he requested? Why would Lucifer believe this is possible? What is the difference between a resurrected angel and an archangel? a God? How much do Adam and Eve really forget when a veil is placed over them? Must they learn to speak again? What is to be gained by repeatedly relearning things that we knew before and by suffering a veil to cover our minds for each probation? Why is it important for Eve to perform the law of Sarah on each earth after a veil has been placed over her- when she has forgotten the joys and blessings of this principle? What is to be understood by modern scriptures that appear to discredit Adam-God teachings? Why is this simple teaching considered a "higher doctrine"? Why is it that these teachings are so difficult for many to accept? Why is plural marriage consistently associated with Adam-God teachings - apart from the clear necessity brought about by Adam siring the savior on each world? At what point do seeds of death produce enough blood to create mortal bodies? Is this connected with the veil? What do Adam-God teachings inform us about the true order of priesthood? How does it make God feel to have His identity essentially unknown among all of His children throughout all time? Is it obvious to the reader how all of these teachings explain the fossil records on this earth? How much more did Joseph and Brigham know that they did not reveal? How are Adam-God teachings integral to understanding the law of consecration? These and many, many other questions have been seriously considered during the course of preparing this volume. However, I felt that these issues were appropriately reserved for more personal settings - reserved for the faithful believer and therefore, this volume is at least a few hundred pages shorter than it otherwise would have been.

interest to the reader. A background of my experience may help to further this end.

I first began compiling the materials in this book because of the rather bitter experience I had reading *Adam-God* by Craig Tholson. As I began reading his book as a member of the LDS Church, I found myself dealing with three burdens: first and foremost, Tholson's tone throughout the book is critical of the modern Church; second, the materials that I was reading were not only new to me, but they contradicted foundational theological teachings that I had learned in the Church; and third, because many of these sources were not readily available for verification and because Tholson's tone was rather anti-mainstream-Mormon,[313] I seriously wondered t*o what degree I could trust his integrity in reproducing these materials.*[314] I only read about a quarter of the book and gave up on the venture because, while I could feel the truthfulness of the teachings of the early brethren, I felt a lack of the presence of the Spirit from Tholson's personal attacks on the modern brethren and thereby became confused with Adam-God teachings in general. After some time passed, I was again presented with the questions surrounding Adam-God teachings and decided that I needed to give these teachings my renewed attention. At that point, I began reading Tholson's book again (it was the only Adam-God book that I knew about at that time). This time, I only read the words of the early brethren and I skipped most, if not all, of Tholson's remaining commentary. At the end of this experience, I found myself heavily enveloped with the love of God and found myself learning that there was something very *sacred and profound* within these teachings - something that needed a more *hallowed treatment* than what I had just read.

I moved on to other areas of scripture study and ultimately discovered that there were more Adam-God publications that had many other interesting statements from the early brethren. However, with each of these books and articles, I found myself wanting to skip over most of the commentaries from the authors because their bias was so strong that I found myself unable to clearly formulate my own understandings as to what the early brethren were teaching - many of the statements found in these other publications have intrusive words inserted into the original statement that were *supposed* to help the reader to interpret the passage in the same manner that the author did. As I only wanted to read the primary words of the brethren themselves, without these interjections, I began compiling the original citations without these interpolations of men - whether I

---

[313] Unfortunately, this trendy approach dominates the tenor of much fundamentalist academia.

[314] In making this observation, I am not accusing Tholson of lacking integrity in producing his book; I am merely recounting my thoughts and concerns at the time that I first read his book - I have since verified much of Tholson's work and believe that his research was ethically reproduced in his book.

agreed with their interpretations or not.[315]

As time passed, I found that the bulk of material that I had far surpassed any previous publication and thought that it was too bad that somebody had not put all of these materials together earlier so that someone like me could read the materials without the intermingling of the doctrines of men. When I had compiled virtually everything that was findable (I later confirmed that with Chris M. Hansen's compilation of Adam-God materials that took decades to compile), I remembered the words of C.S. Lewis who said (I'm paraphrasing) "I write books that I wanted to read but that have never been written before." At that point, I began organizing the materials that I had compiled and began writing this volume. The question at that time was, what should be included in that book? Should I include the controversies? the excommunications? Should I include related teachings about Adam's continued progression in knowledge? materials about Jehovah? Should I cater to members of the Church who have been misinformed about these teachings? to what extent? Would there be enough materials to include a section on Eve? What could I do to make the title of the book appear less controversial? non-contentious?

As I considered these questions and began writing the book, I ran across a third-hand statement from a fundamentalist leader that solidified the course I was taking in preparing *Understanding Adam-God Teachings.* He reportedly said something to this effect: "When we tell the truth, we feel no need to justify our position in telling that truth." When God gives us truth, our duty is to follow the principles behind that truth and to teach those principles and truths to those within our stewardship. While we may take the time to use collateral materials to help individuals within our stewardship fully understand the truths that have been revealed to us, we should not feel threatened by persons who challenge our position because the truths have been revealed to us from heaven. Applying that principle, it was clear to me that *I did not need* to follow the path others had plowed by publishing a volume that carried a defensive posture.

In other words, I believe that previous Adam-God authors have fallen into the trap of trying to justify their position by first *proving* that Adam-God teachings were taught. This *appears* to be necessary because members of the modern LDS Church are adamantly

---

[315] I believe, and I hope that my efforts have borne this out, that when all of the resources on a given subject are considered together, the reader does not need to be spoon-fed these doctrinal interpolations in order to fully understand these doctrines - though there some rare few observations that are more easily presented in this fashion. When most any subsection within this volume is considered as a whole, I believe that the brethren's teachings become quite clear without any further commentary - this is primarily why I have left my commentary to simple, and perhaps overly simplistic, textual analyses.

taught that Adam-God teachings are only taught by "enemies" of the Church - or "stupid people" as Elder Widstoe informs us; however, these proofs presented by Adam-God authors are then supported by several statements by modern LDS priesthood leaders denying that Adam-God teachings were ever taught; then, to seal the tomb of the inaccurate fallacy that Adam-God teachings were never taught, fundamentalist authors have proceeded to discredit, chastise, or contentiously mock the modern leaders of the LDS Church for their allegedly dishonest and falsified statements.[316] Mainstream Mormons, in defensive response, have felt a need to find materials to support the current LDS Church position even when most evidence flies to the contrary conclusion.[317] Some few Mormon authors have fallen in between these two variations of posturing but even then, their conclusions have been rather biased and sometimes rather odd.[318]

As a result of this type of defensive posturing, neither side of the fence has adequately put forth an effort to help readers *understand* Adam-God teachings as they were taught by the early brethren because they were too preoccupied with these and other tangential and contentious issues.[319] It was for this reason that I have made extensive efforts to ignore these issues throughout this volume. In sum, *no one had unblushingly written an Adam-God book to present these teachings without some sort of preemptive, unabashed apologizing for presenting these materials to the reader.*

Initially, I only recognized this as a deficiency for members of the LDS Church and wanted to present them with a volume that would let them read the evidence without these doctrinal whip lashings challenging them at every corner and that would allow

---

[316] Reaction to this publication could theoretically prove me wrong, but I believe that the vast amount of material found within this book does not need the further support of this contentious genre of "nail in the coffin" tactics - can anyone read these materials, spend time verifying the accuracy of these sources, and still remain *unconvinced* that Adam-God teachings were *systematically* and verily taught *as doctrine* by early Mormon leaders?

[317] I have heard, for instance, people declare that Adam-God teachings cannot be treated too seriously because Brigham Young taught *true* doctrines about Adam as well - as examples, they have cited instances where Brigham taught that Adam was Michael, that Elohim was Adam's god, and that Adam was the Ancient of Days. Of course, *none* of these example are *contrary* to Adam-God teachings but this diverting tactic has been convincing to some persons that I have spoken with.

[318] Consider Rodney Turner's position for instance - while concluding that Brigham Young clearly preached Adam-God teachings as a doctrine, he also concluded that the modern LDS position is true because we must follow the living prophet, not a dead prophet.

[319] For instance, they declare that we should not follow the living prophet blindly or that we should follow the living prophet - even if he contradicts previous prophets, that we should learn from some half a dozen Adam-God teachings that the Manifesto was not a revelation, or that the blacks should not have received the priesthood in 1978, or that we should reject Adam-God teachings, even if they were taught because they contradict the scriptures, etc. etc. etc.

them to learn these teachings relatively controversy free. However, as I met more fundamentalists, I realized that they did not have a literary refuge where they could investigate these teachings independent of their peers and family.

I hope that this volume fills this void that I have been describing.

While I have found myself tending to mentally succumb to this same path of defensive posturing, I have made every effort not to allow this tendency to materialize.[320] I even ventured to test the waters and gave some very few persons a copy of "Adam as God the Father" (without analysis) who had previously informed me that there were "only a handful" of statements about the Adam-God "theory". More than one individual informed me that that section was "over-kill" and that the evidence was overwhelming and ought to be cropped down to the more interesting and in-depth statements - and this was before I added more than two dozen statements that I discovered in my later research. It seems, when presented with this evidence alone, this portion of the controversy should be delegated to the status of an academic footnote - an example of the LDS Church's successful propaganda capabilities.

No serious academician, after reading this volume, will be able to lightly dismiss the evidence herein.[321] Likewise, the serious reader will be left with only a few choices as to how to process the contradictions that arise as a result of Adam-God teachings that are now rejected by the modern LDS Church: Either

1)   the LDS Church is "true" (but it is founded upon the authority of a man, who, as President of the Church, incorrectly taught the people to worship a false God for at least twenty-five years) or

2)   the LDS Church is Christ's only "true" church but it is in a state of partial apostasy wherein a portion of it has been severed off to allow some members of the Church to live all of the principles of the gospel without the approval of the "corporate" LDS Church[322] or

3)   the LDS Church is in a state of full apostasy (that began as a result of rejecting Adam-God teachings and plural marriage) and some fundamentalist sect (whether as a

---

[320] I have given a brief response to these issues in the "Miscellaneous Controversies" section, although I view that section as an academic footnote delegated to the end of this volume only as an acknowledgment of this unfortunate historical background to these teachings.

[321] I acknowledge that some statements may have a scrivener's error, an incorrect or incomplete date, a source of disputable reputation, etc. However, the remaining substantive proofs are more than enough to withstand serious academic scrutiny.

[322] This is another issue for another book and I acknowledge it here because there are thousands of fundamentalists who believe in this position - a la John Taylor's September 26/27 1886 visitation.

group or as individual patriarchs) is "true" and continues to maintain proper priesthood succession, or

4)   none of these positions are correct, Mormonism is false, and the truth must be found elsewhere.

None of these propositions are to be lightly treated!

That said, I have not written this volume to attack the current position of the LDS Church; nor have I written this volume for readers to use as a resource for wildly beating upon the Church for turning aside from these teachings. In contrast, I hope that this volume will be used as a tool for fundamentalist readers to divest themselves of any contentious tendencies that they may have in presenting these materials to members of the LDS Church so that they can let the teachings represent themselves and so that they can let the Spirit bear witness of whatever truths may be found therein. I also hope that fundamentalists will use this volume as a tool to teach their children the words of the early brethren instead of teaching them some brand of uninformed interpolation of Adam-God teachings that often plagues fundamentalist literature and fundamentalist culture.

Most importantly, as this material is now readily available, I hope that the reader, along with the author, will feel less apologetic about "Brigham's" Adam-God teachings. As I have read and reread these teachings over the past few years, it has become abundantly clear to me that these early brethren were *very* consistent in their teachings and that *this theological world-view that they presented is a wonderfully rich and inviting area of study* - even if you disbelieve what they were teaching. Although not always directly addressed, many facets of Adam-God teachings were taught under the more generic banner of "the plan of salvation" and were presented on many levels of understanding and in great detail throughout their many publications; as I have read these materials, it has become evident to me that Adam-God teachings are *the very foundation of the plan of salvation* and that more bulky volumes of materials could be compiled to support the teachings found within this book. The vast majority of the questions that I had posed for over a decade in the LDS Church without receiving any satisfactory answer have been answered through Adam-God teachings; inconsistencies have been ironed out, shallow explanations have been replaced by profoundly deep and intimate answers, and the very empty recesses in my soul have been replaced with wellsprings of life-giving sustenance that have enveloped my soul with peace. But even if all of this were dismissed as some psycho-somatic weakness of mine, the intelligent, thoughtful person must still concede that Adam-God teachings provide a very fascinating and groundbreaking theological worldview that is at the very least - academically intriguing - if one is interested in theology at all.

The richness of Adam-God teachings should not be obscured by the posturing that has taken place in the past. If we have been commanded not to be embarrassed in declaring that Jesus is the Christ, ought we to be embarrassed in declaring the identity of God Himself?[323] These teachings are too sacred to be treated lightly - they are too intertwined with divinity to be blithely dismissed - they are of too great of importance to be forgotten or left behind. In echo of Brigham Young, I encourage the reader to solemnly consider these teachings in the most sacred recesses of your soul. Said he in his famous April 9, 1852 discourse when he publicly introduced these teachings for the first time:

Now, let all who may hear these doctrines,
pause before they make light of them,
or treat them with indifference,
for they will prove their salvation or damnation.

Brigham Young, JD 1:51

Lastly, while this hymn may have been written of the Savior, it applies as well to Adam and is worth considering as a final thought to this volume:

W. W. Phelps   *1912*

Sacred Hymns, 16 #11

To Him who made the world,
The sun, the moon and stars,
And all that in them is.
With days and months and years;
To Him who died.
That we might live,
Our thanks and songs
We freely give.

Our hope in things to come.
The Spirit's quick'ning powers
Should turn our hearts to Him
Who makes His blessings ours;
That we may sing

---

[323] I am not suggesting here that Adam-God teachings should be proselyted; I am suggesting that when the topic does arise and where an open heart is present, our posture ought to be one of testimony bearing more than defensive academia that belittles the modern LDS Church.

Of things above,
And always know
That God is love.

When He comes down from heaven,
And earth again is blest,
Then all the ransomed heirs
Will find their promised rest.
With all the just
We then may sing,
God is with us
And we with Him.

Annotated Bibliography

β

I must disclose the fact that the following bibliography is both a compilation of resources that I used to produce this volume and resources from other Adam-God author's bibliographies that were not used for this volume but that may be interesting for the reader to use as a resource[324] to research these other Adam-related materials. I have tried to include all items that would help the reader further research items that are covered in this volume but I have done a significant amount of editing sources (other authors have covered issues that I have not so I have tried to eliminate these sources, etc.). Additionally, the reader may note that the best resource to find many of these materials is in various electronic databases both online and offline. Because I have drawn from other resources to produce this bibliography, some of the citations are not as thorough or as complete as others.

Journals & Diaries

I have listed these in the order of the person or entity keeping the diary or journal instead of listing them alphabetically under "diary", "journal", or "diaries" because some of these sources have been published under multiple names in various pamphlets and/or books. I have italicized the individual's name for the reader's quick reference.

James Beck Journal (Notebook) 1859-1865
Diary of *Thomas D. Brown*. Utah State University Press. Logan, Utah. 1972
"Sayings of Joseph the Prophet," recorded in *Anson Call*'s Journal, 23-24 (Nauvoo period); Church Historian's Office (hereinafter CHO). The following statement precedes the quotes found in the materials above:
I now quote from a certain statement by the Prophet Joseph Smith to certain brethren who promised to cut his wood if he would answer their questions. This statement was recorded at the time by Anson Call: recopied by Patriarch John M. Whitaker of Nauvoo. It was also copied, years later, by B. H. Roberts. A number of copies were also made by John M. Whitaker, the son, and distributed at the B.Y. University by proper consent, in connection with his seminary work. These two copies by Patriarch Whitaker and Roberts are verbatim, circa 1844
Journal of *Abraham H. Cannon*, BYU Library, Special Collections (hereinafter BYUSC)

---

[324] I have been especially selective in not including any anti-Mormon sources. Although I have found useful materials from some of these sources, I have been able to find duplicate research of all materials that I have found via this medium. Therefore, for this reason - and due to their ungodly agenda - I have not knowingly included any of their materials in this Bibliography.

Abraham H. Cannon Diary, CHO

Journal of *Thomas A. Clawson*, 1912-1917 Book, p. 69, 4/8/1912

Journal of *William Clayton*; Utah State Historical Society; also published in George D. Smith, An Intimate Chronicle; The Journals of William Clayton, p.513-515 Appendices A

C. Jess Groesbeck Elder's Journal. Woodland, California

Historian's Office Journal, Church Archives under date and page given. CR/100/1/Reel #1.[The Internet source of this material noted that "The words in parenthesis are transcribed Pitman shorthand entries that I am sure of the transcription. Portions of words in brackets are filled out as context seems to intend. Shorthand entries I could not transcribe are indicated by (sh). Once in the text I have (s) because the shorthand indicated merely the letter s. It should not be considered a mistake in typing (s) instead of (sh). It is not a short-form either for a word I could fit into the context or one with which I am familiar. The blank space after the first time the word Adam appears is in the original. Typed as in the original with no punctuation or capitalization supplied."]

Journal History, School of the Prophets

Journal History of the Church

Oliver B. Huntington Diary BYUSC

Journal of *J. D. T. McAllister*; BYUSC, Mor/M270.1/m/v. 6

J. D. T. McAllister Journal. CHO, Salt Lake City, Utah

Journal of *L. John Nuttall*, BYUSC, Mss 188, Box 5, Folder #11;Letter press copy book #4, p. 290

L. John Nuttall, secretary to three presidents of the LDS Church, pulled material from Clayton's account. He wrote on the inside front cover, "L. John Nuttall his Book 1880."

Journal of *Franklin D. Richards*, CHO, Ms/f/318/ Reel #7

Diary of *Samuel W. Richards*, 1824-19-9: BYUSC, 1946

Journal of *Samuel W. Richards*, 2:214-15; #55, p. 63-64; typed copy in BYUSC

Journal of *Samuel Holister Rogers*, 1:179, BYUSC, Ms 1134

John Lyman Smith Journal; BYUSC; Photocopy of holograph

Diaries and Journals of *Joseph Smith*

Brooks, Juanita, ed. *Journal of the Southern Indian Mission*

Southern Utah Mission Historical Record 1886-1900, Book D. Referred to as the "Annals of the Southern Utah Mission", CHO, 84258, 11/8/1890

Manuscript History of *St. George Stake*, CHO, CR/mh/7836/v. 3

Thomas Evans Jeremy Sr Journal; CHO, 9/30/1852

Diary of *Charles Lowell Walker*, 2:740-741, CHO

Charles L. Walker Journal, 95-6, BYUSC

Jans Christian Anderson Weibye Daybooks

Wilford Woodruff Journal; CHO, Ms/f/115; "MAN KNOW THYSELF": This is a copy from a manuscript found in the possession of N. B. Lundwall; I have found this phrase and the accompanying statement referenced in various places on the web; however, in no case have I been able to authenticate it or to identify the speaker, etc. I have found the identical material found in this statement in Wilford Woodruff's Journal entries so I have placed these items under Wilford Woodruff's Journal throughout this book.
Brigham Young, Jr. "Journal," Apr 4, 1897 - Feb 2, 1899, 30:107. CHO, Ms/f/326

Minutes, Letters, & Other Papers

Similar to the journals, I have alphabetized these sources by the place or group name rather than by the words "letter" or "minute", etc. I have italicized the word or words used to alphabetize any given entry.

Scott Anderson, Letter *to Pres. John Taylor*, 9/22/1884
Minutes of *Bishops Court*, Eleventh Ward School House. 11/20/1885, CHO
Letter of *Bishop Edward Bunker, Jr. to Joseph F. Smith*, CHO, 2/9/1902; 6/11/1892
Coltrin, Zebedee. Papers, CHO
Minutes of a meeting of the *First Presidency and Quorum of the Twelve regarding Orson Pratt*; WWW, recorder
General Conference Report, Monday 10 a.m. 10/9/1865, written and recited for the 35th semi-annual conference
Minutes of the *High Priests Quorum*, 86, Box Elder Stake, 2/24/1880
Minutes of Meeting at *Historian's Office*, Great SLC, 4/4-5/1860
Letter from *Benjamin F. Johnson to G. S. Gibbs*; BYUSC; written sometime between April and October, 1903, this letter was written at the request of the First Presidency in 1903. Bruce R. McConkie recorded in Cultism as Practiced by the So-Called Church of the Firstborn of the Fullness of Times that Benjamin F. Johnson "was asked by the First Presidency of the Church to recount in writing many of his early experiences with the Prophet. This he did, certifying that 'although so many years have intervened, they are still in my mind as fresh as when they occurred.'"
Heber C. Kimball, Memorandum, Sacred History, Solomon F. Kimball, CHO
L. John Nuttall Papers; BYUSC, Mss 188, Container #1, File Folder #1, Red book with gold lining, front and back covers, with the title "Records" on front cover in gold. 19.5 cm x 12.5 cm, 240 pages, Thursday June 19, 1879 - Tuesday December 16, 1879: journal. The following note is found on the inside front cover of the fly leaf and is not in the BYU Typescript of Diaries: "obtained my Second Anointings Sept. 23, 1867 at 9 a.m.

also my wife Elizabeth." Also, found on loose papers at end of the book on the inside back cover "Adam-ondi-Ahman" The Valley of God where Adam dwelt - so say O Pratt Sr Oct/80 [:], 1/13/1880."

E. H. Nye Letter to F. D. Richards. Dec. 4, 1897. E. H. Nye Mission Letter Book, BYUSC

Minutes from *Parowan School of the Prophets* Meeting, CHO, 3/25/1871

Charles Penrose, Conference Address. April 6, 1916. CHO

Letter from *W. W. Phelps to President Brigham Young*; Great SLC, 5/6/1867

Letter from *Orson Pratt to President Young*, cf/1325/Bx 4/fd 3/loose; SLC

Minutes of Meetings Held in *Provo City*, film/979.2/Z99/v.2, BYU Microfilm Room, Provo Bowery

John Pulsipher Papers, Mss 1041, p. 35-37; BYUSC, (p.2) A Scrap - Book Containing Some of the Phraseology- Choice and Select Instruction- & Abridged Speeches of INSPIRED MEN. Observed & Recorded By J. Pulsipher (p. 35) 10-OC-F.; 2. OC- A.

The Reorganized Church of Jesus Christ of Latter Day Saints v. Lucien Williams, Joseph Smith, Sarah F. Videon, Mark H. Forscutt, the Church in Utah of which John Taylor is President and commonly known as the Mormon Church, and John Taylor, President of said Utah Church, Court: Lake County, Ohio, 2/23/1880. A photocopy of the publication of this opinion is in the author's possession. Interestingly, the RLDS Church obtained quiet title to the Kirtland temple by filing a lawsuit in Ohio and by only notifying the Utah LDS Church of the lawsuit by publishing the lawsuit in local Ohio newspapers – effectively keeping the Utah LDS Church from being able to discover and answer the lawsuit in a timely manner. The RLDS Church thereafter won the case by default.

Franklin Dewey Richards Letterbook; Ms/f/318/reel 11

F. D. Richards Letter to E. H. Nye, 12/18/1897. F. D. Richards Letter Book, CHO; President E. H. Nye, 915 Golden Gate Avenue, San Francisco, Cal.

Letter of *F. D. Richards*, Richards Family Collection

Salt Lake School of the Prophet, Minutes, 1883, pp. 69-70; CHO CR/390/1/Box 1, Oct 11, 1883. The account connected to this source took place at New Portage, Ohio - about 50 miles from Kirtland, Ohio, 5/7/1834

Seminary Lectures, BYU, Lecture 10, John M. Whitaker, 6/24/1921

Seminary Lectures, BYU, Lecture 11, Melvin J. Ballard, 6/24/1921

Joseph F. Smith Letter Book, CHO

Joseph F. Smith Letter to Edward Bunker Jr. 2/27/1902

Joseph F. Smith Letter to S. O. Bennion. Salt Lake City: 1912

Joseph F. Smith Letter to Hon. A. Saxey of Provo. Jan. 7, 1897; d1325/Bk4/fd 1

Elder *Lorenzo Snow*, Prest. Salt Lake Temple

CHO. Confidential Research Files, 1950-1974; CR/100/14/#2/Volume 8:16,17; Church Archives Vault. From a Xerox of the original letter. Copy available in: First

Presidency. Letterpress Copybooks, 1877-1949. Jan. 1894--Nov. 1894; CR/1/20/# 23; 28:633-34. Church Archives. 8/31/1894

Minutes of *St. George High Council* of the Trial of Edward Bunker Jr. 12/13/1890, CHO. Salt Lake City, Utah.

Minutes of *St. George High Council of the Trial of Edward Bunker Sr.*, 6/11/1892, CHO

Proceedings of the First *Sunday School* Convention of the Church of Jesus Christ of Latter-day Saints; "Things That Should and Things That Should Not Be Taught In Our Sunday School", Salt Lake City: Deseret Sunday School Union, 1899, CHO; George Q. Cannon, 11/28/1898

John Taylor, "Misc. Minutes" unpublished ms., Brigham Young Collection, Church Archives, Salt Lake City, p.6

Complainant's Abstract of Pleading and Evidence, *Temple Lot Case*, 309

Brigham Young Papers: Brigham Young Addresses 4:134, 1860-1864, by Elden J. Watson, Historical Dept. Church, Ms d 1234, Box 49 fd 8

"A Few Words of Doctrine"; Ms/d/1234/Bx 49/fd 8; an unpublished discourse; SLC Tabernacle, a.m. 10/8/1861

Brigham Young Papers, Ms d 1234, Box 49, fd 13 (5 BYA), 2/19/1854

Brigham Young Papers, Minutes of the Meeting of the Council of the Twelve in Historian's upper room; Great Salt Lake City

Periodicals & Newspapers

I have alphabetized these materials by the newspaper or periodical in lieu of the author because the periodical or newspaper is the source where the reader can find more Adam-God materials. Any specific author's article, etc. is likely already cited somewhere in this volume or in the bonus CD that accompanies it.

Paden, W. M. "Is Mormonism Changing?" *Biblical Review* 14:380-402 (1929)

Jesse, Dean C. "The Early Accounts of Joseph Smith's First Vision," *BYU Studies* 9:275-300

Lyon, Edgar T. "Doctrinal Development of the Church During the Nauvoo Sojourn, 1839-1846," *BYU Studies* 15:435-46

Larson, Stan. "The King Follett Discourse: A Newly Amalgamated Text." *BYU Studies* 18:193-208 (Winter 1978)

Hale, Van. "The Doctrinal Impact of the King Follett Discourse," *BYU Studies* 18:209-23 (Winter 1978)

BYU Studies 19:398-99

The Contributor 17 volumes. Deseret News Publishing Company. Salt Lake City, Utah, Wells, Junius F., 1879-96

Deseret Evening News, Section 3, p. 7; Maricopa Stake Conference; 12/7/1913; Joseph E. Noble, Stake Clerk. Joseph F. Smith, 12/27/1913

Deseret News. Salt Lake City: Deseret New Pub. Co., 1850

Deseret Weekly News 38:19-27; The statements made in connection with this citation were made in the Logan temple; 6/--/1888; they were also published in the CD, Joseph E. Taylor, 12/29/1888; Elder Taylor was in the Salt Lake City stake presidency. Known for his gospel scholarship, he was frequently called upon to lecture throughout the Church and prepared the remarks found in this statement for a meeting in the Logan Temple

Deseret Weekly News 38:675, 676; These statements were given at a general conference

Deseret Weekly News 38:389; These statements were given at a priesthood meeting in Provo - it was published on 3/23/1889

Allen, James B. "The Significance of Joseph Smith's `First Vision' in Mormon Thought," *Dialogue*: A Journal of Mormon Thought 1:29-45 #3

Gary James Bergera, "The Orson Pratt-Brigham Young Controversies: Conflict Within the Quorums, 1853 to 1868," *Dialogue*: A Journal of Mormon Thought 13:7-49 #2 (Summer 1980)

David John Buerger, "The Adam-God Doctrine," *Dialogue*: A Journal of Mormon Thought 15:14-58 #1 (Spring 1982)

Broderick, Carl. "Another Look at Adam-God." *Dialogue* 16:4-7 (Summer 1983)

The *Evening & Morning Star*. Vol I, II. Independence, Mo.: F. G. Williams and Com., 1832-33

Winchester, Benjamin (ed.). *The Gospel Reflector*. Philadelphia Church of Jesus Christ of Latter-day Saints, 1841

The Improvement Era, Salt Lake City: Church of Jesus Christ of Latter-day Saints, 1896

The Improvement Era, William Halls, 11:778, March; The author admitted that this was his own personal understanding of the scriptures and explained "When a passage of scripture taken literally contradicts a fundamental, natural law, I take it as allegorical; and in the absence of divine authority, put a construction on it that seems to harmonize with my experience and reason."

Whitney, Orson F. "Significance of the Fall," *Improvement Era* 19:402-03

The Journal of Discourses. Liverpool : Church of Jesus Christ of Latter-day Saints, 1854-84, Watt, G. D. et. al. (eds.)

Latter-day Saints' Messenger & Advocate. Vol. I. Kirtland, O. F. G. Williams and Com., 1834-37

Latter-day Saint's Millennial Star. Liverpool: Church of Jesus Christ of Latter-day Saints,

1840-1887; only the first 39 volumes are represented in this volume

Liahona, The Elder's Journal 6:33, Chattanooga: Southern States Mission of the Church of Jesus Christ of Latter-day Saints, 1903-1907, Zion's Printing and Publishing Company, Independence, Missouri. 1907-1944. B.F. Cummings editor; there are 42 volumes

Nauvoo Expositor 1:1, Resolution #2, 6/7/1844

The Seer, Washington D. C.: Church of Jesus Christ of Latter-day Saints, 1853-54, published by Orson Pratt; this periodical was named in honor of Joseph Smith, the seer

Kirkland, Boyd. "Jehovah as the Father: The Development of the Mormon Jehovah Doctrine." *Sunstone* 9:36-44 (Autumn 1984)

Alexander, Thomas G. "The Reconstruction of Mormon Doctrine: From Joseph Smith to Progressive Theology," *Sunstone* 5:24-33 #4

Times & Seasons. 6 volumes. Published by the Church of Jesus Christ of Latter-Day Saints. Nauvoo, Illinois. 1839-1846

Truth Teller; Bloomington, Illinois. 1864

"Discourse by President Brigham Young Delivered in the Bowery, Great Salt Lake City, Utah, August 4, 1867," *Utah Historical Quarterly* 29:63-67

Warsaw Message; Warsaw, Illinois. 1843-1844

"The Mormon Endowment Ceremony," *The World Today* 8:166 #2, 2/--/1905

Books etc.

Andrus, Hyrum L. God, *Man and the Universe*. Bookcraft. Salt Lake City, Utah. 1968

Backman, Milton V, Jr., *Joseph Smith's First Vision: Confirming Evidences and Contemporary Accounts*, Salt Lake City, Utah, 1971

Barclay, William. *Jesus As They Saw Him*. Grand Rapids, Mich.: Eerdmans, 1980

Barrett, C. K. "*The Father is Greater Than I.*" *Essays on John*. Philadelphia: Westminster Press, 1982, pp. 19-34

Robert Beckstead, *Origin, Introduction, and Perpetuation in the Mormon Church*

Bennion, Heber. *Gospel Problems, and Supplement to Gospel Problems*, 1855, 1912; While these dates have been used in several Adam-God resources, I have not been able to verify either date. The book was published circa 1920 and I have placed quotes from that book chronologically based upon that date throughout this volume.

Book of Mormon. Translated by Joseph Smith, Jr., Salt Lake City: Church of Jesus Christ of Latter-day Saints, 1947

Borsch, Frederick Houk. *Son of Man in Myth and History*. Westminster Press. Philadelphia, Pennsylvania. 1967

Botterweck, G. Johannes and Helmer Ringgen, ed. Theological

Brigham Young Manuscript Addresses. Church Historian's Office. Salt Lake City, Utah.

Brueggemann, W. "Yahwist." *Interpreter's Dictionary*. Supplementary Vol., Keith Crim, gen. ed. Nashville: Abingdon, 1976, p. 971

Cannon, George Quayle. 1827-1901. *Gospel Truth*: *Discourses and Writing of President George Q. Cannon*. Selected, arranged and edited by Jerreld L. Newquist. Salt Lake City, Utah: Zion's Book Store, 1957

Christensen, Culley K. The *Adam-God Maze*

Clark, James R. *Messages of the First Presidency of the Church of Jesus Christ of Latter-day Saints*. 6 volumes. Bookcraft Inc. Salt Lake City, Utah. 1965

Clement. "*Recognitions of Clement*," *The Ante-Nicene Fathers*, volume 8. Wm. B. Eerdmas Publishing Company. Grand Rapids, Michigan. 1978

Conference Reports of the Church of Jesus Christ of Latter-day Saints. Salt Lake City: Deseret News Print. & Pub. Est., 1880-

DeBuck, A. *The Egyptian Coffin Texts*. 6 volumes. University of Chicago Press. Chicago, Illinois. 1935

The Doctrine and Covenants of the Church of the Latter Day Saints. F. G. Williams and Company. Kirtland, Ohio. 1828, 1835

Harner, Philip B. *The "I Am" of the Fourth Gospel*. Philadelphia: Fortress Press, 1970

Hinckley, Bryant S. *Sermons and Missionary Experiences of Melvin J. Ballard*, 239-240; Melvin J. Ballard, circa 1919-1939

Hippolytus. "*The Refutation of All Heresies*," The Ante-Nicene Fathers, volume 5. Wm. B. Eerdmas Publishing Co. Grand Rapids, Michigan. 1978

History of Wels August Nelson, 1885

Iraneas. *Against Heresies, The Anti-Nicene Fathers*, volume 1. Wm. B. Eerdmas Publishing Co. Grand Rapids, Michigan. 1978

Jeremias, Joachim. *The Prayers of Jesus*. Philadelphia: Fortress Press, 1979

Apostolic Fathers. Translated by Kirsopp Lake. The Shepherd of Hermas. Cambridge: Harvard University Press, 1946

Jessee, Dean C., ed., *The Papers of Joseph Smith*, 2 vols. (Salt Lake City: Deseret Book, 1989-92), 1:102-81; 2:45-124

Lectures on Faith, various editions have been printed in the Doctrine and Covenants (they were taken out of the Doctrine and Covenants in Heber J. Grant's administration) and in separate publications, with and without commentary

Lyon, T. Edgar. "*Orson Pratt, Early Mormon Leader*." Unpublished Master's thesis, Dept. of the Church History, University of Chicago, 1932

Mullen, E. Theodore, Jr. *The Assembly of the Gods; the Divine Council in Canaanite and Early Hebrew Literature*. Chico, Calif.: Scholars Press, 1980

Musser, Joseph W. *The Mormon Conception of Deity*: *Michael Our Father and Our God*. Truth

Publishing Co. Salt Lake City, Utah. 1963
MCD, 117
A correspondent, a Patriarch in the Church, submits the following verses which he states were frequently sung in the "School of the Prophets" during the presidency of Brigham Young, at which time the father of the contributor, a member of the School learned them and sang them in his home.
We Believe in Our God
In "Sons of Michael, He approaches," the second line, where Michael is described as the "eternal" Father was changed to read the "ancient" Father in the latest edition where this song appeared.
Newquist, Jerreld L., ed. *Gospel Truth*, Discourses and Writings of President George Q Cannon. 2 volumes. Deseret Book Co. Salt Lake City, Utah. 1974
Nibley, Hugh. *The Message of the Joseph Smith Papyri an Egyptian Endowment*. Deseret News Press. Salt Lake City, Utah. 1975
Openshaw, Bob. *Openshaw's Notes*
Patai, Raphael. *The Messiah Texts*. Avon Books. New York, New York. 1979
Pearl of Great Price. Salt Lake City: Church of Jesus Christ of Latter-day Saints, 1948
Pratt, Parley P. *Key to the Science of Theology*. Liverpool, England. 1855
Pratt, Orson. *Masterful Discourses of Orson Pratt*, 346; SLC
Richards, Franklin D. *A Compendium of the Faith and Doctrines of the Church of Jesus Christ of Latter-Day Saints*. Liverpool, England. 1855
Richard, Franklin D. (ed.). *Sacred Hymns* and Spiritual Songs for the Church of Jesus Christ of Latter-day Saints. 11th ed. rev.; Liverpool: F. C. Richards, 1856
Roberts, Brigham H. *A Comprehensive History of the Church of Jesus Christ of Latter-day Saints*, 6 volumes. Salt Lake City: Deseret News Press, 1930
Roberts, Brigham H. *Defense of the Faith and the Saints* 2:268,
Roberts, Brigham H. *Mormon Doctrine of Deity*. Salt Lake City: Deseret News, 1930. Salt Lake Herald. June 11, 1907. Salt Lake City: 1870-1920.
Robinson, James M., ed. *The Nag Hammadi Library*. Harper and Row, San Francisco, California. 1977
Sacred Hymns and Spiritual Songs for the Church of Jesus Christ of Latter-day Saints 11th Edition, revised in Liverpool, 1856, by, Apostle Franklin D. Richards
Sacred Hymns and Spiritual Songs for the Church of Jesus Christ of Latter-day Saints. Salt Lake City; The Deseret News Company, 1912; as do Latter-day Saints today, the early saints considered the sacred music of the hymnbook as an expression of their beliefs. The preface to the 1840 edition, reprinted in the 1912 edition, stated "The Saints in this country have been very desirous for a Hymn Book adapted to their faith and worship, that they might sing the truth with an understanding heart, and express their praise, joy,

and gratitude in songs adapted to the New and Everlasting Covenant."

Schroeder, A. T. (ed.). *Zion-Lucifer's Lantern*. Salt Lake City: A. T. Schroeder, 1898-1900

Seaich, Eugene. *Ancient Texts and Mormonism*. Sandy, Utah: Mormon Miscellaneous, 1983

Smith, Joseph Fielding, Jr. (ed). *Teachings of the Prophet Joseph Smith*. Salt Lake City: Deseret News Press, 1946

Smith, Joseph, Jr. *History of the Church* of Jesus Christ of Latter-day Saints. Salt Lake City: Church of Jesus Christ of Latter-day Saints, 1909

Smith, Robert W. *The Last Days*, p. 77

Snow, Eliza R. *Poems of Eliza R. Snow* 2:8-9, 188-89; See also MS 17:320 for a reprint of her poem "The Immortal"

Snow, Eliza R. *Poems, Religious, Historical, and Political*. Salt Lake City: Latter-day Saint Print. and Pub. Est., 1877

Stenhouse, T. B. H. *The Rocky Mountain Saints*. New Your: D. Appleton and Co., 1873.

Stone, Nathan. Names of God. Chicago: Moody Press, 1944

Taylor, John. *The Meditation and Atonement*. Deseret News Company. Salt Lake City, Utah. 1882

Tertullian. "On Prescription Against Heretics. " *The Ante-Nicene Fathers*, volume 3. W. B. Eerdmas Publishing Co. Grand Rapids, Michigan. 1978

Tholson, Craig. *Adam-God*

Tullidge, Edward W. *Life of Brigham Young*, Or Utah and Her Founders. New York: 1877

Tullidge, Edward W. *The Women of Mormondom*. New York: 1877

Turner, Rodney. "The Position of Adam in Latter-Day Saint Scripture and Theology" (*Master's Thesis*, Brigham Young University. 8/--/1953).

Whitney, Orson F. *Elias, An Epic of the Ages*. rev. ed.; Salt Lake City: 1914

Whitney, Orson F. Elias, *Life of Heber C. Kimball*. Salt Lake City: Juvenile Instructor, 1888

Widstoe, John A. (ed). *The Discourses of Brigham Young*. Salt Lake City: Deseret Book Co., 1946

Widstoe, John A. Evidences and Reconciliations. Salt Lake City: Bookcraft, 1943

Gospel Link, CD ROM
New Mormon Studies, CD ROM
http://www.spires.net
http://relarchive.byu.edu/19th/description.html; database includes PDF versions of the
following documents:
  Catechism for children
  Collection of sacred hymns for the Church
  Collection of sacred hymns for the Church in Europe
  Compendium of the faith and doctrines of the Church
  Evening and the Morning Star
  Gospel Reflector
  Interesting account of several remarkable visions
  Journal of Heber C. Kimball
  Key to the science of theology
  Latter Day Saints' Messenger and Advocate
  Latter-day Saints' Millennial Star
  Poems, religious, historical, and political
  Proclamation of the Twelve Apostles
  Seer
  Times and Seasons
  Voice of Warning

Despite my attempts to be exhaustive in my preparation of this volume, there were some
few sources that I was unable to locate in time for the publication of this work. The
following is a list of sources that I have seen referred to as teaching various Adam-God
doctrines but that I have been unable to locate in any significant form (in other words, I
have a citation but no quotation):

Deseret News:
3/11/1857 (This publication date is close enough to the date of the sermon containing
materials in JD 4:217-19 and may just be a reprint of that sermon.)
11/16/1857 (p. 290)
10/26/1859
10/14/1860 (This may just be a reprint of the sermon containing materials in JD 8:208.)
6/18/1874 (This may just be a reprint of the sermon containing materials in JD 17:43.)
9/28/1881

6/2/1888 (38:19-27)

Millennial Star:
64:785-790

The Salt Lake Daily Tribune:
8/17/1877

Wilford W. Woodruff Journal:
1854-69 statement that allegedly says "Adam says 'This is my beloved Son, hear him.'"

Made in the USA
Coppell, TX
02 September 2021